D0914345

A
CHECKLIST of
AMERICAN IMPRINTS
for
1828

Items 31875 - 37342

Compiled by

Richard H. Shoemaker
assisted by
Gayle Cooper

The Scarecrow Press, Inc.
Metuchen, N.J.   1971

Copyright 1971 by Mrs. Richard H. Shoemaker

ISBN 0-8108-0377-1

Z
1215
.55
1828

Preface
Volumes Nine and Ten, 1828 and 1829

Professor Richard H. Shoemaker died on March 3, 1970. He was an outstanding bibliographer and humanist, admired and loved by all who knew him. At the time of Professor Shoemaker's death Volumes Nine and Ten (1828 and 1829) of this Checklist had come through preliminary editing with a number of unresolved problems remaining; and material for Volume Eleven (1830) had been assembled and was about to receive preliminary editing. With the help of Mary Kay Daniels in Washington, D. C. and William Crowe in Boston, Professor Shoemaker's research assistant, Gayle Cooper, went ahead with work on these volumes. Miss Cooper worked under the general supervision of a committee of the Rutgers University Graduate School of Library Service: Dean Thomas H. Mott, Jr., Assistant to the Dean Thomas W. Shaughnessy, and Professors Benjamin Weintraub and Paul S. Dunkin. Work on these volumes has been made possible by grants from the National Endowment for the Humanities and the Rutgers University Research Council. Miss Cooper and the Committee have made every effort to meet the high standards set by Professor Shoemaker.

Paul S. Dunkin

New Brunswick, New Jersey
September, 1970

YOUNGSTOWN STATE UNIVERSITY
LIBRARY

239977

iii

239077

Abernethy, John, 1764-1831
Lectures on anatomy, surgery, and pathology; including observations on the nature and treatment of local diseases... Boston, B. Perkins & co., 1828-29. 2 v. CSt-L; CtMW; DLC; DNLM; GU-M; ICJ; IU-M; KyLoJM; KyLxT; LNOP; LU-Med; MB; MBCo; MdBM; MdUM; MiU; NBuU-M; NbU-M; OC; OCG; OCU-M; OClM; OO; PPC; PU; PPiU-Med; RPM; ScCM; VtU.   31875

Abstract of a correspondence with the executive, relative to the rank or command of Major-Generals Scott and Macomb. [Cincinnati? 1828?] 60 p. OCHP; PPL.   31876

An abstract of the Bible history. See Turner, William.

Académie Classique et Militaire de Mantua.
Prospectus de l'Académie Classique et Militaire de Mantua, (village situé a 2-1/2 milles. Ouest de Philadelphie,) derigee par Victor Value. Philadelphie, P. M. Lafourcade, Imprimeur, 1828. 12 p. PPAmP; PPL.   31877

Academy of Natural Sciences of Philadelphia.
Act of incorporation and by-laws... Philadelphia, J. R. A. Skerrett, 1828. 12 p. DLC.   31878
An account of the proceedings of the meeting at Auburn, on the 23d day of August, 1828; in relation to the measures taken to enforce the observance of the Sabbath, and the attempt to establish a Christian party in politicks. Auburn, Pr. by Richard Oliphant, 1828. 24 p. MWA.   31879

An account of the trial and execution of... John Woods. See Armstrong, James L.

Active benevolence. See American Tract Society, N. Y.

The acts of the days of the Son of Man, from the Passion-week to his Ascension. Philadelphia, Pr. by John Binns, 1828. 72 p. NcWsM; PHi.   31880

Adam, Alexander, 1741-1809
Stereotype edition. Adam's Latin grammar, with some improvements... by Benjamin A. Gould. Boston, Hilliard, Gray, Little and Wilkins; and Richardson and Lord, [Stereotyped at the Boston Type and Stereotype Foundry] 1828. 299, [1] p. GMM; MB; MH; MHi; NNC; PAtM; PPL; BrMus.   31881

Adams, Daniel, 1773-1864
Adams new arithmetic. Arithmetic, in which the principles of operating by numbers are analytically explained and synthetically applied. Illustrated by copious examples. Designed for the use of schools and academies. Keene, N. H., John Prentiss, 1828. 264 p. CSt; CU; CtHT-W; CtY; ICU; MH; MiU.   31882

1

---- Adam's new arithmetic. Arithmetic, in which the principles of operating by numbers are analytically explained and synthetically applied; thus combining the advantages to be derived both from the inductive and synthetic mode of instructing: the whole made familiar by a great variety of useful and interesting examples... Utica, N.Y., Pub. by Hastings & Tracy [Stereotyped at the Boston Type and Stereotype Foundry] 1828. 264 p. MiU; N.   31883

---- Geography; or, a description of the world... 11th ed. Boston, Lincoln & Edmands, 1828. 323, [1] p. CtY; DLC; PP.
31884
---- The scholar's arithmetic; or, Federal accountant... Keene, N.H., [Pr. by John Prentiss] 1828. 224 p. DAU; MB; MH; MeHi; MiU; MnHi; OClWHi.
31885
Adams, John Quincy, 1767-1848
    Letter of the Hon. John Quincy Adams, in reply to a letter of the Hon. Alexander Smyth, to his constituents. Also, the speech of Mr. Adams on the Louisiana treaty, delivered in the Senate of the United States, Nov. 3, 1803. And a letter from Mr. Jefferson to Mr. Dunbar. Relative to the cession of Louisiana. Washington, Pr. by Gales & Seaton, 1828. 16 p. DLC; NcU; PPL.
31886
Adams, Thomas, 1792-1881
    Sermon delivered in Augusta, September 11, 1828, at the annual meeting of the Kennebec Conference of Churches. By Thomas Adams. Augusta, Pr. by Eaton & Severance, 1828. 28 p. CBPac; MBC; MNBedf; MeBaT; MeHi; MeLB.   31887

---- ---- By Thomas Adams, pastor of a church in Vassal-

borough. Augusta, Pr. by Eaton & Severance, 1828. 16 p. MeHi.
31888
An address in regard to the memorial of the surviving officers of the Revolutionary army, now before the representatives of the nation. Washington, 1828. 11 p. Sabin 389.
31889
Address of the Administration standing committee to their fellow-citizens of Indiana. See National Republican Party. Indiana.

Address of the central committee appointed by a convention. See National Republican Party. Massachusetts.

Address of the Central Jackson Committee to the freemen of North Carolina. See Democratic Party. North Carolina.

Address of the General Committee of Republican Young Men of the City of New York. See Democratic Party. New York.

Address of the people of Louisiana. See Democratic Party. Louisiana.

An address of the Republican central committee. See Democratic Party. Indiana.

Address of the Republican committee of correspondence of Philadelphia. See Democratic Party. Pennsylvania.

Address of the Republican young men of the town of Galway, county of Saratoga, to their fellow-citizens. Ballston Spa, Pr. by J. Comstock, 1828. 14 p. DLC; NN.
31890
Address of the state convention of delegates. See National Republican Party. New York.

Address of the Young Men's Association of Trenton, New Jersey. See National Republican Party. New Jersey.

An address, reported by the Committee appointed at Wilkesboro', 5th February, 1828. See Democratic Party. North Carolina.

An address to Methodists, in relation to the Baltimore Union Society, and the periodical called the Mutual Rights. ----By a Layman of the Methodist Episcopal Church. Baltimore, Pub. by Armstrong and Plaskitt, William Woody, pr., 1828. 32 p. Ms-Ar.
31891

An address to the Catholic voters of Baltimore. See Jenkins, William.

An address to the citizens of Connecticut. See Democratic Party. Connecticut.

Address to the electors of Middlesex County. See National Republican Party. Connecticut.

An address to the electors of the ninth ward. New York, J. M. Danforth, pr., 1828. 8 p. MBAt; NNC.
31892

Address to the farmers of Rhode Island, on the subject of the general election of officers in April, 1828. By a Farmer. Providence, H. H. Brown, 1828. 12 p. MBAt; MnU; RP; RPB.
31893

An address to the Federalists of New Jersey. See Hamilton, pseud.

An address to the freeman of Rhode Island, by a Republican Farmer. [Providence, 1828?] 20 p. MBH; MH; RPB.
31894

Address to the freemen of Rhode

Island, on the annual election of state officers to take place April 16, 1828. Providence, 1828. 16 p. MH; RP.
31895

An address to the friends of Andrew Jackson. See Democratic Party. Indiana.

An address to the people of Charles, Calvert, and St. Mary's counties. See Democratic Party. Maryland.

Address to the people of Connecticut. See Democratic Party. Connecticut.

Address to the people of Pennsylvania. [1828] 16 p. DLC.
31896

An address to the people of Rhode Island. See Updike, Wilkins.

Address to the people of the United States. Mt. Holly, Alex A. Young, pr., [1828[1 p. DLC.
31897

An address to the people of the United States. See Brutus, pseud.

Address to the people of the United States. See Colwell, Joseph.

Address to the people of the United States. See Free Trade Convention.

An address to the voters of the electoral district composed of the counties of Anson, Richmond, Robeson, Cumberland, and Moore. Fayetteville, North-Carolina Journal, pr., 1828. 26 p. NcD; NcU.
31898

An address, written for the fiftieth anniversary of our independence, by an old revolutionary soldier of Wrentham... Dedham

[Mass.] Pr. by H. & W. H. Mann, xxiv, 335, [misno. 235] p. PPL.
1828. 19 p. DLC.   31899   31904

Addresse an das Volk von Dau- The affecting history of the
phin County. See Democratic   Duchess of C---; who was con-
Party. Pennsylvania.   fined nine years in a horrid dun-
                              geon under ground, where light
                              never entered... New-York, S.
Addresses; or, The offering of a King, 1828. 1 p. 1., [7]-40 p.
Sunday school teacher to his fel- DLC.   31905
low labourers: containing fifty-
two suitable addresses, to be African Mission School Society.
delivered to the children at the See Protestant Episcopal Church
close of each day's teaching... in the U. S. A. African Mission
2d ed. Philadelphia, William   School Society.
Stavely, 1828. 144 p. NNUT.
                     31900 African Repository & Colonial
Adeline; or, The victim of se- Journal, Washington, D. C.
duction: an affecting tale. Trans- Address of the carrier of the
lated from the French, by Sarah African Repository & Colonial
S. Wilkinson... New York, S. Journal, to his patrons and friends.
King, 1828. 30 p. DLC. 31901 [Washington, D. C., 1828] 1 p.
                              DLC.   31906
Adlum, John, 1759-1836
    A memoir on the cultivation An aged layman, pseud. See
of the vine in America, and the Bradford, A.
best mode of making wine. 2d
ed. Washington, Pr. for the au- Agricola, P., pseud.
thor, by Wm. Greer, 1828. 179,   The New York gardner, or
[1] p. CSmH; ICJ; MB; MNe; Twelve letters from a farmer to
MdBS; MoSHi; NPV; NbU; NcA-S; his son, in which he describes
PPAmP; PPL; PU-V; RNR; T;   the method of laying out and man-
Vi; BrMus.   31902 aging the kitchen-garden. Sara-
                              toga Spring, Pub. by A. C. Cros-
Administration Party. See Na- by, G. W. Davison, pr., 1828.
tional Republican Party.   96 p. MBH; MiD-B.   31907

The adventures of Don Quixote. Agricultural almanac for 1829.
See Cervantes Saavedra, Miguel Lancaster, John Baer [1828] 18 l.
de.   CLU; CtHT-W; DLC; MWA; NN;
                              NNU-H; PHi; PPL.   31908
The adventures of Hajji Baba.
See Morier, James Justinian. ---- Philadelphia, Thomas De-
                              silver [1828] 18 l. CtY; DLC;
Advice to a patriot President... MWA; NBuHi; NHi; NN; PHi.
[1828?] 4 p. DLC; PPL. 31903   31909
                              El aguinaldo para el año de 1829.
Aesopus   Filadelfia, Carey, Lea & Carey
    Fables of Aesop and others, [1828?] 316 p. MWA; NNH.
translated into English: with in-   31910
structive applications: and a [Aikin, John] 1747-1822
print before each fable. By   The farm-yard journal. For the
Samuel Croxall. Philadelphia, amusement and instruction of chil-
Pr. by Simon Probasco, 1828. dren. Cooperstown, Stereotyped,

pr. and sold by H. & E. Phinney,
1828. 31 p. <u>NN</u>.   31911

Alabama (State)
    Acts passed at the ninth an-
nual session of the General Assembly of the state of Alabama,
begun and held in the town of
Tuscaloosa, on the third Monday
in November, one thousand eight
hundred and twenty-seven... [Tus-
caloosa] Pr. by Dugald M'Farlane, state pr., 1828. 176 p.,
[6] p. Ar.   31912

---- An act to establish the
bank of the state of Alabama:
approved December 20th, 1823.
Tuskaloosa, Pr. by Grant and
Mitchell, October 1828. [3] 3-
10 p. Title from McMurtrie.
                           31913
---- Journal of the House of
Representatives of the state of
Alabama, begun and held at the
town of Tuskaloosa on the third
Monday in November, 1827...
Tuskaloosa, Pr. by Dugald M'
Farlane, state pr., 1828. 289 p.
Sc.   31914

---- Journal of the Senate, of
the state of Alabama, begun and
held at the town of Tuskaloosa,
on the third Monday in November, 1827... Tuskaloosa, Pr. by
Dugald McFarlane, state pr.,
1828. 195 p. Sc.   31915

---- Report of the Committee of
Ways and Means. G. W. Gayle,
Chairman. [Tuscaloosa? 1828?]
4 p. Title from McMurtrie.
                           31916
Albany, N. Y. Library
    Catalogue of books in the Al-
bany library July, 1828. Albany,
Pr. by Websters and Skinners,
1828. 81, [1] p. MWA; NjR.
                           31917
Albany Academy for Girls
    Rules, regulations, &c....
passed August, 1828. Albany,

Websters & Skinners, 1828. 11 p.
MB.   31918

Albany Argus, Extra. Sept. 2,
1828. See Democratic Party.
New York.

The Albany directory for 1828-9.
By Ira W. Scott. Albany, Web-
ster & Wood, 1828. 132 p.
MBNEH; N.   31919

Albany Nursery
    Catalogue of fruit trees and of
ornamental trees, shrubs, herbaceous and greenhouse plants culti-
vated and for sale at the Albany
Nursery... Albany, 1828. 24 p.
"From NN imp. catal., but not in
NN." (1932)   31920

Alejandro, ó la satisfaccion gen-
erosa. Por el autor del Evangelio
en Triunfo. Nueva York, En casa
de Lanuza Mendia Y. C. Impresores Liberos, 1828. 128 p.
PPAmP.   31921

Alexander, Archibald, 1772-1851
    A brief outline of the evidences
of the Christian religion. ...4th
ed. Princeton, N. J., Princeton
press, Pub. by Wm. D'Hart, Connolly & Madden, prs., 1828. 231
p. CSmH; GHi; MH; NNU; NjP;
NjR; OrPD; PPLT; PPPrHi.
                           31922
---- The world to be reclaimed
by the Gospel. Missionary paper
No X.   Philadelphia, 1828. 12 p.
IEG.   31923

Alexander, Mark, 1792-1883
    Speech of Mr. Alexander, on
the tariff bill, delivered in the
House of Representatives, April
19, 1828. Washington, Gales and
Seaton, 1828. 28 p. DGU; MoKU.
                           31924
Ali Baba; or, The forty thieves.
A new and improved edition. New-
York, Pub. by W. Whale, 1828.
15 p. DLC.   31925

Alice Bradford. See Goodwin, Ezra Shaw.

All hail to the brave and free! A national song. Written for & dedicated to Miss Clara Fisher, and sung by her with unbounded applause. Adapted to the French air, Le Petit Tambour. Baltimore, John Cole [c1828] 3 p. ViU.   31926

Allegheny County. Jackson Democratic Committee of Correspondence. See Democratic Party. Pennsylvania.

Allegheny County, Pennsylvania Committee of Correspondence. (Circular.) To Charles Shaler, John S. Riddle and Robert Burke of Allegheny- Jonathan Roberts of Montgomery, John S. Weistling and David Karuse of Daulphin... and others, members of the administration committees throughout Pennsylvania. Pittsburgh, May 1st, 1828. Gentlemen: [Election circular] Several of the committee of correspondence for Allegheny County. [Pittsburgh, 1828] 1 p. DLC.
                         31927
Alleine, Joseph, 1634-1668
Alleine on the promises; Containing the voice of the herald, before the great being: the voice of God speaking from Mount Gerazim; being a short view of the great and precious promises of the Gospel, etc. With a sketch of his life and writings by James Nichols. 1st Amer. ed., corr. and amended, with a preface, by a friend. Baltimore, Pub. by Armstrong & Plaskitt, and John Plaskitt & co. Wm. Wooddy, pr. 1828. 240 p. CBPac; GMM; OMC.   31928

---- Solemn warnings of the dead; or An admonition to unconverted sinners... 2d Prince-

ton ed. ... Princeton, N. J., D' Hart, 1828. 160 p. NjP; OO.
                         31929
Allen, Benjamin, 1789-1829
General Stevens; or, The fancy ball, being the third part of Living Manners. Philadelphia, 1828. 72 p. PHi (not loc., 1970).
                         31930
---- Narrative of the labours, sufferings, and final triumph of the Rev. William Eldred... Philadelphia, Pub. at the Church Missionary House [Adam Waldie & Co., prs.] 1828. 80 p. NN; NjMD.   31931

---- An oration, delivered at the request of Phoenix Lodge... Dec. 27, 1827; proving the "great light of Masonry" to be from God. 2nd ed. Philadelphia, L. Johnson, stereotyper, 1828. 24 p. MBFM; NjPT; PPFM.   31932

Allen, Francis D.
[Seventh stereotype edition.] The New York selection of sacred music: containing a great variety of plain, repeating, and fugue tunes. In two parts. New York, Pub. by J. C. Totten, and C. Bartlett, 1828. 168 p. RPB.
                         31933
Allen, Jonathan Adams, 1787-1848
A system of pharmacology; designed for a practical compendium of materia medica and pharmacy and as a text book for students attending medical lectures. Middlebury, Ovid Miner, 1828. 56 p. NNNAM; VtMiS.   31934

[Allen, Joseph] 1790-1873
No. 16. On some corruptions of scripture. Printed for the Unitarian Association. Boston, Bowles and Dearborn [Press of I. R. Butts and Company] 1828. 28 p. CBPac; DLC; ICMe; ICU; MBC; MH-AH; MHi; MeB; MnU; Nh; ScCC.
                         31935

Allen, William, 1784-1868
Brief remarks upon the carnal and spiritual state of man, with some observations upon the nature of true worship and gospel ministry. New York, Samuel Wood and sons, 1828. 31 p. PSC-Hi.   31936

---- A lecture, on the doctrine of universal salvation, delivered in the chapel of Bowdoin College. ...Pub. by request of the students. Brunswick, Pr. by Moore & Wells, 1828. 40 p. ICU; MB; MBC; MH; MeBaT; MeHi; MeLB; PPL.   31937

Alliene, Richard
Heaven opened or, A brief and plain discovery of the riches of God's covenant of grace... Revised and somewhat abridged. New York, American Tract Society, 1828. 388 p. IaPeC.
                              31938
[Allingham, John Till] fl 1799-1810
Tis all a farce. A farce. In two acts, as performed at the Philadelphia Theater. Philadelphia, C. Neal, 1828. 30 p. ICU; MH; NCH; NN; PU.   31939

Almack's revisited. See White, Charles.

Almanac for 1829. Baltimore, William & Joseph Neal; Wm. Wooddy, pr. [1828] 18 l. MWA; NBuHi.   31940

Alonzo and Melissa. See Mitchell, Isaac.

Althans, Henry, 1783-1855
Scripture natural history of quadrupeds, with reflections designed for the young. 1st Amer. ed. Hartford, D. F. Robinson, 1828. 214, 2 p. CtHi; DLC; IObB; PU.   31941

An amateur, pseud.   See Paulding, James Kirke.

An amateur, pseud.   See The Warbler.

American Academy of Arts and Sciences, Boston. A short reply to a pamphlet. See Bigelow, Jacob.

American Academy of the Fine Arts. See New York. American Academy of the Fine Arts.

The American almanac for 1829. By E. A. Lambert. New-Haven [1828] 12 l. Drake 944.   31942

The American almanac for 1829. By E. R. Lambert. New-Haven [1828] 12 l. Ct; CtY.   31943

The American annual register; for the years 1826-7... New-York, Pub. by E. & G. W. Blunt, 1828. 512, 348 p. DLC; KU; MoSpD; NNLI; NjR; RNR.   31944

American Asylum for the Deaf and Dumb, Hartford.
Twelfth report of the directors of the American Asylum, at Hartford, for the Education and Instruction of the Deaf and Dumb, exhibited to the Asylum, May 10, 1828. Hartford, Hudson and Skinner, prs., 1828. 39, [1] p. MBC; PPL.   31945

---- Twelfth report of the directors of the American Asylum, at Hartford, for the education of the Deaf and Dumb...Hartford, W. Hudson and L. Skinner, pr., 1828. 32 p. DLC; IaU; KHi; MiU; OC.
                              31946
American Bible Class Society
First report of the American Bible Class Society, made at Philadelphia, May 22, 1828, with an appendix. Philadelphia, Pr. by W. F. Geddes, 1828. 24 p. DLC;

YOUNGSTOWN STATE UNIVERSITY
LIBRARY

239977

MLow; MnHi; NjR; PPPrHi.
31947

American Bible Society
Twelfth annual report of the
American Bible Society, presented May 8, 1828, with an appendix,
containing extracts of correspondence, list of auxiliaries, &c. &c.
New York, Pr. by Daniel Fanshaw,
1828...xii, 116 p. MeBaT; PPL;
ViRVB.   31948

American Board of Commis-
sioners for Foreign Missions
An appeal to the American
churches...[Missionary Papers,
No. 6. Boston, 1828] 12 p. MHi.
31949
---- Missionary biography...
[Missionary Papers, No. 12. Boston, 1828] 16 p. MHi.   31950

---- Report of the American
Board of Commissioners for
Foreign Missions, compiled from
documents laid before the board,
at the annual meeting, which was
held in the city of Philadelphia,
Oct. 1, 2, and 3, 1828. Boston,
Pr. for the Board by Crocker
and Brewster, 1828. 131 p.
CBPac; IEdS; MA; MeB; TxH.
31951
---- Middlesex Association.
Auxiliary Missionary Society.
Proceedings of the Auxiliary
Missionary Society of the Middlesex Association, for the year
1827, with facts and statements
on the subject of foreign missions... [Middletown, Conn.,
Pr. by E. T. Greenfield, 1828]
12 p. Ct.   31952

The American Chesterfield, or,
Way to wealth, honour, and dis-
tinction; being selections from
the letters of Lord Chesterfield
to his son; and extracts from
other eminent authors, on the
subject of politeness: with alterations and additions, suited to
the youth of the United States.

By a member of the Philadelphia
bar... Philadelphia, J. Grigg,
1828. 286 p. CSmH; CtY; DLC;
KyDC; LNHT; MH; MNe; MiHi;
MnM; NBu; OCHP; OCl; OO; PHi;
PU; TNJ; TxU; Vi; WHi.   31953

American Colonization Society
The eleventh annual report of
the American Society for Colonizing the Free People of Colour of
the United States. With an appendix. Washington, Pr. by James C.
Dunn, Georgetown, D.C., 1828.
120 p. DLC; MA; Ms-Ar; MeBaT;
NN; NbU; NjPT; PPL.   31954

The American common-place book
of prose. See Cheever, George
Barrell.

American Convention for Promoting the Abolition of Slavery.
Address of the American Convention for Promoting the Abolition of Slavery, &c. To the citizens of the United States. [Balti-
more, November, 1828] 4 p.
CtSoP; MdBJ; PHi.   31955

---- Minutes of the adjourned session of the twelfth biennial American Convention for Promoting the
Abolition of Slavery, and improving the condition of the African
race held at Baltimore, Nov. 1828.
Philadelphia, Pub. by order of the
convention, Samuel Parker, pr.,
1828. 68 p. DLC; ICHi; NHi; OC;
PU.   31956

American Education Society
Rules of the American Education Society, August, 1828. [Bos-
ton? 1828] 24 p. CSmH; CtY;
DLC.   31957

---- Twelfth annual report of the
directors of the American Education Society, presented at the annual meeting in the city of New
York, May 8, 1828. Andover, Pr.
by Flagg & Gould, 1828. 56 p.

MA; MNE; MeBaT.   31958

American farmers' almanac for
1829. By Charles F. Egelmann.
Hagers-Town, John Gruber and
Daniel May [1828] 15 l. DLC;
MWA; MdBE; NBuG; NjR; ViU;
ViW.   31959

American Home Missionary So-
ciety.
    The second report of the
American Home Missionary So-
ciety, presented by the execu-
tive committee, at the anniver-
sary meeting, May 7, 1828...
New York, Pr. by Alexander
Ming, Jr., 1828. 90 p. CtSoP;
DLC; GDC; ICN; ICT; IaGG; MB;
MBAt; MHi; MnHi; MoS; NBLiHi;
OClW; OO.   31960

American Institute of the City
of New York.
    Address and resolutions of
the American Institute. At a
meeting of the "American Institute of the City of New-York,
held at Tammany Hall on the 11th
of March 1828, the committee
appointed for that purpose, submitted the following address to
the society... [New York, 1828]
2 p. DLC.   31961

[----] Facts for the consideration of ship-builders, ship-own-
ers, seamen, merchants, &c.
Being an examination of so many
of the tariff laws of the United
States, as have been passed for
their benefit. New-York, Pr.
by Van Winkle & Osborn, 1828.
19 p. CtHT-W; CtY; MH-BA;
MiD; NIC; PPL.   31962

American Mercury, Hartford,
Conn.
    Address of the carrier of the
American Mercury, to his patrons, January 1, 1828. Hartford, Jan. 1, 1828. 1 p. DLC.
                         31963

The American reader, containing
extracts suited to excite a love of
science and literature, to refine
the taste, and to improve the moral character, designed for the use
of schools. Brookfield, E. & G.
Merriam; Boston, Peirce and Williams, 1828. 276 p. CSmH; Ct;
CtHT-W; CtHi; MH; MWA. 31964

--- Hartford, D. F. Robinson,
1828. 274 p. CSmH; CU; CtMMHi;
MH; RPB.   31965

American Society for Colonizing
the Free People of Colour. See
American Colonization Society.

American Society for the Promotion of Temperance
    First annual report of the ex-
ecutive committee of the American Society for the Promotion of
Temperance. For the year ending Nov. 1827. Andover, Pr. for
the Society by Flagg and Gould,
1828. 67, [1] p. DLC; MBC; MeB;
NjR; OCHP; PCC; PHC; PHi; PPL;
PPPrHi; PU; WHi.   31966

American Sunday School Union
    The charter; being a plain state-
ment of facts, in relation to an application to the legislature of
Pennsylvania, to grant a charter
to the American Sunday School
Union, with the statement of the
resident members of the board of
managers, belonging to the Methodist Episcopal Church, in reference to charges made against the
Union by the Christian Advocate
and Journal... Philadelphia, 1828.
22 p. DLC; GDC; ICMcC; MBAt;
MBC; MH; MiD-B; NCH; NNG;
NjPT; NjR; P; PHi; PPAmP;
PPL; PPPrHi; ScU; TNJ.   31967

---- The fourth report... May 20,
1828. Philadelphia, Pr. for the
American Sunday-School Union, by
I. Ashmead & Co., 1828. 22 p.
PPL.   31968

---- ---- Philadelphia, Pr. for
the American Sunday School
Union, by I. Ashmead & Co.,
1828. xxxii, 31, [1] p. MA; MB;
MeB; NRAB. NcWsM; OSW;
PPL.   31969

---- The youth's library; con-
taining the publications of the
American Sunday School Union.
Philadelphia, American Sunday
School Union, 1828. 30 vols.
ScCliTO; ViRVB (vol. 1 only).
                            31970
The American system. See
Hale, Nathan.

The American system. See National Republican Party. Virginia.

The American system. See
Raymond, Daniel.

American taxation. See St.
John, Samuel.

American Tract Society. Boston.
    Fourteenth annual report of
the American Tract Society, Boston, Read May 28, 1828. with
list of auxiliaries, benefactors,
depositories, &c. Boston, T. R.
Marvin, pr., 1828. 47, [1] p.
DLC; MeB; MeBaT; MiD-B; WHi.
                            31971
---- New York.
    No. 4. Active benevolence,
or, Some account of Lucy Careful. New York, Pub. by the
American Tract Society [1828]
32 p. RPB.   31972

---- The Christian drummer.
New York, American Tract Society Publication. Children's
tracts. Series 2, No. 6. [1828]
16 p. MB.   31973

---- Good child's soliloquy.
New York, Pub. by the American Tract Society. Series I, No.
xx. [1828?] 15, [1] p. RPB. 31974

---- No. 2. The history of Jenny Hickling: an authentic narrative. New York, Pub. by the
American Tract Society [1828?]
32 p. RPB.   31975

---- Little verses for good chil-
dren. New York, Pub. by the
American Tract Society, Series
I, No. II [1828?] 15, [1] p. RPB.
                            31976
---- No. 13. Memoir of David
Acheson, Jun., who died Aug.
1826, aged 13 years. New York,
Pub. by the American Tract So-
ciety, [1828?] 36 p. RPB. 31977

---- A new picture book. New
York, Pub. by the American
Tract Society, Series I, No. IV
[1828?] 15, [1] p. RPB.   31978

---- The pleasing instructer [!]
New York, Pub. by the American
Tract Society, Series I, No. VI
[1828?] 15, [1] p. RPB.   31979

---- No. 11. Scripture parables,
'in verse: with notes of explanation, and familiar instruction.
New York, Pub. by the American
Tract Society [1828?] 36 p. RPB.
                            31980
---- The shepherd boy. New York,
Pub. by the American Tract Society, Series I, No. V, [1828?]
15, [1] p. RPB.   31981

---- No. 27. The shipwreck; showing what sometimes happens on the
sea coasts: also giving a particular account of a poor sailor boy
...New York, Pub. by the American Tract Society [1828?] 14+ p.
RPB.   31982

---- Third annual report of the
American Tract Society, instituted
at New-York, 1825. Presented
May, 1828, with a list of auxiliaries and benefactors, the publications of the society &c. Pr. at
the Society's house, New-York, by

D. Fanshaw, 1828. 64 p. DLC; NNS; TNJ. 31983

---- Der Unterschied Zwischen wahren und falschen Bekehrungen. Dargestellt in einer Predigt von Friedr. Wilk Krummacher uber Isaschar, oder: das Lager Zwischen den Grenzen... New York, Herausgegeben von de Amerikanischen Tractat-Gesellschaft [1828?] 20 p. WHi. 31984

American Tract Society. Pennsylvania Branch
First annual report of the Pennsylvania Branch of the American Tract Society, with lists of auxiliaries and benefactors. Philadelphia, Pr. by Martin & Boden, 1828. 24 p. PHi. 31985

American Unitarian Association.
Third annual report to the American Unitarian Association, presented May 27, 1828. Boston, Bowles and Dearborn, [Press of Isaac R. Butts] 1828. 71 p. M; MBC; MMeT-Hi; MiD-B (24 p). 31986

American Watchman, Wilmington, Del.
1828. Address to the patrons of the American Watchman by the carriers. Wilmington, Watchman office [1828] 1 p. DLC. 31987

The American's guide: comprising the Declaration of independence; the Articles of Confederation; the Constitution of the United States; and the constitutions of the several states composing the Union... Philadelphia, Towar & Hogan, 1828. 478 p., 1 l. CU; Ct; DLC; GEU; MB; MH-L; NTR; OAU; OClWHi; OrSC; PPF; ScC; TNJ; WvHu; WyU. 31988

Americanischer stadt und land calender auf 1829. Philadelphia, Conrad Zentler [1828] 18 l. CLU; CtY; DLC; MWA; N; NN; NjP; NjR; P; PDoBHi; PHi; PPG; PPL. 31989

Der Amerikanisch-Teutsche hausfreund und Baltimore calender auf 1829. von Carl F. Egelmann. Baltimore, Johann T. Hanzsche [1828] 18 l. DLC; InU; MWA; PHi. 31990

Amherst Academy
Amherst Academy. Catalogue of the trustees, instructers and students. For the term ending Aug. 19, 1828. Amherst, J. S. and C. Adams, prs. [1828] 8 p. MAJ. 31991

---- Amherst Academy. Catalogue of the trustees, instructers and students. November, 1828. Amherst, Mass. J. S. and C. Adams, prs., [1828] 8 p. MA-H. 31992

Amherst College.
Amherst College. Catalogue of the corporation, faculty and students. October, 1828. Amherst, Mass., J. S. and C. Adams, prs. [1828] 16 p. CSmH; ICN; MA; MeB; NN; NjPT. 31993

---- Amherst College. Order of exercises at commencement. MDCCCXXVIII. August 27, --10 o'clock, A. M. Amherst, Mass. [Amherst], John S. and Charles Adams, prs. [1828] 3, [1] p. CtY; MA; MAJ; MBC. 31994

---- Amherst College. Order of exercises at the Junior exhibition MDCCCXXVIII. July 16, ---two o'clock, P. M. Amherst, Mass. [Amherst], J. S. & C. Adams, prs. [1828] 4 p. CtY; MA. 31995

---- Catalogus senatus academici, eorum qui munera et officia gesserunt quique alicujus gradus laurea donati sunt in Collegio Amherstiensi, Amherstiae, in Republica Massachusettensi. Amherstiae, J. S. et C. Adams, typographis.

MDCCCXXVIII. Rerumpublicarum
foederatarum Americae summae
potestatis anno LIII. 8 p. CSmH;
MA.   31996

---- Alexandrian Society
Amherst College. Order of
exercises at the exhibition of the
Alexandrian Society. Wednesday
evening, October 22, 1828. [Am-
herst], J. S. & C. Adams, prs.
[1828] 4 p. MA.   31997

---- Athenian Society
Amherst College. Order of
exercises at the exhibition of the
Athenian Society 1828. Wednesday evening Nov. 5. Amherst,
J. S. and C. Adams, prs. [1828]
4 p. MA-H.   31998

The ancient order of freemasonry. See Sherman, William.

Anderson, Henry James
Mathematical investigation of
the motion of solids on support-
ing surfaces, with a complete
solution of the cases in which
the oscillations are of small ex-
tent... Philadelphia, J. Kay,
Jun., 1828. 70 p. NN; PU-P;
VtU.   31999

Anderson, John
Speech [of Mr. Anderson, of
Maine] on the proposed increase
of the tariff delivered in the
House of Representatives of the
U. States, March 5, 1828.
Washington [1828] 8 p. DLC; MH.
                                 32000
Anderson, Rufus, 1796-1880
Memoir of Catharine Brown,
a Christian Indian of the Chero-
kee nation. 3d ed. Boston, Pub.
by Crocker and Brewster; New
York, Jonathan Leavitt, 1828.
viii, 144 p. CtY; ICN; MB; MH;
MdBE; NN; NjPT; Nv; OClWHi;
OkU; PHC; PU; RHi; TKL; WHi.
                                 32001

Andover Theological Seminary
Order of exercises at the Anniversary of the Theological
Seminary, Andover, Sept. 24,
1828. 4 p. MNtcA.   32002

Andrew Jackson, an interlude.
See Brice, James Frisby.

[Andrews, Ethan Allen]
Rules of pronunciation, in
reading Latin. New Haven, Pub.
by A.H. Maltby, 1828. 7 p.
CtY.   32003

Animal magnetism. See Inch-
bald, Elizabeth (Simpson).

Anker, Hillel Moses.
An appeal to the citizens of
Baltimore, containing conclusive
evidence of the base conspiracy
entered into by Moses Swarts,
Henry Barnett and several others.
... Baltimore, Pr. by John T.
Hanzsche, 1828. 28 p. MdHi.
                                 32004
Anna Ross. See Kennedy, Grace.

Annotator--Extra. See Democratic Party. Indiana.

Annual state register, of Con-
necticut for 1829. Hartford, John
Russell [1828] 72 l. CLU; Ct;
CtHi; CtW; CtY; InU; MHi; MWA;
MdBP; NjR.   32005

... Another humbug! More gross
falsehoods of the Junto exploded!
The extra-ordinary handbill of
the Antimasonic Central Commit-
tee which made its appearance on
Friday evening. ... Rochester,
Oct. 11th, 1828. Rochester Daily
Advertiser--Extra. Bdsd. NRHi.
                                 32006
... Anthony Rollo, the converted
Indian... Philadelphia, Baptist
General Tract Society [1828?] 12
p. [Baptist General Tract Society.
Tracts, v 3 no. 60] DLC; MiD-
B.   32007

Anti-Jackson convention. See
National Republican Party.

The Anti-Masonic almanac for
1829. By Edward Giddins. Rochester, E. Scrantom [1828] 24
l. CL; CLU; Ct; CtHi; CtNhHi;
CoCC; DLC; InU; MB; MWA;
MeP; MnU; NBuG; NHi; NN;
NRU; NjR; WHi.   32008

Anti-masonic tract, No. 1, Containing: 1. The penalties of masonry, 2. Mr. John R. Mul-
ford's renunciation of freemasonry, 3. Rev. Norman Bentley's
letter. [Boston, Pub. at the office of the Anti-Masonic Free
Press, 1828] 12 p. MB.   32009

Antiquarian and Historical Society of Illinois
    Proceedings of the Antiquari-
an and Historical Society of Illinois, at its first session in December, 1827. With an address
delivered by the Hon. James Hall,
president of the society. Edwardsville, Pr. by Robert K. Fleming
at the office of the Illinois Corrector, 1828. 22 p. ICN; MH;
OC; PPAmP.   32010

---- Vandalia, August 1st, 1828.
Sir: Accompanying this letter,
you will receive a copy of the
proceedings of the Antiquarian
and Historical Society of Illinois.
[Vandalia? 1828] Bdsd. ICN.
                        32011
Anton, Carl Gottlob, 1751-1818
    Historia de la destruccion de
los templarios. Traducida al
español por C. Lanuza. Nueva
York, Lanuza, Mendia y. 1828.
xxiii, 91 p. MB.   32012

The Apostle Paul a Unitarian.
See Stetson, Caleb.

An appeal to the American
churches. See American Board
of Commissioners for Foreign

Missions.

An appeal to the moral & reli-
geious of all denominations; or,
An exposition of some of the in-
discretions of General Andrew
Jackson, as copied from the records, and certified by the clerk
of Mercer County, Kentucky.
New-York, R. Johnson, pr.,
1828. 8 p. MWA; MnH; PPFM.
                        32013
Appeal to the Northern and Eastern churches in behalf of the
South Western Theological Seminary at Maryville, Tennessee.
n. p., 1828. 8 p. MH; PPL; T.
                        32014
An appeal to the people of the
state of Pennsylvania on the
alarming progress of the American Sunday School Union, and its
subordinate institutions. Philadelphia, Pub. for the author,
1828. 16 p. DLC; PHi.
                        32015
An appeal to the unprejudiced
judgment of the freemen of Vermont. [1828?] 16 p. MBC.
                        32016
The application of Christianity to
education. See Flushing Institute.
Flushing, N. Y.

Arbuckle, James
    The sabbatical institute, an
Oration, delivered before the
Orange County Union, auxiliary
to the General Union for Promoting the Observance of the Christian Sabbath... New York, John
P. Haven; E. Conrad, pr., 1828.
23 p. MBAt; MH; NjR; PPiPT.
                        32017
Archbold, John Frederick, 1785-
1870
    A collection of the forms and
entries, which occur in practice,
in the courts of King's Bench and
Common Pleas, in personal actions and ejectment. New York,
E. B. Gould, 1828. xi, [1], 626
p. CU; GU-L; ICL. IaU-L; In-SC;

KyOW; MH-L; MiDU-L; MoU; NIC-L; NNC-L; NNLI; NcD; NjR.
32018

---- The forms of indictment with evidence necessary to support them including the statutes which make many valuable regulations relative to criminal proceedings... New York, Treadway & Bogart, Law Publishers. Boston, Theodore P. Bogart [Gould & Jacobus, prs.] 1828. iv, 412 p. CU; ICLaw; NNLI; NcWsW; NjR; PPB; PU-L; TxWB-L.
32019

Argus extra. See Democratic Party. Kentucky.

Aristotle, pseud.
The works, of Aristotle, the famous philosopher, in four parts, containing I. His complete master-piece;... II. His experienced midwife;... III. His book of problems. ... IV. His last legacy. ... A new edition. New-England, Pr. for the publishers, 1828. 288 p. PPL.   32020

Arithmetic explained. See Beecher, Catharine Esther.

Arithmetical rules and tables of money, weights, measures, and time; together with abbreviations used in writing and printing;... Selected and arranged for the use of schools, and seminaries, and as introductory to T. Smiley's Popular system of arithmetic... Philadelphia, J. Grigg, Stereotyped by L. Johnson, 1828. 48 p. PP.   32021

Arkansas (Territory)
Acts, passed at a special session of the General Assembly of the territory of Arkansas: Which was begun and held at the town of Little Rock, on Monday, the sixth day of October, and ended on Wednesday, the twenty-second day of October, one thousand eight hundred and twenty-eight, pursuant to a proclamation of the governor, dated twentieth June, 1828. Pub. by authority. Little Rock, Pr. by William E. Woodruff, pr. to the territory, 1828. 48 p., 1 l., [2] p. Ar-SC; DLC; Ia-L; M; MH-L; Mi-L; Or-SC.   32022

---- Acts, passed at the fifth session of the General Assembly of the territory of Arkansas: Which was begun and held at the town of Little Rock, on Monday, the first day of October, and ended on Wednesday, the thirty-first day of October, one thousand eight hundred and twenty-seven. Pub. by authority. Little Rock, Pr. by William E. Woodruff, pr. to the territory, 1828. 80, [2] p. Ar-SC; ArU; DLC; Ia-L; M; MH-L; Mi-L; Or-SC.
32023

---- Journals of a special session of the General Assembly of the territory of Arkansas: Begun and held at Little Rock, in said territory, October 6, 1828, pursuant to a proclamation of the governor, dated 20th June, 1828. Little Rock, Pr. by William E. Woodruff, pr. to the territory, 1828. 69 p. ArU.   32024

---- Rules of the superior court of the territory of Arkansas. Adopted at April term, 1828. [Little Rock, Wm. E. Woodruff, pr., 1828?] 14 p. TxU.   32025

[Armstrong, James L.]
An account of the trial and execution of the poor and unfortunate John Woods, a youth about eighteen years old; who was executed at Fort Strother, in the year 1814, under the orders of General Andrew Jackson, as given by eye witnesses of that sickening and heartrending transaction... Russellville, Ky., Pr. by

C. Rhea, 1828. 16 p. DLC.
32026
[----] John Woods. A Tennesseean, No. 1. [n. p. 1828?] 8 p.
WHi.   32027

[----] Reminiscences; or, An extract from the catalogue of General Jackson's 'juvenile indiscre-
tions,' between the ages of 23
and 60. [n. p. 1828?] 8 p. DLC.
32028
Armstrong, Lebbeus, 1775-1860
A sermon, delivered in Northampton, (Montgomery co.) March
6, 1828, on the death of Governor
Clinton. By Lebbeus Armstrong...
Saratoga Springs [N. Y.] Pr. by
G. M. Davison, 1828. 24 p.
CSmH; MB; MBAt; MBC; N; NN;
OCHP.   32029

[Arnold, Samuel James]
My aunt; a petit comedy, in
two acts. New-York, Pr. by R.
Wauchope, 1828. 34+ p. MH.
32030
Arthur Monteith, a moral tale.
See Stoddart, Isabella.

Ashmead, William
The Christian's duty in relation to the contraction and payment of debts: a sermon
preached in the First Prebyteri-
an Church of Philadelphia... Nov.
9, 1828. Philadelphia, D. & S.
Neall, prs., 1828. 18 p. MB;
MH; ScC.   32031

Associate Synod of North America.
A display of the religious
principles of the Associate Synod
of North America. Revised by the
Associate Synod, 1813. 5th ed.
with notes. Albany, Pr. by Webster & Wood, 1828. 177, [1] p.
MH; NN; NNC; NcMHi; NjPT;
OO; PHi; PPL; PPPrHi.   32032

Association for the Relief of Respectable Aged Indigent Females,

New York.
The fifteenth annual report of
the Association for the Relief of
Respectable, Aged, Indigent Fe-
males, established in New-York,
Feb. 7, 1814, presented at the
annual meeting of the Society,
November 27, 1828. New-York,
J. Seymour, pr., 1828. 11, [1]
p. NNG.   32033

The asylum; or Alonzo and Melissa. See Mitchell, Isaac.

Asylum for the Relief of Persons
Deprived of the Use of their
Reason. See Philadelphia.

Friends Asylum for the Insane.

At the state convention of the
friends of Gen'l Jackson. See
Democratic Party. Connecticut.

The Atlantic souvenir, a Christ-
mas and New Year's offering,
1829. Philadelphia, Carey, Lea
& Carey [1828] [12], 360 p.
CSmH; DLC; MB; MWA; MdHi;
NNC; PPL (xii, pr. on one side
of page only; 360 p.); PPi; VtVe;
BrMus.   32034

Atlee, Edwin Augustus, 1776-
1852
Essay at poetry, or A collection of fugitive pieces with the
life of Eugenius Laude Watts...
Philadelphia, T. S. Manning, pr.,
1828. 152, [4] p. CSmH; CtY; IU;
MH; MiD; MnU; PHi; PP; PPL;
PSC-Hi; RPB; BrMus.   32035

Auber, Daniel Francois Esprit
Auber's opera, "Masaniello,"
containing the Italian text, with
an English translation and the music of all the principal airs. Boston, Oliver Ditson; A. B. Kidder's
music typography [1828] 22 p.
NjR.   32036

Auburn Theological Seminary
Catalogue of the officers and

students of the Theological Seminary at Auburn, New York, January, 1828. Auburn, Pr. by T.
M. Skinner, 1828. 8 p. MBC;
MWA; N; NAuT; NN.   32037

---- Order of commencement of
the Theological Seminary, Auburn, August 20, 1828. Richard
Oliphant, pr., Auburn [1828]
Bdsd. NAuT.   32038

Auctions ... [New York, W. A.
Mercein, 1828] 8 p. MH-BA.
                         32039
Auctions. At a large and respectable meeting of citizens,
convened at Masonic Hall, on
Friday evening, 2d inst. for the
purpose of taking into consideration the ruinous effects of the
present auction system... the following resolutions were offered
and unanimously adopted. [New
York, 21 May, 1828] 2 p. PHi.
                         32040
Augsburg Confession
The Augsburgh Confession,
containing the articles of faith of
the Evangelical Lutheran Church,
with notes and observations. By
Rev. E. L. Hazelius, Schoharie
(N. Y.) Pr. at the Western Conference Press, by L. Cuthbert,
1828. 20 p. PPLT.   32041

Augusta College
By-laws and system of education, established at Augusta College in Kentucky: Pub. by order
of the Trustees. Cincinnati, W.
M. & O. Farnsworth, Jun., prs.,
1828. 35 p. ICU.   32042

[Aurora]
Warehousing system and gov-
ernment credits... [Philadelphia,
Philadelphia chamber of com-
merce, 1828] 2 p. l., [7]-57 p.
MH-BA.   32043

[Austin, Benjamin] 1752-1820
Vindication of the land agent,

and refutation of anonymous "Re-
marks, [sic.] addressed to the
Governor, Council, and Legisla-
ture of the state of Maine." By
Honestus [pseud.] Portland,
Thomas Todd, pr., 1828. 34 p.
MH; MWA; MeH; MeHi; MeP;
PP.   32044

Austin, James Trecothick, 1784-
1870
The life of Elbridge Gerry.
With contemporary letters. To
the close of the American Revo-
lution. Boston, Wells and Lilly,
1828-29. 2 vols. CLU; CSmH;
CSt; CtHT-W; CtSoP; CtY; DLC;
IU; IaU; InI; KU; MB; MBAt;
MH; MHi; MWA; MdBE; MdBP;
MeB; MiD-B; MnHi; MoSM;
NBLiHi; NCH; NIC; NSyU;
Nh; NjPT; NjR; OU; PHi; PPAmP;
PPL; PU; RNHi; RPB; TU; Vi;
WHi; WaU; BrMus.   32045

Autumn.   Manhood--The autumn
of life. Woodstock, Pr. and
sold by D. Watson, 1828. 19 p.
VtHi.   32046

Aux Catholiques des Etats-Unis.
See Fenelon, pseud.

Auxiliary Foreign Mission Society. Boston.
Proceedings of the seventeenth
anniversary of the Auxiliary Foreign Mission Society of Boston
and Vicinity. May 29, 1828. Boston, T. R. Marvin, pr., 1828.
32 p. DLC; MHi; WHi.   32047

Auxiliary Foreign Mission Socie-
ty. Brookfield.
Proceedings of the Auxiliary
Foreign Mission Society of the
Brookfield Association at their
fifth annual meeting, Oct. 24, 1828.
Brookfield, E. & G. Merriam,
prs., 1828. 28 p. MBC.   32048

---- Eastern District Fairfield
County, Connecticut.

Fourth annual report... Oct. 2, 1828. New Haven, Pr. by N. Whiting, 1828. CtY (not loc. 1970) 32049

---- Franklin County.
Sixteenth annual report of the Auxiliary Foreign Mission Society, of Franklin County, presented at a meeting held in Ashfield, October 8, 1828. Greenfield, Mass., Phelps & Clark, prs., 1828. 14 p. MHi.   32050

---- Hartford Co., Conn.
Fifth annual report of the Auxiliary Foreign Mission Society of Hartford County, December 1828. Hartford, W. Hudson and L. Skinner, prs., 1828. 30, 1 p. Ct; CtY.   32051

---- New Haven.
Third annual meeting and report of the Auxiliary Foreign Mission Society of New-Haven, October 6, 1828. New-Haven, Baldwin & Treadway, prs., 1828. 12 p. CtY; MBC; MiD-B.   32052

---- New York and Brooklyn.
First annual report of the Auxiliary Foreign Mission Society of New-York and Brooklyn. New-York, Pr. by J. Seymour, 1828. 38 p. DLC; MBC.   32053

Auxiliary Foreign Missionary Society. Farmington, Conn. and Vicinity.
Proceedings at the 4th anniversary, 1827. Hartford, 1828. 12 p. CtY.   32054

Auxiliary Missionary Society of the Middlesex Association. See American Board of Commissioners for Foreign Missions.

Auxiliary Missionary Society of West Association of New Haven County.
Annual report of the ... at a meeting holden in Waterbury, Oc-

tober 8, 1828. New Haven, Pr. by Hezekiah Howe, 1828. 21 p. CtHi.   32055

Auxiliary Union of the City of Boston.
Proceedings in relation to the formation of the Auxiliary Union of the city of Boston, for promoting the observance of the Christian Sabbath, with the address of the General Union to the people of the United States. Boston, T. R. Marvin, pr., 1828. 16 p. CtHT-W; DLC; ICN; ICU; IU; MBAt; MBC; MHi; MNtcA; MWA; MiD-B; NjPT; OCHP; RPB; WHi.   32056

B

Bachmair, John James
A complete German grammar, containing the theory of the language, through all the parts of speech. Philadelphia, Pub. by G. W. Mentz, C. Zentler, pr., 1828. 144 p. MH; MdBS; PAtM; PPG.   32057

Bacon, E.
An essay on infant cultivation: with a compendium of the analytical method of instruction... adopted at Spitalfields infants' school; with general observations on the system of infant tuition, &c. By J. R. Brown, master. To which is added, a manual of the system of instruction pursued at the Infant School, Chester Street, Philadelphia. By E. Bacon. Philadelphia, Clark & Raser, prs., 1828. 56 p. DLC; ICU; MH; MWA; NjR; PHi; PPL.   32058

Bacon, Francis
Essays, moral, economical and political... Stereotyped at the Boston Type and Stereotype Foundry. Boston, Pub. by T. Bedlington, 1828. 218 p. DLC; IObB;

18   Bacon

IcMcC; InRE; MA; MMeT-Hi;
MdBS-P; NN; NbOP; PPL; PU;
ScCoT; TNJ.   32059

Bacon, Leonard, 1802-1881
  A discourse preached in the
Center Church, in New Haven,
August 27, 1828, at the funeral
of Jehudi Ashmun, esq., colonial
agent of the American colony of
Liberia... With the address at
the grave, by R. R. Gurley. New
Haven, Pr. by Hezekiah Howe,
1828. 36 p. CSmH; Ct; CtHT-W;
CtHi; CtY; ICU; MA; MB;
MBAt; MH; MiD-B; NNUT; PHi;
TxH; WHi; BrMus.   32060

Bacon, William, 1789-1863
  Salvation made sure... with an
appendix... Revised ed. Phila-
delphia, Stereotyped by G. J.
Loomis, Pr. for the author, 1828.
156 p. ArBaA; DLC; ICMcC.
                        32061
Bagby, A. P.
  To the public. Tuskaloosa,
Grantland & Mitchell, prs. [1828]
1 p. DLC.   32062

Bailey, B. F.
  An oration, delivered at Burlington, Vt., on the fourth of July,
1828, being the fifty-second anniversary of American independence.
Burlington, Pr. by E. & T. Mills,
1828. 18 p. CSmH; MWA; N;
VtHi; VtU.   32063

Bailey, Ebenezer, 1795-1839
  Review of the mayor's report,
on the subject of schools, as far
as it relates to the High School
for Girls. Boston, Bowles &
Dearborn, 1828. 54 p. CLU;
CSmH; Ct; CtHT-W; DLC; IC;
ICJ; MBAt; MBC; MHi; MiD-B;
NjR; OO; BrMus.   32064

Bailey, Elijah
  Thoughts on the nature and
principles of government, both
civil and ecclesiastical. Pre-

pared for the more immediate
perusal of the Reformed Methodists. Bennington, Darius Clark,
1828. 36 p. MB; MH; ScCoB;
BrMus.   32065

Bailey's Franklin almanac for
1829. By Joshua Sharp. Philadelphia, Lydia R. Bailey [1828] 18 l.
InU; MWA; PHi.   32066

---- By Joshua Sharp. Philadelphia, Thomas Desilver; Lydia R.
Bailey, pr. [1828] 18 l. CtY.
                        32067
Bailey's Washington almanac for
1829. By Joshua Sharp. Philadelphia, Lydia R. Bailey [1828] 18
l. CtY; DLC; MH; MWA; PPL.
                        32068
Baillie, Joanna
  The bride; a drama in three
acts. Philadelphia, Pub. by C.
Neal, Mifflin and Parry, prs.,
1828. 74 p. CSmH; MH; MWA;
NN.   32069

[Baker, Caroline (Horwood)]
  Little Emma and her father.
A lesson for proud children written by Miss Horwood. Philadelphia, Pub. by Morgan & Yeager
[1828] 15 p. DLC.   32070

[Balcom, D. A.]
  The devil on politics, religion,
and other subjects. Pr. at Batavia, N. Y. 1828. 35 p. N.
                        32071
[Baldwin, Charles N.]
  A universal biographical dictionary, containing the lives of
the most celebrated characters of
every age and nation... To which
is added a dictionary of the principal divinities and heroes of
Grecian and Roman mythology;
and a biographical dictionary of
eminent living characters. Hartford, Pub. by S. Andrus, 1828.
444 p. CtHi; DLC; IP; KKcB;
MiU; NCH; PPL; TxU.   32072

Baldwin, Elihu Whittlesey, 1789-
1840
Considerations for the American patriot. A sermon delivered
on occasion of the annual thanksgiving, December 12, 1827....
New-York, John P. Haven, 1828.
24 p. Ct; CtY; DLC; MBC; NBC;
NHi; NIC; NjR.   32073

---- The five apprentices. (Pro-
crastination; or, The history of
Edward Crawford.) Philadelphia,
American Sunday School Union,
1828. 108 p. BrMus.   32074

Balfour, Walter, 1776-1852
A letter to Dr. Allen, President of Bowdoin College, in reply to his lecture on the doctrine
of universal salvation, delivered
in the chapel of Bowdoin College,
and published by request of the
students. Charlestown (Mass.),
G. Davidson, 1828. 72 p. MiD-
B   32075

---- Three essays. On the inter-
mediate state of the dead. The
resurrection from the dead. And
on the Greek terms rendered
judge, judgment, condemned, con-
demnation, damned, damnation,
&c. in the New Testament. With
remarks on Mr. Hudson's letters
in vindication of a future retribu-
tion, addressed to Mr. Hosea
Ballou, of Boston. Charlestown
(Ms.), G. Davidson, 1828. 359,
[1] p. PPL.   32076

Ballou, Hosea, 1771-1852
A candid review of a pamphlet entitled "A candid reply;" the
whole being a doctrinal contro-
versary between Hopkintonian
and the Universalist... 2d ed.
Hallowell, W. F. Lane, 1828.
Williamson: 481. (1st ed. pub.
[1809?])   32077

---- A discourse delivered at the
Universalist Church, in Lombard

Street, Philadelphia, on Monday
evening, June 2, 1828, at the ordination of T. Fisk. Philadelphia,
Charles Alexander, pr., 1828.
14 p. MMeT-Hi; MWA; NhHi;
RPB.   32078

---- A letter to Rev. Dr. Lyman
Beecher. Boston, Bowen & Cush-
ing, 1828. 4 p. MBC; MMeT-Hi;
OClWHi.   32079

---- A review of Dr. Church's
two sermons, on the final condi-
tion of all men; published in the
National Preacher, No. 3, Vol. 3,
Boston, Pr. and pub. by Henry
Bowen, 1828. 24 p. CtHT-W;
CtY; DLC; MBNEH; MMeT; MWA;
PPL.   32080

---- A sermon delivered in the
Second Universalist Meeting in
Boston, on Fast Day morning,
April 3, 1828. Boston, Pub. by
Brown & Cushing, 1828. 12 p.
CtHT-W; DLC; ICMe; MBC; MH;
MeHi; MiD-B; BrMus.   32081

---- ---- Repr. at Gloucester,
[Mass.] 1828. 12 p. CLU; CSmH;
MWA.   32082

---- A treatise on atonement; in
which the finite nature of sin is
argued, its cause and consequences
as such; the necessity and nature
of atonement; and its glorious
consequences, in the final recon-
ciliation of all men to holiness
and happiness... 3d ed., to which
is prefixed a letter of the author
further declarative of his views
upon the same subject. Hallowell,
C. Spaulding, 1828. 240 p.
ICMcC; KWiU; MH; MeB; MeHi;
MiD-B; NcD; PPL; RNHi. 32083

---- The Universalist hymn-book.
By Hosea Ballou and Edward
Turner. 4th ed. Boston, Munroe
and Francis, 1828. 396 p. DLC;
IEG; MBC; MH-AH; MWA;

NjPT.   32084

Balthis, John. See Burnside,
A. (note)

Baltimore (City)
  The ordinances of the Mayor
and City Council of Baltimore,
passed at the extra session in
1827, and at the January session,
1828. To which is annexed, sundry acts of Assembly, a list of
the officers of the corporation,
the summary of the register...
Baltimore, Pr. by Benjamin
Edes, 1828. 212, 58 p. MH-L;
MdBB.   32085

---- Report of the trustees for
the poor of Baltimore city and
county. 1828. [Baltimore, 1828]
7, [11] p. MBAt; MdHi.   32086

Baltimore and Ohio Railroad
  An act... to authorize the Baltimore and Ohio Railroad Company to construct a railroad
through Pennsylvania, in a direction from Baltimore to the Ohio
River [Baltimore] Wm. Wooddy,
pr., [1828] 16 p. MH-BA; BrMus.
                             32087
---- Report of the engineers, on
the reconnoissance and surveys,
made in reference to the Baltimore and Ohio Rail Road. Baltimore, Pr. by William Wooddy,
1828. 188, [1] p. CtY; DBRE;
DIC; DLC; DeGE; ICJ; M; MB;
MBAt; MBC; MH; MdBE; MdBJ;
MdHi; MnHi; NIC; NcD; PHi;
PPF; PPL; BrMus.   32088

---- Second annual report of the
president and directors to the
stockholders of the Baltimore &
Ohio Rail Road Company. Baltimore, Pr. by James Lucas, 1828.
11, 45 p. CtY; IU; MCM; MWA;
NN; NNE.   32089

---- ---- Baltimore, Pr. by
William Wooddy, 1828, 11, 43 p.

CtY; DBRE; DLC; MH-BA; MdHi;
NNE; NjP; WU.   32090

Baltimore and Susquehanna Rail
Road Company
  An act to incorporate the Bal-
timore and Susquehanna Rail
Road Company, passed December
session, 1827. Baltimore, Pr. by
Benjamin Edes, 1828. 16 p. DLC;
MdBE; MdHi; NNE; PHi.   32091

---- Report and proceedings in
relation to a rail road from Baltimore to the Susquehanna. Baltimore. Pr. by B. Edes, 1828.
23 p. DLC; MBAt; MCM; MdHi;
NN; NNC.   32092

---- Report on the Baltimore and
Susquehanna Rail Road. By Gen-
eral J. G. Swift, Chief Engineer.
Also the annual report of the
president and directors to the
stockholders. Baltimore, Pr. by
Lucas & Deaver, 1828. 10, 24 p.
CtY; DBRE; DIC; DLC; IU; MH-
BA; MdBP; MdHi; MiU-T; NIC;
NN; NNE; NjR; PHi; PPL; WU;
BrMus.   32093

A Baltimorean, pseud. See Continuation of the numbers.

Bangs, Nathan, 1778-1862
  An examination of the doctrine
of predestination, as contained
in a sermon, preached in Burlington, Vermont, by Daniel Haskel,
minister of the congregation. 2d
ed. New York, N. Bangs and J.
Emory, Azor Hoyt, pr., 1828.
167 p. MeB; NBuG; OO; T.
                             32094
---- Letters to young ministers
of the Gospel. 2nd ed. New York,
N. Bangs and J. Emory, 1828.
194 p. CtMW; IaMpI; MB; MnSH.
                             32095
Bank of Penn Township
  An act to incorporate the Bank
of Penn Township, in the county
of Philadelphia, and an act to re-

charter certain banks, together
with several acts of Assembly
relating to banks, and the by-
laws of the Bank of Penn Township... Philadelphia, 1828. 56 p.
NjP; PHi.   32096

Bank of the United States, 1816-
1836
Report of the proceedings of
the triennial meeting of the
stockholders of the Bank of the
United States. Held according to
the thirteenth article of the elev-
enth section of the charter, at
Philadelphia... on the first day of
September, 1828. Philadelphia,
Pr. by Garden & Thompson,
1828. 10 p. CSmH; DLC; MH;
MHi; MdBJ; OClWHi; PHi;
PPAmP.   32097

---- ---- Philadelphia, Pr. by
Garden & Thompson, 1828. 18 p.
PPL.   32098

Bank of Virginia
An act for incorporating the
Bank of Virginia, passed the 30th
January, 1804; and, an act extending the charter of the Bank
of Virginia, passed January 24th,
1814. With the rules and regulations for the government of the
bank. Richmond, Va., Pr. by
John Warrock, 1828. 44 p.
CSmH; DLC.   32099

Baptism; an authentic narrative.
By a clergyman of the Church of
England. Hartford, press of the
Episcopal Watchman [F. J. Hunt-
ington] 1828. 17 p. CtY. 32100

Baptism: Objections in miniature to Antipaedo-Baptist views.
Boston, Benjamin Jones, pr.,
1828. 16 p. MBC; NjPT; RPB;
TxHuT.   32101

Baptist Auxiliary Education Society of the Young Men of Boston.

Constitution of the Baptist
Auxiliary Education Society, of
the Young Men of Boston. Instituted and organized February 22,
1819. Boston, Press of Putnam
and Hunt, 1828. 12 p. MWA;
NRAB; NjR.   32102

Baptist Education Society
Eleventh annual meeting of the
Baptist Education Society, of the
state of New-York. Held at Ham-
ilton, June 5, 1828. Hamilton,
N. Y., Pr. by G. Williams &
Co., 1828. 18 p. MB; TxFS.
                             32103
Baptists. Alabama. Baptist As-
sociation
Minutes of the Baptist Asso-
ciation. [1828] Title from the
Huntsville, Ala. Democrat, Nov.
7, 1828.   32104

---- ---- Bethlehem Association.
Minutes of the Bethlehem Bap-
tist Association convened at the
Pidgeon Creek Church, Monroe
County... 1828. Claiborne [Ala.]
Pr. at the Office of the Herald,
1828. 8 p. Ar.   32105

---- ---- Mount Zion Association.
Minutes of the fifth annual
session of the Mount Zion Baptist Association, convened at Hebron Meeting-House, Shelby County, Alabama, from the 20th to
the 23rd September, inclusive,
A. D. 1828... Montgomery, From
the Journal Press, 1828. 8 p.
NRAB.   32106

---- ---- Mulberry Association.
Minutes of the first session of
the Mulberry Baptist Association,
begun and held at the Mulberry
Meeting House, Bibb County, Ala-
bama, from the 15th to the 17th
November inclusive, A. D. 1828.
Selma, Ala., Thomas J. Frow,
pr., 1828. 11 p. Title from Mc
Murtrie.   32107

---- Connecticut. Stonington Union Association.
Minutes of the Stonington Union Baptist Association; held in North Stonington, June 18th and 19th, 1828. Stonington, W. & J. B. Storer, prs., 1828. 8 p. NRAB.
32108

---- Delaware. Delaware Association.
Minutes of the Delaware Baptist Association, held at Brynzion, Kent County, Delaware, on the 31st of May, and 1st and 2d of June, 1828. 7 p. NRAB.
32109

---- Georgia. Chattahoochie Association.
Minutes of the Chattahoochie Baptist Association, convened at Hephzibah Church, Gadsden County, Middle Florida, on the 24th and 26th of October, 1828. 8 p. NRAB.
32110

---- Illinois. Muddy River Association.
Minutes of the (third) Muddy River Baptist Association, begun and held at the East Fork of Muddy River Church, Franklin County, Illinois, Saturday before the third Lord's Day in Sept. 1828, and days following. [1828] 4 p. ISB.
32111

---- Illinois and Missouri. Friends to Humanity.
Minutes of the annual meeting of the Baptized Churches of Christ, Friends to Humanity, held at Cantine Creek, St. Clair County, Illinois, September 19, 1828. [1828] [8] p. ISB.
32112

---- Indiana. Coffee Creek Association.
Minutes. The Coffee Creek Association of Baptists met at Indian Kentucky meeting house 6th September, 1828. [C. P. J. Arion, pr., Madison (Ia.) 1828]
3 p. InFrlC.
32113

---- ---- Flat Rock Association.
Minutes of the Flat Rock Association of Baptists, began and held at Mount Moriah Church, Decatur county, Ind. on the 3d, 4th, and 5th days of October, 1828... 4 p. InFrlC.
32114

---- ---- Indianapolis Association.
Minutes of the Indianapolis Association, begun and held at Liberty Church, Marion County, Indiana, the Friday before the 4th Saturday in August, 1828. [Pr. by John Douglass] 8 p. NRAB.
32115

---- ---- Laughery Association
Minutes of the eleventh annual meeting of the Laughery Association of Baptists, held at the 1st Baptist church in Manchester, Dearborn county, Ind. commencing the 3d Friday in September, 1828. 4 p. InFrlC.
32116

---- ---- Lost River Association.
Minutes of the third annual meeting of the Lost-River Association, held at Lost-River meeting-house, Orange county, Ia. the first Saturday, Lord's day and Monday in September, 1828. [J. Allen, pr., Salem, Indiana] 4 p. InFrlC; TxDaHi.
32117

---- ---- Salem Association.
Minutes of the Salem Baptist Association, held at Harvey's Creek meeting house, Gibson county, Indiana, commencing on Friday, preceding the fourth Lord's day in September, 1828. [Pr. at the office of the New-Harmony Gazette.] 4 p. In.
32118

---- ---- Silver Creek Association.
Minutes of the Silver Creek Association, held at Pigeon Roost

Church, Scott county, Indiana, commencing the fourth Saturday in August, 1828... [Joseph A. Lingan, pr., Charlestown, (Ia.)] 4 p. In.   32119

---- ---- Union Association.
Minutes of the Union Association of Baptists, held at Busreon [sic] meeting-house, Sullivan county, Indiana, on the twentieth, twenty-first and twenty-second of September, 1828. [Pr. at the office of the Wabash Telegraph, Vincennes, Ind.] 4 p. InFrlC.
32120
---- ---- Wabash District Association.
Minutes of the Wabash District Association of Baptists, held at Mount Pleasant Church, in Edgar county, Illinois, commencing the Saturday before the first Lord's day in October, 1828. [From the press of Elihu Stout, Vincennes, Indiana] 4 p. In.   32121

---- ---- White River Association.
Minutes of the White River Association, held at Vernon meeting-house, the second Saturday in August, 1828. 4 p. InFrlC.
32122
---- Kentucky. Bethel Association.
Minutes of the fourth Bethel Baptist Association, held at Little West-fork meeting house, Montgomery county, Tenn. The 27th 28th and 29th days of September 1828. Russellville, Ky., Pr. by Charles Rhea at the office of the "Weekly Messenger." 1828. 2 p. KyBgW; KyU; LNB; NRAB; NcD.
32123
---- ---- Boon's Creek Association.
Minutes of the Boon's Creek Association of Baptists, held at Friendship Meeting House, Clark County, Ky. Commencing on the third Saturday in September,

1828. Lexington, Ky., Smith & Palmer, prs., 1828. 8 p. KyLoS; NRAB.   32124

---- ---- Bracken Association.
Minutes of the Bracken Association of Baptists, held at Wilson's Run meeting house, Fleming County, Ky. on the 1st Saturday in September, 1828, and continued by adjournment until the Monday following, inclusive. Maysville, Pr. at the Eagle Office, 1828. 8 p. NRAB.   32125

---- ---- Convention.
Minutes of the second meeting of the Baptist Association, which commenced on the first Saturday in October, 1828, at Hillsborough Meeting House, in Woodford County, Kentucky. [A. G. Hodges, pr., Commentator Office, Frankfort, Ky.] 6 p. ICU; Ky. 32126

---- ---- Elkhorn Association.
Minutes of the Elkhorn Association of Baptists. [N. L. Finnell, pr., (Georgetown, Ky.) 1828] 8 p. ICU (film); NRAB.
32127
---- ---- Franklin Association.
Minutes of the Franklin Association of Baptists, held at Indian Fork meeting-house Shelby County, Kentucky, on the second Friday in October 1828. 4, 12 p. NRAB.   32128

---- ---- Gasper's River Association.
Minutes of the seventeenth annual meeting of Gasper's River Association, of United Baptists, held at Walton's G. M. H. Ohio County, Kentucky. The 23d, 24th, and 25th days of August, 1828. Russellville, Ky., Pr. by Charles Rhea, 1828. 4 p. NRAB. 32129

---- ---- Licking Association.
Minutes of the Licking Association of Particular Baptists,

held at Bryan's, Fayette County, on the 2nd Saturday in September, 1828, and two succeeding days. [H. Miller, pr., Clarke County, Ky.] 3, [1] p. NRAB.
32130

---- ---- Long Run Association.
Minutes of the Long Run Association of Baptists, held at Salem the first Friday in September, 1828. [D. Hockersmith, pr. Advocate Office, Shelbyville, Ky.] 4 p. NRAB.   32131

---- ---- North Bend Association.
Minutes of the 26th meeting of the North-Bend Association, 1828. At the North-Bend Association of Baptists, begun and held at Dry Creek meeting house, Campbell County, Kentucky, 3d Friday in August, 1828... 4 p. NRAB.
32132

---- ---- Russell's Creek Association.
Minutes of the 24th Russell's Creek Association of Baptists, held at Brush Creek meeting-house, Green County, Ky. on the 20th September, 1828 and days following. 4 p. NRAB.   32133

---- ---- Salem Association.
Minutes of the Salem Association of Baptists, held at Chaplin's Fork Meeting-house, Nelson County, on the 1st Friday and Saturday in October, 1828. 4 p. NRAB.   32134

---- ---- South District Association.
Minutes of the South District Association of Baptists, convened at Cartwrights Creek Meeting house, Washington County, Kentucky the 3rd Saturday in August, 1828. 3 p. NRAB. 32135

---- Maine. Bowdoinham Association.

Minutes of the Bowdoinham Association, held in Bloomfield, Sept. 24 & 25, 1828, together with their circular & corresponding letters. 8 p. NRAB. 32136

---- ---- Convention.
Minutes of the Maine Baptist convention held in Readfield, October 8 & 9, 1828. Hallowell, [Me.] Spaulding & Livermore, prs. [1828] 23 p. MeB.   32137

---- ---- Cumberland Association.
Minutes of the seventeenth anniversary of the Cumberland Association, held at Paris, Wednesday and Thursday, October 1st and 2d, 1828. [Portland, Pr. at the Book & Job Office, 1828] 12 p. MeHi.
32138

---- ---- Eastern Maine Association.
Minutes of the tenth anniversary of the Eastern Maine Baptist Association, holden with the Baptist Church in Cherryfield, on Wednesday and Thursday, September 3 and 4, 1828. 11 p. [Ellsworth, Pr. at the Courier Office] NRAB.   32139

---- ---- Lincoln Association.
Minutes of the Lincoln Association, held at China, September 17th & 18th, 1828. Thomaston, Pr. by Edwin Moody, 1828. 12 p. NRAB.   32140

---- ---- Penobscot Association.
Minutes of the third anniversary of the Penobscot Association, holden at Sommerville, September 10 & 11, 1828, together with their circular and corresponding letters. Bangor, Me., Burton & Carter, prs., 1828. 15 p. MeBa.   32141

---- ---- York Association.

Minutes of the York Baptist Association, which held its anniversary at Berwick, (Maine) June 11th and 12th, 1828. Saco, (Me.), Pr. by Alex C. Putnam, 1828. 8 p. NRAB.   32142

---- Maryland. Baltimore Association.

Minutes of the Baltimore Baptist Association, held by appointment, at Black Rock, Maryland, May 15, 16 & 17, 1828. [Washington City, S. C. Ustick, pr., 1828] 11 p. NRAB.   32143

---- ---- Columbia Association.

Minutes of the ninth annual meeting of the Columbia Baptist Association, held by appointment, at Nanjemoy Meeting-House, in Charles county and state of Maryland, Aug. 21, 22, & 23, 1828. Washington City, Pr. by Stephen C. Ustick, 1828. 28 p. ViRVB.   32144

---- Massachusetts. Boston Association.

Minutes of the seventeenth anniversary of the Boston Baptist Association, held at the First Baptist meeting-house in Cambridge, on Wednesday and Thursday, Sept. 17 & 18, 1828. Boston, Pr. by Lincoln & Edmands, [1828] 24 p. NRAB.   32145

---- ---- Convention.

Minutes of the Massachusetts Baptist Convention, held in Worcester, Oct. 29 & 30, A. D. 1828. Worcester, Spooner and Merriam, prs. , 1828. 16 p. DLC; MWHi; NRAB.   32146

---- ---- Old Colony Association.

Minutes... in Brewster, Mass. October 1st & 2nd, 1828. Plymouth, Allen Danforth [1828] 12 p. NRAB.   32147

---- ---- Salem Association.

Minutes of the convention holden at Salem, October 16, 1827, to organize the Salem Baptist Association. Boston, Pr. by Lincoln & Edmonds, Jan. 1828. 8 p. MNtcA; MWA; NRAB.   32148

---- ---- Worcester Association.

Minutes of the Worcester Baptist Association, held at Templeton, August 20 and 21, 1828. Ninth anniversary. Worcester, Spooner and Merriam, prs. , 1828. 12 p. MWA.   32149

---- Mississippi. Pearl River Association.

Minutes of the Pearl River Baptist Association, convened at the meeting-house of Bethany Church, on Friday the 12th of September 1828. Monticello, Pr. by Samuel Foster, 1828. 8 p. LNB.   32150

---- ---- Union Association.

Minutes of the Union Baptist Association, held at the meeting-house of Fellowship Church, in the county of Jefferson, on the 4th, 5th and 6th of October, 1828. [Natchez, William C. Grissam & Co. 1828] 33 p. KyLoS.   32151

---- New Hampshire. Convention.

Minutes of the convention, held at Portsmouth, N. H. Oct. 29, 1828. Portsmouth, Pr. by Robert Foster, Dec. 1828. NhHi.   32152

---- ---- Meredith Association.

Circular letter of the Meredith Baptist Association holden in the Baptist Meeting-House in Campton, New Hampshire, on Wednesday and Thursday, Sept. 10 & 11, 1828. Concord, Geo. Hough, pr. , 1828. 7 p. NhHi.   32153

---- ---- Milford Association.

Minutes of the first anniversary of the Milford Baptist Association... Oct. 15 & 16, 1828.

Concord, Pr. by Isaac Hill, 1828.
16 p. MB.   32154

---- ---- Salisbury Association.
Minutes of the Salisbury Baptist Association, held at the
North Meeting-House in Weare,
on Wednesday and Thursday, October 8th & 9th, 1828, with their
circular and corresponding letters. [Concord? 1828] 12 p. Nh.
                               32155
---- ---- State Convention.
Third annual report of the
trustees of the Baptist Convention of the state of New Hampshire, held at Chester, June 26,
27, 1828. Pub. by order of the
Convention. Concord, Pr. by
George Hough, for the Convention. 1828. [includes 9th annual
report of N. H. Domestic Mission
Society.] 31, [1] p. NRAB.
                               32156
---- New Jersey. Central Association.
Minutes of the convention at
Hightstown, Middlesex county,
N. J. October 25th A. D. 1828,
for the purpose of organizing a
Baptist Association in this district... Philadelphia, W. Pelking-
ton & Co., prs., 1828. 8 p.
NRAB.   32157

---- ---- New Jersey Association.
Minutes of the New-Jersey
Baptist Association, held by appointment with our sister church
of Amwell, in their meeting-
house at Flemington, Sept. 2d, 3d
& 4th, A. D. 1828. 12 p. NjR.
                               32158
---- New York. Berkshire Association.
Minutes of the Berkshire Baptist Association held with the
First Baptist Church, in Spencer,
N. Y. on the 10th & 11th of June,
1828. Owego, N. Y., 1828. 8 p.
BrMus.   32159

---- New York. Genesee Association.
Minutes of the tenth session of
the Genesee Baptist Association,
held at Middlebury, on the first
and second days of October, 1828;
containing their circular and corresponding letters. Likewise an
appendix, comprising a summary
of the proceedings of the G. B.
M. S. Batavia, Pr. for the society, by F. Follett, 1828. 12 p.
NRAB.   32160

---- ---- Holland Purchase Association.
The annual minutes of the Holland Purchase Baptist Association, held, by appointment, with
the Baptist Church in Eden, Oct.
9th and 10th, 1828. Together with
the circular and corresponding
letters, and the proceedings of
the Missionary and Indian School
Society. Buffalo, Pr. by Salisbury & Snow, 1828. 12 p. NBu;
NHC.   32161

---- ---- Hudson River Association.
The thirteenth anniversary of
the Hudson River Baptist Association... held in the Meeting-House
of the Baptist Church, Hudson,
August 6 & 7, 1828. New York,
Pr. by Gray and Bunce, 1828.
16 p. M.   32162

---- ---- Monroe Association.
Minutes of the organization of
the Monroe Baptist Association,
organized in Rochester, Oct. 18,
1827; and also of its first anniversary, held in Ogden, June 25
and 26, 1828. Rochester, Pr. by
Tuttle & Sprague, 1828. 16 p.
NRAB.   32163

---- ---- New York Association
Minutes of the New-York Baptist Association, held in the
Meeting House of the First Baptist Church in Piscataway, N. J.

May 27, 28, and 29, 1828. 16 p.
NRAB.   32164

---- ---- Niagara Association.
Minutes of the Niagara Baptist Association, holden at Somerset, June 11th & 12th, 1828, with their circular and corresponding letter and progress in missionary business. Lockport, N. Y., Cadwallader, pr. [1828] 8 p. NRAB.   32165

---- ---- Ontario Association.
Minutes of the fifteenth anniversary of the Ontario Baptist association, holden at Palmyra, September 24th and 25th, 1828; together with their circular and corresponding letters. Canandaigua, Pr. by W. W. Phelps, 1828. 8 p. NRAB.   32166

---- ---- St. Lawrence Association.
Minutes of the fourteenth session of the St. Lawrence Baptist Association, convened at Canton, September 10, 1828. Containing their circular and corresponding letters. Canton, N. Y., Pr. by W. W. Wyman, 1828. 8 p. NRAB.   32167

---- ---- Washington Association.
Minutes of the second session of the Washington Baptist Association; convened at Hebron, on the 11th and 12th of June, 1828; containing their circular and corresponding letters, also an account of their missionary concerns. Poultney, Pr. by L. J. Reynolds, 1828. 8 p. NRAB.
                               32168
---- Ohio. Columbus Association.
Minutes of the Columbus Baptist Association, held by appointment at Turkey Run, Fairfield Co., Ohio, Sept. 6, 7, and 8th, A. D. 1828. Newark, (O.), Pr. by Benj. Briggs, 1828. 8 p.

NRAB; OC1WHi.   32169

---- ---- East Fork of the Little Miami Association.
Minutes of the East Fork of the Little Miami Baptist Association, held at East Fork Meeting House, Clermont County, Ohio, on the 6th, 7th, and 8th September, 1828. Cincinnati, Lodge, L'Hommedieu, & Hammond, prs., 1828. 7 p. NRAB; OC1WHi.
                               32170
---- ---- Grand River Association.
Minutes of the twelfth session of the Grand River Baptist Association: Held by appointment in the Baptist Meeting House at Perry, Ohio, September 10th & 11th, 1828; together with their circular and corresponding letter. Ashtabula, Park & Terril, prs., 1828. 12 p. NRAB; OC1WHi.
                               32171
---- ---- Huron Association
Minutes of the seventh annual meeting of Huron Baptist Association, with the Black River Church, Lorain County, Ohio. Norwalk, Ohio, Pr. by Henry Buckingham, 1828. 11 p. NRAB.
                               32172
---- ---- Mahoning Association
Minutes of the Mahoning Baptist Association, convened at Warren, Ohio, on the 29th of August, 1828. Pr. at Bethany, Brooke Co., Va. 1828. 7 p. WvBeC.   32173

---- ---- Miami Association.
Minutes of the Miami Baptist Association, held at Lebanon, Warren county, Ohio, Sept. the 12th, 13th, and 14th, 1828. 8 p. OC1WHi.   32174

---- ---- Mohecan Association.
Minutes of the Mohecan Association of Baptists, held by appointment, with the Union Church, in Richland county, Ohio, on Fri-

day, the 12th of September,
1828... Mansfield, O., Pr. at
the Gazette Office, 1828. 8 p.
OClWHi.   32175

---- ---- Muskingum Association.
Minutes of the Muskingum Baptist Association, held at the Lancaster Baptist Church, Fairfield
county, Ohio, Aug. 22, 23 and
24, A. D. 1828. [Sanderson &
Oswald, prs.] 8 p. OClWHi.
                             32176
---- Pennsylvania. Beaver Association.
Minutes of the Beaver Baptist
Association, held in the Sharon
Church, Mercer County, Pa.
August the 21st, 22nd, and 23d,
1828. Butler, Wm. Stewart, pr.,
1828. 8 p. NRAB.   32177

---- ---- General Association
for Missionary Purposes.
Minutes of the first annual
meeting of the Baptist General
Association of Pennsylvania for
Missionary Purposes, held at
Blockley M. H. Philadelphia Co.,
July 4, 1828: With the constitution, and the annual report of the
board of managers, &c. Philadelphia, Pr. by John Gray, 1828.
8 p. NRAB.   32178

---- ---- Juniata Association.
Minutes of the Juniata Baptist
Association, held in the meeting
house of the Sideling Hill Church,
Bedford County, Pa. Oct. 16,
17 & 18th, 1828. Harrisburg,
Pa., Pr. by Gustavus S. Peters,
1828. 15 p. NRAB.   32179

---- ---- Philadelphia Association.
Minutes of the Philadelphia
Baptist Association, convened in
the meeting-house of the Baptist
Church in Roxborough, Philadelphia County, Oct. 7th, 1828. [Pr.
by S. Siegfried, West Chester,
1828?] 12 p. NRAB.   32180

---- ---- Susquehanna Associa-
tion.
Minutes of the Susquehanna
Baptist Association, held in the
years of our Lord, 1827 & 1828.
Pr. by S. D. Lewis, Wilkesbarre,
Pa. [1828] 8 p. NRAB.   32181

---- Rhode Island. Warren Association.
Sixty-first anniversary. Minutes of the Warren Baptist Association, held at New Bedford,
Wednesday and Thursday, Sept.
10 and 11, 1828. Providence, Pr.
by H. H. Brown, 1828. 16 p. IU;
NRAB; RHi; RPB.   32182

---- South Carolina. Charleston
Association.
Minutes of the Charleston
Baptist Association convened at
Bethel Church, Sumter District,
November 1, and continued to
November 5, 1828. Charleston,
William Riley, 1828. 24 p. MWA.
                             32183
---- Tennessee. Concord Asso-
ciation.
Minutes of the Concord Asso-
ciation of Baptists, Held at Mill
Creek Meeting-House, Davidson
County, September 6, 7 & 8,
1828. Nashville, Pr. at the Whig
and Banner Press, 1828. 16 p.
MWA.   32184

---- ---- Holston Association.
Minutes of the Holston Baptist Association, held at Robinson's Creek Meeting House, Haw-
kins County, E. Tennessee, on
the second Friday in August, 1828
and the following days. [Rogers-
ville [Pr. at the Magazine Office, 1828] Broadsheet. TKL.
                             32185
---- ---- Nolachucky Association.
Minutes of the Nolachucky
Baptist Association, who held
their first anniversary at Bent
Creek Meeting House, Jefferson

County, E. Tennessee, on the first Friday of November, 1828 and days following. [Rogersville, Pr. at the Calvinistic Magazine Office, 1828] Broadsheet. TKL. 32186

---- Vermont. Barre Association.
Minutes of the Barre Association, held at Plainfield, Sept. 10 and 11, 1828. Royalton, Pr. by W. Spooner [1828] 8 p. NRAB. 32187

---- ---- Danville Association.
Minutes of the Danville Association, held at Derby, Vt., June 18 & 19, 1828. Danville, Pr. by E. & W. Eaton, 1828. 8 p. NRAB. 32188

---- ---- Fairfield Association.
Minutes of the Fairfield Baptist Association, held at Fairfield, 17th & 18th Sept., 1828. Burlington, Pr. by E. & T. Mills, 1828. 11 p. NRAB. 32189

---- ---- Vermont Association.
Minutes of the forty-third anniversary of the Vermont Baptist Association, held with the Baptist Church in Bristol, on Wednesday and Thursday, October 1 & 2, 1828. Brandon, Pr. by E. Maxham, 1828. 8 p. NRAB. 32190

---- Virginia. Albemarle District Association.
Minutes of the Baptist Association of the Albemarle District, held at Maple-Creek Church, Amherst County, Virginia, on the 16th of August, 1828. Lexington, Pr. by Valentine M. Mason, 1828. 15 p. ViRVB. 32191

---- ---- Dover Association.
Minutes of the Dover Baptist Association, held at Grafton Meeting-House, York County, on Saturday, Sunday, and Monday, the 11th, 12th and 13th of October 1828. Richmond, Pr. at

the office of the Religious Herald 1828. 12 p. DLC. 32192

---- ---- Ebenezer Association.
Minutes of proceedings... Friday the 24th, and continued on Saturday the 25th of October 1828. Harrisonburg, Rockingham Weekly Register Office [1828] 12 p. NRAB. 32193

---- ---- General Association.
Minutes of the Baptist General Association of Virginia; held in the city of Richmond, Saturday & Monday, May 30th and June 1st, 1828. Richmond, Pr. at the office of the Religious Herald, 1828. 11 p. NRAB; ViRVB. 32194

---- ---- Goshen Association.
Minutes of the Baptist Association, in the district of Goshen: held at County-Line meeting-house, Caroline County, Virginia; commencing on the first Saturday in October, 1828. Pr. at the Herald Office, Fredericksburg, Va. [1828] 12 p. ViRVB. 32195

---- ---- Ketocton Association.
The 62d annual publication. Minutes of the Ketocton Baptist Association, held at Opequon Meeting-house, Berkeley County, Va. August 14, 15, and 16, 1828. [S. H. Davis, pr., Winchester, 1828] 8 p. ViRVB. 32196

---- ---- Middle District Association.
Minutes of the Middle District Association, held at Bethel Meeting-house, Chesterfield County, Virginia. The last Saturday in August, 1828. Richmond, Pr. at the office of the Religious Herald, 1828. 8 p. ViRVB. 32197

---- ---- Portsmouth Association.
Minutes of the Virginia Portsmouth Baptist Association, held

at Rackoon Swamp Meeting-house, Sussex County, Virginia, May 23d, 24th and 25th, 1828. Norfolk [Va.] Pr. by Shields & Ashburn, 1828. 12 p. NRAB. 32198

---- ---- Shiloh Association. Minutes of the Shiloh Baptist Association held at Fiery-Run Meeting-House: Fauquier County, Va., commencing Friday Sept. 6th, 1828. Pr. by James D. Harrow, Fredericksburg, Va., 1828. 12 p. ViRVB. 32199

---- ---- Strawberry Association. Minutes of the Strawberry District Baptist Association, convened at Bethlehem meeting house, in the county of Bedford, October 6th, 1827... and likewise the minutes of the same Association, convened at Timber-Ridge meeting house in Bedford county, on the 24th of May, 1828... Lynchburg, Pr. at the office of The Virginian, 1828. 8 p. ViRVB. 32200

---- ---- Union Association. Minutes of the Union Baptist Association held at Beulah Church, Prunty Town, Harrison county, Va. August 28, 29, 30, and 31st, 1828. Clarksburg, Va., Pr. by Joseph Israel, 1828. 12 p. NRAB. 32201

Barbauld, Anna Letitia (Aikin), 1743-1825 Selections from the works of Mrs. Barbauld: with extracts from Miss Aikin's Memoir of that lady. Arranged for the use of young persons by Mrs. Hughs ... Philadelphia, Pub. by R. H. Small [James Kay, Jun., pr.] 1828. 300 p. CSmH; CoD; MB; MWA; PPL. 32202

Barber, Daniel, 1756-1834 The history of my own times. By the Rev. Daniel Barber, A. M. Washington City, Pr. for the author, by S. C. Ustick, 1828-32. 3 vols. DGU; DLC; InNd; MWA; MdBL; MdBS; MdW; NN; NcD. 32203

Barber, J. Grand march for the piano forte. Composed expressly for & most respectfully dedicated to General Cadwalader by J. Barber. Philadelphia, George Willig, [c1828] [2] p. ViU. 32204

Barber, John Warner, 1798-1885 Historical religious events... being a selection of the most important and interesting religious events which have transpired since the commencement of the Christian era to the present time. Hartford, D. F. Robinson, publisher, 1828. [c1829] 148 p. CSmH; CU; CoFS; Ct; CtHi; CtSoP; CtY; DLC; IObB; MBC; MH; MWA; NBLiHi; NN; NNUT; PP; RPB; WaPS. 32205

---- Interesting events in the history of the United States: being a selection of the most important and interesting events which have transpired since the discovery of this country to the present time. Carefully selected from the most approved authorities. New-Haven, J. W. Barber, 1828. iv, [9]-220, xxiv p. CtW; CtY; DSI; MLow; NNC; NT. 32206

Barber, Jonathan, 1784-1864 Exercises in reading and recitation, founded on an enquiry into the elementary constitution of the human voice. Albany, Pub. by G. J. Loomis, 1828. 300 p. CoU; NjR; NN; PPL. 32207

---- ---- 2d ed. Boston, The author, Providence, Miller & Hammond, 1828. CtMMHi; CtY; InCW; NN; RPB. 32208

Barbour, J. S. Speech of Mr. J. S. Barbour,

of Virginia on the propriety of excluding the agency of the president, in appointing and removing the disbursing and accounting officers of the Treasury Department. Delivered in the House of Representatives of the United States, March 1828. Washington, Pr. by Green & Jarvis, 1828. [3], 40, 4 p. DLC; NjR.   32209

Barclay, Robert
A catechism and confessions of faith approved of and agreed unto by the General Assembly of the Patriarchs, Prophets, and Apostles, Christ Himself chief speaker in and among them... Philadelphia, Pr. by Solomon W. Conrad, 1828. viii, 95 p. DLC; PHi; PPF; PSC-Hi.   32210

Bard, Archibald
A brief statement of certain controversies mentioned and alluded to throughout the Rev. D. Elliott's letters, with a few strictures on church government. Chambersburg, Pa., Pr. for the author by G. K. Harper, 1828. 28 p. DLC; MBAt; NbOP.   32211

Barker, David, 1797-1834
An address in commemoration of the independence of the United States, delivered at Rochester, July 4, 1828... Dover [N. H.] G. W. Ela and co., prs., 1828. 28 p. CSmH; DLC; MB.   32212

Barker, Jacob
Jacob Barker to the electors of the First senatorial district of the state of New-York. [New York? 1828] 20, [1] p. DLC; MB.   32213

Barker, James Nelson, 1784-1858
Sketches of the primitive settlements on the River Delaware. A discourse delivered before the Society for the commemoration of the Landing of William Penn, on

the 24th of October, 1827. Philadelphia, Carey, Lea, and Carey, Mifflin and Parey, prs., 1828 [cover title] 62 p. DLC; PPL.   32214

Barkman, John, Jr. See Burnside, A. (note).

Barnard, Daniel Dewey, 1797-1861
Speech of Mr. Barnard, of New York, on the tariff bill. Delivered in the House of Representatives, March 17, 1828. Washington, Gales & Seaton, 1828. 16 p. Ct; CtY; MH; MWA; NN; PHi; PPAmP.   32215

Barnes, Albert
Church manual, for the members of the Presbyterian Church, Morris-Town, N. J. Compiled by Albert Barnes, pastor; and published by order of the session of said church. Morris-Town, Pr. by Jacob Mann, 1828. 47 p. DLC; NBLiHi; NNUT; NjPT; NjR.   32216
---- Essays on intemperance... Morristown [N. J.] Pr. by Jacob Mann, 1828. 45 p. MH-AH; NN; NjPT; OC.   32217

Barnes, John, M. D. See Jefferson Medical College.

Barnes, John Harbeson
The counting-house tabular tariff sheet. By J. Harbeson Barnes and Elijah A. Carroll. [c 30th Oct. 1828] 1 p. DLC.   32218
---- List of articles free of duty, and tariff, or rates of duties, from and after the thirtieth day of June, 1828, on all goods, wares & merchandise imported into the United States of America ... Collated and compiled by J. Harbeson Barnes & E. A. Carroll. Philadelphia, Pr. for the proprietors [Russell & Martien, prs.] 1828. 128, [1] 135 133, [1]

[i. e. 132 p.] NN.   32219

Barnum, H. L.
The spy unmasked; or, Mem-
oirs of Enoch Crosby, alias Har-
vey Birch, the hero of Mr.
Cooper's tale of the neutral
ground:... New-York, Pr. by J.
& J. Harper; sold by Collins and
Hannay, Collins and co. [etc.];
Philadelphia, Carey, Lea and
Carey; [etc., etc.] 1828. 206, [2] p.
of ads. CSmH; CtHT-W; CtY;
DLC; GU; MBC; MH; MWA;
MWiW-C; MdBP; MeB; MiU-C;
MoS; NN; NcWsW; NjP; OMC;
PPL; PPi; RPB; ViU; BrMus.
                              32220
Barré, Pierre Ives, 1749-1832
Neal & MacKenzie. No. 201
Chestnut Street, between the The-
ater & Arcade. Philadelphia. Le
procés du fandango, ou la fan-
dangomanie. Comedie-vaudeville,
en un acte. Par Mm. Barre,
Radet, et Desfóntaines. [Phila-
delphia, 1828] 20, [1] p. (Also
issued in vol. with covering title:
Collection d'operas et vaude-
villes) ICU; PPL.   32221

Barrett, Ezra
Sabbath school psalmody. Boston, Pub. by Richardson & Lord,
1828. 51 p. NNC-T; RPB. 32222

Barrington, Jonah
Personal sketches of his own
times, by Sir Jonah Barrington,
judge of the high court of admir-
alty in Ireland, &c. &c. &c. In
two volumes. New-York, G. & C.
Carvill; Collins and Hannay; Elam
Bliss; Collins and Co. ; White,
Gallaher, and White [Sleight &
George, prs. , Jamaica] 1828. 2
vols. CtY; MA; MH; MPB; MeB.
                              32223
[Barrymore, William] d. 1845
El hyder: or, Love and bravery. A grand melodramatic romance, in three acts, as performed at the London and New

York theatres, with great success. Got up under the direction
of Mr. Blythe, of Astley's Am-
phitheatre, London and published
from the original manuscript, by
his kind permission. New York,
Pr. and pub. at the Circulating
Library and Dramatic Repository.
1828. 46 p. TxU.   32224

Bartlett, Ichabod, 1786-1853
Speech of Mr. Bartlett, on the
subject of retrenchment. Deliv-
ered in the House of Representa-
tives... February 6, 1828. 2d ed.
Washington city [D. C.] Pr. by
Wm. Greer, 1828. 24 p. CSmH;
DLC; IU; LU; MH; MWA; NhHi;
PHi; PPL; BrMus.   32225

Bartlett, John
A sermon delivered at the or-
dination of the Rev. John M.
Merrick as pastor of the Congre-
gational Church & Society in
Hardwick, Mass. Published by
Bowles & Dearborn, Boston [I.
R. Butts, pr.] 1828. 24 p. ICMe;
MB; MBAU; MBC; MH; MHi;
MWA; RPB; BrMus.   32226

Barton, Cyrus, d. 1855
An address, delivered before
the Republicans of Newport, and
vicinity, July 4, 1828. ... Newport [N. H.] D. Aldrich, 1828. 16
p. DLC; Nh.   32227

Barton, William Paul Crillon
Outlines of lectures on materia
medica and botany, delivered in
Jefferson Medical College, Phila-
delphia. Philadelphia, Pub. by
Jos. G. Auner, T. Town, pr. ,
1828. 246 p. IaAS; KyLxT; MB;
MdBJ; MoSMed; ScCM.   32228

Bartram's Botanic Garden. See
Carr, Robert.

Bascom, Ezekiel Lysander
Parental duties enjoined. A
discourse delivered at Mason,

N. H. , at the close of a Sabbath
school, Nov. 16, 1827. New Ips-
wich, N. H. , Pr. by S. Wilder,
March 1828. 15 p. CtY; MeHi.
                                  32229
Bascom, Henry Bidleman, 1796-
1850
    Inaugural address, delivered
before the Board of Trustees, of
Madison College; Uniontown,
Penn'a-Sept. 15th, 1827. Union-
Town, Pr. at the Office of the
Pennsylvania Democrat, and Lit-
erary Gazette, 1828. 40 p.
CSmH; IEG; KyLx; MB; MBAt;
MH; OCHP.   32230

Bates, Edward, 1793-1869
    Edward Bates against Thomas
H. Benton. St. Louis, Charless
& Paschall, prs. , 1828. 12 p.
CSmH; DLC; MWA; MiD-B; MoHi;
MoSM; NN; PPL (title & p 11-12
only).   32231

Bates, Elisha
    Extract of a letter from ****
**** to a friend in New Jersey,
together with Elias Hick's reply,
and a review of the same by
Elisha Bates. New York, Pr. by
Mahlon Day, 1828. 23 p. MH.
                                  32232
Bates, Isaac Chapman, 1780-
1845
    Speech of Mr. Isaac C. Bates,
of Massachusetts. On the tariff
bill. Delivered in the House of
Representatives, March 26, 1828.
Washington, Pr. by Gales & Sea-
ton, 1828. 26 p. CSmH; Ct; DLC;
DeGE; IU; LU; MBAt; MBC; MH;
MWA; MeB; MoKU; N; NN; BrMus.
                                  32233
Bates, William
    An address, delivered at the
South meeting house in Carver,
on the evening of the 22d Febru-
ary, 1828... Plymouth, Mass. ,
Allen Danforth, pr. , 1828. 24 p.
CSmH; MB; MBC.   32234

Bausset-Roquefort, Louis Fran-

çois Joseph, baron de, b. 1770
    Private memoirs of the court
of Napoleon, and of some publick
events of the imperial reign,
from 1805 to the first of May
1814; to serve as a contribution
to the history of Napoleon...
Translated from the French.
Philadelphia, Carey, Lea &
Carey [etc.] [Griggs & Dickinson,
prs.] 1828. xiv, [9] - 435 p.
CLCM; CtMW; CtY; ICU; InGrD;
MBAt; MH; MWA; MeU; NN; NcU;
OCl; PHi; PPL; PU; TNJ; Vi;
WM; BrMus.   32235

Baxter, Richard, 1615-1691
    The duty of the people of God
to excite others to seek the
saints' rest. Being the ninth chapter of Baxter's invaluable treatise.
Boston, Pr. by Lincoln & Edmands, 1828. 24 p. [1], 154-175,
[1] p. MH-AH.   32236

---- The saints' everlasting rest.
... Abridged by Benjiman Fawcett,
A. M. Stereotyped at the Boston
Type and Stereotype Foundry.
Boston, Pub. by Lincoln & Ed-
mands, [1828] 320 p. DLC; ICU;
MB; MDeeP; MWA; MeBa; MiU;
PPL; PU; TNJ; ViU.   32237

---- ---- New York, John P.
Haven, 1828. 297 p. CSmH; MH;
MWA; NNUT; NcElon; OO; UPB.
                                  32238
---- ---- Philadelphia, T. Kite,
1828. 2 v. CU; IObB; NRAB;
PPeSchw; TNJ.   32239

---- ---- Philadelphia, H. Cow-
perthwait, 1828. 288 p. C-S;
DLC; IaDm; MSo; RNHi; TNJ;
TxAuPT; WMMD; BrMus. 32240

Bayard, Samuel, 1767-1840
    An address delivered on Thurs-
day, the 14th August, 1828, in
the Presbyterian Church, at
Princeton, N. J. at the request
of a committee of the Society

Auxiliary to the General Union,
for the Due Observation of the
Lord's Day. Princeton Press:
Princeton, N. J. Pub. by Wm.
D'Hart, Connolly & Madden, prs. ,
1828. 26 p. DLC; MBAt; MWA;
MiU; NjP; NjR.   32241

Bayle, Antoine Laurent Jessé,
1799-1858
   A manual of general anatomy,
containing a concise description
of the elementary tissues of the
human body. From the French of
A. L. J. Bayle and H. Hollard.
By S. D. Gross, M. D. Philadel-
phia, J. Grigg, 1828. x, 272 p.
CSt-L; CU-M; CtY; DLC; DNLM;
DeGE; GHi; GU-M; ICJ; ICU;
IEN-M; IU; KyLxT; LNT-M; MB;
MBCo; MdBJ-W; MdBM; MdUM;
MeB; MiU; MnU; MoSMed;
NBuU-M; NIC-M; NNC-M;
NNNAM; NbU-M; NhD; NjR; OC;
OClM; PPC; PU; ScCMe; ViU.
                                 32242
[Baylies, Francis] 1783-1852
   The contrast; or, Military
chieftains and political chieftains
... Albany [N. Y.] Pr. by D. M'
Glashan, 1828. 26 p. CSmH;
DLC; MB.   32243

[----] The political character of
John Quincy Adams delineated.
Being a reply to certain observa-
tions in the address of Gen.
Peter B. Porter and others. Al-
bany, Pr. for the Albany Argus
by D. M'Glashan, 1828. 30 p.
CtY; DLC; LNHT; MB; MdHi;
NBLiHi; RP.   32244

[Beaconsfield, Benjamin Dis-
raeli] 1804-1881
   The voyage of Captain Popa-
nilla. By the author of "Vivian
Grey" ... Philadelphia, Carey,
Lea, and Carey [etc. , etc.] 1828.
viii, 243 p. CSmH; CtY; DLC;
IObB; LNHT; LU; MBAt; MMeT;
NCH; NjR; P; PU; TNJ; BrMus.
                                 32245

Bearcroft, William
   The red book. Practical orthography or the art of teaching
spelling by writing... Revised and
enlarged by Daniel H. Barnes...
York, Pr. 1824: New-York, Repr. and sold by Mahlon Day,
1828. x, [2], 347, [1] p. CtHT-
W; DLC; MBAt; MH; MWA; NN;
NNS; NPV.   32246

The beatitudes. See Sedgwick,
Elizabeth Buckminster (Dwight).

Beauties of the souvenirs for
MDCCCXXVIII. Selected by J. W.
Miller. Boston, S. G. Goodrich,
1828. vii [1], 244 p. MB; MWA;
NjR; RPB.   32247

[Beazley, Samuel]
   The lottery ticket, and lawyer's clerk; a farce, in one act.
As performed at the Park, Bow-
ery, and Chatham theatres. New
York, Pr. by R. Hobbs, 1828.
36+ p. [Elton's edition.] MH.
                                 32248
[----] The roue. New York, Pr.
by J. and J. Harper, for Collins
and Hannay [etc. ,] 1828. 2 v.
CtHT; IU; MH.   32249

[Beck, Lewis Caleb] 1798-1853
   Geographical botany of the
United States. [Albany? N. Y.
1828] 13 p. MH; PPL.   32250

Beck, Theodoric Romeyn [1791-
1855]
   Annual address delivered be-
fore the Medical Society of the
State of New-York. February 6,
1828. Albany, Pr. by Webster
and Skinners, 1828. [4], 23 p.
DLC; MB; MWA; N; NN;
NNC; NNNAM; PPAN; PPPrHi;
PU; RNR.   32251

Beckwith, George Cone
   A dissuasive from controversy
respecting the mode of baptism
... 2d ed. Andover, Pr. by Mark

Newman, Flagg & Gould, prs.,
1828. 35 p. PPL.   32252

[Beecher, Catharine Esther]
1800-1878
Arithmetic explained and illustrated, for the use of the Hartford Female Seminary. Hartford,
P. Canfield, pr., 1828. iv, 216
p. Ct; CtHT-W.   32253

Beecher, Lyman, 1775-1863
Letters of the Rev. Dr. Beech-
er and Rev. Mr. Nettleton on the
"New measures" in conducting re-
vivals of religion with a review
of a sermon, by Novanglus. Pub.
by G & C Carvill, New York,
1828. [J. Seymour, pr.] 104 p.
CtHC; CtY; DLC; ICMe; MBAt;
MH-AH; MWA; NCH; NIC; NN;
NNG; NjPT; OClWHi; PPPrHi;
ViRUT; BrMus.   32254

---- The memory of our fathers.
A sermon delivered at Plymouth,
on the twenty-second of Decem-
ber, 1827. Boston, T.R. Marvin,
pr., 1828. 39 p. CSmH; CtSoP;
CtY; DLC; ICU; MBAt; MBC;
MDeeP; MH-AH; MWA; MWey;
NBLiHi; NN; Nh; NjPT; OCHP;
OClWHi; PPL; PPPrHi; RPB;
ScC; VtMiM; WHi; BrMus.
                         32255
---- ---- 2d ed. Boston, T. R.
Marvin, pr., 1828. 30 p. CtSoP;
DLC; IEG; MB; MH; MHi; MWA;
NBLiHi; NCH; NN; NNUT; NjR;
PHi; RPB.   32256

---- A sermon, preached at New-
York, Oct. 12, 1827, before the
American Board of Missions.
Rochester, Pr. by E. Peck &
Co., 1828. 24 p. ICMe; MWA;
NR; NRU.   32257

---- Sermons delivered on various occasions, by Lyman Beecher, D.D. Boston, T.R. Marvin.
Sold by Crocker & Brewster,
Hilliard, Gray & Co... Boston,

Jonathan Leavitt, N.Y., 1828.
367 p. ArBaA; CBPac; CtHT;
CtHT-W; CtY; GDC; ICJ; KyLoP;
KyLoS; LNB; MB; MBC; MH-AH;
MHi; MNtcA; MeBaT; MoSpD;
MsJMC; NGH; NNG; NbCrD;
NhD; NjPT; NmU; OClW; OMC;
OO; OkU; PPPrHi; RPB; ScCoT;
ViRut.   32258

---- Six sermons on the nature,
occasions, signs, evils and remedy of intemperance. 3d ed.
Boston, Pr. by T. R. Marvin,
sold by Crocker and Brewster
[Stereotyped at the Boston Type
and Stereotype Foundry] 1828.
107 p. ICU; PPL.   32259

---- ---- 6th ed. Boston, Sold
by Crocker & Brewster. Stereo-
typed at the Boston Type and
Stereotype Foundry, 1828.
107 p. CU; CtHT-W; CtY;
DNLM; GDC; ICMcC; ICU; IU;
IaPeC; MBC; MH; MNe; MWA;
MeB; MoSW; NN; NcWsW; NjMD;
OClWHi; OO; RPB; ScCliTO;
TN; VtBrt; WHi.   32260

Beers' Carolinas and Georgia
almanac for 1829. Columbia
[1828] Drake.   32261

Beers' Louisiana and Mississip-
pi almanack for 1829. By Samuel
Burr. Natchez, Wm. C. Gris-
sam and Co.; Hotchkiss, Grissam
& Clark; Wm. C. Grissam and
Co., prs. [1828] 18 l. Ms-Ar.
                         32262
---- By Samuel Burr. Natchez,
Henry Moss and Co.; Wm. C.
Grissam & Co., prs. [1828] 18 l.
Ms-Ar.   32263

Bell, John, 1796-1872
On the influence of medicine.
An oration delivered before the
Philadelphia Medical Society, pur-
suant to appointment... February
9, 1828. Pub. by the Society.
Philadelphia, Mifflin and Parry,

prs., 1828. 36 p. CSmH; DLC;
DNLM; GDC; MB; MBAt; MWA;
MiD-B; NNNAM; OC; PHi;
PPAmP; PPL; PPPrHi.   32264

Bell, John, 1797-1869
    Speech of Mr. Bell of Tennes-
see [sic] in committee of the
whole on the bill to relinquish to
the state of Tennessee the lands
belonging to the United States
within the limits of that state,
for the use of common schools.
Washington, 1828. 20 p. CtY.
                            32265
Belot, Carlos
    Observaciones sobre los males
que se esperimentan en esta isla
de Cuba desde la infancia, y con-
sejos dados a las madres y al
bello sexo. Nueva York, Lanuza,
Mendia y c., 1828. 2 v. DLC;
InGrD; NNC-M; PPC.   32266

Bennet, James Arlington
    The American system of prac-
tical bookkeeping... exemplified
in one set of books kept by
double entry. 10th ed. New York,
Collins & Hannay, 1828. [96] p.
IEG; MH-BA.   32267

Bennett, Titus
    Revised impressions... of
practical arithmetic... Philadelphia, Bennett & Walton, 1828. 178,
[26] p. NNU-W.   32268

Bennett & Walton's almanack for
1829. By Joseph Cramer. Philadelphia, D. & S. Neall [1828]
18 l. DLC; InU; MWA; N; NBuG;
NjR; PHi; PP; PPL.   32269

Benton, Jesse
    Murder will out!! Truth is
mighty and shall prevail! Four
years ago I charged General Andrew Jackson, in an address
printed and published in Nashville, with various acts of cruelty
and dishonesty when acting officially... Jesse Benton. City

Hotel, Nashville, Oct. 13th,
1828. Washington, "We the
people." Extra. Oct. 28, 1828.
1 p. DLC.   32270

---- To the public. In September, 1824 I published at this
place, Nashville, some criminal
charges against Gen. Jackson,
the most of which I relied on
proving by public records... [at
end]: Jesse Benton. City Hotel,
Nashville Oct. 30th, 1828. Bdsd.
DLC.   32271

---- ... To the public. The following document, in the form of
a letter to Mr. James Jackson,
has been presented to him, and
he has refused to answer [accus-
ing General Jackson and others
of fraudulent land deals]. Nashville, Banner and Nashville Whig.
Extra Oct. 8, 1828. 1 p. DLC.
                            32272
Benton, Thomas Hart
    Mr. Benton's speeches on the
public lands, delivered in the
Senate of the United States at the
first session of the 20th Congress;
with an appendix. Washington,
Green & Jarvis, 1828. 44 p. KHi;
MH.   32273

---- The substance of Col.
Benton's argument, before the
Supreme Court at Nashville, in
the suit of John Smith, T. ads.
Nicholas Wilson. [Nashville,
1828] 19 p. MoSHi.   32274

Berkshire, pseud.
    Brief remarks on the rail
roads, proposed in Massachusetts. By Berkshire. Stockbridge,
Pr. by Charles Webster, 1828.
23 p. DBRE; M; MB; MCM; MH-
BA; MWA; NN.   32275

The Berkshire agricultural al-
manac for 1829. By Henry K.
Strong. Pittsfield, Henry K.
Strong; J. M. Beckwith, pr. [1828]

12 l. NNUT. 32276

Bernhard, Karl, duke of Saxe-
Weimar-Eisenach, 1792-1862
Travels through North Amer-
ica, during the years 1825 and
1826. Philadelphia, Carey, Lea
& Carey, sold in New York by
G. & C. Carvill [Skerrett, pr.]
1828. 2 v. in 1. CSt; CU; CtY;
DLC; GU-De; ICHi; ICN; IaU;
InHi; KU; KyBgW; KyU; LNHT;
MB; MDeeP; MH; MdBE; MeB;
MiD; MiU-C; MnHi; MoSHi; NNS;
NNUT; NRHi; NT; NWM; NbU;
NcD; NcU; NhHi; NjP; NjR;
OClWHi; OMC; PHi; PLFM; PPL;
PPi; PU; RNR; ScC; ScU; TNJ;
Vi; VtU; WHi; WM; BrMus.
32277

[Berquin, Arnaud] ca 1749-1791
Louisa's tenderness to the lit-
tle birds in winter. New York,
American Tract Society, [1828?]
16 p. (American Tract Society,
Series II, no. 14). RPB. 32278

Berrien, John MacPherson, 1781-
1856
An oration delivered before the
Phi Kappa Society of Franklin
College, at commencement, 1828.
Pr. by O. P. Shaw, at the office
of the "Athenian." Athens, Ga.,
1828. 24 p. A-Ar. 32279

---- Speech of Mr. Berrien, of
Georgia, on the bill for the relief of certain surviving officers
of the revolution. Delivered in
the Senate of the United States.
January 30, 1828. Washington,
Pr. by Gales & Seaton, 1828. 18
p. DGU; DLC; ICN; MoKU; NCH;
PPL; PPi; ScC; WHi. 32280

Bible
Die Bibel, oder Die ganze
Heilige Schrift des Alten und
Neuen Testaments. Nach Dr. Mar-
tin Luther's Uebersetzung. Stereo-
typirt von J. Howe, Philadelphia.
Philadelphia, Geo. W. Mentz,

1828. 828, 272, [1] p. IEdS;
IaOskW; MWA; NStC; OClWHi; P;
PHi; PPG; PPL; PU; ViU.
32281

---- Biblia, Das ist: Die ganze
Heilige Schrift des Alten und
Neuen Testaments, Nach der
deutschen Uebersetzung D. Martin
Luthers; Mit . . . 40 vortrefflichen
bildichen Vorstellungen versehen.
In Stereotypen vertigt von I.
Howe . . . Philadelphia, Kimber und
Scharpless, 1828. 932 p. MiU-C;
NN; P; PHC; PPG; PPeSchw;
PRHi. 32282

---- The Holy Bible . . . with
Canne's Marginal notes and references . . . Apocrypha . . . Stereotyped by B. & J. Collins . . . Pub.
by C. Ewer, T. Bedlington and
J. H. A. Frost, Boston, 1828. 744,
138, [745]-1009, [1], 56 p. CSmH;
GAU; IaU; MWHi; NNAB; NjPT;
PHi (lacks title page). 32283

---- ---- M. M. Teprell, Boston,
[1828] (Collins Stereotype ed. N. T.
title dated 1828) 932 p. NN; NT.
32284

---- ---- Pr. and pub. by Holbrook & Fessenden, Brattleborough, Vt., 1828. 684 p. NN; PP.
32285

---- ---- With Canne's marginal
references . . . Apocrypha . . . Concordance . . . The text corr. according to the Standard of the A-
merican Bible Soc. Stereotyped by
Jas. Conner, New-York . . . Pr.
and pub. by Holbrook & Fessenden,
Brattleborough, Vt. [1828] 527,
78, 168, 14, 56, 124 p. NN;
NNAB; OO; VtHi. 32286

---- ---- With Canne's marginal
references. Also an index, a table
of texts, and what has never before
been added, an account of the lives
and martyrdom of the Apostles
and Evangelists; with plates.
The text corrected according to
the standard of the American

Bible Society. Stereotyped by
James Connor, New York. Brattleborough, Pr. and pub. by Holbrook and Fessenden, 1828. 527,
168, 10 p. MBevHi; NN; OO;
VtHi.   32287

---- ---- Stereotyped, pr. and
pub. by H. & E. Phinney, Cooperstown, 1828. 768 p. NCooHi;
NN; NNAB; NSyHi.   32288

---- ---- Pub. by Hudson and
Skinner, Hartford, 1828. 112 l.
CtHi; NN; NNAB.   32289

---- ---- Stereotyped by J. Howe,
Philadelphia. Silas Andrus, Hartford, 1828. [N. T. dated 1827].
660 p. ICU; MWat; NN; NNAB.
                             32290
---- ---- Containing the Old and
New Testaments: ... Stereotyped
by J. Howe, Philadelphia. Hartford, Pub. by Silas Andrus. Sold
also by the booksellers generally,
1828. 720 p. [N. T. dated 1827]
PPL.   32291

---- ---- trans. out of the original tongues and with the former
translations compared and revised. Hartford, 1828. 681 p.
MH-AH.   32292

---- ---- Hartford, Pub. by
Silas Andrus [Stereotyped by A.
Chandler] 1828. 690, 210, 68 p.
CtHi.   32293

---- ---- Stereotyped by B. and
J. Collins, New-York.... Pub.
by Silas Andrus, Hartford, 1828.
690, 209 p. Ct; CtY; LNHT; MiU;
MoSpD; NHuntHi; NN; WHi.
                             32294
---- ---- [Stereotyped by A.
Chandler] Pub. by Silas Andrus,
Hartford, 1828. (N. T. dated
1826). 824, 251 p. NN; NNAB;
ViU.   32295

---- ---- Pub. and Sold by Ed-

mund Cushing, Lunenburg, Mass.,
1828. 683, 160, 687-930 p.
NNAB.   32296

---- ---- Stereotyped by E. & J.
White, for the Auxiliary New
York Bible and Common Prayer
Society... New York, 1828. O'
Callaghan, p 190.   32297

---- ---- Stereotype ed. New
York, Stereotyped by E. & J.
White, for "The American Bible
Society," [Pr. by D. Fanshaw]
1828. 705, [1], 215 p. MWA;
MiU; PMA.   32298

---- ---- Pub. by the Methodist
Book Concern, New York, 1828.
O'Callaghan, p 191.   32299

---- ---- Stereotyped by J. Howe.
D. D. Smith, New-York, 1828.
615, 192 p. NN; NNAB. 32300

---- ---- With Canne's marginal references. An index, also
references and a key sheet of
questions, geographical, historical, doctrinal, practical and experimental. Accompanied with
valuable chronological harmonies
of both testaments... By Hervy
Wilbur... The text corrected according to the standard of the
American Bible Society... Stereotyped by J. Conner, New York...
Pr. and pub. by Henry C. Sleight,
New York [etc., etc.] 1828. 527,
168, 31 p. NN; NNAB.   32301

---- ---- D. Fanshaw, pr.
Stereotyped for the American
Bible Society by D. & G. Bruce,
New-York, 1828. 837 p. CoD;
MWA; MoSpD; NN; OHi. 32302

---- ---- Stereotype edition...
[D. Fanshaw, pr.]... Stereotyped
by James Conner, for The American Bible Society, New-York,
1828. 486, 162 p. MB; MWA;
MoS; NBatHL; NN; NNAB; NcBe;

RNHi; TNJ.   32303

---- ---- New York, Stereotyped
by J. Connor, for the American
Bible Society, 1828. 824, 251 p.
IaHi.   32304

---- ---- [Stereotyped by Jas.
Conner] ... Pub. by N. Bangs and
J. Emory, for the Methodist
Episcopal Church, New-York,
1828. 486, 162 p. NNAB.   32305

---- ---- Pub. and sold by Daniel D. Smith, ... also by the principal booksellers in the United
States: New-York, 1828. 574, 96,
4, 579-768, 54 p. NjQ; ScC.
                                  32306
---- ---- Pr. for the Bible Society, by the American Sunday
School Union, Philadelphia, 1828.
599, 179 p. NN; NNAB; PHi;
PPDrop; PPFHi; PPeSchw. 32307

---- ---- I. Ashmead & Co., prs.
McCarty & Davis, Philadelphia,
1828. 1073 p. ScGF; WHi. 32308

---- ---- Stereotyped by D. &
G. Bruce, Philadelphia, 1828.
[N. T. dated 1821] 837 p. NNAB.
                                  32309
---- ---- Stereotyped by J. Howe,
Philadelphia; H. Adams, Phila-
delphia, 1828. 852, 259 p. MHa;
NN; NNAB.   32310

---- ---- Trans. from the Latin Vulgat: With Annotations, References, &c. [Stereotyped by J.
Howe] Pub. by Eugene Cummiskey, Philadelphia, 1828. 335,
444, 191 p. DGU.   32311

---- ---- Stereotype Edition...
Canne's Marginal Notes and References... Index... Pr. and pub.
by G. M. Davison, Saratoga
Springs, 1828. 576, [6] 579-768
p. NNAB.   32312

---- ---- Stereotyped by B. & J.

Collins, N. York. Woodstock,
Vt., N. Haskell; Boston, T. Bedlington, 1828. (At head of title:
Stereotype ed.) 1 p. l., 5-792 p.
DLC; MB; NNAB; VtHi; VtMiS.
                                  32313
---- ---- Ka Euanelio a Mataio:
oia ka moo olelo hemolele no ko
kakou haku e ola'i, no Iesu Kris-
to, i laweia i olelo Hawaii.
Hookahi keia o ke pai ana. Rochester, N. Y., Paiia ma ka mea
pai palapala a Lumiki, 1828. 69,
[1] p. CtY; MH; MNe; MWA;
NNAB; NjPT; PPL.   32314

---- A monotessaron: or, The
Gospel of Jesus Christ, according to the four evangelists; har-
monized and chronologically arranged. In a new translation from
the Greek text of Griêsbach, by
the Rev. John S. Thompson...
Baltimore, Pr. by J. Robinson,
1828. 156 p. CU; MdHi; BrMus
(2 pts., 1828-1829).   32315

---- Das neue Testament unsers
Herrn und Heilandes Jesu Christi.
Nach der Deutschen uebersetzung
von Dr. Martin Luther. ...Har-
risburg, Pa. Gedruckt und zu
haben bey Gustav S. Peters,
1828. 511, 5 p. PPL.   32316

---- ---- Philadelphia, Herausgegeben von Georg W. Mentz,
Stereotypirt von J. Howe, 1828.
504 p. NNAB.   32317

---- ---- Philadelphia, J. G.
Ritter, 1828. 542 p. DLC; PPL.
                                  32318
---- ---- Stereotyped by J. Howe,
Philadelphia. Princeton, D. A.
Borrenstein, 1828. 272, [1] p.
NN; NjP; PHi; PPG.   32319

---- Stereotype edition. The New
Testament of Our Lord and Saviour Jesus Christ:... To which is
added Walker's Explanatory Key,
concerning the vocabulary. ...

by Jeremiah Goodrich. Albany,
Pub. and sold wholesale and retail by S. Shaw, 1828. 331 [332-
3] p. NjMD; PP.   32320

---- The New Testament of Our
Lord and Saviour Jesus Christ:
with references and a key sheet
of questions, historical, doctrinal, and practical: designed to
facilitate the acquisition of Scriptural knowledge, in Bible classes,
Sunday schools, common schools,
and private families. By Hervey
Wilbur, A. M. 12th ed. Amherst,
Mass., Pub. by J. S. & C.
Adams, and sold, wholesale and
retail, at the principal bookstores
in the United States. 1828. 334 p.
MAJ; MWA; NN.   32321

---- ---- Pub. by James I. Cutler and Co., Bellows Falls [Vt.]
1828. 270 p. N.   32322

---- ---- Stereotype ed. Boston,
Pub. by Charles Ewer, 1828.
251 p. MEab; MWA.   32323

---- ---- To which is applied
the Orthoepy of the Critical Pronouncing Dictionary... by J. Walker... An Explanatory Key. By I.
Alger, Jun. Stereotyped by T. H.
& C. Carter... Pr. and pub. by
Lincoln & Edmands, Boston, 1828.
304 p. NN.   32324

---- ---- Bridgeport [Con.], Pub.
by J. B. & L. Baldwin. Stereo-
typed by H. & H. Wallis, New-
York, 1828. 270 p. CtHi; NN.
          32325
---- ---- By Hervey Wilbur...
13th ed., with a Harmony and
Tables. B. Perkins & Co., Bos-
ton, 1828. 463, 8, 64 p. CU.
          32326
---- ---- Stereotyped by Baker
& Greele, Boston... Timothy
Bedlington, Boston; and Wm.
Greenough, Lunenburg [Mass.]
1828. 315 p. NNAB.   32327

---- The New Testament in the
Common Version, conformed to
Griesbach's Standard Greek Text
Press of the Boston Daily Adver-
tiser. W. T. Lewis, pr., Bos-
ton, 1828. unpaged. CSmH; DLC;
MB; NN; NNAB.   32328

---- ---- Pub. by H. C. Denison, Jr.: Castleton, Vt., 1828.
336 p. VtHi.   32329

---- ---- Stereotyped by James
Connor: New York. Pr. and pub.
by Horatio Hill & Co., Concord,
N. H., 1828. 226 p. MBU-T;
MoSpD (266 p. ?); Nh; NhHi.
          32330
---- ---- Pub. by Luther Roby,
Concord, N. H., 1828. 335, [1]
p. DLC; NNAB; NhHi.   32331

---- ---- Pr. and pub. by J.
Sanderson, Elizabeth-Town, [New
Jersey] 1828. [4], 335, [3] p.
NN; OS.   32332

---- ---- Stereotype ed. Gardi-
ner, Me., Pr. and Pub. by P.
Sheldon, 1828. 290, [1] p.
NcMHi.   32333

---- ---- Greenfield, Mass.,
Pub. and sold by A. Phelps and
A. Clark; Stereotyped by Baker
& Greele [Boston], 1828. 315 p.
OHi.   32334

---- ---- Hartford, S. Andrus,
Stereotyped by A. Chandler, 1828.
251 p. P.   32335

---- ---- Stereotype ed. New
York, Stereotyped by A. Chandler,
for "The American Bible Society," 1828. [3]-429 p. GDC; LNB;
NcGuG.   32336

---- ---- Stereotyped by James
Connor, New York. New York,
Pub. by N. Bangs and J. Emory,
for the Methodist Episcopal
Church, at the conference office,

Azor Hoyt, pr., 1828. 162, [6] p.
WBur.   32337

---- ---- Stereotype ed. New
York, Stereotyped by J. Conner,
for "The American Bible Society," [D. Fanshaw, pr.] 1828. 237
p. CSt; NSyU; TWcW.   32338

---- ---- New-York, Pr. by
Samuel Marks, 1828. 192 p.
CSmH.   32339

---- ---- Stereotyped by J. Howe,
Philadelphia. Philadelphia, Pub.
by Joseph M'Dowell [1828?] 270 p.
PP.   32340

---- ---- Stereotyped by T. Rutt,
Shacklewell, London, for the
Bible Society at Philadelphia
[Philadelphia] 1828. 304 p. NNAB.
                                 32341
---- ---- [Stereotyped by J.
Howe] M'Carty & Davis' Edition,
Philadelphia, 1828. 239 p. P;
PSt.   32342

---- ---- Stereotyped by L.
Johnson, Philadelphia. Towar &
Hogan, Philadelphia, 1828. 238 p.
NN; NNAB.   32343

---- ---- Stereotyped by L.
Johnson... American Sunday
School Union, Philadelphia, 1828.
288 p. NN.   32344

---- ---- Stereotyped ed. Pub.
by Eugene Cummiskey, Philadelphia, 1828. 346 p. KyLoP.
                                 32345
---- ---- Stereotyped by B. & J.
Collins, New York... Miller &
Hammond, Providence, 1828.
312 [1] p. RPB.   32346

---- ---- To which is added, a
vocabulary of all the Words
Therein Contained... Adapted to
the orthography and pronunciation
of Walker. Likewise a catalogue
of all the proper names... By

Rensselaer Bently... Pr. and pub.
by J. Adancourt, Troy, N.Y.,
1828. 226, 62 p. CSmH; DLC.
                                 32347
---- ---- Stereotyped by H. & H.
Wallis, New York. Utica, Pr.
and pub. by Wm. Williams, 1828.
270 p. NAlf.   32348

---- ---- Stereotyped by J.
Howe, Philadelphia. Pr. and sold
... by R. Porter & Son, Wilmington,
1828. 240 p. DeWI.   32349

---- ---- Stereotyped by Hammond Wallis, New York... Pr.
and sold by Simeon Ide, Windsor
[Vt.], 1828. 372 p. MH; VtMiS;
BrMus.   32350

---- ---- Stereotyped by H. & H.
Wallis, New-York... Rufus Colton, Woodstock, Vt., 1828. 201
p. VtHi; VtU.   32351

---- A practical harmony of the
four Gospels, arranged according
to the most approved harmonies
in the words of the authorized
version, and accompanied with
notes. By Joseph Muenscher.
Northampton, Mass. Pub. by
Elisha Turner. Sold by Crocker
& Brewster, Boston: Jonathan
Leavitt, New-York; Carey, Lea &
Carey, Philadelphia. T. Watson
Shepard, pr., 1828. [8], 326,
[1] p. PPL.   32352

---- The pronouncing Testament.
Boston, Pr. and pub. by Lincoln
& Edmands. Sold also by Cush-
ing & Jewett, Baltimore; Abra-
ham Small, Philadelphia; John P.
Haven, New York; and by book-
sellers generally in the United
States. Stereotyped by T. H. &
C. Carter, Boston, 1828. O'
Callaghan.   32353

---- Psalms adapted to the public worship of the Christian
church... Princeton, N.J., D'

Hart, 1828. 272 p. NjP; NjR; PPPrHi. 32354

---- Psalms carefully suited to the Christian worship in the United States of America. Philadelphia, Pub. by Joseph Marot, 1828. 273 p. NjP; OUrC. 32355

---- The Psalms of David imitated in the language of the New Testament, and applied to the Christian state and worship. By Isaac Watts, D.D. Stereotyped by J. Reed, Boston. Elizabeth-Town, N.J., Pr. and Pub. by James Sanderson, 1828. 282 p. KBB; MA; NjP. 32356

---- ---- By I. Watts... Philadelphia, H. Adams, 1828. 272 p. CSmH. 32357

---- ---- Philadelphia, M. Carty and Davis, 1828. 240 p. CU; CtMW; NSyHi; PPPrHi. 32358

---- ---- Stereotyped by T. H. Carter & Co., Boston. Sanbornton, N.H., Pr. and pub. by D. V. Moulton, 1828. 272 p. MB; MDeeP; MWat; NN; NhHi. 32359

---- Der Psalter des Königs und Propheten David, verdeutscht von Dr. Martin Luther, mit kurzen Summarien oder Inhalt jedes Psalmen. Besonders für Schulen eingerichtet. Philadelphia, Herausgegeben von Georg W. Mentz, Stereotypirt von J. Howe, 1828. 251, [1] p. MH; PPL; PPLT; PPeSchw. 32360

---- The reference Bible,... with references... key sheet of questions... harmonies... maps and highly useful tables... by Hervey Wilbur. 8th ed. Boston, B. Perkins and Co., 1828. 607, 236 p. CtMW; NN. 32361

---- ---- By Hervey Wilbur...

6th ed. [Stereotyped by L. Johnson, Philadelphia] B. Perkins & Co.: Boston, American Sunday School Union, Philadelphia, 1828. 1012, 324, 98 p. MWA; NN; NjPT; WHi. 32362

---- The sacred writings of the apostles and evangelists of Jesus Christ, commonly styled the New Testament. Translated from the original Greek, by George Campbell, James Macknight, and Philip Doddridge... With prefaces to the historical and epistolary books; and an appendix, containing critical notes and various translations of difficult passages. 2d ed. Bethany, Va., Pr. and pub. by Alexander Campbell, 1828. 456 p. CSmH; DLC; ICMcC; InIB; KyLxCB; NN; NNAB; PPL; TNDC; ViU; Wv-Ar; WvBeC; WvU. 32363

---- St. Paul's Epistle to the Hebrews. A new translation, with a commentary by the Rev. Moses Stuart, M.A. Andover, Mass., 1828. O'Callaghan. 32364

---- The whole book of Psalms, in metre; with Hymns... New York, C. Bartlett, 1828. 142 p. NNG. 32365

The Bible-class book, designed for Bible-classes, Sabbath schools and families. Amherst [Mass.] Pub. by J. S. and C. Adams, 1828. 23 p. MB; MeB. 32366

The Bible-class book. Designed for Bible-classes, Sabbath schools and families. 2d ed. ... New York, Pub. by J. Leavitt, 1828. 29 p. MeB. 32367

Bible history. Wendell, Mass., Pr. and sold by J. Metcalf, 1828. 16 p. MA; MWA. 32368

Bible questions. See Nelson, D.

Bible Society of Grafton County. [New Hampshire] Constitution. Hanover [1828] 8 p. MBC; NhHi.   32369

Bible Society of Philadelphia The Twentieth report of the Bible Society of Philadelphia. Read before the Society, 7th May, 1828. Philadelphia, Pr. by order of the Society, by J. W. Allen, 1828. 37, [1] p. <u>PPL</u>.   32370

[Bickerstaffe, Isaac] The |spoil'd child; a farce in two acts. By Prince Hoare. Baltimore, J. Robinson, 1828. 27 p. MH.   32371

Bickersteth, Edward, 1786-1850 Missionary geography; or, The process of religion traced round the world. ... Revised by the Publishing Committee. Boston, Pr. by T. R. Marvin, for the Massachusetts Sabbath School Union, 1828. 106 p. NNC-T; ViRUT.   32372

---- A Scripture help, designed to assist in reading the Bible profitably. ...2d Amer. from the 3d English ed. Richmond [Va.], Pub. by A. Works, and by Jonathan Leavitt, New York [J. Macfarlan, pr.] 1828. [1], 209, 6 p. ArBaA; CSmH; CtSoP; GDC; LNHT; ScCMU; TCSPr; Vi; ViLxW; ViRUT; ViU.   32373

---- A treatise on prayer designed to assist in the devout discharge of that duty: with a few forms of prayer. ...From the 9th London ed. Richmond, Va., Pub. by Pollard & Converse; by Jonathan Leavitt, New York; Wm. Williams, Utica; Towar & Hogan, and John Grigg, Philadelphia [Pr. at the Franklin Press, Richmond] 1828. vi p. 1 l., 302 p. CBPac; CSmH; DLC; GGaB; IObB; ICMcC; KWiU; MWA; MnU; MoS; NBuG;

NcD; NjPT; RNR; ScCoT; TCSPr; Vi; ViRU; ViU.   32374

Bigelow, Andrew Pastoral responsibility. A discourse preached in the Unitarian Church, Washington City, on Sunday, the 26th of October, 1828. Washington, Pr. by Gales & Seaton, 1828. 20 p. DLC; MB; MBAt; MH; PHi; PPAmP; RPB.   32375

---- Signs of the moral age. A sermon preached in Reading, North Parish, on Lord's Day, Jan. 6, 1828; with sundry notes. Boston, Bowles & Dearborn, Press of Isaac R. Butts & Co., 1828. 42 p. DLC; MBAt; MH; MWA; MiD-B; NjPT; PPAmP; <u>PPL</u>; RPB; BrMus.   32376

[Bigelow, Jacob] 1787-1879 A short reply to a pamphlet published at Philadelphia, entitled "A defence of the experiments to determine the comparative value of the principal varieties of fuel used in the United States, and also in Europe... By Marcus Bull ..." By one of the committee of the American Academy. Boston, Hilliard, Gray, Little and Wilkins. New York, G. and C. Carvill. Philadelphia, Carey, Lea, and Carey [Cambridge, Hilliard Metcalf and Co., prs.] 1828. 12 p. CSmH; DLC; DeGE; MB; MH; MHi; MdHi; PPAmP; <u>PPL</u>; RPB; ScU; BrMus.   32377

Bigelow, Jonathan Christians should support and defend the truth. A sermon, delivered March 12, 1828, at the ordination of Rev. Asahel Bigelow, as pastor of the Orthodox Congregational Church in Walpole, Mass. Boston, T. R. Marvin, pr., 1828. 20 p. CBPac; CtSoP; DLC; ICN; MB; MH; MWA; MiD-B;

NCH; NjPT; OClWHi; <u>PPL</u>; RPB;
ViRUT; BrMus.　　　32378

Bigland, John, 1750-1832
A natural history of animals.
Philadelphia, Pub. by John Grigg,
1828. 189 p. CtHi; KU; KyDC;
MA; MH; MeB; NJQ; NcG; NcWsM;
OMC; PHi; RNR.　　　32379

---- A natural history of birds,
fishes, reptiles, and insects...
Philadelphia, J. Grigg, 1828.
179 p. DLC; ICJ; LU; MB; MH;
NNCT; NvHi; OClWHi; PHi; PPi;
RNR; VtB; WBB.　　　32380

Bingham, Caleb, 1757-1817
The Columbian orator; containing a variety of original and selected pieces together with rules;
calculated to improve youth and
others in the ornamental and useful art of eloquence. Stereotype
ed. Boston, Pr. and pub. by J.
H. A. Frost, 1828. 330 p. MH;
OMC; PU.　　　32381

[Binns, John] 1772-1860
Monumental inscriptions. [n. p. ,
1828] 8 l. DLC; MH; WMSF.
　　　32382
[----] ---- These inscriptions
compiled from authentic sources,
but principally from official documents, communicated by the Department of War to Congress, on
the 25th of January, 1828, are in
this form, submitted to the serious consideration of the American people... [n. p. , 1828] 1 p.
CSmH; DLC; NUt.　　　32383

Biographical sketch of the life of
Andrew Jackson. See Walsh, Robert.

Biographical sketches of great
and good men. Designed for the
amusement and instruction, of
young persons. Boston, Putnam
& Hunt, and Thomas T. Ash,
Philadelphia, 1828. 109 p. KU;

MB; MWA.　　　32384

Biography of the signers. See
Sanderson, John.

Bisbe, John, 1793-1829
A sermon delivered in the
Universalist Chapel in Portland,
on the annual Thanksgiving, No-
vember 29, 1827. Portland, Pr.
by Thomas Todd, 1828. 20 p.
CSmH; MH; MMeT-Hi; MWA;
MeB; MeHi.　　　32385

Bishop, Henry Rowley, 1786-
1855.
Oh! no we never mention her.
As sung by Mr. Pearman written
by T. H. Bayly, esq. arranged
by Henry R. Bishop. New York,
Pub. by Dubois & Stodart...
[1828?] [2] p. CSmH.　　　32386

Bisset, Robert, 1759-1805
The history of the reign of
George III. To which is prefixed,
A view of the progressive improvement of England, in prosperity and strength, to the accession of His Majesty... New ed. ,
brought down to the death of the
king... The library ed. Philadelphia, E. Littell, 1828. 3 v. AFlT;
AU; Ar-Hi; DLC; GU; KyDC; LN;
LNB; MChB; MMidb; MWA;
MdBL; MiD; MiU; MoSU; NBuG;
NT; NcU; NdMi; OHi; OO;
PP; PU; ScU; TU; ViL; WvU.
　　　32387
---- ---- New ed. brought down
to the death of the king... Philadelphia, Bennett & Walton, 1828.
3 v. GEU; InGrD; KHi; MoSpD;
TMC; ViU.　　　32388

The black velvet bracelet. By the
author of "The Shower," "Temptation" "Early Impressions," etc.
etc. Boston, Bowles & Dearborn,
Press of I. R. Butts & Co. , 1828.
164 p. KU; MPeaHi.　　　32389

The blackbird, being a choice

collection of the most popular American, English, Irish and Scotch songs. New York, S. King, 1828. 36 p. RPB.   32390

Blackford, Mrs., pseud.   See Stoddart, Isabella.

Blackford, William M.
An address, delivered at the request of the board of managers, before the Fredericksburg Auxiliary Colonization Society, at its anniversary meeting, February 25, 1828. Pub. by the Society. Fredericksburg, [Va.] Pr. at the Arena Office, by Jno. Minor, 1828. 12 p. CSmH; DLC.   32391

Blagden, George Washington, 1802-1884
Effects of education upon a country village. An address delivered before the Brighton School Fund Corporation, March 30, 1828. Boston, T. R. Marvin, pr., 1828. 25, [1] p. CtHT-W; DLC; MB; MBAt; MBC; MDeeP; MH; MHi; MWA; MiD-B; NNUT; NjR; PHi; PU-Penn; BrMus.
                                        32392
Blair, Hugh
An abridgement of lectures on rhetoric. Philadelphia, Towar & Hogan, 1828. 287 p. DLC; KyDC; MiMu.   32393

---- The beauties of Blair, consisting of selections from his works. Boston, N. H. Whitaker, 1828. 160 p. CtMMHi; IU; MB; MBAt; MH; MWA; MiD-B; OMC; PSC-Hi.   32394

Blake, John Lauris, 1788-1857
The historical reader, designed for the use of schools and families. On a new plan... Stereotype ed. Concord, N. H., Pub. by O. L. Sanborn. Boston, Richardson, Lord and Holbrook; Carter and Hendee, and Lincoln and Edmands. New York, N. & J.

White; and Collins and Hannay, Philadelphia; John Grigg and Towar and Hogan. Portland, Samuel Colman, [c1828] 372 p. CSt; CtY; MH; MWA; MiU; NcBe; Nh; RHi; RPB; TxH; TxU-T; ViHaI.
                                        32395
[Blanchard, Joshua P.] 1782-1868
Review of a "Letter from a gentleman in Boston to a Unitarian clergyman of that city." Boston, Wait, Greene, & co. Bowles & Dearborn, Press of Isaac R. Butts & Co., 1828. 24 p. CBPac; ICMe; ICN; MB; MBAU; MH; MHi; MWA; OU; PPL.   32396

[----] ---- 2d ed. Boston, Wait, Greene, & Co., Bowles & Dearborn, Press of Isaac R. Butts & Co., 1828. 24 p. CtSoP; MB; MWA; NjR; PPPrHi; WHi.
                                        32397
[----] ---- 3d ed. Boston, Wait, Greene & Co., Isaac R. Butts & co., pr., 1828. 24 p. NNUT; NjR.   32398

Blatchly, Cornelius C.
Sunday tract. [Philadelphia? 23 d of 12th month, 1828] 7 p. MB.   32399

Bliss, George, 1793-1873
An address, delivered at the opening of the town-hall in Springfield, March 24, 1828. Containing sketches of the early history of that town, and those in its vicinity. With an appendix. Springfield, Tannatt & co., 1828. 68 p. CSmH; DLC; MH.   32400

[Bloodgood, Simeon De Witt]
An Englishman's sketch-book; or, Letters from New-York... New York, G. and C. Carvill, Elliot and Palmer, prs., 1828. 195 p. CSmH; CSt; CtHT-W; CtY; DLC; ICN; MB; MH; NIC; BrMus.
                                        32401

[Bloomfield, Robert, 1766-1823]
Ruth Lee. Written for the
American Sunday School Union.
By the author of "Wild Flowers."
Philadelphia, American Sunday
School Union [c 1828] 195 p. DLC;
NN; PPAmS; PPL.   32402

Bloxham, Wansborough
An address delivered at the
close of the private school in
Dixfield Village, Dec. 22, 1827.
... Pub. by request. Norway, Pr.
at the Observer office by Asa
Barton, 1828. 20 p. Williamson:
1146.   32403

Blue-stocking Hall. See Scar-
gill, William Pitt.

Blunt, Joseph, 1792-1860
An anniversary discourse, delivered before the New-York Historical Society, Thursday, Dec.
13, 1827. New-York, G. and C.
Carvill [Elliott and Palmer, prs.]
1828. 52 p. CSmH; DLC; MB;
MBAt; MWA; NBuG; NN; NSy;
PHi; PU; WHi.   32404

Blythe, James
A sermon on the sinner's in-
ability to obey the law of God...
Frankfort, Pr. by A. G. Hodges,
1828. 23 p. CLSU; CSmH;
PPPrHi; TxU.   32405

The boarding school. See Tri-
olus, pseud.

Bochart, Samuel, 1599-1667
Sacred zoology or, The Scriptures illustrated by the natural
history of animated nature, intended to establish the authenticity of the sacred writings in
connection with zoology. Selected
principally from the most esteemed, authentic, and celebrated
voyages and travels into the East,
by Bochart, Shaw, Irwin, Char-
din, Thevenot, Pitts, and others:
1st Amer. ed., embellished with

plates. [vol. 1] Richmond, Pub.
by Joseph Martin, Pr. by T. W.
White, 1828. Vol. 1 only (viii,
262 p.) [No more published?]
NNC; Vi; ViU.   32406

Boieldieu, François Adrien
Les charmes de New York.
From La dame Blanche. Ar-
ranged as a rondo for the piano-
forte by C. Thibault. New York,
Dubois & Stodart, 1828. 8 p.
MB.   32407

Bolles, William
A spelling book; containing
exercises in orthography, pro-
nunciation and reading. ... 3d ed.
New London, W. Bolles, 1828.
MH.   32408

Bonaparte, Charles Lucien Jules
Laurent, Prince de Canino, 1803-
1857
The genera of North American
birds, and a synopsis of the species found within the territory of
the United States... Extracted
from the Annals of the Lyceum
of Natural History of New York.
New-York, Pr. by J. Seymour,
1828. 1 l., [7]-451 p. KU; MB;
MH; MdBP; NB; NN; PPAN;
PPC; T.   32409

Bond, Alvan, 1793-1882
Memoir of the Rev. Pliny
Fisk, A. M. late missionary to
Palestine. Boston, Pub. by Crock-
er & Brewster; New-York, Jona-
than Leavitt, 1828. 437, [3] p.
ArBaA; CBPac; CU; CtHT-W;
CtY; DLC; GDC; ICMcC; IEdS;
IaHi; KyDC; LU; MA; MB; MBC;
MH; MWHi; MeB; MiD-B; NCH;
NNG; NSyU; NbCrD; NcMHi; NjP;
OClW; OO; PPLT; PPPrHi; PU;
RHi; RPB; VtU; BrMus.   32410

[Bond, Thomas E.]
A narrative and defence of the
proceedings of the Methodist
Episcopal Church in Baltimore

City Station, against certain local preachers and lay-members of said church... To which is added an appendix, containing the Rev. James M. Hanson's Vindication of his official conduct... Baltimore, Pub. by Armstrong & Plaskitt, J.D. Toy, pr., 1828. 135 p. IEG; MWA; MdBBC; MdBE; MdHi; MiD; MsJMC; PPL; PPPrHi; TxDaM.   32411

The book of prices adopted by the house carpenters of the towns of Zanesville & Putnam, March 22, 1828. Zanesville, Pr. by Peters & Pelham, 1828. 15, [2] p. ICN.
                                      32412

Boscawen Academy
A catalogue of the officers and members of Boscawen Academy, spring and summer terms, 1828. Concord, Asa M'Farland, pr., 1828. 6, [1] p. MBAt; MH; PPL.
                                      32413

Bossut, M. L'Abbe, pseud. See Phillips, Sir Richard.

Boston (City)
An address to the board of aldermen and members of the common council on the organization of the city government, January 1, 1828... Boston, N. Hale, city pr., 1828. 19 p. CSmH; DLC; MB; MH; MHi; MWA; MnU; BrMus.   32414

---- City of Boston. In Common Council, June 30, 1828. The joint committee of the city council, who were charged... with the location and general superintendance of the Boston Free Bridge ...report. [Boston, 1828] 8 p. MBAt; MHi.   32415

---- City of Boston. In Common Council, Oct. 6, 1828... The committee of the city council who were directed to consider the expediency of selling... the right of the city to extend a wharf over

the flats, eastward of Faneuil Hall Market, respectfully report. [Boston, 1828] 11 p. MBAt; MHi.   32416

---- City of Boston. Report of the committee of the city council on the memorial of the warden and inspectors of ward no. 9, complaining of the imperfection of the voting lists. [Boston, Dec. 22, 1828] 16 p. MB; MBAt; MHi; MWA.   32417

---- General abstract of the bill of mortality for the city of Boston. From the first of January, 1827, to the first of January, 1828. Agreeably to the records kept at the Health Office... Samuel H. Hewes, Superintendent of Burial Grounds. [Boston, 1828] Bdsd. MB; MHi.   32418

---- List of persons, co-partnerships, and corporations taxed $25 and upwards. [Boston, Hale's Press, 1828?] MB; MBAt; MBB.   32419

---- Report of a sub-committee of the school committee, recommending various improvements in the system of instruction in the grammar and writing schools of this city. Boston, Press of Nathan Hale, city pr., 1828. 37 p. CU; DLC; ICN; ICU; M; MB; MBAt; MBB; MH; MHi; MiD-B; NcD; PHi.   32420

---- Report of the committee for making trial of Monitorial instruction in the primary schools. [Boston, 1828] 15 p. MHi; NIC.
                                      32421

---- Report on compensation of chief engineer of fire dept. [Boston, 1828] 8 p. MBAt.
                                      32422

---- Sixteenth annual report of the receipts and expenditures of the city of Boston and county of

Suffolk. May 1, 1828. Boston,
Nathan Hale, city pr. , 1828. 56
p. DLC; MiD-B; PPL.   32423

Boston. Association of Traders
    Constitution of the Association
of Traders and others, in Boston
and vicinity, for mutual protection against shop lifting and store
breaking instituted, Boston, July
23, 1828. Boston, True & Greene,
prs. , 1828. 6 p. DLC.   32424

Boston Athenaeum. Gallery.
    A catalogue of the second ex-
hibition of paintings, in the A-
thenaeum Gallery [etc.] May 1,
1828. Boston, Press of Wm. W.
Clapp [1828] 8 p. [lists 273 items]
MBAt.   32425

---- ---- Boston, Press of Wm.
W. Clapp, [1828] (with supple.)
8, [1] p. [Lists 318 items.]
MBAt.   32426

---- ---- 2d ed. Boston, Press
of Wm. W. Clapp [1828?] 8 p.
[Lists 318 items] MBAt.   32427

Boston. Citizens
    Report of a committee of the
citizens of Boston and vicinity
opposed to a further increase of
duties on importations. New-
York, Pr. by Clayton & Van Norden, 1828. 196 p. CSmH; CtY;
DLC; IU; InU; MH-BA; MWA;
NIC; Nj; P; PHi; PU; ScU; Vi.
                            32428
---- Report of a committee of
the citizens of Boston and vicinity, opposed to a further increase
of duties on importations. Philadelphia, S. Parker, 1828. 180 p.
P; PPL.   32429

---- ---- Boston, Pr. , Charleston, repr. , A. E. Miller, 1828.
122 p. RPB; ScC.   32430

Boston. Committee for the Relief
of the Greeks.

Address of the Committee appointed at a public meeting held
in Boston, December 19, 1828,
for the relief of the Greeks, to
their fellow citizens. [Boston]
Press of the North American Review, 1828. 18 p. MiD-B.
                            32431
Boston directory; containing
names of the inhabitants; their
occupations, places of business
and dwelling houses; with lists of
the streets, lanes and wharves,
the city officers, public offices
and banks and other useful information. Boston, Hunt & Simpson,
1828. 343 p. MBAt; MBNEH;
MWA; NN.   32432

Boston Evening Bulletin
    Address of the carriers of the
Boston Evening Bulletin. January
1, 1828. [Boston, 1828] Bdsd.
MB.   32433

Boston Fatherless & Widows Society
    Order of exercises at the an-
niversary of the Fatherless and
Widows Society in the Rev. Dr.
Channing's meeting house, Oct.
12, 1828. [Boston, 1828] 1 p.
MHi.   32434

Boston. Federal Street Baptist
Church
    A summary declaration of the
faith and practice of the Federal
Street Baptist Church of Christ in
Boston, adopted June 14, 1827.
Boston, Mass. , Pr. by Lincoln
& Edmands, 1828. 9 p. MNtcA.
                            32435
Boston Female Asylum
    Order of services at the twen-
ty-eighth anniversary... Sept. 26,
1828. Boston, 1828. Bdsd. MHi.
                            32436
Boston Female Monitorial School
    Second report of the instructer
of the Monitorial School, Boston.
Pub. by order of the trustees.
Boston, Munroe & Francis, prs. ,

1828. 20 p. MWA; NIC; PPAmP; PPL.   32437

Boston. King's Chapel.
Liturgy for the use of the church at King's Chapel in Boston; collected principally from the Book of Common Prayer. ... 3d ed. With alterations and additions. Boston, From the press of the Christian Examiner. Hiram Tupper, pr., 1828. 368 p. CBPac; CtHT; ICMe; MB; MBAU; MBAt; MoSpD; MoU; NNG. 32438

Boston Mechanics' Institution
The first annual report of the board of managers of the Boston Mechanics' Institution... with the constitution and a list of the members. Boston, Pr. by John Cotton, 1828. 24 p. M; MBAt; MH; MHi; PP; WHi.   32439

Boston. Methodist Episcopal Church in North Bennett Street.
Plan of the Methodist Episcopal Church in North Bennett Street, Boston. 1828. The pews will be offered for sale at auction, on Friday, September 26, at 2 o'clock, P.M. [Boston, 1828] Bdsd. MHi.   32440

---- Old South Church.
Order of exercises at the installation of the Rev. Mellish Irving Motte, over the South Congregational Society, Wednesday, May 21, 1828. [Boston, 1828] Bdsd. MB.   32441

---- Order of services, at the dedication of the South Congregational Church, Wednesday, January 30, 1828. [Boston, 1828] Bdsd. MB; MHi.   32442

---- Public Latin School
A catalogue of the scholars of the Public Latin School in School-Street, Boston, September, 1828. Boston, Pr. by James Loring,

1828. 12 p. MBAt.   32443

Boston reading lessons. See Hale, Sarah Preston (Everett).

The Boston report and mercantile memorials. See Carey, Mathew.

Boston. Salem Church
The articles of faith and covenant of the Salem Church, Boston, with a list of the members. Boston, T. R. Marvin, pr., 1828. 11, [1] p. MBC; MHi.   32444

---- Scholars Club.
Order of exercises at the annual public declamation of the Scholars' Club, formerly members of the English High School, on Thursday evening Sept. 18, 1828. [Boston, 1828] Bdsd. MH.   32445

Boston Society for the Moral and Religious Instruction of the Poor.
Twelfth annual report of the directors to the Boston Society for the Religious and Moral Instruction of the Poor. Read and accepted, Dec. 4, 1828. Boston, Pr. by Crocker & Brewster, 1828. 32 p. MB; MLow.   32446

Boston Theatre
Playbill. Benefit of Mr. Holland. Feb. 25, 1828. [Boston, 1828] Bdsd. NN.   32447

Boston. Trinity Church
Notification. Boston, April 4, 1828. The special meeting of the Proprietors of Trinity Church for rebuilding their House, stands adjourned to the annual meeting ... [2] p. MHi.   32448

Boston Type and Stereotype Foundry.
Specimen of printing types from the Boston Type and Stereotype Foundry. John G. Rogers, agent. Counting room congress,

corner of Lindall street. Boston,
Dutton and Wentworth, prs.,
1828. [243] p. MAm; MB; NNC.
                                32449
Bostwick, Henry
    A historical and classical at-
las, illustrating... ancient history
and geography... New York,
1828. [40] p. maps. NBLiHi;
NjP.   32450

Botsford, Edmund
    The spiritual voyage, per-
formed in the ship Convert, under the command of Captain God-
ly - fear, from the port of Repentance - unto - life, to the
haven of Felicity on the conti-
nent of Glory. An allegory...
New ed., rev., corr. and improved; to which is prefixed a
sketch of the Life of the author,
by the Rev. Richard Furman...
Charleston, [S. C.] W. Riley,
1828. 120 p. ICN; RPJCB; ViU.
                                32451
---- ---- Harrisburg, Repr. for
D. Barnes, 1828. 126 p. DLC;
NcD; T.   32452

The bouquet; a poetical offering
to lovers of taste and sentiment,
selected from various authors.
Providence, H. H. Brown, pr.,
1828. 32 p. MLex; RHi.   32453

Bouton, Nathaniel, 1799-1878
    The responsibilities of rulers.
A sermon, delivered at Concord,
June 5, 1828 before the consti-
tuted authorities of the state of
New-Hampshire. Concord, Pr. by
Henry E. Moore, 1828. 31 p.
CSmH; CtY; DLC; GDC; MBAt;
MH; MHi; MeBaT; MiD-B; MnHi;
NNG; NhD; NjR; PCC; VtMiM;
BrMus.   32454

---- ---- Concord, Pr. by Henry E. Moore, 1828. 31 p. [Vari-
ant of 32454; cover-title set with
different font.] CSmH.   32455

Bowdoin College, Brunswick, Me.
    Catalogue of the officers and
students of Bowdoin College, and
the Medical School of Maine,
February, 1828. Brunswick, Jos-
eph Griffin, pr., 1828. 16 p.
DLC; MHi; MeB; MeHi; NjP.
                                32456
---- Catalogue of the officers
and students of Bowdoin College,
October, 1828. Brunswick, Geo.
Griffin, pr., 1828. 8 p. MBAt.
                                32457
---- Catalogus senatus academici,
et eorum, qui munera et officia
gesserunt, quique alicujus gradus
laurea donati sunt in Collegio
Bowdeinensi, Republicae Mainen-
si. Brunsvici, E. Typhis Georgii
Griffin, 1828. 21 p. MeB; MiD-
B.   32458

Bowen, William
    Weeping for ourselves the duty
of all men. A discourse, delivered Lord's-day afternoon, at the
house of Zoraida Coffin, occasioned by the death of her daughter, Ann F. Coffin, who died in
the triumphs of faith, aged 18
years, 5 months, and 11 days,
May 11, 1828. New-Bedford,
Benjamin T. Congdon, 1828. 19
p. CtSoP; RPB.   32459

Boyle, Robert, Voyages and adventures of. See Chetwood, William Rufus.

[Bradford, A.]
    The divine unity the doctrine
of the Bible, by a aged layman
...Boston, Bowles & Dearborn,
Press of Isaac R. Butts & Co.,
1828. 35 p. ICMe; MBAt; MDovC;
MWA; MiD-B.   32460

Bradford County. Democratic corresponding committee. See Democratic Party. Pennsylvania.

[Bradstreet, Mrs. Martha]
    Judicial specimens, and brief

explanatory correspondence, submitted to the consideration of a free people, and their legislative representatives... New-York, Pr. for the author, 1828. 15 p. DLC; MB; MBAt; NCH; NjR.   32461

[Branagan, Thomas,] b 1774
The excellency of the female character vindicated; being an investigation relative to the cause and effects of the encroachments of men upon the rights of women, and the too frequent degradation and consequent misfortunes of the fair sex. Pr. from the 2d ed. By the author of the "Beauties of philanthropy." Harrisburg, Pr. by Francis Wyeth, 1828. 280 p. CSmH; CtMW; DLC; P; PHi; PPL; PPi; RPB.   32462

Brazier, Nicolas, 1783-1838
Neal & MacKenzie. No. 201 Chestnut Street, between the Theater & Arcade, Philadelphia. Tony; ou, cinq annees en deux heures, comedie vaudeville en deux actes, par Mm. Brazier, Melesville et Carmouche. [Philadelphia, 1828] 27 p. (Also issued in vol. with covering title: Collection d'operas et vaudevilles) PPL.   32463

Breathitt, John
Circular To the people of Kentucky. By John Breathitt. June 26, 1828. [candidate for the office of Lieutenant Governor] [Louisville] S. Penn, Jr., pr., 1828. 12 p. DLC; KyLoF.   32464

Breck, Samuel, 1771-1862
Address delivered before the Blockley and Merion Agricultural Society on Saturday, September 20th, 1828. On the death of their late president, the Hon. Richard Peters... Philadelphia, Pr. by Lydia R. Bailey, 1828. 27 p. DeWI; ICU; MH; MiD-B; PHC; PHi; PP; PPAmP; PPL;

RPB.   32465

Breckinridge, John, 1797-1841
Ministerial responsibility. A discourse, the substance of which was delivered before the synod of Philadelphia at its late meeting in Harrisburg, (Pa.) Oct. 1827. Baltimore, Armstrong & Plaskitt, John D. Toy, pr., 1828. 56 p. CtY; In; MH-AH; MNF; MoSpD; NjPT; OCHP; PHi; PPPrHi.   32466

Breckinridge, Robert Jefferson
A Masonic oration, delivered before the Grand Lodge of Kentucky, at its annual communication in Lexington, on the 26th August, A.D. 1828, A.L. 5828. Lexington, Ky., Pr. by Joseph G. Norwood, 1828. 14 p. PPPrHi.
                                          32467
[Brent, William L.]
To the voters of the Third Congressional District of the state of Louisiana. [Washington, April 25, 1828] 14 p. PPL.
                                          32468
Brewster, George
An oration on the evils of lotteries... Brooklyn, Pr. for the author, by Piercy and Burling... 1828. 22 p. CSmH; NBLiHi; NN; PLT.   32469

[Brice, James Frisby]
Andrew Jackson, an interlude in three acts. By the author of Democedes. [Annapolis] Pr. by J. Green, April 1828. 12 p. DLC; MWA.   32470

Bridgman, Richard Whalley, 1761?-1820
An analytical digest of the reported cases in the courts of equity, and the high court of Parliament... 1st Amer. from the 3d and last London ed. New York, O. Halsted, pr., 1828. 3 vols. C; DLC; IaDaGL; Md; NjP; NjR; Nm; OCLaw; ViU; WaU.   32471

Brief account of the dreadful occurrence at the laying of the corner stone of the Methodist Church in North Bennet Street, Boston, April 30, 1828. To which is affixed the address delivered on the occasion by the Rev. John Newland Maffit. [Boston, 1828] 11 p. DLC; MWA.   32472

A brief account of the execution of the six militia men. As we soon expect to have official documents in relation to the six militia men, arrested, tried, and put to death under the orders of General Andrew Jackson this may not be an improper time to give to the public some of the particulars of the execution, as we have them from "An Eye Witness."... Extract of a letter to the Editors, dated Washington City. Jan. 30, 1828. 1 p. DLC; NN.   32473

A brief refutation of the slanders ... See Democratic Party. Maryland.

Brief remarks on the rail roads. See Berkshire, pseud.

Brief sketch of the life, character and services of Major General Andrew Jackson. See Hill, Isaac.

A brief statement of facts relating to difficulties in Killingworth, Conn. New Haven, Treadway and Adams, 1828. 15 p. CtHT-W.   32474

A brief summary of Baptist sentiments and practice, at the present day: to which is added, an account of the antiquity of the Baptist sentiments... Danbury [Conn.] For the author, by O. Osburn, pr., 1828. [Signed: A well wisher.] 48 p. CSmH.
                                      32475
A brief view of the government

of the Methodist E. Church, set forth in question and answer, so that by comparing these with the conventional articles, the most ordinary reader will be able to see the difference, and decide between the two systems. Together with conventional articles for the associated Methodist Churches, agreed upon... Nov. 12, 1828. [Imprint blacked out-1828?] PPL.
                                      32476
Briery Presbyterian Church. Hampden District. Prince Edward Co., Virginia
    A manual for the members of the Briery Presbyterian Church, Virginia. Compiled by J. W. Douglas. Richmond, Pub. by order of the session. Pr. by J. Macfarlan, 1828. 60 p. MoS; MoSHi; NcMHi; OFH; ViU. 32477

Brigham, Juan C.
    Atlas adapto al systema nuevo de geografia. Nueva York, White, Gallaher & White, 1828. 5 maps. (Nuevo sistema de geografia pr. in 1827) DLC.   32478

Broad grins of Rochester. See Van Slyck, Albert.

Broaddus, Andrew, 1770-1848
    The Dover selection of spiritual songs: with an appendix of choice hymns, on various occasions: compiled by the recommendation of the Dover Association. Richmond, Pub. by Collins & co., 1828. [var. pag.] DLC; MNtcA; MdBP; NcWsW; ViRU.
                                      32479
Brockway, Diodate, 1776-1849
    A sermon preached in Ellington, January 6th, the first Sabbath in the year 1828. Pub. by those who heard it. Hartford [Conn.] Pr. by Goodwin & co., 1828. 28 p. CSmH; Ct; CtHi; CtY; MWA; NjPT; OO; RPB.
                                      32480
The broken hyacinth. See Sher-

wood, Mrs. Mary Martha (Butt).

Bronson, Asahel
A sermon on the divine decrees, containing a dialogue between Armenians and Calvinists; and also, an explanation of the III chapter of the Presbyterian Confession of faith, preached at Amenia South, N. Y., Feb. 17, 1828. Poughkeepsie, Barnum & Myers, 1828. 18 p. C.   32481

Brooke, Francis
Richmond, February 8th, 1828. My dear Sir, I avail myself of the earliest moment, since the Proceedings and address to the people of Virginia were printed, under the direction of the Central Committee to comply with the resolution of the Convention, requesting me to transmit a copy thereof to each of the gentlemen nominated on its electoral ticket, and to inform them of their several appointments... [Signed in mss. Francis Brooke, President of the Convention.] Richmond, 1828. 1 p. DLC.   32482

Brooklyn (N. Y.)
Ordinances of the village of Brooklyn. [A law to prevent certain animals from running at large in the village of Brooklyn. Passed January 16, 1828.] 40 p. DLC; NBLiHi; NHi.   32483

Brooklyn Apprentices' Library Association
Catalogue of books, belonging to the Brooklyn Apprentices' Library Association. Brooklyn, A. Spooner, 1828. 35 p. NBLiHi.   32484

Brooks, Charles, 1795-1872
Daily monitor, or Reflections for each day in the year... Boston, N. S. Simpkins & co.; Hilliard, Gray, Little and Wilkins [Hingham, Farmer & Brown, prs.] 1828. 374 p. CSmH; ICMcC;

IaHi; MBC; MHi; MWA; Nh.   32485

Brougham and Vaux, Henry Peter Brougham, 1st baron, 1778-1868
Present state of the law. The speech of Henry Brougham, esp., M. P., in the House of commons, on Thursday, February 7th, 1828... Philadelphia, Carey, Lea & Carey, 1828. xii, 146 p., 1 l. A-Ar; CSmH; CtY; DGU; DLC; IaUL; MBAt; MH; MNF; MWA; NIC; NNC-L; NjR; OCLaw; PHi; PPAmP; PPL; ScCC; Vi; ViL.   32486

Broussais, François Joseph Victor, 1772-1838
A treatise on physiology applied to pathology. ... Trans. from the French by John Bell, M. D., and R. LaRoche, M. D. 2d Amer. ed. Philadelphia, Carey, Lea & Carey, publishers. Skerrett, pr., 1828. 600 p. CL; CU; GEU-M; ICU; IEN-M; IU-M; KyLxT; MBU-M; MdBM; MeB; MoU; NNNAM; OCU-M; PPC; PU; RNR; TJaU; ViRA.   32487

[**Brown, Bartholomew**], compiler. 1772-1850
Templi carmina. Songs of the temple; or, Bridgewater collection of sacred music. 18th ed. Boston, Richardson & Lord, 1828. ICN; MH.   32488

Brown, David Paul
Review of the speech of Henry Brougham, Esquire, upon the state of the law. Philadelphia, J. Dobson, Mifflin and Parry, prs., 1828. [3], 64 p. DLC; ICN; MBAt; MH; MdBP; PHi; PPAmP; PPB; PPL; RPB; BrMus.   32489

Brown, Erastus
The trial of Cain, the first murderer, in poetry, by rule of court; in which a Predestinarian, a Universalian and an Armenian argue as attorneys at the bar; the two former as the prisoner's

counsel, the latter as attorney
general. Taunton [Mass.], Repub. by Lorenzo D. Johnson,
Hack and Anthony, prs., 1828.
36 p. CSmH; MB; MHi; MNBedf;
NN; RPB.   32490

Brown, James, 1815-1841
    The American grammar, ab-
breviated and simplified. Chambersburg, Pa., Pr. for the author by Geo. K. Harper, 1828.
144 p. IaHoL; P; PSt.   32491

---- An appeal from the present
popular systems of English phil-
ology to common sense...De-
signed to aid the introduction of
the American system of English
grammar. Carlisle, Pr. at the
"Herald" Office, 1828. 432 p.
PHi.   32492

Brown, Mathew, 1776-1853
    Charge to Rev. Jacob J. Jane-
way, D.D. at his inauguration.
Pittsburgh, Johnston & Stockton,
1828. 12 p. MBC.   32493

[Brown, Paul]
    A dialogue on commonwealths.
Cincinnati, Pr. by S. J. Browne,
1828. 16 p. DLC.   32494

Brown, Thomas, 1778-1820
    Lectures on the philosophy of
the human mind. Cor. from the
last London ed. Stereotyped by
T. H. Carter & co., Boston.
Hallowell [Me.], Glazier & co.,
1828. 2 v. CBPac; CtHT-W;
DLC; GAU; GEU-M; IU; MB;
MeB; MdBL; NNF; NNG; OM; OO;
RPB; ViU.   32495

Brown University.
    Catalogue of the officers and
students of Brown University,
February-1828. Providence, R.I.,
Literary Cadet Office, Smith &
Parmenter, prs., 1828. 12 p.
RPB.   32496

---- Catalogue of the officers and
students of Brown University, for
the academical year 1827-8.
Providence, R.I., F.Y. Carlile
& Co., prs., 1828. 10, [1] p.
RPB.   32497

---- Philermenian Society. Library.
    Catalogue of the books in the
library of the Philermenian Society, with the names of its members. Brown University, Sept.
1828. Providence, Office of the
Christian telescope. John S.
Greene, pr., 1828. 47 p. DLC;
MHi.   32498

Browne, Augusta
    Tyrolese evening hymn. [With
accompaniment for pianoforte.]
Words by Mrs. Hemans. Music
by Miss Browne. Boston, Bradlee, 1828. [2] p. MB.   32499

Browne, David
    A self defence, with a refuta-
tion of calumnies, misrepresentations and fallacies, which have
appeared in several public prints,
evidently intended to convey false
impressions of the "Logierian
diplomatic institution;" as now
established in England, Germany,
France, Spain, East and West
Indies, Africa &c. Also, a review of a pamphlet addressed to
"the musical world;"... by Mr.
Logier. Boston. Browne's Musical Seminary, 1828. 28 p. MB;
MBAt; MH; PPL.   32500

Bruce, Robert
    An address delivered before
the Pittsburgh Philosophical Society. ...July 3, 1828. Pittsburgh, Pittsburgh Philosophical
Society, 1828. 17 p. KyU; MBAt;
NTR; P; PHi; PPAmP; PPi; PU.
                            32501
Brutus, pseud.
    An address to the people of
the United States, being an exam-

ination of a pamphlet, written by "Aristides," and designed to mislead the public mind in favor of General Jackson. By Brutus. Pr. for the author, 1828. 28 p. PHi.
32502

[Bryan, Thomas]
...It has been long the united wish of the most respectable merchants in this country, connected with the silk trade...[New York] 1828. 7 p. (A circular letter, signed: Thomas Bryan. Dated: New-York, January 10th, 1828.) DLC; DeGE; MB; MH-BA; MnD; BrMus.   32503

Buchan, William, 1729-1805
Domestic medicine, or A treatise on the prevention and cure of diseases... From the 22d English ed., with considerable additions, and notes. Exeter, J. & B. Williams, 1828. 495, xlviii p. DLC; MA; MBCo; MiHi; NBM; NcU; OS; RJa; TU-M.
32504

[Buchanan, James]
Report and observations, on the banks, and other incorporated institutions, in the state of New York. With an appendix, and notes. New York, Pr. by W. A. Mercein, 1828. 40 p. CtY; DeGE; ICU; MB; MBAt; MH-BA; MWA; NNS; NjR; OO; PPAmP; PPL; PU.   32505

Buchanan, James, 1791-1868
Bemerkungen von James Buchanan, Esq. Mitlied des Congresses von Pennsylvanien, Gehalten am Montag, den 4ten Februar, 1828, auf Mr. Chiltons Resolution, die Kosten der allgemeinen Regierung zu verringern. Lancaster, 1828. 28 p. Lancaster County Historical Society.
32506

---- ... Remarks of Mr. Buchanan, of Pennsylvania, made on Monday, the 4th February, 1828. On Mr. Chilton's reso-

lution to retrench the expenditures of the general government. Washington, Pr. by Green and Jarvis, 1828. 23 p. United States' telegraph -- Extra. CSmH; DLC; MH; PPL.
32507

Buchanan, William B.
Observations on the silk worm. Baltimore, Pr. by J. D. Toy, 1828. 20 p. DeGE; MdBL; MdHi.
32508

Budd, Thomas Allibon
An oration before the Washington Benevolent Society of Pennsylvania. Delivered in the Olympic Theatre, on the 22d of February, 1828. Philadelphia, Pr. by John Clarke, 1828. 25 p. CSmH; CtY; DLC; MBAt; NjR; PPL.   32509

Bull, Marcus
An answer to "A short reply to 'A defence of the experiments to determine the comparative value of the principal varieties of fuel, &c.' By one of the committee of the American Academy." ... By Marcus Bull... Philadelphia, Judah Dobson, G. & C. Carvill, New-York; Hilliard, Gray, Little & Wilkins, Boston. London, John Miller, Arthus Bertrand, 1828. 16 p. CtY; DLC; DeGE; MB; MH; MWA; MdHi; NjR; PHi; PPAmP; PPL; BrMus.
32510

---- A defence of the experiments to determine the comparative value of the principal varieties of fuel used in the United States, and also in Europe. Containing a correspondence with a committee of the American Academy of Arts and Sciences; their report, and remarks thereon; and animadversions on the manner in which the trust confided to the Academy by Count Rumford has been managed. By Marcus Bull... Philadelphia, Judah Dobson; New York, G. & C. Carvill; [etc., etc.] 1828. 51 p.

CtY; DLC; DNLM; IaDaM; MBAt; MH-BA; MdHi; NN; NjR; PHi; PPAmP; PPF; <u>PPL</u>; RPB; Vt-U; BrMus.   32511

Bumstead, Samuel A.
Token of respect to a departed brother. A sermon delivered ...in the Bedford Street Chapel, Boston, July 20, 1828. On the death of Mr. Frederick Bumstead... Boston, Lyman Gilbert, pr., 1828. 19 p. MH; MiD-B; <u>PPL</u>; RPB; BrMus.   32512

[Bunbury, Selina]
A visit to my birth-place. By the author of The pastor's tales, &c. ...Amer. ed., rev. and imp. Boston, Pub. at James Loring's Sabbath School Book-store [cop. 1828] vii, [5], 137, [3] p. <u>MH</u>.
32513

Bunn, Matthew, b. 1772
Narrative of the life and adventures of Matthew Bunn, (of Providence, R.I.) in an expedition against the northwestern Indians, in the years 1791, 2, 3, 4 & 5. (7th ed., rev. 4000 copies) Batavia [N.Y.] Pr. for the author, by Adams and Thorp, 1828. 59 p. DLC; ICN; MH; MWA; MiD-B; N; OCHP; OClWHi; PPAmP; PPiU; RPB; WHi. 32514

Bunyan, John, 1628-1688
Bunyan's Grace abounding to the chief of sinners; Heart's ease in heart trouble; The world to come, or Visions of heaven and hell; and the Barren fig-tree. Philadelphia, Pub. by J. J. Woodward. Stereotyped by L. Johnson, 1828. 409 p. CoD; CtMW; GMM; KyLoS; MDeeP; MdBL; MiD; MoS; NSsS; Nh; OO; PPPD; RPE.
32515
---- Eines Christen reise nach der seligen ewigkeit, welche in unterschiedlichen artigen sinnbildern den ganzen zustand einer buszfertigen und gottsuchenden

seele vorstellt. In Englischer sprache beschrieben durch Johann Bunyan... Harrisburg (Pa.) Gedruckt und zu haben bey Gustav S. Peters, 1828. 164, 158 p. CSmH; MiU-C; P; <u>PPL</u>; PPLT.
32516
---- Der Himlische Wandersmann, Oder Eine Beschreibung vom Menschen der in Himmel kommt: Sammt dem Wege darin er wandelt, den Zeichen und der Spure da er durchgehet, und einige Anweisungen wie man laufen soll das Kleinod zu ergreifen. Beschrieben in Englischer Sprache durch Johannes Bunyan... Lancaster, Gedruck von Johann Bär, 1828. 68 p. MH; MiU-C; P; PHi; <u>PPL</u>.
32517
---- The pilgrim's progress from this world to that which is to come, delivered under the similitude of a dream; in two parts. ...with original notes by Rev. Thomas Scott, chaplain to the Loch Hospital. Hartford, S. Andrus, publisher, 1828. xv, 360 p. CtHi; CtSoP; CtY; DLC; FU; MH; MWA; MoSU; OClW; PP; TxHuT; Vi; ViU.
32518

---- ---- New York, American Tract Society, 1828. [4]-464 p. ViRVB.
32519

---- ---- New York, Kinnersley, 1828. 2 p. l., [1] iv-viii 447 [1] p. NN.
32520

Burdett, Mrs. C. D.
English fashionables abroad. A novel. In two volumes. Boston, Wells and Lilly, 1828. CtHT; CtY; MH; MeB; PU; RPB. 32521

Burford, Robert, 1791-1861
Description of the panorama of the superb city of Mexico and the surrounding scenery, painted on 2700 square feet of canvas, by Robert Burford, esq., from draw-

ings made on the spot, at the request of the Mexican government, by Mr. W. Bullock, jr. Now open for public inspection at the Rotunda, New-York. New York, Pr. by E. Conrad, 1828. 16 p. CSmH; CtY; DLC; InID; MB; MBAt; MHi; MWA; NN; PHi; TxGR.   32522

[Burges, Mary Anne] 1763-1813
The progress of the pilgrim Good-intent, in Jacobinical times ...2d Amer. ed. New-York, Cornelius Davis, 1828. 188 p. CtY; NN.   32523

Burges, Tristam, 1770-1853
Speech of Mr. Burges, of Rhode Island, delivered in the House of Representatives of the United States, April 21st, A.D. 1828, on the tariff. Washington [D.C.] Way and Gideon, prs., 1828. 90 p. CSmH.   32524

---- Speech of Mr. Burges of Rhode Island, in Committee of the Whole on the state of the union, March 29, 1828, on Mr. Mallary's motion to amend the bill on wool and woollens. 2d ed. Washington, Pr. by P. Force, 1828. 42 p. CSmH; CtHT-W; CtY; DLC; DeGE; IU; LU; MH; MHi; MWA; MeB; MiD-B; OClWHi; RHi; RNR; ScU; BrMus.   32525

Burhans, Daniel
The Scripture doctrine of the election of Jacob, and rejection of Esau, considered. A sermon, preached Sept. 12, 1810... 2d ed. Boston, Pr. at no. 164 Washington-street, 1828. 31 p. Ct; CtY; DLC; MWA; MiD-B; NNG; NjR; Vt; BrMus.   32526

Burhans, Hezekiah
The nomenclature, and expositer of the English language; in which the meaning of each word is clearly explained, and the

orthoepy of every syllable accurately pointed out, according to John Walker's pronouncing dictionary. Compiled for the use of schools in the United States, and Great Britain. Pr. and sold by John Montgomery, New York; Wm. Williams, Utica; Uriah Hunt, Philadelphia... G. J. Loomis, Albany, N.Y., and Peter Cottom, Richmond, Va. Stereotyped by James Conner, New York, 1828. 212 p. ViU.   32527

Burke, Edmund, 1729-1797
The beauties of Burke. Consisting of selections from his works. Boston, N.H. Whitaker, 1828.   CBPac; CtHT-W; LNT; MB; MBAt; MDeeP; MH; MeBaT; MiD; MiU; NjP; OMC; PSC-Hi; PU; TNJ.   32528

Burke, J.A.
A few historical sketches of those that have held or borne testimony that believers' baptism is an institution of our Lord Jesus Christ... Albany, Pr. by A.N. Sherman at the office of Packard and Van Benthuysen, 1828. 72 p. NHC; NNUT; RPB.   32529

Burlington, New Jersey. Endeavour Fire Company.
Articles of the Endeavor Fire Company of the city of Burlington, instituted in the year 1795; revised 1803; again revised 1820. [Burlington? 1828?] (last resolve on p 14 dated "3 mo. 10, 1828") 14 p. PHi.   32530

The Burman slave girl. See Wade, Deborah B.

Burnham, Abraham
Character and prospects of the real Christian. A sermon, preached at Pembroke, New Hampshire, November 2, 1828, Lord's day next day after the interment of Mrs. Mary B. S.

58   Burns

Kittredge... Concord, Geo. Hough,
pr., 1828. 23 p. MB; MBC; Nh;
NhHi; OO; RPB; BrMus.   32531

Burns, Robert
   The works of Robert Burns;
with an account of his life, and
criticism on his writings to which
are prefixed some observations
on the character and condition of
the Scottish peasantry by James
Currie, M. D. Philadelphia, J.
Crissey and J. Grigg, 1828. 2
vols. NCaS; NIC.   32532

Burnside, A.
   The celebrated horse Whip
will stand the ensuing season...
at my stable in Bruceville, Knox
county, and be let to mares...
six dollars to insure a colt...
one dollar & fifty cents the single
leap... A. Burnside Februry [sic]
18, 1828. Bdsd. "In" has 10 others, dated 1828 using same cut and
set in same type as follow: A.
Knox county, March 8th, 1828.
Adam G. Polke advertising Young
Whip. B. Knox county, March 8th,
1828. Noah Purcell advertising Mi-
randa. C. Lawrence county, Ill.,
March 8, 1828. Wilson Lagow advertising Lafayette. D. Daviess
county, March 14, 1828. Josiah
Palmer advertising Young
Eclipse. E. Knox county, Ia.,
March 20, 1828. John Goodman
advertising Whip: F. Carlisle,
March 23, 1828. Wm. Martin
advertising Chester Ball. G. Car-
lisle, Mar. 23, 1828. Wm. Mar-
tin advertising Whip. H. Knox
county, March 24, 1828. John
Balthis advertising Young Farmer.
I. Knox county, Mar. 31, 1828.
John Barkman, jr. advertising
Proud American. J. Knox county,
April 1st, 1828. Jonathan Hornback
advertising Independence. In.
                          32533

Burrowes, J. F.
   The thorough--base primer:

containing explanations and examples of the rudiments of harmony; with fifty exercises. 1st
Amer., imp. from the London
ed. Boston, James Loring,
Book-Seller, 1828. 138 p. InGrD;
NIC; NN; NUt.   32534

Burt, Enoch
   Immersion after believing not
necessary to constitute Christian
baptism, illustrated and established by the conclusive testimony of scripture. Hartford, Pr.
for the author, 1828. 38 p.
CBPac; Ct; CtHi; CtSoP; IEdS;
IaGG; LNB; MBC; MH; NHC-S;
NjPT.   32535

[Bury, Charlotte Maria (Campbell)]
   Flirtation; a novel... New
York, Pr. by J. & J. Harper,
for Collins & Hannay, Collins
and co. [etc.] 1828. 2 v. GHi;
LU; MBAt.   32536

Butler, Frederick
   Elements of geography and
history combined, in a catechetical form, for the use of families
and schools... Accompanied with
an Atlas. 4th ed., rev., corr.,
and brought down to the present
time. Wethersfield, Deming &
Francis, 1828. 420 p. ArCH;
CBPac; CLCM; DLC; IEdS; LNB;
MoS; MoSU; TNJ; UPB.   32537

---- A history of the United
States of America, with a geographical appendix, and a chronological table of contents. 3d rev.
and imp. ed. Wethersfield
[Conn.] Deming & Francis, 1828.
452 p. Ct; CtHi; DLC.   32538

Butler, Samuel
   Hudibras... with a life of the
author, annotations, and an index. New York, Evert Duyckinck,
[W. E. Dean, pr.] 1828. 363
[16] p. CtY; DLC.   32539

Butterworth, John, 1727-1803
A new concordance to the Holy
Scriptures... By the Rev. John
Butterworth. A new ed. Boston,
Pub. by Crocker & Brewster
[Sterotyped at the Boston Type
and Stereotype Foundry] 1828.
516 p. CtHT-W; IEG; IaDmD;
MDeeP; MH-AH; MWA; MeB;
OClW; OO; WaPS.   32540

Bynum, Alfred
An oration, delivered at the
request of the town council, be-
fore the citizens and military of
Columbia, S. C., on the fourth
of July, 1828. Columbia, Pr. by
D. & J. M. Faust, 1828. 24 p.
DLC; MBAt.   32541

Byron, George Gordon Noël Byron, 6th baron, 1788-1824
The beauties of Lord Byron,
selected from his works. To
which is added a biographical
memoir of his life and writings.
By B. F. French. 10th ed. enl.
Philadelphia, 1828. 204 p. CLSU;
CSmH; DLC; NWM.   32542

C

The cabal; or, A peep into Jack-
sonism. A play in one act. By a
Baltimorian. Baltimore, Pr. for
the author, 1828. 18 p. PHi.
                        32543
Cabanis, Pierre Jean Georges
Essay on the certainty of medicine, by P. J. G. Cabanes. Tr.
from the French by R. LaRoche.
... Philadelphia, Desilver, 1828.
[4], 119 p. CoDMS; LN; NcD;
PPHa.   32544

The cabin boy. Boston, Bowles
& Dearborn, 1828. 24 p. (On
cover: Vol. 5. no. 6. Also
paged continuously with preceding
nos. of series: [105]-128 p.) DLC.
                        32545
Calamy, Edmund, 1671-1732

The history of Jonathan
Brown, the bargeman. Philadel-
phia, American Sunday School
Union, [1828?] 12 p. DLC. 32546

---- ---- New York, American
Tract Society, 1828. 12 p. DLC.
                        32547
Caldwell, Charles, 1772-1853
A discourse of the genius and
character of the Rev. Horace
Holley, LL. D. late president of
Transylvania University... with
an appendix, containing copious
notes biographical and illustra-
tive. Boston, Hilliard, Gray,
Little, and Wilkins. Sold by Cot-
tons and Barnard, and O. C.
Greenleaf, Boston; Carey, Lea,
and Carey, Towar and Hogan,
and J. Grigg, Philadelphia; E. H.
Coale, Baltimore, and J. B.
Flint, Cincinnati [Examiner
press. Hiram Tupper, pr.],
1828.   viii, 294 p. CBPac;
CSmH;   CtHT-W;   DLC;
DNLM; ICU; KU; KyLoF; KyLxT;
MB; MBAt; MBL; MH-AH; MHi;
MMeT-Hi; MWA; MdBP; MiD;
MiU; MoHi; NBLiHi; NIC; NN;
NbU; NcD; NjR; OClWHi; PHi;
PPL; PU; RNR; ScCC; TNJ; TxU;
WHi; BrMus.   32548

Caldwell, Joseph
The numbers of Carlton, ad-
dressed to the people of North
Carolina, on a central railroad
through the state. New York, G.
Long, 1828. 232 p. DBRE; MiU-
T; NN; NcD; P; TxU; Vi. 32549

Calef, Robert, 1648-1719
The wonders of the invisible
world displayed, in five parts.
Part 1. An account of the suffer-
ing of Margaret Rule, written by
Rev. Cotton Mather. Part 2.
Several letters to the author.
etc. and his reply relating to
witchcraft... New ed. Boston, T.
Bedlington [David Watson, pr.,
Woodstock, Vt.] 1828. 333 p.

AU; CLU; CtY; DLC; ICMe; MB; MBAt; MdBJ; NHC; NN; NjP; OClWHi; PHi; PU; ViU; Vt. 32550

Der calender eines Christen auf 1829. Philadelphia, Pennsylvanischen Zweig der Amerikanischen Traktat-Gesellschaft; Conrad Zentler [1828] 18 l. MWA; N; P; PAnL; PPL. 32551

The Calvinistic doctrine of predestination unmasked; A sermon preached in Masonic Hall, Andover, Mass. December 30, 1827. By a lay preacher. Boston, 1828. 24 p. RPB. 32552

Cambridge, Mass. Third Church
Order of services at the ordination of Mr Warren Burton over the Third Congregational Society in Cambridge, on Wednesday, March 5, 1828. Press of Isaac R. Butts & Co., Boston [1828] Bdsd. MB; MHi. 32553

Cambridge-Port, Mass. Evangelical Congregational Church
The confession of faith, and the covenant of the Evangelical Congregational Church in Cambridge-Port... Boston, T. R. Marvin, pr., 1828. 8 p. MB; MBC; MH; NRAB; NjR. 32554

Cameron, Mrs. Lucy Lyttleton (Butt), 1781-1858
The fruits of education; or, The two guardians, by Mrs. Cameron. Author of "Emma and her nurse," "Margaret White" "The two lambs," &c. &c. New York, Repr. for W. B. Gilley, 1828. 138 p. DLC. 32555

[----] The lost child. Revised by the Committee of Pulication. Philadelphia, American Sunday School Union, 1828. 6 pts. in 1 vol. ICU; BrMus. 32556

[----] The two lambs; an alle-

gorical history, by the author of Margaret Whyte, etc., etc. New-York, Pr. and sold by Mahlon Day, 1828. 23 p. CtY. 32557

[----] ---- Andover, Ms., Pub. by the American Tract Society, and for sale at the General depository [1828?] 24 p. DLC. 32558

Campbell, Alexander, 1786-1866
Facts and documents confirmatory of the credibility of the debate on baptism, between W. L. M'Calla and A. Campbell. Being a full exposition on a "Unitarian Baptist," created and made by the Rev. W. L. M'Calla. Bethany, Brooke county, [W.] Va., 1828. 24 p. CSmH; KyLxCB; NjPT; TNDC. 32559

---- Psalms, hymns, and spiritual songs, adapted to the Christian religion. Selected by Alexander Campbell. Bethany, Brooke County, Va., 1828. 208 p. PPL. 32560

Campbell, David
Duty and privilege of Christians to devote their all to spreading the gospel. 2d ed. Northampton [Mass.] Pr. by Hiram Ferry, 1828. 16 p. CSmH. 32561

Campbell, James
Tariff, or rates of duties payable after the 30th of June, 1828, on all goods, wares, and merchandise, imported into the United States of America, in American vessels, under the act passed May 19th, 1828, entitled "An act in alteration of the several acts, imposing duties on imports," &c. ... New York, Pub. by Edward B. Gould, 1828. 108 p. CtY; LU; MH; PPL (imperfect) 32562

Campbell, John D.
The American chancery digest being a digested index of

all the important decisions in
equity, in the United States
courts, and in the courts of the
several states... New York,
Gould & Banks; Albany, W.
Gould & Co., 1828. xv, [1], 581
p. CU-Law; IaDmD-L; In-SC;
Md; MnS; NNLI; NNU; BrMus.
32563
Campbell, Thomas, 1777-1844
The pleasures of hope, with
other poems. Providence, Pub.
by A. S. Beckwith, 1828. 76 p.
CSmH; CtHi; DGU; DLC; MH;
NBuCC; RHi; RP; RPB; TMSC.
32564
[Campe, Joachim Heinrich von]
1746-1818
The new Robinson Crusoe.
Designed for youth. Ornamented
with plates. Cooperstown, Stereo-
typed, pr. and sold by H. & E.
Phinney, 1828. 27 p. DLC.
32565
Canandaigua Fire Company
By-laws of the Canandaigua
Fire Company. [Canandaigua,
1828] 7 p. NCanHi.   32566

A candid examination of the
Episcopal Church.   See Strong,
Titus.

A candid man. See Sherman,
William.

A candid view of the presidential
question.   See Kane, John Kintzing.

Canonicus, pseud.   See Shedd,
William.

Capers, William Theodotus,
Bishop, 1790-1855
Six letters to the editor of the
Charleston Observer, vindicating
the sermon of Bishop Soule, a-
gainst "A review" and other publications... To which are added
a further review of the reviewer,
and arguments for the bishop's
doctrine of "The law of liberty."

Charleston, James S. Burges,
1828. 47 p. CSmH; GEU; TxU.
32567
The captivity and sufferings of
Mrs. Mary Velnet, who was sev-
en years a slave in Tripoli,
three of which she was confined
in a dungeon, loaded with irons,
and four times put to the most
cruel tortures ever invented by
man. To which is added, The
lunatic governor, and Adelaide,
or the triumph of constancy. A
tale. Boston, T. Abbot [George
F. Black, pr., Roxbury] 1828.
105 p. MiD-B.   32568

Cardell, William S., d. 1828
Elements of English grammar,
deduced from science and practice. Adapted to the capacity of
learners. 4th ed. Philadelphia,
Russell and Martien, 1828. 144
p. CtHT-W; CtMW; DLC; ICMcC;
MH; RPB; WU.   32569

---- The happy family; or Scenes
of American life: designed for
well instructed children of seven
years old and upwards. 2d ed.
Philadelphia, T. T. Ash, 1828.
177 p. CtY; DLC; ICHi; MB;
OClWHi; OHi.   32570

Carey, John
Latin versification simplified;
Being a graduated series of ex-
ercises in hexameter and penta-
meter verse. ...1st Amer. ed.
with exercises in the principal
lyric and tragic measures. By
Charles Anthon, New York, Pub.
by G. and C. Carvill [W. E.
Dean, pr.] 1828. xii, 82 p. ICN;
InGrD; LShC; MH; NIC; NNG;
PPL; RPB.   32571

[Carey, Mathew]
The Boston report and mercantile memorials. No. 1. [Ham-
ilton, Philadelphia, Feb. 4, 1828]
3 p. ICJ; MB; PU.   32572

[----] Second edition - March 14, 1828. The Boston report and mercantile memorials. No. 1. [Philadelphia, 1828] 3 p. PPL.
32573

---- A brief view of the policy of the founders of the colonies of Massachusetts, Rhode Island, West Jersey, Pennsylvania, Maryland, Virginia and Carolina, as regards liberty of conscience. ...Read before the American Philosophical Society, Nov. 7, 1828. [Philadelphia, 1828] 4 p. DLC; MH; MWA; OOC; PPAmP; PPL; PU.
32574

[----] A common sense address to the citizens of the southern states. No. I - [IV] [Dated May 26-June 4, 1828, signed Hamilton] [Philadelphia, 1828] PU. (...No. II-III [May 31, 1828; June 2, 1828] pp. (5)-12). PU.
32575

[----] ---- No. VI and last. 2d ed. [Philadelphia] July 28, 1828. [21]-24 p. CtY; DLC; MB; MBAt; MdHi; PHi; ScCC.
32576

[----] Common sense addresses. By a Citizen of Philadelphia. Pr. by Clark & Roser, 1828 (Nos. 1-3). DLC; MBAt.
32577

[----] ---- 2d ed. Philadelphia, Pr. by Clark & Raser, 1828 (Nos. 1-6). 24 p. DLC.
32578

[----] Education. [Hamilton, Philadelphia, Oct. 9, 1828] 4 p. MWA; PPL; PU.
32579

[----] Emigration from Ireland and immigration into the United States. Hamilton [Philadelphia, July 18, 1828] 4 p. DLC; MBL; MWA; PHi; PPAmP; PPL; PU.
32580

[----] Essays on the public charities of Philadelphia. [signed Hamilton]...No. I - [VI] [Philadelphia, Nov. 7, 1828] 20 p.

PU.
32581

[----] ---- 2d ed. Philadelphia, 1828. Parsons 1167.
32582

---- ---- 3d ed. Philadelphia, 1828. 25 p. DLC; MB; MBAt; NN; PPAmP; PPPrHi.
32583

[----] A farewell. Philadelphia, Oct. 28, 1828. Sir, You will, I trust, pardon this letter. ... [Philadelphia, 1828] Bdsd. PHi.
32584

[----] Philadelphia, Oct. 24, 1828. Fourth appendix to M. Carey's catalogue. [Philadelphia, 1828] 83-90 p. PPL.
32585

[----] Matter of fact, Versus Messrs. Huskisson & Peel. No. I - [3] [Signed Hamilton dated Sept. 13, 20, Oct. 1, 1828] [Philadelphia, 1828] 12 p. MBAt; MWA; MdHi; PPL; PU; ScCC.
32586

[----] Pennsylvania canals. [Philadelphia, May 15, 1828] 3 p. MWA; PHi; PPL; PU.
32587

[----] Review of "Notions of the Americans, picked up by a travelling Bachelor - In two volumes." Ascribed to J. F. Cooper, Esq. [Philadelphia, 1828] 4 p. PPL.
32588

[----] The revolutionary officers. To the Congress of the United States... [signed at end: Hamilton, May 5, 1828] [Philadelphia, 1828] 5 p. MB; MWA; PU.
32589

[----] ---- 2d ed. corr. [Hamilton, Philadelphia, May 5, 1828] 5 p. PHi; PPL.
32590

[----] Sir. Although I have very recently issued a long circular letter, respecting the extreme irritation of the public mind to the South... [Philadelphia, September 10, 1828] [2] p. PHi.
32591

[----] (Private) Sir, I am induced, by the critical situation of the application for the protection of the woolen and other manufactures, to address a circular to those interested... [Philadelphia, March 13, 1828] 3 p. PHi.
32592

[----] ---- [Philadelphia, 1828] 2d ed. 3 p. MH-BA.   32593

[----] ... Sir, Notwithstanding the very ungenerous, ungentlemanly and ungrateful manner in which I have been treated by some of the wealthy manufacturers here ... [Philadelphia, August 25, 1828] [3] p. PHi.   32594

[----] Some notices of Kentucky, particularly of its chief town, Lexington. [Signed: Hamilton, and dated Philadelphia, Aug. 23, 1828] [2] p. DLC; DeGE; MBL; NN; PPAmP; PPL.   32595

[----] To Messrs. N. Goddard, Shaw, Winslow, W. Goddard, Silsby, Ward, Cruft, Wheelwright, Lee, Shepherd, Swett, Foster, Parker, Baker, and Gray, the Committee of the Boston merchants... [Philadelphia? 1828?] 4 p. CLU; MH-BA. 32596

[----] ---- 2d. ed. Feb. 29 [-March 3] 1828. No. I [-V]. [No. 5 is first ed.] 16 p. ICJ; MWA; PHi; PPL; PU.   32597

[----] To the citizens of the United States. Robert Fulton. [signed Philo Fulton. Philadelhia, 1828] [Philadelphia, Mar. 17, 1828] 2 p. MWA; PPAmP; PPL; PU.   32598

[----] ... To the friends of Ireland, assembled at the Court House. [Philadelphia, Dec. 1, 1828] 4 p. MWA; PHi; PPL; PU.   32599

[----] Second edition - with a

postscript... To the members of the Pennsylvania Society for the Promotion of Manufactures and Mechanic Arts. [Philadelphia, January 14, 1828] 3 p. PHi.
32600

[----] A valedictory address to the members of the acting committee of the Pennsylvania Society for the Promotion of Manufactures and the Mechanic Arts. ...[Philadelphia, July 23, 1828] [2] p. PHi.   32601

[----] When the following letter was written, it was without the slightest idea of its ever being published... Meadville, Dec. 5, 1828. Dear Sir: (letter on financing the construction of canals) [1828?] 8 p. (Signed: H.) MWA; PU.   32602

[Carne, John] 1789-1844
Tales of the West. By the author of Letters from the East. New-York, Pr. by J. & J. Harper. Sold by Collins and Hannay, Collins and co., G. and C. Carvill, Wm. B. Gilley, A. T. Goodrich, O. A. Roorbach, Elam Bliss, C. S. Francis, and Wm. Burgess, Jr. 1828. 2 vols. CSfA; CtY; GauY; MdAS; OAU; OClW; OkU; TNJ; WHi.   32603

Carpenter, George Washington
On the mineralogy of Chester county, with an account of some of the minerals of Delaware, Maryland, and other localities. Philadelphia, Pa., Pub. by Geo. W. Carpenter, 1828. 16 p. DeWI; PHi; PPAN; PPAmP; PPi.
32604

Carpenter, Thomas, of London
The scholar's spelling assistant; wherein the words are arranged on an improved plan, according to their respective principles of accentuation. 3d Charleston ed., corr. and the appendix enl. and imp. Charleston,

Pub. by Philip Hoff, 1828. 156 p.
KyLoS; MH; MWA.   32605

Carr, Benjamin
    The wandering harper. Ar-
ranged for the Spanish guitar by
Franklin Peale. Philadelphia,
Willig [c1828] [1] p. MB.   32606

Carr, Dabney S.
    A short history of a moral &
political scoundrel. To my fellow-
citizens--John S. Tyson than
whom a dirtier scoundrel does
not breathe - a fellow, both mor-
ally and politically corrupt... put
in circulation late Thursday night
...an infamous handbill against
me which calls for some reply...
[Signed] Dabney S. Carr. Baltimore, July 5th, 1828. 1 p. DLC.
                          32607
Carr, Robert
    Periodical catalogue of fruit
& ornamental trees & shrubs,
green house plants, etc. culti-
vated & for sale at Bartram's
Botanic Garden, Kingsessing, nr.
Gray's Ferry-four miles from
Phila.   Rob't Carr, Prop.
Philadelphia, Russell & Martien,
prs., 1828. 47 p. PHi; PPAN;
PU.   32608

The Carrollton march.   See
Corri, Philip Antony.

Carron, Guy Toussaint Julien,
abbé.
    Pious biography for young men:
or, The virtuous scholars. Trans.
from Les ecoliers vertueux, ...
Philadelphia, Pub. by Euene Cummiskey, Garden & Thompson,
prs., 1828. 334 p. DGU; MdBL;
MdBS; MiDSH.   32609

Carson, Alexander
    The truth of the gospel demon-
strated from the character of
God manifested in the Atonement.
In a letter to Mr. Richard Carlisle, by Alexander Carson, A. M.

2d ed., much larger.... New-
York, Pub. from the Dublin ed.,
with notes by a gentleman of this
city. Pr. by Wm. A. Mercein,
1828. 32 p. InID; MBC; NHC-S;
NjR; PPPrHi.   32610

Cartersville Bridge Company
    Documents laid before the
Legislature, at the session of
1827-28, upon the subject of the
application of the Cartersville
Bridge Company, for a loan or
lottery, to re-build the bridge;
with the proceedings thereupon.
Richmond, Va., Pr. by Samuel
Shepherd & Co., 1828. 52 p.
ViU.   32611

Cartersville Bridge Company.
See Harrison, Randolph.

Cary, Mrs. Virginia (Randolph),
1786-1852
    Letters on female character
addressed to a young lady, on the
death of her mother. Richmond,
Va., A. Works, 1828. 2 p. l.,
[iii] - viii, [13] - 199 p. CSmH;
DLC; ICU; KU; MLow; MNS;
MdBC; NNUT; NcU; PPi; Vi; ViU;
ViLRM; ViRUT.   32612

Case, Eliphalet, jr.
    A sermon on the new birth.
By Eliphalet Case, jr. minister
of the gospel; delivered before
the First Universalist Society,
Marietta, Ohio; on the first Sabbath in July, 1827. Pub. by request. Hartford [Conn.] Pr. by
Russell Canfield, at the office of
the Religious Inquirer, 1828. 15
p. CSmH; CtSoP; MBNMHi;
MCM; MMeT-Hi; MiD-B; OCHP;
OMC; PPL.   32613

The case in question 'Doherty's
heirs and others vs. Blake &
Cumings) was in the Federal
Court of Tennessee for June Session, 1828. DLC; T.   32614

The case of Edmund Shotwell and others being a report of the evidence and argument before the Hon. Edward King, with the opinion of the judge. Philadelphia, 1828. 78 p. MiU-C; OClWHi; PHC; PHi; **PPL**.   32615

The case of the public printer. See Dana, James G.

Case of the ship James Birckhead. See Wirt, William.

The case of the six militia men fairly stated. See Democratic Party. North Carolina.

The case of the six mutineers. See Democratic Party. New York.

The casket: a Christmas and New Year's present for children and young persons. MDCCCXXIX. Boston, Bowles and Dearborn [Press of Isaac R. Butts & Co., 1828] viii, 268 p. DLC; ICU; MB; MBMu; MWA; NNC; RPB; WHi.   32616

Castleton Medical College, Castleton, Vermont.
Catalogue of the officers and students, November, 1828. [n. p., 1828] 10 p. CtY; OCHP; VtHi.   32617
The cat. Also, Getting up. In words of four letters. Brookfield, E. and G. Merriam, 1828. 14 p. DLC.   32618

Catalogue of prints, oil paintings, miniatures, electrical machines, philosophical apparatus, &c. &c. to be sold at Columbian Hall, (formerly Museum) Common street, on Friday, June 13, 1828. By order of the administrator on the estate of the late William M. S. Doyle. J. L. Cunningham, auctioneer. [Boston, 1828] 7 p. DLC.   32619

Catalogue of an exhibition of portraits painted by the late Gilbert Stuart. Boston, Eastburn, [1828] 8 p. MB; MBAt; MBMu.   32620

Catholic Church
Ordo divini officii recitandi... Pro anno Domini MDCCCXXIX. Baltimori, J. Robinson, pr. [1828] 48 p. MdBS.   32621

Cato, pseud. See Webster, Ezekiel.

[Catullus] pseud.
To the Federalists of the United States. ... The conduct of John Quincy Adams considered, in his relations, political and moral, towards the Federal Party. Originally printed in the New York Evening Post. [Philadelphia, Pr. at the office of the Philadelphia Gazette, 1828] [Signed: Catullus.] 8 p. CtY; **PPL**.   32622

Cazenove, Lewis A.
To the public. [Alexandria, Va. , 1828] 30 p. MBAt.   32623

Central Jackson Committee. See Democratic Party.

[Cervantes Saavedra, Miguel de] 1547-1616
The adventures of Don Quixote, de La Mancha, knight of the sorrowful countenance, and his humourous squire, Sancho Pancha; with the particulars of his numerous challenges, battles, wounds, courtships, enchantments, feats of chivalry, &c. &c. &c. New-York, S. King, 1828. 22 p. DLC.   32624
---- The life and exploits of Don Quixote de la Mancha. Trans. from the original Spanish of Miguel de Cervants Saavedra, by Charles Jarvis, esq. In four volumes. Exeter, J. & B. Wil-

liams, 1828. 4 vols. DGU;
KyHi; MB; MBC; MWA; Nh; NhD;
OCh.   32625

---- The life and exploits of the
ingenious gentleman Don Quixote
de la Mancha, trans. from the
original Spanish of Miguel De
Cervants Saavedra by Charles
Jarvis Esq. to which is prefixed
a life of the author, in four volumes. Philadelphia, Pub. by H.
Adams, Stereotyped by L. Johnson, 1828. 4 vols. GDC; NNF;
OFH; WyU.   32626

Chaddock, Joseph
    The office work of a mediator
explained, or Active trinity
brought to view. In two parts.
Rochester, Pr. for the author
and pub., 1828. 99 p. DLC;
NAuT.   32627

Chadwick, Jabez
    Candid reasons for becoming
Anti-Trinitarians. Medina, Pr.
by J. Denio & Son, 1828. 35,
[1] p. MMeT-Hi.   32628

---- A sermon delivered at Lansing, Tompkins Co., N.Y. on
the Fourth day of July, 1828, in
commemoration of the Independence of the United States. Cortland Village, Pr. by R. A. Reed
and S. M. Osgood, 1828. 13 p.
ICN.   32629

Chambers, John
    A sermon by the Rev. Mr.
John Chambers, delivered at the
Presbyterian Church in Thirteenth Street Philadelphia on the
evening of December 2, 1827,
from these words, "Ye shall not
surely die." Taken in short hand
by M. T. C. Gould, stenographer.
Philadelphia, 1828. 15 p. NjPT;
OClWHi; PPL.   32630

Channing, William Ellery, 1780-
1842

    A discourse delivered at the
ordination of the Rev. Frederick
A. Farley, as pastor of the
Westminster Congregational So-
ciety in Providence, Rhode Island,
September 10, 1828. Boston,
Bowles & Dearborn, [Examiner
Press. Hiram Tupper, pr.]
1828. 36 p. CBPac; DLC; ICU;
MB; MBAt; MBC; MH; MH-AH;
MHi; MWA; MdHi; MeHi; MiD-
B; NIC; NNS; NjPT; NjR; OClWHi;
PHi; PPAmP; PPL; PPWa; RHi;
RPB; ScCC; BrMus.   32631

---- ---- 2d ed. Boston, Bowles
and Dearborn [Examiner Press.
Hiram Tupper, pr.] 1828. 28 p.
CtHT-W; CtSoP; CtY; ICMe;
ICMcC; MB; MH; MHi; MWA;
MiD-B; NBLiHi; RHi; RNHi;
RPB.   32632

---- A discourse delivered at the
installation of the Rev. Mellish
Irving Motte, as pastor of the
South Congregational Society, in
Boston, May 21, 1828. ...Pub.
by request. Boston, Bowles &
Dearborn [Examiner Press. Hir-
am Tupper, pr.] 1828. 43 p.
CBPac; CSmH; CtSoP; CtY; ICMe;
IU; MB; MBAt; MBC; MH-AH;
MMeT; MWA; MeB; NcD; NjR;
OClWHi; PPL; PU; RHi; RPB;
ScC.   32633

---- ---- 2d ed. Boston, Bowles
and Dearborn [Examiner Press.
Hiram Tupper, pr.] 1828. 22 p.
CSmH; CtSoP; CtY; ICMe; ICU;
MBAU; MH; MWA; MiD-B; NCH;
NjPT; NjR; OClWHi; OO; PPL;
RPB.   32634

---- A continuation of remarks
on the character of Napoleon
Bonaparte, occasioned by the
publication of Scott's Life of Napoleon. From the Christian Examiner, Vol. V. No. 11. Boston,
Bowles & Dearborn [Examiner
Press, Hiram Tupper, pr.] 1828.

23 p. CtHT; CtY; DLC; MB; MH; MHi; MiD-B; NjPT; PHi; PPL; RHi; RPB.   32635

[----] Remarks on the character and writings of John Milton; occasioned by the publication of his lately discovered treatise on Christian doctrine. 3d ed. Boston, Pub. by Benjamin Perkins and Co. [Examiner Press, Hiram Tupper, pr.] 1828. 116, [1] p. ad. ICMe; MB; MH; MMeT; OCX; PPL; RHi; RWe.   32636

Chapin, Horace Billings
    A sermon, delivered before the Congregational Church and Society in Lempster, N. H. September 18, 1828, at the ordination of the Rev. Charles Moulson Brown, as pastor colleague with the Rev. Elias Fisher. Concord, Pr. by Henry E. Moore, 1828. 29 p. CSmH; CtSoP; ICN; MNe; MeBaT; NHi; NhHi; RPB; BrMus.   32637

[Chapman, Ernestine]
    The Scottish exiles. Rendered into prose, from Sir Walter Scott's "Lady of the lake." By a lady of Philadelphia. Philadelphia, Pub. by J. Field, 1828. 180 p. DLC; IObB; MB; MnU; PPL; RPB.   32638

Chapman, George Thomas, 1786-1812
    Sermons upon the ministry, worship and doctrines of the Protestant Episcopal Church and other subjects. Lexington, Ky., Pr. by Smith & Palmer, 1828. viii, 399 p. CtHT; DLC; GEU; ICU; KyLxT; MCET; MPiB; MeBaT; NN; NNG; NjP; OC; OrPD; TN; WBB.   32639

[Chapman, Samuel Henry]
    The red rover, a drama in three acts, founded on the popular novel by J. F. Cooper, esq.

as performed at the London theatres... Philadelphia, F. Turner, [1828] 3 p. 1, 6-52 p. MB; MWA; PU; WaU.   32640

Charless' Missouri almanac for 1829. St. Louis, Charless & Paschall [1828] [Rusk, from an advertisement in the "Missouri Republican." Names of printers assumed, since they entered partnership in mid-1828.] Drake 4565.   32641

Charleston (S. C.)
    Rules for the government of Charleston chamber of commerce. Charleston, Pr. by W. Riley, 1828. 14 p. ScHi.   32642

Charleston. Baptist Church.
    Rules for the admission of members into the Baptist Church in Charleston. Charleston, W. Riley, 1828. 8 p. LNB.   32643

Charleston Bethel Union
    Sixth annual report of the Charleston Bethel Union... Dec. 10, 1827... Charleston, Observer Office Press, 1828. 24 p. MH; PHi.   32644

Charleston Female Seamen's Friend Society
    Second annual report of the Charleston Female Seamen's Friend Society, auxiliary to the American Seamen's Friend Society. Charleston, Observer Office Press, 1828. 14 p. MH; PHi.
                                 32645
Charleston Library Society
    The by-laws and rules and regulations of the Charleston Library Society, ratified at the anniversary meeting, Jan. 16, 1828. Charleston, J. S. Burges, 1828. 24 p. DLC; NcD; OCHP; ScC.   32646

Charleston Port Society for Promoting the Gospel among Seamen,

Charleston, S. C.
Fifth annual report of the
board of managers of the Charleston Port Society. March 1828.
Charleston, Observer Office
Press, 1828. 24 p. MH; PPL.
32647
Charleston Unitarian Book and
Tract Society
Obituary of Jackman J. Davis,
Esq. late of the U.S. Army.
Charleston, [Burges] 1828. 8 p.
MHi.   32648

Charlottesville, Va. Convention
on Internal Improvement.
Convention on internal improvement of the state, July 14,
1828. Proceedings of the Charlottesville Convention. [Richmond,
Va.] 1828. 15 p. NcU.   32649

---- To the honourable the
speakers of the Senate and House
of Delegates of Virginia, the memorial of the Convention assembled at Charlottesville [July 14,
1828], on the subject of internal
improvement... [Charlottesville?
Va.] 1828. Bdsd. DLC; Vi. 32650

Chase, Irah, 1793-1864
Obligations of the baptized;
... A sermon delivered before
the Boston Baptist Association introductory to their session at
Cambridge, Mass., Sept. 17,
1828... Boston, W. R. Collier,
1828. 22 p. CtY; KyLoS; ICN;
LNB; MBAt; MBC; MH; MiD-B;
NCH; NRAB; NjPT; OClWHi; PCC;
RPB.   32651

---- Origin and formation of the
Baptist Church in Granville
street, Halifax, Nova Scotia...
and the motives which induced
a... seperation [sic] from the
Church of England. Boston, Repr.
by Lincoln & Edmands, 1828. 48
p. MWA; MiD-B; NjPT; WHi.
32652
Chase, Philander

The star of the west, or,
Kenyon College, in the year of
our Lord, 1828. 16 p. PPL.
32653
Chastellux, François Jean, marquis de 1734-1788
Travels in North America, in
the years 1780-81-82 by the Marquis de Chastellux... Tr. from
the French by an English gentleman, who resided in America at
that period. With notes by the
translator. Also a biographical
sketch of the author: letters from
Gen. Washington to the Marquis
de Chastellux: and notes and corrections by the American editor.
New York, White, Gallaher &
White, 1828. 416 p. A-Ar;
CSmH; DLC; ICU; KyBgW; LNL;
MHi; MdU; MiD; NRSB; MWA;
OMC; OO; RJa; Vi; VtB.   32654

Chateaubriand, François Auguste
René
Atala y René. Por F. A. de
Chateaubriand. Traduccion hecha
libramente del frances al español
por don T. Toris de la Riva.
Nueva York, Lanuza, Mendia y c.,
impresores libreros, 1828. 180
p. DLC.   32655

Cheever, Charles Augustus
An address on the death of Alfred Mason, delivered at Portsmouth. [Boston, H. Tupper, pr.]
1828. 25 p. CtY; ICN; MB; MBAt;
MH; MWA.   32656

[Cheever, George Barrell] 1807-
1890, comp.
The American common-place
book of prose, a collection of
eloquent and interesting extracts
from the writings of American
authors. Boston, S. G. Goodrich,
1828. 468 p. CSmH; DLC; KU.
32657
---- ---- Boston, Russell, Shattuck, and co. [1828] 468 p.
CStclU; CtHT-W; DLC; IaDaU;
NcU; TxU; BrMus.   32658

Cherokee Nation, (Statutes)
  Laws of the Cherokee Nation,
enacted by the General Council in
1826, 1827 & 1828. Pr. for the
Cherokee Nation: Office of the
"Cherokee Phoenix;" Pr. by
Isaac Heylin Harris, New Echo-
ta, C. N. , 1828. 45 p. NN; NNLI.
                                32659
Chesapeake and Delaware Canal
Co.
  Ninth general report of the
president and directors... June
2, 1828. [Philadelphia, 1828] 15
p. PPL; PU; BrMus.   32660

Chesapeake and Ohio Canal Company
  Acts of Virginia, Maryland,
and Pennsylvania, and of the Congress of the United States, in relation to the Chesapeake and Ohio
Canal Company... Washington,
Pr. by Gales & Seaton, 1828.
102, 6 p. DLC.   32661

---- Chesapeake and Ohio Canal
Company. Acts of the states of
Virginia, Maryland, and Pennsylvania and of the Congress of the
United States, in relation to the
Chesapeake and Ohio Canal Company; with the proceedings of the
convention, which led to the formation of the said company. Also, the acts and resolutions of
the states of Virginia and Maryland concerning the Potomac Company. To which are appended the
by-laws, list of officers, &c. of
the Chesapeake and Ohio Canal
Company. With a copious index.
Washington, Pr. by Gales & Seaton, 1828. 148, 13 p. CSmH; CtY;
DBRE; DLC; DeGE; ICJ; IU;
LNHT; MH-BA; MiU-T; N; NN;
NNE.   32662

---- Laws passed by the legislatures of Maryland, Virginia, and
Pennsylvania and of the Congress
of the United States, in relation
to the Chesapeake and Ohio Canal.

[Washington? 1828] 26 p. DBRE;
DLC; MH-BA; MiD-B.   32663

---- Proceedings of the president and directors of the Chesapeake and Ohio Canal Company,
and of the corporations of Washington, Georgetown, & Alexandria, in relation to the location
of the eastern termination of the
Chesapeake and Ohio Canal. Pr.
by order of the general meeting
of the stockholders; convened on
the 10th September, 1828. Washington, Pr. by Gales & Seaton,
1828. 31 p. DLC.   32664

---- Rules adopted by the president and directors of the Chesapeake and Ohio Canal Company,
for the government of the corps
of engineers. Washington, Gales
& Seaton, 1828. 10 p. DLC;
BrMus.   32665

Chester County Cabinet of Natur-
al Science, West Chester, Pa.
  Report on the progress and
present condition of the Chester
County Cabinet of Natural Science.
March 15, 1828. Pub. by order
of the cabinet. West-Chester, Pa. ,
Pr. by Simeon Siegfried, 1828.
[1], 13, [1] p. DeGE; PPAN;
PPL.   32666

Chesterfield, Lord. See Stanhope, Philip Dormer, 4th earl of
Chesterfield.

[Chetwood, William Rufus] d 1766
  The voyages and adventures of
Capt. Robert Boyle. Exeter (N. H.)
Abel Brown, 1828. 2 vols. CtY;
ViU.   32667

Child, David L. See Political
extracts.

[Child, Mrs. Lydia Maria (Fran-
cis)] 1802-1880
  The first settlers of New-
England: or, Conquest of the Pe-

quods, Narragansets and Pokanokets: as related by a mother to her children, and designed for the instruction of youth. By a lady of Massachusetts. Boston, Munroe & Francis; New York, C. S. Francis [1828?] 282, [1] p. DLC.   32668

The child's botany. See Goodrich, Samuel Griswold.

The child's instructer;... By a teacher of little children in Philadelphia. ... New-York, Pub. by Daniel D. Smith, S. Marks, pr., Peekskill, N. Y., 1828. 108 p. NNC; NNT-C.   32669

Children in the Wood. The children in the wood. A tale. Ornamented with cuts. Binghamton, N. Y., Pr. and sold by Morgan & Canoll, 1828. 31 p. CSmH; MBSi.   32670

---- ---- An affecting tale. Cooperstown, H. & E. Phinney, 1828. 31 p. DLC.   32671

China Academy, China, Me. Catalogue of the officers and students of China Academy, Nov. 1828. August, Pr. by Eaton & Severance, 1828. 7 p. MH.
32672
Chitty, Joseph, d. 1838 A practical treatise on the law of contracts not under seal; and upon the usual defences to actions thereon... With corrections and additional references. By a member of the Massachusetts bar. Boston, Wells and Lilly; Philadelphia, J. Grigg, 1828. xvi, 345 (i. e. 404), [40] p. CL.
32673
---- A treatise on the forms of actions, and on pleading with second and third volumes, containing precedents of pleadings. In three volumes...5th Amer. from the 4th London ed. corr. and enl.,

with notes and additions, By John A. Dunlap, Esq. and additional notes, and references to late decisions By E. D. Ingrahm, Esq. Philadelphia, Pr. for Carey, Lea & Carey and sold by Philip H. Nicklin, 1828. 3 vols. Ct; GU-L; Ky; MBS; Mh-L; MdBP; NjP; PP; PPB; TMeB; TxU-L; WaU.
32674
A choice collection of patriotic and comic songs. Boston, J. Shaw, pr., 1828. 24 p. DLC.
32675
A choice collection of riddles. See Puzzlewell, Peter, pseud.

A choice selection of hymns and Spiritual songs; designed to aid in the devotions of prayer, conference and camp meetings. Concord, Pr. by Isaac Hill, 1828. 168 p. CtY-D.   32676

---- 4th ed. Montpelier, Pr. by E. P. Walton, 1828. 168 p. RPB; VtMiS.   32677

---- New ed. Woodstock, Pr. by David Watson, 1828. 460 p. Not loc. (Gilman, p 135).   32678

The Christian almanac, for Connecticut and Massachusetts for 1829. Hartford, Connecticut Branch of American Tract Society; Charles Hosmer [1828] 20 l. CtB; CtHT-W; DLC; InU; MH; MWA; MiD-B; MnU; N; WHi.
32679
The Christian almanac for 1829. Charleston, South Carolina Tract Society; S. Babcock and Co. [1828] 24 l. ScCC.   32680

---- Pittsburgh, American Tract Society; R. Patterson [1828] 18 l. OClWHi.   32681

---- New York, American Tract Society; Rochester, Repub. by E. Peck & Co. [1828] 18 l. DLC; MiD-B; MnU; NCH; NIC; NR;

NRMA; NRU.   32682

The Christian almanac, for Kentucky for 1829. Lexington, American Tract Society; Danville, Michael G. Young [1828] 18 l. KyLx; OC; OCHP.   32683

The Christian almanac, for Maryland and Virginia for 1829. Baltimore, Baltimore Branch of the American Tract Society; Samuel Young [1828] 18 l. DLC; MWA; OClWHi; PHi.   32684

The Christian almanac, for New England for 1829. Boston, Lincoln & Edmands, [1828] 24 l. CLU; CtY; DLC; ICU; InU; MB; MBAt; MH; MHi; MWA; MeHi; MnU; NHi; NN; NRMA; NjR; OCHP; OClWHi; PHi; RNHi; VtU; WHi.   32685

---- Boston, Lincoln & Edmands [1828] 18 l. Ct; NjR.   32686

The Christian almanac, for New-York, Connecticut, and New-Jersey for 1829. New-York, American Tract Society [1828] 18 l. CLU; Ct; CtY; DLC; IU; InU; MH; MWA; MiD-B; NBLiHi; NBuHi; NN; NjR; OClWHi; OMC; WHi.   32687

The Christian almanac, for New-York, Vermont, and Massachusetts for 1829. Albany, American Tract Society; Oliver Steele [1828] 18 l. CtNhHi; MH; MWA; NHi; NN; NT; VtHi.   32688

The Christian almanac for North Carolina for 1829. Raleigh, American Tract Society; North Carolina Book Company [1828] 18 l. DLC; NcU.   32689

The Christian almanac, for Ohio, Kentucky & Indiana for 1829. Cincinnati, American Tract Society; Auxiliary Tract Society of Cincinnati; George T. Williamson

[1828] 18 l. O; OC; OCHP; WHi.   32690

The Christian almanac, for Pennsylvania and Delaware for 1829. Philadelphia, Pennsylvania branch of the American Tract Society; Nicholas Murray [1828] 36 p. DLC; InU; KHi; MWA; N; PHi; PP; PPL.   32691

The Christian almanac, for Pennsylvania & Ohio for 1829. Pittsburgh, American Tract Society [1828] 18 l. OHi.   32692

The Christian almanack for Rhode-Island for 1829. Providence, American Tract Society; J. Wilcox; Newport, Dr. Phails [1828] 19 l. CLU; DLC; InU; MWA; NBuG; NRU; RHi; RPB; WHi.   32693

The Christian almanack, for South Carolina and Georgia for 1829. By Robert Grier. Augusta, Georgia Religious Tract Society; Timothy Edwards [1828] 21 l. MWA; NN.   32694

The Christian almanac, for South Carolina for 1829. Charleston, South Carolina Branch of the American Tract Society; Horace Utley [1828] 18 l. DLC; GA.   32695

The Christian almanac, for Tennessee for 1829. Nashville, American Tract Society; John Wright [1828] 18 l. MWA; NN.   32696

The Christian almanac, for the state of Connecticut for 1829. New Haven, S. Babcock [1828] 18 l. CtHi; InU; MB; MWA; N; WHi.   32697

The Christian almanac, for the Western District for 1829. Utica, American Tract Society; Utica Auxiliary Tract Society; George S. Wilson [1828] 18 l. CtHi; MiD-B; NUtHi.   32698

The Christian almanac, for Virginia for 1829. Richmond, American Tract Society [1828] 18 1. MWA; ViW.   32699

The Christian and farmers' almanack for 1829. By Zadock Thompson. Burlington, E. & T. Mills [1828] 24 1. CLU; CtU; DLC; MWA.   32700

Christian baptism according to the authority of the Scriptures, both related to the subjects and made. By a minister of the German Reformed Church, Hagerstown, Pr. by Gruber, 1828. 47 p. PLT.   32701

The Christian calendar and New-England farmer's almanack for 1829. Boston, Christian Register Office [1828] 24 1. MB; MHi; MWA; NcD.   32702

The Christian drummer. See American Tract Society, N. Y.

The Christian farmer's almanack for 1829. Louisville, Morton & Co. [1828] 24 1. MWA.   32703

Christian freedom: with remarks on trust deeds... Boston, January, 1828. 12 p. MBAt; MBC; MWA.   32704

Christian martyrs. See Drysdale, Isabel.

Christie, William, 1748-1823
    Dissertations on the unity of God in the person of the Father, and on the Messiahship of Jesus; with proofs and illustrations from Holy Scripture and ecclesiastical antiquity. Philadelphia, R. H. Small, 1828. [8], 260 p. MH.
                                        32705
Christmas, Joseph S.
    Valedictory admonitions; or, A farewell letter, addressed to the American Presbyterian So-

ciety, of Montreal, L. C., Pub. by the American Presbyterian Society. New York, Pr. by E. Conrad, 1828. 36 p. CBPac; CtHi; DLC; GDC; ICMe; MBC; MH-AH; MWA; MeBaT; PPL; PPPrHi; BrMus.   32706

Chronicles of the canongate. See Scott, Walter.

Church, Benjamin, Esq.
    The history of Philip's war, commonly called the great Indian war, of 1675 and 1676... With notes and appendix, by Samuel G. Drake. 2d ed. with plates. Exeter, N. H., Pub. by J. & B. Williams, 1828. 2 vols. NNG.
                                        32707
The churchman, a narrative... Pub. by the "Episcopal Female Tract Society of Philadelphia," for the "Society of the Protestant Episcopal Church for the Advancement of Christianity in Pennsylvania. Philadelphia, Pr. by Wm. Stavely, 1828. (Religious tracts, no. 59.) 23, [1] p. PPL. 32708

Cicero, Marcus Tullius
    M. T. Ciceronis orations quaedam selectae, in usum Delphini, cum interpretatione et historia succinta rerum gestarum et scriptorum M. T. Ciceronis.... By John G. Smart. 2d ed., corr. and imp., with a life of Cicero, in English. Philadelphia, Pub. & for sale by Towar & Hogan, 1828. xvi, 367 p. ABS; CtHT; CtY; IJI; KyBgW; MA; MdBP; MoSU; NjP; OMC; PU; TNJ; ViU.   32709

---- M. T. Ciceronis quaedam selectae, notis illustratae. In usum acadamiae exoniensis. Editio quarta, emendatior, et tabulis analyticis instructa. Bostoniae, Sumptibus Hilliard, Gray, Little, et Wilkins [Hilliard, Metcalf, and co., prs. to the university] 1828. 8, 403, [1] p. CtHT-

W; MeB; RPB; TJaU; BrMus.
                        32710
Cincinnati
    Act incorporating the city of
Cincinnati, and the ordinances of
said city now in force. Pr. by
order of the City council. Cincinnati, Morgan, Fisher, & L'
Hommedieu, prs., 1828. 169,
[69]-76 p. CSmH; DLC; IU; MH-
L; OClWHi.   32711

Cincinnati Academy of Fine Arts
    The act of incorporation of the
Cincinnati Academy of Fine Arts,
with an address to the members
of the institution... Cincinnati,
G. T. Williamson, 1828. 12 p.
OC; OClWHi.   32712

Cincinnati Miami Bible Society
    Report of the managers, read
at the fourteenth anniversary of
the Cincinnati Miami Bible Society: and address, delivered by
Nathaniel Wright, Esq. Cincinnati, Hatch, Nichols & Buxton,
prs., 1828. 12 p. OCHP. 32713

Cinderella
    Cinderella, or, The little glass
slipper... Cooperstown [N.Y.] H.
& E. Phinney, 1828. 30 p. DLC;
MLex; NPV; PV.   32714

Circular.   Linnaean Botanic
Garden. See Prince, William.

Circular on steam mills. See
Embree, Davis.

A circumstantial estimate of the
cost of a railway, followed by
some calculations on its probable
income. (First pub. in the Chronicle and patriot, Feb. 9, 1828)
[Boston, 1828] Bdsd. MB. 32715

Citizen & farmers' almanack for
1829. By Joseph Cramer. Philadelphia, Griggs & Dickinson
[1828] 18 l. NjR.   32716

A citizen of Boston, pseud. See
Henshaw, David.

A citizen of Hagerstown, Maryland, pseud. See Waldo, Samuel
Putnam.

A citizen of Herkimer County,
New York. See A sketch of the
most important events of the life
of Andrew Jackson.

A citizen of Maryland, pseud.
See The rambler.

A citizen of New England, pseud.
See Hill, Isaac.

A citizen of Philadelphia. See
Carey, Mathew.

A citizen of the state of New
York, pseud. See Considerations
which demand the attention.

A citizen of the United States.
See Colwell, Joseph.

A citizen of the United States.
See Niles, John Milton.

A citizen of the United States.
See A universal history of the
United States.

The citizens' and farmers' year-
ly messenger, or New town &
country almanac for 1829. By
Charles F. Egelmann. Baltimore,
John T. Hanzsche [1828] 18 l.
DLC; MWA; MdBE; NcD; NjR;
PYHi.   32717

Claims of Sunday schools upon
churchmen. From the Episcopal
Watchman. Hartford, P. Canfield,
pr., 1828. 36 p. + wrappers.
NNG.   32718

Clancy, James
    A treatise of the rights, du-
ties, and liabilities of husband
and wife, at law and in equity...

1st Amer. from the 3d London ed. New York, Treadway & Bogert, Law Publishers, [etc.] Wm. A. Mercein, pr., 1828. 684 p. C-L; DLC; IaU-L; LNHT; MH-L; MiL; MoKB; N-L; NNC-L; NcU; NhD; OCLaw; PPB; PPL; Sc-SC; WaPS. 32719

Clark, Samuel, comp.
The American orator; selected chiefly from American authors, for the use of schools and private families. Gardiner, Pr. at the Intelligencer Office, 1828. 300 p. CSt; Ia; MB; MH; MeB; MeHi; MeU; PU. 32720

Clark, Thomas, 1775-1859
Tract No. 1. Price 2 cts. Plain reasons why neither Dr. Watts' Imitations of the Psalms, nor any other human composition ought to be used in the praises of the great God our saviour, but, that a metre version of the book of Psalms... ought to be used. Albany, Pr. by Webster and Wood, 1828. 12 p. MH-AH. 32721

Clarke, Adam, 1760?-1832
The doctrine of salvation by faith proved; or, An answer to the important question, what must I do to be saved? New York, Pub. by N. Bangs and J. Emory, for the Methodist Episcopal Church at the Conference Office, Azor Hoyt, pr., 1828. 29 p. MsWJ; Nh. 32722

---- The love of God to a lost world,... A discourse on John III, 16. New-York, Pub. by N. Bangs and J. Emory, A. Hoyt, pr., 1828. 32 p. NcMHi. 32723

Clarke, G. Wallingford
The wreath of the west. [Poems] Philadelphia, Carey, Lea and Carey, 1828. iv, 115 p. MB. 32724

Clarke, Jacob B.

To the Senate and House of Representatives of the United States, in Congress assembled, the memorial of Jacob B. Clarke. New York, Dec. 1, 1828. 2 p. DLC. 32725

Clarke, Samuel
The Christian's inheritance, or A collection of the promises of the Scripture. New York, Pub. by E. Duyckinck, W. E. Dean, pr., 1828. 223 p. MBC. 32726

Clay, Henry, 1777-1852
An address of Henry Clay, to the public; containing certain testimony in refutation of the charges against him, made by Gen. Andrew Jackson, touching the last presidential election. Cincinnati, Repr. by Morgan, Fisher and L'Hommedieu, 1828. 28 p. OCHP. 32727

---- ---- Frankfort, Ky., Repr. by A. G. Hodges, 1828. 72 p. DLC. 32728

---- ---- Louisville [Ky.] Pr. at the office of the Focus, 1828. 48 p. CSmH; DLC. 32729

---- ---- [Louisville, Office of the Focus, Pr. by Lewis Collins, 1828] 82 p. KyBgW; KyLoF; MHi; MNS; NN; OClWHi. 32730

---- ---- Natchez, Pr. at the office of the Ariel, for the administration, Publishing committee, of Adams County, 1828. 52 p. DLC; PHi; PPL. 32731

---- ---- New-Brunswick, By order of the Aministration corresponding committee, D. F. Randolph, pr., 1828. 56 p. CSmH; DLC; MnHi; NjP; ViU. 32732

---- ---- Russellville, Ky., Pr. by Rhea & Atchison, 1828. 63 p. DLC. 32733

---- A supplement to the address of Henry Clay to the public, which was published in December, 1827. Exhibiting further evidence in refutation of the charges against him, touching the last presidential election, made by Gen. Andrew Jackson. Washington, Pr. by Peter Force, 1828. 22 p. CLU; CSmH; DLC; MB; MdHi; NN; NjR; PPFM; PPL; RPB; WMSF. 32734

---- Supplement to the Kentucky Reporter. Lexington, January 23, 1828. An address of Henry Clay, to the public, containing certain testimonials in refutation of charges against him, made by Gen. Andrew Jackson, touching the last presidential election. [Lexington, 1828] 52 p. KyU; MoSHi. 32735

Cleland, Thomas, comp.
Evangelical hymns, for private, family, social, and public worship; selected from various authors. 2d ed. , imp. Lexington, Ky. , Pr. and pub. by T. T. Skillman, 1828. 436 p. ICU; KyBgW; KyHi; NN; NjPT. 32736

Clement, Jonathan
An address delivered before the social fraternity Phillips Academy, Andover... Andover, Pr. by Flagg and Gould, 1828. 23 p. CSmH; MChB; PPL; RPB. 32737

A clergyman. See History of Honest Roger.

A clergyman. See Prayers for children.

A clergyman of England. See The fisherman and his boy.

A clergyman of New England, pseud. See Lucretia and her father.

A clergyman of the Church of England. See Baptism.

Clifton, A. , pseud. See Corri, Philip Antony.

Clinton, De Witt, 1769-1828
Letters of Governor Clinton, and of Colonel L. Baldwin... improved as evidence before the joint committee of the Legislature of Massachusetts, on the petition of Samuel Hinkley and others, for the extension of the Hampshire and Hampden canal. February, 1828. Boston, Dutton & Wentworth, state prs. , 1828. 22 p. CtSoP; DLC; M; MBAt; MH-BA; MWo; MiU-T; N; NhHi. 32738

Clinton, Isaac, 1759-1840
Speech of the Rev. Isaac Clinton, delivered at the court-house, in the county of Lewis, before the Martinsburgh canal convention, held on the 4th of December, 1827. Lowville [N. Y] Pr. by Wm. L. Easton, 1828. 8 p. CSmH. 32739

The closet. By the author of "Early impressions," "Temptation. " Boston. Bowles and Dearborn, 1828. 136 p. WHi. 32740

Clowes, John, 1743-1831
Interpretation of the parable of the unjust steward. Portland, Pr. for the publisher, 1828. 24 p. MH; PBa. 32741

The clubs of London. See Marsh, Charles.

Cobb, Daniel J.
The family adviser; calculated to teach the principles of botany. Compiled with a strict regard to logick. Containing directions for preserving health and curing diseases. For the use of families and private individuals. Rochester, N. Y. , Pr. for the author by

Marshall & Dean, 1828. 131 p.
NR; NRU.   32742

Cobb, James, 1756-1818
    The haunted tower, a comic
opera, in three acts. As performed at the Chestnut-street
theatre. Philadelphia, C. Neal,
1828. 52 p. DLC; NN.   32743

Cobb, Lyman, 1800-1864
    Cobb's spelling book, being a
just standard for pronouncing the
English language; containing the
rudiments of the English language,
arranged in catechetical order...
Rev. ed. Ithaca, Pr. and pub. by
Mack & Andrus, 1828. 168 p.
DLC.   32744

---- ---- Revised ed. Stereotyped by A. Chandler. Watertown,
N. Y , Pr. and pub. by Knowlton
and Rice, 1828. 4, 168 p. FOA.
                                32745
[----] A critical review of Noah
Webster's spelling-book, first
published in a series of numbers
in the Albany Argus, in 1827 and
28 by Examinator. [Albany] 1828.
35 p. CtY; DLC; MA; MB; MH;
MoKU; NjR; NN.   32746

Cobb, Sylvanus
    A discourse delivered in the
meeting-house of the First Parish
in Malden, Mass. on Thanksgiving Day, November 27, 1828.
Boston, Pr. by Geo. W. Bazin at
the Trumpet and Magazine Office, 1828. 16 p. MHi; MMeT-
Hi.   32747

Cobbett, William
    A letter from Mr. William Cob-
bett to Mr. Huskisson, on the
subject of the American tariff;
Intended as a reply to a speech
of the latter, in the British House
of Commons. [Philadelphia, 1828]
John Binns, pr. 16 p. PPL.
                                32748
Cogswell, Jonathan, 1782-1864

A farewell discourse, ad-
dressed to the Church and Society of the First Parish in Saco,
October 12, 1828. Pub. by the
request of the Church and Society. Saco [Me.] Pr. by Alex. C.
Putnam, 1828. 12 p. CSmH;
MBC; MWA; MiD-B; RPB. 32749

Cogswell, William, 1787-1850
    The assistant to family reli-
gion, in six parts: Comprising:
A dissertation on family religion:
A series of resolutions, and of
questions for self-examination:
Select Psalms and hymns, adapt-
ed to family devotion etc. 2d ed.
Boston, Pub. by Crocker &
Brewster,... New York, J. Leav-
itt, 1828. 404 p. CtSoP; GAU;
MA; MB; MBC; MWA; MeB;
NBuG; NcAS; NhHi; NjP; OO.
                                32750
---- Religious liberty. A sermon,
preached on the day of the annu-
al fast in Massachusetts, April
3, 1828. Boston, Peirce and Wil-
liams, 1828. 22 p. CBPac; ICU;
MBC; MH; MHi; MWA; MeBaT;
MiD-B; NhHi; NjPT; NjR; PPPrHi;
OO; RPB; BrMus.   32751

Cohassett Second Congregational
Church.
    The articles of faith and the
covenant adopted by the Second
Congregational Church in Cohassett. Boston, T. R. Marvin,
1828. 12 p. DLC.   32752

Colburn, Warren, 1793-1833
    Arithmetic upon the inductive
method of instruction: being a se-
quel to Intellectual arithmetic.
Stereotyped at the Boston Type
and Stereotype Foundry. Boston,
Hilliard, Gray, Little and Wil-
kins, 1828. 245, [5] p. ArCH;
CtHT-W; CtY; MDeeP; MH; MHi;
MeB; MeHi; MoSpD; NNC; NRHi;
NhD; OCl; PPF; PPL; ScDuE;
TxU-T.   32753

Colburn, Warren, 1793-1833
Colburn's first lessons. Intellectual arithmetic, upon the inductive method of instruction. Stereotyped at the Boston Type and Stereotype Foundry. Baltimore, Cushing and Sons. Boston, Hilliard, Gray, Little and Wilkins, 1828. 172 p. CtHT-W; DAU; DLC; MdHi; NN; NcHiC; OCl; PRHi; TxU-T.   32754

---- ---- Bellows Falls, J. I. Cutler & Co.; Boston, Hilliard, Gray, Little & Wilkins, 1828. 172 p. MH; NN.   32755

---- ---- Boston, Hilliard, Gray, Little, and Wilkins, 1828. 178 p. PPL.   32756

---- ---- Concord, N. H., Pub. by Horatio Hill & Co., Boston, Hilliard, Gray, Little and Wilkins, 1828. 172 p. Nh.   32757

---- ---- Hallowell, Glazier & Co.; Boston, Hilliard, Gray, Little and Wilkins, 1828. 172 p. DLC.   32758

---- ---- New York, R. Lockwood. Boston, Hilliard, Gray, Little and Wilkins, 1828. 172 p. DAU; MH; NN.   32759

---- ---- Philadelphia, Uriah Hunt. Boston, Hilliard, Gray, Little & Wilkins, 1828. 178 p. DAU; MBC; MH; MHi; NjR; OOxM; PU; RHi.   32760

---- ---- Watertown, N. Y., Knowlton & Rice, 1828. 178 p. NNC.   32761

---- An introduction to algebra upon the inductive method of instruction. By Warren Colburn... Boston, Hilliard, Gray, Little, and Wilkins, 1828. 276 p. DLC; MH; MeB; MeHi; MoU; NNCoCi; NjD; OClW; PU; RP.   32762

Colden, Cadwallader D.
An answer to Mr. John L. Sullivan's report to the Manufacturing Society in New-Jersey, in a letter to the directors of the Morris Canal Company, by the president of that company, New-York, Wm. A. Davis, pr., 1828. 39 p. DLC; NN; NjR.   32763

Cole, John, 1774-1855
Sacred melodies, selected from the works of the most celebrated composers, and arranged for one or more voices; with the proper harmony added for the piano forte or organ. [No. 1 Baltimore, Pub. by John Cole, c 1828] 8 p. ("This work will be completed in twelve numbers.") RPB.   32764

Collamer, Jacob, 1791-1865
Oration delivered before the Phi Sigma Nu Society, of the University of Vermont, Burlington, August 6, 1828. Pub. by the Society, Royalton, Pr. by W. Spooner [1828?] 19 p. CSmH; MH; MiD-B; RPB; VtMiS. 32765

Collection d'operas et vaudevilles représentées a Philadelphie par La Troupe Francaise de la Nouvelle Orleans. Philadelphie, Publié par Neal & Mackenzie, 1828. v. p. (each opera separately paginated--the two reported vols. do not include all the same operas in the same order). ICU; PPL.   32766

College of Physicians and Surgeons of the Western District. See Fairfield, N. Y. College...

The Collell claim in Mobile. To the Register and Receiver of the Land Office, at Jackson Court House...Wm. H. Robertson agent for Dusuan De La Croix. District East of Pearl River, 14th April, 1828. [n. p., 1828] 7 p. AMob.   32767

Colman, George
  X, Y, Z. or, The American
  manager. A farce, in two acts.
  ... Correctly marked from the
  Prompt-book, with stage direc-
  tions, &c. Elton's ed. New York,
  Pub. at Elton's Dramatic Reposi-
  tory, and at Whale's Dramatic
  Repository, Wm. Applegate, pr.,
  1828. [3], 2-34 p. MH; MMal.
                                  32768
Colombia, Republic of.
  Manifiesto que hace el Gobier-
  no de Colombia de los fundamen-
  tos quetiene para hacer la guerra
  al Gobierno del Peru; con la
  contestacion que do a los cargos
  el ciudadano M. L. Vidaurre...
  (Spanish and English) Boston [H.
  Tupper, pr.] 1828. 71 p. CtY;
  ICJ; M; MH; MHi.   32769

Colonization Society of the State
of Connecticut
  An address to the public by
  the managers of the Colonization
  Society of Connecticut. With an
  appendix. New-Haven, Pr. by
  Treadway and Adams, 1828. 32 p.
  CtHT; CtY; DLC; ICN; MB; NCH.
                                  32770
Colton, Charles Caleb, 1780?-
1832
  Lacon: or, Many things in few
  words; addressed to those who
  think... From the 8th London ed.
  Concord, N. H., Isaac Hill, 1828.
  DLC; MoS; NSyU; NhD; ViRVal.
                                  32771
---- ---- In two volumes...
  Bridgeport [Conn.] Pub. by M.
  Sherman, 1828. 2 v. CSmH; MB;
  MDeeP; MH-AH; MPiB; MoSU;
  NNS; PPL; RNHi.   32772

Colton, Walter
  Remarks on duelling. Pub. by
  Jonathan Leavitt, New-York,
  Crocker & Brewster, Boston,
  1828. 62 p. CSmH; CtHT-W;
  CtY; DLC; MBC; MHi; MWA;
  MiD-B; NcD; OClWHi; PHi; PU;
  TxU; BrMus.   32773

The Columbian, Georgetown,
D. C.
  Address of the carrier of the
  Columbian. Dec. 25, 1828.
  [Georgetown, D. C. 1828] 1 p.
  DLC.   32774

Columbian almanac for 1829. By
  Wm. Collom. Philadelphia, Jos.
  M'Dowell [1828] 18 l. CtY; DLC;
  DeU; InU; MWA; NBuHi; NHi;
  NjR; PHi.   32775

The Columbian calendar, or New-
  York and Vermont almanack for
  1829. Troy, Francis Adancourt
  [1828] 18 l. CLU; MWA; MnU;
  N; NHi; NT; OMC; PHi.   32776

---- Troy, Francis Adancourt
  [1828] 24 l. MWA; NN.   32777

---- Troy, Francis Adancourt;
  Clark & Hosford; J. Disturnell;
  E. S. Coon [1828] 3d. ed. 12 l.
  NN; NT; OClWHi.   32778

---- 3d ed. Troy, Francis Adancourt; Clark & Hosford; J. Disturnell; E. S. Coon [1828] 24 l.
  DLC.   32779

---- Troy, Francis Adancourt,
  for Wm. S. Parker [1828] 24 l.
  MWA; NbHi.   32780

Columbian Centinel
  Tribute of the muses through
  the carriers of the Columbian
  Centinel, to its generous patrons,
  on the commencement of the New
  Year 1828. [Boston, 1828] 16 p.
  DLC; MH; RPB.   32781

The Columbus almanac for 1829.
  By Wm. Lusk. Columbus, P. H.
  Olmsted [1828] 12 l. MWA.
                                  32782
---- ---- Columbus, P. H. Olm-
  sted [1828] 24 l. O; OHi; Wv-
  Ar.   32783

[Colwell, Joseph]

An address, to the people of the United States, on the subject of the presidential election: with a special reference to the nomination of Andrew Jackson, containing sketches of his public and private character. By a citizen of the United States. [New York?] Pr. for the Proprietor, 1828. 48 p. CtY; DLC; MB; MBAt; NcU; NjR; PHi; PPL; TU; Vi.   32784

Combe, George, 1788-1858
The constitution of man, considered in relation to external objects, by George Combe; Essays on decision of character, by John Foster; Philosophy of sleep and anatomy of drunkenness, by Robert Nacnish; Influence of literature upon society, etc., by Madame De Stael; A treatise on self-knowledge, by John Mason. Hartford, S. Andrus [pref. 1828] 60, 133, 112, 41 p. (Each work has special t. p.) DLC; OO.   32785

Combs, Leslie, 1793-1881
A reply to General Andrew Jackson's letter, of the 31st October, 1828. Published in the Nashville Republican. ...[Nashville, 1828] 8 p. CLU; DLC; ICU; InHi; KyHi; MB; MBAt; MH; MWA; NIC; OCHP; PPL; TxU.
32786
Comly
Comly's primer; or, The first book for children. Philadelphia, Kimber & Sharpless, 1828. 36 p. DLC.   32787

Commentator Extra, June 21, 1828. See A sketch of the life and public services of John Quincy Adams.

Commercial gazette. Extra. See A Republican, pseud.

The Committee of General Correspondence for the State of Mis-souri, appointed by friends of Andrew Jackson. See Democratic Party.

Common sense addresses. See Carey, Mathew.

...Communication from the trustees of Nashoba. Supplement to the New-Harmony Gazette of March 26, 1828. [New Harmony, 1828] 2 p. DLC.   32788

The complete Vermont almanac for 1829. By Marshall Conant. Woodstock, Rufus Colton [1828] 32 l. CtY; NHi; VtHi; VtU.   32789

Comstock, John Lee, 1789-1858
History of the Greek revolution; compiled from official documents of the Greek government, Sketches of the war in Greece, by Philip James Green...and other authentic sources. New York, Wm. W. Reed & co., 1828. 503 p. CU; CtY; GA; ICU; IEG; KyLx;LNHT; MB; MBC; MH; MdBP; MdBS; MiD; MiU; MnHi; NIC; NbU; NjR; OClWHi; PHi; PU; RP; TNJ; ViRU; Wv.
32790

---- ---- New York, W. W. Reed & co., 1828. 498 p. CSmH; DLC.   32791

A concise narrative. See Van Ness, William Peter.

Concord, N. H.
Regulations of the public schools in Concord, New-Hampshire, established November 10, 1828. Concord, 1828. 12 p. NhHi.
32792
---- Report of the superintending school-committee of Concord, presented and read at the annual town-meeting, March 12, 1828... Concord [N. H.] Pr. by George Hough, 1828. 16 p. M; MB; MHi.   32793

Condict, Lewis
An address, delivered by appointment at Morristown, New-Jersey, July 4th, 1828... Morristown [N. J.] Pr. by Jacob Mann, 1828. 36, [1] p. MH; MWA; Nh.
                                        32794
[Congdon, James Bunker] 1802-1880
Information relative to the American Lyceum. What is contained in the following pages, has been principally extracted from the various publications on the subject of the American lyceum. The object is to disseminate information in relation to that interesting institution. New-Bedford, Benj. T. Congdon, 1828. 12 p. MNBedf.   32795

Congregational Education Society. See American Education Society.

Congregational Churches in Connecticut. General Association.
Proceedings of the General Association of Connecticut in session in Meriden, June 1828. Hartford, P. B. Gleason, pr., 1828. 31 p. IEG; IEdS; MHi; NjR.
                                        32796
Congregational churches in Maine. General conference.
Articles of faith. Portland, Shirley & Hyde, 1828. 18 p. DLC; MWA; MeHi; MiD-B.
                                        32797
---- ---- Portland, Shirley & Hyde, 1828. 17 p. MBC; MWA; MeHi.   32798

---- Minutes of the General Conference of Maine, at their annual meeting in Gorham, June, 1828. Portland, Shirley & Hyde, 1828. 24 p. MeBaT; NhHi.   32799

Congregational Churches in Mass. General Association
Minutes of the General Association of Massachusetts, at their meeting in Falmouth, June, 1828.

With the Narrative of the state of religion, and the pastoral address. Boston, Pr. by Crocker & Brewster, 1828. 24, [11] p. MLow; MeBaT.   32800

Congregational Churches in New Hampshire. Piscataqua Association.
Pastoral letter of the Piscataqua conference, for June, 1828. Portsmouth [N. H.] Miller and Brewster, prs., [1828] 8 p. MB; MBC; NhHi.   32801

Congregational Home Missionary Society. See American Home Missionary Society.

Conkling, Alfred, 1789-1874
A discourse commemorative of the talents, virtues and services of the late De Witt Clinton; delivered at Schenectady, before the Society of the Phi Beta Kappa, July 22d, 1828. Albany, Pr. by Websters and Skinners, 1828. 31 p. CtY; DLC; IU; MBAT; MiD-B; MnHi; NN; NNC; NjR; OMC; RPB; BrMus.   32802

Connecticut (Colony)
The code of 1650, being a compilation of the earliest laws and orders of the General Court of Connecticut; also, the constitution, or civil compact, entered into and adopted by the towns of Windsor, Hartford, and Wethersfield in 1638-39; to which is added some extracts from the laws and judicial proceedings of New Haven colony, commonly called blue laws. Hartford, S. Andrus, publisher, 1828. 119 p. AU; CSmH; Ct; CtHi; CtY; MBC; MH-L; MWA; MdBP; MiGr; NIC; NbCrD; NhD; OClWHi; PHi; WaU.
                                        32803
Connecticut (State)
At a General Assembly of the state of Connecticut, holden at New-Haven in said state, on the

first Wednesday of May, in the year of our Lord one thousand eight hundred and twenty-eight. Upon the petition of the Connecticut River Company for an alteration of their charter, as per petition or file... A true copy of record, examined and certified under the seal of the state, by Thomas Day, Secretary. 2 p. Ct.   32804

---- By his Excellency, Gideon Tomlinson, Governor of the state of Connecticut. A proclamation... I do hereby appoint Thursday, the twenty-seventh day of November next, to be observed in this state, as a day of public thanksgiving... Given under my hand, at Fairfield, this thirteenth day of October, in the year of our Lord, one thousand eight hundred and twenty-eight... Gideon Tomlinson. 1 p. DLC.   32805

---- Message of his Excellency Gideon Tomlinson, to the Senate & House of Representatives, of the state of Connecticut, at the commencement of the session of the General Assembly, in New-Haven, May, A. D. 1828. New Haven, Pr. by J. Barber, 1828. 15 p. Ct; MBAt; PPL.   32806

---- The public statute laws of the state of Connecticut, passed at the session of the General Assembly in 1828. Pub. by authority of the General Assembly, under the direction and superintendence of the secretary of state. Hartford, C. Babcock, 1828. 173-211 p. C; CtSoP; DLC; IaT; Mo; NNLI; Nb; Nv; OCLaw; RPB; W-L; Wa-L.   32807

---- Report of the commissioner of the school fund... May session, 1828. New-Haven, Pr. by J. Barber, 1828. CSmH.   32808

---- Report of the directors and warden of the Connecticut State Prison: submitted to the Legislature, May session, 1828. Pr. by order of the Legislature. New Haven, Pr. by Hezekiah Howe, 1828. 20 p. CSmH; Ct; IaHi; MH; NCH; PPAmP; PPL.   32809

---- Report of the joint committee on common schools; submitted to the Legislature, May session, 1828... New Haven, Hezekiah Howe, 1828. 11 p. Ct; CtSoP.   32810

The Connecticut annual register, and United States' calendar for 1829. New-London, Samuel Green [1828] 75 l. Ct; CtHi; CtY; InU; MB; MWA; N; Nh.   32811

Connecticut Baptist Education Society
    Constitution, Connecticut Baptist Education Society; act of incorporation, address, etc. Hartford, P. Canfield, pr., 1828. 15 p. MBC; RWe.   32812

Connecticut Medical Society
    Proceedings of the president and fellows... at their annual convention in May, 1828... Westhersfield, A. Francis, pr., 1828. 14 p. CtHi.   32813

Connecticut River Co.
    Petition to the General Assembly of Connecticut, May 1828. [Hartford? 1828?] 24 p. CtSoP.   32814

Connecticut Sunday School Union
    The annual report of the Connecticut Sunday School Union, presented at the fourth annual meeting of the Society, holden in New-Haven, Thursday, May 8, 1827 [sic] [1828]... New-Haven, Pr. by Treadway & Adams, 1828. 76 p. CtHi.   32815

Considerations which demand the

attention of farmers, mechanics, and friends of the American system ... By a citizen of the state of New York. New York, Sickels, pr., 1828. 16 p. CSmH; DLC; DeGE; IU; MH-BA; NcD; NjR; PHi; TxU.   32816

Consolidated Association of the Planters of Louisiana
Acte pour amender l'acte intitule, "Acte pour incorporer l'Association Consolidée des Cultivateurs de la Louisiane. Feb. 19, 1828. [Nouvelle-Orleans, 1828] 4 p. LNHT.   32817

Conspiracy of the Spaniards. See Saint-Réal, César Vichard de.

A continuation of remarks. See Channing, William Ellery.

Continuation of the numbers of "A Baltimorean;" the first of which were published in the National Intelligencer. Canals. - Railroads. No. 7 [Baltimore, October 21, 1828] [11] p. DBRE; M; MB; MCM; MH-BA; MWA; NN; OClWHi.   32818

The contrast. See Baylies, Francis.

Convention of Delegates Opposed to Free Masonry, Le Roy, N.Y., 1828.
Proceedings of a Convention of Delegates Opposed to Free Masonry, which met at Le Roy, Genesee Co., N.Y., March 6, 1828. Rochester, Weed & Heron, prs., 1828. 23 p. CSmH; DLC; MB; MWA; MeB; NN; NR; NRU; PHi; PPFM; WHi.   32819

Convention of Seceding Masons. Le Roy, N.Y., 1828.
A revelation of Free Masonry, as published to the world by a Convention of Seceding Masons, held at Le Roy, Genesee County, N.Y., on the 4th and 5th of July, 1828: containing a true and genuine development of the mode of initiation... Pub. by the Lewiston committee. Rochester, Pr. by Weed & Heron, 1828. vii, 107 p. CSmH; DLC; MB; MWA; MdW; NIC; NN; NRHi; PHi; PPFM; WHi.   32820

Convention of young men in Rockingham Councillor district. See National Republican Party. New Hampshire.

Conversations on chemistry. See Marcet, Jane (Haldimand)

Conversations on common things. See Dix, Dorothea Lynde.

Conversations on natural philosophy. See Marcet, Jane Haldimand.

Conversations on political economy. See Marcet, Jane (Haldimand).

The conversion and edifying death of Andrew Dunn. See Hughes, John.

Cook, Amos Jones, 1777-1836
Addresses to Sabbath-School scholars, by a superintendent. Portland, Shirley & Hyde, 1828. 108 p. Williamson: 160.   32821

Cooke, Charles Turner
Observations on the efficacy of white mustard seed, in affections of the liver, internal organs, and nervous system... 2d Amer. from 4th English ed. New York, G. & C. Carvill, W. E. Dean, pr., 1828. 116 p. DLC; MBCo; MBM; MNF; NNNAM; NbU-M; PPL.   32822

Cooke, John Esten, 1783-1853
A treatise of pathology and

therapeutics. In three volumes.
Lexington, Ky. [S. H. Davis, pr. ,
Winchester, Va.] 1828. Vol. 1,
2. [Vol. III not pub.] CSmH;
CtY; DLC; DNLM; ICJ; KyBgW;
KyLxT; LNT-M; LU-M; MBCo;
MoSMed; NNNAM; OC; OCG; TxU.
32823
[Cooke, John Rogers] 1788-1854
An earnest appeal to the
friends of reform in the Legisla-
ture of Virginia. (Signed at end
"An uncompromising Friend of
Reform.") [Winchester, Samuel
H. Davis, 1828] 16 p. ViU
(Photocopy)   32824

Cooke, Parsons, 1800-1864
Unitarianism an exclusive system, or The bondage of the
churches that were planted by the
Puritans. A sermon preached on
the occasion of the annual fast,
April 3, 1828. Belchertown, Pr.
at the Sentinel and Journal Office, 1828. 12 p. CtY; MBC;
MDeeP; MH; MHi; MWA; N;
PHi.   32825

---- ---- 2d ed. Boston, Peirce
& Williams, [1828?] 12 p. CBPac;
MH; MHi; PPPrHi; BrMus.32826

Cooke, Thomas Simpson
Singing exemplified in a series of solfeggi [sic] and exercises...New York, Hall, 1828.
97 p. NjP.   32826a

[Cooper, James Fenimore] 1789-
1851
Notions of the Americans:
Picked up by a travelling bachel-
or...Philadelphia, Carey, Lea &
Carey, 1828. 2 v. CL; CSmH;
CoU; CtHT-W; DLC; DeGE; GHi;
GU; IC; KU; Kn; KyLx; LNHT;
MB; MBAt; MH; MPiB; MWA;
MdBE; MdBJ; MdHi; MeB;
MiD; MiU-C; MnHi; MoS; NBuU;
NNP; NSyU; NcU; NcWsW; NjP;
NjR; OHi; OS; PHi; PPL; PU;
RJa; RNR; RP; ScCC; TNJ;

TxDaM; Vi; ViAl.   32827

[----] The pioneers; or, The
sources of the Susquehanna...
5th ed. Philadelphia, Carey, Lea
& Carey, 1828. 2 vols. CtY; MH;
NN.   32828

[----] The prairie; a tale. By
the author of the "Pioneers and
the Last of the Mohicans."...In
two volumes. Philadelphia, Carey,
Lea & Carey, 1828. 2 vols. CtY;
MWA; PJA; PPL.   32829

[----] The red rover, a tale. By
the author of the "Pilot, &c, &c.
...In two volumes. Philadelphia,
Carey, Lea & Carey, 1829, 1828.
2 vols. NjP; PU.   32830

[----] The spy: a tale of the
neutral ground, by the author of
"Precaution;" 6th ed. Philadelphia, Carey, Lea & Carey, 1828.
2 v. MA.   32831

Cooper, Samuel, 1780-1848
First lines of practice of sur-
gery. 3d Amer. ed. from the
3d London ed. , rev. & cor. with
practical notes and observations.
Boston, T. Bedlington, 1828.
447 p. ArU; CSt-L; CtY; GU;
ICJ; KyU; LNOP; MB; MWA;
MdBL; MeB; MeLB; MiD; MnU;
MoSU; MoSW-M; NNNAM; NRAM;
PPC; ScCliP; ViRA.   32832

---- ---- With notes by Alex-
ander H. Stevens...Philadelphia,
T. Desilver & H. Cowperthwait,
J. R. Bailey, pr. , 1828. 2 vols.
ArU-M; CSt-L; CtY; GU-M; Ia;
MBCo; MdBM; MdUM; MeB;
MnU; MoU; NNC-M; NNNAM;
NjR; OCG; PPC; PU; ViRMC;
WKenHi.   32833

Cooper, Phelps and Campbell,
firm, Windsor, Vt.
Fire engines. Windsor (Ver-

mont)March 14, 1828... Cooper,
Phelps & Campbell. [Windsor,
Vt. , 1828] Bdsd. MB.   32834

Coppee, Henry, comp.
The select academic speaker;
containing a large number of new
and appropriate pieces, for prose
declamation, poetical recitation,
and dramatic readings. 6th ed.
Philadelphia, J. H. Butler & co. ,
1828. 572 p. MH.   32835

Copy of a letter from Phillis, to
her sister in the country, describing the riot on Negro Hill.
Bosson, Ulie, 47th, 180028...
[Boston, 1828] Bdsd. MB. 32836

The coquette. See Foster, Mrs.
Hannah (Webster).

Cora; or, The genius of America.
Philadelphia, E. Littell, 1828.
260 p. CtHT; MWA; IUC.   32837

Cordier, Pierre Louis Antoine
An essay on the temperature
of the interior of the earth...
Read to the Academy of Sciences
at their sessions of June 4th,
June 9th and July 23d, 1827.
Trans. from the French by the
Junior class in Amherst College.
Amherst, John S. & Charles
Adams, prs. , 1828. 94 p. CtHT;
CtY; DI-GS; IU; MA; MAJ; MB;
MBAt; MH-Z; MWA; NN; NNM;
NR; PPA.   32838

[Corri, Philip Antony] 1784-1832
The Carrollton march; performed at the ceremony of commencing the Baltimore & Ohio
Railroad, on the fourth of July,
1828. Dedicated by permission to
the Hon. Charles Carroll, of
Carrollton, by A. Clifton. Baltimore, Pub. by John Cole, [1828]
[2] p. DLC.   32839

Cortes, Hernando, 1485-1547
Historia de Mejico, escrita

por ...Hernan Cortes: aumen-
tada con otros documentos y
notas, por D. Francisco Anton-
io Lorenzana... Rev. y adaptada
a la ortografia moderna, por D.
Manuel del Mar. Neuva York,
White, Gallaher y White, 1828.
110, 614 p. CL; CLSU; CU;
CtHT-W; CtY; DLC; MB; MWA;
MnU; MoSM; NN; OC; OCY;
PPDrop; TxH; TxU; WBB;
BrMus.   32840

Cottin, Madame Marie
Elizabeth; or, The exiles of
Siberia. A tale, founded upon
facts. Boston, T. Bedlington,
1828. v, 1-184 p. DGU; DLC;
KU; MB; MH; MWA; MiDSH;
NN; NRU; PU; RNHi.   32841

Cottom's New Virginia & North-
Carolina almanack for 1829.
By Joseph Cave. Richmond,
Peter Cottom [1828] 14 1. ViW.
                          32842
Cottom's Virginia & North Caro-
lina almanack for 1829. By Jos-
eph Cave. Richmond, Peter Cot-
tom; [etc.] [1828] 16 1. NcU;
ViU; ViW.   32843

.... Counterpart to "A strange
thing." Boston, Pub. by Henry
Bowen, 1828. 12 p. [Universal-
ist tract] MH-AH; MMeT-Hi;
VtU.   32844

Cowper, William, 1731-1800
The task: A poem in six books.
Philadelphia, Pub. by D. & S.
Neall, prs. , 1828. 199 p. KWiU;
PU.   32845

Crafts, William, 1787-1826
A selection, in prose and po-
etry, from the miscellaneous
writings of the late William
Crafts. To which is prefixed, a
memoir of his life. Charleston,
Pr. by C. C. Sebring and J. S.
Burges, 1828. 384 p. CSmH;
CtHT; DLC; ICN; ICU; KU; MB;

MBAt; MH; MHi; MWA; MnHi;
NHi; NIC; NN; NcD; PHi; PPAmP;
RPB; ScC; ScCC; ScHi; ScU;
TxU; Vi; ViU; BrMus.   32846

Cramer's magazine almanack for
1829. Pittsburgh, Cramer &
Spear [etc.] [1828] 36 l. DLC;
OC; PPi.   32847

Cramer's Pittsburgh almanack
for 1829. Pittsburgh, Cramer &
Spear [etc.] [1828] 18 l. MWA;
OClWHi; OFH; OHi.   32848

Crary, John
   Speech of the Honourable John
Crary, in the Senate of the state
of New York, March 25, 1828.
On the proposition for appointing
an inquisitor in the case of Wm.
Morgan. With an exposition of
the principles of masonry. New-
York, Pr. and for sale at No.
453 Hudson street [1828] 18 p.
DLC; IaCrM.   32849

Crayon, Geoffrey, pseud.   See
Irving, Washington.

[Creuzé de Lesser, Augustin
François, baron] 1771-1839
   Neal & Mackenzie, No. 201,
Chestnut Street, between the
Theatre & Arcade, Philadelphia,
Le nouveau seigneur de village,
opera-comique, en un acte.
[Philadelphia, 1828] 20 p. (Also
issued in vol. with covering title
"Collection d'Operas et vaude-
villes") ICU; PPL.   32850

The crisis No. 9. See A Republican.

A critical review of Noah Webster's spelling book. See Cobb,
Lyman.

Crocker, Peter
   A sermon, occasioned by the
death of Elizabeth Kilbourn, wife
of Mr. Jonathan Kilbourn; who

departed this life, March 11,
1828. New Haven, Treadway &
Adams, 1828. 14 p. Ct; CtHi.
                            32851
Crocker, Sophia, 1794-1822
   The twins: or, An account of
the happy lives and triumphant
deaths of Sophia Crocker, who
died May 13th, 1822, and her
sister Maria, who died Nov. 3d,
1823... Norwich, Pr. at the Courier office, 1828. 44 p. DLC.
                            32852
Crockford's; or, Life in the
West. See Deale,

[Croker, Thomas Crofton] 1798-
1854
   Fairy legends and traditions
of the south of Ireland... [2nd
ed.] Philadelphia, Carey, Lea &
Carey, 1828. 3 v. CSmH. 32853

Croly, George, 1780-1860
   The church, in the fires of
persecution; or A history of the
sufferings of the church from the
date of Our Saviour. Philadelphia,
Pub. at the Church Missionary
House, 1828. 155 p. IObB. 32854

[----] Salathiel. A story of the
past, the present, and the future.
New York, G. & C. Carvill [etc.]
[Sleight & George, prs., Jamaica,
L.I.] 1828. 2 v. CtY; GHi; MBL;
MH-AH; MNe; NBLiHi; NNCoCi;
NPtw; PHC; WBB.   32855

Cromwell, Oliver, of South Carolina
   The soldier's wreath, or The
battle ground of New Orleans,
and other poems. By Oliver
Cromwell, of South Carolina.
Charleston, Pr. by W. Riley,
1828. 3 p. l., [ix]-xii, [13]-101
p., 1 l. CSmH; DLC; NcD; RPB;
ScC; ScU; BrMus.   32856

[Cruger, Alfred]
   Report on the proposed canal
connecting the Altamaha and Ogee-

chee Rivers, comprising the plan
and estimates of the same. [New
York? 1828] 40 p. GU-DE; GU.
                                32857
Cubi Y Soler, Mariano
  Le traducteur François: or,
A practical system for translat-
ing the French language, to which
are added observations of the
modes generally pursued in learning languages. 2d ed., corr.,
enl. and greatly imp. Boston,
Hilliard, Gray, Little and Wilkins, 1828. xii, 372 p. CoGrS;
CtMW; CtY; MB; MBAt; MH;
MWHi; MdBL; MiOC; Nh; PHi.
                                32858
---- El traductor Español; or,
A practical system for translat-
ing the Spanish language. To
which are added observations on
the modes generally pursued in
learning languages. 2d ed., corr.,
revised and imp. Boston, Hilliard, Gray, Little and Wilkins
[Hilliard, Metcalf, and Company,
Cambridge, pr.] 1828. [8], xvii,
404, [2] p. ABS; ICU; IEdS;
InGrD; LNHT; MB; MH; MdBL;
NbO; RNR; TxU.   32859

---- A new pocket dictionary of
the English and Spanish language
...Spanish and English. Baltimore, Fielding Lucas, Jr., 1828.
2 v. LNHT.   32860

---- A new Spanish grammar,
adapted to every class of learners. 4th ed., rev., corr, simplified and much imp. Baltimore,
Fielding Lucas, jun'r, [J. D. Toy,
pr.] 1828. 542 p. AU; CSfPUC;
CtY; NNH; OMC; PU; RPAt.
                                32861
---- Observations on a practical
system of translation; with a few
remarks on the modes generally
pursued in learning languages...
Boston, Hilliard, Gray, Little,
and Wilkins [Cambridge, Hilliard,
Metcalf and Co., prs. to the Uni-
versity] 1828. 63 p. CtHT-W;

CtY; MBAt; MH; MHi; NN; NNG;
OO; PPAmP; PPL.   32862

Cumberland almanac for 1829.
By W. L. Willeford. Nashville,
John S. Simpson [1828] 18 l.
OClWHi; THi; TMC.   32863

Cuming, Francis Higgins
  A sermon delivered in St.
Luke's Church, Rochester, on
Whitsunday, May 25, 1818...
[Rochester, 1828] 8 p. NRHi.
                                32864
Cummings, Asa, 1791-1856
  A sermon, delivered in Gor-
ham, June 25, 1828, before the
Maine Missionary Society, at
their twenty-first anniversary.
Portland, Shirley and Hyde, 1828.
46, [2] p. CSmH; MH-AH; MWA;
MeB; MeLB; MiD-B; NN. 32865

Cummings, Jacob Abbot, 1773-
1820
  First lessons in geography and
astronomy, with seven plain maps
and a view of the solar system,
for the use of young children,
as preparatory to ancient and
modern geography. 11th ed. New
Haven, S. Babcock, 1828. 82 p.
NN.   32866

---- An introduction to ancient
and modern geography, on the
plan of Goldsmith and Guy: Comprising rules for projecting maps,
with an atlas. 9th ed. Boston,
Pub. and sold by Cummings and
Hillard, Cambridge, Hillard and
Metcalf, 1828. 340 p. KHi; PRHi.
                                32867
---- The pronouncing of the
spelling book, adapted to Walker's Critical pronouncing dictionary...Rev. and imp. from the
4th ed. Boston, Hilliard, Gray,
Little, and Wilkins, 1828. 166 p.
MChB.   32868

Cummins, Francis
  The salvability and church

membership of children and their
right of baptism explained and
vindicated. Milledgeville, Camak & Ragland, prs. , 1828. 24
p. PLT.   32869

Cushing, David, d. 1849
A eulogy, delivered in the
chapel of Williams College, November 6, 1823; on account of
the lamented death of Orren
Ware, a member of the sopho-
more class; who departed this
life October 9, 1823, in the 19th
year of his age. Williamstown,
Pr. by Ridley Bannister, 1828.
12 p. MWiW.   32870

Cusick, David, d. ca. 1840
David Cusick's sketches of ancient history of the Six nations...
2d ed. of 7000 copies. --Embel-
ished with 4 engravings. Tusca-
rora village (Lewiston, Niagara
co.) [Lockport, N. Y. , Cooley &
Lothrop, prs. ,] 1828. 36 p.
DLC; MB.   32871

[Custis, George Washington
Parke]
The Indian prophecy, a national drama in two acts, founded
upon a most interesting and ro-
mantic occurrence in the life of
General Washington. To which is
prefixed a memoir of the Indian
prophecy, from the recollections
and private memoirs of the life
and character of Washington. By
the author of the Recollections.
Georgetown, D. C. , J. Thomas,
pub. , 1828. 35 p. CSmH; IaU;
MH.   32872

Cutler, Benjamin C.
A sermon preached in Christ
Church, Quincy, on completing
a century since its formation, on
Christmas Day, 1827. Cambridge,
Hilliard, Metcalf, and Co. , 1828.
28 [1] p. DLC; MH.   32873

The cypress wreath. See Strong,
Titus.

D

[Dabney, Jonathan Peele] comp.
A selection of hymns and
psalms, for social and private
worship. 8th ed. Boston, Thos.
Wells, 1828. [350] p. CtY; IEG;
IU; LU; MB; MBAt; MHi; NNUT;
Nh; RPB.   32874

[----] ---- 9th ed. Boston, T.
Wells, 1828. [360] p. NNUT;
Nh; RPB.   32875

Daboll, Nathan
Daboll's arithmetic, containing correct solutions to all the
examples and questions, at full
length... to which is added a new
method of solving the irreducible
case of cubic equations, and applied to the extraction of the cube
root... by John D. Williams.
New York, Caleb Bartlett, pub.
and pr. , 1828. 219 p. IaDaP.
                               32876
---- Daboll's schoolmaster's assistant. Imp. and enl. Being a
plain, practical system of arith-
metick. Adapted to the United
States... With the addition of the
Farmers' and mechanicks best
method of book-keeping, designed
as a companion to Daboll's Arith-
metick. By Samuel Green. Middletown, [Con.] Pub. by Wm. H.
Niles, Stereotyped by A. Chandler, New York, 1828. 228, 12 p.
CtHi; TNJ.   32877

---- ---- New London, Pr. and
pub. by Samuel Green, proprietor of the copyright, 1828. 240,
7, [5] p. CoU; CtHT-W; CtMW;
MB; MH; MiU; MtBiP; OClWHi;
RPB.   32878

---- ---- Ithaca, Pr. and pub.
by Mack and Andrus, 1828. 240,
7, [5] p. CSmH; MWA.   32879

---- A key to Daboll's arithmetic... to which is added a new method of solving... cubic equations... New York, C. Bartlett, 1828. 219 p. DLC; NN. 32880

Dagley, Richard
Death's doings; consisting of numerous original compositions in verse and prose; the friendly contributions of various writers, principally intended as illustrations of thirty plates designed and etched by R. Dagley... From the 2d London ed. Boston, C. Ewer, 1828. 2 v. CtHT-W; CtY; DLC; LNHT; MH-AH; MdBS; NNG; PU; TKL; Vi; BrMus. 32881

Damon, David, 1787-1843
A sermon, delivered at Lunenburg December 2, 1827. By David Damon, at the close of his ministry in that town. Lancaster [Mass.] Pr. by Ferdinand and Joseph Andrews, 1828. 22 p. CSmH; DLC. 32882

Dana, Daniel
An election sermon... before his excellency Levi Woodbury, Governor and the honorable council, Senate and House of Representatives of the state [of New Hampshire. Concord, Pr. by J. B. Moore, 1828. 24 p. NjR. 32883

Dana, James G.
The case of the public printer, with some brief illustrations of the testimony, published by Jas. G. Dana... [Frankfort, Ky., 1828] NN (Photostat of 1st page] 32884

Dana, Joseph, 1769-1849
Quaestiones grammaticae: or, Grammatical exercises, by questions only... Particularly adapted to Adam's Latin grammar. With an appendix... 2d ed., corr., etc. Boston, Hilliard, Gray, Little, & Wilkins, 1828. 70 p. DLC; MB; MH; NRHi; OO; BrMus. 32885

Dana's Circulating Library
Catalogue of Dana's Circulating Library, No. 29, Market-Street, Providence, 1828. Providence, Smith and Parmenter, 1828. 40 p. MB; RPB. 32886

Dangell, M. S.
The Cabinet; or, The philosopher's masterpiece, containing a fore-knowledge of future events ... Boston, Repr. from the Dublin ed., 1828. [44] p. MB. 32887

Daniell, William C.
Observations upon the autumnal fevers of Savannah. Savannah, W. T. Williams; New York, Collins, & Hannay, 1828. 152 p. AU; CSt-L; CtMW; GHi; MB; MBCo; MnU; NN; NNNAM; NcU; PPAmP; PPC; PU. 32888

Darby, William, 1775-1854
Lectures on the discovery of America, and colonization of North America by the English... Baltimore [Pub. by Plaskitt & Co.] 1828. 223 p. CSmH; CtHT-W; ICU; LNHT; MB; MdBE; MdHi; MiU-C; MoSM; NNG; NT; OMC; PHi; Vi; WHi; BrMus. 32889

---- A view of the United States, historical geographical, and statistical... Philadelphia, Pub. by H. S. Tanner. [Mifflin & Parry, prs.] 1828. iv, 654, 11 p. (Some copies reported with 622 p. which seem to be the same thing without the index and list of maps.) A-Ar; CtHi; CtY; DBRE; DLC; KHi; ICN; IU; InU; LNHT; MB; MBAt; MH; MdBP; MeB; MiD-B; NIC; NNC; OClWHi; PHi; PPAmP; PPL; RP; TNJ; ViU; WHi; BrMus. 32890

Dartmouth College
A catalogue of the officers and students of Dartmouth College. October-1828. Concord [N. H.], Asa M'Farland, pr.,

1828. 23, [1] p. MBAt; N. 32891

---- Catalogus senatus academici collegii Dartmuthensis in republica Neo-Hantoniensi, eorumque omnium, qui in eodem munera et officia gesserunt, aut alicujus gradus laurea exornati fuerunt. Leuphanae, Typis Thomae Mann, 1828. 44 p. DLC; DNLM; MBNEH; MnHi; Nh; NhD.   32892

---- Laws of Dartmouth College. Hanover, Pr. by Thomas Mann, 1828. 24 p. DLC; M; MBC; MHi; RPB; BrMus.   32893

---- Medical Department. New Hampshire Medical Institution: Dartmouth College, Hanover, 1828. 8 p. MBAt; MBC.
                             32894
Dartmouth College and the state of New Hampshire [from the New Hampshire Statesman and Concord Register, 1828] 23 p. DLC; MBAt; MBC; MH; MHi.   32895

Dashiell, Alfred H.
   Barnabas; or The son of consolation: exemplified in the life and character of the Rev. Joseph Eastburn; late pastor of the Mariners' Church, Philadelphia who departed this life January 30, A. D. 1828: A sermon preached in the Mariners' Church, aforesaid, February 3, 1828. Philadelphia, Pr. by T. S. Manning, 1828. [1], 30 p. MWA; NjPT; PHi; PPPrHi.   32896

Daveiss, Samuel, 1775-1856
   The speech of Samuel Daveiss esq., delivered in the Senate of Kentucky on the 6th day of February 1828, on the resolution offered by Mr. Beatty of Pulaski, as a substitute to the resolutions reported by the committee on internal improvement. [Frankfort? Ky., 1828?] 16 p. DLC.   32897

[Davenport, Rufus]
   The right aim, first, aim to get first principles of right; then trust prevailing with progressive light; while freedom, art, trade, debt, take first the ground, all things for general good, the right aim found. Boston [Dow & Niles, pr.] 1828. 32 p. MHi; NN; RPB.
                             32898
---- To the Legislature of the state of ----one of the United States of America. The undersigned petitioner, with all deference represents to your honorable body, that under coincident misfortunes, he has been a victim to the oppression, harrass and waste against which our debtor laws and customs, do not secure due protection to any citizen of the United States... Equitable principles for free debt rules... Boston, A. D. Dec. 1, 1828. 1 p. DLC; DNA; MB; MBAt.   32899

Davies, Samuel, 1724-1761
   Sermons on important subjects ...to which are prefixed memoirs & character of the author & two sermons on occasion of his death by the Rev. Drs. Gibbons & Finley...4th Amer. ed. containing all the author's sermons ever pub. ...New York, J. & J. Harper, for E. Duyckinck [etc.] 1828. 3 vols. CtMW; CtSoP; FTa; GAGTh; ICMcC; IU; KyBgW; MH-AH; MeBaT; MiD; MoSpD; OO; PLT; PPPrHi; TCU; ViRU.
                             32900
Davis, A. H.
   Observations on the religious instruction of youth, principally with a reference to Sunday schools. Revised by the Committee of Publication. Philadelphia, American Sunday School Union, I. Ashmead & Co., prs., 1828. 165 p. MBC.   32901

Davis, Daniel, 1762-1835
 A practical treatise upon the
authority and duty of justices of
peace in criminal prosecutions,
to which are now added precedents of declarations and pleadings in civil actions. 2d ed. Boston, Hilliard, Gray, Little and
Wilkins, 1828. iv, 471 p. C;
CSt; Ct; DLC; ICLaw; M; MBS;
MH; MHi; MiDU-L; NIC-L; Nj;
PP; RPL; TxU.   32902

Davis, Henry
 Address, commencement of
Hamilton College... 1828. Sabin
18826.   32903

[Davis, John]
 The post-captain, or The
wooden walls well manned; comprehending a view of naval society and manners. Containing also,
a choice collection of sea and
other songs. 4th Amer. from 5th
London ed. New York, Pr. & pub.
by Joseph M'Cleland, 1828. 172,
[8] p. ICU; MH; MWA; PPL.
                       32904
Davis, John, 1787-1854
 Speech of Mr. John Davis, of
Massachusetts, on the tariff bill.
Delivered in the House of Representatives, March 12, 1828.
Washington, Pr. by Gales & Seaton, 1828. 36 p. CSmH; DeGE;
MB; MH; MNF; MNtcA; MeB;
PHi.   32905

[Davis, William M.]
 To the citizens of Ohio county.
[n. p. , 1828] (Cap. title. signed
and dated, William M. Davis,
Frankfurt, Ky. 18th February,
1828. 8 p.) ViU.   32906

Davys, George
 Village conversations on the
liturgy of the Church of England
... Adapted to the Protestant
Episcopal Church in the U. S.
Baltimore, Pr. by the Protestant
Episcopal Female Tract Society

of Baltimore. J. D. Toy, pr. ,
1828. 105 p. MdBP; MdHi.
                       32907
Dawson, Lawrence E.
 An oration delivered before
the Revolution and Cincinnati Societies of Charleston, South-
Carolina on the Fourth of July,
1828... Charleston, Pr. by A. E.
Miller, 1828. 18 p. MWA; ScC.
                       32908
A day after the fair. See Somerset, Charles A.

Day's New-York pocket almanac
for 1829. New-York, M. Day
[1828] 12 l. NHi.   32909

[Deale, --]
 Crockford's: or, Life in the
West... New York, Pr. by J. &
J. Harper, sold by Collins and
Hannay, Collins and Co. , [etc.]
1828. 2 v. CtHT; CtY; DGU;
NN.   32910

Dean, Paul, 1789-1860
 One hundred and twenty rea-
sons for being a Universalist; or,
A conversation between a believ-
er in the final restoration and a
sincere inquirer after truth...
4th ed. Providence, Office of the
Christian Telescope. John S.
Greene, pr. , 1828. 35 p. MB;
MBC; MHi; MMeT-Hi; MWA;
BrMus.   32911

Debate on the revenue. See Johnston, Josiah Stoddard.

The decision. See Kennedy,
Grace.

A defence of the National Administration. See Webster, Ezekiel.

[Defoe, Daniel,] 1660-1731
 The life and adventures of
Robinson Crusoe, of York, mariner. With an account of his
travels round three parts of the
globe. Written by himself. In

two volumes. Exeter, Pub. by
Abel Brown, C. Norris, pr.,
1828. 2 v. DLC; MWA; OClWHi.
32912

Degrand, Peter Paul Francis
Tariff or duties on importations into the United States, revenue laws and custom-house regulations. Compiled by P. P. F. Degrand. 4th ed. Boston, P. P. F.
Degrand, Samuel Condon, pr.,
1828. 117, 119 p. MB; MBAt;
MWA; NhHi; PPi; BrMus.   32913

Dekay, Joseph E.
Letter from Joe Strickland
[pseud.] to Samuel F. B. Morse,
president of the National Academy of the Arts of Design. Mem-
phremagog, From the Graphic
and Picturesque Press [New
York?] 1828. 18 p. MBAt; PPL.
32914

De Lancey, William Heathcote,
bp.
An inaugural address delivered before the trustees, faculty,
and students, in the college
chapel, on Wednesday, September 17th, 1828. Philadelphia,
Carey, Lea & Carey, 1828. 31
p. CtY; KyLx; MH; NCH; NNG;
OrPD; PHi; PPL; PPPrHi; PU;
RPB.   32915

De Lisle; or, The sensitive man
... New-York, Pr. by J. & J.
Harper, Sold by Collins and Han-
nay, Collins and Co., and G.
and C. Carvill, Philadelphia,
Carey, Lea and Carey, R. H.
Small, Towar and Hogan, and U.
Hunt, Boston, Richardson and
Lord, and Hilliard Gray and Co.,
1828. 2 v. DLC; GHi; IaMp;
MBL; MH; MNe; NcU; PPL;
TNJ.   32916

De Lisle - (another ed. of Vol.
I.) New York, Pr. by J. & J.
Harper, Sold by Collins and Han-
nay. Collins and Co., G. & C.
Carvill, William B. Gilley, A.

T. Goodrich, O. A. Roorbach,
Elam Bliss, C. S. Francis, and
William Burgess, Jr., 1828.
PPL.   32917

Delaware and Hudson Canal Co.
Third general report of the
president, managers and company, of the Delaware and Hudson Canal Company, to the stockholders. March 4, 1828. New-
York, Pr. by Elliott and Palmer,
1828. 22 p. CtY; DBRE; MiU-T;
NN; PPL; WHi.   32918

The Delaware and Maryland al-
manac for 1829. Wilmington,
Robert Porter & Son [1828] 18 l.
DLC; PHi.   32919

Democratic convention. (Harrisburg, Jan. 4-5, 1828.) See National Republican Party. Pennsylvania.

Democratic Party. Connecticut.
An address to the citizens of
Connecticut; by the friends of
Andrew Jackson, in Norwich and
vicinity. Norwich, L. H. Young,
1828. 26, [1] p. CtHi; CtY.
32920

---- Address to the people of
Connecticut, adopted at the state
convention, held at Middleton,
August 7, 1828; with the proceed-
ings of the convention. Hartford,
J. Russell, pr., 1828. 24 p.
Ct; CtHT-W; CtHi; CtSoP; CtY;
DLC; MBC; MiD-B; PHi.   32921

---- At the state convention of
the friends of Gen'l Jackson...
were appointed a committee for
the Co. of Hartford... Hartford,
Oct. 14, 1828. Bdsd. CtHT-W.
32922

---- Indiana.
An address to the friends of
Andrew Jackson, in the first
congressional district of Indiana.
To the Democratic Republicans
of the first congressional district

of Indiana. [Salem, July 1st, 1828. Salem, Handy and Allen?] In.   32923

---- Annotator--Extra. An address of the Republican central committee, to the citizens of Indiana: to which is added the letters of General Jackson to Dr. Coleman and Governor J. B. Ray. To the people of Indiana. [Handy & Allen, prs., Salem, Ind., 1828] 8 p. InHi; InU.   32924

---- Kentucky.
Argus extra. To the people of Kentucky. (Frankfort, Ky., Apr. 9th, 1828) 40 p. NcD.   32925

---- Governor's election. The Occupant laws. To the people of Kentucky. [Frankfort, 1828] 24 p. DLC.   32926

---- Louisiana.
Address of the people of Louisiana, in behalf of General Andrew Jackson. [Halifax, Office of the Free press, ca 1828] 7 p. NcU.   32927

---- Maryland.
An address to the people of Charles, Calvert and St. Mary's counties. [n. p., 1828?] 35 p. TxU.   32928

---- A brief refutation of the slanders published in the Coffin handbill and Monumental inscriptions. Baltimore, Pr. by Lucas & Deaver, 1828. 15 p. DLC; MdBP.   32929

---- Massachusetts.
Essex Jackson Meeting. At a convention of the friends of Gen. Jackson in the county of Essex, holden at Haverhill on the 27th day of March, Col. John Johnson, chairman. Capt. William Haseltine, sec'y., the following address and resolutions were

adopted. [Haverhill? Mass., 1828] 8 p. DLC.   32930

---- Missouri.
Address of the Jackson convention to the people of Missouri. Fayette, Pr. at the office of the Western Monitor, 1828. 9 p. MoSHi.   32931

Fayette, 17th July, 1828. The committee of general correspondence for the state of Missouri, appointed by the friends of Andrew Jackson... [Fayette, 1828] 1 p. MoKcU.   32932

---- New Hampshire.
Proceedings and address of the New Hampshire Republican state convention of delegates friendly to the election of Andrew Jackson to the next presidency of the United States, assembled at Concord, June 11 and 12, 1828. Concord, Pr. at the Patriot Office, 1828. 32 p. CSmH; CtY; DLC; IU; InHi; MiD-B; MnU; NNC; NcU; NhHi; T; TKL. 32933

---- New Jersey.
Falsehood and slander exposed. The case of the six militia men stated from official and authentic records. Pub. by order of the Jackson Central Committee. [Trenton, 1828] 15 p. DLC; MiD-B.   32934

---- Proceedings and address of the New-Jersey state convention, assembled at Trenton, on the eighth day of January, 1828, which nominated Andrew Jackson for president, John C. Calhoun for vice-president, of the United States. Trenton, Pr. by Joseph Justice, 1828. 20 p. CSmH; DLC; GDC; IU; MiD-B; MnHi; NIC; Nj; OClWHi; PHi; PPL; PPi; WHi.   32935

---- New York.
Address of the General Com-

mittee of Republican young men
of the City of New York, friendly to the election of Andrew Jackson...[New York, 1828] 1 p.
DLC.   32936

---- Address of the Republican
general committee of young men
of the city and county of New-
York, friendly to the election of
Gen. Andrew Jackson to the
presidency, to the Republican
electors of the state of New-
York. Stereotyped by James Conner, New-York. New-York, Alexander Ming, jr., pr., 1828. 48
p. CSmH; CtY; DLC; NIC; NN;
NbU; NcU; Nh; OClWHi; PPL;
PPiU; WHi.   32937

---- Albany Argus, Extra. Sept.
2, 1828. The reign of terrour.
[A campaign circular favoring
the candidacy of Andrew Jackson
as against John Quincy Adams
for president of the United States,
and giving an account by Henry
Shankwiler of his arrest and
treatment under the alien and
sedition laws, in 1799.] Albany,
1828. 8 p. NN.   32938

---- The case of the six mutineers, whose conviction and sentence were approved of by General Jackson, fairly stated: with
a refutation of some of the falsehoods circulated on this subject.
Pub. by order of the Albany Republican general committee. Albany, Pr. for the Albany Argus,
by Webster and Wood, 1828. 32
p. CLU; CtY; DLC; ICN; MiD-B;
NN; NjR; T; WHi.   32939

---- ---- Albany, Pr. by Webster & Wood, 1828. 32 p. CSmH;
DLC.   32940

---- ---- Geneva [N.Y.], Pr. by
C. S. M'Connell, 1828. 32 p.
DLC; NN.   32941

---- Circular. The Jackson Re-
publican committee of Rochester
... [Rochester, Repr. from the
Daily Advertiser, 1828] [3] p.
McMurtrie, Unpublished check-
list of Rochester imprints.   32942

---- The striking similitude between the reign of terror of the
elder Adams, and the reign of
corruption, of the younger Adams.
An address...Albany, Pr. for
the Albany Argus, by D. M'Glashan, 1828. 8 p. CSmH; CtY;
DLC.   32943

---- Troy Budget-extra. Proceedings of the convention of Republican young men of the state of
New York, friendly to the election of General Andrew Jackson
to the presidency. Held at Herkimer, Oct. 6, 1828. [Troy,
1828] 16 p. NjR.   32944

---- [Text begins]... Young men
of Cortland county [Cortland,
N.Y.] 1828. 4 p. CSmH.   32945

---- North Carolina.
Address of the Central Jackson Committee to the freemen of
North Carolina; electoral ticket
of North Carolina, for president,
Andrew Jackson, for vice-president, John C. Calhoun. Raleigh,
Lawrence and Lemay, 1828. 16
p. NcC; NcU.   32946

---- An address, reported by the
Committee appointed at Wilkesboro', 5th February, 1828, to
the people composing the counties
of Surry, Ashe, Wilkes, and Iredell. Salisbury, Pr. by Philo
White, 1828. 16 p. NcU. 32947

---- The case of the six militia
men fairly stated, with an appendix
of public documents and other papers, in which the imputations
cast upon General Jackson respecting that transaction are

shown to be illiberal and un-
founded calumnies. Pub. by order of the Central Jackson Committee and addressed to the freemen of North-Carolina. Raleigh,
Lawrence & Lemay, 1828. 47 p.
NcU.   32948

---- Ohio.
To sweep the Augean Stable.
For President Andrew Jackson
for Vice-President John C. Calhoun. [16 names of candidates]
[1828] 1 p. DLC.   32949

---- Pennsylvania.
An address of the Jackson
Democratick Committee of cor-
respondence, of Allegheny county.
Pittsburgh, Leonard S. Johns,
pr., 1828. 24 p. DLC.   32950

---- Address of the Republican
Committee of Correspondence of
Philadelphia, to the people of the
United States. Philadelphia, Pr.
by Wm. Stavely, 1828. 12 p. DLC.
InU; NbU; Nh; OC; PPL; Vi.
                                32951
---- Bradford County. Democrat-
ic corresponding committee ap-
pointed by the state convention
on the fourth of March. [1828]
Bdsd. PPL.   32952

---- Addresse an das Volk von
Dauphin County, gehalten vor der
Democratischen Caunty Versamm-
lung, am 25sten letzten July, im
Courthause zu Harrisburg. [Har-
risburg, 1828] 32 p. PHi. 32953

---- Jackson and Liberty. An
address unanimously adopted by
a general meeting of the citizens
of Dauphin County, friendly to
the election of General Andrew
Jackson... Harrisburg, Pr. by S.
C. Stambaugh, 1828. 24 p. NN.
                                32954
---- Letters addressed to John
Sergeant, Manuel Eyre, Lawrence Lewis, Clement C. Biddle,

and Joseph P. Norris, esqs,
authors of An address to the
people of Pennsylvania, adopted
at a meeting of the friends to the
election of John Quincy Adams,
held in Philadelphia, July 7,
1828: containing strictures on
their address. By the committee
of correspondence, of Philadelphia, appointed by a Republican
convention, held at Harrisburg,
January 8, 1828. Philadelphia,
Pr. by William Stavely, 1828.
88 p. CtY; DLC; MWA; MdHi;
MiD-B; NN; NjR; P; PHi; PPL.
                                32955

---- The proceedings of a meeting of the democratic citizens of
North Mulberry Ward, held at
Moody's Hotel on Monday evening,
August 18, 1828 in pursuance of
a public call in the papers of the
city of Philadelphia. Pr. by order of the committee. [Philadel-
phia, 1828] 12 p. PHi.   32956

---- Proceedings of the Demo-
cratic convention, held at Harris-
burg, Pennsylvania, January 8,
1828. [Harrisburg, Pr. by S. C.
Stambaugh, 1828] 16 p. CSmH;
MBAt ("Harrrisburg" in title).
                                32957
---- Vermont.
Proceedings and address of the
Vermont Republican Convention
friendly to the election of Andrew
Jackson to the next presidency of
the United States, holden at
Montpelier, June 27, 1828. Mont-
pelier, Pr. by Geo. W. Hill,
1828. 24 p. CSmH; CtY; DLC;
ICU; MBNMHi; MWA; Nh; VtHi;
VtMiS; VtU.   32958

---- Virginia.
Address of the Jackson Cen-
tral Committee, to the people of
Virginia. [1828] 8 p. DLC. 32959

---- Jackson Ticket. Andrew
Jackson. President. John C. Cal-

houn, Vice President [24 candi-
dates] [Virginia 1828] 1 p. DLC.
32960
---- President, Andrew Jackson.
Vice-President, John C. Calhoun. Virginia. Presidential
electors... [Wheeling? 1828?]
Bdsd. WvWO.   32961

---- Virginia electoral ticket.
Jackson electoral ticket... [Rich-
mond? 1828?] ViU.   32962

Dempster, John
The substance of a sermon,
delivered at the Methodist chapel,
in Cazenovia, on the first Sabbath of the year, 1828. Utica,
Pr. by Wm. Williams, 1828. 16
p. NUt.   32963

A description of the scenery and
incidents in the picturesque and
beautiful spectacle called, Peter
Wilkins; or, The flying islanders,
including copies of the songs,
etc., as presented at the Boston
Theatre. Boston, Pr. by True
and Greene, 1828. 11 p.   MBAt.
32964
Desilver's Philadelphia directory
and stranger's guide, for 1828.
Containing a plan of the city and
suburbs, the names of the citizens alphabetically arranged,
with their occupations and places
of abode; a list of the streets...
Philadelphia, Pub. by Robert Desilver, James Maxwell, pr.,
1828. v.p. DLC; MBAt; MWA;
NN; P; PHi; PP; PPL; BrMus.
32965
Desilver's United States' almanac for 1829. Philadelphia, R.
Desilver; T. Desilver; J. Grigg.
By Seth Smith [1828] 28 l. CLU;
DLC; InU; MB; MWA; NHi; NjR;
P; PHi; PP; PPAmP.   32966

---- Philadelphia, R. Desilver;
T. Desilver; J. Grigg. By Seth
Smith [1828] 36 l. CtY; N; PPL.
32967

Dessaussure, Henry William
Memoirs of the life and eul-
ogy on the character of the late
Judge Waities. Columbia, S.C.,
Pr. by David W. Sims, 1828.
26, 111 p. DLC; MH; NHi; NcU;
PHi; ScC.   32968

Destruction of Jerusalem; a-
bridged. See Josephus, Flavius.

A detailed and correct account
of the grand civic procession in
the city of Baltimore on the
fourth of July, 1828; in honor of
the day, and in commemoration
of the commencement of the Baltimore and Ohio Rail-Road: as
published in the "American."
Baltimore, Pr. by Thomas Murphy, 1828. 46 p. CtY; MdBJ;
MdHi; NN; PHi.   32969

.... Les deux precepteurs. Comedie en un acte. [Philadelphia,
1828] 17 p. (Neal & Mackenzie,
No. 201 Chestnut Street, between
the Theatre & Arcade, Philadelphia.) PPL.   32970

The Devil on politics. See Bal-
com, D. A.

Dewees, William Potts, 1868-
1841
A compendious system of mid-
wifery, chiefly designed to facili-
tate the inquiries of those who
may be pursuing this branch of
study... 3d ed. with additions.
Philadelphia, Carey, Lea &
Carey, 1828. Skerrett, Philadel-
phia, pr. 644 p. ArU-M; CU-
M; CtY; GEU-M; MBCo; MdBM;
MdUM; MeB; MoU; NBM; NNC-
M; NNNAM; OU; PPC; RPM;
ScCM.   32971

---- A treatise on the diseases
of females... 2d ed. rev. and
corr. Philadelphia, Carey, Lea
and Carey [I. Ashmead & Co.,
prs.] 1828. 542 p. CtHT; CtY;

DNLM; GAFM; ICJ; InU-M;
KyLoJM; MBCo; MdBM; MoJK;
NBM; NNNAM; OCG; PPC; PPL;
RPM; ViRA; ViRM; WU.   32972

[Dewey, Orville] 1794-1882
Letters of an English travel-
ler to his friend in England, on
the "Revivals of religion," in
America. Boston, Bowles &
Dearborn [Press of Isaac R.
Butts & Co.] 1828. 142 p.
CBPac; CSmH; CtY; DLC; ICN;
MB; MBAt; MH; MWA; MeB;
MeBaT; NB; NNC; OO; BrMus.
                        32973
[----] No. 17. On tests of true
religion. Pr. for the American
Unitarian Association. Boston,
Bowles & Dearborn [Pr. by I.R.
Butts] 1828. 20 p. CBPac; CtHi;
ICU; MBC; MH-AH; MHi; MMeT;
ScCC.   32974

A dialogue between a colonel of
the militia and a militiaman, in
relation to the rights of militia-
men, and the execution of the
"six-militia-men" shot by the order of General Andrew Jackson.
Russellvile [Ky.] Pr. by Charles
Rhea, 1828. 28 p. CSmH; NN.
                        32975
A dialogue on commonwealths.
See Brown, Paul.

A dialogue on some of the causes
of infidelity. By the author of A
dialogue on Providence, faith and
prayer. Pr. for the American
Unitarian Association. Boston,
Bowles and Dearborn [Stereo-
typed by Lyman Thurston & Co.]
1828. 1st series] [No. 21] 24 p.
ICMe; ICU; IEG; MBAU; MBC;
MH-AH; MHi; RP; ScCC.   32976

Dibdin, Thomas John, 1771-1841
The cabinet, a comic opera...
Philadelphia and New York, Neal
& MacKenzie, 1828. 54 p. DeGE;
MB; MH; PPL.   32977

---- ... The heart of Mid-lothian:
a melo-dramatic romance, in
three acts... As now performed
at the London and American theatres. Baltimore, J. Robinson
[1828?] 47 p. DLC.   32978

---- The reminiscences of Thom-
as Dibdin, of the Theatres Roy-
al, Covent-Garden, Drury-Lane,
Haymarket, &c. ... New-York,
Pr. by J. & J. Harper, for Col-
lins and Hannay; [etc., etc.]
1828. 2 v. in 1. CtY; DLC;
DeGE; FT; GS; IEN; KyLx; LN;
MB; MWA; MiD-B; MoS; NCH;
NRU; NcA-S; NjP; PP; PPL;
PU; TNJ; Vi; WHi; WM.   32979

Dickey, John M.
A brief history of the Presbyterian Church in the state of Indiana. Madison, Pr. by C. P. J.
Arion [1828] 24 p. In; PPPrHi.
                        32980

Dickson, David
Official report. Jackson, 21st
June, 1828. His Excellency,
Gerard C. Brandon [Jackson,
1828] Bdsd. Ms-Ar.   32981

Dickson, Samuel Henry, 1798-
1872
Introductory lecture delivered
at the commencement of the
fourth session of the Medical College of South Carolina, November,
1827. Charleston, Pr. by W.
Riley, 1828. 24 p. NBM; NcD;
ScCM.   32982

A dictionary of select and popular quotations, which are in daily
use; taken from the Latin,
French, Greek, Spanish and Italian languages; together with a
copious collection of law-maxims
and law terms; translated into
English. 5th Amer. ed. Philadelphia, Pub. by A. Finley, Clark
& Raser, prs., 1828. 312 p.
IaBo; NN; PPAmP.   32983

Diderot, Denys, 1713-1784
Thoughts on religion, by M.
Diderot. With a sketch of his life
and writings. New York, Pr. &
pub. by George H. Evans, 1828.
8 p. **PPL**.   32984

Dinner to Mathew Carey, esq.
(and Mr. Carey's address) from
the Pittsburgh Gazette, July 12,
1828. 8 p. MBAt; MWA; PU.
                                  32985
Dinsmoor, Robert, 1757-1836
Incidental poems accompanied
with letters, and a few select
pieces, mostly original, for
their illustration, together with
a preface, and a sketch of the
author's life. Haverhill [Mass.]
A. W. Thayer, pr., 1828. xxiv,
264 p. CSmH; DLC; ICU; MA;
MoSW; PU.   32986

A directory for the village of
Buffalo, containing the names and
residence of the heads of families and householders, in said
village, on the first of January,
1828. To which is added a sketch
of the history of the village,
from 1801 to 1828. Buffalo, Pub.
by L. P. Crary. Day, Follett &
Haskins, prs., 1828. 55 p. DLC;
MiU; NBu; NBuG; NBuHi; NN.
                                  32987
Directory or Guide to the resi-
dences and places of business of
the inhabitants of the city of
Charleston and its environs...for
...1829. Charleston, Pr. by
James S. Burges, 1828. 107,
[1] p. NN; ScC.   32988

A discourse addressed to religious people. See A Pennsylvanian, pseud.

A discourse delivered in the Second Presbyterian Church, Cincinnati. See Root, David.

A discourse on the paramount
importance of spiritual things.

By a Novitiate of the New Jerusa-
lem Church. Philadelphia, Pub.
by "The First New Jerusalem
Church of Philad." [sic] William
Brown, pr., 1828. 24 p. MCNC;
OO.   32989

A disquisition on creation. See
Read, Nathan.

The Divine unity. See Bradford,
A.

[Dix, Dorothea Lynde] 1802-1887
Conversations on common
things; or, Guide to knowledge;
With questions...By a teacher.
3d ed. Boston, Munroe and Francis, 1828. 288 p. CtMW; MBAt;
MH; MWA; NH; RPB.   32990

[----] Evening hours, no VII...
XII. Boston, Munroe and Francis;
New York, C. S. Francis, 1828.
216 p. DLC.   32991

[----] Private hours. By the au-
thor of Evening hours... Boston,
Munroe and Francis, 1828. 80 p.
MB; MH; PHi.   32992

[----] Robert Woodward; or, The
heedless boy. By the author of
"John Williams." Boston, Bowles
& Dearborn, Press of Isaac R.
Butts & Co., 1828. 36 p. (Original
moral tales, vol. 6, no. 1) DLC;
MB.   32993

[----] Sequel to Marrion Wilder.
By the author of "John Williams."
Boston, Bowles & Dearborn, Press
of Isaac R. Butts & Co., 1828. 43
p. (Original moral tales, v. 6, no.
3) MB; MWA; **PPL**.   32994

[----] The storm. By the author of
"John Williams." Boston, Bowles
& Dearborn, Press of Isaac R.
Butts & Co., 1828. 51 p. (Original
moral tales, v. 6, no. 2) CSmH; MB.
                                  32995

Doctor Bolus. A bombastic interlude... New-York, Pub. by E. Dunigan, at the Swamp Dramatic Repository, 1828. 24 p. NN.   32996

Doddridge, Phillip, 1702-1751
Hrn. D. Philip Doddridge, gewesenen oeffentlichen Lehrers der Gottesgelahrtheit und Rectors bey der Academie zu Northampton, Anfang und Fortgang Wahrer Gottseligkeit, in der menschilchen Seele. Nach der vierten Ausgabe, aus dem Englischen ulbersetzt. Erste Amerikanische Anflage. Haerrisburg, John S. Wiestling, 1828. 4 p l. , 400 p. PHi.   32997

---- The life of Col. James Gardiner, who was slain at the battle of Preston - Pans, September 21, 1745. Philadelphia, American Sunday School Union, 1828. 176 p. OMC; PR; BrMus.
                    32998
---- The rise and progress of religion in the soul; illustrated in a course of serious and practical addresses, suited to persons of every character and circumstance: with a devout meditation or prayer, subjoined to each chapter. New-York, American Tract Society, Fanshaw, pr. , [1828?] 280 p. MB.   32999

Dodge, Nehemiah, 1778?-1843
A funeral sermon occasioned by the decease of Mr. Daniel Hutchinson, late of Lebanon... Hartford, R. Canfield, 1828. 16 p. Ct; CtHi; DLC; MB.   33000

Doggett, Simeon, 1765-1852
A discourse delivered to the First Society in Mendon, at the funeral of Richard George, who deceased Oct. 23, 1827. 2d ed. Providence, F. Y. Carlile and Co. , 1828. 15 p. MH-AH; MW; MiD-B; BrMus.   33001

Domestic and Foreign Missionary Society of the Protestant Episcopal Church.
Proceedings of the board of directors of the Domestic and Foreign Missionary Society of the Protestant Episcopal Church ... Philadelphia, Joseph Harding, pr. , 1828. 44 p. CtHC; MBD; PPL.   33002

Domestick Missionary Society of Rhode Island, Providence.
Constitution of the Domestick Missionary Society, of Rhode Island. [Providence, 1828] 4 p. RPB.   33003

Donald Adair, a novel. See Lorraine, A. M.

Dorchester, Mass. Second Church of Christ.
The covenant and declaration of faith of the Second Church of Christ in Dorchester... Boston, T. R. Marvin, pr. , 1828. 36 p. MB; MBC; MH; MWiW; NjPT.
                    33004
Dorr, Benjamin 1796-1869
A sermon preached in Grace Church, Waterford, and Trinity Church, Lansingburgh, Feb. 17, 1828, being the Sunday after the death of his excellency De Witt Clinton. Lansingburgh, N. Y. , Van Cleve, 1828. 20 p. MB; MH; N; OC.   33005

Dorsey, Clement
Speech of Mr. Dorsey, of Maryland, on the subject of retrenchment. Delivered in the House of Representatives of the United States, January, 1828. Washington, Pr. by Gales & Seaton, 1828. 34 p. MWA; NN; BrMus.   33006

Douglas, J. W. , comp. , A manual for the members. See Briery Presbyterian Church.

Douglass, William
An address, delivered at Tinmouth, (Vt.) March 12, 1828, to the Singing School Society, at the request of the Committee. [Rutland, Vt., Pr. by Edward C. Purdy, 1828] 7, [1] p. MWA.
33007

Downing, John
I do certify that a few days ago, Mr. John Downing came into my counting room, and asked me if I thought he ought to be believed in a court of justice on oath... [7 signed testimonials regarding the character of John Downing] Lexington, Oct. 11, 1828. Printed on 1 p. of 4 p. folder, addressed for mailing. DLC.
33008

Doyle, James Warren, bp., 1786-1834
The Right Rev. Dr. Doyle's letters to the Duke of Wellington ... [Philadelphia? 1828?] 10 p. PU.
33009

Drake, Daniel
A discourse on intemperance; delivered at Cincinnati, March 1, 1828, before the Agricultural Society of Hamilton County, and subsequently pronounced, by request, to a popular audience... Cincinnati, Looker & Reynolds, prs., 1828. 96 p. CSmH; CtHC; DNLM; ICU; MWA; NN; OCHP; OClWHi; OMC; PPAmP; PPC; PPL; PPPrHi; ScCC; BrMus.
33010

Draper, Bourne Hall
Conversations on some leading points in natural philosophy; designed to illustrate the perfections of the Deity, and to expand the youthful mind. Utica, Pub. by The Western Sunday School Union; J. Colwell, pr., 1828. 104 p. ICMe; NN.
33011

Drey wunderbare neue Geschich-

ten oder Lieder. Das erste von einem Kleinen Kinde und einem Pudelhund... Ephrata, gedruckt bey J. B., 1828. 11, [1] p. PPL.
33012

Drury, Amos
A sermon preached in Rutland, June 18, 1828, before the Grand Royal Arch Chapter of the state of Vermont. Pub. at the request of the G. R. A. Chapter. Rutland, Pr. by Edward C. Purdy, 1828. 16 p. IaCrM; VtHi; BrMus.
33013

[Drysdale, Isabel]
Christian martyrs, or, Familiar conversations on the sufferings of some eminent Christians; by the author of "Scenes in Georgia;" written for the American Sunday School Union. Philadelphia, American Sunday School Union, 1828. 120 p. P; RNHi; ScCoT; BrMus.
33014

Dudley, J. M.
The soldiers' companion; containing a short drill for company discipline, selected and arranged on the principles of the army regulations, &c. &c. Concord, N. H., Pr. by Manahan, Hoag & Co., 1828. 60 p. NhHi.
33015

Duffie, Cornelius Roosevelt, 1789-1827
A sermon for children, preached at St. Paul's chapel, to the scholars belonging to the New-York Protestant Episcopal Sunday School Society, on Wednesday afternoon, April 18, 1827, being the tenth anniversary of the said society. New-Haven, Pr. for the Bible, Prayer Book and Tract Society by S. Babcock, 1828. 12 p. CtY.
33016

Dunallen. See Kennedy, Grace.

Dunbar, John Richard Woodcock, 1805-1871.

An essay on the structure, functions, and diseases of the nervous system... Philadelphia, J. Dobson, 1828. 80 p. CSt; IEN-M; InU; MB; MBAt; MBCo; MdBM; NNNAM; PHi; PPHi; PPC. 33017

Duncan, James
Polemic disquisitions on four general subjects... Indianapolis, Pr. by J. Douglass, 1828. 215 p. DLC; ICMcC; InGrD; InHi; OOxM; PPPrHi. 33018

Duncan, Joseph, 1794-1844
(Circular.) Fellow-citizens of the state of Illinois: The first session of the term for which you elected me your Representative in Congress having ended on the 26th of May, it becomes my duty... to present to you an account of the proceedings of Congress...[Signed:] Joseph Duncan. Vandalia, June 14, 1828. [Vandalia, 1828] Bdsd. IHi. 33019

Duncan, Thomas Wilson
Catechism exhibiting in questions and answers the fundamental doctrines and duties of the Christian religion; and also the religious experience of a Christian. Portsmouth, Pr. for the author, by Miller & Brewster, 1828. 24 p. NhHi. 33020

Dunn, Henry
Guatimala, or, The United Provinces of Central America, in 1827-8; being sketches and memorandums made during a twelve months' residence in that republic. New York, G. & C. Carvill [Pr. by Vanderpool & Cole] 1828. 318 p., 1 l. CLU; CU; CtY; DLC; ICN; IU; KyLoP; MB; MH; MHi; MWA; MdBE; MdBL; MiU; NBLiHi; NIC; NN; NWM; NbU; NhHi; NjPT; OU; PPL; PU; RPJCB; ViU; WHi; BrMus. 33021

Dwight, Harrison Gray Otis
A dictionary of the proper names in the New Testament, with other helps for teachers in Sabbath schools... Stereotype copy. 2d ed. Utica, Western Sunday School Union; Colwell & Ely, prs., 1828. [6], 66 p. DLC; ICU; MBC; MH-AH; NNUT; NCH; NUt. 33022

[Dwight, Theodore] 1796-1866
The northern traveller; (combined with The northern tour.) Containing the routes to Niagara, Quebec, and the Springs. With the tour of New-England, and the route to the coal mines of Pennsylvania. Embellished with 19 maps and 11 landscapes. 3d ed., rev. and extended. New-York, G. & C. Carvill [Danforth & Penfold, prs.] 1828. 403 p. CtHT-W; DLC; GMM; ICU; IU; MB; MH; MoSM; MoSpD; NCH; NGH; NN; NUt; PHi; PPL; PPi; RPB; TxU; ViU; VtB. 33023

Dwight, Timothy, 1752-1817
Sermons; by Timothy Dwight, D.D., LL.D. late president of Yale college. New Haven, Pub. by Hezekiah Howe and Durrie & Peck. E. & H. Clark, prs., Middletown, 1828. 2 v. CtHi; CtY; IaU; MH; MWA; NBuG; NN; NcD; NjR; OO; OU; PPLT; RPB; TxDaM; WaU. 33024

---- Theology; explained and defended, in a series of sermons ...With a memoir of the author. In four volumes. 5th ed. New York, G. & C. Carvill... Stereotyped by A. Chandler, 1828. 4 vols. CtY; GDC; IaDuU; NNUT; NRU; NSyU; OO; PP; PU; TJaU; USlW; Vi. 33025

Dwyer, John Hanbury
An essay on elocution, with elucidatory passages from various authors... 2d ed. New York,

Pub. by G. & C. Carvill and E. Bliss, 1828. 298 [2] p. CSmH; CtHT-W; CtY; MBAt; NNC; Nj; NjR; OMC.   33026

Dyer, Samuel, 1785-1835
Dyer's New-York selection of sacred music, consisting of about three hundred approved psalm and hymn tunes...4th ed. imp. and enl. New York, The author [c1828] [252] p. ICN.
                                       33027
---- ---- 6th ed., imp. and enl. New-York, Pr. for the author, and sold by J. P. Haven, American Tract Society's House, I. G. Auner, and Carey, Lea & Carey. Philadelphia; F. Lucas, jr., I. Cole, and Cushing & Jewett. Baltimore, Pishey Thompson, Washington City, D. Fanshaw, pr., [c1828] [viii], xxiv p., 244, 44 songs. (Note at end of preface, 4th ed. pub. N.Y., 1828] PPL.
                                       33028
---- Dyer's Philadelphia selection of sacred music...4th ed. enl. New York, Pr. for the author [by] D. Fanshaw, [cop. 1828] 4 p. l., xxiv p., 110 l. CtHT-W; ICN; MHi; MdBS; NN; OO; P.   33029

---- ---- 6th ed. enl. New York, The author, [cop. 1828] 4 p. l., xxiv p., 110 l. NN.   33030

---- ---- 6th ed., improved and enlarged. Philadelphia, Pub. by J. G. Auner [Pr. by T. K. and P. G. Collins, c 1828] [viii], xxiv, p. 244, 44 songs. ICN; NN; OClWHi; PHi; PPL; PPPrHi; RPB; ScCoT.   33031

E

[Earle, William, jr.]
Obi; or, The history of Three-fingered Jack. In a series of letters from a resident in Jamaica to his friend in England... Boston, N. H. Whitaker, 1828. 140 p. CtY.   33032

Early impressions. Boston, Bowles and Dearborn, 1828. 137 p. CtSoP; CtY; KU; MBAt; MWA.
                                       33033
An earnest appeal to the friends of reform. See Cooke, John Rogers.

Eastern Auxiliary Foreign Mission Society of Rockingham County, N. H.
Third annual report of the Eastern Auxiliary Foreign Mission Society... Presented at Portsmouth, June 19, 1828. [Portsmouth] Pr. by T. H. Miller and C. W. Brewster [1828] 8 p. MBC; NhHi.   33034

Eastman, Francis Smith, 1803-1846 or 7
A history of the state of New York, from the first discovery of the country to the present time ...New York, Pub. by E. Bliss, Sold by him, and Collins and Co., White, Gallaher and White [etc., etc.] 1828. viii, 279 [1] p. CSt; CtHT; CtY; MB; MBAt; MH; MWA; MdBJ; MdHi; MiD-B; NBLiHi; NIC; NN; NNC; NR; NhD; NjP; NjR; OCHP; PHi; PPL; ViRU; Vt; BrMus.   33035

---- A history of Vermont, from its first settlement to the present time. With a geographical account of the country, and a view of its original inhabitants. For the use of schools. Brattleboro', Holbrook and Fessenden, 1828. 110 p. DLC; ICJ; MH; MW; MWA; Nh; OSW; VtHi; BrMus.   33036

Eaton, Amos, 1776-1842
Botanical grammar and dictionary; translated from the French,
of Bulliard and Richard. By Prof.
A. Eaton. 3d ed., wholly written
over, and now including the natural orders of Linneus and Jos-
sieu. Albany, Pr. by Websters
and Skinners, 1828. 53 p., 36 l.
CtY; ICMcC; KU; MH; MNS;
MPiB; N; NNC; OClW.   33037

---- Chemical instructor: pre-
senting a familiar method of
teaching the chemical principles
and operations of the most practical utility...3d ed. Albany, Pr.
and pub. by Websters and Skinners, 1828. 274 p. MH; NSyHi;
OBerB; OO; PU-S; TxU-T. 33038

[----] A geological nomenclature
for North America; founded upon
geological surveys, taken under
the direction of the Hon. Stephen
Van Rensselaer. Albany, Pr. by
Packard and Van Benthuysen,
1828. 31 p. CtY; DLC; KyU; MB;
MH; N; NCH; NGH; NWM; NjP;
NjR; OCHP; PPF; PPL.   33039

Eaton, John Henry, 1790-1856
The life of Major General
Andrew Jackson: comprising a
history of the war in the South,
from the commencement of the
Creek campaign to the termination of hostilities before New Orleans. Addenda: containing a
brief history of the Seminole War,
and cession and government of
Florida. 3d ed. rev. and cor. by
the author. Philadelphia, Pub.
by M'Carty & Davis, 1828. 335
p. AB; CtHT-W; DLC; FSaHi;
GEU; ICN; LNHT; MB; MoU;
NcU; OCl; OSW; P; PHi; PLFM;
PPL; PPPrHi; PRA; TN.   33040

[----] Memoirs of Andrew Jackson, late major-general and commander in chief of the Southern
division of the Army of the

United States, comp. by a citizen
of Massachusetts. Boston, Pub.
by Charles Ewer, 1828. 334 p.
A-Ar; AzU; CSmH; CU; CtB;
DLC; FMF; ICN; IHi; IaU; MB;
MBAt; MDeeP; MH; MWA;
MdBS; MiD-B; MoKU; NIC; NN;
NcD; NcU; NhHi; NjMD; OCl;
OClWHi; OMC; OkU; PLFM;
RHi; RPB; ScU; T; TKL; TMC;
TxU; ViU; BrMus.   33041

Eaton, Peter, 1765-1848
A sermon, delivered in the
First parish meetinghouse, in
Haverhill, Lord's day, July 23,
1828. Haverhill, A. W. Thayer,
1828. 15 p. MChB; MHi; PPL.
                          33042
Ebers, John
Seven years of the King's the-
atre. Philadelphia, Carey, Lea
& Carey, Sold in New York, by
G. & C. Carvill, in Boston, by
Munroe & Francis, 1828. 245 p.
GMiW; LU; MB; MH; MWA;
MdBP; MiU; NN; NNC; NNS;
NRU; NcD; NjP; PPL; PPi; RP;
WHi.   33043

Eddowes, Ralph, compiler, 1751-
1833
A selection of sacred poetry
consisting of psalms and hymns
from Watts Doddridge, Merrick,
Scott, Cowper, Barbauld, Steele
and others. 3d ed. with an appendix. Philadelphia, R. H. Small,
James Kay, Jun., pr., 1828.
556 p. IEG; MHi; NNUT; PPAmP;
BrMus.   33044

---- The spirit of orthodoxy, as
exhibited in the proceedings a-
gainst John Biddle, the father of
English Unitarians, in the period
from 1645, to 1662, for imputed
heresy and blasphemy. Abridged
from Dr. Toulmin's Review of
his life, character, and writings.
With correspondent remarks on
certain passages in Dr. Ezra S.
Ely's sermon on the 4th July,

1827. By Ralph Eddowes. [n. p., Feb., 1828] 20 p. PPL. 33045

Eddy, Ansel Doan, 1798-1875
An address, delivered before the Pennsylvania Temperance Society, at their third anniversary. [Philadelphia, 1828] 11 p. MH; PPL. 33046

Edgehill. See Heath, James

Ewell.

Education. See Carey, Mathew.

Edward Duncombe: or, Religion a reality. First American edition, From Edinburgh edition. Worcester, Pub. by Dorr and Howland, 1828. 154 p. MWA. 33047

Edwards, Henry Milne, 1800-1885
A manual of surgical anatomy ... Trans., with notes, by Wm. Coulson... 1st Amer. from the 1st London ed. rev. and cor. with additional notes, by James Webster... Philadelphia, T. Desilver, Pr. by L. R. Bailey, 1828. 382 p. CSt-L; CU; ICJ; IGN-M; IaU; KyLxT; MBCo; MdBM; MdUM; MoSM; NNNAM; NcD; OCG; OClM; OO; PPC; RNR; ScCM; ViRMC; ViU. 33048

Edwards, Jonathan, 1703-1758
A careful and strict enquiry into the modern prevailing notions of that freedom of will, which is supposed to be essential to moral agency, virtue and vice, reward and punishment, praise and blame... New York, G. and C. Carvill, 1828. 2 p. l., [11]-300 p. IaAS; KyLoP; NBLiHi; NjR; OO. 33049

---- The conversion of President Edwards, from an account written by himself. Tract No. 144. Pub. by the American Tract Society... New York, Fanshaw,

pr., [1828?] 16 p. NNU-W. 33050

---- The great Christian doctrine of original sin defended; evidences of its truth produced; and arguments to the contrary answered: ... New-York, G. and C. Carvill, 1828. 283 p. NbOP; NbOU; PPLT; PWW; TWcW. 33051

---- A history of the work of redemption, containing the outlines of a body of divinity including a view of church history, in a method entirely new... New York, G. & C. Carvill, 1828. 1 p l., 276 p. NNPM; OO; PPAmS; PPPrHi. 33052

[----] A treatise concerning religious affections; in three parts. New-York, G. and C. Carvill, 1828. 1 p. l., 344 p. OO. 33053

Eells, James
Conversations on baptism, containing answers to the enquiries of a young convert, respecting the sentiments of those who practice infant baptism. Utica, Pr. by Hastings & Tracy, 1828. 71, [1] p. N. 33054

---- ---- 2d ed. Utica, Pr: by Hastings & Tracy, 1828. 71, [1] p. MBAt; MBC; MWA; NHC-S; NNUT; NjR; OCHP; WHi. 33055

El hyder; or Love and bravery. See Barrymore, William.

Elia, pseud. See Lamb, Charles.

Elliot's annual calendar, and congressional directory for 1828-1829. Washington, Pr. by J. Elliott [1828] 56 p. DLC; MWA. 33056

---- Washington, Pr. by J. Elliot, Dec. 23, 1828. 36 p. DLC. 33057

Elliot's sheet almanac 1829... City of Washington, Pr. and pub.

by S. A. Elliot, December 1828.
1 p. DLC.   33058

Elliott, Mary (Belson)
    Gems in the mine; or Traits
and habits of childhood, in verse.
Lancaster [Mass.] Pr. for James
R. Buffum, Salem; and H. and
G. Carter, and F. and.[!] J.
Andrews, Lancaster, 1828. 104 p.
MB.   33059

Ellis, John, comp.
    A choice selection of hymns,
and spiritual songs, for the use
of Christians. Zanesville, Pr. by
Peters and Pelham, 1828. 40 p.
OC.   33060

... Elspeth Sutherland: or, The
effects of faith. New York, The
American Tract Society [1828?]
48 p. (American Tract Society.
Children's tracts: ser. v, no. 5)
DLC.   33061

Eltinge, Wilhemus
    A sermon on the inability of
man to believe in Jesus Christ
except the Father draw him.
Paterson, Paterson Chronicle,
1828. 16 p. NCH.   33062

[Ely, Elisha]
    Rochester in 1827. With a map
of the village. Rochester, Pr. by
Everard Peck & co., 1828. 155
p. CSmH; NRHi; NRU; RP.
                             33063
Ely, Ezra Stiles
    The duty of Christian Freemen
to elect Christian rulers: a dis-
course delivered on the fourth of
July, 1827 in the Seventh Presby-
terian Church, in Philadelphia...
Philadelphia, Pr. by Wm. F.
Geddes, 1828. 32 p. CSmH;
CtSoP; CtY; DLC; ICU; MBAt;
MBC; MH; MWA; MiD-B; NNC;
NNG; NcU; NjR; OO; PHi; PPL;
PPPrHi; RPB; T; TxDaM; WHi;
BrMus.   33064

Ely, John
    The child's instructor; consist-
ing of easy lessons for children
on subjects which are familiar to
them in language adapted to their
capacities... New York, S.
Marks, 1828. 54 l. PP.   33065

[Embree, Davis]
    Circular on steam mills and
distilleries, containing a description of a patent for the use of
the scape steam of an engine in
distilling, &c. Looker & Reynolds, prs., Cincinnati, 1828. 22
p. PPF.   33066

[Embury, Mrs. Emma Catherine
(Manley)] 1806-1863
    Guido, a tale; sketches from
history, and other poems. By
Ianthe [pseud.] ... New York, G.
& C. Carvill, 1828. iv, 200 p.
CSmH; CtY; DLC; MB; NBLiHi;
NIC; PU; VtMiM; BrMus. 33067

Emerson, Benjamin Dudley, 1781-
1872
    Introduction to the National
spelling-book, with easy and progressive reading lessons; designed
for the use of primary schools...
Boston, Richardson and Lord,
1828. 107 p. DLC.   33068

---- ---- Boston, Richardson
and Lord, 1828. 168 p. CSmH;
CSt; CtHT-W; DLC; MB; MH; MHi;
MNF; MWA; NNC; TxU-T. 33069

Emerson, Joseph, 1777-1833
    The evangelical primer, con-
taining a minor doctrinal catechism
and a minor historical catechism;
to which is added the Westminster
Assembly's Shorter Catechism.
With an appendix. Boston, Crocker & Brewster [etc., etc.] 1828.
72 p.   MH; MWA; PPPrHi.
                             33070
---- Letter to a class of young
ladies, upon the study of the history of the United States. Boston,

Emery 105

Pub. by Crocker & Brewster, 1828. 36 p. CtY; MBC; MiD-B; TxU. 33071

---- Letter to the members of Genesee Consociation, N. Y., [on the subject of masonry.]. [Weathersfield, Conn.] 1828. 20 p. MBC; MH-AH; NhHi; WHi. 33072

---- Question adapted to Whelpley's Compend of history. 8th ed. Boston, Richardson and Lord; New York, Collins and Hannay, 1828. 69 p. CtHT-W; CtY; WGr. 33073

Emery, Stephen, 1790-1863
An address, delivered before the Temperate Society of Buckfield & Vicinity, on Christmasday, 1827. Norway, Me., Pr. at the Observer Office, by Asa Barton, 1828. 14 p. CSmH; MMeT-Hi. 33074

Emigration from Ireland. See Carey, Mathew.

Emmons, Francis Whitefield, 1802-1881
Address delivered in the Baptist Meeting-house of Dudley [Mass.] on Thursday, P. M., June 19, 1828, before the Female Charitable Society of that place. Providence, H. H. Brown, pr., 1828. 15 p. MiD-B. 33075

Emory, John
Defence of "Our fathers" and of the original organization of the Methodist Episcopal Church against the Rev. Alexander Mc Caine and others, with historical and critical notices of early American Methodism... 2d ed. New York, Pub. by N. Bangs & J. Emory, For the Methodist Episcopal Church. Azor Hoyt, pr. 1828. iv, 92 p. CSmH; CtY; GAGTh; GEU; IEG; MH; MiD; MoS; Ms-Ar; NNG; NcMHi; NjMD; PPPrHi; ScSpW. 33076

---- ---- 3d ed. New York, Pub. by N. Bangs and J. Emory, for the Methodist Episcopal Church, A. Hoyt, pr., 1828. 92 p. CSmH; NjMD. 33077

An enemy to creeds, pseud. See Gibbons, William.

[England, John] bishop, 1786-1842
Thirteen letters addressed to the Right Rev. Doctor Bowen, Bishop of the P. E. Church of South Carolina. On the occasion of his sanctioning the publication of a Protestant catechism, by the Charleston Female Episcopal Bible, Prayer Book and Tract Society, written by B. C. To which is prefixed the catechism itself. Revised from the U. S. Catholic Miscellany. Charleston, Pr. by J. Dennehy, at the Office of the Seminary, 1828. [4], 159 p. DCU; MdBL; MdBS; MdW; NcD; PPAmP; PPL. 33078

An Englishman's sketch book. See Bloodgood, Simeon DeWitt.

Epictetus.
Dialogue between the Greek philosopher Epictetus and his son on the Christian religion. New York, Pr. & pub. by George H. Evans, 1828. 8 p. PPL. 33079

An epistle to the quarterly & monthly meetings of Friends. See Woolman, John.

Epitome historiae Graecae. See Siret Charles Joseph.

An epitome of Christian doctrine, in questions and answers, for the instruction of youth in the congregations of the United Brethern. Philadelphia, Pr. by John Binns, 1828. 97 p. PLT. 33080

Erskine, Thomas, 1788-1870
The unconditional freeness of the Gospel: In three essays. ... From the 2d Edinburg ed. Boston, Pub. by Crocker & Brewster, 1828. 249, [2] p. CBPac; CtHT-W; GDC; ICMcC; ICU; MB; MBC; MH-AH; MWA; NBLiHi; NCH; NNG; NNUT; OO; OSW; RNHi; TWcW; ViRUT. 33081

[Erwin, Andrew]
Gen. Jackson's negro speculations, and his traffic in human flesh, examined and established by positive proof. [n. p., 1828] 16 p. CSmH; DLC; OClWHi. 33082

[----] Supplement to Andrew Jackson's negro speculations. From the National Banner. To Gen. Andrew Jackson. [Nashville, 1828] 8 p. DLC; MB. 33082a

Erzählung von etlichen blutigen Thaten des General Jackson. [1828] Bdsd. PPL. 33083

The Esksdale herd-boy. See Stoddart, Isabella.

Essay on the warehousing system and government credits of the United States. Philadelphia, Pr. by order of the Philadelphia Chamber of Commerce, William Brown, pr., 1828. 57 p. Ct; DLC; DeGE; ICU; MB; MH-BA; MWA; MdBP; MiD-B; NBuG; NNC; PPAmP; PPL; PU; ScU; TNM; Vi; BrMus. 33084

Essays on peace and war. See Ladd, William.

Essays on the public charities. See Carey, Mathew.

Essays upon the history, organization and tendency of Free Masonry... Morristown [N. J.] Pr. by Jacob Mann, 1828. 42 p. NN. 33085

Essex Jackson Meeting. See Democratic Party. Massachusetts.

Ettinger, Adam
Der könig Saul von Samuel bestraft und vom Herrn verworfen; in einer Erklaerung ueber 1 Buch Samuel, 15 cap. 17. 18. 19. Vers. Nebst einem ernstlichen Ruf wider den Alter zu Bethel; mit beygefuegtem Anhang, und Zuspruch an das Haus Davids. Aufgesetzt und zam Druck befoerdert durch Adam Ettinger... Harrisburg, Jacob Baab, fuer den Verfasser, 1828. 75, [1] p. PHi; PLFM; PRHi. 33086

Euler, Leonhard, 1707-1783
An introduction to the elements of algebra, designed for the use of those who are acquainted only with the first principles of arithmetic, selected by John Farrar. 3d ed. Boston, Hilliard, Gray, Little & Wilkins, 1828. 213 p. CtY; ICMcC; MH; NhPet; OClW; PMA; RPB; ViRVMI. 33087

An Eutopian, pseud. See Sanford, Ezekiel.

Evangelical Lutheran Church
Verrichtungen einer Conferenz, gehalten zu Woodstock von den Aeltesten und Vorstehern der Lutherischen Gemein den von Woodstock, Zions, Friedens und Strasburg Kirche, den 26sten Jan. 1828; zu welchen die Augsburgische Confession und Dr. Luther's Abhandlung von Glauben and heiliger Taufe, wie auch von heiligen Abendmal, angehangt ist. Neu-Market, Gedruckt in Henkel's Druckerey, 1828. 60 p. DLC; NN; NcD; ViU. 33088

---- Tennessee Synod.
Ecclesiastical annals and evangelical fragments. Report of the

transactions of the Evangelical
Lutheran Tennessee synod during
their ninth session, held in St.
Paul's Church, Lincoln county,
N. C. from Monday the 8th, to
Saturday the 13th of September,
1828; also the constitution which
was then adopted and ratified,
with explanatory remarks. To
which is added a treatise on
prayer. New-Market, Pr. in S.
Henkel's office, 1828. 52 p. NcD.
33089
---- Kirchliches Jahrbuch und
Evangelische Bruchstücke. Bericht
von der Verrichtungen der Evangelisch-Lutherischen Tennessee
Synode, während ihrer neunten
Sitzung, gehalten in der St. Paul-
us Kirche, Lincoln Caunty, N. C.,
angefangen Montags den 8ten, und
geendigt Samstag den 13ten September, 1828; nebst der welche
damahls angenommen und bes-
tätigt wurde, mit erläuternden
Anmerkungen; mit Beifügung eini-
ger Bruchstücke über das Gebet.
Neu-Market, [Va.] Gedruckt in
S. Henkel's Druckerei, 1828. 55
p. CSmH; PPLT.   33090

Evangelical Lutheran Ministerium
of Pennsylvania and Adjacent
States.
    Proceedings of the German
Evangelical Lutheran Synod of
Pennsylvania held at Reading in
Trinity Week 1828. Easton, Pa.,
Pr. by H. and W. Hütter, 1828.
16 p. PPLT.   33091

---- Verhandlungen der Deutsch-
Evangelisch-Lutherischen Synode
von Pennsylvanien gehalten in der
Stadt Reading in der Trinitatis
Woche 1828. Easton [Pa.] Ge-
druckt bey H. und W. Hütter,
1828. 15 p. DLC; ICN; P;
PAtM.   33092

Evangelical Lutheran Synod of
Ohio and Adjacent States.
    Verhandlungen der Elften Sy-

nodal Versammlung der Evangel-
isch-Lutherischen Prediger von
Ohio, und den angränzenden
Staaten. Gehalten zu Canfield,
Trumbull Caunty, Ohio, in der
Trinitatis-Woche, 1828. Lancas-
ter, Ohio, Gedruckt bey Johann
Herman [1828] 25 p. OCoC;
PPLT.   33093

Evangelical Lutheran Synod of
West Pennsylvania.
    Formular für die Regierung
und Disciplin der Evangelisch-
Lutherischen Kirche in West
Pennsylvanien, Gettysburg, Pa.,
H. C. Neinstedt, Drucker, 1828.
19 p. P; PHi; PPL; PPLT.
33094

---- Kleines Liederbuch feur Sonn-
tagsschalen herausgegeben von
einer Committee der Evangelisch
Lutherischen Synode von West
Pennsylvanien. Gettysburg, Pa.,
H. C. Neinstedt, Drucker, 1828.
60 p. MH; P; RPB.   33095

Evans, Evan
    An essay on the doctrines of
foreknowledge, election, and the
divine decrees... Sag Harbour,
Mar., 1828. 10 p. NBLiHi; NEh.
33096
Evans, Henry. See Trial and
dying confession.

Evans, Thomas
    An exposition of the faith of
the Religious Society of Friends,
commonly called Quakers in the
fundamental doctrines of the
Christian Religion; principally
selected from their early writings.
Philadelphia, Kimber & Sharp-
less [etc.] Adam Waldie & Co.,
prs., 1828. xxxvi, 324 p.
CSmH; CtHT-W; GDC; ICMcC;
ICU; IU; IaGG; InRE; KWiU;
MBC; MWA; MdHi; NIC; OClWHi;
OSW; PHC; PHi; PP; PPL;
PPPrHi; PSC-Hi; PU; RNR;
RPAt.   33097

Evening hours.   See Dix, Dorothea Lynde.

Evenings in Boston. First series.
2d ed. Boston, Bowles and Dearborn; Press of I. R. Butts & Co. ,
1828. [1] 125 p. MB; NUt; PP;
BrMus.   33098

---- Second series. Boston,
Bowles & Dearborn, Press of
Isaac R. Butts & Co. , 1828. 108,
107-131 p. MB.   33099

Everett, Edward, 1794-1865
   An address, delivered at the
erection of a monument to John
Harvard, September 26, 1828.
Boston, Pub. by Nathan Hale, Pr.
by Wm. L. Lewis, 1828. 24 p.
CU; CtY; ICMe; MB; MBAU;
MBAt; MBC; MH; MHi; MWA;
MeB; MiD-B; MnHi; MoSW; NhHi;
NjPT; OCHP; OMC; PHi; PPAmP;
PPL; RPB; WHi.   33100

---- An oration delivered before
the citizens of Charlestown on the
fifty-second anniversary of the
Declaration of the Independence of
the United States of America. By
Edward Everett. Charlestown,
Wheildon & Raymond; Boston,
Hilliard, Gray, Little & Wilkins,
1828. 43 p. CLU; CSmH; CU;
DLC; IHi; MH; MiD-B; NNG;
PPL.   33101

---- Remarks of Mr. Everett, of
Massachusetts. House of Repre-
sentatives--March 15. On the bill
for the relief of Susan Decatur.
The question being on striking
out the enacting clause. [Boston?
1828?] 11 p. NN.   33102

---- Speech of Mr. Everett, of
Mass. , on the subject of re-
trenchment. Delivered in the
House of Representatives of the
United States, Feb. 1, 1828.
Washington, Pr. by Gales & Sea-
ton, 1828. 31 p. CSmH; CtY;

MBAt; MH; MHi; MWA; NNC;
PHi; PPAmP; PPL; BrMus.
                                     33103

Everett, L. S.
   Eine Predigt von L. S. Ever-
ett, Prediger des Allgemeinen
Evangeliums, zu Auburn im St.
Neu-York. Aus dem Englischen
übersezt. [Lancaster, Pr. by H.
W. Villee, 1828] 12 p. PHi.
                                     33104

Examination of Joseph Antoine,
Johan Fransoeis Wohlfahrt and
Joanna Wohlfahrt, suspected of
the murder of Samuel Field and
Francis C. Jenkerson, before
Justices Aplin, Staples and Pat-
ten. Providence, Pub. by H. H.
Brown, 1828. 32 p. MoU; ViU-
L.   33105

An examination of the civil administration of Governor Jackson
in Florida. [From the National
Intelligencer, July 3, 1828.] 24
p. DLC.   33106

An examination of the civil administration of Governor Jackson
in Florida... The acts of General Andrew Jackson as a legisla-
tor. [Washington, 1828] 48 p.
CSmH; DLC; ICU; MdHi; OClWHi.
                                     33107
An examination of the reasons,
why the present system of auctions ought to be abolished; as
set forth by the Committee of
New York Merchants, opposed to
the auction system. [Signed: By a
practical man.] Boston, Beals,
Homer and Co. , prs. , 1828. 48 p.
DLC; ICU; MWA; PPL; BrMus.
                                     33108
An examination of the report.
See Fisher, Redwood.

Examinator, pseud. See Cobb,
Lyman.

The excellency of the female
character. See Branagan, Thomas.

Exeter Manufacturing Company
An act... incorporating the
Exeter Manufacturing Company...
Exeter, C. Norris, pr., 1828.
16 p. MH-BA.   33109

The experience of a clergyman
of the Protestant Episcopal
Church, as given by himself in
a sermon to the people of his
charge, in 1827. Philadelphia,
1828. 10 p. NNG; NjR; PHi;
PPPrHi.   33110

Exploder, pseud. See To thinking men.

An exposition of facts connected
with the late prosecutions in the
Methodist Episcopal Church of
Cincinnati, with observations on
a Narrative of facts, &c. by
David Fisher... By a committee.
Cincinnati, Looker & Reynolds,
1828. 60 p. CBCDS; OClWHi.
                                33111
Exposition of the titles to the
lands in Florida, commonly
known by the name of Forbes'
Purchase. Washington, Pr. at the
office of J. Elliot, 1828. 28 p.
PPL.   33112

Extracts from various writers on
cattle. See Noel, Edmund F.

F

Facts and opinions respecting Mr.
John Quincy Adams: and a fair
view of the militia-men story...
[Philadelphia, Pr. by William
Stavely, 1828] 8 p. PHi; PPL.
                                33113
Facts for the consideration of
ship-builders. See American In-
stitute of the City of New York.

A fair and just comparison of
the lives of the two candidates,
Andrew Jackson and John Quincy
Adams. Part I. From their birth

to the year 1814. [n.p., 1828]
1 p. 1., 14 p. CSmH; PPL.
                                33114
Fairclough, Rev. J. W.
An address to the public, with
a letter to the Rev. Wm. Jackson, of Alexandria, D.C. in reply to his assertations against
the Catholic Church in his report
to the Bible Society, which appeared in the Alexandria Gazette
of April 16, 1828. Washington,
Pr. by Way and Gideon, 1828.
15 p. DLC; MdBS; MdHi; MdW;
ScU.   33115

Fairfield, Sumner Lincoln, 1803-
1844
The cities of the plain, with
other poems. 3d ed. Philadel-
phia, Wm. Simpson [Pr. by
James Maxwell] 1828. 300 p.
CtB; KyLx; PHi; PPL; RPB; PU.
                                33116
Fairfield, N.Y. College of Phys-
icians and Surgeons of the West-
ern district.
Circular and catalogue of the
faculty and students... Little
Falls [N.Y.] Pr. by Edward M.
Griffins, 1828. 8 p. NNNAM;
NUtHi.   33117

Fairy legends. See Croker,
Thomas Crofton.

Fall of Babylon; or History of
the Empire of Assyria: com.
from Rollin, Prideaux, and other
authorities. Revised by Committee of Publication. Philadelphia,
American Sunday School Union,
1828. 216 p. NcWsS; PAtM.
                                33118
Falsehood and slander exposed.
See Democratic Party. New Jersey.

Fame Hose Company. Philadel-
phia.
Constitution and by-laws of the
Fame Hose Company, Instituted
Jan. 1st, 1818. Revised 1820.

Do. 1827. Philadelphia, Pr. by
John Young [1828] (last entry
dated 1828) 28 p. PHi.   33119

Familiar description of beasts.
Wendell, J. Metcalf, 1828.
Swann Auction Sale 227, Mar.
17, 1949. No. 11.   33120

A familiar description of birds,
for the entertainment of little
readers. Wendell, Metcalf, 1828.
21 p. MWA.   33121

Fanshawe. See Hawthorne, Nathaniel.

A farewell. See Carey, Mathew.

Farewell hymn on leaving the old
meeting house in Quincy. [1828?]
1 p. DLC.   33122

Farewell to time. See Wright,
Thomas.

The farm yard journal. See Aikin, John.

A farmer, pseud. See Address
to the farmers of Rhode Island.

A farmer, pseud. See Serious
appeal!

[Farmer, John] 1789-1838
   A genealogical memoir of the
family by the name of Farmer,
who settled at Billerica, Mass.
Hingham, Farmer and Brown,
prs., 1828. 20 p. DLC.   33123

The farmer's almanack, and annual register for 1829. By Thomas Spofford. New-York, David
Felt (For Long Island). [1828]
18 1. CtHT-W; DLC; InU; MH;
MWA; NBLiHi; NHi; NN; NSyOHi;
OClWHi.   33124

---- By Thomas Spofford. New-
York, David Felt (For New-York).
[1828] 18 1. NBLiHi.   33125

Farmers' almanac for 1829. Bal-
timore, Wm. & Joseph Neal;
Wm. Wooddy, pr. [1828] 18 1.
DLC; MdBE.   33126

---- Calculated by John Arm-
strong. Pub. by J. F. M'Carty,
Blairsville, Pa. M'Farland &
Murray, prs., [1828] 36 p. Ia-
HA.   33127

---- By Robert B. Thomas,
Boston, Richardson & Lord
[1828] 24 1. AU; CLU; CU; CoU;
CtHT-W; CtHi; CtY; DLC;
FTaSU; GU; ICU; IHi; InU;
MBAt; MH; MHi; MWA; MdHi;
MeHi; MiD-B; MiU-C; MnU;
MoU; NBLiHi; NIC; NN; NHi;
NbU; NhHi; NjP; NjR; OClWHi;
OMC; OrCS; PHi; PPAmP; RNHi;
RPB; TxU; WHi.   33128

---- By Zadock Thompson. Burlington, E. & T. Mills [1828]
12 1. DLC; MWA.   33129

---- By James W. Palmer. Lexington, J. W. Palmer [1828] 14
1. ICU; KyBgW; KyLo; KyLoF;
KyLx; MWA; MoHi; N; NCH.
                              33130
---- Louisville, Morton & Co.
[1828] 11 1. KyU.   33131

---- New-York, C. Brown [1828]
18 1. DLC; MWA.   33132

---- By David Young. New-York,
Caleb Bartlett [1828] 24 1. IU;
MWA; NjR.   33133

---- By David Young. New-York,
Daniel D. Smith [1828] 18 1.
NN.   33134

---- By David Young. New-York,
N. B. Holmes [1828] 18 1. WHi.
                              33135
---- By David Young. Peekskill,
S. Marks & Son [1828] 18 1.
CSmH; NHi.   33136

---- By John Ward. Philadelphia, M'Carty & Davis [1828] 18 1. KU; MWA; NjR; PHi; PPL.   33137

---- By Robert B. Thomas. [Portland] Shirley and Hyde [1828] 25 1. MWelC.   33138

---- By David Young. Poughkeepsie, P. Potter [1828] 18 1. MWA; N; NHi; NP.   33139

The farmer's almanack for 1829 for the state of Maine. By Robt. B. Thomas. Portland, Shirley and Hyde [1828] 26 1. FSaHi; MeP; Vi.   33140

The farmers' and planters' almanack, for the year of our Lord 1829:... Salem, Pub. by John C. Blum. H. S. Noble, pr. [1828] 34 p. (lacks back cover) NcU.
                                          33141
Farmer's calendar or Utica almanac for 1829. Utica, Wm. Williams [1828] Drake 6979.
                                          33142
Farmer's calendar, or Western almanac for 1829. By Edwin E. Prentiss. Ithaca, Mack & Andrus; Cooperstown, H. & E. Phinney, prs. [1828] 18 1. MWA; N; NIC; OClWHi; PScrHi; WHi.   33143

Farmer's diary; or, Catskill almanac for 1829. Catskill, C. Faxon [1828] 12 1. ViU.   33144

The farmer's diary, or, Ontario almanack for 1829. By Oliver Loud. Canandaigua, Bemis & Ward [1828] 18 1. DLC; NRMA.
                                          33145
---- By Oliver Loud. Canandaigua, Morse & Willson [1828] 18 1. DLC; MWA; NCanHi; NHi; NN; NSyOHi.   33146

A farmer's letters. From the Richmond Whig. [Richmond, 1828?] 25 p. ViU.   33147

The farmer's, mechanic's, and gentleman's almanack for 1829. By Nathan Wild. Wendell, J. Metcalf [1828] 24 1. CLU; CSmH; Ct; CtY; DLC; MA; MAJ; MHi; MNF; MWA; N; NBLiHi; NN; NcD; NjR; TxU; WHi.   33148

Farmers of Middlesex... Read this and hand it to your neighbours. A plain unlettered farmer of Middlesex takes leave to address a few words to his brother farmers upon the subject of the approaching election of a member of Congress from this District... Lexington, October 31, 1828. 1 p. DLC.   33149

The farmers' register and Maryland herald - Extra. See United States.

Farmers Tickett. See National Republican Party. New York.

Farrar, John, 1779-1853
    An elementary treatise on the application of trigonometry... Together with logarithmic and other tables, designed for the use of the students of the University at Cambridge, New England. 2d ed. Boston, Hilliard, Gray, Little and Wilkins, [Cambridge, Hilliard, Metcalf & Co., prs. to the University] 1828. viii, 155, [73] p. CtHT; CtY; ICJ; ICMcC; IaHi; MB; MH; NNC; PHC; PPL; PU; RJa.   33150

Farrer, Deerin
    The Christian melodist; containing a selection of tunes in the different meters; together with a great variety of sacred songs and hymns, of approved excellence. Utica, Wm. Williams, 1828. 80 p. MiU.   33151

Fashionable American letter writer; or, The art of polite correspondence: containing a variety

of plain & elegant letters on business, love, courtship, marriage,
relationship, friendship etc. ...
New York, Pr. for the booksellers, 1828. 179 p. ICU; NNC;
PU.   33152

The fashionable letter writer...
Adapted to general use; with forms
of complimentary cards, and a new
and easy English grammar, peculi-
arly applicable to writing letters
with accuracy. Rochester, Pr. and
pub. by E. Peck & Co. , 1828. 179 p.
MiToC; NNC; NR.   33153

The fashionable tour; an excur-
sion to the springs, Niagara,
Quebec, and through the New
England states: interspersed
with geographical and historical
sketches. 3d ed. , enl. and imp.
Saratoga Springs, Pr. and pub.
by G. M. Davison, 1828. 306 p.
Ct; CtY; DLC; GDC; MNe; MiU-
T; NN; NNC; PHC; RP.   33154

The fatal ladder: or, Harry Lin-
ford... Philadelphia, American
Sunday School Union [c1828] 126
p. DLC; BrMus.   33155

Faust, Edwin D.
    A sketch of medical chemis-
try... Columbia, Pr. by D. and
J. M. Faust, 1828. 337 p.
NNNAM; PPF.   33156

Fayette County Corresponding
Committee. See National Republican Party. Kentucky.

Fayette County, Ky. Bible Society.
    First annual report of the
board of managers of the Fayette
Co. Ky. Bible Society, (Auxiliary
to the American Bible Society.)
Read before the Society at Lexington April 14th, 1828. Lexington, Ky. , Pr. for the Society,
by Joseph G. Norwood, 1828. 16
p. ICU.   33157

Fayetteville, North Carolina
    Laws of the town of Fayette-
ville, consisting of all the acts,
and parts of acts now in force,
passed in relation to the said
town, from A. D. 1762 to A. D.
1827, inclusive; and all the ordinances and other proceedings,
now in force passed by the board
of commissioners of the said
town from A. D. 1785 to A. D.
1828, inclusive, with a copious
index, collected and arranged...
under the direction of Louis D.
Henry... by the Rev. Colin Mc
Iver. Fayetteville, Evangelical
Printing Office, 1828. 80 p.
NcU.   33158

Felch, Walton
    The supplement to a lecture
on the stars: being a recapitula-
tion, in verse, of some instructions which are important and
difficult to be remembered. Illustrated by notes and diagrams.
Southbridge [Mass.] From the office of P. E. B. Botham, S. Carr,
pr. , 1828. 15 p. DLC.   33159

Felton, Cornelius Conway
    An address pronounced August
15, 1828, at the close of the second term of the Livingston County High School on Temple Hill,
Geneseo, N. Y. ... Cambridge,
Hilliard, Metcalf, and co. ...
1828. 24 p. CSmH.   33160

Female Bible, Missionary, and
Tract Society
    Third annual report of the Fe-
male Bible, Missionary, and
Tract Society, of New-Utrecht.
February 7th, 1828. A. Spooner,
pr. , Brooklyn. [1828] 10, [1] p.
NBLiHi.   33161

Female Bible Society of Philadelphia
    The fourteenth report of the
Female Bible Society of Philadelphia. Read before the Society,

26th March, 1828... Philadelphia, Pr. by order of the Society, by J. W. Allen, 1828. 19 p. CtHC; PPL. 33162

Female Episcopal Benevolent Society.
Twelfth annual report of the Female Episcopal Benevolent Society. Read before the Society, Nov. 4th, 1828. [Philadelphia, 1828] 7 p. PPL. 33163

Female Episcopal Bible, Prayer Book and Tract Society of Charleston.
The first annual report of the board of managers... made at the anniversary, May 27th, 1828... together with the Constitution & by-laws of the Society, and a list of the members. Charleston, Pr. by A. E. Miller, 1828. ScHi. 33164

[Fenélon] pseud.
Aux Catholiques des Etats-Unis... A la Nouvelle-Orleans, Imprimé pour l'auteur. 1828. 16 p. MB. 33165

Fenning, Daniel
The universal spelling-book or A new and easy guide to the English language. Baltimore, Pub. by Fielding Lucas, Jun'r, 1828. 168 p. MWA. 33166

Der Fertige Rechner; oder des Geschaftsmanns Gehülfe im Kauf und Verkauf. Philadelphia, J. G. Ritter, 1828. 144 p. PPL; PPeSchw. 33167

Fessenden, Thomas Green, 1771-1837
The new American gardener; containing practical directions on the culture of fruit and vegetables; including landscape and ornamental gardening, grape-vines, silk, strawberries &c.&c. Boston, Pub. by J. B. Russell, Sold also by Hilliard & Brown, Cambridge,

Mass., and G. Thorburn & Son, New York [Stereotyped at the Boston Type and Stereotype Foundry] 1828. 306, [6] p. (i. e., [1] index, [2-5] Russell's cat. of seeds.) CSmH; DLC; DeGE; InLP; LNHT; MB; MDeeP; MH; MWA; MdBJ; MiU; NIC; Nh; NjP; PPL; RNR. 33168

Fessenden, Thomas Green
Thoughts on the divine goodness relative to the government of moral agents, particularly displayed in future rewards and punishments. Montpelier, Pr. by Geo. W. Hill, Patriot office, 1828. 148 p. [George B. Reed, Bibliography of Vermont: New and Interesting Titles. Boston, March, 1899.] 33169

A few reflections upon the fancy ball, otherwise known as the city dancing assembly. By a representative of thousands. Philadelphia, Pr. and pub. for the author, by G. R. Lililibridge [sic], 1828. 16 p. PPL. 33170

Field, Alexander P.
Fellow citizens of Johnson, Alexander, & Union counties. My name is again before my fellow citizens, as a candidate for the House of Representatives in the next legislature of your state, and you have a right to expect from me... my views and sentiments... [78 lines]. I am your obedient servant and fellow citizen, A. P. Field. Union County, June 23, 1828. [Shawneetown? 1828.] Bdsd. IHi. 33171

Fielding, Henry, 1707-1754
The history of Joseph Andrews, and his friend, Mr. Abraham Adams... Philadelphia, Pub. by J. J. Woodward. Stereotyped by L. Johnson, 1828. 342 p. RPB. 33172

---- The history of Tom Jones,

114   Finch

a foundling... With a sketch of
the author's life. In four volumes... Philadelphia, Pub. by J.
J. Woodward, 1828. CtY; CtHT-
W; DLC; MdBS; PU; TJoS. 33173

Finch, C.
The gamut and time-table in
verse. For the instruction of
children... New York, S. King
[ca 1828] 18 numb. l. Pr. on
one side of leaf only; the printed
pages facing each other. CSmH.
                              33174
Finney, Charles G.
A sermon, preached in the
Presbyterian Church at Troy,
March 4, 1827... Northampton,
Pr. by Hiram Ferry, 1828. 16 p.
MNF.   33175

The first day of the week. Ster-
eotyped by James Conner, New-
York. New York, Pub. by the
General Protestant Episcopal Sun-
day School Union, and for sale
at their Depository... Edward J.
Swords, pr., 1828. 84 p. MWA.
                              33176
The first settlers of New Eng-
land. See Child, Mrs. Lydia
Maria (Francis).

First Universalist Society in
Boston
An act of incorporation and
by-laws of the First Universalist
Society, in Boston. Boston, Pr.
for William Rutter, 1828. 20 p.
MiD-B.   33177

Fisher, David
A narration of facts, relative
to the proceedings of the Methodist Episcopal Church, against
certain local preachers and lay-
members, in Cincinnati; with
some arguments in favour of the
government of said church. Williamson & Strong, prs., 1828.
48 p. CBCDS; MiD; OCHP.
                              33178
[Fisher, Redwood]

An examination of the Report
of a Committee of the citizens
of Boston and its vicinity, opposed to a further increase of
duties on importation. By a
Pennsylvanian. Philadelphia, Pr.
by J. Maxwell, 1828. 119 p.
CU; CtHT; CtY; DLC; DeGE; ICJ;
IU; MB; MBAt; MH; MWA; MiD-
B; NjR; OO; PHi; PPL; RPB;
BrMus.   33179

Fishback, James
Letters addressed to Thomas
Bullock, moderator of the Elkhorn Association; occasioned by
a publication entitled A response,
&c. ... Lexington, Ky., Pr. by
Norwood & Bradford, Book and
job printers, 1828. 32 p. NNUT;
NRAB.   33180

The fisherman and his boy. By
a Clergyman of England. Also,
John Pascal; or, Temptation re-
sisted. Philadelphia, American
Sunday School Union, 1828. 72 p.
ICU; BrMus.   33181

Fishkill Landing Bible Society
Fishkill Landing Bible Society.
At the annual meeting... held on
the 16th of October, 1828. [n. p.
1828?] 12 p. MHi.   33182

[Fisk, Harvey]
A new series of questions on
the selected Scripture lessons for
Sabbath schools. By a superintendent of a Sabbath school in New
Jersey... Vol. I. Richmond, Va.,
Pub. by A. Works, for Sunday
schools, T. W. White, pr., 1828.
123 p. Vi; ViW.   33183

[----] ---- Princeton, Princeton
Sunday School Union, Borrenstein,
pr., 1828. 135 p. MH; NjR; Vi.
                              33184
Fisk, Theophilus
A hell for all the wicked,
clearly proved. A discourse delivered at the City Hall, Washing-

ton, D. C., on ... Dec. 16, 1827, and repeated at Troy, N.Y. on the first Sunday in August, 1828. Philadelphia, Pr. by John Young [1828] 20 p. NN; NNUT.   33185

---- The pleasures of sin. A discourse delivered in the Capitol, in the city of Washington, on Sunday morning, December 16, 1827. Philadelphia, Charles Alexander, pr., 1828. 22 p. CSmH; IaCrM; MBC; MMeT-Hi; MWA; PPPrHi; ScCoT.   33186

---- The rich man in hell: A discourse delivered at the Lombard Street Church, in the city of Philadelphia, on Sunday evening, March 16, 1828. Philadelphia, 1828. 16 p. CtY; MMeT-Hi; PHi.   33187

---- Die vergnügungen der sünde. Rede gehalten im Capitolium der Foderal stadt Waschington am... Dec. 16, 1827. Lancaster, Pr. by H. W. Villee, 1828. 18 p. PHi.   33188

Fitch, Eleazar Thompson, 1791-1871
    National prosperity perpetuated: a discourse: delivered in the chapel of Yale College; on the day of the annual thanksgiving: November 29, 1827... New Haven, Treadway and Adams, Chronicle Office, pr., 1828. 34 p. CSmH; Ct; CtHT-W; CtHi; ICN; ICMcC; MA; MBAt; MH; MWA; MiD-B; NjPT; OO; RPB; BrMus.   33189

Fitch, Samuel S.
    Remarks on the importance of the teeth, on their diseases and modes of cure; with directions for forming regular and beautiful sets of teeth, and for the preservation of their health and beauty. Philadelphia, Jesper Harding, pr. 1828. 27 p. IEN-D; MBCo; NjR; P; PPL; PPiU-D.   33190

Flavel, John, 1630?-1691
    The balm of the Covenant, applied to the bleeding wounds of afflicted saints: to which is added, a View of the soul of man in the state of separation from the body. Also, a faithful and succinct narrative of some wonderful sea deliverances, remarkable providence, &c. &c. ... 1st Amer., from the 6th London ed. Richmond, Va., Pub. by J. Martin, T. W. White, pr., 1828. [416] p. (Various pagings; errors in paging throughout the book.) DLC; NcD; Vi; ViRU; ViU.   33191

---- The touchstone of sincerity; or, Trial of true and false religion. Written anew from the original. 3d ed. Hallowell, Pr. and pub. by Glazier & Co., 1828. 88 p. NN; OO.   33192

---- A treatise on keeping the heart; selected from the works of the Rev. John Flavel, the style adapted to the present state of improvement. 4th ed. Hallowell, Pr. and pub. by Glazier & Co., 1828. 148 p. MeLB; NN. 33193

Fleetwood, John
    The life of our Blessed Lord and Saviour Jesus Christ: containing a full, accurate, and instructive history of the various transactions in the life of our glorious Redeemer, from His taking upon Himself our sinful nature to His crucifixion, resurrection from the dead, and glorious ascension into heaven. Together with the lives, transactions, and sufferings of the holy evangelists, apostles, and others ...To which is added, a full defence of the Christian religion... New York, Pr. and pub. by Thomas Kinnersley, 1828. 616, xxxi, [4] p.   Ct; PU.   33194

Fleming, Robert
   Remembrance of the righteous.
A sermon delivered in Warren-
ton, Geo. on Sunday, August 3,
1828. Sacred to the memory of
Mrs. Elizabeth Fleming, who de-
parted this life June 25, 1828.
Warrenton, Geo., Pr. by P. L.
Robinson, 1828. 13 p. CSmH.
                                    33195
Fletcher, William
   A discourse delivered in the
city of Edinburgh, in opposition
to the Holy Alliance by William
Fletcher. New-York, Pr. by
Gould & Jacobus, 1828. 13 p.
DLC; MB; P; RPB.   33196

Fleury, Abbe Claude
   A brief summary of the sacred
history, and Christian doctrine.
Published for the use of the Cath-
olic Sunday School, with the ap-
probation of the Right Reverend
Bishop. Boston, Pr. by Ezra
Lincoln. 1828. 52 p. DLC; MWH.
                                    33197
Flint, James, 1779–1855
   A sermon delivered in the
meeting-house of the first parish
of Beverly, June 18, 1828, on
the occasion of the lamented
death of the Rev. Abiel Abbot,
D. D., late pastor of the First
Church and Society in Beverly...
Salem, Salem Gazette press,
1828. 32 p. CSmH; M; MWA.
                                    33198
---- ---- 2d ed. Salem [Mass.]
Pub. by J. R. Buffum [Isaac R.
Butts and co.'s press] 1828. 32
p. CSmH; MH; Nh.   33199

Flint, Joshua Barker, 1801-1864
   An address delivered before
the Massachusetts Society for the
Suppression of Intemperance,
May 29, 1828. Boston, Bowles &
Dearborn, 1828. 43 p. CSmH;
CoCsC; DLC; MBAt; MBC; MH;
MdBJ; MiD-B; NNC; NBM; RPB;
BrMus.   33200

Flint, Timothy, 1780-1840
   A condensed geography and
history of the western states,
or the Mississippi valley. In two
volumes. Cincinnati, Pub. by E.
H. Flint. W. M. and O. Farns-
worth, Jun., prs., 1828. 2 vols.
CSmH; ICHi; ICN; IaB; IaDaM;
IaU; In; InU; KHi; KyBgW; KyLoU;
LNHT; MB; MDeeP; MH; MdBE;
MdBP; MiGr; MiU-C; MoSHi;
MsU; NN; NUt; NbHi; Nj; OCHP;
OClWHi; PPAmP; PPL; PPi;
ScU; TKL; WHi; BrMus.   33201

[----] The life and adventures of
Arthur Clenning... By the author
of "Recollections of ten years in
the valley of the Mississippi,"
"Francis Berrian," &c. ...[A
novel] Philadelphia, Towar &
Hogan, 1828. 2 v. in 1. CSmH;
CtY; DLC; IU; MB; MBAt; MH;
MeU; MnU; OClWHi; PU; TNJ;
BrMus.   33202

Flirtation. See Bury, Charlotte
Maria (Campbell).

Florida
   Acts of the legislative council
of the territory of Florida,
passed at their sixth session,
1827-8. By authority. Tallahas-
see, Pr. by Joseph D. Davenport, 1828. [2], 175, [4] p. FU-
L; IU; MH-L; NNLI; OCLaw.
                                    33203
The Florida pirate; or, An account of a cruise in the schooner
Esparanza; with a sketch of the
life of her commander... New
York, Pub. by S. King and sold
wholesale and retail at his store,
1828. 24 p. DLC.   33204

The flowers of autumn. By the
authoress of the "Cottage minstrel." To which is added, a few
pieces by a young female, late
of this city, dec'd. Philadelphia,
Pr. for the authoress. J. Rich-

ards, pr., 1828. 108 p. IObB;
PHi; PU.   33205

Floyd, John
 Speech of John Floyd, of Virginia, on the bill for the occupation of the Oregon River. Delivered in the House of Representatives, on the 18th December, 1828. Washington, Pr. by
Duff Green, 1828. 7 p. Vi.
                             33206
Flushing Institute, Flushing, N. Y.
 The application of Christianity
to education: being the principles
and plan of education to be a-
dopted in the Institute at Flushing, L. I. Jamaica, L. I., Sleight
& George, prs., 1828. 24 p.
InID; MH; NEh; NHi; NJQ; NNUT.
                             33207
Flute instructor, containing a
plain and easy introduction to the
rules and principles of the German and patent flute; together
with a choice and valuable selection of popular music; consisting
of airs, songs, waltzes, marches,
duets, &c., &c. ...5th ed., corr.
and imp. Hallowell, Glazier,
Masters and Smith, 1828. 47,
[1] p. CtHT-W; DLC.   33208

Follen, Charles Theodore Chris-
tian, 1796-1840
 A practical grammar of the
German language... Boston, Hil-
liard, Gray, Little, and Wilkins
[Cambridge, Hilliard, Metcalf &
Co., Prs. to the University]
1828. xix, [1], 282 p. CU; DLC;
IU; MB; MBAt; MBC; MH; MHi;
MoU; NRU; Nh; PPL; ScCC;
TxU-T; VtU.   33209

Foot, Joseph Ives, 1796-1840
 Two sermons on intemperance.
Brookfield, Pr. by E. & G. Mer-
riam, 1828. 23 p. A-Ar; CSmH.
                             33210
Foreign Missionary Society of
Northampton
 The annual report of the com-

mittee of the Foreign Missionary
Society, of Northampton and the
neighboring towns, at their annual meeting Oct. 9, 1828. Northampton, T. Watson Shepard...
pr. 1828. 11 p. MWA.   33211

The forget-me-not; a New Year's
gift. Philadelphia, Judah Dobson,
Publisher, 1828. 340 p. NN;
NjR; PSC-Hi; RPB.   33212

Forward, Chauncey
 Speech of Mr. Forward, of
Pennsylvania, on the proposed
increase of the tariff, delivered
in the House of Representatives,
U. S. March 26th, & 27th, 1828.
Washington, Pr. by William
Greer, 1828. 24 p. DLC.   33213

Foster, Amos
 A sermon, delivered at Can-
aan, N. H. on Thanksgiving Day,
November 29, 1827. Concord,
Statesman & Register Office, Pr.
by A. M'Farland, 1828. 24 p.
MWA; NhHi; RPB.   33214

[Foster, Mrs. Hannah (Webster)]
1759-1840
 The coquette; or, The history
of Eliza Wharton, a novel...By
a lady of Massachusetts ...10th
ed. Exeter [N. H.], Pub. by
Abel Brown, 1828. 264 p. CSmH;
CtY; MWA; RPB; WU.   33215

[----] ---- 11th ed. Exeter,
Abel Brown, 1828. 264 p. CLO;
DLC; MWA; MWHi; MiU-C; NNC;
NjR; PPL; PU.   33216

Foster, John, 1770-1843
 An essay on the importance of
considering the subject of reli-
gion. Addressed particularly to
men of education. 2d Amer. ed.
Boston, Pub. by Crocker &
Brewster; New York, Jonathan
Leavitt, 1828. 172 p. CBCDS;
CtY; GDC; IU; MB; MnM; NbOU;
NcW; NdU; NjPT; OO;

PPLT; RPAt; TNJ.   33217

Foster, Robert, comp.
Hymn's original and selected,
for the use of Christians. Stereotyped by Smith, Reed & Gaylord,
Boston. Portsmouth, N. H. , Pr.
and sold at the office of the
Christian Herald [etc.] 1828. 448
p. CtY; MDeeP; MeLB; Nh;
NhHi.   33218

---- New selection of reformation melodies. Portsmouth, Pr.
at the Christian Herald Office,
1828. 24 p. NhHi.   33219

The fourth class book, containing
lessons in reading, for the younger classes in school. Brookfield,
E. and G. Merriam, 1828. (cover imprint: Boston, Pierce &
Williams, Brookfield, E. and G.
Merriam, 1828) 136 p. MWA; Nh.
     33220
Fowle, William Bently, 1795-
1865
The French accidence, or
elements of French grammar...
Boston, Hilliard, Gray, Little
and Wilkins [James Loring, pr.]
1828. 88 p. DLC; ICU; MB; MH;
MeB; MoS; NNC; NjP.   33221

---- ---- 2d ed. Boston, Freeman and Bolles, 1828. 88 p.
RPB.   33222

---- The rational guide to reading and orthography: being an attempt to improve the arrangement of words in English spelling books. Boston, Hilliard,
Gray, Little & Wilkins, 1828.
162 p. MH.   33223

Fox, George, 1624-1691
Epistles written by George Fox
and William Penn, describing the
spirit of separation. Hpiladelphia
[sic], Pr. by S. W. Conrad, 1828.
24 p. CSmH; MWA; PHC; PSC-
Hi.   33224

Fox, John
Fox's book of martyrs; or,
The acts and monuments of the
Christian church; being a com-
plete history of the lives, suffer-
ings and deaths of the Christian
martyrs... Rev. and impr. by
Rev. John Malham. New York,
Wm. Borradaile, 1828-1829. 2 v.
in 1. CtHT-W; MnHi; MoSU;
Nj.   33225

Frances, the orphan girl. Trans-
lated from the French, for the
American Sunday School Union.
Philadelphia, American Sunday
School Union [c 1828] 36 p. ICU;
BrMus.   33226

Francis, Convers, 1795-1863
An address delivered on the
Fourth of July, 1828, at Water-
town, in commemoration of the
anniversary of national independ-
ence. Cambridge, Hilliard &
Brown, 1828. 23 p. CSmH; DLC;
PPL; BrMus.   33227

---- A discourse delivered in
Bedford, April 30, 1828, before
the Middlesex Bible Society. Boston, Bowles & Dearborn, Press
of Isaac R. Butts & Co.] 1828.
21 p. CtSoP; MB; MBC; MH-AH;
MHi; MNtcA; NCH; WHi; BrMus.
     33228
---- Errors in education. A discourse, delivered at the anniversary of the Derby Academy, in
Hingham, May 21, 1828... Pub.
by request. Hingham [Mass.]
Farmer & Brown, 1828. 36 p.
CSmH; DLC.   33229

---- ---- 2d ed. Boston, Bowles
& Dearborn, 1828. 28 p. CBPac;
CtSoP; MB; NjPT.   33230

Francke, August Hermann, 1663-
1727
A guide to the reading and
study of the Holy Scriptures.
Philadelphia, Pub. by David Ho-

gan, 1828. xv, 249 p. MBC;
PLT. 33231

---- Der sichere Himmels-Weg
oder Anleitung zum Christenthum
von August Herman Franke, ehe-
maligem Professer in Halle....
Dritte Americanische Auflage.
Zum drittenmal bofoerdert von
Jacob Schweitzer. Ephrata, Gedruckt bey Joseph Bauman, 1828.
36 p. CSmH; P; PPL. 33232

Francoeur, Louis Benjamin,
1773-1849
An introduction to linear drawing; translated from the French
of M. Francoeur; with alterations
and additions to adapt it to the
use of schools in the United
States. To which is added, the
elements of linear perspective;
and questions on the whole. By
William B. Fowle... 2d ed. Boston, Hilliard, Gray, Little and
Wilkins [Monroe & Francis, prs.]
1828. vi, [2], 86, [2] p. CtY;
DLC; IaDaP; MWHi; NhHi;
OClWHi; TxDaM. 33233

Franklin, Benjamin, 1706-1790
The life of Benjamin Franklin.
Written by himself. Cincinnati,
A. Wright ["E. S. and A. S. Buxton, prs."] 1828. 1 p. l., 192
p. DLC; MiU-C; OClWHi; ViU.
33234
---- The works of Dr. Benjamin
Franklin; consisting of essays,
humorous, moral, and literary:
with his life, written by himself
... Boston, T. Bedlington, 1825
[i. e. 1828?] 303 p. CSmH; DLC.
33235
---- Another issue. With added
t. p. engraved: Life of Benjamin
Franklin. To which is added essays &c. Boston, T. Bedlington,
1828. Portrait differs from other
issue. DLC. 33236

Franklin, Sir John, 1786-1847
Narrative of a second expedition to the shores of the polar
sea, in the years 1825, 1826,
and 1827... Including an account
of the progress of a detachment
to the eastward, by John Richardson... Philadelphia, Carey,
Lea, and Carey [etc.] [W. Pil-
kington & Co., prs.] 1828. 318
p. CSmH; CU; CtMW; DeWI;
ICN; MB; MH-Z; MdBE; MdHi;
MiD; MnHi; NBLiHi; NCH;
NbOU; NhHi; NjR; O; OCHP;
OCY; OM; P; PPF; PPL; RP;
ScCC; THi; ViRUT; ViU; VtU;
WHi; BrMus. 33237

Franklin almanac for 1829. Bal-
timore, Armstrong & Plaskitt;
Wm. Wooddy, pr. [1828] 18 l.
MdBE. 33238

---- By Charles Hoffman. Philadelphia, M'Carty & Davis [1828]
17 l. MWA; MiHi; ScSoh. 33239

---- By John Armstrong. Pittsburgh, Johnston and Stockton
[1828] 18 l. CLU; MWA; OMC;
TxF. 33240

---- ---- 30 l. MWA. 33241

---- Richmond, Nathan Pollard
[1828] 24 l. MWA; PHi; ViHi.
33242
Franklin Institute. Philadelphia.
Address of the committee of
premiums of the Franklin Institute of the state of Pennsylvania.
Philadelphia, J. Harding, pr.,
1828. 8 p. MdBJ; RP. 33243

Fraser, Charles, 1782-1860
An address, delivered before
the citizens of Charleston, and
the grand lodge of South Carolina at the laying of the corner
stone of a new college edifice
with Masonic ceremonies, on the
12th January, 1828. Charleston,
Pr. by J. S. Burges, 1828. 24 p.
CSmH; ISC; KyU; MH; MdBJ;
MdHi; NcD; PPAmP; PPFM;

PPL; ScC; ScCC.   33244

[Fraser, James Baellie]
The Kuzzelbash; a tale of
Khorasan. New York, G. & C.
Carvill, 1828. 2 vols. CtHT;
CtY; NNA; PLFM.   33245

Fredericksburg Auxiliary Colonization Society
Proceedings of the Fredericksburg Auxiliary Colonization Society, at its anniversary meeting,
held in the town hall, on Saturday, February 23, 1828. Fredericksburg, Vir., Pr. by John
Minor, 1828. [4] p. (frequently
found with William M. Blackford,
An address, delivered...before
the Fredericksburg Auxiliary
Colonization Society). CSmH;
DLC; PPL.   33246

Fredonia Academy. Fredonia,
N. Y.
Catalogue of the trustees, in-
structors and students, of Fre-
donia Academy, for the year end-
ing Sept. 25, 1828. Fredonia,
H. C. Frisbee, pr., 1828. 7 p.
NFred.   33247

Free masonry. Its pretensions
exposed... See Ward, Henry
Dana.

Free Press, Auburn, N. Y.
New-Year's address, from the
carrier of the Free Press, to
his patrons. Auburn, January 1,
1828. 1 p. DLC.   33248

Free Trade Convention
Address to the people of the
United States. [1828] 8 p. ScU.
                               33249
A freeman, pseud. See Moore,
Jacob Bailey.

The Freeman's almanack for
1829. By Samuel Burr. Cincinnati, N. & G. Guilford; Oliver
Farnsworth; Wm. M. Farnsworth,

pr. [1828] 12 l. InRE; MWA.
                               33250
---- ---- Cincinnati, N. & G.
Guilford; Oliver Farnsworth;
Wm. M. Farnsworth, pr. [1828]
24 l. DLC; In; InU; MWA; OC;
OClWHi; OHi; OMC; WHi.   33251

Freemasons. Alabama. Grand
Chapter
Constitution, laws and regula-
tions, for the government of the
Grand Lodge of Alabama, and the
subordinate lodges under its juris-
diction as amended and adopted at
an annual communication held at
Tuscaloosa, December, A. L. 5827,
A. D. 1827. Huntsville, Pr. by
Dandridge Fariss & Co. 1828. 19
p. CSmH; GL.   33252

---- ---- ---- Proceedings of the
Grand Lodge of Alabama, at its
annual communication in December,
1827. Huntsville, Pr. by Dandridge
Fariss & Co. 1828. 19 p. CSmH;
GL.   33253

---- ---- Royal Arch Masons.
Grand Chapter
Proceedings of the Grand Royal
Arch Chapter of the state of Ala-
bama, at its annual convocation in
December, A. D. 1827. Tuscaloosa.
Pr. by Comp. Dugald M'Farlane.
1828. 7 p. GL.   33254

---- Delaware. Grand Lodge.
Stated communication of the
Grand Lodge of Delaware, held
at Wilmington...June 27, A. L.
5828, A. D. 1828. Wilmington,
Pr. at the Gazette office [1828]
8 p. CSmH.   33255

---- D. C. Grand Lodge
Constitution and by-laws of the
Grand Lodge of the District of
Columbia as amended by the
lodge, Nov. 4, 1828. Washington
(D. C.), 1828. 12 p. IaCrM.
                               33256
---- ---- ---- Proceedings of the

Grand Lodge of the District of Columbia, from December 27, A. L. 5826, to December 27, A. L. 5828, inclusive... Washington, Pr. by Gales & Seaton, 1828. 40 p. LNMas; NNFM; ScU.
33257

---- Indiana. Brookville Harmony Lodge
Bye-laws of Brookville Harmony Lodge, number eleven. Brookville, state of Indiana, A. L. 5828. Pr. by Augustus Jocelyn, Brookville [Ia.], 1828. 8 p. IaCrM.
33258

---- Kentucky. Grand Chapter
Proceedings of the Grand Chapter of the state of Kentucky, at a grand annual convocation, begun and held at Mason's hall in the town of Lexington, on Monday, September 1, A. D. 1828. Frankfort, Pr. by Amos Kendall and company, 1828. 24 p. NNFM.
33259

---- ---- Grand Lodge
Proceedings of the Grand Lodge of Kentucky, at a grand annual communication, in the town of Lexington, August 5828. Lexington, Ken, Pr. by Thomas Tunstall Bradford, 1828. 60 p. IaCrM; KyLxFM; MBFM; NNFM.
33260

---- ---- Knights Templars. Webb Encampment.
The charter of Webb Encampment of Knights Templar [sic] and Knights of Malta, with the by-laws as revised on the 3d Sept. A. L. 5832, A. D. 1828, Y. O. 711. And the constitution of the general grand encampment of the United States of America. Lexington, Ky., Pr. by Joseph G. Norwood, 1828. 13 p. KyBgW.
33261

---- Maine. Grand Lodge
Grand Lodge of the most ancient and honorable Fraternity of Free and Accepted Masons, of the state of Maine... Portland,

Shirley & Hyde, 1828. 28 p. NNFM.
33262

---- ---- Royal Arch Masons. Grand Chapter
Proceedings of the Grand Royal Arch Chapter of Maine... January and August, 1827, and January, 1828. Portland, Pr. by Thomas Todd, 1828. 34 p. NNFM.
33263

---- Massachusetts. Grand Lodge
Annual communication... Grand Lodge of Free and Accepted Masons... Massachusetts, held at Masons' Hall, Boston, Dec. 12, A. L. 5827. Boston, Pr. by E. G. House, 1828. 16 p. IaCrM; NNFM; OCM.
33264

---- ---- ---- Grand lodge, of the most ancient and honourable Fraternity of Free and Accepted Masons, of the commonwealth of Massachusetts. [Annual communication] Boston, Pr. by E. G. House, 1828. 16 p. MWA. 33265

---- ---- Royal Arch Masons. Grand Chapter.
Grand Royal Arch Chapter of Massachusetts. Boston, Nov. 1828. Boston, Pr. by E. G. House, 1828. 23 p. IaCrM.
33266

---- Missouri. Grand Lodge
Proceedings of the Grand Lodge of the state of Missouri, at their several communications, begun and held in the city of St. Louis, on the second day of April, and the first day of October, eighteen hundred and twenty-eight. St. Louis, Pr. by Orr and Keemle, 1828. 20 p. IaCrM; DSC; NNFM.
33267

---- New Hampshire. Royal Arch Masons. Grand Chapter.
A journal of the proceedings of the Grand Royal Arch Chapter

of the state of New Hampshire, at their annual communication, holden in Concord, June 12, A. L. 5828 [1828] Concord, Asa McFarland, pr., 1828. 12 p. LNMas; NNFM.   33268

---- North Carolina. Royal Arch Masons. Grand Chapter.
Sixth annual convocation of the Grand Royal Arch Chapter of North Carolina. Raleigh, Pr. by Lawrence & Lemay, prs. to the state, 1828. 17 p. NcU.   33269

---- Ohio. Grand Lodge
Proceedings of the Grand Lodge of the most ancient and honorable Fraternity of Free and Accepted Masons in the state of Ohio, at the annual grand communication, A. L. 5828. Most worshipful Thomas Corwin, Grand Master. Delaware, O., Pr. by Bro. Ezra Griswold, 1828. 20 p. IaCrM; MBFM.   33270

---- ---- Novae Caesarea Harmony Lodge No. 2.
Proposals for erecting a large and commodious Masonic Hall & city hotel, on their vacant ground, on the corner of Third and Walnut Streets, by Novae Caesarea Harmony Lodge No. 2, Cincinnati. [1828] 8 p. PPFM.   33271

---- Pennsylvania. Grand Lodge
Annual publication. Grand Lodge of the most ancient and honourable Fraternity of Free and Accepted Masons of Pennsylvania... Philadelphia, Pr. by Thomas S. Manning, 1828. [113]-152 p. IaCrM; NNFM; PPFM.
                               33272
---- Rhode Island. Grand Lodge.
Proceedings of the worshipful Grand Lodge of the state of Rhode Island and Providence Plantations, at the annual meeting holden at Lafayette Hall, in Cumberland, June 24th, A. L. 5828.

Providence, Pr. by Bro. Barzillai Cranston, 5828 [1828] 8 p. IaCrM; NNFM.   33273

---- South Carolina. Grand Lodge
Abstract of the proceedings of the Grand Lodge of ancient Free Masons of South Carolina. Charleston, 1828. 45 p. OCM.
                               33274
---- Tennessee. Grand Lodge
Proceedings of the Grand Lodge of the state of Tennessee, at its annual meeting, held in the town of Nashville, for the year 1828. Nashville, Banner Press, Simpson, pr., 1828. 32 p. MBFM.   33275

---- ---- Royal Arch Masons. Grand Chapter
Proceedings of the Grand Royal Arch Chapter of Tennesseee[sic] from October 1826 to March 1828, inclusive. Nashville, Pr. by John S. Simpson, 1828. 32 p. IaCrM; MBFM.   33276

---- United States. General Grand Encampment.
Officers of the General Grand Encampment of the United States of America; of the Grand Encampment of Connecticut; and of Washington Encampment, No. 1, with by-laws and members... in Connecticut. New London (Conn.), Companion Samuel Green, 1828. 20 p. IaCrM.   33277

---- Vermont
A candid appeal to the public, by the members of the Masonick fraternity, connected with the Lodges of Waterford, Concord, Lyndon, St. Johnsbury, Peacham, and Craftsbury, and the Royal Arch-chapter at Danville. Montpelier, Pr. by E. P. Walton, 1828. 15 p. MA; MBFM; VtHi; VtU.   33278

---- Vermont. Royal Arch Masons. Grand Chapter.

Extracts from the proceedings of the Grand Royal Arch Chapter of the state of Vermont, June 18, 1828. Rutland, Pr. by Edward C. Purdy, 1828. 8 p. DSC; IaCrM; LNMas; NNFM.   33279

---- Virginia.

Proceedings of grand commandery of Masonic Lodge, in Virginia: meeting held in 1827. Winchester, Samuel H. Davis, 1828. 12 p. IaCrM.   33280

---- Proceedings of grand commandery of Masonic Lodge, in Virginia: meeting held in 1828. Winchester, Samuel H. Davis, 1828. 10 p. IaCrM.   33281

---- ---- Grand Lodge.

Proceedings of a grand annual communication of the Grand Lodge of Virginia, begun and held in the Masons' Hall, in the city of Richmond, the second Monday in December, being the eighth day of the month, Anno Lucis 5828, Anno Domini 1828. Richmond, Pr. by John Warrock, Pr. to the Grand Lodge, and Grand Chapter of Virginia, 1828. 52 p. IaCrM; MBFM; NNFM; OCM (says pr. by John H. Wynne).   33282

The Freewill Baptist register, and Saint's annual visiter for 1829. Limerick, Samuel Burbank [1828] 27 l. MWA.   33283

Der Freischütz: an opera, in three acts. Altered from the German, by George Soane... As performed at the Philadelphia Theatre. From the prompt book. Philadelphia, Pub. by C. Neal, 1828. 36 p. PPL.   33284

French, Jonathan

A sermon delivered at the funeral of the Rev. Federal Burt, pastor of the Congregational Church, in Durham, New-Hampshire, who died Feb. 9, 1828; Aet, 39. Portsmouth, Pr. by Miller & Brewster, 1828. 16 p. MNe; MWA; Nh; RPB.   33285

The French phrase book. See Phillips, Sir Richard.

The Friend of the Union

Proposals, for publishing in the city of Richmond, a new weekly paper, to be styled The Friend of the Union; to be conducted by Oliver Oldschool: designed for extensive circulation among the people, and to cherish a predominant attachment to the Union of the States, as the only bond of freedom, happiness, and security... January 24th, 1828. 2 p. DLC.   33286

A Friend to the poor. See Infant Education.

Friends of the Administration. See National Republican Party.

Friends, Society of. Baltimore Yearly Meeting.

Extracts from the minutes of our Yearly Meeting, held in Baltimore, for the Western Shore of Maryland, and the adjacent parts of Pennsylvania and Virginia, by adjournments, from the twenty-seventh of the tenth month, to the thirty-first of the same, inclusive, 1828. [Baltimore, Wm. Wooddy, pr., 1828] 16 p. MdBE; PPL; PSC-Hi.   33287

---- [Minutes of the proceedings] of the Yearly Meeting of Friends, held in Baltimore for the Western Shore of Maryland, &c. by adjournments from the 27th of the tenth month to the 1st of the eleventh month, inclusive, 1828. Bdsd. (defective top line & bottom line missing) WHi. 33288

---- Indiana Yearly meeting.

An epistle, from Indiana Yearly Meeting, held at Miami, Ohio,
from the 29th of the 9th, to the
3d of the 10th month, inclusive.
1828. [n. p. , 1828] 5 p. CSmH.
                                    33288a
---- ---- An epistle to the members of the religious society of
Friends, belonging to the yearly
meeting of Pennsylvania, New
Jersey, Delaware, and the eastern parts of Maryland and Virginia. Richmond, Ind. , Pr. by
Samuel B. Walling, 1828. [12?]
p. In.   33289

---- ---- Extracts, &c. from
the minutes of Indiana Yearly
Meeting, held at White-Water,
10th month, 1827. Rochester, E.
Peck & Co. , prs. , 1828. 12 p.
NRU.   33290

---- ---- Indiana yearly meeting
of Friends, held at White-water
in Wayne county, Indiana, on the
sixth-day of the tenth month,
1828. [Richmond? 1828?] 26 p.
In; InRE; InU; WHi.   33291

---- London Yearly Meeting.

The epistle from the yearly
meeting, held in London, by adjournments, from the 21st of the
fifth month, to the 31st of the
same, inclusive, 1828. To the
quarterly and monthly meetings
of Friends, in Great Britain,
Ireland, and elsewhere. [Centre-
ville, In. , Pr. by Finch & Smith,
1828?] [2] p. DLC.   33292

---- New England Yearly Meeting.

An epistle from the yearly
meeting of Friends for New England, to its subordinate meetings
and members. [New Bedford]
1828. 23 p. MH; RPB.   33293

---- New York Yearly Meeting.

An epistle and testimony from
the Yearly Meeting of Friends,
held in New York, by adjournments, from the twenty-sixth of
the fifth month, to the second of
the sixth month inclusive, 1828.
New York, Pr. by Mahlon Day,
1828. 24 p. InRE; MH; MWA;
MeBaT; NGH; NjR; OO; PHC;
PHi; PSC-Hi; ScU.   33294

---- North America. Yearly
Meeting.

Epistles and testimonies issued by the yearly meetings of
Friends, in North America; setting forth their faith respecting
the Holy Scriptures, and in the
divinity and offices of Our Lord
and Saviour Jesus Christ; shewing that the antichristian doctrines of those who have lately
separated from the society, are
repugnant thereto. Philadelphia,
T. Kite, pr. , 1828. 83 p. DLC;
MBC; MH; NcD; NjR; PHC; PHi;
PSC-Hi.   33295

---- North Carolina. Yearly
Meeting.

Epistle of the Yearly Meeting
of Friends of N. C. for the year
1827. Baltimore, Pr. , Providence, Repr. , Brown, 1828.
12 p. NcU; PHC.   33296

---- Ohio, Yearly Meeting.

A declaration of Ohio Yearly
Meeting, held at Mountpleasant
and Short Creek, by adjournments, from the 8th to the 16th
of the 9th mo. inclusive, 1828.
[New-York, M. Day, pr. , 1828]
16 p. MH; OClWHi; WHi. 33297

---- ---- An epistle to the
Quarterly, Monthly, and Prepara-
tive meeting of Friends, within
the compass of Ohio Yearly Meeting. Mount-pleasant, Pr. by direction of the meeting, by Elisha
Bates, 1828. 11 p. OClWHi.
                                    33298
---- ---- ---- [St. Clairsville,

R. H. Miller, pr. , 1828] 4 p.
PSC-Hi.   33299

---- Philadelphia Yearly Meeting.
A declaration of the Yearly
Meeting held in Philadelphia, re-
specting the proceedings of those
who have lately separated from
the Society... New York, Samuel
Wood & Son, 1828. 32 p. MBC;
MH; MWA; NGH; NjR; PSC-Hi;
VtU.   33300

---- ---- ---- Philadelphia, Pr.
by Thomas Kite, 1828. 32 p.
CSmH; DLC; ICU; IEG; IU; MH-
AH; MHi; MiD-B; NBLiHi;
NcWsM; NjR; PHC; PHi; PPAmP;
PPL; PPPrHi; PSC-Hi; VtMiM;
WHi; BrMus.   33301

---- ---- Extracts from the min-
utes of the Yearly Meeting of
Friends, held in Philadelphia...
Philadelphia, Pr. on the Vertical
Press, by D. & S. Neall [1828]
11 p. MM; PHC; PSC-Hi. 33302

---- (Hicksite). Philadelphia
Yearly Meeting
An epistle from the yearly
meeting of Friends, held in
Philadelphia, by adjournments
from the fourteenth of the Fourth
month, to the eighteenth of the
same, inclusive, 1828. To the
Quarterly, Monthly, and Prepara-
tive meetings, thereunto belong-
ing. Philadelphia, Pr. on the
Vertical Press, by D. & S.
Neall [1828] 6 p. CSmH; PHC;
PPL; PSC-Hi.   33303

---- ---- Epistle to Friends with-
in the compass of Ohio and Indi-
ana Yearly Meeting. [Signed:
James Mott, clerk. Philadelphia,
Second month 15, 1828] New York,
Benedict Bolmore, 1828. 8 p.
PHC.   33304

---- ---- ---- Philadelphia, Pr.
by Joseph Parker, 1828. 8 p.

MH; PHC.   33305

---- ---- Rules of discipline of
the Yearly Meeting of Friends
held in Philadelphia... Philadelphia, J. Mortimer, James Kay,
Jun. , pr. , 1828. [vii], 135 p.
InRE; PPL; PSC-Hi; PU. 33306

Frost, John, 1800-1859
The easy reader. Designed to
be used next in course after the
spelling book, in schools and
families. Boston, Bowles & Dearborn, Press of Isaac R. Butts
& Co. , 1828. 142 p. IObB.
                               33307
---- 500 progressive exercises
in parsing. 2d ed. Boston, Hilliard, Gray, Little & Wilkins,
1828. 36 p. ICU; MH; BrMus.
                               33308
---- Questions for the examination of students in Paley's Moral
and political philosophy. Boston,
N. H. Whitaker, 1828. 35 p. TNJ.
                               33309
Fuller, Andrew, comp.
Memoirs of the late Rev.
Samuel Pearce, A. M. with extracts from some of his most interesting letters. To which are
added, an oration, delivered at the
grave, by the Rev. J. Brewer;
A sermon on his death, by Rev.
J. Ryland, and a brief memoir
of Mrs. Pearce. 5th Amer. ed.
Boston, Pr. & pub. by Lincoln
& Edmands, 1828. 267 p. CtHT-
W; GDC; MB; MH; MNtcA;
NNUT; NUt; PHi.   33310

Fuller, Zelotes
The threshing instrument. A
discourse delivered at the Second
Universalist Church in Philadelphia, Sunday evening, November
30, 1828. Philadelphia, 1828. 16
p. MBAt; MMeT; MMeT-Hi;
MWA.   33311

Fulton, Robert, 1765-1815
Report of the practicability of

navigating with steam boats, on the southern waters of the United States, from the Chesapeake to the river St. Mary's, forming part of a line of steam boat communications, now establishing, from the northern extremity of Lake Champlain to east-Florida, a distance of fifteen hundred miles. First published, December, 1813, by Robert Fulton, from the surveys of John D. Delacy. 2d ed. Philadelphia, Pr. by Thomas Town, 1828. 12, 3 p. CSmH; MnHi; NIC; PHi; PPL (imp.); ViU; WHi.   33312

[Furbish, James,] 1796-1878
Some remarks on education, textbooks, etc. By the teacher of the High School for Young Ladies, Portland, Me. Portland, Shirley and Hyde, 1828. 32 p. ArU; MBC.   33313

Furness, William Henry
A discourse preached at the dedication of the First Congregational Unitarian Church, Philadelphia. [James Kay, Jun. & Co. , prs.] Philadelphia, Pub. for the First Congregational Church, Nov. 5, 1828. 40 p. ICMe; MB; MBAU; MH; MHi; MWA; MiD-B; PHi; PPAmP; PPL; RPB; BrMus.   33314

G

Gales's North-Carolina almanac for 1829. By Dr. Hudson M. Cave. Raleigh, J. Gales & Son [1828] 18 l. NcD; NcHiC; NcU; TKL.   33315

Gallaudet, Thomas Hopkins, 1787-1851
An address on female education, delivered Nov. 21st, 1827, at the opening of the edifice erected for the accommodation of the Hartford Female Seminary

... Hartford, H. and F. J. Huntington, P. Canfield, pr. , 1828. 34 p. AU; CSmH; CtHT-W; CtHi; CtY; DLC; MB; MBAt; MBC; MH; MNtcA; MWA; MiU; NCH; NIC; NN; NNG; NjR; OCHP; OClW; PPAmP.   33316

---- A statement with regard to the Moorish Prince Arduhl Rahhahman. Pr. by Daniel Fanshaw, New York, October 22, 1828. 8 p. CtHT-W; CtHi; CtY; DLC; MBAt; MBC; MH; PPAmP. 33317

Gamble, John M.
The memorial of Lieut. Colonel J. M. Gamble, of the United States Marine Corps, to Congress, 1828. New-York, Pr. by Geo. F. Hopkins & Son, 1828. 16 p. MB; MH.   33318

Garcia del Rio, Juan
Documentos relativos a la denegacion de pasaporte para Mejico a J. G. del Rio. New York, Desnoues, 1828. 16 p. NcD; BrMus.   33319

Garden, Alexander, 1757-1826
Anecdotes of the American Revolution, illustrative of the talents and virtues of the heroes and patriots, who acted the most conspicuous parts therein. Second series. Charleston, Pr. by A. E. Miller, 1828. ix, [2], 240 p. CSmH; CtMW; CtSoP; DLC; FTaSU; GHi; GU; ICU; MB; MBAt; MH; MWA; MdBJ; NN; NcA-S; NcD; NcU; OFH; PHi; PPL; ScC; ScHi; ScU; WHi; BrMus.   33320

The gardener's daughter. By the author of "Harriet and her cousin, "... Revised by the Committee of Publication. American Sunday School Union. Philadelphia, 1828. 90 p. BrMus.   33321

Gardiner, W.

Walks in Kent. Containing original moral and interesting histories and narratives for the instruction and amusement of young persons. Portland, Pub. by Shirley & Hyde, 1828. 141, [2] p. WaPS. 33322

Gardner, Matthew
A concise history of the united persecutions against the Church of Christ; by William J. Thompson, a Methodist preacher; and William L. McCalla, a Presbyterian preacher; including an account of a suit for slander, which the author, instituted against William L. McCalla, wherein a verdict was rendered for one cent damages. Likewise, the certificates of the jurors, which show the reason why, and their design in so rendering the verdict. By Matthew Gardner, an elder in the Church of Christ. Georgetown, Ohio, April 16, 1828. 14 p. OC. 33323

Garnett, James Mercer, 1770-1843
...A defense of the Protestant Episcopal Church, against the charges of enmity to the civil institutions of our country. Richmond, Pub. by Peter Cottom, T. W. White, pr., 1828. 11 p. (An Episcopal tract.) CSmH; NN; Vi. 33324

Gaugiran-Nanteuil, P. Charles, 1778- ca 1830.
Neal & Mackenzie, No. 201 Chestnut Street, between the Theater & Arcade, Philadelphia. Les maris garcons, comedie en un acte. Par M. Gaugiran-Nanteuil. [Philadelphia, 1828] 20 p. (Also issued in vol. with covering title: Collection d'Operas et Vaudevilles) ICU; PPL. 33325

Gavin, Antonio
A master-key to popery...

Hagerstown, Md., Pub. for subscribers, 1828. 297 p. MdBP; NN; NcD; TMSC. 33326

Der Gemeinnützige landwithschafts calender auf 1829. Lancaster, Wm. Albrecht [1828] 18 l. CLU; CtY; DLC; InU; MWA; NjP; OC; PDoBHi; PHi; PPL; PPeSchw; WHi. 33327

Das Gemeinschaftliche gesangbuch, zum gottesdienstlichen gebrauch der Lutherischen und Reformirten gemeinden in Nord-America. Auf verlangen der meisten prediger beyder benennungen gesammelt, und von den committeen zweyer ministerien geprüft und genehmiget. Fünfte auflage. Grünsburg [Pa.] Gedruckt und herausgegeben von J. S. Steck, 1828. xviii, 370, [4] p. CSmH; PPL. 33328

Gemeinschaftliches gesangbuch zum gottesdienstlichen gebrauch der Lutherischen und Reformirten Gemeinden in Nord-Amerika. Nebst einem Anhange von anser wählten gebeten. Germania, 1828. iv, 364 p. PPL. 33329

A genealogical memoir of the family by the name of Farmer. See Farmer, John.

Gen. Andrew Jackson and the Rev. Ezra Stiles Ely [New York, Evans, 1828] 8 p. NcU. 33330

The general class book. See Willard, Samuel.

General committee of young men of the city and county of New York. See Democratic Party. New York.

Gen. Jackson's negro speculations. See Erwin, Andrew.

Gen. Metcalffe. To the people

of Kentucky. In a few weeks you will be called on to exercise your right of suffrage by the choice of a Governor and Lt. Governor... July 1, 1828. 1 p. DLC.   33331

General Theological Seminary of the Protestant Episcopal Church. See New York. General Theological Seminary of the Protestant Episcopal Church.

General Union for Promoting the Observance of the Christian Sabbath.
  The address of the General Union for Promoting the Observance of the Christian Sabbath, to the people of the United States, accompanied by minutes of the proceedings in its formation, its constitution and officers. Auburn, Pr. by Richard Oliphant, 1828. 15 p. NBu; OClWHi.   33332

---- ---- New-York, Pr. by Daniel Fanshaw, 1828. 16 p. CtSoP; CtY; GDC; ICU; MB; MBAt; MBC; MH-AH; MNtcA; MWA; MeBaT; MiD-B; NGH; NIC; NN; PHi; PLT; PPPrHi; TxDaM; WHi.
                                    33333
---- Pennsylvania Branch.
  The proceedings and constitution of the Pennsylvania Branch of the General Union for Promoting the Observance of the Christian Sabbath, together with the address of the General Union. Philadelphia, Martin & Boden, 1828. 16 p. Ct; PHi; PPPrHi.
                                    33334
A general view of the rise, progress, and brilliant achievements of the American Navy, down to the present time. Illustrated by biographical sketches, official reports, and interesting views of American commerce. To which is affixed a succinct account of the origin and progress of the Greek Revolution. Terminating

with the glorious victory of Navarino, October 20, 1827. Brooklyn, N. Y., 1828. 484 p. CSmH; CU; CtY; DLC; ICHi; ICN; MBAt; MH; MdAN; MiD; NBLiHi; NN; OClWHi; ViU.   33335

Geneseo, N. Y.   Livingston County High-school.
  View of the Livingston County High-School: on Temple-Hill; Geneseo: under the charge of Seth Sweetser, C. C. Felton, H. R. Cleveland, to which are subjoined, brief remarks on some of the leading topics of popular education. Geneseo, Pr. by J. Percival, 1828. 28 p. CSmH; DLC; MH.   33336

Geneva Catechism
  Abstract of sacred history, being the first part of the Geneva Catechism. 2d ed. Boston, Hilliard, Gray, Little and Wilkins, 1828. 50 p. MB; MBAt; MHi; MiD-B; PPPrHi.   33337

Geneva College. Rutgers Medical Faculty.
  Catalogue of the officers and students of Rutgers Medical Faculty, Geneva College, Duane Street, city of New-York... Session of 1827-28. New-York, Pr. by C. S. Van Winkle, 1828. 7 p. MH; NjR.   33338

---- Catalogue of the officers and students of Rutgers Medical Faculty, Geneva College, Duane street, city of New York, session of 1828-9. Published by the class. New York, Pr. at Grattan's office, 1828. 11 p. NNNAM; NjR.   33339

---- Lectures. The lectures of this institution commence on the 1st Monday in November... New-York, July 10, 1828. Bdsd. NjR.   33340

---- ---- New-York, Sept. 29,
1828. Bdsd. NjR.   33341

---- This college will commence
the course of lectures, for the
ensuing Winter session, on Monday, the third day of November
... New-York, Nov. 1, 1828.
Bdsd. NjR.   33342

Genlis, Stéphanie Félicite Du-
crest de Saint Aubin, comtesse
de, afterwards marquise de Sil-
lery, 1746-1830
    Eugene and Lolotte; A tale for
children. From the French of
Madame De Genlis. Boston, Munroe & Francis, 1828. 79 p. OO;
ScCliTO.   33343

A gentleman of the Baltimore
Bar. See Some account of Gen.
Jackson.

A gentleman of this city. See
Sophia.

Geographical botany of the United
States. See Beck, Lewis Caleb.

A geographical view of the world.
See Phillips, Sir Richard.

A geological nomenclature for
North America. See Eaton, Amos.

George, John D.
    Tariff; or Rates of duty (con-
formably to the existing revenue
laws) on goods, wares and merchandise, imported into the
United States of America, from
and after the thirtieth day of
June, 1828. To which is added
an appendix, containing the acts
of amendment to the tariff of
1824, passed at the last session
of Congress; together with other
useful information to merchants.
By John D. George and Charles
Treichel. Philadelphia, 1828.
116 p. IU; MB; PHi.   33344

Georgia (State)
    Journal of the Senate of the
state of Georgia, at an annual
session of the General Assembly
begun and held at Milledgeville,
the seat of government, in November and December, 1827.
Milledgeville, Pr. by Camak &
Ragland, 1828. 340 p. G-Ar;
GMiW; PU-L.   33345

[Gibbons, William]
    Review of a pamphlet, called
"A testimony, and epistle of advice," lately issued by (or in the
name of) "Indiana Yearly Meeting." Philadelphia, Pr. by Jos.
Parker, 1828. [Signed, "An enemy to creeds."] 16 p. CSmH;
MB; MH; MiD-B; PHC; PSC-Hi.
                                   33346
Gibbs, Josiah Willard, 1790-
1861
    A manual Hebrew and English
lexicon including the Biblical
Chaldee. Andover, Pr. for the
author at the Cidman Press by
Flagg & Gould, 1828. 210 p.
InCW; NN; PPDrop.   33347

[Gibson, John]
    To the public. [New Orleans,
1828] 13 p. DLC.   33348

Gibson, Robert
    The theory and practice of
surveying; containing all the instructions requisite for the skil-
ful [sic] practice of this art...
Newly arranged, improved, and
enlarged, with useful selections,
and a new set of accurate mathematical tables. By James Ryan...
New York, Pr. by J. & J. Harper, For E. Duyckinck, Collins
and Hannay, and O. A. Roorbach;
Philadelphia, John Grigg, Towar
and Hogan; Boston, Richardson
and Lord, and Hilliard, Gray,
Little, and Wilkins, 1828. 385 p.
LNHT; MNBedf; OO; PPF; Vi.
                                   33349

[Gilbert, Ann (Taylor)] 1782-1866
Hymns for infant minds, by the
author of "Original poems, Rhymes
for the nursery," &c ... 2d Hallowell ed. Hallowell [Me.] Pr. &
pub. by Glazier & Co., 1828. 64
p. MB.   33350

[----] Hymns for infant minds...
Rev. by the Committee of Publication of the American Sunday
School Union. Philadelphia, American Sunday School Union, 1828.
85 p. NjP; BrMus.   33351

[----] ---- Windsor, Pub. by P.
Merrifield, 1828. D. Watson,
pr., Woodstock. 77 p. VtHi.
                                33352
Gilbert, Garrit
An address, delivered at a
meeting of the Republican electors of the ninth ward of the city
of New York, friendly to General
Jackson, convened for the purpose of celebrating a festival dinner, on the anniversary of the
glorious battle of New Orleans.
[New York] D. Fanshaw, 1828.
20 p. MH.   33353

Giles, William Branch, 1762-1830
The golden casket; or, The
president's message... New series, no. 9. [dated Feb. 26,
1826] and extract from no. 12.
[Richmond, Va., T.W. White,
1828] 19 p. Vi.   33354

[----] Plain matters of fact, un-
denied and undeniable. One at a
time--"Constructive journies."
From the Richmond Enquirer of
1828. [Richmond, Va., 1828] 57
p. AB; CSt; CU; MdBJ; MH; NcU;
NN; RPB; Vi; ViU; WHi.   33355

[----] To the public. [Re-pub. of
opinions expressed by Giles on
internal improvements] [Richmond,
T. W. White, pr., 1828] 19 p.
DLC; MH-BA; Vi.   33356

Gilles, H. N.
The complete vocal instructor
dedicated to the ladies of Baltimore... Baltimore, Pub. for the
author, by Geo. Willig, Jr.
[1828] viii, 99 p. P; PPL.
                                33357
Gilman, Samuel, 1791-1858
A sermon on the introduction
to the Gospel of St. John. 2d ed.
Boston, Bowles and Dearborn
[Press of Isaac R. Butts & Co.]
1828. 24 p. CtSoP; DLC; ICMe;
MBAU; MH; MWA.   33358

---- Unitarian Christianity free
from objectionable extremes: a
sermon preached at the dedica-
tion of the Unitarian Church, in
Augusta (Geo.), Dec. 27, 1827.
Charleston, (S.C.), Charleston,
James S. Burges, 1828. 43 p.
CSmH; GU-De; MH; MWA; NjPT;
BrMus.   33359

Gilmer, Francis Walker, 1790-
1826
Sketches, essays and translations. Baltimore, F. Lucas, jun.,
1828. 201 p. CSmH; CtHT-W;
DLC; ICU; KyLx; LU; MB; MdBE;
MdBS; MdHi; MiD; NNC; NNNAM;
NcD; PHi; T; ViRU; ViU; WHi.
                                33360
Gilpin, Henry D.
A biographical sketch of Thomas Jefferson. By Henry D. Gilpin. From the Biography of the
signers of the Declaration of Independence. Philadelphia [Wm.
Brown & Charles Peters. W.
Brown, pr.] 1828. [1], [245]-372
p. MdBE; PPL; RPB; Vi. 33361

[Gilpin, Joshua]
A monument of parental affec-
tion to an only son. New York,
N. Bangs & J. Emory, for the
Methodist Episcopal Church, 1828.
102 p. CtW.   33362

Glascott, George Ware
An oration on the present

state of Ireland... Boston, E.
Bellamy, 1828. [3], 8 p. MBAt;
MDovC; BrMus.   33363

The God of the Jews and Chris-
tians, the Great Jehovah; or,
The Trinity in unity. Embellished
with a correct likeness. New
York, Pr. for a Society for the
Promotion of Christian Knowledge
[Geo. H. Evans, pr.] 1828. 8 p.
MBAt.   33364

Goethe, Johann Wolfgang von
   Wilhelm Meister's apprentice-
ship...[Transl. by T. Carlyle]
Boston, Wells & Lilly, 1828.
3 vols. CtHT-W; MBL; MH; MW;
PPL; ViU; VtU.   33365

Goldsmith, Rev. J., pseud. See
Phillips, Sir Richard.

Goldsmith, Oliver, 1728-1774
   Goldsmith's natural history,
abridged for the use of schools.
12th ed. ...New York, Collins
& Hannay [etc.] 1828. xii, 276 p.
DLC.   33366

---- ---- Rev. and corr. by a
teacher of Philadelphia. To
which is added, an appendix. Exhibiting the classification of Lin-
neaus. 12th ed. Philadelphia,
Pub. by Thomas Desilver, 1828.
333, [1] p. CtY; MB; PPeSchw.
                             33367
---- Goldsmith's Roman history;
abridged by himself for the use
of schools. Hartford, S. Andrus,
1828. 316 p. CtY; MiToC. 33368

---- The Grecian history, from
the earliest state to the death of
Alexander the Great. Hartford,
S. Andrus, publisher, stereotyped by H. Wallis, 1828. 2 v.
in 1. [316 p.] CtHi; NT; OCX;
ViAlTh.   33369

---- The vicar of Wakefield, a
tale; with the life of the author,

by Dr. Johnson. Hartford, S.
Andrus, 1828. 252 p. CtHT-W;
CtHi; ICU; MB; MDeeP; MWM;
OCX.   33370

---- ---- A tale to which is annexed, The deserted village.
Exeter, J. and B. Williams,
1828. 288 p. CtHT-W; GAGTh;
MB; MWA; NcA-S; RNHi. 33371

Good, John Mason
   The book of nature... from the
last London ed. New York, Pr.
by J. & J. Harper [etc.] 1828.
530 p. IEN-M; InGrD; KyDC;
KyLx; MB; MWA; MeBa; NBM;
NR; NT; OM; PPC.   33372

Good child's soliloquy. See
American Tract Society. N.Y.

Good examples for children...
New-York, Pr. and sold by Mah-
lon Day, at the new juvenile book-
store. 1828. 17 p. MH; PP.
                             33373
Goodman, John. See Burnside,
A. (note)

Goodrich, Charles Augustus,
1790-1862
   A history of the United States
of America... 21st ed. In which
the historical events are brought
down to the year 1827. And to
which is added A geographical
view of the United States. Boston, Pr. for A.K. White, 1828.
432, 130, [2] p. DLC; OMC.
                             33374
---- ---- 22d ed. Boston, Pr.
for A.K. White, 1828. 432, 130,
[2] p. NcD.   33375

---- ---- A new ed. in which
the historical events are brought
down to the year 1827. Boston,
S. G. Goodrich, Pr. by A.K.
White, 1828. 432 p. CtMW; DLC;
Ia; IaHA; KHi; KyU; MB; MeHi;
NRU.   33376

---- ---- 23d ed. New York, W.
W. Reed & Co. , 1828. 432, 119
p. DLC; ViU.   33377

---- A history of the United
States of America, on a plan
adapted to the capacity of youths,
and designed to aid the memory
by systematick arrangement and
interesting associations. 17th ed.
[Stereotype ed.] Bellows Falls,
J. I. Cutler & Co. , 1828. 296,
20 p. ICU; MH; NhHi; OClWHi;
PSC; VtU.   33378

---- ---- 23d ed. Boston, Pub.
by S. G. Goodrich, 1828. 296,
20 p. CtHT-W; CtHi; MB; PHi.
                                33379
---- ---- 30th ed. Brattleborough, Holbrook & Fessenden,
[etc. , etc.] 1828. 296, 18 p.
KyHi;MH.   33380
---- ---- Greenfield, Mass. , A.
Phelps and A. Clark, 1828. 296,
20 p. MDeeP; MH.   33381

---- Outlines of modern geography on a new plan, carefully
adapted to youth... Boston, Pub.
by Richardson & Lord, 1828.
250 p. MConA.   33382

---- ---- Brattleboro, Holbrook
& Fessenden, 1828. 252 p. ICSX;
MH; VtBrt.   33383

Goodrich, Chauncey Allen, 1790-
1860
  Elements of Greek grammar.
4th ed. , enl. and imp. Hartford,
O. D. Cooke, publisher [c1828]
247 p. CtHT-W; CtMW; IaHoL;
InTR; KBB; MB; MBC; MH;
MWiW; MiDSH; MsJMC; NN; NcU;
OCl; PLF; RPB; TxU; ViRU;
ViU.   33384

[Goodrich, Samuel Griswold]
1793-1860
  The child's botany... Boston,
S. G. Goodrich, 1828. 115 p.
CSmH; DLC; KU; MB; MH;

PU.   33385

[----] Outlines of chronology,
ancient and modern; being an
introduction to the study of history. On the plan of the Rev.
David Blair. 4th ed. Boston,
Pub. by Richardson & Lord,
and Samuel G. Goodrich, 1828.
232 p. CtHT-W; MB; MH;
PPPrHi; RPB.   33386

[----] Outlines of political economy. On the plan of the Rev.
David Blair; adapted to the use
of schools in the United States
of America. Boston, S. G. Goodrich [Dutton & Wentworth, prs.]
1828. 216 p. ICMcC; KU; M;
MW; NjR.   33387

[----] Outlines of the history of
ancient Rome, embracing its
antiquities; on the plan of the
Rev. David Blair. Adapted to
schools in the United States.
With engravings. Boston, S. G.
Goodrich [Press of Isaac R.
Butts & Co.] 1828. x, 312 p.
MB; MNe.   33388

[----] Outlines of the history of
England, on the plan of the Rev.
David Blair. Adapted to the use
of schools in the United States.
Boston, S. G. Goodrich [Exam-
iner press. Hiram Tupper, pr.]
1828. 391 p. TNJ.   33389

[----] The tales of Peter Par-
ley about America. Boston,
Carter, Hendee and Co. [1828]
[Info. on p 4 "Note to the sec-
ond ed... Boston, 1828"] 160 p.
MH.   33390

[----] The tales of Peter Parley
about Europe. Boston, S. G. Goodrich [Isaac R. Butts & Co. , prs.]
1828. 136 p. DLC; KU; MB; NSYU.
                                33391
[Goodwin, Ezra Shaw]
  Alice Bradford, or The birth

day's experience of religion.
Boston, N. S. Simpkins & Co.,
1828. 51 p. MH.   33392

Goody Two Shoes
The history of Goody Two
Shoes. Cooperstown, Pr. and
sold by H. and E. Phinney,
1828. 31 p. DLC.   33393

The gooseberry bush. Portland,
Shirley and Hyde, 1828. 24 p.
MCNC.   33394

Gordon, Thomas Francis, 1787-
1860
A map of the state of New
Jersey with part of the adjoining states. Compiled under the
patronage of the Legislature of
said state by Thomas Gordon.
Engraved by H. S. Tanner, assisted by E. B. Dawson & W. Allen. Trenton, The author; Philadelphia, H. S. Tanner, 1828.
Col. map. 138 x 81 cm. DeGE;
NjT; PHi; PPAmP.   33395

Gother, John
A papist misrepresented and
represented; or, A twofold char-
acter of popery. ... From the
19th London ed. Rev. by a Cath-
olic clergyman of Baltimore.
Philadelphia, Pub. by Eugene
Cummiskey. Stereotyped by L.
Johnson, 1828. 86 p. MBC;
MChB; MdW.   33396

Gould, Marcus Tullius Cicero.
See Report of the trial of Friends.

The governor of Florida. [Phila-
delphia, 1828] [4 p.] [Acts of the
governor of Florida. "By their
fruits ye shall know them."]
PPL.   33397

Governor's election. See Democratic Party. Kentucky.

Graham, Mrs. Isabella (Marshall) 1742-1814

The power of faith: exemplified in the life and writings of
the late Mrs. Isabella Graham
of New York. 6th ed. Stereotyped by E. White... New York,
Pub. by Jonathan Leavitt; Boston. Crocker & Brewster. Wm.
A. Mercein, pr., 1828. 304 p.
Me; NhHi; PSC; ViL.   33398

Graham, John Andrew
Memoirs of John Horne Tooke,
together with his valuable speech-
es and writings; also, containing
proofs identifying him as author
of the celebrated letters of Jun-
ius. New York, Pr. by A.
Gould & L. Jacobus, for Steph-
en Gould, 1828. 238 p. CSmH;
CU; CtHC; CtHT-W; CtY; GDu;
IU; IaDa; MB; MH; MWA;
MdBE; MdBJ; MeLB; MiD; MiU-
C; MoK; NGH; NN; NNC; NNUT;
NWM; NjR; OO; PPL; PPi; RNR;
TNJ; VtMiM; WHi; BrMus.
                             33399

Graham, T., and Dye, K.
Saddlery. The subscribers
respectfully inform their friends
and the public, that they have
entered into partnership, under
the firm of Graham & Dye, for
the purpose of carrying on the
saddlery business, in all its
branches... T. Graham, K. Dye.
Washington, Ia. Feb. 1828. Bdsd.
In.   33400

[Graham, Thomas John] 1795?-
1876
Sure methods of improving
health, and prolonging life... 1st
Amer. ed., with additions.
Philadelphia, Carey, Lea &
Carey; New York, G. & C. Car-
vill; [etc., etc.] 1828. 248 p.
[2] ads. CSmH; CtMW; CtY;
KyLx; IU-M; LU; MPB; MdBM;
MoS; OC; PHi; PPL; RPB.
                             33401

A grammar of the Greek language: with an appendix: originally composed for the college-

school at Gloucester: and now re-
published with additions.   First
Cambridge ed. Cambridge, Pub.
by Hilliard and Brown, Hilliard,
Metcalf & Co., prs., 1828. viii,
156, 132, viii p. RPB.   33402

Grandpapa's drawer opened. New-
York, Pr. by W. B. Gilley, 1828.
141 p. DLC; KU; MdHi; WHi.
                            33403
Granger, Gideon
   Reasons for voting against the
grant of $11,870.50 to Governor
Tompkins. [E. & E. Hosford,
prs., Albany Apr. 10, 1828] 12
p. NN.   33404

Grant, Duncan
   An address delivered in the
Gaelic Chapel, Aberdeen, to the
children attending the Aberdeen
Sabbath Evening Schools... Rev.
by the Committee of Publication
American Sunday-School Union.
Philadelphia, I. Ashmead & Co.,
prs., 1828. 134 p. IaDuU;
MMeT; NHuntL.   33405

Grayson, William John, 1788-
1863
   An oration, delivered in the
College Chapel before the Clario-
sophic Society incorporate, and
the inhabitants of Columbia on
the 3rd Dec. 1827. Charleston,
A. E. Miller, 1828. 19 p. DLC;
ScU.   33406

Great Britain
   Cases argued and decreed in
the High Court of Chancery...
[1660-1697] From the 2d London
ed., carefully corr. from the
many gross errors of the former
impression. To which are also
added proper references to the
ancient and modern books of the
law. New York, O. Halsted.
Philadelphia, J. Grigg, 1828. 3
v. in 1. CSt; DLC; ICLaw; L;
MiDB; MnU; NNLI; NcD;
NjR; Nv; OClW; PPV; PU-L;

U.   33407

---- Reports of cases argued and
determined in the English courts
of common law. With tables of
the cases and principal matters.
Edited by Thomas Sergeant and
John C. Lowber, Esqrs., of the
Philadelphia Bar. Vol. XI [-XIII]
Containing cases in the courts of
King's Bench and Common Pleas,
and in the Circuit, in 1823
[-1827]. Philadelphia, Philip H.
Nicklin, law bookseller, 1828.
[Mifflin & Parry, prs.] 3 vols.
Ia; In-Sc; LNT-L; MdBB; MdUL;
Ms; PScrLL; U.   33408

---- Reports of cases argued and
determined in the High Court of
Chancery during the time of Lord
Chancellor Eldon, by James Rus-
sell... New York, Gould &
Banks, 1828. vii, 623 p. C;
CoU; In-SC; KyLxT; KyU-L; MH-
L; Md; MiDu-L; Ms; NIC-L; Nj;
OClW; OrSC; PP; Sc-SC; ViU;
VtU.   33409

---- The reports of the most
learned Sir Edmund Saunders...
of several pleadings and cases in
the Court of King's Bench in the
time of the reign of... King
Charles the Second [1666-1672]...
4th Amer. from the 5th London
ed. by John Patteson and Edward Vaughan Williams, Philadelphia, John Grigg, 1828. 2 vols.
in 3. Ct; F-SC; ICLaw; IEN-L;
ICI-L; LNT-L; MH-L; MiD-B;
NjP; PPiAL; PU-L; WaU.
                            33410
---- A supplement to Vesey,
junior's reports of cases in
chancery, containing notes occa-
sionally illustrated by cases decided by Lords Hardwicke, King
&c. from the mss. of Mr. For-
rester. By John E. Hovenden.
Philadelphia, Philip H. Nicklin
[E. &G. Merriam, prs., Brook-
field] 1828.   IaDaGL; In-SC;

KyLxT; MiD-B; NNC-L; Nj;
OCLaw; P; PP; PPiAl; Sc-SC;
ViU; WaU; WvW.   33411

Great Republican meeting. See
National Republican Party. New
York.

Green, Ashbel, 1762-1848
    Memoirs of the Rev.
Joseph Eastburn, stated preacher/in the
Mariner's church, Philadelphia...
By Ashbel Green, D. D. Phila-
delphia, Pub. by G. W. Mentz,
1828. vi, 208 p. CSmH; CtHT-
W; CtY; IC; ICN; KHi; MB;
MBAt; MH; MWA; MiD-B; MnHi;
MoS; NBLiHi; NNC; NRAB; NjP;
NjPT; NjR; OClWHi; PHi; PP;
PPL; PPPrHi; PU; RPB; TMSC;
BrMus.   33412

Green, Joseph C.
    An appeal to the Christian pub-
lic; containing the discipline of
the Trinitarian Church in Concord, Mass., with Joseph C.
Green: also his Defence... Boston, 1828. 36 p. ICU; MB; MBD;
MH-AH; MHi; MWA.   33413

Green, Roland
    A treatise on the cultivation of
ornamental flowers... with directions for the general treatment of
bulbous flower roots... Boston,
Pub. by John B. Russell, press
of I. R. Butts & Co., 1828. 60 p.
IaBo; LNHT; MB; MBH; MWA;
NIC; NNNBG; PMA; BrMus.
                         33414
Green, Samuel
    The practical accountant, or,
Farmers' and mechanicks' best
method of book-keeping... Middletown (Conn.), Pub. by Wm. H.
Niles. Stereotyped by A. Chandler, New York, 1828. 12 p. (Part
of Daboll's schoolmaster's assistant.) TNJ.   33415

Greene, Daniel, comp.
    Conference hymns; selected
from various authors, for the use
of the pious of every denomination...2d ed. Providence, R.I.,
Pub. by Hutchens and Cory [R.
Meacham, pr.] 1828. 47, [1] p.
CSmH; DLC; MH.   33416

Greene, Nathaniel
    An address, delivered at Fan-
euil Hall, Boston, January 8,
1828. Boston, Pub. by Richardson & Lord, 1828. 22, [1] p.
MWA; MdBJ; MiD-B; NhHi; RPB;
T; BrMus.   33417

Greene county almanack for 1829.
By Edwin E. Prentiss. Catskill,
Nathan G. Elliott; Hudson, Rural
Repository [1828] 18 l. NCooHi.
                         33418
Greenleaf, Abner
    Address delivered at Jefferson
Hall Portsmouth, N. H. Jan. 8,
1828, being the thirteenth anniver-
sary, of Jackson's victory at
New Orleans. Portsmouth, N. H.,
Gideon Begs, pr., 1828. 13 p.
MnHi; NhD; NhHi.   33419

Greenleaf, Jeremiah, 1791-1864
    Grammar simplified; or, An
ocular analysis of the English
language. 20th ed., corr., enl.,
and imp. by the author... Hartford, D. F. Robinson, publisher,
1828. 50 p. COMC.   33420

---- ---- 20th ed., corr., enl.
and imp. by the author. Brattleboro, Holbrook & Fessenden,
1828. 2 p. l. [7]-50 p.
CtMW; CtY; DLC; MH; OO; PU;
TxU; VtMiS.   33421

Greenleaf, Jonathan, 1785-1865
    A doctrinal catechism. Port-
land, Shirley & Hyde, prs., 1828.
31 p. Williamson: 3916. 33422

The green-room remembrancer,
or The actor's jest-book. ...
New-York, Elton's theatrical
play, print and song store, 1828.

34 p. MH.   33423

Greenwood, Francis William Pitt
    The classical reader; a selec-
tion of lessons in prose and
verse from the most esteemed
English and American writers.
Intended for the use of the higher
classes in public and private
seminaries. Boston, Lincoln &
Edmands, 1828. 408 p. CtHT-W;
MH; MWA; MdBP; Nh.   33424

---- Lives of the twelve apostles;
with explanatory notes. Boston,
Hilliard, Gray, Little and Wil-
kins [Examiner Press, Hiram
Tupper, pr.] 1828. 148 p. FTU;
ICMe; KWiU; MBAU; MBAt; MBC;
MH-AH; MNtcA; MWA; MoS;
MoSC; NB; ScSp.   33425

---- The prospects of Christian-
ity. A sermon delivered at the
ordination of the Rev. Warren
Burton as minister of the Third
Congregational Society in Cam-
bridge. Boston, Pub. by Bowles
& Dearborn, Isaac R. Butts, pr.
1828. 22 p. CtY; ICMe; MBAU;
MH; MHi; MWA; MiD-B; PHi;
RPB; BrMus.   33426

---- A sermon delivered at the
ordination of the Rev. Wm. Par-
sons Lunt... New York, Pub. by
David Felt [Boston-Examiner
Press. Hiram Tupper, pr.] 1828.
50 p. CBPac; CtY; DLC; ICMe;
ICN; ICU; MB; MBAt; MBC; MH;
MHi; MNtcA; MW; MiD-B; MnHi;
NIC; NjPT; OClWHi; PHi;
PPAmP; BrMus.   33427

Gregg, Daniel H.
    An address delivered before
the Newton Temperance Society,
July 4, 1828... Pub. by the Society. Boston, True & Greene,
prs., 1828. 26, [2] p. MBAt;
MH; MWA; NjPT; BrMus. 33428

Gregg, J.

An apology for withdrawing
from the Methodist Episcopal
Church; and a blow at the roots
of partyism. By J. and J. Gregg.
Lexington, Ky., Pr. by J.G.
Norwood, at the "Old Hotel."
1828. 23 p. KyU (not located)
                          33429
Grew, Henry, 1781-1862
    Address delivered before the
Peace Society of Hartford and
vicinity, Sept. 7, 1828. Hart-
ford, Pub. by the Society, P.
Canfield, pr., 1828. 22 p. Ct;
CtHT-W; ICT; MH-AH; MNBedf;
WHi.   33430

Gridley, Saleh, 1767?-1826?
    The mill of the muses... Ex-
eter [N.H.] T. Gridley, 1828.
267 p. CSmH; CtY; DLC; ICU;
IU; MB; NhD; NhHi; PU; RPB;
Vt.   33431

[Grierson, Miss]
    The student's walk; or A Sab-
bath in the country... Baltimore,
Armstrong and Plaskitt, R.J.
Matchett, pr., 1828. 116 p. DLC;
MNS.   33432

[----] A visit to the Isle of
Wight. By the author of "Pierre
and his family," "The catachist,"
&c. Rev. by the Committee of
Publication of the American Sunday School Union. Philadelphia,
1828. 87 p. CtY; IObB; BrMus.
                          33433
Griffin, Edward Dorr, 1770-1837
    Building the walls of Zion. A
sermon preached before the annual convention of the Congregational ministers of Massachusetts, in
Boston, May 29, 1828. Lexington, Ky., Repr. and sold by
Thomas T. Skillman, 1828. 23 p.
ICMcC; MdBM; PPPrHi. 33434

---- A sermon preached before
the annual convention of the Congregational ministers of Massachusetts, in Boston, May 29,

1828. Boston, T. R. Marvin, pr.
1828. 24 p. CBPac; CSmH; CtY;
DLC; ICU; InCW; MBAt; MH-AH;
MHi; MNtcA; MWA; MeBaT;
MiD-B; NCH; NjPT; NjR; OClW;
PLT; RPB; BrMus.   33435

---- A sermon preached September 2, 1828, at the dedication of
the new chapel connected with
Williams College, Mass. ... Williamstown, Pr. by Ridley Bannister, 1828. 37 p. CSmH; MWiW.
                           33436

Griffith, Isaac
   Galanthe, the angel of the ruby
tower: in six cantos. To which
are added the adventures of
Francisco. .. Philadelphia, E.
Littell, Wm. Brown, pr., 1828.
84 p. RPB.   33437

Griffiths, Elijah
   Observations on fevers, &c.
... Read before the College of
Physicians, Philadelphia, the last
Tuesday in April, and the last
Tuesday in June, 1828. [From
Vol. xv. No. xliv of the American Medical Recorder.] 46 p.
[Philadelphia, 1828] PPL. 33438

Griggs & Dickinson's American
primer improved: being a selection of words the most easy of
pronunciation; adapted to the capacities of young beginners...
Philadelphia, Griggs & Dickinson,
1828. 36 p. DLC.   33439

Grimke, Thomas S.
   Resolutions submitted to the
Senate by Thomas S. Grimke,
one of the members from St.
Philip's and St. Michael's, 12th
December, 1828. [Washington?
1828] 1 p. DLC.   33440

Grimm, Jakob Ludwig Karl
   German popular stories, translated from the Rinder und Hans
Märchen. Collected by M. M.
Grimm, from oral tradition. New

York, Charles S. Francis, and
Monroe & Francis, Boston, 1828.
214 p. VtMiM.   33441

Grimshaw, William, 1782-1852
   History of France, from the
foundation of the monarchy, by
Clovis, to the final abdication of
Napoleon. Philadelphia, Pub. by
J. Grigg [pr. by Lydia R. Bailey]
1828. 410 p. DLC; GMiW; KyDC;
LU; MNe; MSo; MoS; NCH;
PPL; TxD-T.   33442

Griswold, Alexander Viets, bp.,
1766-1843
   Address to the diocesan convention, held at Bellows Falls,
Vt., Sept. 24, 1828. Middlebury,
Pr. by J. W. Copeland, 1828.
8 p. MBC.   33443

Griswold, Charles
   An address, delivered at Hadlyme, Oct. 21, 1828, before the
Middlesex Association, for the
Promotion of Temperance. Middletown, Conn., From the Gazette Press. By Parmelee &
Greenfield [1828?] 18 p. Ct;
CtHi; PPL.   33444

Groves, John
   A Greek and English dictionary, comprising all the words in
the writings of the most popular
Greek authors; With the difficult inflections in them and in
the Septuagint and New Testament:
Designed for the use of schools
and the under graduate course of
a collegiate education. ... With
corr. and additional matter, by
the American editor. Boston,
Hilliard, Gray, Little, and Wilkins, 1828. vii, 644 p. KyHi;
MH; OMC.   33445

Guido. See Embury, Mrs. Emma
Catherine (Manley).

Gummere, John, 1784-1845
   A treatise on surveying...

Particularly adapted to the use of schools... 5th ed. imp. Philadelphia, Kimber & Sharpless, Adam Waldie and Co., prs., 1828. 216 p. DLC; In; MnU; NP; OCU; OOxM; PHC; PHi; PSC; ScC.
33446

Gummere, Samuel R.
Elementary exercises in geography, for the use of schools... 6th ed., corr. and imp. Philadelphia, Kimber and Sharpless, A. Waldie & Co., prs., 1828. 180 p. PPL; PU.
33447

Gurley, Henry Hosford
Speech of Mr. Gurley, of Louisiana, delivered in committee of the whole house in support of his motion to amend the bill for the relief of Marigny d'Auterive, January 11, 1828. Washington, Pr. by Peter Force, 1828. 16 p. MH.
33448

Guyon, Jeanne Marie (Bouvier de La Motte) 1648-1717
Die heilige liebe Gottes und die unheilige naturliebe nach ihren unterschiedenen wirkungen, in xliv anmuthigen sinnbildern und erbaulichen versen vorgestellet. Aus dem französischen der Madame I. M. B. de la Mothe Guion truelich verdeutschet und mit ferneren betrachtungen, aus ihren sämmtlichen biblischen schriften erläutert, von G. T. St. Lancaster, Jacob Schweitzer, 1828. Gedruckt von Johann Bär. 360 p. MH; MdW; MiU-C; P; PHi; PLFM; PLT; PP; PPG; PPL; PPLT; PPeSchw; PU.
33449

H

H., See Carey, Mathew.

Hack, Maria, 1778-1844
Familiar illustrations of the principal evidences and design of Christianity. Philadelphia, Pr.

and pub. by Thos. Kite, 1828. 202, [1] ad. p. InRE; MB; PHC; PHi; PPL; PSC-Hi. 33450

---- Harry Beaufoy; or, The pupil of nature... Philadelphia, Pr. and pub. by Thos. Kite, 1828. iv, [1]-95 p. PHC; PSC-Hi.
33451

The Hagerstown town and country almanack for 1829. By Charles F. Egelmann. Hagerstown, J. Gruber and D. May [1828] Drake 2563.
33452

Haile, William
Speech of Mr. Haile, of Mississippi, on the proposed alteration of the tariff. Delivered in the House of Representatives of the United States, April 7, 1828. Washington, Green & Jarvis, 1828. 7 p. OClWHi.
33453

[Hale, Nathan] 1784-1863
The American system, or the effects of high duties on imports designed for the encouragement of domestic industry; with remarks on the late annual treasury report. Boston, From Nathan Hale's press, 1828. 86 p. CtHT-W; CtY; DLC; DeGE; ICJ; IU; MBAt; MH; MHi; MWA; MiD-B; NNS; Nh; OO; PHi; RPB; WHi.
33454

[Hale, Sarah Preston (Everett)]
Boston reading lessons for primary schools... Boston, Richardson & Lord, 1828. 142, [2] p. CSt; DLC; KU; MB; MH; NNC-T; PU.
33455

Halen, Juan Van, conde de Peracamps, 1788-1864
Narrative of Don Juan Van Halen's imprisonment in the dungeons of the Inquisition at Madrid... New York, Pr. by J. & J. Harper for Collins and Hannay [etc.] 1828. xv, [25]-388 p. CSmH; PPL.
33456

---- ---- Ed. from the original Spanish manuscript by the author of "Don Esteban" and "Sandoval." New York, J. and J. Harper [etc.] 1828. 2 v. in 1. CtMW; CtY; GDC; ICMe; ICU; KyLx; MB; MWA; MWiW; MiU; NNS; NcA-S; Nh; NhHi; O; OCY; P; PU; RPB; ScC. 33457

[Hall, Edward Brooks]
A sketch of the life and character of the Hon. Samuel Howe. From the Christian Examiner, Vol. V, No. III. Boston, Hiram Tupper, pr., 1828. 20 p. M; MH; NNC; OCHP; RPB; BrMus. 33458

Hall, Frederick
An oration, on the importance of cultivating the sciences: delivered at Dartmouth College, before the New Hampshire Alpha of the Phi Beta Kappa, Aug. 21, 1828. Baltimore, Pr. by J. Robinson, 1828. 28 p. CSmH; CtY; DLC; MH-AH; MdBS; MdHi; MiD-B; NCH; NNC; NjPT; OC; PPL; PPPrHi; BrMus. 33459

Hall, Harrison, b. 1785.
The American ornithology, with seventy-six splendid coloured engravings. By Alexander Wilson. [Announcement of new edition being prepared by Harrison Hall. Philadelphia, 1828] 3 p. PPL. 33460

Hall, Willard, 1780-1875
A defence of the American Sunday School Union against the changes of its opponents, in an address delivered at the 1st anniversary of the New Castle County Sabbath School Union, March 26, 1828. Philadelphia, Pr. by J. Clarke, 1828. 18 p. CtY; DeWI; MBC; MH; MWA; NCH; PHi; PPAmP; PPPrHi; BrMus. 33461

[Hamilton,] pseud.
An address to the Federalists of New-Jersey. [Trenton? 1828] 8 p. PPL. 33462

---- Review of a late pamphlet, under the signature of "Brutus." By Hamilton... Charleston, Pr. and pub. by James S. Burges, 1828. 1 p. l., [5]-105 p. CSmH; DLC; MBAt; MH; MHi; PPAmP; PPL; ScC; ScU. 33463

---- See Carey, Mathew.

Hamilton, James, 1786-1857
Speech of Mr. Hamilton, of S. Carolina on Mr. Randolph's motion indefinitely to postpone the tariff bill; delivered in the House of Representatives of the U. S., April 19th, 1828. Washington, Green & Jarvis, 1828. 15 p. NHi; NN; NjR; PPAmP; ScCC; ScU. 33464

---- A speech on the operation of the tariff on the interests of the South, and the constitutional means of redressing its evils: delivered at Walterborough, on the 21st Oct. 1828, by James Hamilton, jun., at a public dinner given to him by his constituents of Colleton district. Charleston, Pr. by A. E. Miller, 1828. 24 p. CtY; DLC; ICU; IU; MH; NN; NcD; PHi; PPAmP; RPB; ScC; ScU. 33465

[Hammon, Charles] 1779-1840
...View of General Jackson's domestic relations, in reference to his fitness for the presidency. [Washington? 1828] 20 p. DLC; MiD-B; NSyU; OClW. 33466

Hampshire and Hampden Canal Company
...An act to authorize the Hampshire and Hampden Canal Company to construct a canal from Northampton to the North line of this commonwealth. [Boston? 1828?] 22 p. DLC. 33467

Hampshire Bible Society
    The twelfth annual report of
the directors of the Hampshire
Bible Society, presented at the
annual meeting Oct. 8, 1828.
Northampton, T. Watson Shepard,
pr., 1828. 12 p. MWA.   33468

Hampshire Education Society
    Report of the directors of the
Hampshire Education Society, at
their fourteenth annual meeting,
Oct. 8, 1828. Northampton, T.
Watson Shepard, pr., 1828. 12 p.
MWA.   33469

Hampshire Missionary Society
    The twenty-sixth report of the
trustees of the Hampshire Missionary Society, presented at the annual meeting, Oct. 11, 1827.
Northampton, Pr. by H. Ferry &
Co., 1828. 16 p. MNF.   33470

Handbuch fur Deutsche; Enthaltend
Formen zu Handschriften, welche
den Burgern der Vereinigten
Staaten nutzlich und dienlich seyn
Konnen... Zweyte und verbesserte
Auflage. Reading, Johann Ritter
und Comp., 1828. viii, 108, [17]
p. MH; P; PHi; PPL; BrMus.
                              33471
Handel, Georg Friedrich, 1685-
1752
    The words of the Oratorio of
the Messiah, by Handel; As performed by the Musical Fund Society of Philadelphia... Philadelphia, Pub. by the Musical Fund
Society, 1828. 20 p. 10 1. on v.
of title. MH; PHi; PPL.   33472

---- ---- Another issue. Philadelphia, Pub. by the Musical
Fund Society, 1828. 20 p. 9 lines
on verso of title "Leader, Mr.
Hupfeld" omitted. PPL.   33473

Hannah Jane: or, First reading
lessons for children, in words of
one syllable. Boston, Bowles
and Dearborn, 1828. 13 p.

MB.   33474

Hanney, W.
    Massachusetts quickstep. Bos-
ton, Pub. for the author by C.
Bradlee [1828] 2 p. MB.   33475

Harbison, Massy (White) "Mrs.
J. Harbison," b. 1770.
    A narrative of the sufferings
of Massy Harbison, from Indian
barbarity, giving an account of
her captivity, the murder of her
two children, her escape, with
an infant at her breast; together
with some account of the cruel-
ties of the Indians, on the Allegheny River, &c., during the
years 1790, '91, '92, '93, '94.
Communicated by herself. Pittsburgh, Pr. by D. & M. Mac
Lean, 1828. 98 p. DLC; MH;
MWA.   33476

Hare, Robert, 1781-1858
    A compendium of the course
of chemical instruction in the
medical department of the University of Pennsylvania. ... For
the use of his pupils. Philadelphia, J. G. Auner [etc.] 1828.
xiv, 2,310, 46 p. CSt; CtHT;
DNLM; GU-M; IEN-M; KU; MH;
MdU; MiU; MnU; NGH; NNG;
OCLloyd; P; PPAmP; PPC; PU;
TNJ; WaSK.   33477

Harmon, Joel, 1773-1833
    The Sacred minstrel, contain-
ing a concise introduction to music... and a selection of Psalm
and hymn tunes... Also, several
anthems and set-pieces; designed
for worshipping assemblies and
singing societies. Carlisle [Pa.]
Pr. by Geo. Fleming, 1828. 162
p. RPB.   33478

The harp of Delaware. See Lofland, John.

Harriet and her scholars; a Sabbath school story. Revised by

the Committee of Publication. 2d
ed. Philadelphia, American Sunday School Union, 1828. 90 p.
NcU.   33479

Harris, Samuel, 1814-1899
Questions on Christian experience and character... Haverhill,
[N. H.] Pr. by A. W. Thayer,
1828. 24 p. NhD; WHi.   33480

Harris, Wiley P.
A defence of Thomas B. Reed,
against the charges prefered a-
gainst him by Wiley P. Harris,
of Holmesville. Natchez, Pr. by
Wm. C. Grissam & Co., 1828.
22 p. MWA; WHi.   33481

Harrison, H.
Hydraulicus; or improvement
of the Mississippi; offering a
plan for the reduction of its over-
flow, and of that of its alluvial
tributary streams. The expense
arising from the execution of this
plan, the apportionment of that
expense, and the distribution of
it among the different parties who
may receive permanent benefits
from the effectuation of it. To
which is subjoined, a brief enu-
meration of some of the most
important consequences which
will result. Cincinnati, Geo. T.
Williamson, pr., 1828. 67, [1]
p. CSmH; ICJ; MB; MHi; MWA;
O; PPL; BrMus.   33482

Harrison, Jesse Burton, 1805-
1841
A discourse on the prospects
of letters and taste in Virginia,
pronounced before the Literary
and Philosophical Society of
Hampden-Sydney College at their
fourth anniversary, in September,
1827. Cambridge, Pub. by Hilliard and Brown, 1828. 42 p.
DLC; PPL; RPB.   33483

Harrison, Randolph
To the speakers and members

of both houses of the General Assembly of Virginia. Randolph
Harrison begs leave to offer a
respectful memorial... in relation to the Cartersville Bridge
Company...[1828] 4 p. Vi.
                          33484
Harrison, William Henry, 1773-
1841
Gen. Harrison's address. The
following able address was delivered by Gen. Harrison, our
senator in congress, at a meeting held by the friends of the administration, at the circus in the
city of Cincinnati, in September
last. We recommend it to the at-
tentive perusal of every friend to
his country. Editor Crisis & Em-
porium [Cincinnati, 1828?] 7 p.
OCHP.   33485

Harry Hobart; or A friend in
need is a friend indeed. Pub. by
Wait, Greene & Co., 1828. Boston, Press of Isaac R. Butts &
Co., 1828. 36 p. MLow; NNC.
                          33486
Hart, J. C.
A modern atlas of fourteen
maps. Drawn and engraved to illustrate Hart's geographical exercises...5th ed. rev. and corr.
New York, R. Lockwood; Philadelphia, J. Grigg & A. Finley,
1828. 1 p. l., 14 fold. maps.
DLC.   33487

Hartford city directory, for
1828. [Hartford] Pub. by Ariel
Ensign [1828] 60 p. CtHi; MWA;
NHi.   33488

Hartford County Sabbath School
Union
First annual report... pre-
sented April 9, 1828. Hartford,
Canfield, 1828. 26 p. CtHi.
                          33489
Hartford Library Company
Catalogue of books belonging
to the Hartford Library Company,
January 1, 1828; and extracts

from the by-laws of said company. Hartford, Goodwin, 1828. 43 p. Ct; CtHT-W; CtHi; CtSoP; ICN; MB.   33490

Hartshorn, John
    Decimal interest table. Calculated for the use of merchants and bankers, at six per cent. Embracing calculations of interest, from 1 dollar to 9900 dollars, from 1 day to 6 months. Contained in 6 small folio pages. Also a table of interest from 1 day to 66 days, and on 1 dollar to 9900 dollars, from 1 month to 9 years upon one page. ... Stereotyped. Containing 17,523 calculations of interest at 6 per cent. On banking principles with rules... Boston, Pub. by the author, 1828. [16] p. CSt; MH.
                                33491

Harvard University
    A catalogue of the officers and students of Harvard University, for the academical year 1828-9, Cambridge, Hilliard and Brown, 1828. 24 p. MH.   33492

---- The second annual report of the president of Harvard University to the overseers on the state of the university, for the academical year 1826-7. Cambridge, Hilliard, Metcalf, and co. , pr. to the university, 1828. 52 p. MH.   33493

Harvest Home meeting of Chester and Montgomery Counties, at the Valley Forge Encampment Ground. July 26, 1828. With remarks and explanations. [Philadelphia? 1828] 29 p. PHi; PPAmP; PPL.
                                33494
Haskett, William J.
    Shakerism unmasked, or, The history of the Shakers; including a form politic of their government as councils, orders, gifts, with an exposition of the five orders of Shakerism, and Ann

Lee's grand foundation vision, in sealed pages. With some extracts from their private hymns which have never appeared before the public. Pittsfield, Pub. by the author, E. H. Walkley, pr. , 1828. 300 p. CSmH; DLC; MA.
                                33495
Hassard, Samuel.
    An oration, delivered at the Union meeting house, in Westerly, R. I. , July 4th, 1828. Pub. by the Committee of Arrangements. Stonington, Pr. by W. & J. B. Storer, 1828. 28 p. NCH; RPB.   33496

Hassler, Ferdinand Rudolph, 1770-1843
    Elements of arithmetic, theoretical and practical; adapted to the use of schools, and to private study. A new stereotype ed. , rev. and cor. New-York, C. Bartlett, 1828. 215, [1] p. CtHT-W; DAU; DLC; ICU; MH; MiU; NIC; NNC; NjR.   33497

---- Elements of the geometry of planes and solids. With four plates. Richmond, The author, 1828. 159 [1] p. DLC; CtY; GU; KHi; LNHT; MB; MiU; NBuG; NCH; NNC; NWM; NjP; OClW; PPAmP; PU; RPB; Vi; ViU.
                                33498
---- A popular exposition of the system of the universe, with plates and tables. New York, G. & C. Carvill, [Gratten, pr.] 1828. x p. , 1 l. , 230 p. , 1 l. CtY; DLC; GU; KHi; LShC; MB; MH; MdAN; MtBu; NN; NNUT; NjR; OClW; PPAmP; VtMiM; VtNN.   33499

Hastings, Thomas
    Musica sacra; or, Utica and Springfield collections united: consisting of Psalm and hymn tunes, anthems, and chants: arranged for two, three or four voices, with a figured bass for the organ

or piano forte... 7th rev. ed.
Utica, Wm. Williams, 1828. 262
p. CtY; NCH.   33500

[----] Selection for the musica
sacra: Being the words of the
set pieces, &c. in that collection of music, together with a
number of other hymns, from
various authors, with references
to tunes suitable for each. Geneva, Pr. by James Bogert, and
for sale at his Bookstore. 1828.
64 p. NN.   33501

Hatin, Jules
Compendium of operative mid-
wifery... New York, Charles S.
Francis, Munroe and Francis,
Boston, [George H. Evans, pr.]
1828. 171 p. CSt-L; DLC;
DNLM; IEN-M; Ia; MBCo; MiHM;
MsU; NBM; NBuU-M; NbU-M;
Nh; PPC; RPM; VtU.   33502

---- A manual of practical ob-
stetrics: arranged so as to afford a concise and accurate description of the management of
preternatural labours; preceded
by an account of the mechanism
of natural labour... With an appendix, containing a physiological
memoir upon the brain. From
the French of M. Magendie, by
Joseph Gardner, M.D. Philadelphia, J. Grigg, 1828. 2 p. l.,
198 p. CtY; DLC; DNLM; ICU-R;
IaU; GDC; GU-M; MB; MdBJ;
MdU-H; MeB; MiKa; MnU;
MoSW-M; NBM; NBuU-M; NNNAM;
OCG; OClM; PPC; PU; RPM;
ScCM.   33503

Haven, Nathaniel Appleton, 1790-
1826
An address delivered before
the teachers of the South Parish
Sunday School in Portsmouth,
New-Hampshire, April 23, 1823.
To which is prefixed a letter on
Sunday Schools. 2d ed. Boston,
Hilliard, Gray, Little and Wil-

kins [Cambridge, Hilliard, Metcalf and Co., Prs. to the Uni-
versity] 1828. 36 p. MH; MHi;
NhHi; VtU; BrMus.   33504

---- The remains of Nathaniel
Appleton Haven. With a memoir
of his life, by George Ticknor.
2d ed. Boston, Hilliard, Gray,
Little and Wilkins, 1828. viii,
368 p. DLC; MB; MBL; MH;
MWA; RPB; TxU; VtMiM.
                           33505
Hawes, Joel, 1789-1867
Lectures addressed to the
young men of Hartford and New-
Haven. Hartford, O.D. Cooke,
publisher, P. Canfield, pr.,
1828. 142 p. CBPac; CtHC;
CtHT-W; CtY; ICN; IaHoL; KWiU;
MB; MPB; MiOC; MsU; NBuU;
NIC; NN; NjP; OClWHi; OMC;
PWcHi; RPB; ViU.   33506

---- ---- 2d ed. Hartford, Pub.
by Oliver D. Cooke and Co.,
Sold also by Hezekiah Howe, New-
Haven. -- Jonathan Leavitt, New-
York, and Croker and Brewster,
Boston. Hudson and Skinner, prs.
1828. 142 p. DLC; KWiU; MA.
                           33507
[Hawthorne, Nathaniel] 1804-1864
Fanshawe, a tale... Boston,
Marsh & Capen, 1828. 141 p.
CSmH; CtY; InU; MB; MBAt; MH;
NBuU; NN; PU; BrMus.   33508

Haynes, Andrew
Reflections on the vanity of all
things under the sun, in a series
of letters, written after the death
of a young lady. Philadelphia, Pr.
for the author by Geo. Siegfried,
1828. 56 p. DLC; NN; BrMus.
                           33509
Haynes, Lemuel, 1753-1833
An interesting controversy between Rev. Lemuel Haynes, minister of a Congregational church
in Rutland, Vt., and Rev. Hosea
Ballou, preacher of the doctrine
of universal salvation. Rutland,

Vt., Pr. by Wm. Fay, 1805; Middlebury, Repub. by Ovid Miner, 1828. 23 p. CtY; MBC; VtMiM; TNF.   33510

[Haywood, John] 1753-1826
Appendix 1818-1828 [to: A. Manual of the laws of North Carolina, Raleigh, 1819] [Raleigh, 1828?] [3]-202 p. DLC; MnU; NIC.   33511

Hazzi, Joseph Ritter von, 1768-1845
Treatise on the culture of silk. See United States. Letter from James Mease--and United States: Silk-worms.

The heart of man; either a temple of God, or a habitation of Satan, represented in ten emblematical figures. Calculated to awaken and promote a Christian disposition. Translated from the fourth German ed. Harrisburg, Pa., Pr. and pub. by Gustavus S. Peters, 1828. 57 p. CSmH.
                                33512
[Heath, James Ewell] 1792-1862
Edge-hill, or, The family of the Fitzroyals. A novel. By a Virginian... Richmond, T.W. White, 1828. 2 v. in 1. CSmH; CtHT-W; DLC; ICU; IU; MBAt; MH; MWA; NIC; NcD; OClWHi; OU; PU; Vi; ViU.   33513

Heber, Reginald, 1783-1826
Narrative of a journey through the upper provinces of India, from Calcutta to Bombay, 1824-1825... In two vols. Philadelphia, Carey, Lea & Carey, [etc.], [Adam Waldie & Co., prs.] 1828. 2 vols. CL; CtHC; CtHT; DeGE; DeWI; GHi; ICU; IU; MB; MDeeP; MsU; NBLiHi; NGH; NNG; NSyU; NcWsW; Nh; NjP; OM; PPF; PPL; PPLT; RNR; ScC; ScU; TNF; TNJ; UU; Vi; ViRVal; VtMiM.   33514

---- Palestine, and other poems.

By the late Right Rev. Reginald Heber, D.D. Lord Bishop of Calcutta. Now first collected. With a memoir of his life. Philadelphia, Carey, Lea and Carey--Chestnut Street. Sold in New York by G. & C. Carvill--Boston by Monroe & Francis [Adam Waldie & Co., prs.] 1828. [4] lxxi [1] 245 p. CtHT; CtY; DLC; ICMe; IEG; MB; MeB; NN; NNG; NcD; Nh; NjP; PHi; PPL; PU; ScC.   33515

Hedge, Levi, 1766-1844
Elements of logick; or, A summary of the general principles and different modes of reasoning. Stereotype ed. Boston, Hilliard, Gray, Little and Wilkins, 1828. 178 p. CoOrd; IU; MC; MQ; MiU; PAtM.   33516

Heeren, Arnold Hermann Ludwig 1760-1842
History of the states of antiquity... Northampton, Mass., Pub. by S. Butler, and G. & C. Carvill. New York, T. Watson Shepard, pr., 1828. vi, 487, [1] p. DLC; IaPeC; LNHT; MeLB; PPL.   33517

Helen Maurice: or, The benefit of early religious instruction exemplified. By a Sunday School teacher. Written for the American Sunday School Union. Philadelphia, American Sunday School Union, 1828. 144 p. DLC; MChiA; NcWsS; BrMus.   33518

Hellenbroek, Abraham
A specimen of divine truths... Rutgers Press, New York, Pr. and pub. by Wm. A. Mercein... And for sale at the office of the Missionary Society, 1828. 48 p. NN.   33519

Hemans, Mrs. Felicia Dorothea (Browne), 1793-1835
Poems by Mrs. Felicia He-

mans. A new collection. Boston, Hilliard, Gray, Little and Wilkins, 1828. 2 v. GU; KyDC; MB; MH; MS; TxU.   33520

---- The poetical works of Mrs. Felicia Hemans. 4th Amer. ed. To which is added many pieces not contained in any former ed. In two volumes. New-York, Evert Duyckinck [W. E. Dean, pr.] 1828. CLCM; CU; CtHC; CtHT-W; DLC; KWiU; MWA; MdBL; MsJMC; TBriK; BrMus.
                                        33521
---- ---- 5th Amer. ed. To which is added many pieces not contained in any former ed. New Haven, Nathan Whiting, 1828. 2 v. CtY; DLC; MH; MiU; NNC; PU.   33522

---- Records of woman: with other poems. Boston, Hilliard, Gray, Little and Wilkins [Cambridge, Hilliard, Metcalf, and Company, prs. to the University] 1828. [4], vi, 253 p. DLC; IaCrM; MB; MH; MdBL; MeB; MoK; MoSW; NcA-S; ViU. 33523

---- ---- New York, Wm. B. Gilley, Sleight & George, pr., 1828. 324 p. C; CtY; ICA; MBAt; NBLiHi; NHi; NNS; NNUT; OO; PP; WHi.   33524

Henderson, E. A.
    Grammar made easy and interesting; or, A practical grammar of the English language... Dover, Inquirer office, 1828. 80 p. WU.   33525

Hendricks, William
    Speech of Mr. Hendricks on the bill to graduate the price of the public lands. Delivered in the Senate... January 28, 1828. Washington, Pr. by Gales & Seaton, 1828. 26 p. DLC; MH.
                                        33526
Henry, Matthew, 1662-1714

A church in the house. A sermon concerning family religion. Preached in London, April 16, 1704. Pittsburgh, Pub. by the Rev. Jos. Patterson, 1828. 36 p. OClWHi.   33527

---- The communicant's companion... Boston, Pub. by Crocker & Brewster; New-York, Jonathan Leavitt [Pr. by Dutton & Wentworth, Boston] 1828. 280 p. ABS; CBPac; ICMcC; KyLoS; MB; MBC; NN; NNG; NbOP; OO.
                                        33528
---- A discourse concerning meekness. 2d Amer. ed. Plymouth, Ezra Collier, 1828. 144 p. KBB; MBC; MH; OO; PSC.
                                        33529
---- An exposition of the Old and New Testaments... with practical remarks and observations by Matthew Henry, edited by the Rev. George Burder and the Rev. Joseph Hughes, A. M. with the life of the author by the Rev. Samuel Palmer. 1st Amer. ed. to which is prefixed a preface, by Archibald Alexander, D. D. ... John P. Haven, New York; Robt. Patterson, Pittsburgh; Towar & Hogan, Philadelphia, 1828-29. 6 vols. CoD; DLC; KSalM; OO.   33530

Henry, Thomas Charlton, 1790-1827
    Etchings from the religious world... Charleston, Observer Office Press, 1828. 215 p. CtHC; CtY; GDC; ICMcC; NcMHi; NjP; PPPrHi; ScCoT; ScU; BrMus.   33531

[Henshaw, David] 1791-1852
    Observations occasioned by the remarks, on the character of Napoleon Bonaparte, pub. in the Christian Examiner vol. IV, no. V. By a citizen of Boston [pseud.] Boston, True & Greene, prs., 1828. 56 p. CSmH; Ct; CtY;

KWiU; MB; MHi; MWA; MiD-B;
MnHi; NN; NjR; PHi; RPB;
BrMus.   33532

Herbert, John C.
    An address delivered in St.
Anne's church, Annapolis, on the
22nd February 1828 at the request of the Society of the Alumni of St. John's College. Annapolis, Pr. by Jeremiah Hughes,
1828. 15 p. CSmH; Md; MdAS;
BrMus.   33533

Herbert Lacy.   See Lister,
Thomas Henry.

Herodotus.
    Herodotus: Translated... By
Rev. William Beloe. In three
volumes. The 2d Amer. from the
last London ed. New York, Pub.
by P. P. Berresford, 1828. 3
vols. AzU; CSt; CtHT; CtY; KBB;
KyU; MB; MBC; MH; MdW;
MeBaT; MiU; MoSU; NNC;
NcWsS; OCX; OMC; OrPD; PP;
PU; PV; ScCliJ; ViU.   33534

Herttell, Thomas
    The demurrer: Or, Proofs
of error in the decision of the
supreme court of the state of
New-York, requiring faith in
particular religious doctrines as
a legal qualification of witnesses;
thence establishing by law a religious test, and a religious
creed. ... New York, Pr. and
pub. by E. Conrad, Sold also at
the bookstores of John Montgomery, Gould & Banks, and Abner
Kneeland, 1828. 158 p. CtHT-W;
DLC; ICMe; MH-AH; MMeT; MWA;
MdBP; MdHi; MiD-B; MiU-L;
NNC; NjR; OCLaw; OO; P;
PPAmP; PPL; RHi; ScU; ViRU.
                                33535
Hertz, Daniel, comp.
    Poetischer himmelsweg, oder
Kleine, geistliche lieder sammlung, zum gebrauch des offentli-
chen und hauslichen gottesdiens-

tes und erbauung aller gottlieben-
den seelen jeder confession. Zusammengetragen von Daniel Hertz
...1. aufl. Lancaster, Gedruckt
bey H. W. Villee, 1828. 4 p. l.,
295, [10] p. CtHT-W; DLC; PHi;
PPL.   33536

Hewitt, John Hill, 1801-1890
    A soldier's the lad I adore
written for and dedicated to Miss
Rock, and sung by her with universal applause adapted to the
original French air of Le petit
tambour. Words & accompaniment by J. H. Hewitt. Baltimore,
Pub. & sold by Geo. Willig,
Junr. [c1828] 3 p. CSmH; CtY.
                                33537
Hibernicus; or, Memoirs of an
Irishman, now in America; containing an account of the principal events of his life, both before and since his emigration;
and interspersed with anecdotes
and observations, humorous, political, and moral. With a supplement. Pittsburgh, Pr. for the
author by Cramer & Spear, 1828.
251 p. ICN; KyU; MB; MdW;
MoSHi; PPi; PPiU.   33538

Hickox, B. H.
    Sermon, preached at Manlius
Square, Feb. 22d, 1828, on the
news of the death of His Excellency, the governor, De Witt
Clinton, by the request of the
committee of arrangements; by
the Rev. B. H. Hickox, A. B.
minister of Christ's church,
Manilus. Onondaga C. H. [N. Y.]
Pr. at the Journal office, 1828.
11 p. CSmH.   33539

Hicks, Elias, 1748-1830
    Letter of Elias Hicks. From
the Friend. Extract from a letter of... ... to a friend in New
Jersey, dated New York, 6 mo.
2nd, 1828. Elias Hicks' reply.
[n. p. , n. d.] 6 p. PSC-Hi.
                                33540

---- Sermons, by Elias Hicks, Ann Jones, and others, of the Society of Friends, at the quarterly meetings of Nine Partners and Stanford, and first day preceding, in fifth month, 1828. Taken in short hand, by Henry P. Hoag, stenographer, Washington, Dutchess county. Brooklyn, Pr. for the proprietor, by Piercy & Burling, (Cover title as above; title page as above except after New-York, pr. for the proprietor.) 1828. 98 p. NJQ; PSC-Hi.
33541

High-School Society of New York
Fourth annual report of the trustees of the High-School Society, of New York, made on Saturday, November 29, 1828, pursuant to the act of incorporation. New York, Pr. by Wm. A. Mercein, 1828. 25 p. DLC; MB; MBAt; OClWHi; PHi; PP; PPL.
33542

Hill, Isaac, 1788-1851
An address, delivered at Concord, N. H. January 8, 1828, being the thirteenth anniversary of Jackson's victory at New-Orleans. Concord, N. H. , Pr. by Manahan, Hoag & Co. , 1828. 44 p. CL; CSmH; DLC; ICN; MB; MBAt; MH; MHi; NN; Nh; NjR; OCHP.
33543

---- An address delivered before the Republicans of Portsmouth and vicinity, July 4, 1828... Concord [N. H.] |H. Hill & Co. , 1828. 14 p. DLC; MBAt; MiD-B; Nh; OCHP; OClWHi; PHi.
33544

[----] Brief sketch of the life, character and services of Major General Andrew Jackson, by a citizen of New-England [pseud.] Concord, N. H. , Pr. by Manahan, Hoag & co. , for Isaac Hill, 1828. 51 p. InHi;MH; MWA; NN; Nh; OCl; OClWHi; WHi.
33545

---- The wise sayings of the

Honorable Isaac Hill. [Concord, N. H. , New Hampshire Journal office, Jan. 8, 1828] 8 p. CSmH; MB; MH; Nh.
33546

Hilliard, Timothy
A sermon preached Oct. 24, 1787... in Hingham. 2d ed. Cambridge, Hilliard, Metcalf and Company, 1828. 22 p. MWA.
33547

Hilliard, Gray, Little, and Wilkins, firm, publishers, Boston.
A catalogue of school and classical books, published by Hilliard, Gray, Little, and Wilkins, Boston [Pr. by T. R. Marvin] 1828. 32 p. DLC; MB; MWA.
33548

Hilton, John T.
An address, delivered before the African Grand Lodge, of Boston, No. 459. June 24th, 1828... on the annual festival of St. John the Baptist. Boston, Pr. by David Hooton, 1828. 16 p. MB; MHi; RPB.
33549

Hinde, Thomas S.
The pilgrim's songster: or A choice collection of spiritual songs, from the best authors. A new ed. , corr. and enl. , with many songs never before in print. Pub. by A. Wright & A. Wolliscroft. Cincinnati, Morgan, Fisher & L'Hommedieu, prs. , 1828. 236 p. OCHP.
33550

Hindmarsh, Robert
A compendium of the true Christian religion. Cincinnati, Repr. from the Manchester ed. by the Western New Jerusalem Printing Society [Looker & Reynolds, prs.] 1828. 197, 3 p. DLC; OUrC.
33551

Hines, William
Address, delivered at the Methodist Chapel in Norwich, December 22, 1827, at the request

of the Norwich Falls Society for the Promotion of Temperance... Norwich, J. Dunham, pr., 1828. 20 p. CSmH; CtHi; MWA. 33552

Hints on female education. See Marks, Elias.

Historical and descriptive lessons, embracing sketches of the history, character and customs of all nations; designed as a companion to Goodrich's, Woodbridge's, and other school geographies, with numerous engravings. Brattleboro, Holbrook & Fessenden, 1828. 336 p. CtY; DLC; IaDaP; NIC. 33553

History of animals. Wendell, J. Metcalf, 1828. 12 l. MWA (14 p.); PP. 33554

History of beasts and birds. Cooperstown, Stereotyped, pr. and sold by H. & E. Phinney, 1828. 30 p. DLC. 33555

The history of fair Rosamond; mistress to Henry II king of England; showing how she came to be so: with her life, remarkable actions and unhappy end. To which is added, the surprising adventures of Henry Twisdon... Philadelphia, Pr. for the booksellers, 1828. 72 p. CSmH; DLC. 33556

History of Goody Two Shoes. See Goody Two Shoes.

History of honest Roger. Founded on fact. By a Clergyman. New-Haven, Pr. for the Bible, Prayer Book and Tract Society, by S. Babcock, 1828. 24 p. CtHi. 33557
...The history of Jacob Newman, the shipwrecked Irish boy. New York, The American Tract Society [1828?] (American Tract Society. Children's tracts: ser. iv, no. 6) 36 p. DLC; MB. 33558

The history of Jenny Hickling. See American Tract Society. New York.

The history of Joe Bennett. Philadelphia. American Sunday School Union, 1828. 31 p. BrMus. 33559
The history of Sindbad the sailor; containing an account of his surprising voyages and miraculous escapes... Boston, Pr. for the publisher, 1828. 95 p. KU; RPB. 33560
History of the Bible. Cooperstown, Pr. by H. & E. Phinney, 1828. 192 p. MWA; NN. 33561

A history of the Indian wars. See Sanders, Daniel Clarke.

A history of the life and public services of Major General Andrew Jackson. Impartially compiled from the most authentic sources. [Philadelphia] 1828. [1], 37 p. PPL. 33562

---- [n. p.] 1828. 1 p. l., 36, [1] p. CSmH; DLC; PPL; WHi; BrMus. 33563

---- Partially [sic] compiled from the most authentic sources. 1828. 32 p. NjR. 33564

History of the Patriarch Abraham. See Simes, William.

[Hitchcock, Edward] 1793-1864
    Pulpit exchanges between the Orthodox and Unitarians. Boston, Pierce & Williams, 1828. 34 p. CBPac; CtHC; CtY; MBC; MLexHi; MWA; NNUT; PPL. 33565
Hitchcock, Calvin, 1787-1867
    The wisdom of God in the selection of his ministers. A sermon, delivered at Sharon, June 11, 1828. Before the Norfolk County Education Society. Boston, Pr. by Crocker and Brewster,

1828. 32 p. CoU; CtHC; DLC;
MB; MBC; MHi; MeBaT; MiD-B;
NNUT; NhD; OO; RPB; BrMus.
                              33566
Hoare, Prince, pseud. See Bick-
erstaffe, Isaac.

Hobart, John Henry, bp. , 1775-
1830
    An address delivered to the
students of the General Theological Seminary of the Protestant
Episcopal Church, in the chapel
of the said Seminary, in the city
of New York, on Sunday, the 27th
of January, A. D. 1828. . . New-
York, Pub. by T. & J. Swords,
1828. 22 p. Ct; CtHT; DLC;
MB; MBAt; NBLiHi; NCH; NIC;
NNG; NNUT; NcU; PHi; TCU;
BrMus.   33567

---- The clergyman's companion,
containing occasional offices of
the Protestant Episcopal Church
with prayers suitable to be used
by the clergy of the said church
in the discharge of their parochi-
al duties. 2d ed. New York, T.
& J. Swords, 1828. 2 v. CBDP;
CtY; IES; MnHi; NNG; NSyU;
ViAlTh; WNaE.   33568

---- The man of God; a sermon,
preached in St. Thomas' Church,
in the city of New-York, at the
institution of the Rev. George
Upfold, into the rectorship of the
said church, on Thursday, the
6th of March, 1828. . . New York,
Pub. by T. and J. Swords, 1828.
26 p.   CtHT; CtY; MH; MHi;
MWA; MiD-B; MnHi; NBLiHi;
NGH; NIC; NNG; NNS; NcU; NjR;
PHi; RPB; WHi; BrMus.   33569

Der Hoch-Deutsche Americanische
calender auf 1829. Von Carl
Friederich Egelmann. German-
taun, M. Billmeyer [1828] 18 l.
DLC; InU; MH; MWA; NN; PHi;
PLF; PPG; PPL; PPeSchw; WHi.
                              33570

Hoch-deutsches Lutherisches
ABC-und namen-büchlein, für
kinder, welche anfangen zu ler-
nen. Verbesserte Ausgabee.
Philadelphia, Gedruckt bey Con-
rad Zentler, 1828. [30] p. MnU.
                              33571
Hodge, Hugh L.
    Essay on expansibility. . . From
the North American Medical and
Surgical Journal. Philadelphia,
J. Dobson, agent, Pr. by James
Kay, Jun. , 1828. 37, 10 p. DLC;
NNNAM.   33572

Hoffman, David
    Memorial and argument in the
case of the ship Blairean, praying
a return of tonnage and duties,
erroneously paid in 1823; addressed to the Senate of the United
States. Baltimore, Pr. by John
D. Toy, 1828. 26 p. DLC; DNA;
MBAt; MH; OOC; ScU.   33573

Hofland, Mrs. Barbara (Wreaks)
Hoole.
    Integrity, a tale. . . Philadel-
phia, Pub. by Thomas T. Ash,
1828. [1], 212 p. MNBedf; MWA;
PHi.   33574

---- Self-denial. A tale. . . . New
York, Gilley, 1828. 194 p. CL;
CtY; RPB.   33575

---- The young cadet; or, Henry
Delamere's voyage to India, his
travels in Hindostan, his account
of the Burmese War, and the wonders of Elora. . . New York, O. A.
Roorbach, W. E. Dean, pr. ,
1828. x, 206 p. CSt; CtHT; LU;
MB; MPB; MWHi; NCanHi; NjP;
OkU; TBriK; TNJ.   33576

---- The young pilgrim, or, Al-
fred Campbell's return to the
East; and his travels in Egypt,
Nubia, Asia Minor, Arabia Pe-
traea, &c. &c. New-York, O. A.
Roorbach, 1828. xii, 211 p.
CtHT; DLC; MB; NcU; NjN;

OClWHi; PHi; ScNC; ViRVal;
WHi.   33577

Hohman, Johann Georg
   Der lange Verborgene Freund,
oder Getreuer und Christlicher
Unterricht fuer jedermann, enthaltend, Wunderbare und prob-
maessige Mittel und Kuenste.
Ephrata, Gedruckt bey J. B.,
1828. 94 p. P; PPL.   33578

A hole in the wall. or, A peep
at the creed-worshipers. [Phila-
delphia] 1828. 36 p. DLC; IC;
MB; MH; PHC.   33579

Holland, Mrs. Mary
   The modern family receipt
book... Philadelphia, R. Desilver,
1828. xiii p., 1 l., 230 p. DLC.
                           33580
Holley, Myron, 1779-1841
   An initiatory discourse, delivered at Geneva, 27th November, 1828, before an assembly
from which, on that day, was
formed the Domestic Horticultural Society of the western parts
of the state of New York. By
Myron Holley... Geneva, Pr. by
James Bogert, 1828. 27 p. NN;
PPL.   33581

[----] Memorial. To the Hon. the
Legislature of the state of
N. Y. in Senate and Assembly convened. [New York? January 9th,
1828] 21 p. NN.   33582

Home, John
   Douglas; a tragedy. With pref-
atory remarks. Marked with the
stage business, and stage direc-
tions, as it is performed at the
Theatres Royal, by W. Oxberry.
New-York, W. Whale [etc., etc.]
1828. 64 p. (Oxberry's ed.) MH.
                           33583
Homer, Jonathan, 1759-1843
   A sermon delivered before the
Massachusetts Society for Pro-
moting Christian Knowledge, at

their anniversary, May 29, 1828.
Boston, Pr. by Crocker & Brew-
ster, 1828. 40 p. CBPac;
CtSoP; CtY; DLC; ICU; MBC;
MH-AH; MMeT-Hi; MWA; MeBaT;
MiD-B; NN; NjPT; RPB; BrMus.
                           33584
Homerus
   The Odyssey. Translated from
the Greek, by Alexander Pope.
Philadelphia, James Crissey,
1828. 2 v. CLSU; IEG; LNHT;
MB; MH; MdBS; MdW; MiD-U;
MoSW; PHi; PP; PU; TNJ.
                           33585
Honestus, pseud.   See Austin,
Benjamin.

Hood, Thomas
   Whims and oddities, in prose
and verse; with forty original
designs... Philadelphia, Carey,
Lea & Carey. Sold, in New York,
by G. & C. Carvill, in Boston by
Monroe & Francis, 1828. 144 p.
CSmH; MNBedf; MdBP; ScSoh.
                           33586
Hopkins, Jesse
   The patriot's manual; compris-
ing various standard and miscel-
laneous subjects, interesting to
every American citizen... Comp.
by Jesse Hopkins. Utica, W. Wil-
liams, 1828. 220 p. CSt; DLC;
IU; KyLxT; MH; MdBLC; MiKC;
NBuG; NCH; NIC; NN; NSyU;
OClW.   33587

Hopkinton Academy
   A catalogue of the officers,
instructers, and students, of
Hopkinton Academy. Fall term
Oct. 1828. Concord, Geo. Hough,
pr., 1828. 8 p. Nh.   33588

Horatius Flaccus, Quintus
   Horacio Español, ó poesias
liricas, de Q. Horacio Flacco;
traducidas en prosa española...
por el P. Urbano Campos.
Nueva edicion. Nueva-York,
White, Gallaher y White, 1828.
xv, 548 p. MB.   33589

---- [Stereotype edition] Quinti Horatii Flacci Opera. Interpretatione et notis illustravit Ludovicus Desprez. ... Editio quinta in America stereotypis impressa: cum novissima Parisiensi diligenter collata, ceterisque hactenus editis longe emendatior. ... E stereotypis a D. & G. Bruce fabricatis. Philadelphia, Pub. by Joseph Allen, Sold by J. Grigg, 1828. xv, [1] 559, 61 p. IEG; IaAt; MA; MB; MdBJ; MdBS.   33590

---- Quinti Horatii Flacci Opera. Accedunt clavis metrica et notae anglicae juventuti accommodatae Cura B. A. Gould. Bostoniae, Hilliard, Gary, Little, et Wilkins, 1828. iv, 380 p. CtY; MB; MH.   33591

Horn, Charles Edward, 1786-1849
Ode to Washington. Composed & dedicated to the Handel & Haydn Society, of Boston... New York, Pub. by Dubois & Stodart [c1828] 31 p. CSmH; MB. 33592

Hornback, Jonathan. See Burnside, A. (note).

Horry, Elias, 1743-1834
An address delivered in Charleston before the Agricultural Society of South Carolina, at its anniversary meeting on Tuesday, the 19th August, 1828. Charleston, Pr. by A. E. Miller, 1828. 40 p. CSmH; ICN; MHi; NcD; PPAmP; ScC; ScCC; ScU; TxU.   33593

Horwood, Miss. See Baker, Caroline (Horwood).

Hotchkin, Jedediah H.
A candid appeal to the professors of religion, upon the subject of speculative free-masonry. New York, Pr. for the publisher, 1828. 16 p. ICU; NNG; PPL.   33594

[Howard, William]

Report on the survey of a canal from the Potomac to Baltimore. Baltimore, Pr. by B. Edes, 1828. 14 p. MdHi; NNC; WHi; BrMus.   33595

Howard Benevolent Society, Boston
Order of services at the anniversary of the Howard Benevolent Society. Jan. 10, 1828. [Boston, 1828] Folder (3, [1] p.) MB.   33596

---- Report of the standing committee, presented at their annual meeting, October 29, 1828. Pub. by vote of the Society. Boston, T. R. Marvin, 1828. 12 p. MBAt; MWA; PPL.   33597

Howe, Samuel Gridley, 1801-1876
An historical sketch of the Greek revolution. New York, White, Gallaher and White, 1828. xxxvi, 452 p. CSmH; CU; CtHC; CtHT-W; DLC; GDC; ICMe; ICN; IaDaM; InCW; KU; MB; MBAt; MBC; MH; MNtcA; MWA; MdAS; MeU; MiU; MnHi; MoSpD; NBLiHi; NGH; NNG; NcU; NhHi; NjPT; OCHP; OHi; PPAmP; PPL; RPB; ScSoh; Vi; WHi; Wv; BrMus.   33598

---- ---- 2d ed. New York, White, Gallaher and White, 1828. A-Ar; CSt; CU; CtY; GU; IGK; IaGG; LNHT; MdBE; MiD; MnU; MoSU; NNG; NNUT; NbU-M; NjP; OClW; P; PPiW; RPB; ScC; TNJ; VtU.   33599

Howell, O. V.
An address; delivered at the opening of Campbell Academy; in Wilson County, Tennessee. January, 1828. Gallatin, Pr. by H. Strange & co. , 1828. 12 p. NNG; T.   33600

Hoyt, O. P.
A sermon, delivered at the dedication of the First Congrega-

tional Meeting House, Malone,
N. Y. , Feb. 7, 1828. Fort Covington, Pr. by Long and Hoard,
1828. 16 p. MBC.   33601

Hubbard, Austin O.
    Christian character. A sermon,
preached at Hawk's Church, Frederick County, Md. , May 11,
1828. Baltimore, Pr. by J. D.
Toy, 1828. 30 p. PPPrHi. 33602

Hubbard, Simeon. See Democratic Party. Connecticut.

Hudson, Charles
    A system of divine truth; ex-
hibited in a sermon... Providence,
John S. Greene, pr. , 1828. 16 p.
MMeT-Hi; MWA; RHi.   33603

The Hudson river port folio.
See Wall, William G.

[Hughes, John]
    The conversion and edifying
death of Andrew Dunn: or, A
guide to truth and peace. Philadelphia, Mifflin and Parry, prs. ,
1828. 36 p. ArLSJ; InNd; MdBS;
MoSU; PPL.   33604

Hughs, Mrs. Mary Robson
    Family dialogues; or Sunday
well-spent. By Mary Hughes.
Philadelphia, Pr. by Joseph
Rakestraw, for the Tract and
Book Society of the Evangelical
Church of St. John, 1828. 48 p.
PPPrHi.   33605

---- The life of William Penn com-
piled from the usual authorities
and also many original manu-
scripts. Philadelphia, Pr. by
James Kay, Jun. for Carey, Lea
& Carey, Towar & Hogan, John
Grigg, Uriah Hunt, Robert H.
Small, M'Carty & Davis, Kimber
& Sharpless, J. Crissy. Boston,
Munroe & Francis, 1828. 224 p.
DLC; IC; ICMc; InRE; MB;
MBAt; MH; MWA; Mi; NN; Nj;

NjR; P; PHC; PPAmP; PPF;
PPL; PSC-Hi; BrMus.   33606

Hugo, Abel
    Historical summary of the
events which placed Joseph Napoleon, on the throne of Spain.
(From the American quarterly
review) No. 6. [Philadelphia,
1828] 31 p. DLC.   33607

Hull, Joseph Hervey
    English grammar, by lectures:
comprehending the principle and
rules of syntactical parsing on a
new and high improved system;
intended as a text book for students; containing exercises in
syntax rules for parsing by trans-
position, critical notes, and a
lecture in rhetoric. 4th ed. Boston, Lincoln & Edmands, 1828.
59 p. CtY; MH; RPB.   33608

Humara Y Salamanca, Rafael
    Ramiro, conde de Lucena,
Obra original en seis libros.
Por Don Rafael Humara Y Sala-
manca. Paris, Bossange padre;
Nueva Yorck, Lanuza, Mendia Y
Cia, 1828. 286 p. MH; ViU.
                          33609
Hume, David, 1711-1776
    The history of England, from
the invasion of Julius Caesar, to
the Revolution, in 1688. In four
volumes... Philadelphia, E. Lit-
tell, Clark & Raser, prs. , [vols.
III-IV Jesper Harding, pr.] 1828.
4 vols. CBDP; CtHT; GMM; IaK;
KyDC; MdAN; MiD; MoS; NdHi;
OClW; OU; PLFM; PPL; PP-W;
PU; ScCC; TBriK; TxDaM; ViL;
WvW.   33610

---- ---- Philadelphia, Bennett
& Walton [c1828?] 4 vols. CLSU;
GHi; KyWa; MoSpD; ViU; WM.
                          33611
---- Hume and Smollett's history
of England, abridged, and con-
tinued to the accession of George
IV. By John Robinson... Exeter,

Hummel   153

[N. H.] J. & B. Williams, 1828.
2 v. CoU; DLC; IU; KyHi;
MDeeP; MH; NbCrD; Nh; OSW;
TNJ; ViU.   33612

Hummel, Johann Nepomuk, 1778-1837
Hummel's Waltz epitomised
for the piano-forte by P. K. Moran. New York, Dubois & Stodart,
1828. 3 p. CtY; MB.   33613

The humourist; or, Choice selections of anecdotes, wit and
sentiment. Comp. by a laughing
philosopher. Philadelphia, Sold
by C. Alexander, 1828. 72 p.
DLC; PPL.   33614

The humours of Eutopia. See
Sanford, Ezekiel.

[Humphrey, Ch.]
Mentor, or Dialogues between
a parent and children; on some
of the duties, amusements, pursuits and relations of life... Lexington [Ky.] Pr. by Thomas
Smith, 1828. 203 p. DLC; ICN;
ICU; LNT; NN; PPL. ("Presented to Math. Carey Esq. by
the author Ch. Humphrey")
                            33615
Humphrey, Heman
Parallel between intemperance
and the slave trade: an address
delivered at Amherst College,
July 4, 1828. Amherst, J. S. &C.
Adams, 1828. 40 p. CBPac;
CSmH; Ct; CtHC; DLC; IaGG;
MBAt; MBC; MH; MHi; MNtcA;
MWA; MeBaT; MiD-B; MnU;
NCH; NN; NNC; OClWHi;
PPPrHi; RPB; TNF; TxU; WHi.
                            33616
The hundred pound note. See
Peake, Richard Brinsley.

Hunt, Leigh, 1784-1859
Lord Byron and some of his
contemporaries, with recollections of the author's life, and of
his visit to Italy. Philadelphia,

Carey, Lea & Carey, Sold in
New York, by G. & C. Carvill,
1828. 440 p. CLU; CtMW; GMiW;
IaU; InGrD; KyLo; MB; MBAt;
Md; MeLB; NBLiHi; NN; NNS;
NR; NWM; NbO; NcA-S; NhHi;
NjR; OC; P; PP; PPL; PU;
RPB; ScU; TMC.   33617

Hunt, William Gibbes
An address on the character
and services of De Witt Clinton,
delivered at Nashville, March 11,
1828, at the request of the grand
chapter of Tennessee. Nashville,
Pr. by John S. Simpson, 1828.
20 p. CBPac; CSmH; DLC; DSC;
IU; In; MB; MBAt; MBFM; MH;
MHi; MWA; NNFM; NNS; RPB;
T; THi; WHi; BrMus.   33618

Hunter, Henry
Sacred biography, or, the History of the Patriarchs to which
is added the history of Deborah,
Ruth and Hannah, and also the
history of Jesus Christ. Being a
course of lectures, delivered at
the Scots Church, London-Wall...
3d Amer. ed. Complete in seven
volumes. Pub. by Glazier & Co.,
Hallowell, Me; Richardson &
Lord, Hilliard, Gray & Co.,
Boston; O. A. Roorbach, W. Burgess, Jr. and Collins & Hannay,
New York; Towar & Hogan, John
Grigg, Philadelphia; Glazier &
Co., prs., 1828. 7 vols.
ICU; KyBrU; MNe; MH; NGH;
WM.   33619

Huntingford, George Isaac
Huntingford's Greek syntax,
with examples. J. Griffin, pr.,
Brunswick (verso t. p.) [1828]
24 p. PPL.   33620

Huntington, Conn. Congregational Church.
Confession of faith & covenant,
as revised & adopted by the
church in Huntington, April 13,
1826. New-Haven, Intelligencer

Office, 1828. 12 p. Ct.   33621

Hurlbut, Martin Luther
Presumptive arguments in favor of Unitarianism. Boston, Bowles & Dearborn, [Press of Isaac R. Butts & Co.] 1828. 42 p. CBPac; MBAU; MH-AH; MWA.
33622

Huchings' improved almanac for 1829. By David Young. New-York, John C. Totten [1828] 18 l. NHi; NWhpHi.   33623

Huchings' revived almanac for 1829. By David Young. New-York, John C. Totten [1828] 18 l. N; WHi.   33624

Hutchings' almanac for 1829. By David Young. New York, Daniel D. Smith [1828] 18 l. MWA; NBLiHi.   33625

---- ---- New York, James A. Burtis [1828] 18 l. MWA; NjR.
33626
---- ---- Peekskill, S. Marks [1828] 18 l. Ct.   33627

---- ---- Poughkeepsie, P. Potter [1828] 18 l. DLC; NHi; NN; NP.   33628

Hutchings' (Revived) almanac for 1829. By Poor Old Richard. New-York, C. Brown [1828] 18 l. NB.
33629
---- By David Young. New-York, Daniel D. Smith [1828] 18 l. MWA; NN.   33630

---- ---- Poughkeepsie, P. Potter [1828] 18 l. MWA.   33631

Hutchins' improved almanac and ephemeris for 1829. New-York, Caleb Bartlett [1828] 24 l. CtHi; DLC; InU; MB; MWA; N; NBLiHi; NHi; NN; NjMo; WHi.
33632
---- New-York, Caleb Bartlett; N. B. Holmes [1828] 24 l.

NN.   33633

Hutchinson, Samuel
A Scriptural exhibition of the mighty conquest, and glorious triumph of Jesus Christ, over sin, death, and hell; and His exaltation, His second coming, the day of judgment, and the capacity, equality, and success of His reign; and the ultimate triumph of His ransomed... Norway, Me., Pr. at the Observer office, by A. Barton, 1828. 144 p. CSmH; CtHT; DLC; IEG; MBC; MH; MMeT; PPL.   33634

Hutin, Philippe, b 1802
Manual of the physiology of man; or A concise description of the phenomena of his organization. Trans. from the French, with notes, by Joseph Togno... Philadelphia, Carey, Lea & Carey, 1828. 309 p. DLC; DNLM; ICJ; ICU-R; InGrD; KyLxT; MB; MBC; MdBL; MdUM; MeB; MnU; NBM; NBU-M; NNNAM; NbU-M; OC; OMC; PLFM; PPAmP; PPC; PPL; ScCM; VtU.   33635

Hymns for infant minds. See Gilbert, Ann (Taylor).

Hymns for little children. Wendell, J. Metcalf, 1828. 23 p. MBrZ; MWA; WHi.   33636

Hymns for Sunday schools. Pr. for the trustees of the publishing fund, and approved by the Boston Sunday School Society. 3d ed. Boston, Wait, Green & Co., 1828. 66 p. MBAt; RPB. 33637

Hymns sung at a union meeting of Sunday schools in Wheeling, January 1, 1828. Bdsd. WvWO.
33638

I

I'll risk it! Boston, Bowles &
Dearborn, Press of Isaac R.
Butts and Co., 1828. 20 p. DLC;
MH; NNC.   33639

Ianthe, pseud. See Embury,
Mrs. Emma Catherine (Manley).

Illinois
    A bill for an act repealing
certain acts. [1828?] 3 p. I-Ar.
                            33640
---- A bill for "An act to provide for the construction of the
Illinois and Michigan Canal."
[1828?] H. R. No. 2. 3 p. I-Ar.
                            33641
---- List of lands entered on the
books of the auditor of public accounts, for the state of Illinois,
subject to taxation for the several years set forth, (with interest
and costs) and upon which the
taxes have not been paid, in conformity to the provisions of the
several laws for levying and col-
lecting a tax on land. The Illinois Intelligencer Extra. [Van-
dalia, 1828] 34 p. CtY; I-Ar.
                            33642
An illustration of the present
pernicious mode of fashionable
practice of medicine. With plates.
Accompanied with A dialogue, between an apothecary and a physician, on the subject of the statute regulating the practice of
physic and surgery. After which
is added a few brief anecdotes.
Albany, 1828. 36 p. DNLM; RPB.
                            33643

Illustrations from the Spy, the
Pioneers, and the Waverley
novels, with explanatory and critical remarks. Philadelphia, H.
Hall, 1828. [14] p. DLC. 33644

Illustrations of Shakespeare. New
York, W. Borradaile, 1828. 37
plates. MH.   33645

Immorality. Fellow citizens. Can
we vote for the man who openly
sets the laws of the great Jehovah at defiance, thereby showing
a bad example to our children?
Some few Sundays past, Mr.
Adams passed through Providence
galloping and running his horse,
and at every tavern stopping to
receive the salutes and huzzas of
the federal party. I have always
been an Adams man, until he violated and trampled on the laws
of God...I therefore shall choose
Andrew Jackson, one who keeps
holy the Sabbath day. A professor of religion. Kittery-Point,
Sept. 8, 1828. 1 p. DLC.
                            33646
...An impartial and true history
of the life and services of Major
General Andrew Jackson. n. p.
[1828] [Begins "Military men,
above all others..."] 40 p. PPL.
                            33647
---- [n. p., 1828?] 36 p. CSmH;
PPL.   33648

---- [n. p., 1828?] 31 p. CSmH;
DLC; MB.   33649

In honor of the election of our
distinguished fellow-citizen General Andrew Jackson, to the
presidency of the United States,
you are respectfully invited to
attend a ball in Nashville...
Nashville, December 10, 1828.
1 p. DLC.   33650

In relation to the Baltimore and
Ohio Rail Road Company. See
Warfield, Charles.

In the matter of William Kenner
& Co. See Mazureau, Étienne.

[Inchbald, Elizabeth (Simpson)]
1753-1821
    Animal magnetism. A farce...
Philadelphia, & New York, Neal
& MacKenzie, Mifflin & Parry,
prs., 1828. 31 p. DeGE; MH;

PU; RPB.   33651

Independence, pseud. See To the
free voters of the state of Maryland.

The Indian prophecy. See Custis,
George Washington Parke.

Indiana
    Journal of the House of Rep-
resentatives of the state of Indiana, being the twelfth session of
the General Assembly; begun and
held at Indianapolis, in said
state, on Monday the third day of
December, 1827. Indianapolis,
Ind. Smith & Bolton, state prs.,
1827 [i. e. 1828] 483 p. In; InU.
                                 33652
---- Journal of the Senate of the
state of Indiana; being the twelfth
session of the General Assembly;
begun and held at Indianapolis,
in said state, on Monday the
third day of December, 1827.
Indianapolis, Ind., Smith & Bolton, state prs., 1827 [i. e. 1828]
265 p. In; InU.   33653

---- Laws of the state of Indiana, passed and published at the
twelfth session of the General
Assembly, held at Indianapolis,
on the first Monday in December,
one thousand eight hundred and
twenty-seven. By authority. Indianapolis, Smith & Bolton, state
prs., 1828. 165 p. In; InHi; InU;
N.   33654

---- Message of His Excellency
James Brown Ray; delivered in
person, to both houses of the
General Assembly of the state of
Indiana, on Tuesday the 2d of
December, 1828. Indianapolis,
Smith & Bolton, state prs., 1828.
12 p. CSmH.   33655

Indiana Journal
    Address of the carrier of the
Indiana Journal, to its patrons,

on the commencement of the new
year... Thomas Brown. Jan. 1,
1828. Bdsd. InHi.   33656

Indigent Widows' and Single Wom-
en's Society.
    Constitution of the Indigent
Widows' and Single Women's Society of Philadelphia. With rules
for the regulation of the board
of managers and for the government of the asylum. Philadelphia,
Lydia R. Bailey, 1828. 12 p.
IU; MiD-B; PHi.   33657

---- The eleventh annual report,
for the year 1827 of the managers
of the Indigent Widows' and Single
Women's Society; with a list of
the officers and managers...
Philadelphia, Pr. by order of
the Society. Lydia R. Bailey,
pr., 1828. 8 p. PPL.   33658

Infant education; or, Remarks on
the importance of educating the
infant poor, from the age of
eighteen months to seven years;
with an account of some of the
infant schools in England, and
the system of education there
adopted. Selected and abridged
from the Works of Wilderspin
and adapted to the use of infant
schools in America. By a friend
to the poor. Portland, Shirley
and Hyde, prs., 1828. 108 p.
MH; MeHi; PPAmS.   33659

The infant school and nursery
hymn book... New York, Sold by
W. Carey and R. Lockwood, 1828.
126 p. MH-AH.   33660

Infant School Society. Boston.
    Constitution and by-laws of the
Infant School Society of Boston.
Boston, Press of the Daily Ad-
vertiser, 1828. 16 p. DLC.
                                33661
Infant School Society of South-
wark, Philadelphia.
    To all whom it may concern.

This is to certify, that----is
duly authorized to collect the
names of subscribers for "The
Infant School Society of Southwark..." [Philadelphia, 1828]
Pr. by Wm. F. Geddes. 8 p.
(pp. 2-4 are blank, pp 5 to end
contain Constitution of the Society, dated June 10th, 1828).
PPL.   33662

Infant School Society of the City
of New York.
The constitution and by-laws
of the Infant School Society of
the City of New-York, with the
subscribers' names, etc. Instituted May 23, 1827. New York,
J. Seymour, pr., 1828. 18 p.
DLC; IEG; KHi; MHi; MnHi; PHi.
                          33663

Infant School Society of the North-
ern Liberties and Kensington,
Philadelphia.
Constitution of the Infant
School Society of the Northern
Liberties and Kensington. Phila-
delphia, Pr. by D. & S. Neall
[1828] 8 p. PPL.   33664

Infant School Society. Philadelphia.
First annual report of the Infant School Society of Philadelphia. Philadelphia, Pr. by Lydia
R. Bailey, 1828. 12 p. PHi;
PPAmP; PPL; PPPrHi.   33665

Information relative to the American Lyceum. See Congdon,
James Bunker.

Ingersoll, Charles M.
Conversations on English
grammar; explaining the principles and rules of the language.
Illustrated by appropriate exercises, adapted to the use of
schools. 6th ed. Portland, Shirley & Hyde; James Adams, Jun.,
pr., 1828. iv, [13]-264 p. MFiHi;
MH; MeHi.   33666

---- ---- 7th ed. Portland,
Shirley & Hyde, 1828. 248 p.
MH; P; WU.   33667

Ingersoll, Joseph Reed, 1786-
1868
An address delivered in the
church at Princeton, the evening
before the annual commencement
of the College of New-Jersey,
September 23, 1828... Pub. at the
request of the American Whig
and Cliosophic Societies. [Prince-
ton, N.J.] Princeton Press: Pr.
for the Societies by Connolly &
Madden, 1828. 26 p. CSmH;
CtY; MB; MiD-B; NNG; NjP;
NjR; PHi; PPAmP; PPL; PPPrHi;
TNJ.   33668

Ingham, Samuel Dulucenna
An exposition of the political
character and principles of John
Quincy Adams, showing by historical documents and incontest-
ible facts, that he was a mon-
archist; has been hostile to popular government, and particularly to its great bulwark, the right
of suffrage; and that he affected
to become a Republican only to
attain the power to pervert and
degrade the Democratic party;
and to pave the way for such a
change of the Constitution as
would establish in these United
States an aristocratical and he-
reditary government... Pub. by
the Jackson Committee of Hamilton County, Ohio. [Cincinnati]
Wm. Hill Woodward, pr., 1828.
30 p. OCHP.   33669

Ingraham, Edward Duffield, 1793-
1854
An address delivered before
the Law Academy of Philadelphia,
at the opening of the session of
1828-9. ... Philadelphia, Pub. by
the Law Academy, 1828. [James
Kay, Jun., pr.] (NN and Who
Was who in America say "Edward Duffield Ingraham;" DLC

and MH say "Edward Duncan Ingraham;" both give birth and death dates as above). 24 p. MH; MHi; MiD-B; NN; PHi; PPL; BrMus.   33670

Ingraham, Joseph Wentworth, 1799-1849
   An historical map of Palestine; or, The Holy Land, exhibiting a correct and masterly delineation of the peculiar geographical features of the country and of all places therein; ... Originally delineated by J. T. Assheton, London. Boston, Pub. by Thos. B. Wait and Jos. W. Ingraham, Peirce & Williams, prs., 1828. 96, 8 p. CBPac; CtY; DLC; IP; MH; MHi; MWA; MiD; NBLiHi; NNG; NNUT; NjPT; OCl; PPF; WHi; BrMus.   33671

An inhabitant of Florida, pseud. See Kingsley, Zephaniah.

Inman, James, 1776-1859
   An introduction to naval gunnery. Portsea, Pr. and sold by W. Woodward; [etc., etc.], 1828. 52 p. DLC; NWM.   33672

The Intelligencer and Petersburg Commercial Advertiser. Petersburg, Va.
   To the friends and patriots of The Intelligencer and Petersburg Commercial Advertiser, the carrier, with the compliments of the season, respectfully presents the following Christmas address. Christmas, December 25, 1828. [Petersburg, Va., 1828] 1 p. DLC.   33673

The interesting life, travels, voyages, and daring engagements of the celebrated Paul Jones; containing numerous anecdotes of undaunted courage, in the prosecution of his bold enterprizes. To which is added, the song written on the engagement between the

Good Man Richard, and the English frigate Serapis. New-York, S. King, 1828. 28 p. DLC.
                                   33674
Investigator. See McNemar, Richard.

The invincibles. See Morton, Thomas.

Irving, Edward
   Babylon and infidelity foredoomed of God: A discourse on the prophecies of Daniel and the Apocalypse. Philadelphia, Church Missionary House. Stereotyped by L. Johnson, 1828. 118 p. CtHC; GDC; IObB; MBAt; MiU; PPPrHi; WBB.   33675

Irving, Washington
   A history of the life and voyages of Christopher Columbus... In 3 vols. New York, Pr. by Elliot & Palmer, Pub. by G. & C. Carvill [1828] 3 vols. CSmH; CSt; CoCsC; CtHT; CtMW; CtY; DLC; FSa; GHi; GU; ICHi; InNd; KHi; KWiU; KyLx; LNHT; MB; MBAt; MBC; MDeeP; MH; MNF; MdAN; Mi; MoSHi; MoSW; NFred; NN; NWM; Nh; Nj; OCHP; PP; PPAmP; PPF; PU; RPB; ScU; TNJ; ViU; VtU; WMMD; WvW.
                                   33676
[----] The sketch-book of Geoffrey Crayon, gent. [pseud.]... 6th Amer. ed. Philadelphia, Carey, Lea & Carey, 1828. 2 vols. CSmH; IEN; MA; MH; PPL; PPFHi.   33677

Is it a lie? A comic piece, in one act. Boston, Richardson & Lord, 1828. 36 p. MB; MH.
                                   33678
Isabella; or, Filial affection. A tale by the author of "The prize." "Self conquest." &c. &c... Boston, Bowles and Dearborn. Press of Isaac R. Butts and Co., 1828. 160 p. CtY; DLC; MWA; PU.
                                   33679

The Italian and English phrase-
book. See Phillips, Sir Richard.

Ithaca and Owego Railroad Company
    An act to incorporate the Ith-
aca and Owego Railroad Company.
Passed Jan. 28, 1828. [Albany?
1828?] 19 p. NIC; NN.   33680

The itinerant sketch book; or Select tales of fiction and real life,
poetry, scraps, &c. Philadelphia,
Pub. by Woodward & Spragg,
and sold by David Clark, 1828.
140 p. DLC; ICU.   33681

                J

Jack Halyard, and Ishmael Bar-
dus. Wendell, J. Metcalf, 1828.
8 p. PP.   33682

Jackson, Charles, 1775-1855
    A treatise on the pleadings
and practice in real actions; with
precedents of pleadings... Boston,
Wells & Lilly, 1828. xx, 396 p.
CU; Ct; DLC; ICLaw; IaDaGL;
IaU-L; In-SC; MB; MH-L; MHi;
MNe; Me-LR; MoKU; MoU; NIC;
NNLI; NcD; Nv; OCoSc; PPAmP;
PU-L; WU-L; BrMus.   33683

Jackson, Daniel, jr., pseud.
See Mitchell, Isaac.

Jackson, Samuel C.
    A sermon, delivered in the
West Parish of Andover, Dec.
30, 1827. Being the last Sabbath
in the year. Andover, Pr. by
Flagg and Gould, 1828. 30 p.
PPL.   33684

Jackson and Liberty. See Democratic Party. Pennsylvania.

Jackson and the people's ticket.
[1828] 1 p. DLC.   33685

Jackson Convention. See Demo-

cratic Party. Missouri.

Jackson delegate ticket...[1828?]
1 p. DLC.   33686

The Jackson Republican Committee of Rochester. See Democratic Party. New York.

Jackson Ticket. See Democratic
Party. Virginia.

Jackson triumphant in the great
city of Philadelphia. Jos. Hemp-
hill, a federalist of high Tory
principles, and of the blood and
carnage times of 1798 and 1799
...[James City County, Va.,
1828] 1 p. DLC.   33687

Jacobs, Friederick
    An expeditious method of
learning the Latin language, exemplified in a literal interlineary
translation of the first part of
Jacobs' Latin reader. Salem,
Foote & Brown, 1828. [Pr. at
the Salem Gazette Office] 197,
[1] p. MH; PPL.   33688

---- Stereotyped ed. The Latin
reader. Part second. Chiefly
from the 4th German ed. of F.
Jacobs and F. W. Doering. Bos-
ton, Hilliard, Gray, Little and
Wilkins, 1828. [Stereotyped at
the Boston Type and Stereotype
Foundry.] iv, [1]-148 p. CtHT-
W; KyLxT; MH; MNF; NN; OMC;
TxU-T.   33689

Jahn, Friederich L.
    A treatise on gymnasticks,
taken chiefly from the German of
F. L. Jahn. Northampton, Mass.
Pub. by Simeon Butler... T.
Watson Shepard, pr. 1828. xxiii,
179 p. MA; MNF.   33690

Jahn Johann, 1750-1816
    Jahn's History of the Hebrew
commonwealth; translated from
the German by Calvin E. Stowe

...Andover, Pr. at the Codman Press by Flagg & Gould, for G. & C. Carvill, New York, 1828. xii, [9]-512, DXIII-DXVIII [513]-692 p. DLC; KyLoS; LNB; MBL; MdBS; NN; NbOP; OClW; PPL.
33691

James, John Angell
The Sunday-School teachers guide. Philadelphia, American Sunday-School Union, 1828. 90 p. IEdS.   33692

James, William
The debt of nations to Christianity. A discourse delivered in Rochester, June 8, 1828. Rochester, Pr. by E. Peck & Co., 1828. 20 p. CSmH; MB; MBC; NN; NRHi; NRU; NjPT; PPPrHi.
33693
---- The moral responsibility of the American nation. A discourse delivered in Rochester, July 4, 1828. By Wm. James, pastor of the Brick Presbyterian Church. Pub. by request. Rochester, N.Y., Pr. by Everard Peck & Company, 1828. 17 p. CSmH; CtHC; MBC; NCH; NN; NRHi; NRU; NjPT; PPPrHi; RPB.
33694

Jameson, Horatio Gates
An introductory lecture... at the opening of Washington Medical College of Baltimore, 1827. Baltimore, R.J. Matchett, 1828. 18 p. DLC.   33695

Janeway, James
Invisible realities, demonstrated in the holy life and triumphant death of John Janeway. Philadelphia, Pr. by J. Young, 1828. 118 p. DLC.   33696

[----] A token for children. Wendell, J. Metcalf, 1828. 15, [1] p. MA; MWA.   33697

Jaquith, Andrew
The wonderful dealings of God to Andrew Jaquith, Junior, from a child up to the twenty-sixth year of his age, who professes to be called of God to preach the gospel. Clinton, 1828. 34 p. Williamson: 4907.   33698

Jarman, George B.
The life and confessions of George B. Jarman, who was executed for murder in New-Brunswick, N.J. on Friday the 8th of August 1828... New Brunswick, Pub. by Jacob Edmonds, Wm. Packer & Aaron Slack [1828?] 8 p. DLC.   33699

Jaudon, Daniel
The English orthographical expositor: being a compendious selection of the most useful words in the English language... 15th ed. Philadelphia, Towar & Hogan, 1828. 223 p. OClWHi.
33700
---- The union grammar, in three parts. 4th ed. Philadelphia, Towar & Hogan, 1828. 216 p. DLC; MB; NNC; PHi.   33701

Jay, William, 1769-1853
The Christian contemplated in a course of lectures, delivered in Argyle Chapel, Bath. 1st Amer. from the 2d London ed. Boston, Pr. and pub. by Lincoln & Edmands, 1828. 382 p. CtHC; CtY; ICMcC; ICU; KyLoS; MBC; MH; NGH; OCl; RPB; ScSp.
33702
---- Morning exercises, for every day in the year... From the ed. of his works rev. by himself... New York, Boston, American Tract Society, D. Fanshaw, pr. [pref. 1828] 653 p. CtY; DLC; ICU; IU; MH; MiU; NN; NNG; NSyU; NcD; OO; ScCliTO; ViRU; TxAuPT.   33703

---- Prayers for the use of families; or, The domestic minister's assistant. Hartford, S. Andrus, publisher, 1828. 266 p.

CSmH; LNB.   33704

Jefferson, Thomas, 1743-1826
A manual of parliamentary
practice, composed originally for
the use of the Senate of the
United States... To which are
added the rules and orders of
both houses of Congress. Cincinnati, Pub. by Drake and Con-
clin. Geo. T. Williamson, pr.,
1828. 162 p. CSmH; MB; MdBG;
OC; OCHP; ViU.   33705

The Jefferson almanac for 1829.
Baltimore, Geo. McDowell &
Son; Wm. Wooddy, pr. [1828] 18
l. PPi.   33706

Jefferson, in reply to the Richmond anti-Jackson address. To
the editors of the Richmond Inquirer. [Richmond, 1828] 39 p.
ViU.   33707

Jefferson Medical College: a representation of the conduct of the
trustees and members of the faculty, and circumstances connected therewith, in relation to
John Barnes, M. D. ... Philadelphia, 1828. 38 p. DLC; DNLM;
MH; NNNAM; PHi; PPC; PPL;
PU.   33708

Jelleff, Joseph
Jelleff & Hull's patent pocket
interest tables. Utica, Pr. for
the proprietors, by Wm. Williams, 1828. 47 p. CSmH. 33709

Jenkins, Warren
An oration delivered 4th July,
1828, before a very numerous
assembly of the friends of the
general and state administrations,
in the borough of Towanda, Bradford County, Pa. Pub. by request
of the hearer. Towanda, Burr
Ridgway, 1828. 15 p. P.   33710

[Jenkins, William]
An address to the Catholic

voters of Baltimore. Baltimore,
Pr. by Lucas & Deaver, 1828.
15 p. DGU; DLC; MdBE; MdHi;
OCX; PHi; PPL.   33711

[----] Vindication of An address
to the Catholic voters of Baltimore. Baltimore, Pr. by Lucas
& Deaver, 1828. 25 p. DGU;
DLC; MdBS.   33712

Jennings, Samuel Kennedy, 1771-
1854
An address, intended when
written, to have been delivered
before the district conference of
the Baltimore district... Its ob-
jectives, to shew, that the prosecutions... against the local
preachers... are unreasonable
and unjust. Baltimore, Pr. by
Samuel Sands, 1828. 28 p.
MdBBC; MdBE; MdBP; PPL.
                           33713
[Jennison, William] 1757-1843
An outline of political economy, designed for seminaries,
and intended to explain the principles of this important science,
by familiar examples, and to ex-
hibit more particularly the great
importance of agriculture, min-
ing industry, manufactures, and
internal improvments, to national wealth and prosperity. Philadelphia, Pr. for the author,
1828. 2 p. l. 78 p. CtHT-W;
CtY; DLC; DeGE; ICU; MH;
MdBJ; NN; PHi; PPAmP; PPL;
PU.   33714

Jess, Zachariah
The American tutor's assistant, improved; or A compendious
system of decimal, practical
arithmetic... Containing also, a
course of book keeping, by single
entry... Pittsburgh, L. Loomis
& co., 1828. 188, ii, 10, [1],
3 p. DLC.   33715

Jim Crow. A celebrated comic
song or ballad as sung by all

the comic singers, composed and
arranged for the piano forte.
New York, Atwill's Music Sa-
loon, [1828?] [2] p. DLC.   33716

Jocelyn, N. , & S. S. , publisher,
New Haven.
    Map exhibiting the Farmington
& Hampshire & Hampden canals,
together with the line of their
proposed continuation through the
valley of the Connecticut River
to Canada. Engraved and pub.
by N. & S. S. Jocelyn. New
Haven, 1828. map 121 x 39 cm.
CtY; ICJ; MB.   33717

Joe Miller's almanac for 1829.
Baltimore, Wm. and Joseph
Neal [1828] 18 l. NBuHi.   33718

John Grigg's almanack for 1829.
By Joseph Cramer. Philadelphia,
D. & S. Neall [1828] 18 l. DLC;
InU; MWA; NBuHi; NjR; PHi;
PPL.   33718a

John Randolph. See Rush, Richard.

John Woods. A Tennesseean.
See Armstrong, James L.

Johnson, Alexander Bryan, 1786-
1867
    The philosophy of human
knowledge, or A treatise on language. A course of lectures delivered at the Utica [N. Y.] lyceum, [1825-26] New York, G. &
C. Carvill, 1828. vi, [3]-200 p.
CtY; DLC; KyLxT; MH; MHi;
NIC; NUt; NWM; PU; TNJ. 33719

Johnson, James, 1777-1845
    An essay on morbid sensibility
of the stomach and bowels...
Philadelphia, Pub. by Thos. Kite,
1828. 155 p. CtMW; DNLM; IC;
LU-Me; MBCo; MeB; NNNAM;
PU; RPM; ScCM.   33720

Johnson, John, 1777-1848

An abridgment of Johnson's
Typographia, or The printers'
instructor: with an appendix. Boston, C. L. Adams, print. , 1828.
2 p. l. , 316 p. DeGE; ICN; IaU;
MB; MWA; MdBP; NNC. 33721

Johnson, Samuel
    The farewell sermon of Rev.
Samuel Johnson, preached at Alna
on the afternoon of July 6, 1828.
With an appendix. (Published by
request.) Wiscasset, Pr. by Amos C. Tappan, 1828. 24 p. MBC;
MeBaT; MeHi; MWA.   33722

Johnson, Samuel, 1709-1784
    The beauties of Johnson, con-
sisting of selections from his
works. Boston, N. H. Whitaker,
1828. 160 p. CtY; MB; MBAt;
MH; MeBaT; MiD; OHi; PSC-Hi;
RJa.   33723

---- Johnson's English dictionary,
as improved by Todd and a-
bridged by Chalmers; with Walker's pronouncing dictionary, combined... Boston, Charles Ewer &
T. Harrington Carter. [Stereo-
typed at the Boston Type and
Stereotype Foundry] 1828. xxx,
[1], 1156 p. DLC; ICF; MB; MH;
MWA; MdW; NNC; PPL; PU;
RPB; ScC; ViU.   33724

---- ---- Boston, B. Perkins &
Co. , 1828. xii, 444 p. NN.
                              33725
[Johnston, Josiah Stoddard] 1784-
1833
    Debate on the revenue. [Wash-
ington, 1828] 8 p. PPL. 33726

---- Speech of Mr. Johnston, of
Lou. , on the public debt. Deliv-
ered in the Senate of the U.
States, March 3, 1828. Washing-
ton, Gales & Seaton, 1828. 16 p.
CSmH; DLC; DeGE; MWA; MeB;
MiD-B; NN; PPL.   33727

---- Speech of the Hon. Josiah

S. Johnston, of Louisiana, on the report of the select committee respecting the powers of the vice president. Delivered in the Senate of the United States, February 14, 1828. Washington, Pr. by Gales & Seaton, 1828. 18 p. DGU; IU; MWA; MoKU; NcD; ScU.   33728

Jones, Elijah
Addressed delivered at the fifth anniversary of the Peace Society of Minot, November 5, 1826. Portland, Shirley and Hyde, prs., 1828. 23 p. DLC; MBC; MeB; MeHi; MiD-B.   33729

Jones, Elizabeth C.
Fugitive poems. Providence, Smith & Parmenter, 1828. 59, [1] p. CSmH; CtHT-W; CtY; DLC; ICU; MH; MWH; MnU; NNC; RPB; TxU; BrMus.   33730

Jones, L.
An eulogy on the Rev. Abiel Carter, A. M. Rector of Christ Church and chaplain of the Georgia Charter no. III, delivered on the festival of St. John the Evangelist, December 27, 1827, at the request of said charter. Savannah, W. T. Williams, 1828. 16 p. NGH.   33731

Jones, Thomas Ap Catesby, Master Commandant U. S. N.
To the Honorable Samuel L. Southard, Richard Rush, and James Barbour, Board of Commissioners for the management of the Navy Pension Fund. [Washington, 1828] [2] p. **PPL**.   33732

Jones, William, 1746-1794
An essay on the law of bailments... 3d London ed., with notes and references on the subject of carriers, innkeepers, warehousemen, and other bailees. By William Nichols... With additional notes and references to

American decisions, by Wm. Halsted, jun., esq. New-York, O. Halsted and John Grigg, Philadelphia, 1828. xv, 123 (i. e. 222), xix, [8] p. CSt; Ct; DLC; ICLaw; LNP; MoU; NIC-A; OrU; PU-L; TxU-L; ViU.   33733

Jones, William, 1760-1831
Remarks on the proposed breakwater at Cape Henlopen. Communicated, by request of the secretary of the Treasury, by Wm. Jones... To which are added, the report of the Board of engineers, and Captain Bainbridge of the navy; the memorial of the Chamber of commerce of Philadelphia, proceedings of a town meeting, shipwrecks, loss and disaster, &c. &c. 3d ed. Philadelphia, Pr. by order of the Chamber of commerce of Philadelphia, 1828. 24 p., 1 l. CtY; DLC; MB; MWA; BrMus. 33734

Josephus, Flavius
Destruction of Jerusalem; abridged from the history of the Jewish wars by Josepheus; together with sketches of the history of the Jews, since their dispersion. By the author of Pierre and his family. Philadelphia, American Sunday School Union, [c1828] vi, 234 p. CtY; GDC; IObB; InRE; MA; MS; NH; NHuntL; NcWsS; OMC; P; ScCliP; ScCliTO; WHi; BrMus.
                                    33735
---- The genuine works of Flavius Josephus by the late Wm. Whiston, M. A. Revised & illustrated with notes in two volumes. New York, Pub. by Wm. Barradaile, 1828. 2 vols. CtY; IGK; KyLoF; MeAU; NNG; PSC-Hi.
                                    33736

---- ---- Bridgeport, M. Sherman, 1828. 6 v. CL; DLC; GMM; GMW; IU; IaCrM; KyDC; MdW; MoSpD; NGH; OCX; OO; OUr;

164 Journal

PWW; RPA; TJaL; TxAuPT. 33737

Journal of the convention of young men, of the state of New York, assembled at Utica. See National Republican Party. New York.

Judicial specimens. See Bradstreet, Mrs. Martha.

[Judson, Albert]
A series of questions on the selected scripture lessons. Designed for five yearly courses of instruction. Philadelphia, American Sunday School Union, 1828. 5 vols. [I= 3rd ed.; II-V = 7th ed.] RPB. 33738

[----] ---- Designed as a second annual course of instruction. In five volumes. Vol. II. ...3d ed. Philadelphia, American Sunday-School Union, 1828. Vol. II only, 220, [3] p. MH. 33739

Julius, pseud. See Rush, Richard.

Junius, pseud.
To the people of Kentucky. Will you stand quietly by and see the constitution of your country wantonly violated by the ambitious leaders of a desperate faction?... Junius. [Kentucky, 1828?] 2 p. DLC. 33740

Junius unmasked; or, Lord George Sackville proved to be Junius. With an appendix, showing, that the author of the letters of Junius was also the author of 'The history of the reign of George III,' and author of 'The North Briton,' ascribed to Mr. Wilkes... Boston, Hilliard, Gray, Little, and Wilkins, [Cambridge, Hilliard, Metcalf, and Co.] 1828. 2 p. l., v, [7]-187 p. CtY; DGU; DLC; IU; KU; MA; MB; MBC; MBS; MH-AH; MNBedf; MWA; MiD-B; NCH; NNS; NhHi;

OO; PPL; WHi; BrMus. 33741

A jurisprudencial [sic] enquiry into the ground of the old and new grant controversy, with some remarks and observations on the correctness of Judge Haywood's Decisions in relation to the doctrine of retracing land surveys in a forest of fraudulent land jobbers. By a reflecting and critical observer of Nashville interested in the said conflict. [Nashville? 1828?] 12 p. T. 33742

Juvenalis, Decimas Junius
D. Junii Juvenalis Satirae expurgatae, Accedunt notae Anglicae in usum Scholae Bostoniensis Cura F. P. Leverett. Bostoniae, Hilliard, Gray, Little et Wilkins, 1828. 2 p l., 257 p. CtY; DLC; MB; MH; MdW; PPLT; TxU; ViL; WBB. 33743

The Juvenile forget me not; or, Cabinet of entertainment and instruction. By the author of "The rival crusoes." "The Young emigrant," etc. New York, Repr. for W. B. Gilley, 1828. 144 p. DLC; ICN; KU; KWiU; MHad; MPlyA. 33744

Juvenile poems. Wendell, Mass., J. Metcalf, 1828. 16 p. DLC; MWA; RPB. 33745

The juvenile sketch book: containing original and select stories. Boston, N. S. Simpkins & co.; J. H. Eastburn, pr., 1828. 211 p. DLC; ICN; KN; MB; MH; MWA; NjR. 33746

K

[Kane, John Kintzing] 1795-1858
A candid view of the presidential question, by a Pennsylvanian. Philadelphia, Pr. by William Stavely, 1828. 22 p. DLC; MdHi;

NN; OCHP; P; PHi; PPL. 33747

Kathleen O'Moore, an Irish air,
the poetry by S. Woodworth.
Sung by Miss L. Gillingham.
With an accompaniment for piano
forte. New York, E. Riley, 1828.
2 p. DLC. 33748

Kearney, Ravaud
An appeal to the candid of all
denominations; in reply to one
Peter Gough of St. Mary's coun-
ty Maryland. Baltimore, William
Wooddy, 1828. 83 p. NNG.
33749
Kecht, J. S.
Der verbesserte praktische
Weinbau in Gärten und vorzüglich
auf Weinbergen. Mit einer an-
weisung den Wein ohne presse zu
keltern. Von J. S. Kecht. Den
amerikanischen Weinbauern ge-
widmet von Heinrich B. Sage.
Reading, Gedruckt bey G. Adolph
Sage, 1828. viii, 84 p. IU; P;
PHi; PPG; PPL. 33750

Kelley, Hall J.
Kelley's first spelling book: or,
Child's instructor, designed for
Sunday and common schools; containing lessons in orthography
and reading made easy by the division of words and an improved
use of figures and letters, agreeably to Walker's critical pronouncing dictionary. 8th ed. Concord,
N. H. , Horatio Hill, 1828. 84 p.
InTI. 33751

Kendall, J.
On man's accountableness.
[Keene, 1828] 147 p. MB. 33752

[Kennedy, Grace]
Anna Ross; a story for children. By the author of "The Decision,"... New York, Pub. by
Wm. Burgess, Jr. [J. S. Anderson & Co. , prs.] 1828. 156 p.
DLC; IU. 33753

[----] The decision; or, Religion
must be all, or is nothing. 6th
Amer. ed. Exeter, Pr. & Pub.
by J. C. Gerrish, 1828. 152 p.
MH. 33754

[----] ---- 6th Amer. ed. New-
York, W. Burgess, jr. , 1828.
108 p. CtY; GAGTh; MB. 33755

[----] Dunallen; or, Know what
you judge. In two volumes. By
the author of "The Decision,"
"Father Clement," &c. &c. New-
York, Collins & Hannay; Collins
and co.; J. P. Haven; White, Gallaher and White; E. Bliss, and
W. B. Gilley [Sleight & George,
prs. , Jamaica] 1828. 2 vols.
NBLiHi; NJQ. 33756

[----] ---- New York, Orville
A. Roorbach [W. E. Dean, pr.]
1828. 2 vols. IU; NBLiHi; NN;
NjR. 33757

[----] ---- Exeter, Pr. for the
publishers, 1828. 2 vols. ICU;
MBAt; MWA; Nh; NhHi. 33758

[----] Profession is not principle;
or, The name of Christian is not
Christianity... 4th Amer. ed.
Exeter [N. H.] Pub. by John C.
Gerrish, 1828. 224 p. CSmH;
NhHi; NjR. 33759

Kennedy, John Herron, 1801-
1840
Sympathy, its foundation and
legitimate exercise considered,
in a special relation to Africa:
A discourse delivered on the
Fourth of July 1828... Philadelphia, Pr. by W. F. Geddes
[1828] 11 p. CtHC; DeWI; MB;
MdW; MsJS; NjPT; PPL;
PPPrHi. 33760

Kenney, James
Turn out, a musical farce in
two acts. Baltimore, J. Robinson, 1828. 36 p. MH; NN. 33761

Kenrick, Francis Patrick
    The letters of Omega and
Omicron on transsubstantiation:
or, Two "Unanswerable" letters
written by a Pr. minister "Eulo-
gized" in twenty one. Louisville,
Pr. by W. W. Worsley, 1828. 71
p. DGU; ICL; ICU; InNd; KyLo;
MdBL; MdBS; MoSU; PPCCH.
                                    33762
Kenrick, Timothy, 1759-1804
    An exposition of the historical
writings of the New Testament,
with reflections subjoined to each
section... With a memoir of the
author, From the 2d London oc-
tavo ed. ... Boston, Munroe &
Francis, 1828. 3 v. CBPac;
CtHC; CtY; DLC; GAuY; ICU;
IEG; KyBrU; MB; MBAt; MBC;
MH; MWA; MeAu; NBLiHi; NCH;
NNG; TBriK; ViRUT; VtU; WHi;
BrMus.   33763

Kent, Benjamin
    Address delivered at the fu-
neral of the Hon. George Partridge, July 9, 1828; and a sermon preached in the First Congregational Church in Duxbury on
the next Sabbath. Boston, Press
of Isaac R. Butts and co., 1828.
36 p. CtY; DLC; ICMe; MB;
MBAU; MBAt; MH; MHi; MWA;
MeBaT; PPL; RPB; BrMus.
                                    33764
Kent, James
    Commentaries on American
law. New York, Pub. by O. Halsted [Clayton & Van Norden, prs.]
1828. 3 vol. IP; KyLxT; MeU;
MoSW; MsU; RNR; TU; W. 33765

Kentuckian - Extra.   See Major
Barry's hostility.

Kentucky
    Acts passed at the first ses-
sion of the thirty-sixth General
Assembly for the commonwealth
of Kentucky, begun and held in
the town of Frankfort, on Monday, the third day of December,

in the year eighteen hundred and
twenty seven... Frankfort, Jacob
H. Holeman, state pr., 1828.
247 p. Ar-CS; In-SC; IaU-L;
KyLoF; KyLxT; KyU-L; MdBB;
MiD-B; NNLI; Nb; Nc-S; Nj; Nv;
OrSC; RPL; T; W; Wa.   33766

---- Journal of the House of
Representatives of the commonwealth of Kentucky. Begun and
held in the town of Frankfort, on
Monday the third day of December, in the year of Our Lord
1827. ... Frankfort, Pr. by Jacob
H. Holeman, pr. for the state,
1827 [i. e. 1828] 429 p. Ky;
KyBgW; KyHi; KyLxT; KyU-L.
                                    33767
---- Journal of the Senate of the
commonwealth of Kentucky. Begun and held in the town of
Frankfort on Monday the third
day of December, in the year of
our Lord 1827... Frankfort, Pr.
by Jacob H. Holeman, pr. for
the state, 1827 [i. e. 1828] 451 p.
Ky; KyLoF; KyLxT; KyU-L.
                                    33768
---- Reports of cases at common
law and in equity argued and decided in the Court of Appeals of
the commonwealth of Kentucky.
By Thomas B. Monroe... Vol.
IV. Commencing with the Reap-
pointment of Geo. M. Bibb,
Chief Justice; January, 1827, and
ending with the first session of
Spring Term of that year. Frank-
fort, Albert C. Hodges, pr.,
1828. xii, 594, 644 p. Az; KyBgW;
KuHi; KyLxT; MH-L; MdBB; N-
L; Nc-S; Nd-L; RPL; W; BrMus.
                                    33769
Kersey, Jesse
    Lectures on agriculture, de-
livered before the Downingtown
Society for the Acquisition and
Promotion of Natural Knowledge.
West-Chester, Penn., Pr. by
Simeon Siegfried. 1828. [3], 80 p.
DeGE; P; PHi; PPL; PPi.
                                    33770

Kilbourn, John
    Public documents, concerning
the Ohio canals... comprising a
complete official history... Columbus, Compiled and pub. by John
Kilbourn. Olmsted, Bailhache &
Camron, prs., 1828. 403 + 1
blank + [1] p. N; NN; O; OCHP;
OCoSc; OHi; BrMus.   33771

Kilham, Mrs. Hannah (Spurr),
1774-1832
    Family maxims... No. 31.
New-York, For sale at the bookstores of Samuel Wood and Sons,
and Mahlon Day. M. Day, pr.,
1828. 12 p. MeU.   33772

Kimpton, F.
    He "lies like truth," a comic
interlude, in one act. Tr. and
adapted from the French, by F.
Kimpton... Baltimore, J. Robin-
son, 1828. 28 p. DLC; MH.
                          33773
King, Thomas F.
    The Lord's supper, a sermon,
delivered in the Universalist
meeting-house in Portsmouth,
N. H., on the morning of the first
Sabbath in November, 1828...
Portsmouth [N. H.] Pr. by Gideon
Beck, 1828. 16 p. CSmH; MBAt;
MMeT-Hi.   33774

King, William, abp. of Dublin,
1650-1729
    A discourse, concerning the
inventions of men in the worship
of God. Philadelphia, Pr. by J.
Harding, 1828. 112 p. CBDP;
CtHT; DLC; IObB; MdHi; MeBaT;
MoS; NNG; NjR; OCHP; RNR;
ScCC.   33775

[Kingsley, Zephaniah]
    A treatise on the patriarchal,
or co-operative system of society, as it exists in some governments, and colonies in America,
and in the United States, under
the name of slavery... By an inhabitant of Florida. [no place]

1828. 16 p. OCU; TxH.   33776

Kinsley, A. W. & Co., Albany,
N. Y.
    A specimen of printing types,
cast in the Franklin letter foundry of A. W. Kinsley & Co. ...
[Albany] Webster & Wood [1828?]
unpaged. MB.   33777

Kippis, A.
    A narrative of the voyages
round the world, performed by
Captain James Cook. With an ac-
count of his life, during the pre-
vious and intervening periods.
Boston, Pub. by N. H. Whitaker
[Pr. by J. H. A. Frost] 1828. 2 v.
CtHT-W; GAGTh; MBC; MH;
MdBP; PWW; RJa; ViU.   33778

Kirkham, Samuel
    English grammar in familiar
lectures accompanied by a compendium embracing a new systematick order of parsing... 6th ed.
Cincinnati, N. & G. Guilford,
Farnsworth, Jr., pr., 1828. 192
+ p. KyBgW; KyU; OClWHi.
                          33779
---- ---- 8th ed., enl. and imp.
Philadelphia, Pub. and sold by
Towar and Hogan, 1828. 190 p.
VtVe.   33780

---- ---- 6th ed. enl. and imp.
Pittsburg, Pub. & sold by Johns-
ton and Stockton, 1828. 192 p.
PMA.   33781

---- ---- 10th ed. enl. and imp.
Rochester, Pr. and sold by Mar-
shall & Dean, 1828. 216 p. NIC;
NRHi.   33782

Kirkland, John Thornton, 1770-
1846
    Valuable private library. Cata-
logue of the library of the Rev.
Dr. Kirkland, containing many
valuable theological, classical
and scientific books, in Greek,
Latin and English. To be sold

on Thursday, May 22, 1828, at Cunningham's Auction. Room... Boston, Condon, pr., 1828. 20 p. PPL.   33783

Kite's town and country almanac for 1829. By William Collom. Philadelphia, Thos. Kite [1828] 18 l. MWA; MiU-C; NBuHi; PHi.   33784

Kittredge, Jonathan, 1793-1864
It is every man's duty to read this address. Address upon the effects of ardent spirits. Delivered in the Town-hall of Lyme, N. H. January 8, 1827... Hartford, Pub. by Silas Andrus, 1828. 23 p. CBPac; CtHi; CtY; KyLoF; MH.   33785

---- An address upon the effects of ardent spirits. Delivered in the Town-Hall of Lyme, N. H. January 8, 1827. New-York, Pr. by D. Fanshaw, Pub. by John P. Haven, 1828. 24 p. A-Ar; CtY; DLC; MHi; MWA; MWo; MnU; NCH; NcMHi; NjPT; NjR; OO; PPiW; ScCC.   33786

---- ---- Rochester, Pr. by Elisha Loomis, 1828. 24 p. NRU.
                              33787
---- ---- 2d Rochester ed. Rochester [N. Y.] Pr. by Elisha Loomis, 1828. 24 p. CSmH; NN; NRHi.   33788

---- ---- [3d ed.] Rochester, Pr. by Elisha Loomis, 1828. 24 p. CSmH; RPB.   33789

---- ---- Westfield [N. Y.] Pr. by John B. Eldredge, 1828. 24 p. CSmH.   33790

---- An address, upon the subject of intemperance, delivered in the Town Hall of Lyme, New-Hampshire, January 8, 1827. Ithaca, Pr. by Mack & Andrus, 1828. 24 p. NIC.   33791

---- An address upon the subject of temperance, delivered in the Town Hall of Lyme, New Hampshire, January 8, 1827... Watertown, Pr. by H. L. Harvey, 1828. 12 p. N.   33792

Knapp, Samuel Lorenzo, 1783-1838
A discourse on the life and character of DeWitt Clinton, delivered before the Grand chapter and Grand lodge of the District of Columbia, the Grand chapter of Maryland, the Blue lodges of Washington, Georgetown and Alexandria, and other masons of the vicinity, and the brethren sojourners in the city of Washington, on the twenty-ninth of March, 1828. Washington, Pr. by William Greer, 1828. 36 p. CSmH; CtHT; DLC; IaCrM; LNHT; MBAt; MH; MdHi; NjPT; OCHP; PHi; PPL; RPB; BrMus.   33793

---- The genius of masonry; or, A defence of the order, containing some remarks on the origin and history; the uses and abuses of the science, with some notices of other secret societies in the United States, in three lectures. Providence, Cranston and Marshall, prs., 1828. 107 p. DLC; IaCrM; MB; MH; MdBFM; NB; NN; OCM; PPFM; PPL; RHi; RP; RPMA; TxWFM; BrMus. 33794

Knickerbocker's almanac for 1829. By David Young. New-York, Caleb Bartlett [1828] 24 l. CtHi; CtY; MWA; N; NN.   33795

---- ---- Poughkeepsie, Platt & Parsons [1828] 24 l. MWA; NjR.
                              33796
The knights of the orange grove; a farce in two acts. New-York, Pub. by John M. Danforth, 1828. 32 p. NNC.   33797

Knowles, James Davis, 1798-1838

Perils and safeguards of American liberty. Address, pronounced July 4, 1828, in the Second Baptist meeting-house in Boston at the religious celebration of the anniversary of American independence, by the Baptist churches and societies in Boston. Boston, Pr. by Lincoln & Edmands [1828] 27, [1] p. CSmH; CtY; DLC; MB; MBAt; MH; MW; MWA; MiD-B; NN; NjPT; PHi; RHi; RPB; BrMus.   33798

Knowles, James Sheridan, 1784-1862
    Brian Boroihme, or, The maid of Erin, a historical Hibernian melo-drama, in three acts, as performed at the Theatres Royal, Dublin, and Belfast; also at the Philadelphia and New-York theatres. Now first printed.... New-York, E. M. Murden, 1828. 40 p. DLC; MH; NN.   33799

---- William Tell: a play in five acts. Philadelphia, C. Neal, 1828. 89 p. CSmH; MH.   33800

Koecker, Leonard, 1785-1850
    An essay on the diseases of the jaws, and their treatment; with observations on the amputation of a part or the whole of the inferior maxilla; tending to prove that such operation is seldom, if ever, necessary... Philadelphia, H. C. Carey & I. Lea, 1828. 95 p. MdU-H; MiU; BrMus.   33801

Kuffner, J.
    Boston Independent Cadets' grand march composed by J. Kuffner. Arranged for piano-forte by J. Worsley. Boston, C. Bradlee, 1828. 2 p. KU; MB.   33802

Kurtz, Benjamin, 1795-1865
    Christ blesses little children. A sermon preached before the Sunday school in Funks-town on the 16th November, 1828...

Hagers-town, Md. , Pr. by Wm. D. Bell, 1828. 20 p. CSmH; PPLT.   33803

Kurtzgefasste Anweisung über die Anlegung von Weinbergen, die Behandlung des Mostes und des Weines und andere dahin gehörigen Gegenständen mit besonderer Rücksicht auf die Vereinigten Staaten. Von einem praktischen teutschen Weingärtner. Baltimore, Johann T. Hanzsche, 1828. Seidensticker 236.   33804

The Kuzzelbash. See Fraser, James Baellie.

Kynaston, Humphrey
    The life and adventures of Humphrey Kynaston, with the Surprising adventures of Capt. Redmond O. Hanlon, a celebrated robber. New York, 1828. Sabin 38373.   33805

L

L. , A.
    Little Ellen, and other pleasing poetical tales. By A. L. of New-port, R. I. New York, Pr. by Mahlon Day, 1828. 23 p. OClWHi.   33806

Lacey, William B.
    An illustration of the principles of elocution; designed for the use of schools. Albany, Pr. by Websters and Skinners, 1828. 300 p. **PPL**.   33807

[Ladd, William]
    Essays on peace and war. By Philanthropos. In two vols. Pub. by John T. Burnham, Exeter, N. H., 1828. 2 vols. DLC; ICU; MeBaT; VtU.   33808

A lady, pseud. See Tuthill, Louisa Caroline (Huggins).

The Lady at the farm house; or, Religion the best friend in trouble. Revised by the committee of publication. Philadelphia, American Sunday School Union, 1828. 141 p. ICU; BrMus.   33809

A lady of Boston.   See Tales of the Emerald Isle.

A lady of Massachusetts.   See Child, Mrs. Lydia Maria (Francis).

A lady of Massachusetts.   See Foster, Mrs. Hannah (Webster).

A lady of New Jersey.   See A plain and easy catechism.

A lady of Philadelphia. See Chapman, Ernestine.

A lady of Philadelphia. See Leslie, Eliza.

A lady of Philadelphia. See The mirror.

A lady of Richmond.   See Littleford, Mrs.

A lady of Virginia.   See Rives, Judith Page Walker.

Lafayette almanac for 1829. Baltimore, Lovegrove [1828] PP; TKL.   33810

Lafitte; or, The Baratarian chief. A tale. New York, 1828. 106 p. CtY; MH; MWA; NN; PU; RPB.
                                   33811
Lagow, Wilson.   See Burnside, A. (note).

Lamb, Jonathan
    The child's primer, or First book for primary schools. Burlington [Vt.] C. Goodrich, 1828. 72 p. DLC.   33812

[Lamb, Charles]

Elia. Essays... First series. 2d ed. Philadelphia, Carey, Lea, & Carey, Mifflin and Parry, prs., 1828. 292 p. CSmH; PPL.
                                   33813
[----] ---- 2d series. Philadelphia, Carey, Lea and Carey, J. R. A. Skerrett, pr., 1828. 230, [2] p. CLU; CSmH; KyU; MH; MdBP; NN; NNS; NjP; OClStM; PPL; PU; BrMus.   33814

Lamson, Alvan
    No. 20. On the doctrine of two natures in Jesus Christ. Pr. for The American Unitarian Association. Boston, Bowles & Dearborn,[Isaac R. Butts, pr.] 1828. 36 p. CBPac; CtHC; DLC; ICMe; ICU; IEG; MB; MBAU; MBC; MH-AH; MHi; MMeT-Hi; MWA; MeB; Nh; RP; ScCC.   33815

A Landholder, pseud.   See Updike, Wilkens.

Lansing, John V. S.
    Address to the friends of sound doctrine, experimental piety, and ministerial faithfulness in the true Reformed Dutch Church. New York, Sam'l. Marks, 1828. 43 p. NjR; PPPrHi.
                                   33816
Lardner, Dionysius, 1793-1859
    Popular lectures on the steam engine, in which its construction and operation are familiarly explained; with an historical sketch of its invention and progressive improvement... With additions by James Renwick... New-York, Pr. for Elam Bliss, 1828. [Gray & Bunce, prs.] xi, 171 p. CSmH; CtHC; CtMW; DBRE; GDC; IaHi; MB; MH; MiU-T; MWA; NCH; NGH; NNC; NNE; NSyU; NWM; PPF; PPL; Vi.   33817

The last day of the week. New York, Pub. by the General Protestant Episcopal Sunday School Union. Edward J. Swords, pr.,

1828. 88 p. NNC-T.   33818

Lathrop, Leonard Elijah
    The farmers' library: or Es-
says designed to encourage the
pursuits, and promote the science of agriculture... 3d ed.,
corr. and enl. Rochester, N.Y.,
Pr. by Marshall & Dean, 1828.
344 p. CSmH; MNe; NGH; NIC;
NNC; NR; NRHi; NRU; PHi;
PPAmP; PPL.   33819

Latourette, James
    Letters from James Latour-
ettee [!] of New York, to his
friend Charles Crook, of Baltimore... [Baltimore] [R. J.] Matchett, pr. [1828] [9]-16 p. MdHi.
                             33820
A Laughing Philosopher. See The
humorist.

Laura Somerville; or, Indolent
habits overcome. Boston, Bowles
& Dearborn, 1828. 17 p. (Vol.
v, no. 5.) DLC.   33821

Law, Thomas, 1756-1834
    An address to the Columbian
Institute, on a moneyed system
... Washington, Pr. by Gales &
Seaton, 1828. 95 p. CtY; DLC;
MB; NNC; PPL; PU.   33822

Law Association of Philadelphia
    Catalogue of the books belong-
ing to the Law Association of
Philadelphia. To which are added,
the charters, regulations, and a
list of the members. Philadelphia, 1828. 39, [1] p. NN; PHi.
                             33823
Lawrence, William
    Lectures on physiology, zool-
ogy, and the natural history of
man, delivered at the Royal College of Surgeons... Salem, Pr.
and pub. by Foote & Brown,
1828. 495 p. CSmH; KyLxT; Md;
NcD; PPL.   33824

Lawrence & Lemay's North-

Carolina almanack for 1829. By
William Collom. Raleigh, Law-
rence & Lemay [1828] 18 l.
MWA; NcD; NcHiC.   33825

Lay, William
    Narrative of the mutiny on
board the ship Globe, of Nantucket, in the Pacific Ocean, Jan.
1824. And the journal of a residence of two years on the Mul-
grave islands; with observations
on the manners and customs of
the inhabitants. New-London, Pub.
by Wm. Lay and C. M. Hussey
[S. Green, pr.] 1828. 168 p.
CSmH; Ct; CtHi; DLC; IEdS; IHi;
MB; MBC; MH; PP; PPL; TxH;
BrMus.   33826

A lay preacher, pseud. See The
Calvinistic doctrine.

A layman, pseud. See Lowell,
John.

A Layman, pseud. See Scott,
Walter.

A layman of the Methodist Episcopal Church. See An address to
Methodists.

A Layman of the Reformed
Dutch Church. See Remarks on
liberty of conscience.

Lea, Pryor
    Circular of Mr. Lea to his
constituents. Fellow-citizens...
[1828] 14 p. McMurtrie 269.
                             33827
Leavitt's improved New-England
almanack for 1829. By Dudley
Leavitt. Concord, Jacob B.
Moore [1828] 12 l. CLU; CtHi;
DLC; InU; MB; MBAt; MBC; MH;
MWA; MdBJ; MiD-B; N; NCH;
NhHi; NjR; PPL; WHi.   33828

LeBlanc, H.
    The art of tying the cravat...
From the 2d London ed. Phila-

delphia, Robert Desilver, [T.
Town, pr.] 1828. vii, 72 p. MB;
NNC-T; P; ScC.   33829

Lecture delivered in the Holy
Royal Arch Chapter, no. 91,
Philadelphia, on the evening of
August 20, A. L. 5828. Philadel-
phia, T. S. Manning, 1828. 12 p.
IaCrM.   33830

Lee, Chauncey, 1763-1842
     The remembrancer; a farewell
sermon delivered in Colebrook
[Conn.] on the first sabbath in
February 1828. Hartford, Pr. by
Philemon Canfield, 1828. 16 p.
CBPac; Ct; CtHC; CtHi; CtY;
MBC; MWA; OClWHi; WHi.
                          33831
Lee, Henry. Report of a com-
mittee. See Boston, Citizens.

Lee, Henry, 1787-1837
     A vindication of the character
and public services of Andrew
Jackson... Boston, True & Green,
prs., 1828. 51 p. CU; CtY; DLC;
MB; MBAt; MH; MWA; Nh; Nh-
Hi; OClWHi; ScCC; WHi. 33832

Lee, Isaac
     No. IV. Description of six new
species of the genus Unio, embracing the anatomy of the ovi-
duct of one of them, together with
some anatomical observations on
the genus. By Isaac Lea. Read
before the American Philosophical Society. November 2d, 1827.
[Philadelphia? 1828?] 15 p. PPL.
                          33833
Lee, Thomas J.
     A spelling-book... 2d ed. Bos-
ton, Pub. by Munroe & Francis,
1828. 180 p. NNC.   33834

Leech, Richard T.
     Address delivered by Richard
T. Leech, Esq. on the 4th July,
1828, to the friends of the administration, assembled on the
island opposite Harrisburg: [Har-

risburg, Pr. at the Intelligence
Office, 1828] 24 p. PHi; T.
                          33835
---- ---- Another ed. [Harris-
burg, Pr. at the Intelligence Office, 1828] 16 p. PPL.   33836

The Legendary. See, Willis Nathaniel Parker.

Legendre, Adrien Marie, 1752-
1833
     Elements of geometry and
trigonometry; with notes. Trans-
lated from the French of A. M.
Legendre... By David Brewster
... Rev. and altered for the use
of the Military Academy at West
Point. New York, J. Ryan, 1828.
xvi, 316 p. CSt; CtY; IaU; KU;
MH; MnHi; NRU; NWM; NcU;
NjR; PMA; RPB; ScCliP; TxGR;
ViRVal; ViU; WaU.   33837

Le Guire, Amos
     A juvenile poem, entitled The
Heliad; or, Christ, the light of
the world. In numbers, at different intervals... Haverstraw
[N. Y.] Pr. by E. Burroughs,
1828. 53, [1] p. ICU.   33838

Lehigh Coal and Navigation Company
     Report of the board of man-
agers of the Lehigh Coal and
Navigation Company, presented
to the stockholders, January 14,
1828. Philadelphia, Pr. by S. W.
Conrad [1828] 12 p. DLC; NN;
MH-BA.   33839

Le Sage, Alain Rene, 1668-1747
     The adventures of Gil Blas of
Santillane. Translated from the
French of Le Sage. By T. Smollett, M. D.   To which is prefixed
a memoir of the author, Philadelphia, J. Harding, 1828-29.
4 v. IU; OFH; ViPet.   33840

[Leslie, Eliza] 1787-1858
     Seventy-five receipts for pas-

try, cakes, and sweetmeats. By
a lady of Philadelphia. Boston,
Munroe and Francis, C. S. Francis, New York, 1828. viii, [1],
[7]-88 p. CtHT-W; MB; MH;
PPL; RPB.   33841

Le Tellier, Charles Constant,
1768-1846
    Grammaire françoise a l'usage
des pensionnats; 1. éd. ameri-
caine d'après la 40. éd. de Paris. New York, De Behr, 1828.
192 p. CtMW; CtY; IGK.   33842

Let it alone till tomorrow. In
two parts. 1st Amer. ed. Boston, Peirce and Williams, 1828.
36 p. MB.   33843

Letter from a gentleman in Boston. See Tappan, Lewis.

A letter from a German doctor
of the University of Strasburg,
to a Protestant gentleman. St.
Louis, Pr. by Charles Keemle,
1828. 31 p. DGU; ICN.   33844

Letter from Joe Strickland. See
Dekay, Joseph E.

Letter to a convert, by Sacerdos.
To it is added, A net for the
fishers of men; by way of dilem-
na. By two late converts. Baltimore, Pub. by James Myres.
Matchett, pr. [1828] 101, [3], [2]
p. MdW.   33845

A letter to Edward Livingston,
Esq. delegate from Louisiana to
the general congress at Washington City, on the subject of the
speech delivered by him, at
Washington, at the late celebration of the anniversary of the 8th
of January, 1815. Natchez, Pr.
for the author, 1828. 21, 3 p.
Signed "W." Dated "Natchez, 10th
March, 1828." CtY; DLC; LU;
PPL.   33846

Letter to the Methodists of central Virginia... Staunton, Va.,
Spectator Office, pr., 1828. 24
p. PLT.   33847

Letter to the Rev. Parsons
Cooke. See Parker, Isaac.

Letters addressed to John Sergeant, Manuel Eyre, Lawrence
Lewis, Clement C. Biddle, and
Joseph P. Norris. See Democratic Party. Pennsylvania.

... Letters and documents of distinguished citizens of Tennessee
on the buying and selling of human beings... New York, Sickels,
pr., 1828. At head of title:
"Hear him and his neighbours."
16 p. CSmH; MnHi; PHi; WHi.
                              33848
Letters from Europe, in 1828.
See Sprague, William Buell.

Letters of an English traveller.
See Dewey, Orville.

The letters of David and John;
containing animadversions upon
the lectures of Dr. Woods on infant baptism. First pub. in The
Columbia Star. Philadelphia, W.
Wilkins & Co. [Pilkington & Co.,
pr.] 1828. 106 p. CtY; KyLoS;
LNB; NRAB; NjPT; RPB. 33849

Letters to the Rev. William E.
Channing. See Shedd, William.

Levins, Thomas C.
    A discourse delivered on the
17th of March, 1828, in St. Pat-
rick's Cathedral, New York.
New-York, Pr. at the office of
"The Truth Teller," 1828. 47 p.
CtY; DGU; NN.   33850

Levizac, Jean Pons Victor Le-
coutz de
    A theoretical and practical
grammar of the French tongue:
in which the present usage is

displayed, agreeably, to the decisions of the French Academy...
6th Amer. from the last London ed., rev. and corr. by Mr. Stephen Pasquier... New-York, Evert Duyckinck, Collins & co., Collins & Hannay, and O. A. Roorbach [W. E. Dean, pr.] 1828. 444 p. CU; CtHT-W; DLC; InGrD; MB; MH; MeBaT; TxU-T.
33851

Lewis, Enoch
The Child's companion. A new primer, containing easy and familiar lessons. Philadelphia, Pub. by Thomas Kite, 1828. 36 p. PHi.
33852

Lewis, Freeman, 1781-1859
Revised edition. The beauties of harmony; containing the rudiments of music on an improved plan, a musical dictionary, or glossary of musical terms, with their explanations, and an extensive collection of sacred music, consisting of tunes, fugues, and anthems. 5th ed. rev. and enl. Pittsburgh, Johnston & Stockton, 1828. 208 p. MiU-C; NN; OClWHi.
33853

Lewis, John, 1784-1858
Tables of comprative etymology and analogous formations in the Greek, Latin, Spanish, Italian, French, English, and German languages; or, The student's manual of languages. Philadelphia, Carey, Lea & Carey, Mifflin and Parry, prs., 1828. 12 p., 1 l., 38 tab. (part double). DLC; MB; MWA; MdBP; MiD; NB; NIC; NN; NNC; PPL; ScU; ViU. 33854

Lewis, Matthew Gregory
The castle specter, a dramatic romance in five acts. New York, Samuel French [1828] 46 p. MLex.
33855
---- Raymond and Agnes; or, The bleeding nun or[!] the castle of Lindenberg. New York, S.

King, 1828. 38 p. DLC. 33856

---- ---- Philadelphia, Pub. and sold by Freeman Scott, 1828. 70+ p. CSmH.   33857

Lexington and Fayette County Auxiliary Colonization Society
Second annual report of the managers of the Lexington and Fayette County Auxiliary Colonization Society, made at the annual meeting, July 8, 1828. Pub. by order of the Society. Lexington, Ky., Smith & Palmer, prs., 1828. 15, [1] p. KyBgW; KyU; PPPrHi.   33858

Lhomond, Charles François, 1727-1794
De viris illustribus urbus Romae, a romulo ad Augustum, ad usum sextae scholae;... Editio duarta Novi-Eborachi, juxta ultimam Parisiensem stereotypam... By James Hardie, A. M. Rev. and corr. by Thos. S. Joy... New York, Pr. and pub. by Geo. Long, 1828. iv, 252 p. CSt; KyLoP; MWHi; NNC; PRHi; PU.   33859

Liberal principles of Mr. Adams, An attempt has been made to create an impression that Mr. Adams, the President of the United States, is hostile to Catholics. The following extract of a letter from a Catholic of high standing and unimpeachable character, in Washington City, will put this matter straight. Extract of a letter from a gentleman in Washington City, to his friend in Hagerstown, Md. dated August 5, 1828. 1 p. DLC.   33860

Life and adventures of Arthur Clenning. See Flint, Timothy.

The life and adventures of Peter Wilkins. See Paltock, Robert.

Life and adventures of Robinson

Crusoe. See Defoe, Daniel.

The life and confessions of
George B. Jarman. See Jarman,
George B.

Life and death of Isabella Turnbull. See Wilson, Samuel.

The life of Bamfyld Moore Car-
ew, some time King of the Beggars, containing an accurate history of his travels, voyages, and
adventures. New-York, Pub. by
S. King, and sold wholesale and
retail at his store, 1828. 29,
[3] p. CSmH; MBNEH; NN; NcHiC;
OCHP.   33861

The life of Joab the son of Ze-
ruiah, compared with that of
Andrew Jackson. Addressed to
the sober and reflecting people of
the Western Country. By an old
farmer. [n. p. 1828] 8 p. DLC;
MH.   33862

The life of Mansie Wauch. See
Moir, David Macbeth.

The life of Napoleon Buonaparte.
See Scott, Sir Walter.

The life of Saint Patrick, Apostle
of Ireland. To which is added
the celebrated hymn, composed
above twelve hundred years since,
by his Disciple, St. Fiech; comprehending a compendious history
of his life... Philadelphia, E. Cum-
misky, 1828. 191, [1] p. MBtS;
MdW; PRosC.   33863

The life of the late... Dr. Cotton
Mather. See Mather, Samuel.

Life of William Caxton. See
Stevenson, William.

The light of truth; an account of
some of the deeds of Andrew
Jackson. [Washington, Pr. at
the office of J. Elliot, 1828?]

8 p. DLC; MBAt.   33864

Light and shades of English life.
From the New Monthly Magazine. Philadelphia, Pub. by
Carey, Lea & Carey, 1828. 2
vols. MBAt; NGH.   33865

Linnaean Botanic Garden. See
Prince, William.

Linsley, Joel Harvey, 1790-
1868
    Lectures on the relations
and duties of the middle aged.
Hartford, D. F. Robinson, pub-
lisher; Hudson and Skinner,
prs., 1828. 180 p. ArCH;
CBPac; CtHC; CtSoP; CtY; ICT;
ICMcC; IObB; InCW; MB; MBAt;
MBC; MH; MWA; MeBaT; MiU;
NNUT; Nh; ODW; OHi; OMC;
VtMiS.   33866

Lintner, G. A.
    A discourse, delivered be-
fore the Western Conference of
Lutheran Ministers, in the state
of New-York, at the installation
of the Rev. J. D. Lawyer, A. M.
Pastor of the Associate Evangelical Lutheran Churches in
Stone-Arabia, Minden and Pala-
tine. In Trinity Church, at
Stone-Arabia, January 1, 1828
... Schoharie, L. Cuthbert, pr.,
1828. 31 p. CSmH; N; NCH; NN.
                                   33867
[Lister, Thomas Henry] 1800-
1842
    Herbert Lacy. By the author
of Granby... Philadelphia, Carey,
Lea & Carey, 1828. 2 v. in 1.
DLC; MBAt; MBL; MH. 33868

Litchfield Law School
    Catalogue of the Litchfield
Law School from 1798 to 1827
inclusive. Litchfield, Pr. by S.
S. Smith, 1828. 27 p. CSmH;
CtY; MB; MBC.   33869

Little, William
    Revised and enlarged edition.
The easy instructor; or, A new
method of teaching sacred harmony. Containing 1. The rudiments of music on an improved
plan. wherein the naming and the
timing of the notes are familiar-
ized to the weakest capacity. II.
A choice collection of Psalm tunes
and anthems from the most celebrated authors, with a number
composed in Europe and America,
entirely new; suited to all meters
sung in the different churches in
the United States. Pub. for the
use of singing societies in general, but more particularly for these
who have not the advantage of an
instructor. Albany, Pr. by Websters & Skinners and Oliver Steele,
and sold at their respective bookstores, 1828. 127 p. CLCM; DLC;
MWA; NRAB.   33870

Little Agnes and blind Mary.
Boston, Bowles and Dearborn,
1828. 54 p. MWatP.   33871

Little Anne, a true story; and
other pleasing poetical pieces for
children. New York, Pr. and
sold by Mahlon Day, 1828. 23 p.
RPB.   33872

The little boy who minded trifles.
Designed for children from six to
eight years old. By the author of
'Fruit and flowers.' Boston, Hilliard, Gray, Little & Wilkins,
1828. 19 p. MH.   33873

The little Eagle containing a short
description of a tract of land situated in Clearfield County, Pa....
Also, a proposal for laying out a
new town... Harrisburg, Pa., 1828.
14 p. PPL.   33874

Little Edward, or Lessons in
reading for children between four
and six years old. Boston,
Bowles & Dearborn, 1828. 56 p.

MB; MH.   33875

Little Emma and her father. See
Baker, Caroline Horwood.

Little Henry's Sunday lesson.
Boston, Hilliard, Gray, Little &
Wilkins, 1828. 15 p. MH.
                             33876
Little Jack and his rocking
horse. Hartford, H. Benton,
1828. 12 plates. MnS.   33877

Little poems for little readers.
Wendell, J. Metcalf, 1828. 23 p.
MA; MWA.   33878

The little present. Wendell, J.
Metcalf, 1828. 8 p. MWA.
                             33879
Little Susan. Designed for chil-
dren two or three years old. By
the author of 'Fruit and Flowers.'
Boston, Hilliard, Gray, Little,
and Wilkins, 1828. 15 p. MH;
MWal.   33880

Little traveller. Boston, Bowles
and Dearborn, Press of Isaac R.
Butts & Co., 1828 [Original
moral tales, v. 6, no. 4] 32 p.
MB.   33881

Little verses for good children.
See American Tract Society.
New York.

Little Wentworth's morning lesson. Designed for children two
or three years old. By the auth-
or of 'Fruit and Flowers.' Boston, Hilliard, Gray, Little and
Wilkins, 1828. 9 p. MH. 33882

[Littleford, Mrs.]
    The wreath; or, Verses on
various subjects. By a lady of
Richmond. 2d ed., enl. ... Richmond, Pr. by Samuel Shepherd
& co., 1828. 5 p. l., [7]-132 p.
CSmH; DLC; PHi; PU; Vi; ViU.
                             33883
Livermore, Jonathan, 1770-1845

An address, pronounced at Wilton, before the friends of the national administration, at the celebration of American independence, July 4, 1828. Dunstable, N. H. , Pr. by Thayer & Wiggin, 1828. 16 p. CSmH; DLC; MBAt; MBC. 33884

Livermore, Samuel, 1786-1833
Dissertations on the questions which arise from the contrariety of the positive laws of different states and nations... No. 1, containing two dissertations. New Orleans, Pr. by Benjamin Levy, 1828. 172, [1] p. CSmH; IaU-L; LNHT; MB; MBAt; NN; NNC; OClWHi; PPL. 33885

Liverpool Packet Company
Articles of association of the Liverpool Packet Company, established July 25, 1827. Boston, N. Hale's press, 1828. 17 p. MH. 33886

The lives of Clemens Romanus, Ignatius, and Polycarp. By the author of Salome, &c. Philadelphia, American Sunday School Union, 1828. 126 p. MoSMa; BrMus. 33887

Livingston, Edward, 1764-1836
Letter from Edward Livingston, Esq. to Roberts Vaux, on the advantages of the Pennsylvania System of prison discipline, for the application of which the new Penitentiary has been constructed near Philadelphia, &c. &c. Philadelphia, Jesper Harding, pr. , 1828. 15 p. CLU; CU; Ct; ICLaw; MB; MH; MHi; MiD-B; NN; NNC; NjP; NjR; PHi; PPAmP; PPL; PU; RP; BrMus. 33888
---- A system of penal law for the United States of America... Pr. by order of the House of Representatives. Washington, Pr. by Gales & Seaton, 1828. 142,

187, 51, 45, 21 p. CU; CtHT; DLC; GU; IaU-L; MB; MH; MWA; MiU; MnU; NN; NNC-L; NNLI; Nb; NjP; OCLaw; WU-L; WaU; BrMus. 33889

Lochman, Johann Georg, 1773-1826
Hinterlassene predigten, von Johann Georg Lochman... Zum druck befördert von Augustus H. Lochman. A. M. Harrisburg, Gustav S. Peters, 1828. 332, [2] p. DLC; MH; MiD; P; PPL; PPLT. 33890

Locke, John, 1632-1704
Philosophical beauties selected from the works of John Locke, esq. ...with several other subjects treated on by this great philosopher, to which is prefixed some account of his life. 1st Amer. ed. New York, Pub. by J. Langdon, 1828. [5], 258 p. MB; MeBa; PSC-Hi. 33891

No entry. 33892

---- A treatise on the conduct of the understanding. Boston, Timothy Bedlington, 1828. 218 p. CtHC; ICL; IU; InRE; MH; MeAu; NNC; NbOP; PU-Penn; PWW; ScCoT. 33893

Locke, John 1792-1856
Problems to illustrate the most important principles of geography and astronomy, performed by the inclinable orrery, an instrument invented by J. Locke, M. D. and made by A. Willard, jr. Cincinnati, Morgan,

Fisher and L'Hommedieu, 1828.
14 p. DLC.   33894

[Lofland, John] 1798-1849
   The harp of Delaware; or, The
miscellaneous poems of the Milford bard... Philadelphia, Atkinson & Alexander, 1828. xi, 212
p. DLC; DeGE; Ia; IaHA; MB;
MH; MdBJ; MiKT; NjP; PHi;
PPL; PU; BrMus.   33895

Long, John
   To the free-men of the tenth
Congressional district in North
Carolina. Washington, 1828. 6 p.
NcU.   33896

Long, Stephen Harriman, 1784-
1864
   Rail road manual, or, A brief
exposition of principles and de-
ductions applicable in tracing the
route of a rail road... Baltimore,
W. Wooddy, pr., 1828-1829. 2
pt. in 1 v. CSmH; DBRE; DLC;
MH-BA; MdHi; MiU-T; NN;
NNC; NNE; NjP.   33897

Long Island Bible Society
   The twelfth annual report of
the Long-Island Bible Society.
Brooklyn, December 5, 1827.
Brooklyn, N.Y., Pr. by Alden
Spooner, 1828. 28 p. NBLiHi;
NHi; NJQ; NRivHi; NSmB. 33898

---- The thirteenth annual report
of the Long Island Bible Society.
Brooklyn, September 17, 1828.
Brooklyn, N.Y., Pr. by Alden
Spooner, 1828. 24 p. NBLiHi.
                              33899
Long Island Education Society
for the Reformed Dutch Church
   The constitution and address
of an Education Society, for the
Reformed Dutch Church, on Long-
Island. Instituted May, 1828.
Brooklyn, Alden Spooner, pr.,
1828. 18 p. NBLiHi; NEh; NHi.
                              33900
Longden, Henry

   The life of Henry Longden,
Minister of the Gospel; Compiled
from his own memoirs, diary,
letters and other authentic documents. 3d Amer. ed. Baltimore,
Armstrong & Plaskitt, and Plaskitt & co., [John D. Toy, pr.]
1828. 172, [2] p. IObB; MdHi.
                              33901

Longworth's American almanac,
New-York register and city di-
rectory, for the fifty-third year
of American Independence... New
York, Pub. by Thomas Longworth,
[J. Seymour, pr.] 1828. 652 p.
DLC; ICN; MWA; NHi; NN; NjR;
PPL.   33902

Lord, Nathan, 1793-1870
   An address delivered at Han-
over, October 29, 1828, at the
inauguration of the author as
president of Dartmouth College.
Windsor, Pr. by Simeon Ide,
1828. 28 p. CSmH; CtHT-W; CtY;
DLC; GDC; IEG; MA; MBAt;
MBC; MeB; MH; MHi; MMeT;
MoSpD; NCH; Nh; NjR; OCHP;
OO; RBr; RPB; VtMiM; VtU.
                              33903
Loring, Levi, 1784-1860
   The origin, evils, and remedy,
of intemperance. An address de-
livered in Buxton, April 10, 1828.
Pub. by request. Portland, Shir-
ley & Hyde, prs., 1828. 21 p.
MBC; MH; MeLB; Nh; RPB.
                              33904
[Lorraine, A. M.]
   Donald Adair: a novel, by a
young lady of Virginia... Rich-
mond, Pub. by Peter Cottom,
1828. 2 v. CSmH; MH; PU.
                              33905
The lost child. See Cameron,
Mrs. Lucy Lyttleton (Butt).

The lottery ticket. See Beazley,
Samuel.

Louisa's tenderness. See Ber-
quin, Arnaud.

Louisiana

Acts passed at the second session of the eighth Legislature of the state of Louisiana, begun and held in the city of New Orleans, on Monday [Jan. 7, 1828]... By authority. New Orleans, John Gibson, state pr., 1828. 199 p. IU; LNHT; LU.   33906

---- A general digest of the acts of the Legislature of Louisiana: Passed from the year 1804, to 1827, inclusive, and in force at this last period... By L. Moreau Lislet, Esq., counselor at law. Pub. according to an act of the Legislature... New Orleans, Benjamin Levy, 1828. 2 v. L; LNB; M; Nb; OCLaw; W.   33907

---- Journal de la chambre des representans de l'état de la Louisiane. (2nd session of eighth legislature) Nouvelle Orleans, Imprime par John Gibson, 1828. 96 p. DLC.   33908

---- Journal de la chambre des representans de l'état de la Louisiane. Neuvieme législature, premiere session. Nouvelle-Orleans, imprimé par John Gibson, imprimeur de l'état, 1828. 110 p. LNHT; LU.   33909

---- Journal du senat pendant la seconde session de la huitième législature de l'état de la Louisiane. Par autorité. Nouvelle Orleans, imprime par John Gibson, imprimeur de l'état, 1828. [64] p. L.   33910

---- Journal of the House of Representatives during the second session of the eighth Legislature of the state of Louisiana... New Orleans, Pr. by John Gibson, state pr., 1828. 111 p. DLC; LNHT.   33911

---- Journal of the House of

Representatives of the state of Louisiana. Ninth Legislature, first session. New Orleans, Pr. by John Gibson, state pr., 1828. 111 p. IU.   33912

---- The journal of the Senate during the second session of the eighth Legislature of the state of Louisiana. By authority. New Orleans, Pr. by John Gibson, state pr., 1828. 68 p. LNHT; LU.   33913

---- Journal of the Senate during the first session of the ninth Legislature of the state of Louisiana. New Orleans, Pr. by John Gibson, state pr., 1828. 82 p. LNHT.   33914

The Louisiana almanack for 1829. By Wm. Collom. New Orleans, Wm. M'Kean [1828] 24 l. MWA.   33915

Love of admiration. See Tuthill, Louisa Caroline (Huggins).

Loveland, Samuel C.
A Greek lexicon, adapted to the New Testament, with English definitions. Woodstock, Vt., Pr. by D. Watson, 1828. vi p., 1 l., 376 p. DLC; MH; MiD; NNC; Nh; NhHi; VtMiS; VtU; BrMus.   33916

---- Influence of hope and fear with regard to future objects. A sermon, ... [Woodstock? 1828?] 8 p. DLC; WHi.   33917

Lovell, John Epy, 1795-1892
Introductory arithmetic; prepared for the pupils of the Lancastrian school, New-Haven, Accompanied by a Key for the use of the monitor. Part first. ... 2d ed. New-Haven, Pub. by S. Wadsworth. N. Whiting, pr., 1828. 240 p. CtHT-W; CtHi; CtY; DAU; MoS; PPF.   33918

---- A key to introductory arithmetic; prepared for the pupils of the Lancasterian School, New-Haven. Part first... 2d ed. New Haven, Pub. by S. Wadworth [N. Whiting, pr.] 1828. 203 p. CtHT-W; CtHi; CtY; DAU; MH; MoS; PPF. 33919

Lowell, Charles, 1782-1861
The name of Christian the only appropriate name for believers in Christ. A sermon... Boston, N.S. Simpkins & Co., prs., 1828. 18 p. ICMe; RPB. 33920

---- ---- Cambridge [Mass.] Hilliard, Metcalf and company, prs. to the University, 1828. 24 p. CSmH; ICMe; MWA; NjPT. 33921
---- The trinitarian controversy, a discourse delivered at the ordination of Mr. Daniel M. Stearns... Boston, Pub. by N.S. Simpkins & Co. and N.S. Simpkins, Barnstable [press of the Barnstable Journal] 1828. 35 p. MBAU. 33922

---- ---- Boston, Pub. by N.S. Simpkins & Co. [Freeman & Bolles, prs.] 1828. 40 p. CBPac; CtSoP; ICMe; ICN; ICU; MB; MBAt; MBC; MDeeP; MH-AH; MHi; MMeT; MWA; MiD-B; NjPT; PHi; RPB; BrMus. 33923

[Lowell, John] 1769-1840
The recent attempt to defeat the constitutional provisions in favour of religious freedom, considered in reference to the trust conveyances of Hanover Street Church. By a layman. Boston, Wells & Lilly, 1828. 24 p. CtHC; ICMe; MB; MBAt; MBC; MH-AH; MHi; MWA; MiD-B; MnHi; NIC; NNS; RPB; WHi; BrMus. 33924

[----] ---- 2d ed. Boston, Hilliard, Gray, Little & Wilkins, 1828. 24 p. CBPac; CSmH;

CtHT-W; ICMe; DLC; MB; MH; MHi; MWA; MiD-B; NIC; NcD; PPPrHi. 33925

Lucinda; a dramatic piece in two acts. New-York, Pub. by John M. Danforth, 1828. 42 p. NNC. 33926

Lucretia and her father. A narrative founded on fact. By a clergyman of New England. Approved by the board of managers. 2d ed. Hartford, D.F. Robinson & co., 1828. 96 p. CSmH; CtHT-W; CtHi; CtY; DLC; KU; MWA. 33927

Luther, Martin
Der kleine Catechismus... Philadelphia, Gedruckt und zu haben bei Conrad Zentler, 1828. 142 p. MH; PPL; PRHi. 33928

---- Der kleine Catechismus... Lancaster, Pa. Gedruckt und zu haben bey H.W. Villee, 1828. [4], 121, [2] p. PPL. 33929

---- ---- Lancaster, Pa. Gedruckt und zu haben bey H.W. Villee [1828] [4], 121, [2] p. PPL. 33930

---- ---- Lancaster, Pr. by Johann Baer, 1828. 125, [1] p. MiU-C; P; PPL; PU. 33931

Lycoming Navigation, Rail Road and Coal Company. Lycoming County, Pa.
A brief description of the property belonging to the Lycoming Coal Company, with some general remarks on the subject of the coal and iron business. Poughkeepsie, Pr. by P. Potter, Dec. 1828. 32 p. CSmH; DIC; DLC; MH; N; NHi; NN; NNE. 33932

Lyman, Theodore, 1792-1849
The diplomacy of the United States. Being an account of the

foreign relations of the country,
from the first treaty with France,
in 1778, to the present time. 2d
ed. , with additions. Boston,
Wells & Lilly, 1828. 2 v. CSmH;
CU; CtMW; DLC; GAU; IaU; MB;
MH; MHi; MLy; MdBJ; MdBP;
MiD-B; MnHi; MoSHi; NB; NCH;
NNC; NNLI; NR; NUt; NbU;
NcA-S; NjP; OClWHi; PHC; PHi;
PPL; RP; RBP; ScC; WHi;
BrMus.   33933

Lyman, Theodore, defendant.
See Report of a trial in the su-
preme judicial court, holden at
Boston.

Lyon, D. S.
   Tariff, or rates of duties payable from and after June 30,
1828. On all goods and merchandise, imported into U. S. of
America... New York, O. Halsted, 1828. 180 p. IHi; MH; MH-
BA.   33934

[Lytton, Edward George Earle
Lytton Bulwer-Lytton, 1st baron]
   Pelham; or, The adventures
of a gentleman... New York, Pr.
by J. & J. Harper for Collins
and Hannay [etc. , etc.] 1828. 2
v. CSmH; CtMW; LNB; MH;
MdBP; NNS; NRU.   33935

                M

Macbeth, John
   A dissertation on the Sabbath,
in which the nature of the institution and the obligations to its
observance, are stated and illustrated. Philadelphia, Pr. by John
Clarke, 1828. 254 p. CtHC; GAU;
GDC; ICMcC; MBC; MnSM; NjR;
PLT; PPL; ViRUT.   33936

McCall, John C.
   Fleurette and other rhymes...
Philadelphia, Carey, Lea & Carey,
1828. [Adam Waldie & Co. , prs.]

[3], 68 p. PPL.   33937

M'Calla, William Latta, 1788-
1859
   A discussion of Christian Baptism, as to its subject, its mode,
its history... Philadelphia, Pub.
by George M'Laughlin [Russell
& Martien, prs.] 1828. Vol. I.
398, [1] p. (Vol. II not printed
according to note at end of Vol.
I) CtMW; ICU; KyLoP; KyLoS;
KyU; MoInRC; NNG; PLT; PPL;
PPPrHi; ViRUT.   33938

---- The psalmists and hymnists,
in answer to a pamphlet of Mr.
Rankin. 1828. Philadelphia, Pr.
by John Young [1828] 14 p. PHi;
PPPrHi.   33939

M'Carter's country almanac for
1829. By David Young. Charleston, J. J. M'Carter [1828] 18 1.
DLC.   33940

M'Carty's American primer. Being a selection of words the most
easy of pronunciation. Intended to
facilitate the improvement of children in spelling. Philadelphia,
Pub. and sold by M'Carty and
Davis. Stereotyped by J. Howe
[1828] 36 p. CSmH; CtSoP; DLC;
ICHi; IU; InU; MH; MWA; NHi;
NNC; PPL; ViU.   33941

McDowell, John, 1780-1863
   Questions on the Bible. By
John M'Dowell. Elizabethtown,
Sanderson, 1828. 138 p. NPV.
                           33942

McDuffie, George, 1790-1851
   Speech of Mr. McDuffie, of S.
Carolina, against the prohibitory
system; delivered in the House
of Representatives, April 1828...
Washington, Pr. by Green & Jar-
vis, 1828. 31 p. CSmH; MBAt;
MH; PPL; TxU.   33943

M'Farland, John
   A series of letters, on the re-

lation, rights, priveleges[!] and
duties of baptized children. Lex-
ington, Ky. , Pr. by J. G. Nor-
wood, 1828. 173 p. , 1 l. CSmH;
DLC; ICMcC; ICU; IaDuU; InCW;
KyDC; KyLoP; KyLxT; LNB; NN;
NjP; PPiPT; PPPrHi; TxHuT;
TxU.   33944

MacGavin, William, 1773-1832
    Maternal instructions; or The
history of Mrs. Murray and her
children. Boston, Pr. by T. R.
Marvin, for the Massachusetts
Sabbath School Union, 1828. 180
p. MB; MWA.   33945

Macgowan, John
    The shaver; a sermon... Lon-
don, Pr. , Philadelphia, Repr. ,
1828. 40 p. PPL.   33946

M'Henry, James, 1785-1845
    An ode, written by request, on
the opening of the exhibition at
the Franklin Institute of Philadelphia, October, 1828. [Philadel-
phia, 1828] Bdsd. PPL.   33947

---- The pleasures of friendship
and other poems... 3d Amer. ed.
Philadelphia, John Grigg, 1828.
120 p. PPL; RPB.   33948

M'Ilvain, James, 1769-1850
    ...Memorial of James M'Ilvain,
praying that the aid of government may be extended to the
growers of wool, and the manufacturers of woollen goods...
Washington, Pr. by Gales & Seaton, 1828; Wilmington, Del. ,
Repr. by order of a number of
Friends of National Industry, at
the Advertiser Office [1828] 8 p.
DeGE.   33949

McIlvaine, Charles Pettit, bp.
1799-1873
    Rev. Mr. M'Ilvaine in answer
to the Rev. Henry U. Onderdonk,
D. D. 2d ed. with appendix. New
York, John P. Haven [Sleight &

George, prs.] 1828. 48 p. CtMW;
ICU; MBC; MCE; MdHi; NCH;
NJQ; NN; NNUT; NjR; PHi; PPL.
                              33950
McKeen, Silas, 1791-1877
    The right object and use of
religious investigation; an ad-
dress to the Society for Religi-
ous Inquiry in the University of
Vermont, August 5, 1828. Bur-
lington, Pr. at the Free Press
Office, 1828. 11 p. CtHC; MBC;
MH.   33951

---- A sermon, delivered at
Montpelier, October 15, 1828,
before the Vermont Colonization
Society. Montpelier, Pr. by E. P.
Walton, 1828. 22 p. CSmH; CtHT;
CtY; DLC; MBAt; MBC; NcD;
NjR; TxU; VtHi; VtMiM; WHi;
BrMus.   33952

McKenney, Thomas Lorraine,
Reports and proceedings. See
United States. Reports and pro-
ceedings.

McKenney, Thomas Lorraine
    To the public. July 18, 1828.
16 p. DLC.   33953

MacKenzie, Henry
    The man of feeling... With a
life of the author. Boston, Pub.
by J. P. Peaslee. J. H. Dix, pr. ,
1828. 208 p. MHi; NNS; PPL.
                              33954
McKnight, Laird & Company
    Sea bathing at Long Branch,
deal or squam on the Atlantic
Ocean. Through in a day. Stage
fare $3, by steam boats and
stage... [Philadelphia] July 1,
1828. Bdsd. DeGE.   33955

Maclaurin, Robert
    The pious shepherd; or Life
and character of James Wait...
Philadelphia, Presbyterian Board
of Publication [1828] 199 p.
GMiM; ICMcC; ViRUT.   33956

M'Lean, Alexander

An appeal to the public, or,
An exposition of the conduct of
Rev. Isaac Jennison and others,
in Ludlow, in the months of February and March, 1828. Also, an
address to the local preachers
of the Methodist Episcopal Church;
with remarks on the government,
discipline and monied system of
said church. Belchertown [Mass.]
Pr. by C. A. Warren, 1828. 56 p.
CBPac; CtHT-W; DLC; MA;
MBAt; MBC; MH; MiD-B; NhHi;
NjPT; NN; Vt; BrMus.   33957

M'Lean, C. G.
   The glory of Christ given to
the ministry; a sermon preached
at the ordination of the Rev.
Robert B. Kerr. Chambersburg,
Pa., Pr. by J. Pritts, 1828. 39
p. IObB; PAnL; PLT; PPLT;
PPPrHi.   33958

MacMahon, Bernard
   The American gardener's calendar, adapted to the climates
and seasons of the United States,
containing a complete account of
all the work necessary to be done
in the kitchen-garden, fruit-gar-
den, orchard, etc., for every
month in the year. 7th ed., imp.
Philadelphia, A. M'Mahon, 1828.
MH.   33959

McNairy, Boyd
   Dr. M'Nairy's circular To the
citizens of the seventh electoral
district, in the state of Tennessee, composed of the counties of
Rutherford, Davidson and Williamson. [Nashville, September 22d,
1828] Bdsd. McMurtrie 273.
                            33960
---- Jackson, a negro trader.
From the Nashville Banner and
Whig. To the public. [Signed]
Boyd McNairy. 14th July 1828.
1 p. DLC.   33961

[McNemar, Richard] 1780-1839
   Investigator: or A defence of
the order, government & econ-
omy of the United Society called
Shakers, against sundry charges
& legislative proceedings ad-
dressed to the political world.
By the Society of believers at
Pleasant Hill, Ky. ...Lexington,
Pr. by Smith & Palmer, 1828.
47 p. CSmH; Ct; DLC; ICJ; ICN;
KyBgW-K; MHi; MWA; MWiW;
NN; Nh; OClWHi; BrMus. 33962

Macnish, Robert, 1802-1837
   The anatomy of drunkenness...
1st Amer., from the 2d London
ed. Philadelphia, Carey, Lea and
Carey. Sold in New-York, by G.
and C. Carvill; in Boston, by
Monroe and Francis, 1828. 198
p. CSmH; DLC; DNLM; GDC;
MBAt; MH-AH; NNNAM; OCG.
                            33963
M'Phail, Leonard Cassell
   Oration delivered by Leonard
Cassell M'Phail, in the City-
Council Chamber, before the Jefferson and Franklin Associations
of Young Men, ...July the 4th,
1828. On the return of the civic
procession from laying the first
stone for the commencement of
the Baltimore and Ohio Railroad.
Baltimore, Pr. by R. J. Matchett,
1828. 12 p. MHi.   33964

Madison, James, 1751-1836
   Letters on the constitutionality
of the power in Congress to impose a tariff for the protection
of manufactures. Washington City,
Pr. and pub. by S. C. Ustick,
1828. 24 p. DLC; DeGE; MH-BA;
MNF; MWA; N; NNLI; PU; ScCC;
BrMus.   33965

---- A memorial and remonstrance on the religious rights of
man; written in 1784-5 at the request of the Religious Society of
Baptists in Virginia. By Ex-
President Madison. Washington
City, Pr. and pub. by S. C. Ustick, 1828. 12 p. DLC; IHi; MB;

MH; MWA; MdHi; NCH; NHC-S; PPL; ViRU.   33966

---- Mr. Madison on the Constitution. [From the National Intelligencer.] [Washington, 1828] Gales & Seaton, prs. (colop.) 16 p. PPL.   33967

Maelzel's exhibition... To commence with the celebrated automaton chess-player... [Boston] W. W. Clapp, pr. [1828] 1 p. DLC.   33968

Maffitt, John Newland, 1794-1850
An address delivered before the Hibernian Relief Society, at their first anniversary, April 7, 1828. Boston, T. R. Marvin, pr., 1828. 16 p. MBAt; MdBL; MnHi; NN; PHi; PPL.   33969

---- Pulpit sketches, sermons, and devotional fragments. Boston, T. R. Marvin, 1828. 300 p. CtHC; DLC; GAGTh; IEG; LNP; MB; MBAt; MBC; MdBE; MnH; MoSpD; OMC; RP; TxU; BrMus.   33970

Magdalen Society of Philadelphia
Report of the managers of the Magdalen Society, for 1827. [Philadelphia, 1828] 12 p. DNLM; PPL; PU.   33971

Magendie, François, 1783-1855
Formulary for the preparation and employment of many new medicines... by F. Majendie ... Trans. from the 5th ed., rev. and augm., by John Baxter... With notes and additions. 2d ed. New York, G. H. Evans, 1828. x, 138, [2] p. CSt-L; MB; MeB; NBM; NNC-M; OClM; PPC; ViRA.   33972

---- A physiological memoir upon the brain, read in a public sitting of the Royal Academy of Sciences, on the 16th of June, 1828. From the French, by Jos-

eph Gardner [Philadelphia, 1828] 198 p. MdBM; RPM.   33973

Maine
Governor's speech. [Communication of Gov. Enoch Lincoln to the Legislature of Maine, Jan. 3, 1828] [Portland? 1828] 16 p. DLC; ViU.   33974

---- Laws of the state of Maine containing the public acts, 1822-1828... Hallowell, Pr. and pub. by Glazier & Co., 1828. ii, 196, 22, 15 p. Ia; MWCL; Me; Nb; OCLaw.   33975

---- Private acts of the state of Maine, passed by the Eighth Legislature at its session held in January, 1828. Pub. agreeably to the resolve of the 28th of June 1820. Portland, Pr. by Thos. Todd, pr. to the state, 1828. [5], 816-926, [57], 614-826, [40] p. IaHi; IaU-L; In-SC; Me-LR; MeU; Mo; Ms; Nb; Nv; PU; TxU-L.   33976

---- Private or special laws of the state of Maine from 1820 to 1828 inclusive. Vol. I. Pub. agreeably to the resolve of the 28th of June, 1820. Portland, Pr. by Thos. Todd, pr. to the state, 1828. [56 p.] IaHi; MS; MeU; Nb.   33977

---- Private or special laws of the state of Maine passed by the Eighth Legislature, at its session held in January, 1828. Pub. agreeably to the resolve of the 28th June, 1820. Portland, Pr. by Thos. Todd, pr. to the state, 1828. [4], 815-926 p. Ia; In-SC; MWCL; Me-LR; Nb; TxU-L.   33978

---- Public acts of the state of Maine passed by the Eighth Legislature, at its session held in January, 1828. Pub. agreeably to the resolve of the 28th of June,

1820. Portland, Pr. by Thos.
Todd, pr. to the state, 1828. In-
SC [2], 1141-1183, [4] p.; Me-
LR [5], 1142-1182, [6] p.; MeBa
[4], 1141-1182, [1] p.; MeU [4],
1142-1182, [6] p.; Nb [4], 1142-
1182, [6] p.; TxU-L; [1137]-
1182, [5] p.   33979

---- Public laws of the state of
Maine, January, 1828. Hallowell,
Glazier & Co., 1828. 169-196,
16 p. R.   33980

---- Report of Charles S. Daveis,
esq., agent appointed by the executive of the state of Maine, to
inquire into and report upon certain facts relating to aggressions
upon the rights of the state, and
of individual citizens thereof, by
inhabitants of the province of New
Brunswick. Pr. by order of the
Legislature. Portland, T. Todd,
pr. to the state, 1828. 35, [2] p.
DLC; ViU.   33981

---- Report of the joint select
committee of the Senate and
House of Representatives of the
state of Maine [in relation to the
North eastern boundary of the
state]. Pr. by order of the Legislature. Portland, T. Todd, pr.
to the state, 1828. 60, 56 p.
(Jan. sess. 1828. Doc. no. 13).
DLC.   33982

---- ---- Portland, T. Todd, pr.
to the state, 1828. 59, 56 p.
(Jan. sess. 1828. Doc. no. 13).
DLC.   33983

---- Reports of cases argued
and determined in the Supreme
Judicial Court of the state of
Maine. By Simon Greenleaf,
Counsellor at Law. Vol. IV. Port-
land, James Adams, Jr., 1828.
562 p. Az; FDeS; LNBA; MeBa;
NNU; Nd-L.   33984

---- Resolves of the state of

Maine, from 1820 to 1828,
[1829-1835; 1836-1839] inclusive.
Pub. agreeably to the resolve of
June 28, 1820. Portland, Pr. by
Thos. Todd, pr. to the state,
1828-1839. 3 vols. MWCL.
                                33985
---- State of Maine. By the governor of the state of Maine. A
proclamation for a day of public thanksgiving and praise. By
the advice of the Council, I appoint Thursday, the thirteenth
day of November next, a day of
thanksgiving and praise. Enoch
Lincoln. By the Governor. Portland, October 15th, 1828. Bdsd.
MeHi.   33986

The Maine farmers' almanac for
1829. By Daniel Robinson. Hallowell, Glazier & Co. [1828] 24 l.
DLC; MB; MH; MWA (three varieties); MeBa; MeHi.   33987

---- ---- Hallowell, Glazier,
Masters & Co. [1828] 24 l.
MAtt; MeB.   33988

---- ---- Portland, Shirley &
Hyde [1828] 24 l. MDedHi; MWA.
N.   33989

The Maine primer; or, Child's
second book. Boston, A. B. Parker; Belfast [Me.] E. Fellowes,
1828. [5]-36 p. DLC.   33990

The Maine register, and United
States calendar for 1829. Hallowell, Glazier, Masters & Co.
[1828] 89 l. DLC; MHi; MWA;
MeBa; MeU; Nh.   33991

Maine Sabbath School Union.
   Sabbath school addresses.
Portland, Shirley & Hyde, 1828.
Williamson: 8791.   33992

---- Second annual report of the
Maine Sabbath School Union,
auxiliary to the American Sunday
School Union. Portland, Shirley

& Hyde, prs. , 1828. 36 p. MBC.
33993

Maine Wesleyan Seminary
Reports of the trustees of the
board of overseers, December,
1828, Maine Wesleyan Seminary.
Portland, Pr. by Thos. Todd,
1828. [3], 7 p. Me.   33994

Mair, John
Mair's introduction to Latin
syntax. From the Edinburgh
stereotype ed. Rev. and corr.
by A. R. Carson... To which is
added, copious exercises upon the
declinable parts of speech; and an
exemplification of the several
moods and tenses. By David Patterson... New York, Collins &
Hannay, and Collins & co. [W. E.
Dean, pr.] 1828. 248 p. ICMcC;
ICU; MH; MWHi; MoMM; NjR;
PHi; PV.   33995

... Major Barry's hostility to the
occupant and Green River settler,
proved conclusively by his votes
recorded on the journals, and
certified by the Secretary of
State. Frankfort, Ky. , Jacob H.
Holeman, 1828. [Kentuckian...
Extra] 24 p. ICU.   33996

Malan, César Henri Abraham,
1787-1864
The image boys. Abridged
from the French of Rev. C. Malan, of Geneva. New York, Pub.
by the Amer. Tract Soc. , [ca
1828] 16 p. NNC-T.   33997

[Malcolm, John] 1769-1833
Sketches of Persia. From the
journals of a traveller in the
East. Philadelphia, Carey, Lea
& Carey [etc.] [Adam Waldie &
Co. , prs.] 1828. 316 p. CoU;
CtHC; CtHT; DeGE; InRE; KyLx;
MdHi; NjR; O; P; PPDrop; PPL;
PU; PWW; RP; ScSoh; ViAl.
33998

Mallary, Rollin Carolus, 1784-
1831

Debate on the tariff. Speech of
Mr. Mallary of Vermont. House
of Representatives, March 3
[1828] [Washington, D. C.] National Journal 1828. 2 p. DLC.
33999

---- Speech of Mr. Mallary, of
Vt. , on the tariff bill. Delivered
in the House of Representatives
of the U. S. March 3, 1828.
Washington, Pr. by Gales & Seaton, 1828. 34 p. CSmH; DLC;
DeGE; MBAt; MH; MWA; MeB.
34000

Malte-Brun, Conrad, 1775-1826
A new general atlas, exhibiting the five great divisions of
the globe, Europe, Asia, Africa,
America and Oceanica, with their
several empires, kingdoms, states,
territories and other subdivisions,
corrected to the present time.
Drawn and engraved, particularly
to illustrate the Universal geography... Philadelphia, J. Grigg,
1828. 2 p. l. , 40 colored maps.
DLC; DeGE; MNF; NBLiHi; OO;
PP; PU; RPB; WaU.   34001

---- System of geography, by M.
Malte-Brun... with additions and
corrections by James G. Percival
... Stereotyped by James Connor,
New York. Boston, Pr. and pub.
by S. Walker, 1828-29. 2 vols.
in 3. ICA; ICMcC; KyHi; LNHT;
MChB; MdW; MnHi; NNA; NjR;
OCMtSM; OO; PP; PPF; WHi.
34002

Manley, James R.
An eulogium on De Witt Clinton,
late governor of the state of New-
York. Delivered at the request
of a joint committee of the Medical Society and College of Physicians and Surgeons, in the hall of
Columbia College, on Friday,
11th July, 1828. New-York, Pr.
by Gould & Jacobus, 1828. [4],
22 p. CSmH; DLC; ICU; IaU;
MBAt; MH; MWA; MiD-B; MnHi;
NN; NjR; OMC; PHi.   34003

[Mann, Charles]
A new interest table; by which the interest of any sum, from one dollar to one million, for one day to ten years, can be readily and correctly ascertained. Calculated at seven per cent, and adapted to general use. Rochester, Pub. by the author, 1828. 1 p. DLC.   34004

Mann, Cyrus, 1785-1859
Ruinous consequences of profaning the Sabbath. A sermon, delivered at Westminster, Massachusetts, July 6, 1828. Pub. by request. Lancaster [Mass.] Pr. by Carter, Andrews & co., 1828. 20 p. CSmH.   34005

Mann, Joel, 1789-1884
Intemperance destructive of national welfare. An essay by Joel Mann, minister of the Gospel in Suffield, Connecticut. [Suffield] July 1828. 12 p. WHi; BrMus.   34006

Mannock, John, 1677-1764
Poor man's catechism; or, The Christian doctrine explained. With short admonitions. Stereotyped from the 5th London ed. Philadelphia, Pub. by Eugene Cummiskey, 1828. 272 p. DGU; PPCCH.   34007

Manual of court forms containing the forms most in use in the supreme court, district court, courts of common pleas, courts of quarter sessions and mayors court. Philadelphia, Pr. and pub. at No. 24 Arch St., A. Walker, Agt. 1828. 248 p. C; Ia; IaDmD-L; PAtM; PP; PPB; PU.   34008

Manwaring, Christopher
Essays, historical, moral, political and agricultural...New London, Samuel Green, 1828. 204 p. DLC.   34009

[Marcet, Jane (Haldimand)] 1769-1858
Conversations on chemistry... 10th Amer. from the 8th London ed., rev., corr., and enl. To which are now added explanations of the text; directions for simplifying the apparatus; and a vocabulary of terms; together with a list of interesting experiments. By J. L. Comstock. Together with a new and extensive series of questions, by Rev. J. L. Blake. Hartford, O. D. Cooke, publisher, 1828. 348 p. Also ascribed to Mrs. Margaret Bryan. CSt; CoU; CtHT; CtHT-W; CtHi; CtMW; DLC; InLW; MH; MWH; MeB; MeHi; NBM; NNE; NRU; OClWHi; OMC; PPAA; PPi; PPiU; PU-S.   34010

[----] Conversations on natural philosophy...Improved by... questions...by Rev. J. L. Blake. 8th Amer. ed. Boston, Pr. and pub. by Lincoln & Edmands, Stereotyped by T. H. Carter & Co., Boston. 1828. 252 p. MH; OO.   34011

[----] Conversations on political economy; in which the elements of science are familiarly explained. By the author of conversations on chemistry and natural philosophy corr. and imp., and adapted to the use of schools. By Rev. J. L. Blake, A. M. Boston, Bowles & Dearborn [Isaac R. Butts, pr.] 1828. 330 p. CtHT-W; DLC; ICU; LNL; MB; MH; MS; MiU; NNC; NRU; NcSalL; OSW; PMA; RP; TxU-T; VtU.   34012

Maria; or the good girl. Wendell, J. Metcalf, 1828. 16 p. MNF; MWA.   34013

Marks, David
The conference meeting hymn

book, for the use of all who love
our Lord and Saviour Jesus
Christ. Compiled by Elder David
Marks. 2d ed. Rochester, Pr.
by E. Peck & Co. for D. Marks,
Jr. , J. Bignall, and Asa Dodge,
1828. 160 p. MeBaT.   34014

---- ---- 3d ed. Rochester, Pr.
for friend Marks by E. [Peck &
Co.] 1828. 160 p. (t. p. defective). NRU.   34015

[Marks, Elias]
Hints on female education;
with an outline of an institution
for the education of females,
termed the So. Ca. Female Institute, under the direction of Elias
Marks. This institute, situated
at Barhamville, will go into operation, Oct. 1st, 1828. Columbia, D. W. Sims, 1828. 44 p.
MH.   34016

Marques Y Espejo, Antonio
Anastasia o La recompensa
de la hospitalidad; anecdota his-
torica de un casto amor contra-
riado. Nueva York, Lanuza Mendia y c. , 1828. MBC; MH.
                           34017
A marriage in high life. See
Scott, Lady Caroline Lucy.

Marryat, Thomas, 1730-1792
Dr. Marryat's therapeutics,
or The art of healing... 21st
English, and 1st Amer. ed. ;
carefully rev. , corr. , and con-
siderably enl. by the proprietor.
To which are added, a glossary,
explaining all the difficult words;
with recipes for several popular
medicines now in use. New York,
Pub. by Hugh Evans, surgeon;
and may be purchased at the
principal book stores in New-
York, Albany, & Utica, 1828.
240, [i. e. 224] p. MBCo; NUt;
OCx.   34018

[Marsh, Charles] 1774?-1835?

The clubs of London; with
anecdotes of their members,
sketches of character, and con-
versations. Philadelphia, Carey,
Lea & Carey [etc.] 1828. 2 v.
Ct; DLC; LNHT; MAnP; MdBP;
MeHi; MeU; NT; OT; P; PPL;
PU; RNR; TxU.   34019

Marsh, John
An epitome of general ecclesi-
astical history, from the earli-
est period to the present time,
with an appendix, giving a con-
densed history of the Jews,
from the destruction of Jerusa-
lem to the present day. 2d ed.
New York, Pr. by Vanderpool
& Cole, 1828. 449 p. CtMW;
GMM; ICMcC; IU; IaMp; MBAt;
MS; NBuG; NN; NR; NcCJ; OCl;
OMC; OO; OkHi; PCC; PPiW;
ScCliJ; TMSC.   34020

Marshall, Mrs.
A sketch of my friend's fam-
ily, intended to suggest some
practical hints on religion and
domestic manners... Sanbornton,
N. Y. , Pr. and pub. by D. V.
Moulton, 1828. 160 p. CSmH;
Nh.   34021

Marsollier des Vivetières, Benoit
Joseph, 1750-1817
Neal & Mackenzie, No. 201,
Chestnut Street, between the The-
atre & Arcade, Philadelphia.
Adolphe et Clara, comedie en un
acte, par B. J. Marsollier.
[Philadelphia, 1828] 24 p. (also
issued in vol. with covering title.
"Collection d'Operas et Vaude-
villes.") ICU; PPL.   34022

Martin, William. See Burnside,
A. (note).

[Martineau, Harriet] 1802-1876
Principle and practice, or The
orphan family; a tale. New-York,
Repr. for W. B. Gilley, 1828.

144 p. MH; MWatP.   34023

Mary and Betsey. Wendell, J.
Metcalf, 1828. 8 p. MWA. 34024

Mary and her cat. Words of two
syllables. Portland [Me.] By
Shirley and Hyde, Exchange-
Street, 1828. 21 p. DLC; MB.
                             34025
Mary Jones: A little girl who
learned to be always happy and
always good, from the thought that
God was near her. Boston,
Bowles and Dearborn, 1828.
MHi (unavailable 1970)   34026

Maryland
    A communication from the ex-
ecutive; relative to the Chesapeake and Delaware Canal. Feb.
7, 1828. Annapolis, Pr. by Jeremiah Hughes, Jan. [sic] 1828.
7 p. PPL.   34027

---- First annual report of the
superintendent of public instruction to the legislature of Maryland made on the 31st December,
1827. Annapolis, J. Hughes, pr.,
1828. 37 p. ICU; MB; MBAt;
MdBE.   34028

---- The general report... of the
Treasurer of the Western Shore.
Annapolis, Pr. by Jeremiah
Hughes, 1828. 2 l. MdBP.
                             34029
---- Journal of the proceedings
of the House of Delegates of the
state of Maryland, at a session
of the General Assembly, begun
and held at the capitol in the city
of Annapolis... on the last Monday of December, the 31st day of
the month, A. D. 1827... Annapolis, Pr. by J. Green, 1828. 638
p. Md; MdBB; MdBE; MdHi.
                             34030
---- Laws made and passed by
the General Assembly of the state
of Maryland at a session begun
and held at the city of Annapolis,

on the last Monday of December,
eighteen hundred and twenty sev-
en. Pub. by authority. Annapolis, J. Hughes, 1828. [3]-379 p.
A-SC; IaU-L; L; MWCL; MdBB;
MdHi; Mi-L; Mo; Ms; NN; NNLI;
Nb; Nc-S; Nj; Nv; R; T. 34031

---- Message of Joseph Kent,
esq. Governor of Maryland.
Transmitted to the Legislature on
Wednesday, 2d January, 1828.
Annapolis, Pr. by Jeremiah
Hughes, Jan. 1828. 12 p. MdHi.
                             34032
---- Report of the committee on
internal improvement, to the
House of Delegates. Annapolis,
Pr. by Jeremiah Hughes, 1828.
23 p. MdHi.   34033

---- Report of the committee on
internal improvement. December
session, 1827. [Annapolis, J.
Green, 1828] 22 p. NIC. 34034

---- Report of the committee appointed by the board of directors
of the Maryland penitentiary, to
visit the penitentiaries and prisons in the city of Philadelphia
and state of New York. Baltimore, Lucas & Deaver, 1828.
26 p. DNLM; MB; MBAt; Md;
MdBE; MdBP; MdHi; Vi. 34035

---- Reports of cases argued and
determined in the Court of Ap-
peals of Maryland in 1826 &
18[29]. By Thos. Harris, clerk...
Richard W. Gill, attorney at law.
Annapolis, Pr. by Jonas Green,
1828 [-1829] 2 v. Az; CU-Law;
Ct; F-SC; Ia; In-SC; KyU-L; LU-
L; MWA; MdBE; MiD-B; MoW;
Ms; NCH; NNLI; Nb; Nc-S; Nj;
OCLaw; PU-L; RPL; Sc-SC; TU-
L; Tx-SC; Vi-L; BrMus. 34036

---- A supplement to the act, entitled, An act for the promotion
of internal improvement. [Balti-
more, Wm. Wooddy, pr., 1828]

16 p. CtY; MdHi; NN.   34037

Maryland Colonization Society
    Proceedings of a meeting of
the friends of African colonization, held in the city of Baltimore, on the seventeenth of October, 1827. Baltimore, Pr. by
B. Edes, 1828. 27 p. MdHi;
MdToH; OO.   34038

Maryland Sunday School Union
    Report of the Sunday School
Union for the state of Maryland,
presented December 16, 1828.
Baltimore, Pr. by Lucas &
Deaver, 1828. 16 p. MdHi.
                            34039
Mason, Henry M.
    A compend of ecclesiastical
history, for the use of the laity
... New York, Pub. by G. & C.
Carvill, 1828. 464 p. CtSoP; ICU;
IEG; MWH; MWiW; MeBaT; NCH;
NNUT; OO; PPiW; RPB; ViAlTh;
BrMus.   34040

Mason, John
    An appeal to the churches; to
defend them against the encroachments of associations. Pr. by
Finch & Smith, Centreville, Ind.,
1828. 35 p. Byrd 359.   34041

Mason, John, d 1694
    Select remains of the Rev.
John Mason, with a preface giving some account of the author.
New York, Wm. Burgess, Jr.,
1828. 179 p. MB; ScNC.   34042

Mason, John, 1706-1763
    A treatise on self knowledge;
showing the nature and benefit of
that important science, and the
way to attain it.   Intermixed with
various reflections and observations on human nature. With which
are connected, questions adapted
to the work; for the use of
schools, with notes. Windsor,
Simeon Ide, 1828. viii, 144 p.
MB; MH; MWA; NN; OO;

OCxW.   34043

Mason, John, 1734-1792
    ... Conversations with a young
traveller. [New York, American
Tract Society, 1828?] 8 p.
([American Tract Society. Publi-
cations] no. 203) DLC.   34044

Mason, John M.
    A brief outline of the mode of
instruction pursued by the Rev.
John M. Mason, D. D. in the
Theological Seminary lately un-
der his care in the city of New
York. New York, John P. Haven,
1828. 22 p. NjR; OO; PLT;
PPPrHi.   34045

Mason, Lowell, ed.
    Choral harmony: being a se-
lection of the most approved anthems, choruses, and other
pieces of sacred music; suitable
for singing societies, concert and
various public occasions. The
vocal parts in score; the instru-
mental accompaniment adapted
to the organ. Edited by Lowell
Mason. Vol. I. By the Boston
Handel and Haydn Society. Boston, Richardson & Lord, 1828.
1-32, 61-84, 85-108 [Vol I, Nos.
1, 3 & 4] NRU.   34046

Mason, Richard
    The gentleman's new pocket
farrier, comprising a general
description of the noble and useful animal the horse; together
with the quickest and simplest
mode of fattening; necessary
treatment while undergoing excessive fatigue... Also, a concise
account of the diseases to which
the horse is subject; with such
remedies as long experience has
proved to be effectual... 4th ed.,
enl. and imp. ... Richmond, Pr.
by Peter Cottom, 1828. DLC;
MNF; MiU-C; NNNAM; NcD; PPL;
PPeSchw; T; ViW.   34047

Mason, Thomas, comp.
Zion's songster; or, A collection of hymns and spiritual songs
... 2d ed. New York, Pr. for the compiler at the Conference Office, A. Hoyt, pr., 1828. 320 p.
CtHT-W; IEG.   34048

The Masonic obligations from an entered apprentice to Knights Templar, (inclusive) as attested to at the Masonic anti-masonic convention, holden at Le Roy, N.Y., Feb. 19, 1828. Danville, E. & W. Eaton, 1828. 24 p.
IaCrM.   34049

A Mason's daughter.   See Reason versus prejudice.

Massachusetts
An act of the commonwealth of Massachusetts... 1827, to provide for the instruction of youth; together with the by-laws of the town of Groton, in relation to schools. Boston, Christian Register office, 1828. 22 p. DLC; IU; MBAt; MH; MiU; OO.   34050

---- An act to incorporate the Berkshire and Hudson Rail Road Company. [Boston, Dutton & Wentworth, 1828] 14 p. DBRE; DLC; M; MBAt; MH; NN.
                                34051

Massachusetts. Address of the central committee appointed by a convention of both branches of the legislature. See National Republican Party. Massachusetts.

---- Annual report of the number of convicts in the Massachusetts state prison, their employment &c. with a view of the expences and income of the institution for one year ending Sept. 30, 1828...
[Boston] G. Davidson, pr. [1828]
1 p. DLC.   34052

---- Commonwealth of Massachusetts. By His Excellency Levi

Lincoln, Governor of the Commonwelath of Massachusetts, A proclamation for a day of public fasting, humiliation, and prayer. Given at the Council Chamber in Boston, this twenty-sixth day of February, in the year of our Lord one thousand eight hundred and twenty-eight, and of the Independence of the United States the fifty-second. Thursday, April 3, 1828.
Bdsd. MAtt.   34053

---- Detail of evolutions and manoeuvres, to be performed on the 14th of October inst. by the 6th Regiment, 1st Brigade and 6th Division of Massachusetts Militia, in Worcester, 1828. 8 p.
MWHi.   34054

---- Documents relating to the north eastern boundary of the state of Maine. Boston, Dutton & Wentworth, prs. to the state, 1828. 275 p. CSmH; CtHT-W; CtMW; DLC; GHi; LNHT; MB; MBAt; MBC; MH-L; MHi; MeU; MiD-B; MnHi; NBLiHi; NN; Nh; OClWHi; OO; RNR; TNJ; BrMus.
                                34055

---- [Governor's message transmitting accounts of the commissioners and engineer on the Western Railway and also of the Board of Internal Improvement, together with the record of the doings of the Executive Council, in auditing and allowing these accounts, and their advice thereon, to be prepared... Feb. 13, 1828] [Boston, 1828] 26 p. DBRE; M; MB; MBAt; MCM; MH; MH-BA; MWA; NN.
                                34056

---- H. R. ...No. 8 Commonwealth of Massachusetts. House of Representatives, January 5, 1828. Ordered, that so much of the message of His Excellency the Governor as relates to the bestowment to this Commonwealth, and the location, of the statue of

Washington, within the State House, together with His Excellency's second Message on the same subject, be committed to Messrs. Baylies, of Taunton, Worthington, Lenox, and Taylor, Northampton. Attest, P. W. Warren, Clerk. [Boston 1828] 7 p. MB.   34057

---- Laws of the commonwealth of Massachusetts, passed by the General Court, at their session, which began on Wednesday, the second of January, and ended on Thursday, the thirteenth of March, one thousand eight hundred and twenty-eight. Boston, Dutton & Wentworth, prs. to the state, 1828. 627-884 p. IaU-L; MH-L; Mi-L; Mo; NNLI; Nj; TxU-L.   34058

---- Laws of the commonwealth of Massachusetts, passed by the General Court, at their session, which commenced on Wednesday, the twenty-eighth of May, and ended on Thursday, the twelfth of June, one thousand eight hundred and twenty-eight. Boston, True and Greene, prs. to the state, 1828. 50 p. MBevHi; MH-L; MdBB; Mo; Nj; Wa-L. 34059

---- Message of His Excellency Levi Lincoln, communicated to the two branches of the Legislature January 2, 1828. Boston, Dutton & Wentworth, prs., 1828. 32 p. M; MH; MHi; MWHi.
                                       34060
---- ... Message of Levi Lincoln [transmitting a memorial of the Troy (N. Y.) Common Council to the Legislature of the commonwealth of Massachusetts in regard to the construction of a railroad from the city of Boston to the eastern shore of the Hudson river. Boston? 1828] 7 p. DBRE; M; MB; MBAt; MH-BA; MWA; MiU-T; NN.   34061

---- Militia report of William H. Sumner, Adjutant General and acting Quarter Master General, to His Excellency Levi Lincoln, Governor and Commander in chief of Massachusetts... Boston, Dutton & Wentworth, 1828. 31 p. DLC; MBAt; MHi; OClWHi; WHi; BrMus.   34062

---- Report of the board of commissioners, of internal improvement in relation to the examination of a route for a canal, from Boston to the Blackstone Canal, and thence to the line of Connecticut: &c., &c. Boston, Dutton & Wentworth... prs. to the state, 1828. 18 p. DLC; IU; MB; MH-BA; NbO; RPB.   34063

---- ...Report of the board of commissioners, of internal improvement in relation to the examination of sundry routes for a railway from Boston to Providence. With a memoir of the survey. Boston, Dutton & Wentworth, 1828. 72 p. (At head of title: Senate no. 4). CSmH; MA; PPL.
                                       34064
---- ---- Boston, Dutton & Wentworth, prs. to the state, 1828. 72 p. (This edition has no document note on title-page.") CSmH; CSt; DBRE; DLC; IU; M; MB; MH-BA; MWA; N; NNE; NRU; PPAmP.   34065

---- Report of the board of commissioners, for the survey of one or more routes for a railway from Boston to Albany. Boston, Dutton & Wentworth, 1828. 56 p. CSmH; CSt; DBRE; DLC; ICJ; ICU; IU; KU; M; MB; MBAt; MCM; MH; MH-BA; MWA; MiU-T; NN; NNC; NNE; NRU; NbO; NjP; NjR; OO; PPL; RPB.
                                       34066
---- [Report of the committee instructed, by an order of the House of Representatives, "to in-

quire into the expediency of reducing the salaries of the several officers of this commonwealth, and other expenditures attending the administration of the government thereof..." Boston, 1828] 13 [2] p. (General Court, 1828. House Doc. 50) DLC.   34067

---- [Report of the Committee on Roads and Railways on the report of the Board of Commissioners for the Survey of One or More Routes for a Railway from Boston to Albany, and also the report of the Board of Commissioners of Internal Improvements in relation to the examination of sundry routes for a railway from Boston to Providence...] Feb. 15, 1828. [Boston, 1828] 11 p. DBRE; DLC; M; MBAt; MH; MH-BA; MWA; NN.   34068

---- ...Report of the joint committee on the state prison... Boston, Dutton & Wentworth... state prs., 1828. 35 p. CSmH; MB; MBC; MH-L; NNC.   34069

---- ...Report [on the organization of the board and on the prosecution of the surveys for proposed railroads in Massachusetts]. [Boston, 1828] 15 p. CtY; DBRE; DLC; M; MB; MBAt; MH; MWA; MiU-T; NN.   34070

---- Reports of cases argued and determined in the supreme judicial court of the commonwealth of Massachusetts... From September, 1804, to [March term, 1822]...both inclusive...With notes and references to the English and American cases, by Benjamin Rand. Boston, C. C. Little and J. Brown, 1828-1853. 17 vols. DLC.   34071

---- Resolves of the General Court of the Commonwealth of Massachusetts, passed at their

session, which commenced on Wednesday, the twenty-eighth day of May, and ended on Thursday, the twelfth of June, one thousand eight hundred and twenty-eight. Boston, True & Green, prs. to the state, 1828. 68 p. iii p. IaU-L; MBevHi; MKiTH; Nb.   34072

---- Speech of His Excellency Levi Lincoln, delivered before the two branches of the Legislature in Convention. June 2, 1828. Boston, Dutton & Wentworth, prs. 1828. 22 p. IU; M; MB; MBAt; MH; MHi; MWA; WHi.   34073

---- A statement showing, in detail, the particulars of the item of $240, 75*59, which appears in the report of the 30th January, 1828, on the claim of the state of Massachusetts, under the head "Miscellaneous." [Boston, 1828?] 53 p. MB; MHi.   34074

Massachusetts Charitable Eye and Ear Infirmary, Boston.
     Fourth annual report of the surgeons of the Massachusetts Charitable Eye and Ear Infirmary. Supported by private contributors. Boston, T. R. Marvin, pr., 1828. 10, [2] p. DLC; MB; MHi; WHi.   34075
---- Statement of a committee of the Eye and Ear Infirmary, Boston. Boston, T. R. Marvin, pr., 1828. 8 p. CtHT-W; DLC; DNLM; MB; MBAt; MBCo; MHi; MWA; MiU; NN.   34076

Massachusetts Episcopal Missionary Society
     Address to the members of the Episcopal Church, Oct. 11, 1828. Boston, 1828. 4 p. Sabin 45842.   34077
Massachusetts General Hospital, Boston
     Massachusetts General Hospital Annual report of Board of Trustees. A. D.... 1828. [Boston,

1828] 8 p. DNLM; MHi; BrMus.
34078
Massachusetts Missionary Society
Twenty-ninth annual report of
the Massachusetts Missionary Society, presented by the executive
committee at the anniversary
meeting in Boston, May 27, 1828.
Boston, Pr. by Crocker & Brewster, 1828. 34, [2] p. ICN; MA;
MHi; WHi.   34079

Massachusetts Peace Society
Twelfth annual report of the
Massachusetts Peace Society.
Boston, 1828. 8 p. MiD-B.
34080
The Massachusetts register and
United States calendar for 1829.
Boston, Richardson & Lord,
James Loring [1828] 252 p.
CtHT-W; ICU; InU; MB; MHi;
MWA; MdBP; MeB; MnU; NBLiHi;
NN; Nh; OClWHi; PPL; RPB;
ViHi.   34081

Massachusetts Sabbath School
Union
Third annual report of the
Massachusetts Sabbath School
Union, presented at the third an-
nual meeting, May 29, 1828.
Boston, T. R. Marvin, pr., 1828.
64 p. MBC; MNtcA; MWA.
34082
Mather, Cotton, 1663-1728
Corderius americanus. A dis-
course on the good education of
children, &c. &c. delivered at
the funeral of Ezekiel Cheever,
principal of the Latin school in
Boston... Boston, Pr. by Dutton
& Wentworth, 1828. 32 p.
CSmH; DLC; ICN; ICU; KHi; MB;
MBC; MH-AH; MHi; MMeT; MWA;
MiD-B; MiU; NN; NNC; NNG;
NhHi; PHi; RPB; TxU; BrMus.
34083
[Mather, Samuel] 1706-1785
The life of the late Reverend
and learned Dr. Cotton Mather,
of Boston, New England... 2d ed.
Philadelphia, American Sunday

School Union, 1828. 115 p.
ICMcC; ICN; NNG; NR; NcWsS.
34084
Matter of fact. See Carey,
Mathew.

Matthews, Elizabeth
Memoir of Elizabeth Matthews.
New-York, Pub. by J. Emory
and B. Waugh for the Tract Society of the Methodist Episcopal
Church, Azor Hoyt, pr., 1828.
18+2 p. NBLiHi.   34085

Matthews, John, 1772?-1848?
The divine purpose, displayed
in the works of providence and
grace; in a series of twenty letters. Addressed to an inquiring
friend. Lexington, Ky., Pr. and
pub. by T. T. Skillman, 1828.
[4], 224 p. CSmH; ICU; IEG;
KyBgW; KyLxT; MnSM; NbOP;
BrMus.   34086

Maxwell, Wright & Co.
Commercial formalities of
Rio de Janeiro... Baltimore, Pr.
by Benjamin Edes, 1828. 69 p.
MB; MH-BA.   34087

Maynard, Sampson
The experience of Sampson
Maynard, local preacher of the
Methodist Episcopal Church.
(Written by himself) To which is
prefixed, an allegorical address
to the Christian world, or, A
thimble full of truth, to blow up
the world of error... New-York,
Pr. for the author, by Wm. C.
Taylor, 1828. 252 p. CtMW;
CtY-D; NN.   34088

Mazro, (Mrs.) Sophia
Turkish barbarity. An affecting narrative of the unparalleled
sufferings of Mrs. Sophia Mazro,
a Greek lady of Missolonghi, who
with her two daughters, (at the
capture of that fortress by the
Turks,) were made prisoners by
the barbarians... Taken from her

own mouth and translated by Mr.
Kelch, the Greek agent in Lon-
don. Providence, Pr. for G. C.
Jennings, [1828] 38 p. C-S;
CSmH; DLC; MB; MH; MHi;
OCHP; PPL; RHi; RP; RPB; WHi;
BrMus.   34089

[Mazureau, Étienne] 1777-1849
    In the matter of William Ken-
ner & co. and of Richard Clague
and John Oldham, versus their
creditors; C. Price & Morgan,
and others, appellants. Appeal
from the Court of the parish and
city of New-Orleans. To the Supreme court of the state of Louisiana. [New Orleans? B. Levy,
1828?] 100 p. MH-BA.   34090

Mead, Charles
    American minstrel consisting
of poetical essays on various sub-
jects. Philadelphia, Pub. by J.
Mortimer, 1828. 174 [1] p.
CSmH; DLC; MB; MH; NBuG; NIC;
P; PU; RPB; TxU.   34091

Meade, William, bp., 1789-1862
    Sermon at the opening of the
convention of the Protestant Epis-
copal Church of Virginia, in
Petersburg, May the 15th, 1828.
Richmond, Pr. by John Warrock,
1828. 24 p. DLC; MB; MBC;
NNG; NcU; PPPrHi; RPB;
ViAlTh; ViU.   34092

Mease, James, 1771-1846
    Observations on the peniten-
tiary system, & penal code of
Pennsylvania: with suggestions for
their improvement. Philadelphia,
Clark & Raser, prs., 1828. vi,
95 p. Ct; MBAt; MH; NIC; NNC;
Nj; PHi; PPB; PPL; ScU; BrMus.
                        34093
---- A reply to the criticisms
by J. N. Barker, on the historical facts in the Picture of Philadelphia. By James Mease. Philadelphia, Clark & Raser, pr.,
1828. 18 p. CSmH; DLC; DeGE;

MB; MBAt; MH; MWA; MdHi;
NhHi; NjP; NjR; PHC; PHi;
PP; PPAmP; PPL; RPB; ScC;
WHi; BrMus.   34094

    The mechanic's and working
man's almanac for 1829. Philadelphia, Mechanic's Free Press
[1828] 18 l. MWA.   34095

Medical College of Ohio, Cincinnati
    Catalogue of the officers and
students, in the Medical College
of Ohio, during the session of
1827, '8. Cincinnati, Pr. by S.
J. Browne [1828?] 8 p. CSmH;
OCHP; OClWHi.   34096

Medical Society of the County of
Albany
    By laws of the Medical Society
of the County of Albany, July
1828. Albany, Pr. by Websters
and Skinners, 1828. 10 p.
DNLM; MBCo; NNNAM. 34097

Medical Society of the County of
New York
    Statutes regulating the prac-
tice of physic and surgery in the
state of New York and the by-
laws of the Medical Society of
the County of New-York, adopted
July 14, 1828... New York, Pr.
by J. Seymour, 1828. 63 p.
DNLM; IU-M; MBCo; NNNAM;
PPL.   34098

---- Transactions of the Medical
Society of the State of New York
... with the annual address, by T.
Romeyn Beck, M. D. ... Albany,
Pr. by Websters and Skinners,
1828. 64 p. NjR; NN; NNNAM.
                        34099
Medical State Convention, Columbus.
    The proceedings of the Medi-
cal State Convention, begun and
held in the town of Columbus
December 10, A. D. 1827. Pub.
by order of the convention.

Zanesville, Pr. by Adam Peters,
1828. 7 p. Copy on file in the office of the Secretary of State,
Columbus.   34100

Meeker, Eli
Sermons, on philosophical,
evangelical, and practical sub-
jects. Designed for the use of
various denominations of Chris-
tians. Ithaca, Pr. by Mack &
Andrus, 1828. 408 p. IU; N; NIC.
                             34101
Meigs, Charles
The Philadelphia practice of
midwifery. Philadelphia, James
Kay, Jun. & brother; Pittsburg,
John I. Kay & Co., 1828. 370 p.
KyLoJM.   34102

Meineke, Christopher, 1782-1850
Exercises for the piano forte,
being a supplement to Meineke's
Instruction. Philadelphia, Geo.
Willig [c1828] 3 p. ViU.   34103

---- The rail road, a character-
istic divertimento for the piano
forte; in which is introduced a
variety of national and popular
airs... Baltimore, Pub. by John
Cole, 1828. 8 p. NN.   34104

---- Rail road march--for the
Fourth of July--dedicated to the
directors of the Baltimore & Ohio
Rail Road... Baltimore, Pub. &
sold by Geo. Willig, 1828. 3 p.
Thompson.   34105

---- ---- 2d ed. Baltimore, Geo.
Willig Junr, c1828. 3 p. DLC;
MiU-T; MNF; NN; ViU.   34106

Melford, Charlotte. See The
twin sisters.

[Mellen, Grenville] 1799-1841
Sad tales and glad tales; by
Reginald Reverie [pseud.]... Bos-
ton, S. G. Goodrich [Press of I.
R. Butts & Co.] 1828. vi, 185 p.
CSmH; CtY; DLC; ICU; InCW;

MB; MH; MWA; MiU-C; NIC;
NWM; OC; BrMus.   34107

A member of the bar. See
The Right of the Universalist to
Testify.

A member of the Enon Baptist
Church. See A vindication of
the truth.

Memoir of David Acheson, Jun.
See American Tract Society,
N. Y.

Memoir of Samuel Hooker
Cowles. See Richards, John.

Memoirs of Andrew Jackson.
See Eaton, John Henry.

Memoirs of Lafitte, or the Bar-
ritarian pirate; a narrative
founded on fact. New York, J.
M. Danforth, 1828. 106 p. RPB.
                             34108
Memoirs of Miss Eliza J. Drysdale... 2d ed. Charleston, Pr.
and pub. by W. Riley, 1828.
120 p. CSmH.   34109

Memoirs of the illustrious citizen and patriot, Andrew Jackson. See Waldo, Samuel Putnam.

Memoirs of the Rev. William
Tennant, formerly of Freehold,
New Jersey. Philadelphia, A.
Claxton, John Gray, pr., 1828.
72 p. NjT; PPPrHi.   34110

Memoranda of Maryland. [For
1828:] Designed as an annual repository for whatever most immediately regards the state. No.
1. Annapolis, From the Press of
J. Hughes, 1828. 2 p. l., 146
p. MdHi.   34111

Memorial of the owners of real
estate in the vicinity of the
Washington Military parade
ground for relief from the as-

sessment for enlarging the same.
New York, Clayton & Van Norden,
1828. 8 p. MH-BA.   34112
A memorial, remonstrating a-
gainst a certain act. See Shakers.

Memorial. To the Hon. the Legislature. See Holley, Myron.

The mental guide, being a compend of the first principles of
metaphysics... predicated on the
analysis of the human mind...
Boston, Pub. by Marsh & Capen
and Richardson & Lord. J. H. A.
Frost, pr., 1828. 384 p. CtHT-
W; MB; MH.   34113

Mentor, or Dialogues. See
Humphrey, Ch.

Merchant, A. M.
The American school grammar
of the English language; simplified and improved. Comprising
rules and exercises in orthography, syntax and punctuation,
principally selected from Murray
...Stereotyped by A. Chandler.
New-York, Pr. and pub. by John
C. Totten, and sold by the principal booksellers in the Union.
1828. 216 p. CtHT-W; NNC-P.
                         34114
Methodist Episcopal Church
A collection of hymns, for the
use of the Methodist Episcopal
Church, principally from the collection of the Rev. John Wesley
...New York, Pub. by J. Emory
and B. Waugh, for the Methodist
Episcopal Church, 1828. 544 p.
IEG; MoK; RPB.   34115

---- The Methodist harmonist...
New-York, Pub. by N. Bangs
and J. Emory, for the Methodist
Episcopal Church. Azor Hoyt,
pr., 1828. [xii], 247 p. RPB.
                         34116
---- Minutes of the annual conferences of the Methodist Episco-

pal Church, for the year 1828.
New-York, Pub. by J. Emory
and B. Waugh, for the Methodist Episcopal Church, J. Col-
lord, pr., 1828. 35, [1] p.
CoDI; TNJ; TxGeoS.   34117

---- A report of the committee
on petitions and memorials,
adopted, we believe, without a
dissenting vote, by the late general conference, on motion of
the Rev. Asa Shinn. Cincinnati,
Pub. by C. Holliday, for the
Methodist Episcopal Church
[1828?] 8 p. MiD (not loc.,
1970)   34118

---- Baltimore
Proceedings, statements, and
resolutions, of "A very large
meeting" of members of the Methodist Episcopal Church, opposed
to the late proceedings against
members of the Baltimore Union
Society. Baltimore, R. J. Matchett, 1828. 16 p. MdBBC.
                         34119
---- Cincinnati. Union Society.
Report of the committee appointed by the Union Society of
Cincinnati, to receive the communication from the last General
Conference, in relation to reform
in the government of the Methodist Episcopal Church, and to report thereon. Cincinnati, Lodge,
L'Hommedieu & Hammond, prs.,
1828. 10 p. CBDP; OCHP.
                         34120
---- Conferences. Maine.
Articles of faith and a church
covenant, reported by the committee of the General conference
of Maine: and adopted by the
church in Gorham as a formula
of admission. Portland, Shirley
and Hyde, prs., 1828. 17 p.
CSmH.   34121

---- ---- Portland, Shirley &
Hyde, 1828. 18 p. CSmH.
                         34122

---- Missionary Society.
Ninth annual report of the Missionary Society of the Methodist Episcopal Church. New York, Pr. at the Conference Office, Azor Hoyt, pr., 1828. 36, 4 p. Ms-Ar.   34123

Mexico. Congreso. Camara de Diputados
Semblanzas de los miembros que han compuesto la Camara de diputados del congresso de la union de la Republica Mexicana en el bienio de 1827 y 1828. Nueva York, Inprenta fraternal, 1828. 23 p. BrMus; CU-B.   34124

Miami University. Oxford
Catalogue of the officers and students of the Miami University, Oxford, Ohio. July, 1828. Oxford, Ohio, Pr. at the Societies' Press, 1828. 12 p. OOxM.34125

Michigan (territory)
Acts passed at the first session of the third legislative council of the territory of Michigan. Detroit, Pr. by H. L. Ball. 1828. 102 p. C-L; DLC; MH-L; Mi; MiD-B; MiGr; MnHi; Mo; Ms; NNB; Nj; OCLaw; RPL; WHi; WaU-L.   34126

---- No. 6. Third council. First session. May 19, 1828. Read the second time and laid on the table. A bill, concerning grand and petit jurors. I Sect. I. Be it enacted by the legislative council of the Territory of Michigan... [Detroit, 1828] 11 p. MiD-B.
                                    34127
Middlebrook's almanack for 1829. By Elijah Middlebrook. Bridgeport, J. B. & L. Baldwin [1828] 12 l. Ct; CtB; CtHi; CtY; MWA.
                                    34128
---- ---- New Haven, S. Babcock, Sidney's press [1828] 12 l. CRedl; Ct; CtLHi; DLC; MWA.
                                    34129
---- ---- 2d ed. New Haven,

S. Babcock [1828] Drake 952. 34130

---- ---- 3d ed. New Haven, S. Babcock [1828] Drake 953.
                                    34131
---- ---- 4th ed. New Haven, S. Babcock [1828] 12 l. CtY.
                                    34132
---- ---- 5th ed. New Haven, S. Babcock [1828] 12 l. CtHi; CtY; MWA.   34133

Middlebury College. Middlebury, Vermont
Catalogue of the officers and students... for November, 1828. Middlebury, Press of the Vermont American, 1828. 11 p. CSmH.   34134

Middlesex Law Library Association.
A catalogue of books belonging to Middlesex Law Library Association. Concord, Pr. by Herman Atwill, 1828. 10 p. MHi. 34135

Mikve Israel.
No. 195. An act to enable the Hebrew Congregation known by the name and style of Kaal Kadosh Mickve [sic] Israel, of the city of Philadelphia, in the commonwealth of Pennsylvania, to lease on ground rent a lot of ground, in the city of Philadelphia, belonging to said Congregation. Passed 14th April, 1828. Bdsd. Collection of Dr. A. S. W. Rosenbach, Philadelphia.
                                    34136

Mildrum, James
To the honourable Superior Court of the state of Connecticut, to be holden at Haddam in and for the county of Middlesex, on the fourth Tuesday of August A. D. 1828. The petition of James Mildrum [requesting the court to judge him an insolvent debtor] Dated at Middletown July 24th, A. D. 1828. 1 p. DLC.   34137

The Milford bard, pseud. See
Lofland, John.

Milledoler, Philip
Address delivered before the
alumni of Columbia College, on
the seventh of May 1828. In the
chapel of the College... Rutgers
Press. Pub. by Terhune & Let-
son, New Brunswick. Terhune &
Letson, prs., 1828. 23 p. MBAt;
MH-AH; NN; NNC; NjR; PHi;
PPPrHi.   34138

The millennium. Extracts from
vol. III of the Moral Advocate.
A monthly publication, edited by
Elisha Bates, at Mt. Pleasant,
Ohio... Wethersfield, Con. Pr.
by Deming & Francis, 1828. 144
p. CtHi; PSC-Hi.   34139

Miller, Jonathan P., 1797-1847
The condition of Greece, in
1827 and 1828... As contained in
his journal, kept by order of the
executive Greek committee of the
city of New York... New York,
Pr. by J. & J. Harper, 1828.
300 p. C-S; CSmH; CtHT; DLC;
ILM; LNT; MBAt; MH; MNe;
MW; MdBE; Me; MeLB; MiD;
MiGr; NCH; NGH; NNUT; NT;
NjP; OCX; OClW; P; PPA; PSC;
VtB; VtU; BrMus.   34140

Miller, Orren
(Second edition) A funeral sermon, preached on the occasion
of the death of Mrs. Hannah Miller, consort of the Rev. Jonathan
A. Miller, September 14, 1819,
at Mount-Morris, (Genesse Co.,
N.Y.) Rochester, Elisha Loomis,
1828. 16 p. MiD-B; PPL. 34141

Miller's planters' & merchants'
almanac for 1829. By Joshua
Sharp. Charleston, A. E. Miller
[1828] 24 1. AU; GEU; InU; NN;
ScC.   34142

---- ---- 2d ed. Charleston,

A. E. Miller [1828] 24 1. ScC.
                               34143
---- ---- [3d ed.] Charleston,
A. E. Miller [1828] 24 1. MWA;
RPB.   34144

Milnor, James, 1773-1844
Sermon, occasioned by the
death of his excellency Dewitt
Clinton, late governor of the
state of New-York, Preached in
St. George's Church, N.Y. on
Sunday, February 24, 1828...
New-York, Pr. by Gray and
Bunce, 1828. 26 p. CtHC; ICU;
IEG; MH; NBLiHi; NIC; PHi;
WHi.   34145

Miltiades, pseud. See Shannon,
James.

Milton, John, 1608-1674
Paradise lost: A poem, in
twelve books. Philadelphia, J.
Locken, 1828. 176 p. 2 v. in 1.
IObB; MH; OClWHi; OO. 34146

Miner, Charles, 1780-1865
Speech of Mr. Miner, on the
constitutional power of Congress
to make internal improvements.
Delivered in the House of Rep-
resentatives, Monday, February
25, 1828. Washington, Pr. by
Gales and Seaton, 1828. 19 p.
DGU; DLC; DeGE; ICN; MBAt;
MH; MoKU; PPL; ScU.   34147

Ming's Hutchins' improved almanac and ephemeris for 1829.
New York, Alexander Ming
[1828] 18 1. DLC; MWA; N; NHi;
NN.   34148

Miniature almanack for 1829.
Boston, Richardson & Lord
[1828] 14 1. MHi; NN.   34149

---- Boston, Richardson & Lord,
[1828] 20 1. InU; MB; MWA.
                               34150
A minister of the German Reformed Church. See Christian

baptism.

The minstrel: A collection of
popular songs. Philadelphia, Pr.
& pub. by William W. Weeks,
1828. 356, [iii]-xiv p. PPL.
34151
The mirror; or, Eighteen juvenile tales and dialogues. By a
lady of Philadelphia. Boston,
Munroe and Francis and Charles
S. Francis, New York, 1828. 288
p. RPB; ScCliTO.   34152

A mirror for politicians. Moral
beauty of consistency illustrated
by Sunday extracts from the leading prints now engaged in advo-
cating the election of General
Jackson to the presidency...[New
York? 1828] Bdsd. MB.   34153

Missionary biography. See
American Board of Commissioners for Foreign Missions.

Mississippi
    Auditor's report. Auditor's
office, Jackson, Jan. 10th, 1828.
[Jackson, 1828] Bdsd. Ms-Ar.
34154
---- Documents, accompanying
the governor's message, transmitted to the senate. [Jackson,
1828?] Bdsd. Ms-Ar.   34155

---- Governor's message. [Jack-
son, Office of the State Journal,
1828] Bdsd. Ms-Ar.   34156

---- Head Quarters, Jackson,
August 23, 1828. General orders.
The Commander in Chief of the
Militia of the state of Mississippi, intending as far as practicable,
to review the various Regiments
composing the same, during the
ensuing autumn, the Regiments
will therefore parade at their respective places of muster, armed
and accoutred according to law:
and be prepared for Review and
Inspection, at twelve o'clock, on

the days designated as follows:
By order of the Commander in
Chief. James Smith, Adjutant
General. [Jackson, 1828] Bdsd.
Ms-Ar.   34157

---- Journal of the House of
Representatives of the state of
Mississippi, at their eleventh
session, held in the town of Jack-
son. Jackson, Miss., Pr. by
Peter Isler, 1828. 368 p. DLC;
M; Ms; MsU; NN; WHi.   34158

---- Journal of the Senate of the
state of Mississippi, at their
eleventh session, held in the
town of Jackson. Jackson [Miss.]
Pr. by Peter Isler, 1828. 254 p.
Ms; MsU; MsWJ.   34159

---- Laws of the state of Mis-
sissippi, passed at the eleventh
session of the General Assembly,
held in the town of Jackson.
Jackson, Peter Isler, state pr.,
1828. 147, viii, [10] p. C-L;
DLC; I; ICLaw; Ia; In-SC; MH-
L; MdBB; Mi-L; Ms-Ar; MsU;
NN; NNLI; Nb; Nj; Nv; O-SC;
OCLaw; Or-SC; RPL.   34160

---- Legislature of the state of
Mississippi. Mr. Harris, from
the Joint-Committee appointed to
meet General Andrew Jackson,
and welcome him within the bor-
ders of this state, Reported--
That they had performed that
duty, by delivering him an Address, in the following words, to
wit: January 20, 1828. [Jackson,
1828] Bdsd. Ms-Ar.   34161

---- Legislature of the state of
Mississippi. Mr. Runnels, from
the Joint-Committee appointed to
meet General Andrew Jackson,
and welcome him within the bor-
ders of this state, Reported--
That they had performed that
duty, by delivering him an Address, in the following words,

to wit: January 20, 1828. [Jackson, 1828] Bdsd. Ms-Ar. 34162

---- Treasurer's report. [Jackson, 1828] Bdsd. Ms-Ar. 34163

Mississippi Bible Society
Report of the Mississippi
Bible Society, presented at the
fourteenth anniversary meeting,
held in Trinity Church at Natchez, March 29, 1828. Natchez,
Pr. by Wm. C. Grissam & Co.,
1828. 16 p. MsJPED.   34164

Mitchell, Elisha, 1793-1857
[No. 3] Professor Mitchell's
report on the geology of North-
Carolina: with C. E. Rothe's remarks on the gold country: and
a report on the subject of manufacturing establishments, and the
raising of sheep. Pub. by order
of the Board of Agriculture.
Raleigh, Pr. by J. Gales & Son,
1828. 60 p. NcU.   34165

[Mitchell, Isaac] d. 1812.
Alonzo and Melissa; or, The
unfeeling father. An American
tale... By Daniel Jackson, jr.
Exeter [N. H.?] Pub. by Abel
Brown, 1828. 240 p. CSmH; MB;
MWA; PPL.   34166

Mitchell, Thomas Rothmaler,
1783-1837
Speech of Mr. Mitchell, of
South Carolina, on a motion to
postpone, indefinitely, the tariff
bill, delivered in the House of
Representatives, April 15, 1828.
Washington, Pr. at the office of
Jonathan Elliot, 1828. 16 p. ScHi.
                         34167
Mitchill, Samuel Latham, 1764-
1831
A chymical examination of the
mineral water of Schooley's
Mountain [N. J.]; together with a
physical geography of the first
range of mountains extending a-
cross New Jersey, from the Hud-

son to the Delaware. Morristown,
[N. J.] Pr. by Jacob Mann, 1828.
23 p. DNLM; NBLiHi; PHi.
                         34168
---- ---- New York, Sickels,
pr., 1828. 24 p. NNNAM; NjR;
PHi; PPL.   34169

---- A discourse on the character and scientific attainments of
De Witt Clinton, late Governor of
the state of New York; Pronounced at the Lyceum of Natural History... 14th July, 1828...
New York, Pr. by E. Conrad,
1828. 28 p. CSmH; ICU; IU;
MBAt; MH; MnHi; NNC; NNG;
PHi; PPAmP; PPL; WHi. 34170

---- A discourse on the life and
character of Thomas Addis Emmit, pronounced, by request, in
the New-York city-hall, on the
first day of March, 1828. New
York, E. Conrad, 1828. 26 p.
CSmH; ICN; MH; NNG; NNNAM;
PHi; WHi.   34171

---- A lecture on some parts of
the natural history of New-Jersey, delivered before the Newark
Mechanic Association for Mutual
Improvement in the Arts and Sciences, on Tuesday, June 3, 1828.
New-York, Pr. by Elliott and
Palmer, 1828. 34 p. CSmH;
NBLiHi; NHi; NNNAM; NjR;
PPAmP; PPL; PPPrHi.   34172

[----] Some of the memorable
events and occurrences in the
life of Samuel L. Mitchill, of
New York, from the year 1786 to
1826... [1828?] 8 p. NNC;
PPAmP.   34173

Mitford, Mary Russell, 1787-
1855
Our village... From the 4th
London ed. New-York, E. Bliss
[J. Seymour, pr.] 1828. 3 vols.
CtHT-W; MB; NCH; NNC;
NjR; PPL; RJa; ScU;

WHi.   34174

The Modern martyr. A fragment.
With other interesting extracts
from "The Spirit and Manners of
the Age." Originally selected for
and published in the 'Philadelphia Recorder'." Philadelphia,
Pub. by Wm. Stavely, 1828. 221
p. MB.   34175

[Moir, David Macbeth] 1798-1851
The life of Mansie Wauch,
tailor in Dalkeith. Written by him-
self. New-York, Pr. by J. & J.
Harper; Philadelphia, Carey, Lea
and Carey; [etc., etc.] 1828. 223
p. CSmH; DLC; LNHT; LU; MB;
MBL; MH; NjP; NjR; RPB.
                             34176
Moncrieff, William Thomas
Paris & London; or, A trip to
both cities, an operatic extrava-
ganza in three acts... New York,
Murden, 1828. 54 p. MA; MH;
PU.   34177

Monfort, David
A farewell sermon, delivered
at Bethel... eleventh of Novem-
ber, 1827... Oxford, O., J. D.
Smith, pr., 1828. 12 p. ICMcC.
                             34178
Monroe, James, 1758-1831
The memoir of James Monroe,
esq. relating to his unsettled
claims upon the people and gov-
ernment of the United States.
Charlottesville, Va., Pr. & pub.
by Gilmer, Davis and co., 1828.
60 p. CSmH; CtHT-W; DLC; IHi;
KyU; MB; MBAt; MBC; MH; MHi;
MdHi; NBu; NN; NcD; Nh; NhHi;
PPL; PU; TxU; Vi; ViU; ViW;
WHi.   34179

...Monsieur Botte, comedie-
vaudeville en trois actes. [Phila-
delphia, 1828. 34 p. (Neal &
MacKenzie. No. 201 Chestnut
Street, between the Theater &
Arcade, Philadelphia.) (Also issued in vol. with covering title:

Collection d'operas et vaudevilles.) PPL.   34180

Montgomery, Robert, 1807-1855
The omnipresence of the Deity:
A poem. Philadelphia, Carey,
Lea and Carey. Sold in New
York, by G. & C. Carvill; in
Boston by Monroe and Francis
[Thos. Kite, pr.] 1828. 192 p.
DLC; GHi; MB; MBC; MH; NGH;
NCWsS; OCY; PP; PPL; PU.
                             34181
A monument of parental affec-
tion. See Gilpin, Joshua.

Monumental inscriptions. See
Binns, John.

[Moore, Jacob Bailey]
The principles and acts of Mr.
Adams' administration, vindicated
against the aspersions contained in
the address of the Jackson Convention, assembled at Concord,
on the 11th and 12th of June,
1828. By a Freeman. Concord,
Pr. at the N. H. Journal Office.
1828. 40 p. CSmH; DLC; MH;
MWA; MiD-B; NIC; NNC; NRHi;
NhHi; PHi; RPB; TxD-W. 34182

Moore, Thomas, 1779-1852
Llalla Rookh. New ed. Boston,
S. G. Goodrich, 1828. 302 p.
CtHT; DLC; MH; NjR; OClW;
ViAlTh.   34183

---- ---- Cabinet ed. Providence,
Pub. by H. Le Barron and Co.,
1828. [5], 208 p. CSmH; PU.
                             34184
---- Melodies, songs, sacred
songs, and national airs.
Bridgeport, Sherman, 1828. 284
p. NjP.   34185

---- ---- New York, Pub. for
the booksellers, 1828. 273 p.
DGU.   34186

[----] Odes upon cash, corn,
Catholics, and other matters.

Selected from the columns of the
Times Journal... Philadelphia,
Carey, Lea & Carey, 1828. 191
p. CtHT-W; LNHT; LU; MB;
MBAt; MdBP; MeBaT; MoSM;
NPV; P; PHi; PPL; BrMus.
34187
---- The poetical works of
Thomas Moore, including his
melodies, ballads, etc. Complete
in one volume. Stereotyped by L.
Johnson, Philadelphia, Pub. by J.
Crissey and J. Grigg, Philadel-
phia, 1828. 419 p. MeAug.
34188
Moral and religious souvenir.
Boston, N. S. Simpkins & co.,
1828. 288 p. DLC; MB; MBC;
MH; MWA; NN; NjR; RPB; WU.
34189
A moral inquiry into the charac-
ter of man. Part I. New York,
Pub. for the Author by E. Bliss
[J. Seymour, pr.] 1828. 78 p.
MBC; PPAmP.   34190

Moral stories, for boys and girls.
Wendell, J. Metcalf, 1828. 23 p.
MWA.   34191

More, Hannah
The shepherd of Salisbury
plain. [New York, J. Emory and
B. Waugh, 1828] 36 p. [Sunday
School biography. 1828-1829 no.
9] ICU.   34192

Morgan, Mordecai
Biographical memoir of Dr.
John Davis, late of Chester
County, Pennsylvania. Philadel-
phia, 1828. 15 p. DLC; PHi.
34193
Morgan, Sydney (Owenson) Lady
The O'Briens and the O'Fla-
hertys; a national tale. By Lady
Morgan... Philadelphia, Carey,
Lea & Carey, 1828. 4 vols. in
2. DLC; MH; MHa; MNS. 34194

Morgan, William, 1774-ca. 1826.
Erlaeuterung der frey-maure-
rey, wie geschrieben von capt.

William Morgan, aus der englischen in die deutsche sprache
uebersetzt, nebst einem meister
schluessel zu den geheimnissen
des hoehern ordens... Von einem
freymauren, welcher der institution viele jahre gewidmet hat.
Waterloo, Gedruckt bei W. Child,
1828. 96 p. DLC.   34195

---- Masonry, by William Morgan. One of the fraternity, who
has devoted thirty years to it.
Rochester, N. Y., Pr. for the
author, 1828. 24 p. PPFM.
34196
Morganiana, or The wonderful
life and terrible death of Morgan.
Written by himself. Illustrated
with gritholaphic plates, by Has-
san Straightshanks, Turkey. First
Amer. ed., tr. from the original Arabic manuscript. By Baron
Munchausen, jr. ... Boston, Pr.
and pub. by the proprietors,
1828. 92 p. CSmH; CtY; DLC;
MBNEH; MHi; MWA.   34197

Morgridge, Charles
A discourse on the reciprocal
duties of a minister and his
people: delivered at the opening
of the Christian Chapel in Salem,
Mass. May 1, 1828. Boston,
Wait Greene & Co. [Press of
Isaac R. Butts & Co.] 1828. 24
p. CSmH; ICMe; MB; MBAU; MH;
MiD-B; RPB; BrMus.   34198

[Morier, James Justinian] 1780?-
1849
The adventures of Hajji Baba,
of Ispahan, in England. In two
volumes. New-York, Pr. by J.
& J. Harper. Sold by Collins and
Hannay, Collins and co., G. and
C. Carvill, A. T. Goodrich, O. A.
Roorbach, and Wm. B. Gilley; -
Philadelphia, Carey, Lea, and
Carey, John Grigg, M'Carty &
Davis, and U. Hunt; - Boston,
Richardson and Lord, and Hilli-
ard, Gray, and co., 1828. 2 v.

CtHT; LU; MBAt; NGH; PPL; RPB; TNJ; ViAl; VtU.   34199

Morse, Jedediah
Modern atlas, adapted to Morse's School geography. New York, Collins & Hannay, 1828. 8 col. maps. DLC; NPV.   34200

---- A new system of geography, ancient and modern for the use of schools, accompanied with an atlas, adapted to the work. 26th ed. Boston, Pub. by Richardson and Lord, 1828. 300, 21 p. CSt; CtHT-W; MH; MWHi; MtHi; NBuG; NPV.   34201

---- ---- 26th ed. New-York, Pub. by Collins & Hannay. J. & J. Harper, prs., 1828. 228, 23 p. CtHT-W; NNC; TNJ.   34202

Morse, Samuel Finley Breese, 1791-1872
Fine arts. A reply to article X, no. LVIII, in the North American Review, entitled "Academies of arts," &c. New York, G. & C. Carvill [John M. Danforth, pr.] 1828. 45 p. CSmH; DLC; MA; MB; MBAt; MH; MdHi; MiD-B; NIC; NNC; NNUT; NbU; PPAmP; PPL; PPPM; PPPrHi; ScCC; WHi.   34203

[Morton, Thomas] 1764?-1838
The invincibles, or, Carnival crotchets; a musical farce in two acts. Philadelphia, Neal & Mackenzie; New York, Mifflin & Parry, 1828. 43 p. MH.   34204

Morton; a tale of the revolution... Cincinnati, Hatch, Nichols & Buxton, 1828. 331 p. DLC; NN; OSW.   34205

Morton, Daniel Oliver, 1788-1852
"Wine is a mocker, strong drink is raging." A discourse, delivered at Montpelier, Oct. 16, 1828, on the formation of the Vermont Temperance Society. Mont-

pelier, Pr. by E. P. Walton, Watchman Office, 1828. 16 p. MH; PPPrHi; VtHi; VtU.   34206

Motherless Mary: or the Interesting history of a friendless orphan... New York, Pub. by S. King, 1828. 16 l. PP.   34207

Mott, James, 1788-1868
Brief hints to parents on the subject of education. New York, M. Day, pr., 1828. Tract No. 17 [Amer. Tract Society?] 24 p. MB.   34208

Mott, John, fl. 1827
An epistle to Friends within the compass of Philadelphia Yearly Meeting, by John Mott. Philadelphia, Pr. on the vertical press, by D. & S. Neall, [1828] 18 p. CSmH; MB; PHC; PPL; PSC-Hi.   34209

Motte, Mellish I.
Simplicity in the Christian faith alike scriptural and powerful. A sermon delivered... July 1, 1827, at the Second Independent Church in Charleston, S. C. Boston, Pr. by Dutton & Wentworth, 1828. 23 p. MB.   34210

Mt. Holyoke, or, The travels of Henry and Maria, a tale. Amherst, Mass., J. S. and C. Adams, 1828. 70 p. DLC; MAJ; MB. NN.   34211

Mount Pleasant Classical Institution. Amherst, Mass.
Mount Pleasant Classical Institution. Amherst, Mass. Catalogue &c. January, 1828. Amherst, John S. and C. Adams, prs. [1828] 16 p. CLU; DLC; MAJ; MBAt; MBC; MH; MeB; NN; P; PHi.   34212

Mournful tragedy [Cuts] or, The death of Jacob Webb, David Morrow, John Harris, Henry Lewis,

David Hunt, and Edward Lindsay,
six militia men who were condemned to die, the sentence approved by Major General Jackson,
and by his order the whole six
shot. Boston, July 1828. 1 p.
DLC. 34213

Mulkey, William
Analytical spelling book, being
a practical illustration of the
principles of pronunciation, as
laid down in Mr. Walker's Critical pronouncing dictionary: containing two hundred and fifty principles, exemplified by one hundred lessons, and upwards of one
hundred and fifty tables.... Tuscaloosa, Pr. by Grantland and
Robinson, 1828. 167 p. DHEW;
DLC; MH. 34214

Munchausen, Baron, Jr. See
Morganiana.

Munroe and Frances
Proposals for printing, by
subscription, an Exposition of the
historical writings of the New
Testament... by the Late Rev.
Timothy Kenrick... Boston, Munroe & Francis, 1828. [2] p. +
sample pages 12-16. PPL.
34215

Murray, John
A system of materia medica
and pharmacy including translations of the Edinburgh, London,
and Dublin pharmacopoeias by
John Murray, M.D. from 4th and
last Edinburgh editions with notes
and additions by John Beck, M.D.
New York, Pub. by Evert Duyckinck and others, W. E. Dean,
pr. 1828. 2 v. in one. CSt-L;
CU-M; ICJ; IaU; KyLxT; MBCo;
MdBM; MeB; NIC; NNC-P;
NNNAM; OkU; PPC; RPM; ScCM;
VtU; WU. 34216

Murray, Lindley
...An abridgment of Murray's
English grammar with an appendix, containing exercises in orthography, in parsing, [etc., etc.]
Designed for the younger classes
of learners... Stereotyped by T.
H. & C. Carter. Baltimore,
Pub. by Armstrong & Plaskitt,
and John Plaskitt & co., 1828.
105 p. MdHi; WU. 34217

---- ---- Bellows Falls, James
I. Cutler, 1828. 108 p. DLC;
MH. 34218

---- Putnam's Murray. Improved
stereotype ed. An abridgment of
Murray's English grammar. Containing also puncutation, the notes
under rules in syntax, and lessons in parsing: to the latter of
which are prefixed, specimens illustrative of that exercise, and
false syntax to be corrected. All
appropriately arranged. To all
which is adapted, a new system
of questions. From the second
Portsmouth ed., enl. and imp.
Boston, Hilliard, Gray, Little
and Wilkins, 1828. 108 p. MH;
NNC. 34219

---- Alger's Murray. English
grammar. Improved stereotype
ed. Abridgment of Murray's
English grammar, with an appendix, containing exercises in
orthography, in parsing, in syntax, and in punctuation. Designed
for the younger classes of learners. Rev., prepared and adapted
to the use of "English exercises."
By Israel Alger, Jr. Boston,
Pub. by Lincoln & Edmands;
Stereotyped by S. Walker, & co.
1828. 122 p. MH; TxU-T.
34220

---- ---- Containing also punctuation, the notes under rules in
syntax, and lessons in parsing:
to the latter of which are prefixed, specimens illustrative of
that exercise, and false syntax
to be corrected. All appropriately arranged to all which is

adapted, a new system of questions. From the 2d Portsmouth ed. enl. and imp. By Samuel Putnam. Dover, N. H. , Pub. by Samuel C. Stevens, 1828. 108 p. , 2 l. CSmH.   34221

---- An abridgment of Murray's English grammar, and exercises, with improvements, designed as a text book for the use of schools in the United States. By the Rev. J. G. Cooper... Philadelphia, Pub. by Judah Dobson, 1828. 200, [4] p. LShC; NNC Plimpton.   34222

---- The duty and benefit of a daily perusal of the Holy Scriptures in families. Philadelphia, Waldie, 1828. 30 p. PPAmP.
                              34223
---- English exercises, adapted to Murray's English grammar... Designed for the benefit of private learners, as well as for the use of schools. Baltimore, Pub. by Cushings & Jewett, F. Lucas, Jr. and Armstrong & Plaskitt; Benjamin Edes, pr. , 1828. 192 p. MdBE.   34224

---- Murray's exercises - Improved stereotype ed. Murray's English exercises. Rev. , prepared, and particularly adapted to the use of schools... by Israel Alger, Jun. Boston, Lincoln & Edmands, 1828. 252 p. IEdS; MH; NNC.   34225

---- English exercises adapted to Murray's English grammar designed for the benefit of private learners as well as for the use of schools. By Lindley Murray. Boston, Pr. by James Loring, 1828. 213 p. MB.   34226

---- English grammar, adapted to the different classes of learners... Stereotyped by B. and J. Collins, from the last English

ed. Bridgeport, J. B. & L. Baldwin, 1828. 312 p. IU; MiD-B; NjR; OClW.   34227

---- ---- With an appendix... for assisting the more advanced students... Philadelphia, T. Desilver, Jr. , 1828. 339 p. MH; OCHP; PHi.   34228

---- ---- With an appendix, containing rules and observations, for assisting the more advanced students to write with perspicuity and accuracy... Utica, W. Williams, 1828. 264 p. (Stereotype ed.)   DLC.   34229

---- Murray's English grammar simplified; designed to facilitate the study of the English language, comprehending the principles and rules of English grammar, illustrated by appropriate exercises. To which is added a series of questions for examination. Abridged for the use of schools. By Allen Fisk, author of Adam's Latin grammar simplified. 2d ed. Hallowell, Me. , Pr. and pub. by Glazier, Masters & Co. , 1828. 124 p. NNC.   34230

---- The English reader... Bridgeport, Pub. by J. B. & L. Baldwin, 1828. 263 p. CtSoP; NN.   34231

---- ---- Concord, N. H. , Pr. and pub. by Horatio Hill & co. , 1828. 252 p. MH; MWA; MiU; Nh; PU-Penn; TCU; VtRoc.
                              34232
---- ---- Elizabeth Town, N. J. , T. O. Sayre, 1828. 252 p. AzU; IaHA; NSyU; ViRVal.   34233

---- New-England stereotype ed. The English reader; or, Pieces in prose and poetry, selected from the best writers. Designed to assist young persons to read with propriety and effect, to im-

prove their language and sentiments, and to inculcate some of
the most important principles of
piety and virtue. With a few preliminary observations on the principles of good reading. Stereotyped by B. & J. Collins, New-
York. Hallowell, Me., Pub. by
Glazier & Co., 1828. 263 p.
NNC.   34234

---- ---- Stereotyped by B. &
J. Collins, N. Y. Hallowell, Me.,
Pub. by Glazier, Masters & Co.,
1828. 252 p. CtHT-W; MeAu;
OClWHi.   34235

---- ---- Improved by the addition of a concordant and synony-
mising vocabulary... according
to the principles of John Walker.
By Jeremiah Goodrich. Middletown, Conn., Pr. and pub. by
E. & H. Clark, 1828. 304 p.
CtHi.   34236

---- ---- With a few preliminary
observations on the principles
of good reading. Stereotyped by
B. & J. Collins from the late
English ed. Philadelphia, D. &
S. Neall, 1828. 263 p. P;
PPeSchw.   34237

---- ---- Pittsburgh, Henry
Holdship, 1828. 204, [60] p.
OClWHi; PPi.   34238

---- ---- By Jeremiah and Anna
F. Goodrich. Saratoga Springs,
Pr. at the Sentinel Office [1828?]
72 p. MH.   34239

---- ---- Utica, Press of Hastings and Tracy, 1828. 263 p.
PSC-Hi.   34240

---- ---- To which are prefixed,
the definitions of inflections &
emphasis and rules for reading
verse, with a key... By M. R.
Bartlett... Utica, W. Williams,

1828. 252 p. CtY; DLC; MiD-B;
NUt; OClWHi; OO.   34241

---- ---- Improved by the addition of a concordant and synony-
mising vocabulary. The words
pronounced according to the principles of John Walker, by Jeremiah Goodrich. Windsor, Simeon
Ide, 1828. xxiii, 304 p. MH;
VtMiM; VtMiS; BrMus.   34242

---- ---- Stereotyped by J.
Howe. Zanesville, Pub. and sold
by William Davis. Wholesale and
retail. 1828. 252 p. DGU; PU.
                               34243

---- Introduction to the English
reader, or a selection of pieces,
in prose and poetry, calculated
to improve the younger classes
of learning in reading, and to
imbue their minds with the love
of virtue, to which are added,
Rules and observations for assisting Children to read with propriety. From the last English ed.
Baltimore, Pub. by Cushing &
Jewett, Benjamin Edes, pr.,
1828. 166 p. ICMcC.   34244

---- ---- Boston, Stereotyped
at the Boston Type and Stereo-
type Foundry. Pub. by N. S. and
S. G. Simpkins: Hilliard Gray,
Little and Wilkins, 1828. 216 p.
MPlyA.   34245

No entries.   34246-34345

---- ---- Cincinnati, N. & G.
Guilford, 1828. 156 p. ICN.
                               34346

---- ---- Philadelphia, Pub. by
David Clark, 1828. 166 p. PPL.
                               34347

---- ---- Philadelphia, Pub. by
P. M. Lafourcade, 1828. 166 p.
IaAt; PAtM; PLFM; TCU. 34348

---- ---- Raleigh, Gales, 1828.
179 p. NcU.   34349

---- Key to the exercises adapted to Murray's English grammar, calculated to enable private learners to become their own instructers [sic] in grammar and composition. By the author of the exercises. Baltimore, Cushing & Jewett, and F. Lucas, jr., 1828. viii, 151 p. ICU.   34350

---- The power of religion on the mind, in retirement, affliction, and at the approach of death: exemplified in the testimonies and experience of persons distinguished by their greatness, learning, or virtue... New York, Richard and George S. Wood, 1828. 288 p. GDC; IObB; InRE; MiD; NRF; PHC; PPFHi.   34351

---- Sequel to the English reader; or, Elegant selections in prose and poetry, designed to improve the highest class of learners in reading; to establish a taste for just and accurate composition, and to promote the interests of piety and virtue. Woodstock, 1828. 299 p. MBarn.   34352

Murray, M. C.
    Murray's sure guide to the English language; comprising a comprehensive guide for all public and private schools, and the public in general. Boston, Pub. and pr. by I. Thomas, Jr., 1828. 80 p. IaPeC.   34353

Muse, Joseph Ennalls
    An address upon the dominant errors of the agriculture of Maryland, delivered... before the Dorchester Agricultural Society... at the third exhibition and fair, held in Cambridge, Oct. 29, 1827... Baltimore, Pr. by J. D. Toy, 1828. 25 p. MB; MdBP; MdHi; BrMus.   34354

Museum of foreign animals; or, History of beasts... New Haven, S.

S. Babcock [1828?] 16 p. DLC.
                                  34355
Music of the church. See Wainwright, Jonathan Mayhew.

Musical Fund Society of Philadelphia.
    15th concert... Wednesday, January 30, 1828. [Philadelphia, 1828] Bdsd. PPL.   34356

---- Seventeenth concert of the Musical Fund Society of Philadelphia, December 11, 1828. [Philadelphia, 1828] 4 p. PPL. 34357

Musical Institute of the City of New York.
    Constitution of the Musical Institute of the City of New-York. New-York, Pr. by Edward Grattan, 1828. 12 p. Whi.   34358

Mussey, Reuben Dimond, 1780-1866
    An address on ardent spirits, read before the New Hampshire Medical Society at their annual meeting June 5, 1827. Hanover, Pr. by Thos. Mann, 1828. 24 p. CtSoP; CtY; DNLM; MB; MH; MHi; MiD-B; NNNAM; NhHi; OC; OCG; OO; RPB; VtMiM; WHi; BrMus.   34359

Mutius.   See Rives, Judith Page Walker.

My aunt; a petit comedy. See Arnold, Samuel James.

N

Nantucket, Mass. First Congregational Church
    The articles of faith, the covenant and rules of discipline of the First Congregational Church in Nantucket. Boston, T. R. Marvin, pr., 1828. 8 p. MBC.   34360

Narragansett Bay Company

Charter of the Narragansett
Bay Company. Granted at October session A.D. 1828. Providence, 1828. 8 p. RHi.   34361

A narrative and defence. See
Bond, Thomas E.

A narrative of the facts and circumstances relating to the kid-
napping and presumed murder of
William Morgan: and of the attempt to carry off David C. Miller, and to burn or destroy the
printing-office of the latter, for
the purpose of preventing the
printing and publishing of a book
entitled "Illustrations of masonry." Prepared under the direction of the several committees
appointed at the meetings of the
citizens of the counties of Genesee, Livingston, Ontario, Monroe, and Niagara in the state of
New-York: with an appendix...
disclosing many particulars of
the transaction, not in the narrative. 3d ed. Rochester, N.Y.,
Pr. by E. Scrantom, 1828. 72
p. CSmH; DLC; IaCrM; MB;
MHi; NN; PHi; PPFM.   34362

Nashville, Tenn.
The laws of the corporation of
Nashville, as revised, re-enacted
and passed 20th December, 1827.
To which are added the acts of
North Carolina and Tennessee,
relating to the town of Nashville.
Nashville, Pr. by John S. Simp-
son, 1828. 70 p. T.   34363

Natchez, Mississippi
Natchez, January 7th, 1828.
Sir, At a meeting of Persons
"opposed to the election of gen-
eral Jackson,"...[Natchez, 1828]
Bdsd. Ms-Ar.   34364

The national calendar and gentleman's almanac for...1829. Baltimore, Pub. by Henry Vicary...

Wm. Wooddy, Pr. [1828] 18 l.
DLC; MWA; PP.   34365

The national calendar for 1829.
By Peter Force. Washington
City, P. Force [1828] 144 l.
CtY; DLC; MBAt; MdHi; N; NjP;
PHi; PU; RNHi; RNR; THi; WvU.
34366

National Journal, Washington,
D.C.
Address of the carriers of the
National Journal. January 1st,
1828. [Washington, D.C., 1828]
1 p. DLC.   34367

National Republican Party. Con-
necticut.
Address to the electors of
Middlesex County. [Middletown?
Conn., 1828] 6 p. DLC. 34368

---- Indiana.
Address of the Administration
standing committee to their fellow-citizens of Indiana. [Indian-
apolis? 1828] 22 p. DLC; InHi.
34369
---- Proceedings of the Administration convention held at Indianapolis, January 12, 1828. [In-
dianapolis, pr. at the office of
the Indiana Journal, 1828] 16 p.
DLC.   34370

---- ---- [Indianapolis, Indiana
Journal office, 1828] 24 p. In;
InHi; MB; OCHP.   34371

---- Kentucky
Supplement to the Kentucky
Reporter. Address, of the Fay-
ette County Corresponding Com-
mittee, on the proceedings in the
Senate of Kentucky, against the
President, Secretary of State and
Members of Congress; and on oth-
er subjects connected with the ap-
proaching Presidential election.
Lexington, Thomas Smith, pr.
[1828] 48 p. DLC; ICU; KyLo;
KyLoF; MBAt; NN; PPL; T;
WHi.   34372

---- Louisiana.
Address of the Central Committee, of the friends of the administration to the voters of Louisiana. On the subject of the approaching presidential election. New Orleans, Pr. by John Gibson at the Argus Office, 1828. 15, [1] p. DLC.   34373

---- Maine.
Proceedings of a convention of the people of Maine, friendly to the present administration of the general government... [n. p., 1828] 12 p. DLC.   34374

---- Maryland.
Address of the Administration Convention in Baltimore County. [Baltimore? 1828?] 4 p. DLC.
34375

---- Massachusetts.
Address of the central committee appointed by a convention of both branches of the Legislature friendly to the election of John Q. Adams, as president and Richard Rush as vice-president of the U. States, held at the statehouse in Boston, June 10, 1828, to their fellow citizens, [Boston, 1828] 24 p. Page 1, line 12 of text ends: "to this." CLU; CSmH; DLC; ICN; IU; MB; MBAt; MH; NNUT; OCLaw; PHi; PPAmP; PPL.   34376

---- ---- [Boston, 1828] Page 1, line 12 of text ends: "to this Com-" PPL.   34377

---- Administration convention.
At a convention of members of both branches of the Legislature of Massachusetts, holden in the hall of the House of Representatives, in Boston on Tuesday the 10th day of June, 1828, for the purpose of designating suitable persons to be recommended as candidates for presidential electors at the ensuing election...

[Boston, 1828] 1 p. DLC; WHi.
34378

---- Missouri.
Administration meeting in Cooper County, Feb. 2, 1828. [Jefferson City? 1828] MoHi.
34379

---- Proceedings and address of the Anti-Jackson Convention of Missouri, to their fellow-citizens. [Fayette, Pr. by Nathaniel Patten, 1828] 47 p. I; MB; MoSM; BrMus.   34380

---- New Hampshire.
Address of the great state convention of friends of the administration, assembled at the capitol in Concord, June 12, 1828, with the speech of Mr. Bartlett, in reply to the charges which have been made against Mr. Adams. Concord, Pub. by order of the convention, 1828. 24 p. CSmH; DLC; ICU; IU; MH; MHi; MiD-B; NNC; NhD; NhHi; OClWHi; PHi.
34381

---- Proceedings and address of the Convention of young men in Rockingham councillor district, Epping, Sept. 10, 1828. [Epping? N. H.] Miller & Brewster, prs., [1828] 8 p. CSmH; MBC; MH; MiD-B.   34382

---- New Jersey.
Address of the Young Men's Association of Trenton, N. J. favorable to the present administration to the young men of the state. [Trenton? 1828?] 11 p. NjP; PHi.   34382a

---- Proceedings and address of the New Jersey delegates in favor of the present administration of the general government assembled in convention at Trenton, February 22, 1828. Wm. L. Prall, pr., Trenton [1828] 18 p. CSmH; DLC; NN; WHi.   34383

---- New York.

Address of the state convention of delegates from the several counties of the state of New-York, to the people, on the subject of the approaching presidential election. Albany, Pr. by Beach, Denio & Richards, 1828. 16 p. CLU; DLC; MB; MBC; PU.
34384

---- Address to the republican citizens of the state of New York. Albany, Pr. for Beach, Denio & Richards by Webster and Wood, 1828. 8 p. CSmH; DLC; MBC; WHi.
34385

---- Administration convention of young men. Address of the general committee of Republican young men of the city of New York, to the republican young men of the state of New York, recommending a state convention to be held at Utica, on ... August 12, 1828. New York, 1828. 8 p. OClWHi; TxDaM.
34386

---- Farmers tickett. John Quincy Adams a heddwch, llwyddiant ag happisrwydd. Andrew Jackson a rhyfel, trethu, ag ymrafelion. Dewyswch pa un or rhai hyn yr ydych yn ei ethol. Os ydym yn dymyno Uwyddo gochelwn ryfel a threthu. Maen gwlad yn awr yn ddedwydd na ddyoddefwn ddun rhyfelgar i rwystro eun llyddiant. Ticket llwyddiant a heddwch. Ebenezer B. Sherman elector for President. Henry R. Storrs for Congress. [Utica? 1828?] Bdsd. NBuHi.
34387

---- Great Republican meeting Rochester. At a meeting of the citizens of Rochester friendly to the Administration... at J. G. Christopher's, on the 28th of June... [Rochester, 1828] 8 p. MB; NRHi; NRU.
34388

---- Journal of the convention of young men, of the state of New-

York, assembled at Utica, on the 12th day of August, 1828. Utica, Northway & Porter, pr., 1828. 29 p. CSmH.
34389

---- New York state convention. [Albany? 1828] 33 p. CSmH; DLC.
34390

---- Report of the state convention held at the capitol in the city of Albany, to select suitable candidates for president and vice president of the U. S. A. New York, Sickels, pr. to the General Republican Committee. [1828] 42 p. ICMe; MB.
34391

---- Resolutions and addresses of the convention of delegates from the counties of New York, held at Albany June 10, 11, 1828, nominating John Quincy Adams and Richard Rush for president and vice president, in opposition to General Andrew Jackson. [Albany, 1828] 33 p. DLC; KU; MH; OCL; PHC; PHi; VtU; WaS; WaU; WyU.
34392

---- [St. Lawrence Co. --County Corresponding Committee. Letter dated Ogdensburgh, October 27, 1828, written to urge voters to attend election and cast their vote for Mr. Adams. Ogdensburgh, 1828] 4 p. fold. with writing on p. 1. WHi.
34393

---- State convention. Proceedings and address of the Republican young men... on the 12th day of August, 1828. Utica, Northway & Porter, prs., 1828. 24 p. CSmH; MB; MH; MMeT-Hi; MdBJ; NBu; NUt; PHi; PPL.
34394

---- Utica. October 16, 1828. Sir, The Central corresponding committee, appointed by the friends of the administration in convention on the 23d July last, having received communications

from gentlemen in all parts of
the state, in answer to letters
addressed to them cheerfully sub-
mit the result to their friends.
Utica, 1828. 3 p. DLC.   34395

---- North Carolina.
Address of the administration
convention, held at Raleigh, Dec.
20, 1827. To the freemen of
North Carolina. [Raleigh, 1828]
8 p. NcU.   34396

---- ---- Raleigh, Pr. by J. Gales
and son, 1827. [i. e. 1828] [3]-
15 p. NcU.   34397

---- To the people of Cayuga
County... Cayuga County, April,
1828. Address of the administration convention, held in the capitol at Raleigh, December 20,
1827. [Auburn, 1828] 8 p. NN.
                          34398
---- Ohio.
Verhandlungen und Addresse
von der Convention der Delegaten,
welche sich den 28sten December,
1827, in Columbus, Ohio ver-
sammelten, um ein Electoral
Ticket zu gunsten der Wieder-
Erwählung von John Quincy
Adams, President der Vereinigten Staaten, zu formiren, welches
bey der Electoral Wahl in 1828
unterstützt werden soll. German-
town, Ohio, Gedruckt in der
Druckerey der National Zeitung
der Deutschen von Eduard
Schäffer, 1828. 24 p. MBAt.
                          34399
---- Pennsylvania.
Democratic convention. [Har-
risburg, Pr. at the office of the
Harrisburg Argus, 1828] iv, 20
p. DeGE; MBAt (20 p.)   34400

---- Virginia.
The American system. Internal improvements and domestic
manufactures. For President,
John Quincy Adams. Vice-President, Richard Rush. Virginia

Electoral Ticket... [Wheeling?
1828] Bdsd. WvWO.   34401

---- At a meeting of the friends
of the present administration,
held at the house of Paul L.
Evans, in the town of Winchester,
on the 29th of March 1828... To
the people of Clarke County.
[n. p. 1828] 32 p. DLC.   34402

---- People's ticket. For Presi-
dent, John Quincy Adams of
Mass. For Vice-President, Rich-
ard Rush of Pa. Electoral ticket
... [Wheeling? 1828?] Bdsd.
WvWO.   34403

---- Plain truth. The following
documents are submitted to the
consideration of a candid public,
as conclusive evidence that Andrew Jackson, a candidate for the
presidency of the United States,
has been a trafficer in human
flesh... From the Knoxville [Ten-
nessee] Enquirer. To the public.
[Wheeling, 1828] 15 [1] p. "Published by the Ohio County, Va.
Committee of Vigilence [sic]"
MB; WvU.   34404

---- Plain truth. The following
documents are submitted to the
consideration of a candid public,
as proofs that Andrew Jackson,
a candidate for the presidency
of the United States, was associated with Aaron Burr... [Wheel-
ing, 1828] 15 p. "Published by
the Ohio County, (Va.) Committee of Vigilance." MB.   34405

---- Proceedings of the Anti-
Jackson convention held at the
capitol in the city of Richmond,
with their address to the people
of Virginia (accompanied by documents). Richmond, Pr. by S.
Shepherd & Co., at the Franklin press, 1828. 38 p. CSmH;
ICU; IU; M; MBat; MnU; NcD;
NcU; PHi; Vi; ViL; ViU;

WHi.   34406

---- Verhandlungen der Anti-
Jackson Convention gehalten in
dem Capitolium in der Stadt Richmond; nebst ihrer Zuschrift an
das Volk von Virginien, und den
dazu gehörigen Dokumenten. Hagerstaun, Johann Gruber und Daniel May, 1828. 35 p. NN. 34407

---- The Virginia address.
[Richmond? 1828] 8 p. CtY; DLC;
ICN; MB; MH; MnHi; NHi; NN;
PPL; TxU; Vi.   34408

---- The Voice of Virginia! In
offering to the citizens of New-
Hampshire, the following eloquent address of the convention
at Richmond, in Virginia, it need
only be stated that it was unanimously adopted by the Convention,
consisting of one hundred and
eighty delegates... It is hoped
that every citizen of New Hampshire will read it with care and
attention... Adress of the Virginia
Anti-Jackson Convention to the
people of Virginia. [1828] 2 p.
DLC.   34409

A native American. See Reflections on the character and public
services of Andrew Jackson.

Nautical almanac for 1829. Pub-
lished by order of the Commis-
sioners of Longitude. New York,
N.Y., Repub. by Richard Pat-
ten [1828] 205, 23, [6] p. MWA.
                            34410
Neal, John, 1793-1876
    Rachel Dyer: a North Ameri-
can story. Portland [Me.] Shir-
ley and Hyde, 1828. 276 p. CLU;
CSmH; CtHT-W; DLC; ICN; ICU;
KU; MB; MH; MHi; MWH; MdHi;
MeBa; MeHi; MeU; MnU; NT; NjR;
OClW; OOxM; PU; RPB; ViU.
                            34411
Neele, Henry, 1798-1828
    The romance of history. Eng-

land. Philadelphia, Carey, Lea
& Carey, 1828. 2 v. DLC; LN;
LU; MH; MW; MnSS; NGlo; RJa.
                            34412
Negrēs, Alexandros
    A grammar of the Modern
Greek language; with an appendix
containing original specimens of
prose and verse. Boston, Hilli-
ard, Gray, Little & Wilkins,
1828. 2 p. l., [88] p. 1 l.
DLC; KyU; MB; MBAt; MH;
MdBS; MeBaT; NCH; NN;
NNC; OMC; RPB; TxU; ViU;
VtU; BrMus.   34413

[Nelson, D.]
    Bible questions. [Pr. at the
Transylvania Press, by Jos. G.
Norwood, Lexington, Ky. 1828?]
15 p. ICU; KyU.   34414

Nelson, David P.
    Meditations on various religi-
ous subjects, at the conclusion
of which is affixed a treatise on
some important diseases. Louisville, Ky., 1828. 300 p. ICU;
KyLo; KyRE; MoSM; NN; OCHP;
TxHuT.   34415

Nelson, John, 1786-1871
    The influence of the Christian
ministry. A sermon, delivered
at the ordination of Rev. Benson
C. Baldwin, over the Norwich-
Falls Church, [Conn.] January
31, 1828... Boston, T.R. Marvin, pr., 1828. 22 p. CBPac;
Ct; CtSoP; ICN; MBC; MH-AH;
OClWHi; RPB; BrMus.   34416

Nettleton, Asahel
    Village hymns for social wor-
ship. Selected and original. De-
signed as a supplement to the
Psalms and hymns of Dr. Watts.
New York, E. Sands, publishers,
1828. 488 p. CBPac; Ct; CtHC;
CtHT; DLC; FStP; IEG; LNHT;
MB; MBC; MDeeP; NRU; NSyU;
OClWHi; OMC; OO; PPPrHi;
ViRU; WHi; WaPS; BrMus. 34417

Der Neue Americanische Land-
wirthschafts-Calender auf 1829.
Von Carl Friedrich Egelmann.
Reading, Johann Ritter u. Comp.
[1828] 18 l. DLC; InU; MWA;
NHi; NjP; PHi; PPL; PRHi.
34418
Der Neue Hochdeutsche Orwigs-
burger Calender auf 1829. Or-
wigsburg, Thoma und May [1828]
18 l. MWA; NN; PHi; PPL.
34419
Der Neue Pennsylvanische Stadt-
und Land-Calender auf 1829.
Allentaun, Heinrich Ebner und
Comp. [1828] 18 l. CLU; CtY;
DLC; MWA; N; PPL; PRHi.
34420
Das neue und verbesserte gesangbuch, worinnen die Psalmen
Davids, samt einer sammlung
alter und neuer Geistreicher
Lieder... Nach einen Synodal
Schluss zusammen getragen und
eingerichtet vor die Evangelisch-
Reformirten Gemeinen in den
Vereinigten Staaten von America.
Sechste auflage. Germantaun,
Gedruckt bey M. Billmeyer, 1828.
402, [8] p. NcMHi; PHi; PPL.
34421
Neuman, Henry
    Neuman and Baretti's diction-
ary of the Spanish and English
languages... Stereotype ed., carefully rev., and enl. ...to which
are added, directions for finding
the difference between the ancient
and modern orthography... Boston,
Hilliard, Gray, Little, and Wilkins, 1828. 2 v. CtMW; DLC;
GDC; KyLoN; MH; MeBaT; MoS;
NNE; OClW; ViU. 34422

Nevin, John Williamson, 1803-
1886
    A summary of Biblical an-
tiquities; compiled for the use of
Sunday-school teachers, and for
the benefit of families... Rev.
and corr. by the author for the
American Sunday School Union.
Philadelphia, American Sunday

School Union, [1828-30] 2 v.
WaPS. 34423

---- ---- Utica, Western Sun-
day School Union, Northway &
Porter, prs., 1828. 2 v. DLC;
MB; MiToC; NCH; NUt; NbCrD;
OBerB; OO; PWW. 34424

The New Brunswick (N. J.) al-
manack for 1829. By Joseph
Cramer. Philadelphia, Griggs &
Dickinson, for Joseph C. Griggs,
New Brunswick [1828] 18 l. CtY;
MWA; NjR; PHi. 34425

The new casket, containing rich
treasures for young minds.
Portland, Shirley & Hyde, 1828.
144 p. ICN; OHi. 34426

The New-England almanack, and
farmer's friend for 1829. By
Nathan Daboll. New-London, Sam-
uel Green [1828] 16 l. CLU; CtHi;
CtY; DLC; InU; MB; MWA; NHi;
NNC; NjR; OClWHi; WHi. 34427

The New England almanack and
Masonic calendar for 1829. Bos-
ton, Marsh & Capen [1828] 30 l.
DLC; MB; MBC; MH; MHi; MWA;
NN; OClWHi. 34428

---- Concord, Horatio Hill &
Co. [1828] 28 l. MWA; PPFM.
34429
The New England Anti-Masonic
almanac for 1829. By Edward
Giddings. Boston, Anti-Masonic
Free Press [1828] 12 l. CLU;
IaCrM; MB; MH; MHi; MWA;
NHi; NIC; PPFM; RP. 34430

The New England farmer's al-
manack for 1829. By Thos. G.
Fessenden. Boston, John B. Rus-
sell; Bowles & Dearborn [1828]
25 l. CLU; Ct; CtY; DLC; ICHi;
InU; MBAt; MBC; MH; MHi;
MWA; NN; NPV; NhHi; NjP; NjR;
RPB; VtU; WHi. 34431

---- By Truman Abell. Windsor, Simeon Ide [1828] 24 l. CLU; DLC; MH; MWA; NCooHi; NhHi; Vt; VtHi.   34432

The New England primer, or an easy and pleasant guide to the art of reading. Brookfield, E. & G. Merriam, 1828. 32 l. CtSoP.   34433

The New-England primer improved: or, An easy and pleasant guide for children to the art of reading. To which is annexed, the shorter Catechism, as composed and agreed upon by the reverend Assembly of divines at Westminster in England. Concord, N. H., G. Hough, pr., 1828. 70, [2] p. DLC; NNC; Nh.   34434

The New-England primer, improved. Being an easy method to teach young children the English language. To which is added, the Assembly of divines' and Episcopal catechisms. New-York, Pr. and sold by C. Brown, 1828. 70 p. MH; RPB.   34435

New Hampshire
    Journal of the House of Representatives of the state of New Hampshire, at their session, holden at the capitol in Concord, commencing Wednesday, June 4, 1828. Pub. by authority. Concord, [N. H.], Pr. by Jacob B. Moore, for the state, 1828. 192 p. DLC; IaHi; MHi; PPL. 34436

---- Journal of the Senate of the state of New Hampshire, at their session, holden at the capitol in Concord, commencing Wednesday, June 4, 1828. Pub. by authority. Concord (N. H.), Pr. by Jacob B. Moore, for the state, 1828. 115 p. DLC; IaHi.   34437

---- Laws of the state of New-Hampshire, passed June Session 1828. Pub. by authority. Con-

cord, Pr. by Jacob B. Moore, for the state, 1828. [2], 263-290 p. [1] p. Ar-SC; IaU-L; In-SC; MdBB; Mo; Nb; Nv.   34438

---- Laws of the state of New-Hampshire, passed November Session 1828. Pub. by authority. Concord, Pr. by Jacob B. Moore, for the state, 1828. [2] p. 293-480 p. Ar-SC; IaU-L; In-SC; MdBB; Mo; Nb; Nj; Nv; T.   34439

---- Message from His Excellency the Governor to both Houses of the Legislature November 19, 1828. Pub. by order of the House of Representatives. Concord, Pr. by Jacob B. Moore, 1828. 7 p. NhHi.   34440

---- Report of commissioners appointed to settle the line between New-Hampshire and Maine. [Concord, N. H., A. M'Farland, pr., 1828] 18 p. DLC; MH; NhHi; BrMus.   34441

---- Rules and orders of the House of Representatives of the state of New-Hampshire, with the joint rules of the two Houses, a list of standing committees, and the names of the members and officers of the different branches of government, A. D. 1828. To which is added the constitution of New-Hampshire. Concord, 1828. WHi.   34442

---- State of New-Hampshire. A proclamation for a day of public fasting and prayer... I therefore ... appoint Thursday, the third day of April next as a day of public fasting and prayer throughout this state... Given at Hillsborough, this first day of March, in the year of our Lord, one thousand eight hundred and twenty eight, and of the Independence of the United States the fifty-second Benjamin Pierce. By His Excellency the Governor, with the advice of the Council. Richard Bartlett, Secretary of State [1828] 1 p. DLC.   34443

The New-Hampshire annual register, and United States calendar for 1829. By John Farmer. Concord, Jacob B. Moore [1828] 72 l. CtY; ICN; MB; MHi; MWA; MdBP; MiD-B; N; NHi; NhHi.   34444

New Hampshire Auxiliary Colonization Society
    Fourth annual report of the New Hampshire Auxiliary Colonization Society, presented and read at the meeting of the Society, holden in the Brick Meeting-House in Concord, June 5, 1828. Pub. by order of the Society. Concord, Pr. by Geo. Hough, 1828. 12 p. MH; Nh; WHi.   34445

New Hampshire Bible Society
    The seventeenth report of the New-Hampshire Bible Society, communicated at the annual meeting of the Society, holden at Salisbury, September 3, 1828. Concord, Pr. by Geo. Hough, for the Society, 1828. 39 p. CtHC.   34446

New Hampshire Branch of the American Education Society
    Second annual report of the directors of the... for the year ending Sept. 2, 1828. Hanover, Pr. by Thos. Mann, 1828. 22, [2] p. CSmH; MBC; NjR.   34447

New Hampshire Missionary Society.
    Twenty-seventh annual report of the New Hampshire Missionary Society... holden at Salisbury... Concord, Pr. by Geo. Hough, 1828. 32 p. MB; MiD-B.   34448

New Hampshire Patriot-Extra. See A voice from Kentucky.

New Hampshire Republican State Convention. See Democratic Party. New Hampshire.

New Hampshire Society for the Promotion of Temperance
    Constitution of the New-Hampshire Society for the Promotion of Temperance, auxiliary to the American Society; together with a list of the officers, elected June, 1828. Concord [N. H.] A. M'Farland, pr., 1828. [4] p. DLC; MB; Nh; NhHi; OC.   34449

New Harmony Gazette Supplement. See Communication from the trustees of Nashoba.

New Haven Gymnasium. New Haven, Conn.
    Catalogue of the... November, 1828. [New Haven, H. Howe, pr. 1828] 8 p. CtHi; CtY; MH; Nh; PHi; PPL.   34450

New-Haven town and city register for 1829. [New Haven, 1828] 1 l. CtY.   34451

A new interest table. See Mann, Charles.

New Jersey
    Acts of the fifty-second General Assembly of the state of New Jersey, at a session begun at Trenton on the twenty-third day of October, one thousand eight hundred and twenty-seven. and continued by adjournments. Being the second sitting. Trenton, Pr. by Wm. L. Parall, 1828. [3] 217 p. In-SC; Ky; Ms; Nb; NjR; T.   34452

---- Acts of the fifty-third General Assembly of the state of New Jersey. At a session begun at Trenton on the twenty-eighth day of October, one thousand eight hundred and twenty-eight, and continued by adjournments:

being the first sitting. Trenton,
A. W. Phillips, pr., 1828. 13 p.
IaU-L; In-SC; MdBB; Mi-L; Ms;
NNLI; Nb; Nj; NjR; Nv; T; W.
34453

---- Journal of the proceedings
of the Legislative Council of the
state of New Jersey, convened at
Trenton, the 23d day of October,
1827... Woodbury, N. J., Pr. by
P. J. Gray, 1828. 123, 36 p.
M̲H̲; NN; Nj; NjR.   34454

---- Message of His Excellency
the governor, together with the
report of the commissioners appointed on the part of the state
of New Jersey, to settle the question of territory and jurisdiction
in dispute with the state of New-
York, &c. &c. February, 1828.
Trenton, Pr. for the state by J.
Justice, 1828. 64 p. CSmH; DLC;
MH-L; NjP; NjR; RPB.   34455

---- Report of the commissioners appointed by the Legislature
of the state of New Jersey for
the purpose of exploring the route
of a canal to unite the river Delaware, near Easton, with the
Passaic, near Newark, with accompanying documents. Morristown, Pr. by J. Mann, 1828.
148 p. NNE.   34456

---- Report of the joint committee of Council and Assembly appointed to view the Morris canal
and inclined planes. [Trenton?
1828] 27 p. DLC; Nj.   34457

---- Rules and orders of the
Supreme court of judicature of
the state of New-Jersey, published under the authority and
direction of the court. By Zachariah Rossell, clerk. With an
appendix. Trenton, Pr. by J.
Justice, 1828. 46 p. DLC; MH-
L; Nj; NjN; NjT.   34458

---- Votes and proceedings of the

fifty second General Assembly
... session begun... twenty-third
day of October, one thousand
eight hundred and twenty-seven.
Being the first sitting. Woodbury, N. J., Pr. by P. J. Gray,
1828. 320 p. NN.   34459

New-Jersey almanac for 1829.
By David Young. Newark, Ben-
jamin Olds [1828] 18 l. CtY;
DLC; MH; MWA; NHi; NjHi;
NjR; ViHi.   34460

---- Trenton, Geo. Sherman
[1828] 18 l. DLC; MBC; MWA;
MdBJ; NjHi; NjR; NjT.   34461

New Jersey Bible Society
Statement of what has recent-
ly been done to supply the desti-
tute of New Jersey with sacred
Scriptures. Princeton, Princeton
Press, 1828. 37 p. NjP; NjR;
PPPrHi; RPB.   34462

New Jersey State Convention.
See Democratic Party. New Jersey.

The new lover's instructor, or,
Whole art of courtship. Being
the lover's complete library and
guide; and containing full and
complete instructions concerning
love, courtship, and marriage.
Including... the most ingenious
love letters... calculated for the
use of persons of all ranks and
conditions of life. Published under the direction and inspection
of Chas. Freeman, esq., & Mrs.
Charlotte Dorrington... New-
York, S. King, 1828. 36 p.
DLC.   34463

The new mirror for travellers.
See Paulding, James Kirke.

New Norwood gipsy; or, Complete art of fortune telling by
cards, moles, the wheel of fortune, lines in the hands, features

of the face, colour of the hair, and by the grounds of tea or coffee-cups, together with the evil and perilous days throughout the year... New-York, S. King, 1828. 1 p. l. , [9]-34 p. DLC.   34464

A new picture book. See American Tract Society. N. Y.

New riddle book... New York, Pr. and sold by Mahlon Day, at the new juvenile book store, 1828. 19 p. MH.   34465

The new Robinson Crusoe. See Campe, Joachim Heinrich von.

New Salem Academy
    Catalogue of the trustees, instructors and students... Oct. 1828. Athol, Alonzo Rawson? [1828] Bdsd. MWA.   34466

A new series of questions. See Fisk, Harvey.

New York (City)
    Annual report of deaths in the city & county of N. York, for the year, 1827. Published by order of the Common council. New-York, P. Van Pelt, pr. , 1828. 12 [2] p. PHi; ScU.   34467

New York (State)
    An act authorising the construction of a rail road from the state prison at Auburn, to the Erie Canal. [Albany, 1828] 2 p. NN.   34468

---- An act concerning the revised statutes, submitted to the Legislature, December 5, 1828. Albany, Pr. by Croswell and Van Benthuysen, 1828. 27 p. IaU; MB; NNB ([2], 27 p.); NNLI; NjR; RPL.   34469

---- An act to facilitate the construction of a rail-road from the city of Boston to the Hudson

river. [Albany, 1828] [1] p. NN.
                                34470
---- An act to incorporate the Catskill and Ithaca Rail-Road Company. [Albany, 1828] 4 p. NN.   34471

---- An act to incorporate the "Great Sable Rail Road Company. " [Albany, 1828] 3 p. NN.
                                34472
---- An act to incorporate the Hudson and Berkshire Rail-Road Company. [Albany, 1828] 5 p. NN.   34473

---- An act to incorporate the Watervliet Turnpike Company passed March 31, 1828... Albany, Pr. by Websters and Skinners, 1828. 15 p. NBC; OCHP. 34474

---- Amendment offered by Mr. Speaker, while in committee of the whole, on Chapter V. , entitled "of suits relating to real property. " [Albany, Pr. by Croswell and Van Benthuysen, 1828] 2 p. NNB.   34475

---- Amendments to chapter I. Of the third part of the proposed revision, relating to the Court of Chancery. Prepared by the revisers, pursuant to a resolution of the Senate and Assembly. Albany, Pr. by Croswell and Van Benthuysen, 1828. 20 p. NN; NNB; NNLI; NjR; RPL.   34476

---- The annual report of the canal commissioners of the state of New York, presented to the Legislature, the 19th January 1828. Albany, Pr. by Croswell and Van Benthuysen, 1828. 31, [1] p. MWo; NRom.   34477

---- Annual report of the superintendent of common schools; made to the Legislature of the state of New York. January 29, 1828. Albany, Pr. by Croswell and Van Benthuysen, 1828. 61, [1] p. IaHi; MH; P; PPL. 34478

---- Article second of Title III. Chapter IX. of the third part of writs of certiorari and error in special cases. Sections 66-76. [Albany, Pr. by Croswell and Van Benthuysen, 1828] 70*-73* p. (*these pages to be substituted for pp. 70-76 in Chapter IX of the third part.) NNB; NjR. 34479

---- Chapter I. Of the second part of the proposed revision of the statute laws of the state of New-York. Albany, Pr. by Croswell and Van Benthuysen, 1828. [4], 90 p. NNB. 34480

---- Chapter I. Of the third part of the proposed revision of the statute laws of the state of New York. Albany, Pr. by Croswell and Van Benthuysen, 1828. iv, 93 p. IaU-L; NNB; NNLI; NjR; RPL. 34481

---- Chapter II. Of the third part of the proposed revision of the statute laws of the state of New-York. Albany, Pr. by Croswell and Van Benthuysen, 1828. 85 p. IaU-L; NNB; NNLI; NjR; RPL. 34482

---- Chapter III. Of the third part of the proposed revision of the statute laws of the state of New-York. Albany, Pr. by Croswell and Van Benthuysen, 1828. 20 p. IaU-L; N; NNB; NNLI; NjR; RPL. 34483

---- Chapter IV. Of the third part of the proposed revision of the statute laws of the state of New-York. Albany, Pr. by Croswell and Van Benthuysen, 1828. [3], 20 p. IaU-L; NNB; NNLI; NjR; RPL. 34484

---- Chapter V. Of the third part of the proposed revision of

the statute laws of the state of New-York. Albany, Pr. by Croswell and Van Benthuysen, 1828. [3], 86 p. IaU-L; NNB; NNLI; NjR; RPL. 34485

---- Chapter VI. Of the third part of the proposed revision of the statute laws of the state of New-York. Albany, Pr. by Croswell and Van Benthuysen, 1828. 4, 69 p. IaU-L; NNB; NNLI; NjR; RPL. 34486

---- Chapter VII. Of the third part of the proposed revision of the statute laws of the state of New York. Albany, Pr. by Croswell and Van Benthuysen, 1828. 4, 102 p. IaU-L; NNB; NNLI; NjR; RPL. 34487

---- Chapter VIII. Of the third part of the proposed revision of the statute laws of the state of New-York. Albany, Pr. by Croswell and Van Benthuysen, 1828. v, 203 p. NNB; NNLI; NjR. 34488

---- Chapter IX. Of the third part of the proposed revision of the statute laws of the state of New-York. Albany, Pr. by Croswell and Van Benthuysen, 1828. [3], 1-70, 70*-73*, 71-81 p. NNB; NNLI; NjR (copy seen contains pp. 70*-73* as described above no. 34479. Also found in original form, [3] 81 p.); RPL. 34489

---- Chapter X. Of the third part of the proposed revision of the statute laws of the state of New-York. Albany, Pr. by Croswell and Van Benthuysen, 1828. [3], 73 p. NNB; NNLI; NjR; RPL. 34490

---- Chapter I. Of the fourth part of the proposed revision of the statute laws of the state of New York. Albany, Pr. by Croswell & Van Benthuysen, 1828.

vi, 95 p. MB; NNB; NNLI; NjR;
RPL.   34491

---- Chapter II. Of the fourth
part of the proposed revision of
the statute laws of the state of
New York. Albany, Pr. by Croswell and Van Benthuysen, 1828.
iv, 84 p. IaU-L; NNB; NNLI;
NjR; RPL.   34492

---- Chapter III. Of the fourth
part of the proposed revision of
the statute laws of the state of
New York. Albany, Pr. by Croswell and Van Benthuysen, 1828.
[3], 38 p. IaU-L; NNB; NjR;
PPL.   34493

---- Charter and by-laws of the
New York Chamber of Commerce.
Instituted 5th April, 1768-Incor-
porated 13th March, 1770. New
York, Pr. by Vanderpool & Cole,
1828. 24 p. NIC; PHi; WHi.
                            34494
---- A complete analysis of the
several acts and chapters em-
braced in the revised statutes.
Albany, Pr. by Croswell and Van
Benthuysen, 1828. 30 p. IaU-L;
NNB; NNLI; NjR; RPL.   34495

---- Constitution and by-laws of
the LaFayette Guards, of the
211th Reg't, 13th Division, &
13th Brigade. Designed for members of the company. Utica, Pr.
by Northway & Porter, 1828. 8,
[2] p. N.   34496

---- The constitution of the state
of New-York; together with a law
of the state respecting elections,
other than for militia & town officers. Published by order of the
corporation of the city of New-
York. New-York, Pr. by P. Van
Pelt, 1828. 37 p. NNC.   34497

---- The constitution of the
United States and the state of
New York, together with the

rules and orders, standing committees and list of members of
the Senate and Assembly for
1828. Albany, Croswell & Van
Benthuysen, 1828. 161 p. NCH.
                            34498
---- In Assembly, Mar. 28,
1828. Memorial of upwards of
one hundred physicians and surgeons of the City of New-York,
praying for the incorporation of
Manhattan College...[Albany,
1828] 2 p. NNNAM; NjR. 34499

---- In the court for the trial
of impeachments and the correction of errors. Between Richard
Abraham, Impleaded with Jonathan Thompson. Appellant; and
Charles Berners Plestow, and
others: Respondents. New York,
Alexander Ming, pr. [1828?] 25,
[1] p. NN.   34500

---- Joint rules of the Senate
and Assembly, respecting the
order of business and mode of
proceeding in considering the revised statutes. [Albany, Pr. by
Croswell and Van Benthuysen,
1828?] 2 p. NNB; NjR.   34501

---- List of acts omitted in the
revision of the statutes; and table
of references of provisions re-
vised. Prepared by the revisers.
Albany, Pr. by Croswell and
Van Benthuysen, 1828. 156 p.
IaU-L; MH-L; NNB; NNLI; NjR;
RPL.   34502

---- ...Memorial of the inspectors of the Auburn state prison,
&c. praying the construction of a
rail-road from the said prison
to the Erie canal. To...the Legislature of the state of New-
York...[Albany, 1828] 5 p. NN.
                            34503
----...Message from the Governor. [Albany, Jan. 1, 1828] 9 p. NN.
                            34504
---- Signs of the Times--Extra.

Message of His Excellency De Witt Clinton, to the Legislature of the state of New-York, on the opening of the session, January 1, 1828. Albany, Pr. by D. M' Glashan, 1828. 12 p. MB; N; NbU.   34505

---- New school act. Revised statute. Relating to common schools. Passed at the extra session of the Legislature of the state of New-York, December 3, 1827. With the forms and regulations prepared by the Superintendent of Common Schools... Hudson, Pub. by Wm. E. Norman, 1828. 48 p. ViRUT. 34506

---- Remarks of Gershom Powers, agent and keeper of the state prison at Auburn, on chapter third of the fourth part of the revision of the statute laws, relating to state prisons. Submitted to the Legislature, November 17, 1828. Albany, Pr. by Croswell and Van Benthuysen, 1828. 25 p. CSmH; NCH; NNB; NNLI; RPL.   34507

---- Report, in relation to the instruction of the deaf and dumb, in the city of New York made to the Senate, Apr. 14, 1828. [Albany] Croswell, 1828. 68 p. MB; NCH; WHi.   34508

---- Report of Gershom Powers, agent and keeper of the state prison, at Auburn. Made to the Legislature, Jan. 7, 1828. Albany, Pr. by Croswell and Van Benthuysen, 1828. 126 p. ICJ; IU; MB; MH; MHi; NHi; NNC; NjR; OO; PPAmP; PPL; PU; WHi.   34509

---- Report of the Commissioners appointed to revise the statute laws of this state. Made to the Legislature, January 2, 1828. Albany, Pr. by Croswell and Van

Benthuysen, 1828. 16 p. NNB; NNLI; NjR; PPL; RPL.   34510

---- ---- Made to the Legislature, September 9, 1828. Albany, Pr. by Croswell and Van Benthuysen, 1828. 20 p. NNB; NLitf; NNLI; NjR; RPL.   34511

---- ---- Made to the Legislature, October 15, 1828. Albany, Pr. by Croswell and Ven Benthuysen, 1828. 10 p. NNB; NNLI; NjR; RPL.   34512

---- ... Report of the commissioners of New York, relative to the boundary line between this state and the state of New-Jersey. Made to the Senate, January 26, 1828. [Albany? 1828] 17 p. CSmH; NjN.   34513

---- Report of the committee on canals and internal improvements, relative to the construction of a rail-road from the Auburn state prison, to the Erie canal. [Albany, Feb. 26, 1828] 4 p. NN.   34514

---- Report of the committee on roads and bridges, on the petition of inhabitants of the county of Columbia. [Albany, March 17, 1828] 2 p. NN.   34515

---- Report of the select committee, appointed to inquire into the expediency of repealing the charter of the Life and Fire Insurance Company and other chartered institutions. Made to the Senate, March 31st, 1828. Albany, Pr. by Croswell and Van Benthuysen, 1828. 44 p. N.   34516

---- ... Report of the select committee, on the engrossed bill from the Assembly, relative to the construction of a rail-road from the Auburn state prison to the Erie canal. [Albany, April 15, 1828] 3 p. NN.   34517

---- ...Report of the select committee, relative to the construction of a rail-road from Port Kent to the Sable river. [Albany, February 25, 1828] 2 p. NN. 34518

---- ...Report of the select committee, relative to the construction of a rail-road from the Hudson river to Ithaca. [Albany, March 27, 1828] 2 p. NN. 34519

---- ...Report of the select committee relative to the incorporation of the Susquehannah Navigation and Rail Road Company. [Albany, March 10, 1828] 4 p. NN. 34520

---- Revised statute relating to elections, other than for militia and town officers; being chapter VI. passed at the extra session of the Legislature of the state of New-York, December 3, 1827... Albany, Pr. by Croswell & Van Benthuysen, 1828. 43 p. MH-L; P. 34521

---- Rules of practice in the Superior Court of the city of New York. New York, Pub. by Gould & Banks, 1828. 36 p. NNLI. 34522

---- Substitute for Titles I, II, & VI, of Chapter V. (As printed) of the third part of the revised statutes. Prepared by the revisers, pursuant to a resolution of the Assembly of the 18th of September. [Albany, Pr. by Croswell and Van Benthuysen, 1828] 18 p. NNB; NjR. 34523

---- Substitute offered by Mr. Cheever, for a part of article 10, of the 4th title of chapter II. [Albany, Pr. by Croswell and Van Benthuysen, 1828] 4 p. NNB; NjR. 34524

---- Supplement to Chapter II. - Third part. [Albany, Pr. by Croswell & Van Benthuysen, 1828] 3 p. NNB. 34525

---- Third part. - Chapter I. Title II. Article sixth. Sections 112 to 120 inclusive, as amended by the Assembly. [Albany, Pr. by Croswell and Van Benthuysen, 1828] 3 p. NNB. 34526

---- Title IV. Of Chapter II of the Third part, as passed in committee of the whole of the Assembly. [Albany, Pr. by Croswell and Van Benthuysen, 1828] 67 p. NNB. 34527

New York. American Academy of Fine Arts
Catalogue of paintings and sculpture, exhibited by the American Academy of the Fine Arts, May, 1828. The fourteenth exhibition. New-York, Rutgers Press, 1828. Wm. A. Mercein, pr. to the Academy. 16 p. NBLiHi. 34528

New York. Auxiliary New York Bible and Common Prayer Book Society
The thirteenth annual report of the managers of the Auxiliary New York Bible and Common Prayer Book Society. New-York, Pr. by T. & J. Swords, 1828. 14 p. NNG. 34529

No entry. 34530

New York City Tract Society
The first annual report of the New-York City Tract Society, auxiliary to the American Tract Society, with the constitution and by-laws. New-York, Pr. for the

Society, by D. Fanshaw, 1828.
22 p. CSmH; CU; DLC; MiD-B.
                                    34531
New York. College of Physicians
and Surgeons.
    Copy of a memorial from the
trustees of the College of Physicians and Surgeons of the City
of New-York, to the regents of
the University... Albany, Feb.,
1828. Bdsd. NjR.   34532

---- Outlines of the lectures on
chemistry, delivered in the College of Physicains and Surgeons
of the University of the state
of New-York. Pr. by A. Ming,
[New York?] 1828. 12 1. DNLM.
                                    34533
New-York consolidated lottery,
class no. eleven to be drawn...
August 12th, 1828... J. Booth &
Sons, prs., New-York. [1828]
Bdsd. NN.   34534

New York Daily Advertiser. New
York.
    Address of the carrier of The
New-York Daily Advertiser. To
his patrons. January 1, 1828.
[New York, 1828] 1 p. DLC.
                                    34535
New York Female Auxiliary Bible
Society
    The twelfth annual report of
the New-York Female Auxiliary
Bible Society... New York, J.
Seymour, pr., 1828. 22 p. MB;
NjR.   34536

The New York gardner.   See
Agricola, P., pseud.

New York. General Theological
Seminary of the Protestant Episcopal Church.
    New York, July 21, 1828.
Sir, In compliance with the direction of the standing committee
of the General Theological Seminary of the Protestant Episcopal
Church in the United States, I
have the honour of sending to

you the annexed Resolutions.
Jonathan W. Wainwright, Secretary. [New York, 1828?] Pr. on
pages 1 and 2 of a 4-page fold.
WHi.   34537

---- Proceedings of the board of
trustees of the General Theological Seminary of the Protestant
Episcopal Church in the United
States at their annual meeting,
held in the city of New-York,
from the 24th to the 27th of June,
1828. Published by order of the
trustees. New York, Pr. by T.
& J. Swords, 1828. 23 p. CtHT.
                                    34538
New York. Greek Committee.
    Address of the Greek commit-
tee to the public... [Dated] New
York, March 6, 1828. [Followed
by] (Circular.) Present state of
Greece. [New York, 1828] 3 p.
DLC.   34539

---- A voice from Greece, in
appeal to the sympathies and
charities in America. Published
by order of the New-York Greek
Committee, for distribution.
June, 1828. 20 p. CtY; MH; NN;
NjR; MA; RPB.   34540

New York Horticultural Society
    Proceedings of the New-York
Horticultural Society, at the cele-
bration of its tenth anniversary,
August 26, 1828. New-York, Pr.
by E. Conrad, 1828. 24, [1] p.
MBH; MiD-B; PPL; WU-A.
                                    34541
New York. House of Refuge.
    Rules and regulations for the
government of the House of Ref-
uge. [New York, 1828] 15 p.
PPL.   34542

New York. Institution for the Instruction of the Deaf and Dumb.
    Ninth annual report of the di-
rectors of the New-York Institution for the Instruction of the
Deaf and Dumb, to the Legisla-

ture of the state of New-York; for the year ending 31st Dec. 1827. To which is added: The report of the Female Association to Aid in Giving Support and Instruction to the Indigent Deaf and Dumb, &c. &c. New-York, Pr. by E. Conrad, 1828. 56 p. MoHi; NbU; PPL.   34543

New York. Laight Street Presbyterian Church.
Church manual, No. 4, for the communicants of the Laight St. Presbyterian Church, city of New York. [New York, 1828?] 35 p. PPPrHi.   34544

New York. Mercantile Library Association.
Catalogue of the books belonging to the Mercantile Library Association of the city of New York; to which are prefixed, the constitution, and the rules and regulations of the same. New-York, Pr. by J. & J. Harper, 1828. 188 p. NNS; RPA.   34545

New York Merchants
Reasons why the present system of auctions ought to be abolished. New York, Pr. by Alexander Ming, Jr., 1828. [1], 16 p. CSt; CtHT; DLC; DeGE; MH-BA; MWA; MdBJ; MiD-B; NCH; NN; NNC; PHi; PPL; WHi; BrMus.
                                      34546
New York Protestant Episcopal Sunday School Society
The eleventh annual report of the board of managers of the New York Protestant Episcopal Sunday School Society. Instituted in 1817. New-York, Pr. by T. & J. Swords, 1828. 20 p. DLC; NNG; NNS.   34547

The New York reader, no. 3: being selections in prose and poetry, from the best writers: designed for the use of schools, and calculated to assist the schol-

ar in acquiring the art of reading, and at the same time to fix his principles, and inspire him with a love of virtue. New York, Pub. by Samuel S. & William Wood, [c1828] 238 p. CSmH; CtHT-W; IObB.   34548

New York. St. Thomas's Church. Theological Scholarship Society.
Second annual report of the Theological Scholarship Society of St. Thomas' Church, New York, attached to the General Theological Seminary of the Protestant Episcopal Church in the United States. New York, Pr. by T. & J. Swords, 1828. 8 p. NNG.   34549

New York State convention. See National Republican Party. New York.

New York Sunday School Union
The twelfth annual report of the New-York Sunday School Union, auxiliary to the American Sunday School Union, to the year ending May, 1828. New York, Pr. for the Society by Gray and Bunce, 1828. 11, [3], [12]-13 p. MBC.   34550

New York. University.
Annual report of the regents of the University, to the legislature of the state of New-York. Made to the Senate Feb. 29, 1828. Albany, Pr. by Croswell and Van Benthuysen, 1828. 24 p. PPL; WHi.   34551

Newton, Hubbard
An address, on the use of ardent spirit, pronounced before the Society for the Promotion of Temperance, August 26th, A.D. 1828 at Newport, New-Hampshire ... Newport, Pr. by Aldrich & Barton, 1828. 23, [1] p. DLC; OC.   34552

Newton, John
  Memoirs, of Eliza Cunningham, by John Newton; of Jane
Lucy Benn, by Basil Woodd; and
of Caroline Elizabeth Smelt, by
Dr. Waddell, Rev. by the Committee of Publication of the American Sunday School Union. Philadelphia, American Sunday School
Union, 1828. 90 p. IEdS; NPV;
ScRhW; BrMus.   34553

Newton, John, 1725-1807
  The works of the Rev. John
Newton. Late Rector of the United
Parishes of St. Mary Woolnoth
and St. Mary Woolchurch Haw,
London. From the last London ed.
Pub. by direction of his execu-
tors. In four volumes. New
Haven, Pr. and pub. by Nathan
Whiting, 1828. 4 vols. GColu;
IJI; KyHe; TBriK; ViRU.   34554

Newton Theological Institution
  Anniversary of the Newton
Theological Institution, Sept. 11,
A.D. 1828. [Boston? 1828] Bdsd.
NN.   34555

The Newtonian reflector, or New
England almanac for 1829. By
Anson Allen. Hartford, H. Burr
Jun. [1828] 12 l. CLU; Ct; CtB;
CtHi; CtY; DLC; InU; MB; MWA;
MiD-B; MnU; N; NN; WHi.
                           34556
Nichols, Ichabod, 1784-1859
  Address delivered before the
Portland Association for the Pro-
motion of Temperance, Feb. 22,
1828... Portland, Hill and Ed-
wards, prs., 1828. [3], 32 p.
CBPac; CSmH; ICN; MB; MBC;
MH; MHi; MMeT-Hi; MWA; MeB;
MeHi; MiD-B; NN; Nh; OC; PHi.
                           34557
[Niles, John Milton] 1787-1856
  A view of South America and
Mexico, comprising their history,
the political condition, geogra-
phy, agriculture, commerce, &c
of the republics of Mexico, Gua-

tamala[sic], Colombia, Peru, the
United Provinces of South-Ameri-
ca and Chile. By a citizen of the
United States. New York, Huntington, 1828. 2 v. in 1. MB.
                           34558
Noah, Mordecai M.
  City of New York--ss. Mordecai M. Noah, of No. 57, Frank-
lin-street, being duly sworn, de-
poseth and saith, that on the 20th
day of June, 1828, at the 2d
ward of the city of New York,
he was violently assaulted by
Elijah J. Roberts who attacked
him on the steps and cow-skinned
him!!...Sworn before me this
20th day of June 1828. J. Hop-
son. [New York, 1828] Bdsd.
DLC.   34559

Noble, Samuel, 1779-1853
  Brief remarks on the atone-
ment and mediation of Jesus
Christ extracted from "An appeal,"
&c. in behalf of the doctrines of
the New Jerusalem. ...Boston,
Adonis Howard, 1828. 20 p.
MBAt.   34560

---- The plenary inspiration of
the Scriptures asserted, and the
principles of their composition
investigated, with a view to the
reputation of all objections to
their divinity. In six lectures,
(very greatly enlarged,) delivered
at Albion Hall, London Wall.
With an appendix, illustrative and
critical... From the London ed.
Boston, Crocker & Brewster;
Hilliard, Gray and Co. ; Cottons
and Barnard; and Benjamin Perkins and Co. [Boston, John Cotton, pr.] 1828. xvi, 439, lxviii
p. CU; CtMW; GDC; ICMcC;
KWiU; KyHe; MBC; MH-AH;
MdBP; MeLB; MiU; MoS; NIC;
NNG; Nh; PPiW; PU; VtU.
                           34561
---- The true object of Christian worship demonstrated...
Boston, Adonis Howard, 1828.

35 p. ICMe; MBAt; MBC; VtU; BrMus. 34562

Noel, Edmund F.
Extracts from various writers on cattle, &c. &c. By Edmund F. Noel, Essex County, Va. Baltimore, Pr. by Jos. Robinson, 1828. 112 p. NcU.   34563

Norfolk, Va. Athenaeum
Catalogue of the books belonging to the Norfolk Athenaeum; with a brief compend of the laws of the institution. Norfolk, Pr. by Shields & Ashburn, 1828. 28 p. PHi (with 8 p. "Addenda" pr. 1829 or 1830).   34564

The North American calendar, or The Columbian almanac for 1829. By W. Collom. Wilmington, R. Porter & Son [1828] 18 l. DLC; InU; MWA; NHi; NN; NjR. 34565

North Bank, Boston
North Bank. You are hereby notified, that agreeable to a vote of the stockholders...you are entitled to half as many shares... Boston, 1828. [Circular letter.] MB.   34566

North Carolina
An act to redeem the paper currency in circulation, and to establish a bank, by the name and title of the State Bank of North-Carolina, passed December, 1810; an act in addition to the preceding passed December, 1811, also, An act to amend the charter, passed in 1816, to which are subjoined the by-laws of the corporation. Raleigh, Pr. by J. Gales & son, 1828. 36 p. NN; NcU.   34567

---- Acts passed by the General Assembly of the state of North-Carolina, at the session of 1827-28. [Raleigh] Pr. by Lawrence & Lemay, prs. to the state, 1828. 100 p. L; MdBB; Mi-L; NN;

NNLI; NcU; Nv; T; W.   34568

---- ...Annual report of the Board for Int'l Improvements. November 29, 1828. Raleigh, Pr. by Lawrence & Lemay, prs. to the state, 1828. 43 p. NcU.   34569

---- Journals of the Senate & House of Commons of the General Assembly of the state of North-Carolina, at the session of 1827-28. Raleigh, Pr. by Lawrence & Lemay, prs. to the state, [1828] 246 p. NcU.   34570

---- ...Message of His Excellency Governor Iredell, to the General Assembly of North-Carolina. 1828. Raleigh, Pr. by Lawrence & Lemay, prs. to the state, 1828. 14 p. MWA; NcU.   34571

---- ...Report of General R. M. Saunders, on the subject of Cherokee lands. 1828. Raleigh, Pr. by Lawrence & Lemay, prs. to the state, 1828. 8 p. NcU.   34572

---- ...Report of the adjutant general of North-Carolina. 1828. Raleigh, Pr. by Lawrence & Lemay, prs. to the state, 1828. 16 p. NcU.   34573

---- ... Report of the joint select committee on the subject of a penitentiary & lunatic asylum. December 30, 1826[!] Raleigh, Pr. by Lawrence & Lemay, prs. to the state, 1828. 8 p. NcU; PPL.   34574

---- ... Report of the president and directors of the Literary Fund 1828. Raleigh, Pr. by Lawrence & Lemay, prs. to the state, 1828. 12 p. NcU. 34575

---- ...Report of the representatives on behalf of the state at the meeting of the stockholders of the Cape-Fear Bank. 1828.

Raleigh, Pr. by Lawrence & Lemay, prs. to the state, 1828. 7
p. NcU.   34576

---- ...Report of the select committee on the division of Haywood
County. Senate, Nov. 28, 1828.
Raleigh, Pr. by Lawrence & Lemay, prs. to the state, 1828. 4
p. NcU.   34577

---- ...Report of the surviving
commissioner appointed to superintend the sale of the property of
the late treasurer. Raleigh, Pr.
by Lawrence & Lemay, prs. to
the state, 1828. 18 p. NcU.
                                 34578
---- ...Report of the treasurer
of the state of North Carolina.
1828. Raleigh, Pr. by Lawrence
& Lemay, prs. to the state,
1828. 34 p. NcU.   34579

---- Report on an additional appropriation for the improvement
of Cape Fear River below Wilmington, 1828. Raleigh, Lawrence & Lemay, 1828. 6 p. NcU.
                                 34580
---- ...Report on the improvement of the navigation of Neuse
River. 1828. Raleigh, Pr. by
Lawrence & Lemay, prs. to the
state, 1828. 4 p. NcU.   34581

---- Report on the subject of
cotton and woollen manufactures,
and on the growing of wool in
North Carolina. 1828. Raleigh,
Pr. by Lawrence & Lemay, prs.
to the state. Philadelphia, Repr.
by Wm. Brown, 1828. 16 p.
DLC; MH; MWA; PPAmP. 34582

---- Reports and minutes of
proceedings...on so much of the
Governor's message as relates
to the banks. Raleigh, Lawrence
& Lemay, pr., 1828. 28 p. NcU.
                                 34583
---- Statement of the accounts of
the banks of North-Carolina with

the state. Raleigh, Pr. by Lawrence & Lemay, prs. to the
state, 1828. 31 p. NcU.   34584

---- A statement of the revenue
of North Carolina. [Raleigh]
1828. Bdsd. NcU.   34585

The North eastern coast of North
America from New York to Cape
Canso; including Sable island.
By Edmund Blunt. New York, E.
& G. W. Blunt [1828] map 38 x
75 cm. DLC.   34586

The Northern traveller. See
Dwight, Theodore.

Norwich University. Northfield,
Vt.
    Catalogue of the officers and
cadets of the American Literary,
Scientific, and Military Academy,
Norwich, Vermont. Windsor,
1828. 20 p. Sabin 58963A note
                                 34587

The Norwood gypsy, or Complete
art of fortune-telling. New York,
Pub. by S. King, 1828. 34 p.
DLC.   34588

Notions of the Americans. See
Cooper, James Fenimore.

Nott, Samuel, 1788-1869
    An appeal to the temperate,
on the vice of intemperance...
Albany, Webster & Wood, prs.,
1828. 1 p. l., [v]-vii, [8]-8
(i. e. 98) p. DLC; ICMcC; MB;
MH-AH; MnHi; MnU; NNUT.
                                 34589
---- ---- Hartford, Pub. by D.
F. Robinson & Co. and sold by
Hilliard, Gray and Co. Richard-
son and Lord, and Crocker and
Brewster, Boston; [etc., etc.]
1828. 120 p. CSmH; IU; KyBB;
MBC; MNan; NN; NRom; OCHP;
PMA; ViU.   34590

---- Sermons for children; de-

signed to promote their immedi-
ate piety... New York, Leavitt;
Boston, Crocker and Brewster,
Gray and Bruce, prs., 1828. 3
vols. CtHC; GDC; ICMcC; MH-
AH; NcD; ScCliJ!   34591

Le nouveau seigneur. See
Creuzé de Lesser, Augustin
François, baron.

A novitiate of the New Jerusalem
Church. See A discourse on the
paramount importance.

Nutting, Rufus, 1793-1878
A practical grammar of the
English language; accompanied
with notes, critical and explanatory. 4th ed., rev. by the author.
Montpelier, E. P. Walton, proprietor of the Copyright, 1828.
144 p. MH; NNC; BrMus. 34592

O

Obi; or the history of Three-
fingered Jack. See Earle, William, Jr.

Observations occasioned by the
Remarks. See Henshaw, David.

Observations on the efficacy of
white mustard seed. See Turnor,
John.

Observations on the report...
See Pennsylvania Society for the
Promotion of Manufactures and
the Mechanic Arts.

Observations upon the memorial
and report of the citizens of Boston, opposed to a further increase of duties on importations
... Providence, F. Y. Carlile &
Co., 1828. 8 p. MH-BA. 34593

An observer. See A peep into
the banks...

Odes upon cash. See Moore,
Thomas.

O'Flaherty, Thomas J.
A medical essay on drinking.
Hartford, W. Hudson and L.
Skinner, pr., 1828. 46 p. CSmH;
CtHi; MBAt; MWA; OC; NjR.
34594
Ogden, Aaron
Circular. Washington. July 19,
1828. Dear Sir: Being desirous
to give you entire satisfaction, in
regard to the commissions which
have been charged by the agents
who prosecuted your claim before
Congress, for Revolutionary services, I must now request your
particular attention... [Signed by]
Aaron Ogden] 3 p. DLC. 34595

Ogden, David Longworth
The excellence of liberality.
A sermon delivered at Farming-
ton, before the Auxiliary Foreign
Mission Society, of Farmington
& Vicinity, Oct. 22, 1828. New
Haven, Hezekiah Howe, 1828. 20
p. C; CtHi; CtY; MB; MWA;
MiD-B; PPPrHi; BrMus. 34596

Ohio
Acts and proceedings of the
government of the state of Ohio,
relating to the navigation of the
Muskingum River and its connection with the Ohio and Erie canal.
Zanesville, 1828. 20 p. RPB.
34597
---- Cases decided in the Supreme Court of Ohio, upon the
circuit, and at a special session
in Columbus, December, 1827
[-1828] Reported in conformity
with the Act of Assembly. By
Charles Hammond, attorney at
law. Volume III. Pub. by Morgan, Fisher, and L'Hommedieu.
1828 [-1829]. 2 pts. in 1 vol.
CtY-L; DLC; MH-L; MdBB; MiU-
L; NNB; OCLW; OCLaw; PPiAL.
34598
---- Catalogue of books in the

Ohio State Library. December 1, 1828. Pub. by authority. Columbus, Pr. by Zechariah Mills, Librarian State Library, at the office of the State Journal [1828] 23 p. OMC.   34599

---- Journal of the House of Representatives. Columbus, P. H. Olmsted, state pr. , 1827 [i. e. 1828] 403 p. O.   34600

---- Journal of the Senate of the state of Ohio; being the first session of the twenty-sixth General Assembly, begun and held in the town of Columbus, in the County of Franklin; Monday, December 3, 1827, and in the twenty-sixth year of said state. Columbus, P. H. Olmsted, state pr. , 1827 [i. e. 1828] 418 p. DLC.   34601

---- Report of the Board of canal commissioners. [Columbus, January 17, 1828] 13 p. DLC.
            34602
---- Report of the committee, to whom was referred the report of the commissioners, of common schools. Pub. by authority. Columbus, Pr. at the Office of the Columbus Gazette by P. H. Olmsted, 1828. 12 p. DLC.   34603

Ohio County, Virginia. Committee of Vigilance. See National Republican Party. Virginia.

Ohio magazine almanack for 1829. By John Armstrong. Zanesville, William Davis [1828] 28 1. MWA; NHi; OHi.   34604

Old and young; or, The four Mowbrays. A farce, in one act. . . New York, Neal & Mackenzie, [S. H. Jackson] 1828. 28 p. MH; NjR; PU.   34605

An old farmer, pseud. See The life of Joab.

An old revolutionary soldier of Wrenthem. See An address, written for the fiftieth anniversary.

Oliver, Benjamin Lynde, 1788-1843
    Forms of practice; or, American precedents in actions, personal and real, interspersed with annotations. Boston, Hilliard, Gray, Little, and Wilkins, 1828. 47, 48a-48th, [49]-628 p. CSt; ICLaw; MBS; MH-L; MiD-B; N-L; TU; TxWB-L; Vi-L; ViU; WML.   34606

[Olmstead, Denison] 1791-1859
    Outlines of the experimental lectures in natural philosophy, delivered at Yale College. For the use of the students. New Haven, Pr. by Lucius K. Dow, 1828. 39 numbered leaves, pr. on verso only. CtY-M; CtMMHi.   34607

Olney, Jesse, 1798-1872
    A practical system of modern geography: or, A view of the present state of the world. . . Hartford, D. F. Robinson & Co. , 1828. 270 p. CtHT-W; DLC; OClWHi; ViHaI.   34608

On confirmation. Questions to be proposed to those who are about to receive the holy sacrament of confirmation. With the answers to the same. Washington, Pr. by Peter Force, 1828. 4 p. DGU.
            34609
On some corruptions of scripture. See Allen, Joseph.

On tests of true religion. See Dewey, Orville.

On the evidence. See Thacher, Samuel Cooper.

On the peace of God, which passeth all understanding. No. 14. New York, For sale at the bookstores of Samuel Wood and Sons,

and Mahlon Day. M. Day, pr.,
1828. 12 p. MeU.   34610

Onderdonk, Benjamin Tredwell,
1791-1861
An address, delivered in St.
Stephen's Church, New York, at
the funeral of the Rev. Henry J.
Feltus, D. D. ... Monday, Aug.
25, 1828. Pub. by request of
wardens and vestrymen of St.
Stephen's Church. New York, Pr.
by T. & J. Swords, 1828. 15 p.
IU; NBLiHi; NGH; NNG.   34611

102. Or, The veteran and his
progeny. Boston, Richardson and
Lord, 1828. 33 p. DLC; ICU;
IaU; NN.   34612

One of the people. See The
Patriot.

Oneida Academy. Utica, N.Y.
First report of the trustees
of Oneida Academy. March, 1828.
Utica, Pr. by Hastings & Tracy,
1828. 9, [3] p. MiU-C; PPPrHi.
                           34613
An operative citizen.   See The
principles of aristocratic legislation.

Opie, Amelia, 1764-1853
Detraction displayed. New
York, Pub. by Orville A. Roor-
back, W. E. Dean, pr., 1828.
251 p. CU; CtHT; GHi; ICMcC;
IaHi; MB; MBAt; MH; MeB; PU;
TNJ.   34614

---- ---- Philadelphia, Carey,
Lea, and Carey... 1828. [2], 256
p. MH; MW; NBLiHi; NNS; OMC;
PHC; PU; ScSoh.   34615

---- Illustrations of lying, in all
its branches.   Boston, S. G. Goodrich, press of I. R. Butts & co.,
1828. 172 p. NjR; PHi.   34616

---- ---- From the 2d London

ed. Hartford, S. Andrus, pub-
lisher, 1828. 283 p. CSmH;
CtY; MoS; NcMHi; OU; PMA;
PPL.   34617

---- ---- New York, Evert Duyckinck, 1828. 286 p. CtHT-W;
CtMW; LNHT; OCC.   34618

Ord, George, 1781-1866
Sketch of the life of Alexander
Wilson, author of the American
Ornithology. Philadelphia, Pub.
by Harrison Hall, 1828. iv, ix-
cxcix p. ArU; DLC; DeWI; ICN;
LNHT; MB; MH; MiD; NNS;
NcA-S; OCHP; ODa; PHi; PP;
PPL; PPi; TxU; BrMus.   34619

Order of performances at the
celebration of American independence, July 4, 1828. by the citizens of Charlestown. Performances in the Rev. Mr. Fay's
meeting-house. Wheildon and
Raymond--Aurora Press, Charlestown [Mass., 1828] Bdsd. MB.
                           34620
Order of procession for the funeral of Maj. Gen. Brown...R.
Jones, Adjutant General. [Wash-
ington, D. C. February, 1828]
1 p. DLC.   34621

Orme, William, 1787-1830
Memoirs, including letters
and select remains, of John Ur-
quhart, late of the University of
St. Andrew's. Philadelphia, A.
Claxton, Wm. Stavely, pr.,
1828. 2 vols. CtMW; MH; NNC;
NcSalL; PPL (V. I only); TNJ;
ViU.   34622

---- ---- Boston, Pub. by
Crocker & Brewster; New York,
Jonathan Leavitt, 1828. 2 vols.
CtHC; CtHT; DLC; GDC; IEdS;
ICMcC; IEG; MB; MBC; MWiW;
MdAS; MiD; MoSpD; NGH; NNG;
NPV; NhD; NjR; PHi; PU;
ScCliTO; ViAl; ViRUT; VtU;
WBB.   34623

Orphan Society of Philadelphia
   Thirteenth annual report of the
Philadelphia Orphan Society, read
at the Anniversary meeting, January 1, 1828... Philadelphia, Pr.
by Lydia R. Bailey, 1828. 5,
[5] p. PPL.   34624

Orton, Job
   Memoirs of the life, charac-
ter and writings of the late Rev.
Philip Doddridge, New ed. Boston,
Pub. by Peirce and Williams,
1828. 310 p. GDC; ICMcC; ICMe;
IU; LNHT; MBC; Nh; NhHi; OO;
ViRUT; WBB.   34625

Osbourn, James
   Good news from a far country,
or Epistles of love to men of
truth... Baltimore, Pr. by John
D. Toy, 1828. 408 p. CSmH;
ICMcC; MBC; NcD.   34626

Ostrander, Tobias
   The mathematical expositor;
containing rules, theorems, lem-
mas, and explanations of various
parts of the mathematical science,
in a series of lectures, calculated for the use of teachers and
students of schools and academies
in the United States. Palmyra,
Pr. by E. B. Grandin, for the
author, 1828. 92, [2] p. CSmH;
NNC-T; NRMA.   34627

O'Sullivan, B.
   A series of lectures on female
education by B. O'Sullivan comprised in twelve numbers No. 1.
Washington, Pr. for the author,
1828. 30 p. DLC; MB; MH.
                                34628
Oulton, Walley Chamberlain
   Botheration; or, A ten year's
blunder. A farce. In two acts.
Philadelphia, Weikel & Bunn,
1828. 36 p. MH; PU.   34629

Our country, and its laws. The
execution of the unfortunate militiamen, fairly stated, and sup-
ported by official documents...
[n. p. , 1828?] 40 p. CSmH.
                                34630
An outline of political economy.
See Jennison, William.

Outline of the history of England.
See Goodrich, Samuel Griswold.

Outlines of chronology. See
Goodrich, Samuel Griswold.

Outlines of political economy.
See Goodrich, Samuel Griswold.

Outlines of the experimental lectures. See Olmstead, Denison.

Outlines of the history of ancient
Rome. See Goodrich, Samuel
Griswold.

An overture to the general assembly of the Presbyterian
Church in the United States for
an improved organization of the
board of missions, under the direction of the said general assembly. Philadelphia, Clark and
Raser, prs. , 1828. [3], 15 p.
GDC; NcMHi; PPPrHi.   34631

P

Pacific overtures for Christian
Harmony. See Worcester, Noah.

Page, John
   Twelve letters on the energies
of the human mind... New York,
Sickels, pr. , 1828. 55 p. CSmH;
NN; PHi.   34632

Paley, William , 1743-1805
   Paley's Moral philosophy, a-
bridged and adapted to the constitution, laws and usages of the
United States of America. By B.
Judd... New York, Collins & Hannay [Wm. E. Dean, pr.] 1828.
180 p. CBPac; CtHT-W; CtW;
GHi; MoSpD.   34633

---- The principles of moral and political philosophy... With questions for the examination of students, by John Frost... Boston, N. H. Whitaker, 1828. 2 v. ICU; GHi; MB; MBC; MH; OMC; PU; TNJ; ViU.   34634

Palmer, Josiah. See Burnside, A. (note).

Palmer, William Pitt, 1805-1884
A poem, spoken July 4, 1828, before the Anti-Slavery Society of Williams College... Pub. by request of the Society. Williamstown [Mass.] Pr. by Ridley Bannister, 1828. 24 p. CSmH; MB; MWiW.   34635

[Paltock, Robert] 1697-1767
The life and adventures of Peter Wilkins, containing an account of his visit to the Flying Islanders, taken from his own mouth, in his passage to England, from off Cape Horn, in America, in the ship Hector. By R. S. a passenger in the Hector. Imp. ed. Boston, Pub. by J. Shaw & J. Q. Adams, 1828. 2 p l., 263 p. MBedf; MNS; RJa; RNHi.
                                34636
[----] ---- Boston, Baker and Alexander, 1828. 2 v. CtHT-W; GEU; ScC.   34637

A parent, pseud. See Tuckerman, Joseph.

Paris, John Ayrton, 1785-1856
Pharmacologia. 3d Amer. from the 6th London ed., corr. and extended, in accordance with the London pharmacololia of 1824, and with the generally advanced state of chemical science ... New York, E. Duyckinck, Collins & co. [etc.] [W. C. Dean, pr.] 1828. 3 p. l., iii, 544 p. ICU-R; IaU; InU-M; KyLxT; KyU; MB; MdBJ; MdBM; MeB; MoSMed; NIC-M; NNNAM; NRU-M; NcU;

NhD; OU; PPC; PPF; ViRA; ViU; WMAM.   34638

---- Philosophy in sport. Philadelphia, Carey, Lea and Carey, 1828. 2 vols. LNHT; NjP.
                                34639
---- A treatise on diet: with a view to establish, on practical grounds, a system of rules for the prevention and cure of the diseases incident to a disorderd state of the digestive functions. New York, E. Duyckinck, Collins & Co., Collins & Hannay, and O. A. Roorbach, 1828. [W. E. Dean, pr.] iv, 210 p. CtHT-W; ICJ; KyLoJM; MA; MBCo; MdBJ; MdBM; MoSU; OC; OO; PPC; PPL; ViU. 34640

Parker, Daniel
The improved arithmetic, newly arranged and clearly illustrated... 1st ed. New York, Pr. and sold by J. & J. Harper, 1828. 348 p. NjR; PIndT. 34641

Parker, Isaac
Address of Chief Justice Parker to the Bar of the county of Suffolk at a meeting held for the purpose of testifying their respect for the memory of the Hon. Samuel Howe one of the justices of the Court of Common Pleas for the commonwealth. Boston, Press of N. Hale, 1828. 14 p. CSmH; CtSoP; DLC (Another listing: From the press of Nathan Hale); ICU; LNHT; M; MBAt; MH; MHi; MWA; MiD-B; NjR; OCHP; PHi; PPL; WHi.
                                34642
[----] Letter to the Rev. Parsons Cooke. From the Christian Examiner, for July and August, 1828. 11 p. CBSK; MB; MH; MWA.   34643

Parker, Joel
The signs of the times. A sermon delivered in Rochester,

December 4, 1828, being the day
of public thanksgiving. Rochester,
Pr. by Everard Peck & Co.,
1828. 16 p. CSmH; CtHC; NRHi;
NRU; NcD; NjR; PPPrHi; BrMus.
34644

Parkes, Mrs. William
Domestic duties: or Instruc-
tions to young married ladies...
1st Amer. from the 3d London
ed. New-York, Pr. by J. & J.
Harper, 1828. 400 p. IC; MB;
MS; MoKU; NNC; NPV; NRHi;
NcU.   34645

Parley, Peter, pseud. See Goodrich, Samuel Griswold.

Parmelee, Linus
Address, pronounced at Had-
dam, December 1, 1828; at the
request of the Association for the
Promotion of Temperance...
Middletown, Conn., From the
Gazette Press by Parmelee &
Greenfield, 1828. 16 p. CtHi.
34646
Parnell, M. H.
All hands, unmoor! unmoor!
In the Red rover. [Song. T.,
with pianoforte accomp.] Boston,
Bradlee [1828] [2] p. MB. 34647

---- The king and the country
man. A favorite comic song...
arranged for the pianoforte by
Mr. Parnell, leader of the or-
chestra at the Theatre, Boston,
Boston, Pub. by C. Bradlee,
[1828] 3 p. MB; MNF.   34648

Parrish, Joel
To the public. It will be re-
collected, that in a publication
which I felt it my duty to make
on the 9th of April last, in relation to the punishment of John
Wood, I spoke of Doctor James
L. Armstrong, the reputed author of "A Tennessean," as "an
infamous man"...Nashville,
Tenn. June 23, 1828. 1 p. DLC.
34649

Partridge, [Alden] 1785?-1854
Capt. Partridge's lecture on
education. [Middletown, Conn.,
1828] 12 p. CtHi; PPL. 34650

Parveliers, A.
The stations of devotions on
the passion of our Lord Jesus
Christ crucified, as they are
made in Jerusalem. From the
French of A. Parveliers, S. J.
Aposotolic Missionary at the
Holy land. To which are annexed
the prayers of St. Bridget, and
other devotions on the same subject. Philadelphia, Stereotyped
for E. Cummiskey, 1828. 125 p.
NRSB.   34651

Pascal, Blaise
Provincial letters, containing
an exposure of the reasoning and
morals of the Jesuits... New
York, Pub. by J. Leavitt; Boston, Crocker & Brewster [Van-
derpool & Cole, prs.] 1828. 319
p. ABS; CBPac; CU; CtHC; GDC;
ICU; IaHi; KyDC; LNHT; MH;
MdBS; MnU; MoSU; NIC; NNG;
Nh; OClW; RBr; TNF; WHi.
34652
The patriot; or, People's companion: consisting of five essays
on the laws and politics of our
country...By one of the people.
Hudson, Pr. by A. Stoddard,
1828. 24 p. MWA; N.   34653

Paul, John, 1771-1846
A refutation of Arianism; or,
Defence of the plenary inspira-
tion of the Holy Scriptures, the
supreme deity of the Son and
Holy Ghost...in reply to Drs.
Bruce, Mant, Millar, and
Graves...to which is added a
defence of creeds and confes-
sions. New York, Pr. for and
pub. by Robt. Lowry [J. Sey-
mour, pr.] 1828. 319 p. CLSU;
CtMW; ICMcC; IEG; MBC; MH-
AH; MiU; NNUT; NbOP; OCX;
OHi; PPLT; PPPrHi.   34654

[Paulding, James Kirke] 1778-1860
The new mirror for travellers; and guide to the springs. By an amateur... New York, G. & C. Carvill [Sleight & George, prs., Jamaica, L. I.] 1828. 292 p. CSmH; CU; CtY; DLC; ICU; Ia; MB; MH; MWA; MdBP; MiU; MnU; NIC; NNS; NPV; Nh; NjP; NjR; OC; OO; PPL; PU; RPB; ScSoh; TNJ; WHi; BrMus. 34655

Payne, J. W. H.
The true history of Zoa, the beautiful Indian, (Daughter of Henrietta de Belgrave;) and of Rodomond, an East Indian merchant... New York, S. King, 1828. 36 p. RPB. 34656

---- ---- Philadelphia, Pub. and sold wholesale only, by Freeman Scott, 1828. 72 p. IObB. 34657

---- The unfortunate lovers: or, The affecting history of Selim and Almena. A Turkish tale: from "The bride of Abydos," of Lord Byron... New York, S. King, 1828. 26 p. RPB. 34658

Payson, Edward, 1783-1827
Sermons; by the late Rev. Payson, D. D., pastor of the Second Church in Portland. Portland, Shirley & Hyde, sold by Pierce and Williams, Boston; John P. Haven, New York; and E. Littell, Philadelphia, 1828. 503 p. CBPac; CtHC; CtSoP; GAGTh; GDC; ICU; IEG; IaCrM; InU; MB; MBC; MH; MWiW; MeHi; MiU; MnSH; MoS; NCH; NPV; NhHi; NjP; NjR; OM; OO; OClW; RPB; TBriK; ViAl; ViRU. 34659

Peabody, Nathaniel
The art of preserving teeth. 2d ed. Salem, Pr. by W. and S. B. Ives, 1828. 28 p. MH-AH. 34660

Peabody, William Bourn Oliver, 1799-1847
An address, delivered at Springfield, before the Hampden Colonization Society, July 4th, 1828. Pub. by request of the society. Springfield, Pr. by S. Bowles, 1828. 16 p. CSmH; DLC. 34661

[Peake, Richard Brinsley]
The hundred pound note. A farce, in two acts. As performed at the Covent-Garden, Theatre London, and at the New York Theatre. Now first printed. New York, E. M. Murden, 1828. CSmH; MH; MWA; PU; TxU. 34662

Pearce, Aaron
Candid reasons assigned for a belief in the saintship of Judas Iscariot. Hartford, Norton & Russell, pr., 1828. 16 p. MBAt. 34663

Pearson, Richmond Mumford, 1805-1878
To my friends. [Salisbury, May 15, 1828] 7 p. NcU. 34664

Peck, John Mason, 1789-1858
A sermon, preached at Edwardsville, Illinois, December 25, 1827: in reference to the death of Daniel P. Cook. Edwardsville, Pr. by R. K. Fleming, at the office of the Illinois Corrector, March, 1828. 14 p. I-Ar; IGK; IHi. 34665

[Pedder, James] 1775-1859
The yellow shoe-strings, or, The good effects of obedience to parents. By the author of "Frank," or, Dialogues between a father and son, on the subjects of agriculture, husbandry and rural affairs. 2d Amer. ed. Philadelphia, J. Kay, jun. & bro. [etc.]; Pittsburgh, C. H. Kay & co. [1828?] 48 p. DLC; MH; MdBP; PU-Penn. 34666

A peep into the banks, and a glance at the consequences of creating monied institutions. By an observer. New York, Pr. and pub. by Vanderpool & Cole, 1828. 48 p. DLC; MdBJ; NN; NNC; PHi; PU.   34667

Pelham. See Lytton, Edward G. E. L. B. -L.

Pengilly, Richard, 1782-1865
    The Scripture guide to baptism; or, A faithful citation of all the passages of the New Testament which relate to this ordinance, with the sacred text impartially examined, and the sense supported by numerou[!] extracts from the most eminent and learned writers. To which is added, a short examination of the rise and grounds of infant baptism. By R. Pengilly...3d Boston ed. Boston, Lincoln & Edmands, 1828. 48 p. CBPac; Ct; DLC.   34668

Penington, Isaac, 1616-1679
    Letters of Isaac Penington, an eminent minister of the Gospel in the Society of Friends...from the 2d London ed. Philadelphia, Friends' book store [1828] 283 p. CL; CLSU; ICMcC; InMuB; NjR; PLT; PP; PPiW.   34669

Penitent Females' Refuge. See Refuge in the city of Boston.

Penn, pseud.
    Presidential election. No. xiv [-xvi]. To the People of the United States. n. p. [1828] 32 p. PPL.   34670

Pennock, Caspar Wistar
    Observations and experiments on the efficacy and modus operandi of cupping-glasses, in preventing and arresting the effects of poisoned wounds. Philadelphia, Pr. by J. R. A. Skerrett, 1828.

20 p. PPL.   34671

Pennsylvania
    An act for the regulation of the militia, of the commonwealth of Pennsylvania...Harrisburg, Pr. at the office of the "Reporter," 1828. 72, 9 p. DLC; P; PHi.   34672

---- An act passed by the Legislature of Pennsylvania to authorize the Baltimore & Ohio Rail-Road to construct a rail road through Pennsylvania in the direction from Baltimore to the Ohio river. [Harrisburg, 1828] [7] p. MB.   34673

---- A compilation and digest of the road laws, and the election laws, together with certain forms. Prepared and pub. under authority of an act of Assembly of Pennsylvania, passed the first day of February, Anno Domini 1827. Harrisburg, Office of the Reporter, 1828. 141, 16 p. CU-Law; MB; MH-L; P; PPB; PPi; PPiHi.   34674

---- Documents accompanying the report of the canal commissioners, of the commonwealth of Pennsylvania, for promoting the internal improvement of the state, with the exception of those relating to the surveys made the past season. Read in the Senate, January 4, 1828. Vol. 2. Harrisburg, Pr. by S. C. Stambaugh, 1828. 180, 3 p. MH-BA; MiU-T; NN; P; PPAmP; PPF; PPL.
                                  34675
---- Journal of the Senate...of the session 1827-28. Containing the appendix. Vol. II. Harrisburg, Pr. by Samuel O. Stambaugh, 1828. 914, 9 p. CSmH.
                                  34676
---- Journal of the thirty-eighth House of Representatives...[Dec. 4, 1827-Apr. 15, 1828] Vol. I.

Harrisburg, Pr. by Samuel C. Stambaugh, 1827 [i. e. 1828] 836, 12, 56 p. CSmH.   34677

---- Laws of the General Assembly of the state of Pennsylvania, passed at the session of 1827-28. In the fifty-second year of independence. Pub. by authority. Harrisburg, Pr. at the office of the Reporter, 1828. 506, 39 p. IaU-L; In-SC; L; MdBB; Mi-L; Ms; NNLI; Nb; Nj; Nv; P; PAtM; R; RPL; TxU-L; W.   34678

---- The laws relating to the relief and employment of the poor, in the city of Philadelphia, the district of Southwark, and the townships of the Northern Liberties and Penn. Philadelphia, Pr. by Thos. Kite for the Board of Guardians, 1828. 55 p. PPL.
                              34679
---- Letter, report and documents on the penal code ʳrom the president and commissioners appointed to superintend the erection of the Eastern Penitentiary, adapted and modelled to the system of solitary confinement; read, in the Senate, January 8, 1828. Harrisburg, Pr. by S. C. Stambaugh, 1828. [1], 51 p. Ct; In-SC; MB; MH-L; MWA; MiD-B; MnU; NNC-L; Nj; P; PHi; PP; PPAmP; PPL; PPi; PU; RPB; WaU.   34680

---- Message from the governor, accompanied with the report of the canal commissioners. Read in the House of Representatives, December 13, 1828. Harrisburg, Pa. , S. C. Stambaugh, pr. , 1828. 326 p. DLC; ICJ; MB; MWA; NN; P; PPAmP; PPF; PPL.
                              34681
---- ---- Read in the Senate, December 15, 1828. Harrisburg, S. C. Stambaugh, pr. , 1828. 12 p. DLC; DeGE; ICJ; MiU-T; P; PPL.   34682

---- Minutes of the proceedings of the Electoral College of Pennsylvania, held in the Senate chamber of the state capitol, Harrisburg, on the third day of December, in the year of our Lord one thousand eight hundred and twenty eight... Harrisburg, S. C. Stambaugh, 1828. 15 p. P; PHi; PPiU.   34683

---- Report of the canal commissioners of the commonwealth of Pennsylvania. Accompanied with documents. Read in the House of Representatives, January 4, 1828. Harrisburg, Pr. by Samuel C. Stambaugh, 1828. 325 p. CtY; DBRE; DLC; P; PPF.   34684

---- Report of the canal commissioners, of the commonwealth of Pennsylvania, for promoting the internal improvement of the state. With the documents relating to the surveys made the past season. Read in the Senate, January 4, 1828. Harrisburg, Pr. by Samuel C. Stambaugh, 1828. 145 p. MH; MiU-T; NN; P; PPAmP. PPF; PPL.   34685

---- Report of the canal commissioners, relative to a railroad from the mouth of the Swatara by Columbia to Philadelphia. Philadelphia, [1828] 18 p. CSmH; MH-BA; P; PPAmP.   34686

---- Report of the commissioners on the penal code, with the accompanying documents. Read in the House of Representatives, Jan. 4, 1828. Harrisburg, Pr. by S. C. Stambaugh, 1828. 192 p. PPL.   34687

---- ---- Read in the Senate January 4, 1828. Philadelphia, Pr. by John Clark, 1828. [1], 77 p. IaHi; PPL.   34688

---- Report of the committee of ways and means relative to the Union Canal Lottery, and to prevent the sale of foreign lottery tickets... Harrisburg, S. C. Stambaugh, 1828. 7 p. P.   34689

---- Report of the committee on banks, relative to restraining the circulation of notes under the denomination of five dollars, as are not authorized by laws of this state. Read in the House of Representatives Feb. 25, 1828. [Harrisburg? 1828] 7 p. PPAmP.
34690

---- Report of the committee on education. Read in the Senate, January 18, 1828. Mr. Kelley, chairman. Harrisburg, Pr. by S. C. Stambaugh, 1828. 5 p. P; PPL.   34691

---- Report of the committee on internal improvement relative to the extension of the Pennsylvania Canal and the construction of a railroad. Read in the House of Representatives Feb. 4, 1828. Harrisburg, Pr. by S. C. Stambaugh, 1828. 7 p. DLC; P.
34692

---- Report on punishments and prison discipline: by the commissioners appointed to revise the penal code of Pennsylvania... 2d ed. Philadelphia, Pr. by John Clarke, 1828. [1], 77 p. A-Ar; MB; MWA; MdHi; MiD-B; MnU; NcU; P; PHi; PPAmP; PPL; PU; Vi; BrMus.   34693

---- Report on the finances of the commonwealth of Pennsylvania, for the year 1828, made to the Legislature, by the auditor general, agreeably to law. Harrisburg, Pr. at the Office of the Reporter, 1828. 38 p. PPL.
34694

---- Rules of the Supreme Court of Pennsylvania, of the Circuit courts & of the District court,

and court of common pleas for the city and county of Philadelphia. Revised and adopted, 1828. Philadelphia, A. Walker, [1828] 43, [1] p. Ct; DLC; ICU; MH-L; P; PPL.   34695

---- Tagebuch des neun und dreyssigsten Hauses der Representanten, der Republik von Pennsylvanien, Eröffnet in der Stadt Harrisburg. Harrisburg, Gedruckt bey Jacob Baab, 1828-1829. 1101, 15, 36 p. PPAmP.
34696

---- Tenth annual report of the controllers of the public schools of the first school district of the state of Pennsylvania. With their accounts. Philadelphia, Pr. by order of the Board of Control. Garden & Thompson, prs., 1828. 15 p. PPL.   34697

Pennsylvania almanac for 1829. By John Ward. Lancaster, Wm. Allbright [1828] 18 l. InU; MWA; PYHi.   34698

---- ---- Philadelphia, M'Carty & Davis [1828] 18 l. CtY; PDoBHi; PP.   34699

---- ---- Philadelphia, M'Carty & Davis and Geo. W. Mentz [1828] 18 l. DLC; DeGE; InU; MWA; PHi; PPL.   34700

Pennsylvania Canal Boat Company
List of freights charged by the Pennsylvania Canal Boat Company to and from Middletown and Philadelphia. [Philadelphia, 1828] 2 l. DeGE.   34701

Pennsylvania canals. See Carey, Mathew.

Pennsylvania Hospital
State of the accounts of the Pennsylvania Hospital, as adjusted by the managers, being a summary of the receipts and pay-

ments for the year ending 4th mo.
1828, and laid before the con-
tributors at their annual meeting
5th mo. 5th, 1828. [Philadelphia,
1828] Bdsd. PPL.   34702

---- Some account of the origin,
objects, and present state of the
Pennsylvania Hospital. Philadelphia, Pr. by Thos. Kite, 1828.
24 p. ICU; IEN-M; MB; PHi;
PPWa; PU; RPA.   34703

Pennsylvania Society for Discouraging the Use of Ardent Spirits.
 Report of a committee appointed by the Pennsylvania Society, for Discouraging the use
of Ardent Spirits, to examine and
report what amendments ought to
be made in the laws of the said
state, for the suppression of
vice and immorality, particularly those against gaming. Read
and adopted, February 14, 1828.
Pr. by order of the said Society.
Philadelphia, Pr. by Atkinson &
Alexander, 1828. 17 p. CSmH;
KyLx; PHi; PPAmP; PPC; PPL;
PPPrHi; PPiW.   34704

Pennsylvania Society for Promoting the Culture of the Mulberry
Tree and the Raising of Silk
Worms.
 At a meeting of the subscribers to the plan... held at the Indian Queen, April 2, 1828... The
following constitution was read,
and, after due consideration,
adopted. [Philadelphia, 1828] 4 p.
PPL.   34705

---- Directions for the rearing
of silk worms, and the culture
of the white mulberry tree...
Philadelphia, Clark & Raser,
prs., 1828. 25 p. DeGE; MB;
MWA; P; BrMus.   34706

Pennsylvania Society for the Promotion of Internal Improvements
in the Commonwealth.

 Published by the Society for
the Promotion of Internal Improvement. From the Pennsylvania Gazette of March 4, 1828.
Delaware Canal. 12 p. DLC;
NN; PPAmP.   34707

Pennsylvania Society for the Promotion of Manufactures and the
Mechanic Arts.
 Observations on the report of
the Committee of ways and
means, made at Washington, 12th
March, 1828. Philadelphia, 1828.
27 p. DLC; MH-BA; MWA;
NNNAM; OClWHi; PHi; PPL.
                    34708
Pennsylvania Society for the Promotion of Public Schools.
 The first report on the state
of education in Pennsylvania,
made to the Pennsylvania Society
for the Promotion of Public
Schools, to which is added the
Constitution of the Society. Philadelphia, Pr. on the Vertical
Press, by D. & S. Neall [1828]
9 p. PPL.   34709

---- Proof of Circular for consideration at an early meeting of
the council. Sir, In this en-
lightened age, we presume it
would be wholly superfluous to
undertake to prove the great importance of establishing a general system of Public Schools...
Philadelphia, Aug. 7, 1828. [An-
nounces formation of Penn. Soc.
for Promotion of Public Schools]
Bdsd. PPL.   34710

Pennsylvania, University of
 Annual statement of the funds
of the University of Pennsylvania,
as reported by the committee of
finance. Philadelphia, 1828. 8,
[2] p. PPL.   34711

---- Commencement. University
of Pennsylvania. Order of exercises... [Philadelphia, 1828]
Bdsd. PU.   34712

---- Laws for the government of the collegiate department of the University of Pennsylvania. Revised and amended, Nov. 1828. Philadelphia, Joseph R. A. Skerrett, 1828. 8 p. MH; NN. 34713

Pennsylvania. Washington Grays. Constitution and by-laws of the Light Artillery Corps of Washington Grays. Philadelphia, 1828. 12 p. PHi. 34714

A Pennsylvanian, pseud. See Fisher, Redwood.

A Pennsylvanian, pseud. See Kane, John Kintzing.

A Pennsylvanian, pseud. A discourse addressed to religious people of all denominations by a Pennsylvanian... Philadelphia, Pr.; Repr. at Dover, Del., by J. Robertson, 1828. 12 p. DLC; NN; PU. 34715

Penobscot County, Maine The rules and regulations of the Bar, in the county of Penobscot, established in the year, 1828. Bangor, Pr. at the Republican Office, 1828. 11 p. PPL. 34716

Pensacola Gazette & West Florida Advertiser, Pensacola, Fla. Address of the carrier of the Pensacola Gazette & West Florida Advertiser, on the first day of January 1828. [Pensacola, 1828] 1 p. DLC. 34717

People's ticket. See National Republican Party. Virginia.

Perkins, Elisha Backus, 1792-1863 Address delivered before the Peace Society of Windham County, at its annual meeting in Brooklyn August 20th, 1828. Brooklyn, Con., Advertiser Press. Wm. H. Bigelow, 1828.

32 p. Ct; CtHi; ICME; MBC; MeB; MiD-B; PPAmP. 34718

---- ---- 2d ed. Brooklyn, Con., Advertiser press, Wm. H. Bigelow, 1828. 32 p. CSmH; CtHi; PPL. 34719

Perkins, Henry Sermon preached at the funeral of George Holcombe... with a brief sketch of his life annexed. Trenton, Geo. Sherman, 1828. 31 p. IEN-M; MWA; NNNAM; Nj. 34720

Perkins, Jonas A sermon, delivered before the Palestine Missionary Society, at their seventh annual meeting, held at Bridgewater, Mass. June 20, 1828. Boston, Pr. by Crocker and Brewster, 1828. 24 p. MBC; MLex; MiD-B; RPB. 34721

Perkins, La Fayette, 1786-1874 A poem, delivered on the celebration of Independence, in the free Meeting-House at Wilton, Maine, July 4, 1828. Hallowell, Spaulding & Livermore, prs., 1828. 16 p. CSmH; MB; MnHi. 34722

Perkins, Samuel, 1767-1850 General Jackson's conduct in the Seminole War, delineated in a history of that period, affording conclusive reasons why he should not be the next president. Brooklyn, Con., Advertiser press, John Gray, Jr., 1828. 39 p. CSmH; DLC; MBAt; NIC; NhHi; PHi; PPL; WHi. 34723

Perrin, Jean Baptiste The elements of French and English conversation: with new, familiar, and easy dialogues, each preceded by a suitable vocabulary, in French and English, designed particularly for the use of schools. (Stereotyped by A. Chandler, New York.) New York,

Pub. by Evert Duyckinck, W. E.
Dean, pr. , 1828. 216 p. CtHT-
W; CtMW; MH; NjR.   34724

---- Fables amusantes, avec une
table generale et particuliers des
mots et de leur signification en
anglais selon l'ordre des fables,
pour en rendre la traduction plus
facile a l'écolier... Ed. , rev. et
cor. par un maitre de langue
francaise. Stereotype de A.
Chandler New York, E. Duyckinck, 1828. 180 p. DLC; MNF;
MdBS; TNJ.   34725

---- A selection of one hundred
of Perrin's fables, accompanied
with a key; containing the text,
a literal and a free translation
... The whole preceded by A
short treatise on the sounds of
the French language, compared
with those of the English. By A.
Bolmar. Philadelphia, Pr. for
the Author, 1828. iv, 22, 61,
181 p. GHi; MB; MH; PHi;
PPL; PPeSchw; RPB; TNJ.
                          34726
Perry, Gardner Braman, 1783-
1859
   An address, delivered before
the Society for Promoting Temperance, in Haverhill and Vicinity,
Feb. 5, 1828, at its organization.
Haverhill [Mass.] Pr. by A. W.
Thayer, 1828. 24 p. DLC; MB.
                          34727
Perry, Gideon Babcock
   A sermon on religious and
moral brotherhood... funeral of
Mr. Asher Coats. January 20,
1828. Stonington, Pr. by W. &
J. B. Storer, 1828. 24 p. RPB.
                          34728
Perry, Ichabod
   A brief history of the life and
services of Ichabod Perry, dur-
ing the Revolutionary War. With
an account of his sufferings on
board the prison ships at New
York, as well as during several
most severe actions in defence

of his country. Written by himself. Rochester, Pr. for the author by E. Scrantom, 1828. 69,
10 p. NHi.   34729

Perry, William
   Alger's Perry. The orthoepi-
cal guide to the English tongue
being Perry's Spelling book revised and corrected, with Walker's pronunciation precisely applied on a new scheme... By Israel Alger Jun. A. M. Boston,
Pub. by Richardson and Lord,
1828. 168+ p. CtY (Imperfect)
                          34730
Petigru, Charles
   An oration, prepared for delivery on the occasion of laying
the corner stone, of a monument,
erected to the memory of Kosci-
uszko at West Point, by the
corps of cadets. July 4, 1828.
Newburgh (N. Y.), W. M. Gazlay,
1828. 15 p. DLC; MH; N; NN;
NbU; NcU.   34731

Petitpierre, Ferdinand Oliver,
1722-1790
   Thoughts on the divine good-
ness relative to the government
of moral agents, particularly dis-
played in future rewards and pun-
ishments. Translated from the
French of Ferdinand Oliver Petit-
pierre. Montpelier, Pr. by Geo.
W. Hill, 1828. 148 p. DLC; IGK;
MMeT-Hi; MsCLiM; VtHi; VtU.
                          34732
Pettengill, Amos, 1780-1830
   Stellarota. Invented by Rev.
Amos Pettengill. Projected and
drawn by C. M. Doolittle and S.
B. Munson. [New Haven] En-
graved by N. & S. S. Jocelyn for
A. Goodyear & son, 1828. 1 map
mounted and moveable in frame.
                          34733
Pettibone, H. R.
   Oration, delivered before St.
Mark's lodge, No. 36, at the
celebration of the Festival of St.
John the Baptist at Simsbury

(Tariffville) Conn. June 24,
1828... Hartford, Pr. by J. Russell, at the Times office, 1828.
14 p. Ct; CtHi.   34734

Pettis, Peter
   Address, delivered before the
fourth company, eighteenth regi-
ment, Connecticut militia, in
Franklin, on the first Monday in
May, 1828... Norwich, Pr. by
J. Dunham, 1828. 17 p. CtHi.
                                   34735

Pettit, Thomas M'Kean
   An annual discourse delivered
before the Historical Society of
Pennsylvania, November 19, 1828.
Philadelphia, Carey Lea & Carey,
1828. 38 p. DLC; ICN; MB; MH;
MdHi; MiD-B; NNC; NhHi; NjR;
PHi; PP; PPAmP; PPL; BrMus.
                                   34736
The pharmacopoeia of the United
States of America. By the au-
thority of the medical societies
and colleges. 2d ed. Boston, C.
Ewer, 1828. 272 p. C; CLSU;
CSt; CtMW; ICU-R; MBCo;
MdUM; MiU; MnSM; MoSU-M;
MsU; NBuU; NNC-P; NNNAM;
Nh; OU; OkU; PU; RNR; RPB;
TxU-M; WU; WaPS; WaU. 34737

Phelps, Dudley
   Faith and works inseparable:
a sermon, delivered in the First
Parish Meetinghouse, Haverhill,
Lord's day, Nov. 9, 1828. Hav-
erhill, Pr. by A. W. Thayer,
1828. 32 p. CSmH; DLC; MA;
PPL.   34738

Philadelphia (City)
   Accounts of the corporation of
the city of Philadelphia from
April 1, 1823 to January 1, 1828.
[Philadelphia, 1828] 64 p. PP.
                                   34739
---- An act for the relief and
employment of the poor of the
city of Philadelphia, the district
of Southwark, and the townships
of the Northern Liberties and

Penn. Philadelphia, Pr. by order
of the Board of Guardians, 1828.
18 p. NjP; PPL.   34740

---- An act of incorporation for
the Kensington District of the
Northern Liberties; with rules
and regulations for the government of the board of commissioners. Philadelphia, Pr. for
the board, by Jos. Rakestraw,
1828. 80, [1] p. NIC; PHi; PPL.
                                   34741
---- A digest of the ordinances
of the corporation of the city of
Philadelphia & of the acts of Assembly relating thereto. Pub.
under the authority of the councils. By C. S. Miller. Philadelphia, Pub. by Robert Desilver,
1828. [2], 348 p. PHi; PP;
PPAmP; PPB; PPL; PU.   34742

---- Laws and ordinances respecting the markets, in the city
of Philadelphia to June, 1828.
Pub. by R. Desilver, 1828. 55
p. IU; MiD-B.   34743

---- Memorandum of the different loans to the mayor, alderman
and citizens of Philadelphia,
showing the date of ordinances
authorizing them, the period of
their becoming due and their respective amounts. [Philadelphia,
1828] Bdsd. PPL.   34744

---- Report of the Watering Committee, to the Select and Common Councils. Read January 10,
1828. Pub. by order of the Councils. Philadelphia, Pr. by Lydia
R. Bailey, 1828. 27 p. THi.
                                   34745
---- Report of the Watering Committee, to the Select and Common Councils of the city of Philadelphia, relative to the dam at
Fair Mount. Read and adopted
September 25, 1828. Philadelphia,
Pr. by L. R. Bailey, 1828. 22 p.
DeGE; PHi.   34746

---- Rules for the government of the board of guardians, its officers, business and affairs; and for regulations and controlling the alms-house and house of employment. Philadelphia, Pr. by Thomas Kite, 1828. 46, [1] p. PHi; PPL.   34747

Philadelphia almanack for 1829. By Joseph ramer [sic]. Philadelphia, Uriah Hunt; D. & S. Neall, prs. [1828] 18 1. PHi.   34748

---- By Joseph Cramer. Philadelphia, Uriah Hunt; D. & S. Neall, prs. [1828] 18 1. CtY; DLC; InU; MBC; MWA; NN; Nj; WHi.   34749

Philadelphia. Arch Street Theatre [Playbills] October 2, -Dec. 27, 1828. [Philadelphia, Pr. by Thos. Desilver, 1828] 52 items. PPL.   34750

Philadelphia Cabinet and Chair Maker's Union.
    The Philadelphia Cabinet and Chair Makers' Union Book of prices for manufacturing cabinet ware. Established January, 1828. By a committee of employers and journeymen. Philadelphia, Pr. for the Cabinet and Chair Makers, by Wm. Stavely, 1828. [1] p. 1. [5]-93, [1] p. MiGr; PPL.   34751

Philadelphia Citizens
    Address of a meeting of citizens of the city and county of Philadelphia, friends of the civil and religious freedom of Ireland, held in the city of Philadelphia, on the 5th of February, 1828. To the Roman Catholics of Ireland. [Philadelphia, 1828] 4 p. PPL.   34752

---- The memorial and resolutions of the citizens of Philadelphia, opposed to an increase of the du-

ties, on woollens, and other imported goods. Philadelphia, 1828. 8 p. P.   34753

---- Philadelphia City tavern Jan. 31st, 1828. A meeting of a number of citizens was held...[to appoint a committee to draft an] Address to the public [on the question of establishing a line of stages & steamboats from Norfolk to Charleston.] Philadelphia, Feb. 4th, 1828. (Signed by the Committee). 3 p. MH; MWA; PPAmP; PPL.   34754

Philadelphia. Committee for the Relief of the Greeks.
    Address of the Greek committee to the citizens of the state of Pennsylvania [dated April 2, 1828] [Philadelphia, 1828] 4 p. KHi; MBC; MH; MWA; MdHi; PPAmP; PPL; PU.   34755

---- To the citizens of the commonwealth of Pennsylvania. [Philadelphia, Jan. 1, 1828] 7 p. PPL.   34756

Philadelphia, Dover and Norfolk Steam-Boat and Transportation Company.
    Philadelphia, August, 1828. Philadelphia, Dover and Norfolk Steam-Boat and Transportation Company. At a meeting of stockholders...held August 28th, 1828 ...the following paper was read. [Philadelphia, 1828] 4 p. MWA; PPL.   34757

Philadelphia. Friends Asylum for the Insane.
    Eleventh annual report on the state of the Asylum for the Relief of Persons Deprived of the Use of their Reason. Philadelphia, Pr. by Solomon W. Conrad, 1828. 24 p. RPB.   34758

---- The rules for the management...adopted by the board of

managers, ninth month 8th 1828. Philadelphia, 1828. DLC; MHi.
34759

Philadelphia Gazette
Address of the carriers of the Philadelphia Gazette, to its patrons, on the commencement of the year 1828. [Philadelphia, 1828] Bdsd. PU.   34760

Philadelphia House of Refuge
An address from the managers of the House of Refuge, to their fellow citizens. Philadelphia, Pr. by Solomon W. Conrad, 1828. 8 p. MB; PHC; PHi; PPL.
34761

Philadelphia. Loganian Library
Catalogue of the books, belonging to the Loganian Library. Vol. I Part 2. Philadelphia, J. Dobson, 1828. 23, 3 p. MHi; PPL; PU.   34762

Philadelphia. Manual Labour Academy of Pennsylvania.
A report on the subject of connecting manual labour with study. Presented to the trustees of the Philadelphia Manual Labour Academy. At a meeting held Dec. 11, 1828. Philadelphia, Pr. by Wm. F. Geddes, 1828. 15 p. DLC; PPL; PPPrHi; PU. 34763

Philadelphia Medical Society
First report of the Committee of the Philadelphia Medical Society on quack medicines. Read on the 15th December, 1827, and ordered to be published by the Society. Philadelphia, Judah Dobson, Agent, 1828. 37 p. DLC; GDC; MHi; MdBM; MeB; NNNAM; NjR; P; PP; PPL; ScC; ScCC; BrMus.   34764

Philadelphia. Mercantile Library Company
Catalogue. [Philadelphia] Pr. by I. Ashmead & co., 1828. 76 p. MH; PHi; PPi; PU.   34765

Philadelphia Museum Company
Charter and by-laws of the Philadelphia Museum Company. Philadelphia, Pr. by James Kay, Jun., 1828. 12 p. PHi.   34766

Philadelphia. Northern Dispensary for the Medical Relief of the Poor.
Rules and regulations of the Northern Dispensary... and the annual report for 1827. [Philadelphia, 1828] 11 p. PPL.
34767

Philadelphia. Northern Sunday School Union.
Second annual meeting of the Northern Sunday School Union, held... on the second of April, 1828. Philadelphia, Pub. by Shadrach Taylor, 1828. [cover title: Second report... read at annual meeting...] 15 p. PPPrHi.
34768

Philadelphia. St. James' Church.
The holders of pews and sittings in St. James's Church are respectfully requested to meet at the Church, on Thursday the 18th instant at 3 o'clock P.M., in reference to the proposed plan for the separation of the said church from the United Churches. Dec. 16, 1828. [Philadelphia, 1828] Bdsd. PPL.
34769

Philadelphia Society for Alleviating the Miseries of Public Prisons.
Memorial of the Society for Alleviating the Miseries of Public Prisons, in favour of the adoption of a penal code, based upon a plan of solitary confinement. Read in the Senate, January 12, 1828. [Philadelphia, 1828] 4 p. P.   34770

Philadelphia Society for the Establishment and Support of Charity Schools.
Annual report of the board of managers of the Philadelphia So-

ciety for the Establishment and Support of Charity Schools. Philadelphia, Pub. by order of the Society, Garden & Thompson, prs., 1828. 11 p. PPL.   34771

Philadelphia Theatre [Playbills] July 3 - July 18, 1828. 10 items. PPL.   34772

Philadelphia. Town meeting. Report of the proceedings of the town meeting in the city of Philadelphia. July 7th, 1828. [Philadelphia 1828] [2], 22 p. DLC; MBAt; NjR; PHi; PPFM; WMSF.   34773

Philadelphia. United Churches of Christ Church, St. Peter's and St. James's. To the members of the United Episcopal Churches of Christ Church, St. Peter's Church, and St. James' Church, in the city of Philadelphia. Philadelphia, Dec. 11, 1828. 4 p. PPL.
                                        34774
Philanthropus, pseud. See Ladd, William.

Phillips, C. E. My soul is dark! By Lord Byron. Composed by C. E. Phillips... Boston, Oliver Ditson [Bouvé & Sharp Lithrs, c1828] 5 p. MB; MNF; ViU.   34775

Phillips, Cyrus B. The musical self instructer, containing five hundred questions and answers relative to the science of music, with appropriate examples, tables, &c. Comprising about twenty chapters; and designed chiefly for students... Burlington, N. J., Pr. for the author, by J. L. Powell, 1828. 4 p. l., [7]-57 p. CSmH; PPL.
                                        34776
[Phillips, Sir Richard] The French phrase book, or key to French conversation...

By M. L'Abbe Bossut. 2d ed. Boston, Hilliard, Gray, Little and Wilkins [Jas. Loring, pr.] 1828. 96 p. MH; NNC.   34777

[----] A geographical view of the world, embracing the manners, customs, and pursuits of every nation... by Rev. J. Goldsmith... ed. by J. C. Percival. 12th ed. Boston, Reed & Jewett, 1828. 406, 46 p. OO.   34778

[----] ---- 13th ed. Boston, Pr. for Reed and Jewett, 1828. 406, [3] 46 p. MH.   34779

[----] The Italian and English phrase-book: serving as a key to Italian conversation. By M. l'abbe Bossut. With improvements. Boston, Hilliard, Gray, Little and Wilkins, 1828. 128 p. DLC; MB; MH.   34780

Phillips, Sylvanus To the public. Fellow citizens: I ask your indulgence. [Little Rock, 1828] [2] p. CtY.   34781

Phillips, Willard, 1784-1873 A manual of political economy, with particular reference to the institutions, resources, and condition of the United States. Boston, Hilliard, Gray, Little, and Wilkins, [Press of Isaac R. Butts and Co.] 1828. 278 p. C; DLC; DeGE; FU; GHi; GU; ICU; InU; MB; MBAt; MH; MWA; Md; MiD-B; NNC; NbU; NcD; NjR; OClW; OO; PPL; PU; RPB; ScU; WvU.   34782

Phillips, Zalegman To the electors of the Second Congressional district of the state of Pennsylvania. [Philadelphia, 1828] 15 p. PPL.   34783

Phillips Exeter Academy Catalogue of the officers and students of Phillips Exeter Acad-

emy, 1827-28. Exeter, John C.
Gerrish, pr., 1828. 12 p.
NhExP.   34784

Phillis. See Copy of a letter
from Phillis.

Philo Fulton, pseud. See Carey,
Mathew.

Phinney's calendar, or Western
almanac for 1829. By Edwin E.
Prentiss. Cooperstown, H. & E.
Phinney [1828] 18 l. CtY; DLC;
FSpHi; InU; MWA; NHi; NN;
NUt; PHi; WHi.   34785

---- ---- Cooperstown, H. & E.
Phinney]1828] ["Almanack" in title]
18 l. NCooHi; NNFM.   34786

---- ---- Little Falls, J. C.
Dann & Co. [1828] 18 l. Drake
7001.   34787

---- ---- Utica, H. E. Phinney
& Co. [1828] 18 l. Drake 7002.
                           34788
[Phipps, Constantine Henry of
Normandy, 1st Marquis]
   Yes and no: A tale of the day.
By the author of "Matilda." Phil-
adelphia, Carey, Lea & Carey.
Sold in New York, by G. & C.
Carvill. In Boston by Hilliard,
Gray & Co. and Richardson &
Lord, 1828. 2 vols. MBAt; PPL;
ViAl.   34789

Phoebus, William
   Memoirs of the Rev. Richard
Whatcoat, late bishop of the
Methodist Episcopal Church. New-
York, J. Allen, 1828. 118 p.
CtMW; CtY; DLC; ICU; IEG; MH;
MdBE; NNUT; NcD; NjMD; TxU.
                           34790
Phrenological Society of the City
of Washington
   A report submitted to the
Phrenological Society of the City
of Washington on the 14th of
March 1828 and printed by order.

Washington, E. DeKrafft, pr.
[1828] 8 p. DLC; ICN.   34791

Pickering, David, 1788-1859
   Address delivered before the
citizens of Providence, in the
Universalist Chapel, on the fifty-
second anniversary of American
independence. 2d ed. Providence,
Literary Cadet Office, Smith &
Parmenter, prs., 1828. 24 p.
MH; MWA; NCH; NNC; RHi; RPB.
                           34792
[Pickering, John] 1777-1846
   Review of Johnson's English
dictionary... From the American
Quarterly Review. Vol. IV. No.
VII. [Boston, 1828] 36 p. MH;
MHi (reported as 32 p); MWA;
PPAmP.   34793

Picket, Albert, 1771-1850
   American school class book,
no. 1. Picket's juvenile spelling
book or analogical pronouncer of
the English language; conformable
to the standard orthography of
Johnson, and classic pronunciation of Walker; with appropriate
definitions and reading lessons.
Cincinnati, G. T. Williamson,
publisher, 1828. 214 p. OCHP.
                           34794
---- Juvenile mentor, or select
readings, American Class Book
No. 3. Cincinnati, 1828. 258 p.
(Title from Smith Book Co. List
89)   34795

The picture of New-York, and
Stranger's guide to the commer-
cial metropolis of the United
States. New-York, Pub. by A. T.
Goodrich, [1828] viii, 492 p.
CSmH; DLC; IaDaM; NN; NNC;
NNS; PHi; TxU; BrMus.   34796

Pictures of Bible history, with
suitable descriptions. Wendell,
J. Metcalf, 1828. 23 p. PP;
WHi.   34797

Pidgin, William, 1771-1848
  A compendious system of English grammar; comprising all
that is necessary in the work of
this kind. Norway, Pub. by the
author, pr. at the Observer Office, by Asa Barton, 1828. 76 p.
Williamson: 7474.   34798

Pierpont, John, 1785-1868
  The American first class book;
or, Exercises in reading and
recitation... Boston, Hilliard,
Gray, Little, and Wilkins [etc.]
1828. 480 p. CtMW; DLC; MB;
MH; MHi; MeU.   34799

---- As you sow, so must you
reap. A sermon preached at the
ordination of the Rev. Samuel
Presbury, over the Second Con-
gregational Society in Northfield,
Mass. Feb. 27, 1828. By John
Pierpont. 2d ed. Boston, Bowles
and Dearborn [Press of Isaac R.
Butts & Co.] 1828. 24 p. CtSoP;
ICMe; MB; MH-AH; MHi; MWA;
MiD-B; RPB; BrMus.   34800

---- Pierpont's introduction. Introduction to the national reader;
a selection of easy lessons, designed to fill the same place in
the common schools of the United
States, that is held by Murray's
introduction, and the compila-
tions of Guy, Mylius, and Pin-
nock, in those of Great Britain.
Boston, Richardson and Lord,
1828. 168 p. CSt; DLC; MH;
TxU-T.   34801

---- The national reader... Pub.
by Hilliard, Gray, Little and
Wilkins, and Richardson and
Lord, Boston, 1828. 276 p.
IaGG; LNHT; MBAU; MDeeP; MH;
MeBa; NPV; NSyHi; PPAmP;
TxU-T.   34802

---- The object of the resurrection of Jesus Christ. A sermon,
preached in the Congregational

Church in Federal Street, Boston,
January 6, 1828. The Sunday eve-
ning lecture. Boston, Bowles and
Dearborn, Press of Isaac R.
Butts & Co., 1828. 15 p. ICMe;
MA; MB; MH-AH; MWA; MiD-B;
BrMus.   34803

---- "Who goeth a warfare at his
own charges?" A discourse de-
livered before the Ancient and
Honorable Artillery Company of
Massachusetts on the celebration
of their 190th anniversary.
Bowles & Dearborn, publishers.
[I. R. Butts & Co., prs.] Bos-
ton, 1828. 24 p. CSmH; CtHT;
CtSoP; DLC; ICMe; MB; MBC;
MH; MHi; MeB; MiD-B; NCH;
NhHi; OClWHi; OMC; PHi;
WHi; BrMus.   34804

---- ---- Pub. at the request
of the company. Boston, Bowles
& Dearborn, 1828. 28 p. CSmH.
                              34805
Pike, John Deodatus Gregory,
1784-1854
  Persuasives to early piety in-
terspersed with suitable prayers.
1st Amer. from the 5th London ed.
Limerick, Me., Pub. by Hobbs,
Woodman & Co., W. Burr, pr.,
1828. 290 p. CSmH; MB; Me;
MeLB.   34806

Pindar, Paul
  The Creekiad; or, A free version or narrative of a talk to the
Creek Indians, delivered by a
certain envoy extraordinary &
minister plenipotentiary to that
nation: with much other incidental and accidental matter; in English
Octosyllabic, Hudibrastic doggerel
... By Paul Pindar. Washington, Pr.
for the author, 1828. 34 p. DLC.
                              34807
Pinistri, Salvader
  Instruction. In the Italian and
Spanish languages, and in all
branches of drawing and painting,
taught according to the Italian

School. [Philadelphia, 1828] Bdsd.
PPL.   34808

Pinkney, Frederick
    To the public. The undersigned
having entered into a correspondence with Dabney S. Carr, has
to inform all honorable men that
he has found him altogether destitute to the qualities of a gentleman. Frederick Pinkney. Baltimore, Oct. 15, 1828. 1 p. DLC.
                            34809
The pioneers. See Cooper,
James Fenimore.

Piscataqua Association of Ministers, Portsmouth, N. H.
    Pastoral letter of the Pisca-
taqua Association, to the churches of the Piscataqua conference,
for June, 1828. Portsmouth
[N. H.] Miller & Brewster, prs.
[1828] 8 p. CSmH.   34810

Pitkin, Timothy, 1766-1847
    A political and civil history
of the United States of America,
for the year 1763 to the close of
the administration of President
Washington, in March, 1797: including a summary view of the
political and civil state of the
North American colonies, prior
to that period. New Haven, Pub.
by Hezekiah Howe and Durrie &
Peck. [Pr. by Hezekiah Howe,
New Haven] 1828. 2 v. CL; CSmH;
DLC; DeGE; ICN; ICU; MB; MH;
MiD-B; NN; OO; PPL; PPi; PU;
RPB; WHi; BrMus.   34811

Pittsburgh
    By-laws and ordinances of the
city of Pittsburgh, and the acts
of assembly relating thereto: with
notes and references to judicial
decisions thereon, and an appendix, relating to several subjects
connected with the laws and police of the city corporation. (Pub.
under the authority of the city
councils.) Pittsburgh, Pr. and

pub. by Johnston and Stockton,
1828. 531 p. CSmH; MH-L;
NBuG; PPL; PPi; PU; BrMus.
                            34812
Pittsburgh, Administration Publishing Committee.
    The presidential contest. To
the thinking and reflecting sup-
porters of Gen. Andrew Jackson,
particularly to his advocates in
Pennsylvania this authentic history, of some of his acts of op-
ression[!] and cruelty, is respectfully dedicated and addressed: by the Administration Publishing Committee of the city of
Pittsburgh, September 16, 1828.
[Pittsburgh] 1828. 20, [1] p.
DLC.   34813

---- ---- 2d ed.[Pittsburgh]
1828. cover-title, 20, [1] p.
DLC; MiU-C.   34814

Pizarro, José Antonio
    Select dialogues, or Spanish
and English conversations, for
the use of those who study the
Spanish language. Middletown,
Conn., Pr. by E. & H. Clark,
1828. 225, [1] p. PPL.   34815

A plain and easy catechism, suitable for children of a tender age.
And adapted to the use of families and Sabbath schools. By a
lady of New-Jersey. Princeton,
N. J., Pub. by the Princeton S.
School Union. D. A. Borrenstein,
pr., 1828. 16 p. NjP; OCH;
PP; PPL.   34816

Plain and easy directions for
forming Sunday schools, present-
ing complete and approved plans
for their management and instruction. New York, Sunday School
Depository, 1828. 179 p. NNG.
                            34817
Plain hymns for Sunday schools,
Bible classes, and family worship. Boston, Samuel H. Parker,
1828. 60 p. MB.   34818

Plain matters of fact. See Giles, William Branch.

A plain practical man. See Remarks upon the auction system.

Plain truth. See National Republican Party. Virginia.

Plain Truth-Extra. See To thinking men.

Plainfield Academy, Plainfield, Conn.
Catalogue of the trustees, instructors, and students of Plainfield Academy. Plainfield, [Con.] August 1828. Brooklyn, Conn. Advertiser pr. John Gray, jr. 1828. 10 p. MA. 34819

Plantou, Anthony
Ode sur le combat naval de Navarin, entre L'Escadre Combinée Anglaise, Française, et Russe, et L'Escadre Turque; Par Mr. A. Plantou. Philadelphia, par J. F. Hurtel, 1828. 8 p. PPL; RPB. 34820

Playfair, John, 1748-1819
Elements of geometry, containing the first six books of Euclid---New York, E. Duyckinck, publisher, W. E. Dean, pr., 1828. 333 p. CSt; CtY; IaGG; MB; MH. 34821
The pleasing instructer. See American Tract Society. N. Y.

A pleasing toy, for girl or boy. Wendell, Mass., Pr. and sold by J. Metcalf, 1828. 16 p. MB; MWA. 34822

Plumer, William, 1789-1854
An address, delivered at Portsmouth, N. H., on the Fourth of July, 1828. Portsmouth, T. H. Miller and C. W. Brewster, prs., 1828. 24 p. CSmH; DLC; IEG; MB; MBAt; MH; Me; MiD-B; NCH; NhHi; NjR; RPB; BrMus. 34823

Plutarchus
Plutarch's Lives, translated from the original Greek; with notes, historical and critical; and a life of Plutarch. By John Langhorne, M. D., and William Langhorne, M. A. Carefully corrected, and pr. from the last London ed.... Philadelphia, J. Crissy, 1828. 4 v. FH; FSa; GEU-M; IaScM; LNL; M; MAnHi; MCM; NNG; NbU; NjR; PHi; PPF; PU; WvW. 34824

A pocket expositor; selected from Doddridge's family expositor, Philadelphia, Towar & Hogan, John Gray, pr., 1828. 232 p. OMC; OWoC; UU. 34825

The pocket lawyer, or self-conveyancer: containing all the most useful forms, rendered so plain, that every man can draw any instrument of writing, without the assistance of an attorney. In a method entirely new. Harrisburg, Gustavus S. Peters, 1828. 107 p. P. 34826

Poesias de un Mexicano. Nueva York, En Casa de Lanuza, Mendia y C, 1828. 2 vols. C-S; NN; PPL. 34827

Poetry for schools. See Robbins, Eliza.

The political character of John Quincy Adams delineated. See Baylies, Francis.

Political tables, shewing the population of the different states, and exhibiting the return of votes at the elections in 1823 and 1826, and in several of the states in 1828. with remarks. New York, Pr. by Elliott and Palmer, 1828. 72 p. CSmH; DLC; OClWHi; WHi. 34828

Polke, Adam G. See Burnside, A. (note).

Pollok, Robert
The course of time, a poem.
Exeter, Pub. by Leonard W.
Kimball, 1828. 240 p. MNe;
MWHi; Nh.   34829

---- ---- Boston, Pub. by
Crocker & Brewster, New York,
J. Leavitt, 1828. [3], [13]-295
p. PPL.   34830

---- ---- 3d Amer. from the
3d Edinburgh ed., Pub. by Crock-
er & Brewster, Boston; Jonathan
Leavitt, New York; John Grigg,
Philadelphia; Cushing & Jewett,
Baltimore. Stereotyped at the
Boston Type and Stereotype Foun-
dry, 1828. 247 p. CSmH; MA;
PPL.   34831

---- ---- Another ed. xx, 247 p.
(completely different title page
setting from copy without the xx
introductory pages.) PPL. 34832

---- ---- 2d Amer. from the 3d
London ed. New York, J. P.
Haven; E. Bliss, [etc.] [Sleight
& George, prs., Jamaica, L. I.]
1828. 227 p. NJQ; NN; NNS.
                             34833
---- ---- Philadelphia, A. Clax-
ton, J. Harding, pr., 1828. 228
p. MB; MdW; MeLB; P; PRHi.
                             34834
---- Pollok's Course of time.
With an introductory notice, an-
alysis and index. 4th Amer. ed.
Amherst, Mass., Pub. by J. S.
and C. Adams, 1828. 7 p. l.,
[9]-300, [4] p. CoCsC; CtHC;
MAJ; MB; MDeeP; MH; MWA;
MiD; NN; OClWHi; OSW; PU.
                             34835
Poor Richard's almanack for
1829. By Poor Richard, Jr.
Rochester, Marshall & Dean
[1828] 12 l. MWA; MnM; NRMA;
NRU; NUtHi.   34836

Poor Will's almanac for 1829.
By William Collom. Philadelphia,

Kimber & Sharpless [1828] 18 l.
DLC; MWA; NBuHi; PPL.
                             34837
---- ---- Philadelphia, J. Rake-
straw [1828] 18 l. InU; MB; MWA;
N; NHi; NjR; PHi; PPL; WHi.
                             34838
Poor Will's pocket almanack for
1829. Philadelphia, Kimber &
Sharpless [1828] 24 l. DLC;
MWA; NN; NjR; PHi; PP; PPL.
                             34839
Pope, Alexander, 1688-1774
An essay on man, in four
epistles to H. St. John, Lord
Bolingbroke; to which is added
the Universal prayer. Hartford,
S. Andrus, 1828. ix, 67 p.
CSmH; MH; OO; TxU. 34840

---- ---- With notes illustrative
of the grammatical construction,
designed as a text-book for parsing. By Daniel Clarke. Portland,
Me., Pub. by Shirley & Hyde,
1828. 53 p. CSmH; MH. 34841

---- ---- Woodstock, Pr. by
David Watson, 1828. 47 p. MH.
                            34841a
---- The poetical works of Alex-
ander Pope: to which is prefixed
the life of the author. New York,
Pub. for the booksellers [John
Dixon, pr.] 1828. 2 v. MChi;
MPeaHi; MdW; NbOP; OClWHi.
                             34842
---- ---- Princeton, D. A. Bor-
renstein, pub., 1828. 3 v. CSmH;
CtHT; CtY; GEU; IU; MH; NN;
NjP; NjR; PHi; TxDaM; ViU.
                             34843
---- The political works of Alex-
ander Pope... New York, E. Duy-
ckinck & G. Lord, 1828. 206 p.
CSmH.   34844

Porter, Ebenezer, 1772-1834
Analysis of the principles of
rhetorical delivery as applied in
reading and speaking. 2d ed.
Andover, Mark Newman, 1828.
404 p. Tuttle.   34845

Porter, Jane, 1776-1850
Coming out, and The field of forty footsteps, by Jane and Anna Maria Porter... New York, Pr. by J. & J. Harper, 1828. 3 v. CtHT; NbOU; O; WU.   34846

Portland, Maine
Great democratic and anti-tariff meeting of the young men of Portland. Office of the Eastern Argus, Portland, Sept. 3, 1828. 1 p. DLC.   34847

Portland. Athenaeum.
Catalogue of books in the Portland Athenaeum, with the by-laws and regulations of the Institution. Portland, Shirley & Hyde, prs., 1828. 52 p. [i.e. 53] p. NN.   34848

---- Female Orphan Asylum.
Constitution and by-laws, &c., of the Female Orphan Asylum of Portland. [Portland] Shirley & Hyde, prs. [1828] 33 p. Williamson: 7984.   34849

---- Gymnasium.
Constitution of the Portland Gymnasium, with the rules and regulations, and the names of the subscribers. Portland, Pr. by James Adams, Jun., 1828. 15 p. MeHi.   34850

---- Monitorial School.
Catalogue of Monitorial School, No. 2, Portland, March 10, 1828. Samuel Kelley, master. 16 p. MH; MiD-B.   34851

Portland Mutual Fire Insurance Company.
By-laws of the Portland Mutual Fire Insurance Company, incorporated February 21, 1828. Together with the act of incorporation. Portland, Pr. by Thos. Todd, 1828. 18 p. MeHi. 34852

Portsmouth, N. H.

Report of the school committee of the town of Portsmouth, March 25, 1828. [Portsmouth, Miller & Brewster, prs., 1828] 8 p. NhD; OO.   34853

---- First Church of Christ.
Names of the members of the First or North Church of Christ in Portsmouth. Jan. 1828. [Portsmouth, N. H.] Miller & Brewster, prs. [1828] 14 p. ICN.   34854

---- Lyceum.
Portsmouth Lyceum. Prospectus. [Portsmouth, New-Hampshire, January, 1828] 8 p. MBC; NhHi.   34855

---- North Parish Library.
North Parish Library, 1828. While the library consisted of only a few volumes... It is therefore necessary at this time to print a catalogue of those books only which have been added to the Library in the course of the year. 2 l. [made up of above covering letter and p 13, a supplement to be added to earlier printed catalogues of the Library.] MBC.   34856

The post-captain. See Davis, John.

The post-chaise companion. See Socio, Clio Convivius, pseud.

Posthumous papers, facetious and fanciful. See Webbe, Cornelius.

Potter, Henry, 1766-1857
The office and duty of a justice of the peace, and a guide to sheriffs, coroners, clerks, constables, and other civil officers. According to the laws of North-Carolina, with an appendix. Containing the Declaration of rights and constitution of this state, the

Constitution of the United States,
with the amendments, thereto;
and a collection of the most approved forms. Corr. to the present time. 2d ed. Raleigh, J.
Gales & son, 1828. 448 p. MH-
L; NcU.   34857

Potter, W. W.
    First letter of W. W. Potter,
to the committee of the Philadelphia Medical Society, on quack
medicines. Read on the 12th February, 1828. Philadelphia, 1828.
7 p. NIC.   34858

Potts, William Stephens, 1802-
1852
    A masonic discourse delivered
before the Missouri lodge no. 1,
on St. John's day... 1828. St.
Louis, 1828. Sabin 64691. 34859

Powell, Benjamin F.
    The Bible of reason; or,
Scriptures of modern authors.
Selected and written by B. F.
Powell. New York, Geo. H.
Evans, pr. and publisher, 1828.
2 pts. DLC; MNS.   34860

Powell, John Joseph, 1755?-1801
    A treatise on the law of mort-
gages... Reprinted from the 6th
English ed., much enl. and imp.
with copious notes, by Thos.
Coventry... Boston, Wells &
Lilly, 1828. 3 v. C; CU; CoU;
CtMW; GU-L; IU; KU; KyLxT; MH-
L; MdBB; Me; Ms; NIC-L; NNLI;
NcD; NjR; OCLaw; PU; Sc-SC;
ViU; BrMus.   34861

Powers, Grant
    Essay upon the influence of
the imagination on the nervous
system, contributing to a false
hope in religion. Andover, Pr.
and pub. by Flagg & Gould, 1828.
118 p. DLC; KWiU; MA.   34862

Practical arithmetic, prepared
for the use of Mrs. Okill's Fe-

male Boarding-School. New York,
Pr. by Daniel Fanshaw, 1828.
251, [1] p. N.   34863

A Practical Man, pseud.   See
An examination of the reasons...

Practical morality. See Stanhope,
Philip Dormer, 4th earl of
Chesterfield.

The prairie. See Cooper,
James Fenimore.

Pratt, Horace S.
    Sermon, delivered at Frye-
burg, Maine, on the 4th of July,
1828... Portland, Shirley & Hyde,
prs., 1828. 31 p. MH; MHi;
RPB.   34864

Pratt, Luther
    A defence of Freemasonry in
a series of letters addressed to
Solomon Southwick, Esq. and
others. In which the true principles of the order are given,
and many late misrepresentations
corrected. With an appendix containing explanatory notes and Masonic documents. Troy, Pr. for
the author, by Francis Adancourt, and sold by him and various other book-sellers in the
United States. 1828. 216 p.
IaCrM.   34865

Prayers for children. By a
clergyman. Boston [1828?]
BrMus.   34866

Preble, William Pitt, 1783-1857
    Report of the school commit-
tee of the town of Portland, 1828,
by W. P. Preble. Portland, Pr.
by Thos. Todd, 1828. 7 p. MiU.
                           34867

[Prentiss, Sophia]
    Remains of my early friend.
Keene, N.H., 1828. 55 p. ICU;
MB; MH; N; Nh; BrMus. 34868

Presbyterian Church in the
U. S. A.
Minutes of the General Assembly of the Presbyterian Church in the United States of America: with an appendix. A. D. 1828. Philadelphia, Pr. by Lydia R. Bailey, 1828. [3], 220-360 p. InU; KyLoP; MsJS; NcMHi; TxDaM.   34869

---- Presbytery of Chillicothe.
A pastoral letter, from the Presbytery of Chillicothe, to the churches under their care. Georgetown, Pr. at the office of the Western Aegis. 1828. 8 p. PPPrHi.   34870

---- Synod of Pittsburgh.
Address of the board of education to the churches under the care of the synod of Pittsburgh. Pittsburgh, 1828. 12 p. PPiW.
                               34871
Presbyterian Education Society of Kentucky
Constitution of the Presbyterian Education Society of Kentucky ... Danville, Feb. 28, 1828.[2] p. PPPrHi.   34872

A present from New-York: containing many pictures worth seeing, and some things worth remembering. New-York, M. Day, 1828. 23 p. DLC.   34873

The president, directors and company of the Bank of the United States vs. Solomon Etting, removed from the Circuit Court, U. S. December term, 1827, to the Supreme Court of the United States, on a certificate of division of the judges. Baltimore, Pr. by John D. Toy, 1828. iv, 133 p. PPL.   34874

Presidential election. See Penn, pseud.

... The presidential question. Ad-

dressed to the people of the United States. New York, Sickels, pr. , 1828. ["Lend this to your neighbour" at head of title.] 16 p. MnH; NIC; NcU.
                               34875
... The presidential question. To the friends of equal rights. [Philadelphia, 1828] ["Supplement to the Democratic Press.] Philadelphia, Sept. 13, 1828. 8 p. MBC.   34876

Preston, Lyman, b. 1795.
Preston's complete time table: showing the number of days from any date in any given month to any date in any other month; embracing upwards of ten thousand combinations of dates. By Lyman Preston... New York, Pr. by Elliott & Palmer, 1828. [3], 12 p. CtHT; copy seen at Mass. Old Sturbridge Village (Bank); WHi.
                               34877
---- Preston's tables of interest, showing the interest on any sum from one dollar to five hundred dollars, inclusive; proceeding from five hundred to one thousand dollars, by hundreds; and from one thousand to five thousand dollars, by thousands: computed at seven per cent... together with a perfect cent table... Utica [N. Y.] Pr. for the author by W. Williams, 1828. 96 p. DLC; NUt.   34878

Preston, Richard, 1763-1850
An elementary treatise on estates... with preliminary observations on the quality of estates. New York, O. Halsted; Philadelphia, W. A. Halsted, 1828. 2 v. in 1. Ct; DLC; IaU-L; In-SC; KyLxT; MH-L; MHi; Md; MnU; NIC-L; NcU; OCLaw; PPB; PPiAL; PU-L; ViU; W.   34879

---- An essay in a course of lectures on abstracts of title; to facilitate the study, and the application of the first principles, and general rules of the laws of property; stating in detail, the duty of solicitors in preparing, etc., and of counsel in advising, on abstracts of title. New York, O. Halsted [etc.] 1828. 3 v. Ia; KyLxT; MH-L; Md; MdBB; NIC-L; NNLI; NRAL; OCLaw; PPB; TJaU; Vi-L; W.   34880

Pretty pictures, with pretty verses. Wendell, Mass., J. Metcalf, pr., 1828. 8 p. DLC; MWA.   34881

Priest, Josiah, 1790-1850
A view of the expected Christian millenium which is promised in the Holy Scriptures, and is believed to be nigh...4th ed. Albany, Pub. for subscribers. Loomis Press, 1828. 408 p. ICU; IU; MiU; MPB; NN; NNC; OClWHi; PCA; TxH.   34882

---- ---- 5th ed. Albany, Pub. for subscribers, Loomis' Press, 1828. ICMcC; NBu; NNUT.
34883
---- ---- 6th ed. Albany, Pub. for subscribers, Loomis' Press, 1828. 408 p. CtHT-W; NCH; NN; NhHi; OClWHi; PPPrHi; RPB.
34884
Primary dictionary.   See Robbins, Eliza.

Prince, Joseph Hardy
An address, delivered at Fanueil Hall, July 4, 1828, at the Jackson Celebration, in Boston. Boston, True & Greene, prs., 1828. 35, [1] p. CSmH; CtSoP; DLC; M; MBNEH; MHi; MWA; NNC; NcU; ScCC.   34885

[Prince, William] 1766-1842
Circular. Linnaean Botanic Garden and Nurseries, New York, October 1, 1828. Bdsd. DNA.
34886
---- A short treatise on horti-

culture: embracing descriptions of a great variety of fruit and ornamental trees and shrubs, grape vines, bulbous flowers, green houses, trees and plants, etc., nearly all of which are at present comprised in the collection of the Linnaean Botanic Garden, at Flushing, near New-York. ...By Wm. Prince... New-York, Pr. by T. and J. Swords, 1828. ix, 196 p. ArU; CU; DeGE; IU; IaAS; InLP; KU; MB; MBH; MH; MHi; MdU; MiU; MnU; NBLiHi; NIC; NN; NNC; NSyU; NcU; NjR; OHi; OU; PPL; RP; TNJ; WU.   34887

Princeton University. Philological Society of Nassau-Hall.
Catalogue of books belonging to the library of the Philological Society of Nassau-Hall, together with those deposited for the use of its members. [Princeton] Princeton Press, Pr. by Connolly and Madden, 1828. [5]-60 p. PPAmP; WMSF.   34888

Principle and practice.   See Martineau, Harriet.

The principles and acts of Mr. Adams' Administration. See Moore, Jacob Bailey.

The principles of aristocratic legislation, developed in an address, delivered to the working people of the district of Southwark, and townships of Moyamensing and Passyunk. In the Commissioner's hall, August 14, 1828. By an operative citizen. Philadelphia, J. Coates, Jr., pr., 1828. 16 p. ICN.   34889

Prindle's almanack for 1829. By Charles Prindle. New-Haven, A. H. Maltby [1828] 12 l. CtHi; CtY; DLC; MBAt; MWA; N; OClWHi.   34890

Prison Discipline Society. Boston.
   Second annual report of the
board of managers of the Prison
Discipline Society, Boston, June
1, 1827. Stereotyped at the Bos-
ton Type and Stereotype Foundry.
Boston, T.R. Marvin, pr., 1828.
100 p. CU; CtHT-W; DLC;
MBAt; MHi; NCH; NNC; Nj;
OCHP; OU; PPL; RPA; RPB;
ScCC.   34891

---- Third annual report of the
board of managers of the Prison
Discipline Society, Boston, 1828.
Boston, T.R. Marvin, pr., 1828.
iv, 83, [1] p. CU; CtHT-W; MW;
MWA; MeBaT; NGH; NbHi;
NcMHi; Nj; OU; PPL; RPA; RPB.
                               34892
Private character of General
Jackson. [Philadelphia?] 1828.
Bdsd. PPL.   34893

Private hours. See Dix, Dorothea Lynde.

Proceedings and address of the
New Hampshire Republican State
Convention. See Democratic
Party. New Hampshire.

Proceedings and address of the
New Jersey delegates. See Na-
tional Republican Party. New
Jersey.

Proceedings and address of the
New Jersey State Convention. See
Democratic Party. New Jersey.

Proceedings of a convention of
the people of Maine. See National Republican Party. Maine.

The proceedings of a meeting of
the democratic citizens of North
Mulberry Ward. See Democratic
Party. Pennsylvania.

Profession is not principle. See
Kennedy, Grace.

The progress of the pilgrim
Good-intent. See Burges, Mary
Anne.

Proposals for a new school for
boys... [Charlottesville, 1828]
2 p. ViU.   34894

Proposals, for publishing in the
city of Richmond, a new weekly
paper. See Friend of the Union.

Protestant Episcopal Church in
the U.S.
   The book of common prayer,
and administration of the sacra-
ments... together with the Psalter
...of David...Baltimore, Pub.
by E.J. Coale, 1828. 360, 80,
7, 50 p. MdHi.   34895

---- ---- Boston, Massachusetts
Episcopal Missionary Society,
1828. 405 p. MB.   34896

---- ---- Hartford, S. Andrus,
publisher, stereotyped by A.
Chandler, 1828. [c1826] 575 p.
IEG; MH; NbOP; ViAlTh. 34897

---- ---- 2d Stereotype ed. New
York, White, Gallaher & White,
1828. 222, 70, [8] p. CSmH.
                               34898
---- ---- Philadelphia, Samuel
F. Bradford, 1828. 304 [2] 305-
381, 135 p. MBD; MiU-C; NN;
NNG; NjMD.   34899

---- ---- Philadelphia, Church
Missionary House, 1828. 479, 91,
[9], 135 p. (Sep. titles for
Psalms and for Hymns). NNG;
PU.   34900

---- A denial of certain charges
made against the Protestant Episcopal Church. Carlisle, The Republican Office, 1828. 8 p.
PPPrHi.   34901

---- Hymns of the Protestant
Episcopal Church in the United

States of America, set forth in
general conventions of said
church, in the years of our Lord
1789, 1808 and 1826. Stereotyped at the Boston Type and
Stereotype Foundry. Boston, Pub.
by the Massachusetts Episcopal
Missionary Society, 1828. [1]
223-358, [1] p. MBC; RNR; ScU.
34902

---- ---- Stereotyped by James
Conner. New York, Pr. and pub.
by Caleb Bartlett, 1828. 2 l.,
31-129, [140-142] p. TxU. 34903

---- ---- Philadelphia, Pub. by
S. F. Bradford, 1828. 50 p. MH;
NN; NNG. 34904

---- Second annual report of the
executive committee of the board
of managers of the General Protestant Episcopal Sunday School
Union: presented to the board of
managers, at their second annual meeting, held in the city of
New York, June 26, 1828. With
an appendix, containing a list
of contributions and other documents. New-York, Pub. at the
Depository, Edward J. Swords,
pr., 1828. 56 p. DLC; MBD;
MHi; NNG. 34905

---- African Mission School Society.
Address of the executive committee of the African Mission
School Society; together with the
record of the proceedings at the
formation of said society. Hartford, J. F. Huntington, 1828. 11
p. CSmH; CtHT; ICJ; MB; MBC;
MHi; MeB; NNG; NjPT. 34906

---- Connecticut (Diocese)
Journal of the proceedings of
the annual convention of the
Protestant Episcopal Church, in
the diocese of Connecticut, held
in St. Paul's Church, Norwalk,
June 4th and 5th, 1828. Middletown, Pr. by Wm. D. Starr,

1828. 50 p. CtHC. 34907

---- Delaware (Diocese of)
Journal of the convention of the
Protestant Episcopal Church of
the diocess[!] of Delaware, held
at Dover, June 7, 1828. Dover,
Del., Augustus M. Schee, pr.,
1828. 16+ p. PPL. 34908

---- Maryland (Diocese of)
Journal of a convention of the
Protestant Episcopal Church of
Maryland, held in St. Ann's
Church, Annapolis, June 4th, 5th,
and 6th, 1828. Baltimore, Pr.
by J. Robinson, 1828. 34, [2] p.
MBD; NNG. 34909

---- Mississippi (Diocese of)
Journal of the proceedings of
the third annual convention of the
Protestant Episcopal Church, in
the diocese of Mississippi, held
on Wednesday the 7th day of May,
1828. In Christ Church, Jefferson County. Natchez, Pr. by
William C. Grissam & Co., 1828.
18 p. CtHT; Ms-Ar; MsJPED;
MsLE; NN. 34910

---- New Jersey (Diocese of)
Journal of the proceedings of
the forty-fifth annual convention
of the Protestant Episcopal
Church in the state of New Jersey held in St. Mary's Church,
Burlington...New Brunswick, Pr.
by Terhune & Letson, 1828. 29,
[3] p. NjR; PPL. 34911

---- New York (Diocese of)
Constitution and canons of the
Protestant Episcopal Church in
the state of New-York, together
with an appendix, containing directions for candidates for orders.
New York, Pr. by T. & J.
Swords, 1828. 20 p. CtHT; WHi.
34912

---- ---- Journal of the proceedings of the forty-third convention
of the Protestant Episcopal

Church in the state of New-York; held in Trinity Church, in the city of New-York, on Tuesday, October 16th, and Friday, October 17th, A. D. 1828. To which is prefixed, a list of the clergy of the diocese of New-York. New-York, Pr. by T. & J. Swords, 1828. 72 p. MBD; TSewU.   34913

---- New York (Diocese of). Missionary Society.
The twelfth annual report of the board of managers of the New-York Protestant Episcopal Missionary Society at the anniversary meeting held in Oct. 1828. . . New-York, Pr. by T. &J. Swords, 1828. 35 p. NNG; NjR.   34914

---- North Carolina (Diocese of)
Journal of the proceedings of the twelfth annual convention of the Protestant Episcopal Church in the state of North Carolina. . . 1828. Fayetteville, Pr. by Edward J. Hale, 1828. 48 p. ICU; MBD; NcU.   34915

---- Pennsylvania (Diocese of)
Journal of the proceedings of the forty-fourth convention of the Protestant Episcopal Church in the state of Pennsylvania. held in St. Peter's and St. James's Churches, in the City of Philadelphia, on Tuesday, May 20th Wednesday, May 21st- Thursday, May 22nd, and Friday, May 23d, 1828. Philadelphia, Pub. by order of the convention. Jesper Harding, pr. , 1828. 16 p. DLC; MBD; MiD-B; PPL; BrMus.
                                  34916
---- South Carolina (Diocese of)
Journal of the proceedings of the 40th annual convention of the Protestant Episcopal Church in the diocese of South Carolina, held in St. Michael's Church, Charleston, on the 13th, 14th and 15th, of February, 1828. Charleston, Pr. by A. E. Miller, 1828. 46 p. MBD; NN; NNG;

TSewU.   34917

---- Vermont (Diocese of)
Journal of the proceedings of the convention of the Protestant Episcopal Church in the state of Vermont. Woodstock, Pr. by David Watson, 1828. 12 p. MB; MBD; MHi.   34918

---- Virginia (Diocese of)
The constitution of the Protestant Episcopal Church in the United States; and the constitution and canons of the Protestant Episcopal Church in the diocese of Virginia, to which is prefixed, an address to the friends and members of the Church. Richmond, Pr. by John Warrock, 1828. 20 p. MB.   34919

---- ---- Journal of the proceedings of convention of the diocese of Virginia, which assembled in the town of Petersburg, on Thursday the fifteenth day of May, 1828. Richmond, Pr. by John Warrock, 1828. 36, [1] p. DLC; ViAlTh; ViU; WHi.
                                  34920
Protestant Episcopal Clerical Association of the City of New York.
Constitution of the Protestant Episcopal Clerical Association of the City of New-York; and forms of prayer used by the Association. New-York, Pr. by E. Conrad, 1828. 16 p. NNC; NNG.
                                  34921

Protestant Episcopal Sunday and Adult School Society of Philadelphia.
The annual report of the Protestant Episcopal Sunday and Adult School Society of Philadelphia. Read December 28th, 1827. Philadelphia, Pr. by Wm. Stavely, 1828. 28 p. MnHi.   34922

Protestant Episcopal Tract

Society
   The eighteenth annual report of the board of trustees of the New York Protestant Episcopal Tract Society. J. H. Hobart president. New-York, T. &J. Swords, 1828. 9 p. NNG.   34923

Proudfit, Alexander
   Agency of God in the elevation of man. A sermon, commemorative of the eminent talents, and private virtues, and public services of his excellency De Witt Clinton, late governor of the state of New-York: preached at Salem, N. Y. March 11, 1828. Salem, N. Y. , Pr. by Dodd & Stevenson, 1828. 28 p. ICMe; MH; MdHi; MiD-B; N; PHi; PPPrHi.   34924

Prout, William
   An inquiry into the nature and treatment of diabetes, calculus, and other affections of the urinary organs: with remarks on the importance of attending to the state of the urine in organic diseases of the kidney and bladder ... From the 2d London ed. , rev. and much enlarged: With notes and additions by S. Calhoun, Philadelphia, Pub. by Towar & Hogan, W. Brown, pr. , 1828. xi, 308 p. ViRA.   34925

Providence (City)
   Plan of the city government, reported by the committee, to be considered by the Freemen of Providence, in Town Meeting Assembled, on the first day of October, 1828. Pr. for the use of the Freemen, by order of the Town. [Providence, 1828] 11 p. CSmH; NN; RHi; RPB.   34926

---- Report of the Committee on Public Schools. 1828. [Providence, 1828] 11 p. MH; PU-Penn; RHi; RPB.   34927

---- Baptist Society.
   Minutes of the early proceedings of the Baptist Society; also the charter of incorporation and by-laws of the Charitable Baptist Society, in Providence, R. I. Providence, H. H. Brown, pr. , 1828. 16 p. MNtcA; NRAB; RHi; RPB.   34928

---- Citizens.
   Report of a committee at a meeting of the citizens of Providence, friendly to the promotion of temperance... Providence, F. Y. Carlile and Co. , prs. , 1828. 16 p. MB; MBC; MWA; OCU-L; RPB.   34929

---- Dexter Asylum.
   Rules and regulations for the government of the Dexter Asylum established at a town meeting of the freemen of the town of Providence, on the 26th day of July, 1828. Providence, Smith & Parmenter, prs. , 1828. 13 p. RHi; RNHi.   34930

The Providence directory; containing names of the inhabitants, their occupations, place of business and dwelling houses, with lists of the streets, lanes, wharves, etc. , Also banks, insurance offices and other public institutions; the whole [carefully] collected and arranged. Providence, Pub. by H. H. Brown, 1828. 116, 5 p. CSmH; DLC; MBNEH; MWA; MWHi; RHi; RP.   34931

Providence. First Universalist Society.
   Charter and by-laws of the First Universalist Society, incorporated June 1827. Providence, 1828. 8 p. RHi.   34932

---- Forcing Stationary Engine Co. No. 2.
   By-laws... Providence, H. H. Brown, pr. , 1828. 8 p.

RPB.   34933

---- Mechanic Banks.
Charter... Providence, Miller
and Hammond, prs. , 1828. 8 p.
MiD-B.   34934

Providence Young Men's Bible
Society.
Annual report of the Providence Young Men's Bible Society
...1828. Providence, 1828. Sabin 66339.   34935

Provident Society for the Employment of the Poor, Philadelphia.
Fourth annual report of the
Provident Society for Employing
the Poor. Presented at their
annual meeting held January 8th,
1828. Philadelphia, Pr. by Samuel Parker, 1828. 10 p. PPL.
                          34936
Pryor, Abraham
A sketch of the practice of
physic, containing a remedy for
epilepsy and cancer, and a new
theory...[Pittsburgh, 1828] 8 p.
PPHa.   34937

Ps and Qs. Boston, Bowles &
Dearborn, 1828. 200 p. ICU; MB;
MH; MW; MWA; NN; RPB.
                          34938
Public School Society of New
York.
An address of the trustees of
the Public School Society in the
city of New-York, to their fel-
low-citizens, respecting the ex-
tension of their public schools.
New York, Pr. by J. Seymour,
1828. 18, [1] p. CBPac; CU; MB;
MHi; PHi; PPL.   34939

---- Twenty-third annual report
of the trustees of the Public
School Society of New York. New
York, Pr. by Mahlon Day, 1828.
17 p. MiD; NjR; PPL.   34940

Pulpit exchanges. See Hitchcock,
Edward.

Purcell, Noah.   See Burnside,
A. (note).

Putnam, John March
English grammar with an im-
proved syntax... 2d ed. Concord,
N. H. , J. B. Moore, 1828. 180 p.
MH; NhHi; PU.   34941

Putnam, Samuel
The introduction to the analytical reader... Salem, Pub. by
Whipple and Lawrence [T. H. Miller and C. W. Brewster, prs. ,
Portsmouth Journal office]
1828. 144 p. MHaHi; MeHi.
                          34942
---- Sequel to the analytical
reader, in which the original design is extended, so as to em-
brace an explanation of phrases
and figurative language. Portland, Shirley & Hyde; Boston,
Hilliard, Gray, Little & Wilkins,
1828. 300 p. CU; DLC; MBAt;
MH; Nh; OClW; OClWHi; OMC;
RPB.   34943

Puzzlewell, Peter [pseud.]
A choice collection of riddles
& charades, by Peter Puzzlewell, Esq. ... Cooperstown, Pr.
and sold by H. & E. Phinney,
1828. 30 p. 1 l. DLC.   34944

Q

Quincy, Josiah. An address to
the board of aldermen. See
Boston.

Quincy, Mass. , Congregational
Church.
Order of service, at the dedication of the New Stone Congregational church in Quincy. November 12, 1828. 1 p. DLC.
                          34945
Quotations from the British poets, being a pocket dictionary

of their most admired passages.
The whole alphabetically arranged
according to the subjects. Philadelphia, J. P. Ayres, 1828. 338
p. CtHT-W; CtY; NAlf.   34946

R

Radcliffe, Ann (Ward), 1764-
1823.
    The mysteries of Udolpho. A
romance. Interspersed with some
pieces of poetry. In three volumes. Philadelphia, Pub. by J.
& J. Woodward, 1828. 3 vols.
CSmH; MdBS; NRMA; PHi; ScU.
                             34947
Radet, Jean Baptiste, 1752-1830
    Neal & Mackenzie. No. 201
Chestnut Street, between the
Theater & Arcade, Philadelphia.
Gaspard l'Avisé, Comedie-anec-
dote, en un acte. Par Mm. Radet, Barre, et Desfontaines.
[Philadelphia, 1828] 20 p. ICU;
PP L. (Also issued in vol. with
covering title: Collection d'Operas
& vaudevilles.)   34948

Radford, William
    To the public. To the gross
charge of John Hambden Pleas-
ants, in his hand bill of yester-
day, which he alleges is founded
upon documents in the hands of
another person, and which he has
not seen, I can only reply by
calling for the proofs. It is the
conclusive struggle of an expiring
man. I have given the best evidence of my innocence, by publishing his letters to Mr. Higgin-
botham. . . Wm. Radford. January
7th, 1828. 1 p. DLC.   34949

Rafinesque, Constantine (Schmaltz)
Samuel, 1783-1840
    Medical flora: or, Manual of
the medical botany of the United
States of North America. . . Phila-
delphia, Pr. & pub. by Atkinson
& Alexander, 1828-30. 2 v. A-

GS; CSmH; CtHT-W; DLC; GEU-
M; ICN; IU; IaU; InNd; InU; KU;
KyBgW; LNHT; MB; MBHo; MH;
MWA; MdBP; MoS; N; NBM;
NBuB; NIC-A; NNNBG; NNNAM;
NbOU; NbU; NcA-S; NcU; OC;
OCG; OCLloyd; OClW; OMC; OO;
P; PHi; PPAmP; PPC; PPL; PU;
TNJ; WHi; WU; BrMus.   34950
Rail-road meeting. Chatham
County, N. C. August 1, 1828.
Agreeably to previous notice, a
number of citizens of the coun-
ties of Chatham, Randolph, Guil-
ford and Orange. . . [Hillsborough,
D. Heartt, pr. , 1828] 8 p. NcU.
                             34951
Ramamohana Raya, 1774-1833
    Final appeal to the Christian
public in defence of the "Pre-
cepts of Jesus." Boston, S. B.
Manning, 1828. 316 p. KWiU;
MBAt; MBC; MH; MMeT-Hi;
MeBaT; NCH; NNC; OO; PSC-Hi.
                             34952
---- The precepts of Jesus, the
guide to peace and happiness, extracted from. . . the New Testament
. . . to which are added, the First,
the Second, and Final appeal to the
Christian public, in reply to the observations of Dr. Marshman. . .
from the London ed. Boston,
Christian Register office, 1828.
xix, 318 p. ICMcC; MB; MBAU;
MBC; MDeeP; MH-AH; MiDU;
NNC; RNR; RPA.   34953

The rambler, or, A tour through
Virginia, Tennessee, Alabama,
Mississippi and Louisiana; describing the climate, the manners,
customs and religion of the inhabitants. Interspersed with geographical and political sketches.
By a Citizen of Maryland. Annapolis, J. Green, 1828. 41, [1] p.
DLC; ICN; MdBP; MdBS; WHi.
                             34954
Ramsey, David
    The life of George Washington,
commander in chief of the Armies

of the United States of America,
throughout the war which established their independence: and
first president of the United
States. 7th ed. Baltimore, Pub.
by Cushing and Jewett, Benjamin
Edes, pr. , 1828. 234 p. CSmH;
KMcPC; MB.   34955

Randel, John
Description of a direct map
for the Erie canal, at its eastern
termination... Albany, Pr. by G.
J. Loomis and company, 1828.
72 p. NjR.   34956

Randolph, John, 1773-1833
Speech of the Hon. John Randolph, of Virginia, on the retrenchment resolutions. Delivered
in the House of Representatives
of the United States, Feb. 1,
1828. Boston, 1828. 31 p. CSmH;
CtHC; CtHT-W; DLC; ICU; MB;
MH; MHi; MWA; MiD-B; NcD;
PPAmP; PPL; ViU; WHi.   34957

---- Substance of a speech of
Mr. Randolph, on retrenchment
and reform, delivered in the
House of Representatives of the
United States on the first of Feb-
ruary, 1828. Washington, Pr. by
Green and Jarvis, 1828, 32 p.
CSmH; DLC; ICU; IU; In; MB;
MWA; NNC; NjR; RNR; Vi.
                          34958
---- ---- 2d ed. with the latest
corr. Washington, Pr. by Green
and Jarvis, 1828. 35 p. DLC;
MB; MWA; MdHi; PPL; TxU.
                          34959
Randolph, Mrs. Mary
The Virginia housewife: or,
Methodical cook... Stereotyped
ed. , with amendments and addi-
tions. Baltimore, Pub. by Plas-
kitt, & Cugle, 1828. 180 p. LU;
NUtHi.   34960

---- ---- 3d ed. , with amendments and additions. Washington,
Pub. by P. Thompson. Way &

Gideon, prs. , 1828. 240 p. OMC.
                          34961
[Raymond, Daniel] 1786-1849
The American system... Balti-
more, Pr. by Lucas & Deaver,
1828. 42 p. DLC; DeGE; MB;
MH-BA; MdBP; MdHi; PPAmP;
PU.   34962

Rayner, Menzies, 1770-1850
Divine love, the source of all
Christian virtue; illustrated in a
sermon by Rev. Menzies Rayner,
pastor of the First Independent
Universalist Church in Hartford,
Ct. [Feb. 10, 1828] Hartford,
1828. 18 p. CtHi; CtSoP; CtY;
MMeT-Hi; MWA; NcD.   34963

[Read, Nathan] 1759-1847
A disquisition on creation, an-
nihilation, the future existence,
and final happiness of all senti-
ent beings. Belfast, Maine, Pr.
by Ephraim Fellowes, 1828. 23,
[1] p. CSmH; DLC; MB; MWA;
MiU.   34964

Reason versus prejudice, Morgan refuted; or, A defence of the
ancient and honorable institution
of Masonry. By a Mason's daughter. Philadelphia, Pub. for the
authoress, by R. Desilver, 1828.
25 p. PPFM; PU.   34965

Reasons why the present system
of auctions. See New York (City)
Merchants.

The recent attempt to defeat the
constitutional provisions. See
Lowell, John.

Records of the Spanish Inquisi-
tion, translated from the original
manuscript. Boston, Samuel G.
Goodrich [Examiner Press, Hir-
am Tupper, pr.] 1828. 280 p.
CU; ICMcC; IaCrM; InU; MBL;
MS; MdBP; MeB; NIC; NNG; O;
P; RPA; BrMus.   34966

The red rover. See Chapman, Samuel Henry.

The red rover. See Cooper, James Fenimore.

Reed, Isaac
The Christian traveller... New York, Pr. by J. & J. Harper, 1828. 242, [1] p. ICN; IHi; IU; In; MiToC; OClW.   34967

Reed, John
Speech of Mr. John Reed, of Massachusetts, on the tariff bill. Delivered in the House of Representatives U. S. April 3d, 1828. Washington, Pr. by Wm. Greer, 1828. 31 p. DLC; LU; MBAt; MH; MWA.   34968

Reed, Philip
Speech ... delivered in the United States House of Representatives, on the Seminole War in 1819. [Washington, 1828] 8 p. MBAt.   34969

Reese, David Meredith
Strictures on health; or, An investigation into the physical effects of intemperance upon the public health... New York, N. Bangs and J. Emory, Azor Hoyt, pr., 1828. viii, 160 p. OC.   34970
A reflecting and critical observer of Nashville. See Jurisprudencial enquiry.

Reflections on the character and public services of Andrew Jackson with references to his qualifications for the presidency with general remarks; by a native American. New York, Pr. and sold by Geo. F. Hopkins, 1828. 48 p. MB; MH; MiD-B; NjR; PPAmP; RPB; TxU; WHi.   34971

Reformed Church in America
The acts and proceedings of the extra and stated sessions of the general synod of the Reformed Dutch Church in North America, at Albany, April & June, 1828, With an appendix containing the plan of the Theological School, as amended by synod. New York, Pr. by Vanderpool & Cole, 1828. [81]-143 p. IaPeC; NcMHi; NjR.   34972

---- Board of Education
Address of the board of education to the Reformed Dutch Churches. New York, Pr. by Daniel Fanshaw, 1828. 16 p. DLC; MB; NNUT; NjR.   34973

---- Missionary Society
The sixth annual report of the Missionary Society of the Reformed Dutch Church in North America... New York, Vanderpool & Cole, 1828. 56 p. NjR.   34974

Reformed Church in the U. S. Synod.
The acts and proceedings of the Synod of the German Reformed Church of the United States of North America, held at Mifflinburg, Union County, Pennsylvania, September, 1828. Chambersburg, Pa. , Pr. by Henry Ruby, 1828. 40 p. DLC; P; PHi; PLT; PPLT.   34975

---- The proceedings of the Synod of the German Reformed Church in North America, at York, Pa. , September, 1827. With an appendix. Hagerstown, Pr. by Gruber and May, 1828. 56 p. PLT.   34976

---- Synodal Verhandlung der Hoch Deutschen Reformirten Kirche in Der Vereinigten Staaten Von Nord Amerika, Gehalten in New York den 30sten September, 1827... Philadelphia, Gedruckt Bey Conrad Zentler, 1828. 95 p. PLERC-Hi; PPeSchw.   34977

---- Verhandlungen der Synode

der Hochdeutschen Reformirten Kirche in den Vereinigten Staaten von Nord-Amerika, gehalten zu Mifflinburg, Union County, vom 29sten September bis zum 4ten October, 1828. Chambersburg, [Pa.] Gedruckt bey Heinrich Ruby, 1828. 42 p. DLC; PLERC-Hi; PPL.   34978

The Reformed Methodist pocket hymn book... 2d ed. Taunton, Mass., Pr. by Stephen Carr, 1828. 430 p. CSmH.   34979

Reformer's discipline. 5th ed. Rev. by the Conference and pr. for the Society. Bennington, Darius Clark [1828?] 249 p. Vt.
                                        34980
Refuge in the City of Boston
    Ninth annual report of the directors of the Penitent Females' Refuge. Read at the annual meeting. Boston, T. R. Marvin, pr., 1828. 18, [2] p. DLC; ICMcC; MWA; NUtHi; PPL.   34981

A refutation of sundry written charges, made by the Rev. Ravaud Kearney, of the Protestant Episcopal Church, against Peter Gough. Baltimore, Wm. Wooddy, 1828. 81 p. NNG.   34982

A register of officers and agents, civil, military, and naval, in the service of the United States on the 30th of September, 1827... Washington, Pr. by Peter Force, 1828. 140, 180 p. InU; MB; MeHi; MiD-B; R.   34983

Reid, Robert
    The seven last plagues; or, The vials of wrath of God: a treatise on the prophecies, in two parts. Consisting of dissertations on various passages of Scripture, particularly on the VII, VIII, IX, and XII chapters of Daniel, and on the XI, XII, XIII, XIV; XV and XVI, chapters of

the book of Revelation... Pittsburgh, D. & M. Maclean, 1828. xxviii, 305 p. ICMcC; IObB; InU; NjR; OClWHi; OHi; P; PHi; PPi.
                                        34984
The reign of terror. See Democratic Party. New York.

Rejected addresses. See Smith, James.

Rejected plays... New York, J. M. Danforth, 1828. 102 p. ICU; MH; NNC; PU.   34985

Religious Conference of Grafton County, N. H.
    Constitution of the Religious Conference of Grafton County, N. H. Adopted by a convention of clergy and delegates from Congregational Churches, holden at Orford, January 2, 1828. T. Mann, pr., Hanover, N. H. [1828] 8 p. MBC.   34986

Religious discourses. See Scott, Walter.

The religious informer; being a selection of numbers [Vol. IV, no. 1-Vol. VI, 12) from a periodical work, bearing the above title, containing accounts of revivals of religion among different denominations of Christians, a general statement of the people called Freewill Baptists in the United States... By Ebenezer Chase. Enfield, 1828. BrMus.
                                        34987
Religious Tract Society, Washington, D. C.
    Ninth annual report of the managers of the Religious Tract Society of the city of Washington. City of Washington, Pr. by Peter Force, 1828. 14 p. DLC.
                                        34988
Remains of my early friend. See Prentiss, Sophia.

Remarks on liberty of conscience,

human creeds, and theological schools, suggested by the facts in a recent case. By a layman of the Reformed Dutch Church... New York, Pr. by J. & J. Harper, 1828. 102 p. CBPac; CtY; DLC; IU; MB; MH-AH; MH-L; NNUT; NjR; PLT; PPL; PPPrHi.
34989
Remarks on our inland communications, with a view to steamboat navigation. [Schenectady, 1828] 12 p. NN.   34990

Remarks on the character and writings of John Milton. See Channing, William Ellery.

Remarks on the constitution of the Supreme and Circuit Courts of the state of New-York. New-York, Pr. by Edward Grattan, 1828. 36 p. MB; NIC; PPL; ScU.
34991
Remarks on the Farmington Canal, &c. By an original stockholder. The construction of canals is the proper work of the sovereign power, and should never be committed to private stock companies. New-Haven, 1828. 16 p. CtHT-W; CtHi.   34992

Remarks on the letter from a gentleman in Boston, to a Unitarian clergyman of that city. And the reply, and review of the same. 2d ed. Boston, J.Q. Adams, 1828. 21 p. CBPac; CtHC; MB; MBAU; MMeT; MWA; MiD-B; NNUT; RPB.   34993

Remarks on the Lord's prayer. See Worcester, Samuel.

Remarks on the two last reports of the land agent together with some particulars of his conduct while in office; addressed to the Governor, Council, and Legislature of the state of Maine. [Bangor? 1828] 13, [1] p. MH-BA.
34994

Remarks upon the auction system, as practised in New-York, to which are added numerous facts in illustration. By a plain practical man. New-York, 1828. 56 p. DLC; DeGE; ICU; KyU-L; MWA; MdHi; MiD-B; NCH; NN; NNC; NbU; Nh; OCHP; PHi; PPAmP; PPL; ScU; WHi; BrMus.
34995
Remarks upon the use of anthracite... See Vaux, James.

Reminiscences. See Armstrong, James L.

Renwick, James, 1790-1863
An account of some of the steam-boats navigating the Hudson River in the state of New York. In a letter from Mr. Renwick, Professor... in Columbia College, to Capt. Edward Sabine, R.A., Secretary of the Royal Society, [n.p. 1828?] 24 p. NN.
34996
Repertory, St. Albans, Vt.
Address of the carrier of The Repertory to its patrons. Jan. 1st, 1828. St. Albans, Vt., 1828. 1 p. DLC.   34997

Reply of a Unitarian clergyman to the "Letter of a gentleman in Boston." Boston, Wait, Greene & Co. & Bowles & Dearborn, Press of Isaac R. Butts & Co., 1828. (Attributed to Henry Ware Jr. by CBPac; to W.E. Channing by MB.) CSmH; CtY; ICMe; M; MHi; MMeT; MWA; PPL. 34998

---- 2d ed. Boston, Wait, Greene & co. [etc.] 1828. 23 p. CtHC; MB; MH; MiD; MiD-B; NNUT.
34999
---- 3d ed. Boston, Wait, Greene & co.; Isaac R. Butts and co., prs., 1828. 23 p. MB; NCH; NjR; PPPrHi.   35000

---- 4th ed. Boston, Wait, Greene & Co., 1828. 23 p.

CBPac; CtHC; MHi; OO; RPB; WHi. 35001

Report and observations, on the banks. See Buchanan, James.

Report of a committee of the citizens of Boston. See Boston. Citizens.

Report of a trial in the Supreme judicial court, holden at Boston, Dec. 16th and 17th, 1828, of Theodore Lyman, jr., for an alleged libel on Daniel Webster, a senator of the United States, published in the Jackson Republican, comprising all the documents and testimony given in the cause, and full notes of the arguments of counsel, and the charge of the court. Taken in short hand. By John W. Whitman. Boston, Pub. by Putnam and Hunt, 1828. 76 p. CSmH; DLC; MBC; MBS; MH-L; MWA; MdBB; MdHi; MiU; NIC; NN; Nh; NPV; NhHi; OCLaw; PHi; PPB; PPL; RPB; WHi; WaU; BrMus. 35002

The report of the committee appointed at a public meeting of the friends of education, held at the State house, in Trenton, on the night of the eleventh of November, 1828; exhibiting a succinct account of the state of common schools in New-Jersey. Derived from the reports of the central and sub-committees of several counties and townships in the state. Trenton, N. J., D. Fenton, 1828. 46 p. DLC; MHi; Nj; RPB. 35003

Report of the state convention held at the Capitol in the city of Albany. See National Republican Party. New York. 35004

Report of the trial of Friends, in the city of Philadelphia, June, 1828, before the Honourable Edward King, Esq. president judge of the court of common pleas, for the first judicial district of Pennsylvania; or The case of Edmund Shotwell, Joseph Lukins, Charles Middleton and two others, who had been, by the mayor of the City, committed to prison, whence they were brought up by Habeas Corpus, June 9th, 1828. Taken in short-hand by M. T. C. Gould, stenographer. Philadelphia, J. Harding, pr., 1828. 154 [1] p. CSmH; DLC; DeWI; MB; MH; MdBB; MiD; N-L; PHC; PHi; PP; PPB; PPL; PSC-Hi. 35005

Report of the trial of Friends at Steubenville, Ohio, from the 15th to the 26th of October, 1828, before the Hon. Jeremiah H. Hallock. ...By Marcus T. C. Gould, stenographer. Philadelphia, J. Harding, 1828. 340 p. PSC-Hi. 35006

Report, on the origin and increase of the Paterson manufactories. See Sullivan, John Langdon.

Report on the proposed canal. See Cruger, Alfred.

A report on the subject of connecting manual labour with study. See Philadelphia. Manual Labour Academy of Pennsylvania.

Report on the survey of a canal. See Howard, William.

Reports and proceedings of Col. McKenney. See United States. Reports and proceedings.

A representative of thousands. See A few reflections.

Republican, A.
 Commercial Gazette extra. Boston. For the Gazette. The

crisis No. 9. The proclamation. The meeting at Faneuil Hall, The American revolution. [Signed A republican] [Boston, 1828] 1 p. DLC.   35007

A republican farmer, pseud. See An address to the freemen of Rhode Island.

A republican of the Jefferson school, pseud. See A voice from the interior.

The republican sentiment of New-Hampshire, July 4, 1828; exhibited in her anniversary celebration. 31 p. DLC.   35008

Republican young men of the City of New York friendly to ... Jackson. See Democratic Party. New York.

Resolutions and addresses of the convention of delegates from the counties of New York. See National Republican Party. New York.

The resolutions of Virginia and Kentucky; penned by Madison and Jefferson, in relation to the Alien and sedition laws... Charleston, Repr. and sold by A. E. Miller, 1828. 68 p. DLC; PPAmP; ScC; ScU.   35009

Revelation of free masonry. See Convention of seceding masons.

Reverie, Reginald, pseud. See Mellen, Grenville.

A review and refutation. See Vindex, pseud.

Review of a late pamphlet. See Hamilton, pseud.

Review of a "Letter from a Gentleman" See Blanchard, Joshua P.

Review of a pamphlet called "A testimony." See Gibbons, William.

Review of a pamphlet, entitled "An epistle." See Truth, pseud.

Review of a pamphlet on the trust deed of the Hanover church. Boston, T. R. Marvin, pr. , 1828. 37 p. (Boston Athenaeum gives Beecher as author. Sabin gives Wisner.) CBPac; CSmH; Ct; CtHT-W; DLC; ICU; IEG; IU; M; MB; MBAt; MH; MWA; MeBaT; MeHi; MiD-B; N; NjR; PHi; PPL; PPPrHi; VtU; BrMus.   35010

A review of "An appeal to the Christian public from the unprovoked attacks of the Reverend George Duffield, against the Methodist Episcopal Church by A. G. ... Carlisle, Pa. , Pr. at the Herald Office, 1828. 26 p. DLC; MWA; MiU; NjR; PPPrHi.
                                    35011
Review of Johnson's English dictionary. See Pickering, John.

Review of "Notions of the Americans." See Carey, Mathew.

Review of Rev. Mr. Whitman's discourse on regeneration. Boston, Pierce and Williams, 1828. 20 p. CBPac; MBC; MeBaT; MiD-B; NH; BrMus.   35012

Review of the battle of the Horse Shoe, and of the facts relating to the killing of sixteen Indians, on the morning after the battle, by the orders of Gen. Andrew Jackson. [n. p. , 1828] 8 p. CSmH; DLC.   35013

Review of the report of a committee of the citizens of Boston and vicinity, opposed to a further increase to duties on importations. Philadelphia, Pr. by John Young, 1828. 87 p. DLC; DeGE;

ICJ; ICU; M; MBAt; MH; MHi;
MoSHi; Nh; OO; PHi; PPAmP;
PPL; PU; TKL.   35014

---- Another printing. Philadelphia, J. Young, 1828. 87 p. MH-
BA.   35015

Review of Webster's American
dictionary. From the North American Review vol. xxviii, -No.
lxiii. [New York, S. Converse,
1828] 47 p. NjR.   35016

The Revolutionary officers. See
Carey, Mathew.

Rhode Island
   At the General Assembly of
Rhode Island and Providence Plan-
tations, held at Providence, Janu-
ary 1828. 54, [2] p. CU; Ia;
MdBB; Mi.   35017

---- At the General Assembly of
Rhode Island and Providence
Plantations, held at Providence,
October, 1828. 72, [2] p. Ia;
MdBB; Mi.   35018

---- Debate on the bill establishing free schools, at the January
session of the Rhode Island Legislature, A.D. 1828. Reported for
the Rhode Island American. Providence, By F.Y. Carlile and Co.,
American Office, 1828. 24 p.
CSmH; RHi; RNHi; RP.   35019

---- Laws passed at the General
Assembly: May, 1828. [Provi-
dence? 1828] 63 p. Ia; Mi.
        35020
The Rhode-Island almanack for
1829. By Isaac Bickerstaff. Provi-
dence, H.H. Brown [1828] 12 l.
CLU; CU; DLC; ICN; InU; MB;
MWA; N; NHi; NcD; NjR; PHi;
RHi; RPB; WHi.   35021

No entry.   35022

The Rhode-Island register and
United States calendar for 1829.
Providence, H.H. Brown [1828]
48 l. InU; MWA; NN; RHi; RP;
RPB.   35023

Rhode Island Sunday School Union
   Third annual report of the
board of managers of the R.I.
Sunday School Union, read at the
annual meeting of the association
in Providence, April 2, 1828.
Providence, Francis Y. Carlile
& Co., prs., 1828. 21 p. RHi;
RP.   35024

Rice, D.
   The mirror, reflecting the
light of truth on the subject of
manufactures; in which will be
seen the impolicy and injustice of
increasing the present tariff of
duties on woollens, and the great
and growing evils which will nec-
essarily result from a too extended manufacturing system.
Part 1. Boston, Samuel G. Andrews, pr., 1828. 16 p. MWA.
        35025
Rice, John Holt, 1777-1831
   Correspondence between the
Rev. John H. Rice, D.D. and
James M. Garnett, Esq., on the
subject of the tendency of Episcopal principles. [Richmond, Pr.
by John Warrock, 1828?] 16 p.
Vi.   35026

---- The power of truth and love.
A sermon preached at Philadelphia, Oct. 1, 1828, at the nineteenth annual meeting of the
American Board of Commissioners for Foreign Missions. Boston, Pr. by Crocker & Brewster,
1828. 28 p. CLU; ICU; IaDuU;
MB; MBAt; MBC; MWA; MeBaT;

NCH; NN; PHi; PLT; PPPrHI; RPB; Vi; VtMiM; BrMus. 35027

Rice, Roswell, b 1803
Mental vision on the ruins of the fall; the atonement of Christ; the general resurrection, and final judgment. With the addition of some poetry on religious subjects. 1st ed. Bennington, Pr. for the Proprietor, 1828. 249, [3] p. NSyU; OClWHi; Vt; VtU. 35028

Richard, Gaspard
A petition and memorial, addressed to the honourable Legislature of the state of New York, and to the congress of the United States. The plan and invention of Gaspard Richard. New York, Pr. for the author, 1828. 20, 24 p. DLC. 35029

[Richards, John]
Memoir of Samuel Hooker Cowles. [From the Christian Spectator] New Haven, Pr. by Durrie, Peck & Co., [1828] 16 p. CtY. 35030

Richardson, Joseph, 1778-1871
Calumny refuted. The unexpected and very singular attack upon Mr. Richardson, the candidate for congress from Plymouth District, which appeared in the Massachusetts Journal of Tuesday has been promptly met and we trust will be effectually put down by the following letter from Mr. R. to D. L. Child, Esq. the editor of the Journal... Hingham, 1828. 1 folded page. DLC. 35031

---- An oration, delivered in the South parish, in Weymouth, July 4, 1828. Being the fifty-second anniversary of American independence. Pub. by request of the Committee of arrangements. Hingham, Press of Farmer and Brown, 1828. 23 p. CSmH; DLC; MH; MdBP. 35032

---- Sermon on conversion delivered to the First Parish in Hingham, Lord's Day, July 20, 1828. Hingham, Caleb Gill, Jr., Boston, Bowles & Dearborn, 1828. 35 p. CSmH. 35032a

Richardson, Josiah
The New England farrier and family physician... comp. by Josiah Richardson. Exeter, Josiah Richardson, 1828. 444, 24 p. CSmH; DNLM; MBCo; MWA; MeU (468, 24 p.); NhD; NhHi. 35033

Richmond, Legh, 1772-1827
Annals of the poor, Narratives of the dairyman's daughter, The negro servant, and The young cottager, by Rev. Legh Richmond, M. A. New York, the American Tract Society. Boston [1828] 320 p. Ct. 35034

---- La hija del lechers... [Nueva York. Sociedad Americana de tratados. 1828] 28 p. MB. 35035

---- Das Milchmädchen... [Neu-York. Amerikanische Tract-Gesellschaft, 1828] 32 p. MB. 35036

---- The Rev. Legh Richmond's counsels to his children: selected from his Memoir and 'Domestic portraiture," with an account of the closing scene of his life written by his daughter. New York, American Tract Society, [1828?] 201, 3 p. MdBE. 35037

Richmond and Manchester Colonization Society.
Fifth annual meeting of the Richmond and Manchester Colonization Society [Held Dec. 17, 1827] [Richmond, 1828?] 15 p. Vi. 35038

Rickman, Joseph, d 1810
Religious & moral poems. Philadelphia, Pr. for the proprietor, 1828. 34 p. DLC; PHC;

PHi; PSC-Hi; BrMus.   35039

[Rickman, William]
Friends' asylum, 1st day morning, 10th Mo. 7, 1827. To the members of the Society of Friends ... residing in... Cecil County, Maryland. [Baltimore, 10th mo. 1828] 18 p. PPL.   35040

Rickman, William
Observations on insanity, education, and presumed improvements on Robert Owen's System of mutual co-operation. Philadelphia, Pr. for the Author, 1828. 16+ p. MBAt; PHC; PHi (imp.); PSC-Hi.   35041

The right aim. See Davenport, Rufus.

The right of Universalists to testify in a court of justice vindicated. By a member of the bar. Boston, Bowles & Dearborn, 1828. 28 p. CtHT-W; MWA; RHi; RPB.   35042

Ripley, Henry Jones, 1798-1875
Characteristics of the minister's work; A sermon preached October 22, 1828, at the ordination of Mr. Calvin Newton as pastor of the Baptist Church and Society in Bellingham, Mass. Boston, Collier, pr., 1828. 11 p. MB; MBC; MW; MWA; OO; RPB.   35043

Ripley, Thomas B.
Christian deportment. A discourse addressed to the Baptist Church in Portland, Lord's-day, March 30, 1828. Boston, Lincoln & Edmands [1828] 25 p. Ct; MWA; WHi.   35044

Rishel, Jonas
The Indian physician, containing a new system of practice, founded on medical plants.... Together with a description of their properties, localities and method of using, and preparing

them... New Berlin, Penn., Pr. for the author and proprietor, by Jos. Miller, 1828. xii, 132 p. ICJ; ICN; IEN-M.   35045

Ritchie, William
A sermon, preached at the dedication of the Congregational Church at the Upper Falls, Newton, 1828. Dedham, By H. & W. H. Mann, 1828. 19 p. CtHT-W; MBD.   35046

[Rives, Judith Page Walker] 1802-1882
Mutius: an historical sketch of the fourth century... by a lady of Virginia. Written for the American Sunday School Union. Philadelphia, American Sunday School Union, 1828. 180 p. ICU (attribution made by OHi for 1829 ed.)   35047

Rives, William Cabell
Speech of Mr. Rives, of Virginia, on retrenchment and reform: delivered in the House of Representatives of the United States on the 5th February, 1828. Washington, Pr. by Green and Jarvis, 1828. 21 p. DLC; ICN; InHi; MWA; NcD; PPL.   35048

The robber's daughter. Portland, by Shirley & Hyde, 1828. 24 p. DLC.   35049

Robbins, Archibald, 1792-1865
A journal, comprising an account of the loss of the Brig Commerce, of Hartford (Con.) James Riley, Master, upon the Western coast of Africa, August 28, 1815 ... 20th ed. Hartford, Pub. by Silas Andrus, 1828. 275 p. CSmH.   35050

[Robbins, Eliza] comp.
Poetry for schools designed for reading and recitation. The whole selected from the best poets in the English language by

the author of American popular lessons. New York, Pub. by White, Gallaher & White. Elliot & Palmer, prs., 1828. 396 p. CoGrS; MBAt; MH; MWHi; NH.
35051

[----] Primary dictionary, or, Rational vocabulary... 3d ed., stereotyped. By the author of American popular lessons. New-York, Pub. by R. Lockwood, at his school book depository [1828] 5, 257 p. IEG; MHi; NNC.
35052

Robbins, Thomas
Century sermon, delivered at Danbury January 1, A. D. 1801. Being the first day of the nineteenth century, since the Christian aera. In which is exhibited a brief view of the most remarkable events of the eighteenth century: with a sketch of the town of Danbury, from the first settlement, to the present time... Danbury, Pr. and sold by Nichols & Rowe. Danbury, Repr. and sold by O. Osborn, Feb. 1828. 22, [1] p. CtHT-W; CtHi; CtSoP; OClWHi.
35053

Robert Woodward. See Dix, Dorothea Lynde.

Roberts, Nathan S.
Reports relative to the Chenango Canal, by N. S. Roberts & H. Hutchinson, Civil engineers. Made to the Senate, April 7th, 1828. Albany, Pr. by Croswell and Van Benthuysen, 1828. 38 p. NN.
35054

Roberts, Robert
The house servant's directory. Or, A monitor for private families: comprising hints on the arrangement and performance of servants' work... 2d ed. Boston, Munroe and Francis; New York, C. S. Francis, 1828. 180 p. CtHT-W; DLC; MBAt; MH; OCX; PPL.
35055

Roberts, William L.
Submission to "The powers that be," scripturally illustrated: a discourse in three parts. Rochester, Pr. for the author by E. Peck & Co., 1828. 139 p. NNUT; NcMHi.
35056

Robertson, Archibald
Conversations on anatomy, physiology, and surgery. Philadelphia, Towar & Hogan, publishers, 1828. 2 vols. CSt-L; GU-M; MBCo; MW; MeB; MiDW-M; MoKJM; NNNAM; NRAM; OC; OCG; PPC.
35057

Robertson, William, 1721-1793
Harper's edition, with copperplate engravings. The history of the discovery and settlement of America... With an account of his life and writings. New York, Pr. by J. & J. Harper; sold by E. Duyckinck, [etc.] 1828. xxxii, 539 p. CSt; DLC (lists a copy [variant?] with imprint, Pr. by J. & J. Harper]; KyLoF; LNHT; MoS; NNG; NbOP; PP; RHi; Wv.
35058

Robin Hood
The extraordinary life and adventures of Robin Hood, captain of the robbers of Sherwood Forest. Interspersed with the History of Little John and his Merry Men All. New York, Pub. by S. King, 1828. 15 l. PP.
35059

Robinson, Isaac, 1780-1854
A brief examination of Rev. Mr. Sullivan's reply to the review of his remarks upon a sermon, illustrating the human and official inferiority and supreme divinity of Christ. Keene, N. H., Pr. by John Prentiss, 1828. 24 p. CSmH; MH; Nh; BrMus.
35060

Roche, Mrs. Regina Maria (Dalton), 1764?-1845
The children of the abbey. A tale... Exeter [N. H.] J. & B.

Williams, 1828. 3 v. CtHT; NNF;
ViLRM.   35061

---- Contrast... New York, Pr.
by J. & J. Harper, 1828. 2 vols.
DLC; NCaS; NcU; PU.   35062

Rochester. African Church
Report of the trustees...[cut]
...with an address to the publick.
Rochester, N.Y., Marshall &
Dean, 1828. 12 p. NRHi.   35063

Rochester Daily Advertiser-Extra.
See Another humbug!

Rochester in 1827. See Ely,
Elisha.

Rogers, Isaac
On cultivating a spirit of universal peace. A sermon delivered
before the Peace Society of
Temple, in the Methodist meeting-house, on Tuesday Oct. 28,
1828. it being the anniversary of
said society. Portland, Shirley
and Hyde, prs., 1828. 19 p.
DLC; MH-AH; MeB.   35064

Rogers, J.
A discourse delivered on the
4th of July, 1828, in Carlisle,
Ky. on the subject of civil & re-
ligious liberty, by J. Rogers,
(pastor of a Christian Church in
Carlisle). N. L. Finnell, pr.,
Georgetown, Ky., 1828. 36 p.
ICMcC.   35065

Rollin, Charles, 1661-1741
The ancient history of the
Egyptians, Carthaginians, As-
syrians, Babylonians, Medes and
Persians, Macedonians and Gre-
cians. Trans. from the French
...From the latest London ed.,
carefully rev. and cor. New-
York, G. Long, pr. and pub.,
1828. 4 v. CBPac; CSt; CtMW;
In; KyHi; LN; MB; MDeeP; MWA;
MiU; MoSF; NN; NjR; OClW;
PHC; RP; ScCliJ; ViU; WMC;

WaPS; WvC.   35066

---- The ancient history of the
Greeks...New York, Geo. Long,
1828. 4 v. MWA; NN.   35067

Roorbach, Orville Augustus,
1803-1861
A catalogue of historical, scientific, law, medical, chemical,
biographical, theological, juvenile, novels, school, classical,
and miscellaneous books, for
sale at O. A. Roorbach's ...sign
of the Bible...November 15th,
1828. Charleston. 43 p. ScU.
                         35068
[Root, David]
A discourse delivered in the
Second Presbyterian Church, Cincinnati, Aug. 31, 1828. Occasioned by the death of Robert
Wallace, senior and pub. by request of friends...Cincinnati,
Pr. by S. J. Browne, 1828. 12 p.
OCHP; OClWHi.   35069

The roue. See Beazley, Samuel.

Rowe, Elizabeth
Devout exercises of the heart,
in meditation and soliloquy,
prayer and praise. By the late
pious and ingenious Mrs. Elizabeth Rowe. New York, Pub. by
N. Bangs and J. Emory, for the
Methodist Episcopal Church, at
the Conference Office. A.Hoyt,
pr., 1828. 147 p. OBerB.
                         35070
Rowlandson, Mrs. Mary (White)
fl. 1682
Narrative of the captivity and
removes of Mrs. Mary Rowlandson, who was taken by the Indians at the destruction of Lancaster, in 1676. Written by herself. 5th ed. Lancaster [Mass.]
Pub. by Carter, Andrews, and
co., 1828. xii, 81 p. CSmH.
                         35071
---- ---- 6th ed., 2d Lancaster
ed. Lancaster [Mass.] Carter,

Andrews, and co., 1828. 100 p.
CSmH; DLC.   35072

Rowson, Susanna (Haswell) 1762-
1824
    Charlotte Temple, a tale of
truth. Hartford, S. Andrus, 1828.
138 p. CtY; MWA; MWH; NN; OU.
                              35073
---- Charlotte's daughter; or,
The three orphans. A sequel to
Charlotte Temple... To which is
prefixed, a memoir of the author.
Boston, Richardson & Lord,
1828. 184 p.   CSmH; CtHT-W;
DLC; ICU; MB; MBAt; MH; MWA;
MeU; MnU; NcD; PU; RPB.
                              35074
Royall, Mrs. Anne (Newport)
1769-1854
    The black book; or, A continu-
ation of travels in the United
States... Washington City, Pr. for
the author, 1828. 2 vols. CtMW;
CtY; DGU; DLC; ICN; MB; MH;
MWA; MdBP; NNC; NjP; OMC;
PHi; PPL; RPB; ViU; WHi.
                              35075
---- ---- Another ed. Washing-
ton City, Pr. for the author,
1828. Has "Note" at bottom of
index in vol. I. PPL.   35076

The ruinous tendency of auction-
eering, and the necessity of restraining it for the benefit of
trade, demonstrated in a letter
to the Right Hon. Lord Bathurst,
president of the board of trade.
Pub. in London, repub. in New-
York, 1828. 23 p. MH; MWA;
NNC; NT; NbU; Nh; PPL. 35077

Rules and regulations of medical
practice, adopted by the physicians of Portland, [Maine], Nov.
19, 1828. Portland, Day &
Fraser, 1828, 12 p. NNNAM.
                              35078
Rules of pronunciation, in reading Latin. See Andrews, Ethan
Allen.

[Rush, Richard] 1780-1859
    John Randolph, abroad and at
home. Being the only accurate
delineation ever published of that
distinguished orator. Philadelphia, Pr. for the purchaser,
1828. [Signed: Julius] CtY; DLC;
MB; PPAmP; PPL.   35079
[----] ---- By Julius [pseud.]
Washington, Pr. by Peter Force,
1828. 29 p. DLC; MB; MH; NjR;
OO; PPL; RPB; Vi; BrMus.
                              35080
[Rush, Richard]
    Sketch of the character of Mr.
Canning. From the National Intelligencer of Sept. 15, 1827.
Washington, Pr. by Gales & Seaton, 1828. 22 p. DLC; MB; MHi;
PHi; PPAmP.   35081

Russell, John B.
    Catalogue of kitchen garden,
herb, tree, field and flower
seeds... for sale at the seed store
connected with The New England
Farmer... Boston, by John Russell... 2d ed. Boston, Pr. at the
New England Farmer Office,
1828. 47, [1] p. PPL; BrMus.
                              35082
Ruter, Martin, 1785-1838
    The juvenile arithmetick and
scholar's guide; wherein theory
and practice are combined... Cincinnati, Pub. and sold by N. &
G. Guilford. W. M. and O. Farnsworth, Jr., prs., 1828. 166,
[2] p. KU; MH; OCHP.   35083

Rutgers College
    The statutes of Rutgers Col-
lege, in the city of New-Brunswick, N.J. March, 1828. Rutgers Press. Pr. by Terhune &
Letson, New-Brunswick, 1828.
15 p. DLC; MBC; PPPrHi.
                              35084
Rutgers Medical College, New
York. See Geneva College. Rutgers Medical Faculty.

Ruth Lee. See Bloomfield, Robert.

Rutledge, Edward, 1798-1832
The family altar; consisting of prayers for family worship, and for the sick and the mourner... New Haven, Pub. by A. H. Maltby [Durrie, Peck & Co., prs.] 1828. 300 p. Ct; CtHT-W; ICU; MBD; PPA; PU. 35085

Ryan, James
The differential and integral calculus... New York, White, Gallaher and White, W. E. Dean, pr., 1828. viii, 328 p. DLC; DeGE; GU; InCW; InTR; KyLxT; LU; MH; NBuG; NN; NjP; OClW; PSC. 35086

---- The mathematical diary, containing new researches and improvements in the mathematics; with collections of questions, proposed and resolved by ingenious correspondents. New York, James Ryan, 1828. 1 p. l., [43]-144 p. MdBJ; NIC; PPAmP. 35087

S

The Sabbath school directory. Containing instructions for the formation and management of Sabbath schools. Middlebury, Pub. by the Vermont Sabbath School Union; pr. by Ovid Miner, 1828. 24 p. MiD-B; NNC-T. 35088

Sabina ó Los Grandes sin disfraz. Por el autor del evangelio en triunfo. Nueva York, En casa de Lanuza, Mendia YC. impresores liberos, 1828. 96, 80 p. InGrD. 35089

Sabine, James
The glory of the latter house. A sermon, on the dedication of the First Presbyterian Church, in the city of Boston. Delivered January 31, 1828. Boston, Pub. by request of the Congregation, 1828. 20 p. CtSoP; DLC; ICN; MB; MBC; MH; MHi; MWA; NN; OOC; PHi; PPL; RPB; BrMus. 35089a

Sacerdos, pseud. See Letter to a convert.

Sacred poetry... Selected and prepared by the committee of publication of the American Sunday School Union. Philadelphia, Pub. by The American Sunday School Union, 1828. 180 p. ICT; MeBaT; NN; NNUT; PPAmS; BrMus. 35090

Sad tales. See Mellen, Grenville.

The sagacity of dogs. Boston, Marsh and Capen... Press of Putnam & Hunt, 1828. 18 p. NN. 35090a

[St. John, Samuel]
American taxation. The Primrose Hill. Hudson, Ashbel Stoddard, 1828. 8 p. RPB. 35091

St. Lawrence County--County Corresponding Committee. See National Republican Party. New York.

St. Louis
The acts of assembly, incorporating the city of St. Louis, and the ordinances of the city, which are now in force. Revised and pub. by order of the Mayor and Board of Aldermen. 1828. St. Louis, Pr. by Orr and Keemle. 1828. 143, xix p. MH-L. 35091a

Saint-Pierre, Jacques Henri Bernardin de, 1737-1814
Adventures, love and constancy of Paul and Virginia, who were reared in the sequestered valley of Port Louis, in the Isle of France, the history of their rural life and friendship; Vir-

ginia's compulsive visit to her aunt beyond the sea; her return and the miraculous preservation from a watery grave through the extraordinary exertions of Paul. New York, S. King, 1828. 32 p. NPV.   35092

[Saint-Real, César Vichard de] 1639-1692
Conspiracy of the Spaniards against Venice and of John Lewis Fiesco against Genoa. Boston, Hilliard, Gray, Little, & Wilkins, 1828. 171 p. CU; DLC; IEG; MB; MeB; NhHi; OC; OClWHi.   35092a

Salathiel. See Croly, George.

Salazar, José Maria, 1785-1828
Observaciones sobre las Reformas Politicas de Colombia. Filadelfia, Imprinta de Guillelmo Stavely, 1828. 54 p. MHi; MWA; PPL; ScU.   35093

---- Observations on the political reforms of Colombia... Trans. from the manuscript, by Edward Barry. Philadelphia, Pr. by Wm. Stavely, 1828. 47 p. DLC; MB; MHi; PHi; PPAmP; ScU; TxU.
                                 35093a
Salem, Mass. North Church.
Two-hundredth anniversary of the first settlement of Salem. Order of exercises at the North church. [Salem] Foote & Brown, prs. [1828] Bdsd. CSmH.   35094

Sales, Francis, 1771-1834, compiler
Seleccion de obras maestras dramatics. Por Calderon de la Barca, Lope de Vega, y Moreto... Por F. Sales... Boston, de la imprenta de Munroe y Francis, 1828. [4], 255 p. CLCM; IEN; MB; MWA; MdW; NIC.   35095

Sampson, Ezra, 1749-1823

Remarks on troubles of our own making and on habitual discontent, arising from imaginery wants. From "The brief remarker on the ways of man," New York, 1828. MH (missing 1970)
                                 35096
Sanborn, Reuben
Freemasonry, a covenant with death: a discourse, delivered at a public meeting in Hornby, Steuben County, June 3, 1828... Bath, N.Y., Pr. by D. Ramsey, 1828. 11 p. DLC; IaCrM; MW; NN; OClW.   35097

[Sanders, Daniel Clarke] 1768-1850
A history of the Indian wars with the first settlers of the United States, to the commencement of the late war; together with an appendix, not before added to this history, containing interesting accounts of the battles fought by Gen. Andrew Jackson... Rochester, N.Y., Pr. by E. Scrantom, 1828. 196 (i.e. 192) p. CLU; CSmH; DLC; ICN; KHi; MH; MHi; MdBE; MiU-C; NN; PPi; T; WHi.   35098

[Sanderson, John] 1783-1844, ed.
Biography of the signers to the Declaration of independence. 2d ed. Revised, improved, and enl. Philadelphia, Wm. Brown, and Charles Peters, 1828. [W. Brown, pr.] CLU; CSmH; CtB; DLC; DeGE; GEU; GU; ICU; IaDu; InU; KyBgW; KyHi; LNHT; MB; MHi; MdBC; MiD-B; MoSU; MsJMC; NBu; NCH; NNC; NRU; NcG; NjP; OCHP; OClWHi; PHC; PP; PPL; PSC; PU; RP; ScU; TNJ; Vi; WHi; BrMus.   35099

Sandford, Peter P.
Help to faith; or, A summary of the evidences of the genuineness, authenticity, credibility, and divine authority of the Holy Scriptures... New-York, Pr. by

J. & J. Harper, 1828. 270 p.
ArCH; CtHT; CtMW; DLC;
ICMcC; IEG; NCH; NSyU; OO.
35100

[Sanford, Ezekiel] 1796-1822
The humours of Eutopia: A
tale of colonial times. By an
Eutopian. . . Philadelphia, Carey,
Lea & Carey, 1828. 2 v. CSmH;
CtY; DLC; IObB; MB; MBAt; MH;
NIC; NRU; PPAmP; PU; RPB.
35101

Sasse, Bernhard Henrich, fl.
1775
Geistliche Lieder. . . Erste und
zweyte Sammlung. Minden, gedruckt, 1781, und nachgedruckt
bey Heinrich Ruby in Chambersburg. Chambersburg, Pa., H.
Ruby, 1828. 156 p. PHuJ; PPL.
35102

Savannah Republican, Savannah,
Ga.
Address of the carriers of the
Savannah Republican to its pa-
trons on the commencement of
the new-year, 1828. Savannah,
January 1, 1828. 1 p. DLC.
35103

Say, Thomas, 1787-1835
American entomology, or de-
scription of the insects of North
America. Philadelphia Museum.
Pub. by Samuel Augustus Mitch-
ell. For sale by Anthony Finley.
Wm. Brown, pr., 1828. vol. III.
Plates 37-54. PPL.   35104

[Scargill, William Pitt] 1787-1836
Blue-stocking Hall. . . New-
York, Pr. by J. & J. Harper,
for Collins & Hannay; [etc.,
etc.] 1828. 2 v. DLC; LU; MB;
MdBP; NGH; NjR.   35105

Schenck, Abraham H.
A reply of Abraham H.
Schenck, in vindication of his
character against the slanderous
charges made on the floor of
Congress, by Churchill C. Cambreleng, a member from the city
of New-York, as published in the

Evening Post, 9th May, 1828.
[New York] October, 1828. 9
p. MB; NN; PHi.   35106

Schiller, Johann Christopher
Frederich von, 1759-1805
The robbers: a tragedy in five
acts from the German of Fred-
erich Schiller. . . Baltimore, J.
Robinson, 1828. 60 p. CU; ICU;
MH.   35107

Der Schlüssel zur Offenbahrung
von Jesus Christus selbst aufge-
schlossen und entsiegelt. Philadelphia, d. 12 August 1825.
Laodiceae [i. e. Philadelphia]
gedruckt im Jahr Christi, 1828.
54 p. PLT; PPG.   35108

Scholar's guide to chirography,
containing writing-book, copies,
rules and general directions to
the art. By a teacher. Portsmouth, Pub. by Childs & March,
1828. No. 4. NhHi.   35109

The school of good manners.
Providence, 1828. 22 p. RPB.
35110

Schrevel, Cornelis, 1608-1664
Cornelii Schrevelii Lexicon
Manuale Graeco-Latinum et La-
tino-Graecum: Studio Atque Opera
Jospehi Hill, Joannis Entrick,
Gulielmi Bowyer, nec non Jacobi
Smith, S. T. P. Adactum. Insuper
quaque, ad calcem adjectae sunt
Sententiae Graeco-Latinae, Quibus
Omnia Graecae Linguae Primi-
tiva Comprehenduntur: item Trac-
tatus Duo, alter de Resolutione
Verborum, de Articulis alter ut-
erque perutilis, et aeque desi-
deratus. Hanc Editionem xxii
Curvait et auctiorem fecit Petrus
Steele, A. M. Editio Haec Ameri-
cana, cum nitida illa (xxii) edi-
nensi nuperrima, accurate Com-
parata et emendata. New York,
Stereotyped by Hammond Wallis.
Pub. by Collins and Hannay, 1828.
531, 122 p. CoPu.   35110a

Schroeder, John Frederick, 1800-1857
    Death, judgment, and eternity:
A sermon for children, preached
in St. Paul's Chapel, in the city
of New York, on Wednesday, April 9th, 1828, being the eleventh
anniversary, of the New York
Protestant Episcopal Sunday
School Society. New York, E.
Bliss, 1828. MH; NGH; NNG;
PPPrHi; RPB; BrMus.   35111

---- The intellectual and moral
resources of horticulture. An
anniversary discourse, pronounced before the New-York
Horticultural Society... August
26, 1828... New-York, Pub. at
the request of the society [E.
Conrad, pr.] 1828. 40 p. CtHT;
DLC; MB; MBHo; MH; MdBP;
NNC; NNG; NNNAM; NjP; NjR;
PHi; PPAmP; PPL; PPPrHi;
RPB; BrMus.   35112

Der Schulpsalter. Vierte Auflage.
Reading, Pr. by Johann Ritter u.
Comp., 1828. Seidensticker p.
239.   35113

Schuylkill Navigation Co.
    Report of the president and
managers... to the stockholders.
Jan. 7, 1828. [Philadelphia] Pr.
by Lydia R. Bailey, 1828. 9 p.
IU; PHi.   35114

[Scott, Lady Caroline Lucy]
    A marrige in high life. Edited by the authoress of "Flirtation!" Philadelphia, Carey, Lea,
and Carey, 1828. 252 p. MdBP.
                          35115
Scott, John
    The life of the Rev. Thomas
Scott, D.D. Rector of Ashton
Sandford, Bucks: Including a narrative drawn up by himself, and
copius extracts of his letters...
By John Scott... New York,
White, Gallaher & White, [Sleight

& George, prs., Jamaica, L.I.]
1828. 418 p. DLC; IEdS; MB;
NNUT; RPA; WHi.   35116

Scott, Sir Walter, 1771-1832
    The beauties of Sir Walter
Scott, and Thomas Moore, Esq.;
selected from their works; with
historical and explanatory notes.
10th ed. Philadelphia, 1828. [5],
[3], 1-204 p. CSmH; DLC;
PU.   35117

[----] Beauties of the Waverley
novels. Boston, Pub. by Samuel
G. Goodrich, 1828. 456 p. CSmH;
DLC; MdHi; MeB; NN; OClW.
                          35118
[----] Chronicles of the Canongate. Second series. New York,
Pr. by J. & J. Harper, 1828.
2 vols. MFiHi; NIC; NN; NjR;
OM; PPL.   35119

[----] ---- Philadelphia, Carey,
Lea, and Carey, 1828. 2 vols.
MWA; NCH; PPL; RPB; ViU;
WU.   35120

[----] The life of Napoleon Buonaparte, emperor of the French.
With a preliminary view of the
French revolution. By the author
of "Waverley," In three volumes.
New-York, Pr. and pub. by J.
& J. Harper, 1828. 3 vols. ANA;
CtHC; IG; IJI; IaU; GHi; KyBgW;
KyHe; MBev; MeB; MoSU;
NBLiHi; NBuU; NN; RPA; ViAl.
                          35121
[----] ---- Exeter [N.H.] J. &
B. Williams, 1828. 2 v. CtMW;
GEU; ICU; MB; MDeeP; MWH;
NT; OClW; OO; PLT; PPLT;
ViU.   35122

---- The poetical works of Sir
Walter Scott. In VII volumes.
Boston, Pub. by Timothy Bedlington, 1828. 7 vols. CSmH;
DLC; KU; KyLoP; KyU; MB;
ScCM.   35123

[----] Religious discourses. By a Layman. New York, J. & J. Harper, Sold by Collins & Hannay, [etc.] 1828. 48 p. DLC; GDC; MB; MBC; MH-AH; MMeT-Hi; MdBJ; MeBaT; MiDSH; MoKU; NCH; NN; NRAB; NcU; OO; RP.
35124

[----] ---- Philadelphia, Carey, Lea and Carey, Sold in New York by G. and C. Carvill - in Boston by Munroe and Francis, 1828. 79 p. DLC; GHi; LU; MB; MH; NIC; NNS; PPL.   35125

[----] Tales of a grandfather, being stories taken from Scottish history. Boston, Hiram Tupper, pr., 1828. 2 vols. PPL.   35126

[----] ---- New-York, Pub. by William Burgess, jun., 1828. 2 v. CtHT; GDC; IaDmD; MdBL; NBuU; NN; NjP; PPL.   35127

[----] ---- Philadelphia, Carey, Lea & Carey, 1828. 2 vols. DLC; GHi; LN; MBAt; MW; MWi; NCH; NIC; Nh; OClWHi; PHi; PPL; PU.   35128

The Scottish exiles. See Chapman, Ernestine.

The Scottish orphans. See Stoddart, Isabella.

Scribe, Augustin Eugène, 1791-1861
    Neal & Mackenzie. No. 201 Chestnut Street, between the Theatre & Arcade. Philadelphia. La Charlatanisme, comedie-vaudeville en un acte. Par Scribe. [Philadelphia, 1828] 24 p. (Also issued with covering title: Collection d'operas et vaudevilles...) ICU; PPL.   35129

---- ---- Le coiffeur et le perruquier, vaudeville en un acte, par Mm. Scribe, Mazere, et St. Laurent. [Philadelphia, 1828] 18

p. (Also issued in vol. with covering title. Collection d'operas et vaudevilles). ICU; PPL.
35130

---- ---- Le secretaire et le cuisinier; comedie-vaudeville en une acte, par Mm. Eugene Scribe et Melesville. [Philadelphia, 1828] 20 p. (Also issued with covering title: Collection d'operas et vaudevilles.) ICU; PPL.
35131

---- ---- La somnambule, comedie-vaudeville en deux actes. Par Mm. Eugene Scribe et G. Delavigne. [Philadelphia, 1828] 23 p. (Also issued in vol. with covering title: Collection d'operas & vaudevilles.) ICU; PPL.
35132

---- ---- Une visite a bedlam. Comedie en un acte. Par Mm. Scribe et Delestre-Poirson. [Philadelphia, 1828] 18 p. (Also issued in vol. with covering title: Collection d'operas et vaudevilles...) ICU; PPL.
35133

Scripture history, abridged, In which it is designed to give children such a taste of the writings of the inspired penmen, as may engage them diligently to study the sacred scriptures. Waterville, Pub. and sold by Wm. Hastings, 1828. 54 p. DLC; NN; PP.   35134

Scripture parables. See American Tract Society. N. Y.

Seabrook, Whitemarsh Benjamin, 1795-1855
    An address delivered at the first anniversary meeting of the United Agricultural Society of South Carolina, in the hall of representatives at Columbia on 6th Dec., 1827. Pub. at the request of the society. Charleston, A. E. Miller, 1828. 40 p. CLU; CtY; MH; NcU; PPAmP; RPB; ScC; ViU.   35135

Seaman's Friend Society of the
City of Boston
   Address of the directors... to
the Christian public. [Boston,
Oct. 12, 1828] 12 p. MB; MBAt;
MHi; NjR; PPL.   35136

Searle, Moses Colman
   On slander. A sermon,
preached in Grafton, September
9, 1827, and also in Westborough,
Oct. 7, 1827... Pr. by request of
committees from churches in
Westborough and Grafton. Worcester, Wm. Manning, pr., 1828. 16
p. CBPac; MB; MBC; MWA;
MWHi; MWo.   35137

Sears, James H.
   A standard spelling book; or,
The scholar's guide to an accurate pronunciation of the English
language: accompanied with easy,
familiar and progressive reading
lessons. Designed as an introduction to the use of Walker's critical pronouncing dictionary of the
English language. The revised ed.
Bridgeport [Conn.], Pub. by J.
B. & L. Baldwin, 1828. 144 p.
CSmH.   35138

---- A standard spelling book;
or, The scholar's guide to an
[accurate] pronunciation of the
English language: ... Compiled
for the use of schools. Rev. ed.
Providence, Pub. by Hutchens
and Cory, 1828. 144 p. RHi.
                              35139

Secondary lessons. See Willard,
Samuel.

[Sedgwick, Catharine Maria] 1789-
1867
   ...A short essay to do good.
By the author of Redwood. Repub-
lished from the Christian teacher's
manual. Stockbridge, Pr. by
Webster and Stanley, 1828. 24 p.
N.   35140

[Sedgwick, Elizabeth Buckminster (Dwight)] 1791-1864
   The beatitudes. Boston, Bowles
and Dearborn, Press of Isaac R.
Butts and Co., 1828. 144 p.
([Original moral tales, v. 6, no.
5]). MB; PMA.   35141

   Select anecdotes of animals; accompanied with descriptions and
engravings, intended for the instruction and amusement of young
persons. By the author of "Evenings in Boston." Boston, Bowles
& Dearborn, Press of Isaac R.
Butts and Co., 1828. 227, [1] p.
KU; MH-Z; MNBedf.   35142

   Select poems for small children,
embellished with cuts. Portland,
Me., Shirley & Hyde, 1828. 18
p. CtNwchA.   35143

Selection for the musica sacra.
See Hastings, Thomas.

A selection of hymns and psalms.
See Dabney, Jonathan Peele.

Sellon, John
   A series of sermons, on the
doctrine of everlasting punish-
ment, as revealed in the Holy
Scriptures. Canandaigua, Pr. by
Morse & Willson, 1828. 106 p.
NBuG; NCanHi; NN; NNUT; NRHi;
PPL.   35144

A sentimental journey through
France and Italy. See Sterne,
Laurence.

Sequel to Marrion Wilder. See
Dix, Dorothea Lynde.

Sergeant, John, 1779-1852
   An address delivered before
the citizens of Philadelphia, at
the House of Refuge, on Saturday, the twenty-ninth of November, 1828. Pub. by order of the
Board of managers. Philadelphia,
Jesper Harding, pr., 1828. 56 p.

DLC; ICN; KyLx; MB; MBC; MH;
MdHi; MiD-B; MnHi; NN; NjP;
NjR; OClW; PHC; PHi; PPAmP;
PPL; PPPrHi; RPB; ViL; BrMus.
                                35145
---- Observations and reflections
on the design and effects of punishment...in letters, addressed
to Roberts Vaux...Also, the
opinion of the keepers of the
penitentiary and Bridewell at
Philadelphia, on the separate confinement of criminals. [Philadel-
phia] Jesper Harding, pr., 1828.
10 p. DLC; DNLM; GDC; MB;
MWA; NjP; P; PPL; PU; PPPrHi;
RPB.   35146

---- Remarks of Mr. Sergeant,
of Penn., House of Representatives. --Feb. 2, 1828. [Washing-
ton? 1828?] 24 p. ICU; MH-BA;
MWA.   35147

A series of questions. See Judson, Albert.

Serious appeal! Read and reflect!! Fellow-citizens- The following letter, being one of a series from the pen of a distinguished statesman of Virginia, is
recommended to the serious consideration of every man who has
a stake in the welfare of his
country. Although addressed to
the people of Virginia, we are
convinced it will be read with
deep interest by the citizens of
New-York... [Signed] A farmer.
[1828] 1 p. DLC.   35148

Sermons, or homilies, appointed
to be read in churches in the
time of Queen Elizabeth, of famous memory. Baltimore, Pub. by
E. J. Coale & Co. Benjamin Edes,
pr., 1828. 565 p. ICMcC;
MsJMC; PHi; ViAlTh.   35149

Sessford, John
    City affairs. To the editors.
Messrs. Gales & Seaton: I en-
close you for publication an ex-
hibit of the improvements made
within the year 1827, and also a
tabular statement of the number
of deaths in each month, during
the same period, &c. J. Sessford. [Washington, 1828] 1 p.
DLC.   35150

Seventy-five receipts. See Leslie,
Eliza.

Sewall, Jotham
    Cause, evils and remedy of
intemperance. A sermon delivered
at New Castle, Maine, April 3,
1828. Wiscasset, Pr. by Herrick
& Co., 1828. 19 p. MeLB.
                                35151
Sewall, Thomas
    A charge delivered to the grad-
uating class of the Columbian
College, D. C., at the medical
commencement, March 22, 1827
...Washington, Pr. by D. Green,
1828. 12 p. DLC; DNLM; IEN-
M; MH; MnHi; PPC; TxU.
                                35152
Seymour, Caleb Perkins, 1808-
1875
    A eulogy, delivered in the
chapel of Williams College, on
account of the lamented death of
Harry Ware, a member of the
freshman class; who departed this
life November 19, 1827, in the
22d year of his age. Williamstown, R. Bannister, 1828. 11 p.
MWiW.   35153

Seymour's almanac for 1829. By
Matthew Seymour. Danbury, O.
Osborn [1828] 12 l. CtY; MWA.
                                35154
---- ---- Norwalk, P. Price
[1828] 12 l. NHi.   35155

Sganzin, Joseph Mathieu, 1750-
1837
    An elementary course of civil
engineering. Trans. from the
French of M. I. Sganzin... From
the 3d French ed. with notes and

applications adapted to the United States. 2d ed. Boston, Hilliard, Gray, Little and Wilkins, 1828. viii, 232 p., illus. DLC; GU; LNL; MB; MdBJ; MdBS; MiU-T; MnS; MoSpD; NBu; NCH; NNE; OCX; OCl; OO; PPAmP; PU; BrMus.   35156

Shakers
     A memorial, remonstrating a-gainst a certain act of the legis-lature of Kentucky, entitled "An act to regulate civil proceedings against certain communities hav-ing property in common" and de-claring "that it shall and may be lawful to commence and prose-cute suits, obtain decrees and have execution against any of the communities of people called Shakers, - without naming or designating the individuals, or serving process on them, other-wise than by fixing a subpoena on the door of their meeting-house, &c. Approved Feb. 11, 1828. [Harrodsburg, Ky., Pr. at the Union Office, 1828] 8 p. CSmH; DLC; In; KyLoF; NN; NNUT; OClWHi.   35157

Shakspeare, William
     The dramatic works of William Shakspeare. Pr. from the text of the corrected copy left by the late George Steevens, esq. With a glossary, and notes, and a sketch of the life of Shakspeare. New York, W. Borradaile, 1828. 2 v. GHi; MH; NjP; OCl.   35158

Shanarai-Chasset
     The constitution and bye-laws of the Israelite Congregation of Shanarai-Chasset (Gates of Mercy) of the city of New Orleans... New Orleans: Pr. by F. Delaup, pr. of the Congregation, 1828. 16 p. Dr. Meyer Solis-Cohen.   35159

[Shannon, James]
     Kentucky Gazette - Extra. Let-ters of Miltiades to the people of Kentucky, on the subject of the gubernatorial election. Lexington, Ky., Pr. by J. G. Norwood, 1828. 35 p. ICU.   35160

Sharp, Daniel, 1783-1853
     The memory of the just. A discourse delivered in the First Baptist meeting house in Provi-dence, August 20, 1828, at the interment of Rev. Stephen Gano ... Boston, Lincoln & Edmands, 1828. 20 p. MB; MBC; MH; MNtcA; MWA; MiD-B; NHC-S; NhHi; OClWHi; RPB; BrMus.   35161
---- The selection and use of acceptable words. A sermon de-livered at the ordination of Mr. Ebenezer Thresher, Jr., to the pastoral charge of the First Bap-tist Church, Portland. Portland, Pr. by Day & Fraser, 1828. 18 p. MH; MeB; RPB.   35162

---- The tendency of evil speak-ing against rulers, illustrated in a discourse delivered on fast day, in the Third Baptist meeting house in Boston, April 3, 1828. Boston, Beals, Homer & Co., prs., 1828. 20 p. MB; MH-AH; MHi; MNtcA; MWA; MiD-B; NCH-S; PHi; RPB.   35163

Shaw, Benjamin
     The fatal looking-glass; or, Universalism looked in the face. Woodstock, David Watson, 1828. 56 p. MMeT-Hi; Nh; OCHP.
                                       35164
---- A key to the revelation; or, Revelation revealed. In which all the dark passages, and most of the others, are briefly illustrated, and the book made to explain it-self. Woodstock, Pr. by Davis Watson, 1828. 28 p. MMeT-Hi; NN; Nh; OCHP.   35165

Shaw, John A.
     An oration delivered before

the citizens of Plymouth, July 4,
1828. Pub. by request. 2d ed.
Boston, Munroe & Francis, 1828.
24 p. ICN; MH; MWA; PPL;
BrMus.   35166

[Shedd, William] 1798-1830
    Letters to the Rev. William
E. Channing, D. D. on the exis-
tence and agency of fallen spirits.
By Canonicus. Boston, T. R. Mar-
vin, Sold by Crocker and Brew-
ster, [etc.] 1828. 156 p. CU;
CtHT; GDC; ICMcC; IEdS; IaU;
KyLoP; LNHT; MB; MBAt; MH;
MMet-Hi; MeBaT; MoSpD; NNUT;
NbOU; OU; PPL; PPPrHi; PU;
RPB; WHi.   35167

Sheet almanack for 1829. New
London, Samuel Green. [1828]
Advertised in the "New London
Gazette," December 17, 1828.
Drake 962.   35168

Shelby, James
    Kentucky reporter extra.
Chichasaw Treaty. An attempt to
obtain the testimony of James
Jackson, Esq. to prove the connection of Gen. Andrew Jackson
with a company of land specula-
tors, while acting as United
States commissioner, and to sustain the statement on that subject
of the Late Governor Shelby, by
his son, James Shelby. October,
1828. [Lexington, 1828] 8 p.
DLC; ICU; KyU.   35169

Shepard, Samuel W.
    Erie & Junction canal direc-
tory; containing a list of the
principal places on said canals,
with their distance from each
other, and from the several collectors' of ice. Little-Falls,
Griffing's Press, 1828. 1 p.
DLC.   35170

The shepherd boy.   See American Tract Society. N. Y.

Sherburne, Andrew, 1765-1831
    Memoirs of Andrew Sherburne:
a pensioner of the navy of the
Revolution. Written by himself.
Utica, William Williams, 1828.
262 p., 1 l. CL; CSmH; CtHC;
DLC; ICHi; IaU; MB; MH; MWA;
MdBE; MdHi; MeHi; MiD-B;
MiU-C; MoU; NCH; NN; NUt;
NhD; NjP; OClWHi; PHi; PP;
PPL; PPPrHi; PU; RHi; Vi;
ViRU; VtMiM; WHi; BrMus.
                                 35171

Sherman, Eleazer, b. 1795
    The narrative of Eleazer Sher-
man, giving an account of his life,
experience, call to the ministry
of the gospel and travels as such
to the present time. Vol. I.
Providence, Pr. for the author,
1828. 108 p. (Pr. at the end of
volume: The author has it in con-
templation to publish another volume in a short time.) DLC; GU;
LNB; M; MH; RHi; RPB. 35172

Sherman, John, 1772-1828
    A description of Trenton Falls,
Oneida County, New-York. Utica,
Pr. by Wm. Williams, 1828.
18, [1] p. MB; NBuG; PPL.
                                 35173
---- ---- Utica, Pr. by Wm.
Williams, 1828. 18 p. PPL.
(Completely diff. type & setting)
                                 35174
[Sherman, William]
    The ancient order of freema-
sonry and liberty of conscience,
opposed to bigotry and supersti-
tion, exemplified by plain and in-
dubitable facts and reasoning, deduced from scripture and common sense. By a candid man...
New-York, Pr. for the author,
1828. 40 p. IaCrM; MWA.
                                 35175
Sherwood, Mrs. Mary Martha
(Butt) 1775-1851
    The Ayah and lady. An Indian
story. By Mrs. Sherwood, author
of "Little Henry and his bearer,
&c. &c. Philadelphia, Towar and

Hogan, John Gray, pr. , 1828. 86 p. IObB.   35176

[----] The broken hyacinth, or, Ellen and Sophia... Revised by the Committee of publication. Philadelphia, American Sunday School Union, 1828. 106 p. CSmH.
                                   35177
---- The children of the Hartz mountains; or The little beggars ...Philadelphia, American Sunday School Union Depository, 1828. 36 p. DLC; OO.   35178

---- The history of Henry Milner. A Sabbath-school book. Portland, Shirley & Hyde, 1828. Williamson, 4425.   35179

---- History of Lucy Clare, as related by a clergyman, being intended for the use of young women. Hartford, D. F. Robinson, 1828. 108 p. Ct; CtHi; DLC; NNUT.   35180

---- History of Susan Gray. A Sabbath-school book. Portland, Shirley & Hyde, 1828. Williamson, 4564.   35181

---- The history of the Fairchild family; or, The child's manual: being a collection of stories calculated to show the importance and effects of a religious education. New-York, J. P. Haven, C. and G. Carvill, E. Bliss, Collins and Hannay, Collins and Co. , 1828. Pr. by Sleight and George, Jamaica, L. I. 2 v. in 1. NBLiHi.   35182

---- ... The history of Theophilus and Sophia. By Mrs. Sherwood... New York, The American Tract Society [1828?] 44+ p. DLC.
                                   35183
---- The infant's progress, from the valley of destruction, to everlasting glory... Philadelphia, Pub. by A. Claxton. J. Harding, pr. ,

1828. 254 p. KWiF; MH. 35184

---- The lady of the manor: being a series of conversations on the subject of confirmation. Bridgeport, M. Sherman, 1828. 8 v. CtHT-W; CtY; GDC; NCH; NN; OM; RNHi.   35185

---- The orphans of Normandy; or, Florentin and Lucie... 2d Amer. ed. Hartrord, D. F. Robinson, 1828. 106 p. CtY; MnS; NNC.   35186

---- The pilgrim of India on his journey to Mount Zion. ...the whole exhibiting traits of Hindoo character. Revised Boston ed. Boston, Pub. at James Loring's Sunday School Book-store. [c1828] 110 p. IObB; NcWsS.   35187

---- ... Primer; or, First book for children. Hartford, Pub. by H. & F. J. Huntington. P. Canfield, pr. , 1828. 48 p. CtHi; OO.   35188

---- Stories explanatory of the church catechism. From the 9th London ed. Philadelphia, E. Bacon, Clark & Razer, prs. , 1828. iv, [1]-308 p. LNB.   35189

Shiel, Richard
   The apostate. A tragedy in five acts. Philadelphia, Mifflin and Parry, 1828. 60 p. LNHT; MH; MWA.   35190

Shinn, Asa
   A defence before the Christian public, against certain charges and specifications brought before that tribunal by the Methodist prosecuting committee of Baltimore. Baltimore, Pr. by Richard J. Matchett, 1828. 32 p. MdHi.   35191

Shinn, Joshua
    The new Ohio arithmetic, or,
A new and complete calculator;
adapted to the juvenile understanding, in which the use of pounds,
shillings, and pence, (except in
the rule of exchange,) &c. is
omitted, and others inserted in
the room of them... New-Garden,
The author, 1828. H. J. Howard,
pr. 1 p. l, [11]-251, [1] p.
DLC; InHi; OClWHi; PPi.   35192

Shipherd, John Jay, 1802-1844
    The Sabbath school guide; or,
A selection of interesting and
profitable scripture lessons, illustrated and applied by questions
and answers. Designed as a
permanent system of Sabbath
school instruction. No. I. Burlington, Chauncey Goodrich, Pr.
by Ovid Miner, 1828. 60 p. MH;
OCHP; VtHi; VtMiS; VtU.   35193

---- ---- No. II. Middlebury,
Vermont Sabbath School Union;
pr. by Ovid Miner, 1828. 62 p.
MnU.   35194

The shipwreck. See American
Tract Society, N. Y.

Shoberl, Frederic, 1775-1853
    Austria; containing a descrip-
tion of the manners, customs,
character and costumes of the
people of that empire. Philadelphia, Pub. by C. S. Williams.
W. Brown, pr., 1828. [iv], 108
p. CtHC; DeWI; GU; ICMe; KU;
LNHT; MB; MDeeP; MH; NSy;
NbOU; NjR; PHi; PU.   35195

---- Persia; containing a description of the country, with an account of its government, laws,
and religion, and of the character, manners and customs, arts,
amusements, etc. of its inhabitants... Philadelphia, J. Griggs,
1828. 181 p. CtHC; CtHT;
GU; ICU; IaMu; KyLoS; MB;

MDeeP; MH; MiToC; NBuG;
NhHi; OMC; PLFM; RPB; TNJ;
TxU.   35196

---- Present state of Christianity, and of the missionary establishments for its propagation
in all parts of the world... New
York, Pr. by J. & J. Harper,
for Collins and Hannay. Boston,
Crocker & Brewster, 1828. viii,
[13] 260 p. CtHT-W; CtMW;
ICMcC; KWiU; LNHT; MB; MBC;
MH; NSyU; OClWHi; P; RPA;
ScCC; TNJ; VtU; WBB.   35197

Short, Charles Wilkins
    Biographical memoir of Doctor
Frederick Ridgely; late of Lexington, Kentucky. (From the
Transylvania Journal of Medicine,
&c. No. III. August, 1828) Lexington, Ky. Pr. by Jos. G. Norwood, 1828. 8 p. DLC; KyLoF;
KyU.   35198

...A short essay to do good.
See Sedgwick, Catharine Maria.

A short reply to a pamphlet.
See Bigelow, Jacob.

Short stories, moral & religious:
for the benefit of the young.
Portland, Shirley & Hyde, 1828.
36, 12 p. DLC.   35199

The sick monkey. Wendell,
Mass., J. Metcalf, pr., 1828.
8 p. ICU.   35200

Signs of the Times - Extra. See
New York. (State). Message.

Silliman, Benjamin, 1779-1864
    An introductory lecture, de-
livered in the laboratory of Yale
College October, 1828. New
Haven, Pr. by Hezekiah Howe,
1828. 48 p. MH; NNC; NjR; P;
PPL; PPPrHi; PU-S; WHi.
                           35201
[Sime, William]

History of the Patriarch Abraham. By the author of the life of Martin Luther. Philadelphia, American Sunday School Union, 1828. 86 p. MiDSH; BrMus.
35202

Simmons, John
The juvenile class book... No. 1. Philadelphia, Sold by Isaac Pugh... Bennett & Walton... Elijah Weaver... Stoddart & Atherton ... Kimber & Sharpless... Shadrach Taylor... Thomas Wallace... B. Redman... Joseph Rakestraw... and by the editor... 1828. 215 p. DLC; PAtM.
35203

Simon, Barbara Allan
A view of the human heart... To which is added, an appendix, containing thoughts on the scriptural expectations of the Christian church. Philadelphia, Pr. by L. R. Bailey, 1828. [2nd title - p [3] - A series of allegorical designs, representing the human heart from its natural to its regenerated state. Philadelphia, Pr. by Lydia R. Bailey, 1828] 228 p. PHi.
35204

Simons, Thomas Young, 1798-1857
Observations on mental alienation and the application of its phenomena to the illustration of subjects connected with medical jurisprudence. Charleston [S. C.] A. F. Cunningham, 1828. 50 p. CSmH; DLC; NBM; NN; ScCM.
35205

Sir, Although I have very recently issued. See Carey, Mathew.

...Sir, I am induced... See Carey, Mathew.

...Sir, Notwithstanding the very ungenerous... See Carey, Mathew.

...Sir, You will, I trust... See Carey, Mathew. A farewell.

[Siret, Charles Joseph] 1760-1830
Epitome historiae Graecae, cum appendice de Diis et Heroibus Poeticis auctore Josepho Juvencio. S. J. Accedit dictionarium Latineo-Anglicum. Editio secundo Americana, Priore longe emendatior. New Haven, Pub. by A. H. Maltby. Boston, Hilliard, Gray, Little, and Wilkins. Philadelphia, John Grigg, 1828. 152, 128 p. MH.
35206

A sister's gift; consisting of conversations on sacred subjects. First American from 2d London ed. New York, W. B. Gilley, [Gray & Bunce, prs.] 1828. 195, [1] p. PPL.
35207

The skaters. Boston, Bowles & Dearborn, Press of Isaac R. Butts and Co., 1828. 23 p. ("Vol. V, no. 4" of an unidentified series.) MB.
35208

The sketch-book. See Irving, Washington.

Sketch of the character of Mr. Canning./ See Rush, Richard.

A sketch of the life and character of the Hon. Samuel Howe. See Hall, Edward Brooks.

... A sketch of the life and public services of John Quincy Adams, president of the United States. To which is added, 1, An exposition of Mr. Adams' views and wishes upon the acquisition of Louisiana. 2, A correct statement of his conduct at Ghent, touching the navigation of the Mississippi, and the fisheries. 3, A critical examination of the votes of the people at the polls at the last presidential election ... Frankfort, Ky., Commentator office [1828] 48 p. "Commentator - Extra June 21, 1828" at head of title. DLC; ICHi. 35209

A sketch of the life and service of
John Quincy Adams... New York,
Sickels, pr., 1828. 16 p. CtY;
DLC; MdBJ; MnHi; NBLiHi; NBuG.
                                35210
---- 1828. 16 p. CSmH; NjR.
                                35211
A sketch of the life of General
Thos. Metcalfe. [Lexington? Ky.,
1828?] 27 p. DLC.   35212

A sketch of the most important
events of the life of Andrew Jackson, of Tennessee, from his birth
up to the present time. By a citizen of Herkimer Co. N.Y. Utica,
Dauby & Maynard, prs., 1828. 31
p. MiD; NCH; NUtHi; PPFM.
                                35213
A sketch of the theory of protecting and prohibitory duties, with
a few practical applications to the
present state of the Union. Charleston [S.C.] A.E. Miller, 1828.
32 p. CSmH; MH-BA; PPAmP.
                                35214
Sketches of character; or Facts
and arguments, relative to the
presidential election, 1828; ear-
nestly, and anxiously, submitted
to the feelings and judgments of
the people of Pennsylvania, by
one of themselves, who as a husband, a father, and a citizen,
has a deep stake in the freedom
and happiness of his country.
Philadelphia, 1828. 24 p. DLC;
NjR.   35215

Sketches of Moravian missions:
containing the most interesting
portions of the missionary labours of the United Brethren, a-
mong the Greenlanders, Esqui-
maux, North American Indians,
and Hottentots. Revised by the
Committee of publication of the
American Sunday School Union.
Philadelphia, American Sunday
School Union, 1828. 179 p.
ICMcC; OHi; BrMus.   35216

Sketches of Persia. See Mal-

colm, John.

Slack, Elijah
    A key to the technical lan-
guage, and a few other difficulties of chemistry, or chemical
nomenclature. Together with a
concise view of the doctrine of
definite proportions and chemical equivalents. For the use of
students in the Medical College of
Ohio. Cincinnati, Pr. by G.T.
Williamson, 1828. 25 p. OCHP.
                                35217
Slade, William, 1786-1859
    An oration delivered at Bur-
lington, Vt., on the anniversary
of American Independence, July
4, 1828. Burlington, Pr. by E.
& T. Mills, 1828. 13 p. MiD.
                                35218
Sloane, John
    The following letter from Mr.
Sloane, a member of Congress
from Ohio and accompanying
comments, are taken from the
Richmond Whig of October 1
[1828] and addressed to the people
of Hanover, Henrico, New Kent,
Charles City, and the city of
Richmond, by several freeholders.
1 p. DLC.   35219

---- Mr. Sloane's view. [To the
Editor of the National Journal]
...View of the report of the committee of military affairs, in relation to the proceedings of a
court martial, ordered for the
trial of certain Tennessee militia-
men. [Washington, 1828] 16 p.
NjR.   35220

Slocomb, William
    The federal calculator, or, A
concise system of practical arith-
metick; containing all the rules
necessary for transacting the common business of life. Together
with questions for examination,
under each of the rules... To
which is added, a short system
of book-keeping. Wheeling, The

author, [R. J. Curtis, pr.] 1828.
137, [7] p. DLC; InU; OClWHi;
WvU.   35221

Sloman, John
    Sloman's drolleries. 2d ed.,
imp. and corr. New York,
Eton's Theatrical play, pr. and
song store, 1828. 33 p. MH.
                              35222
Smiley, Thomas Tucker, d 1879.
    A complete key to Smiley's new
federal calculator; or, Scholar's
assistant... Philadelphia, J.
Grigg, 1828. 177 p. MiDSH.
                              35223
---- An easy introduction to the
study of geography, ...accom-
panied by an improved atlas...
6th ed., imp. Philadelphia, Pr.
for the author and for sale at J.
Griggs, Clark & Raser, prs.,
1828. 252 p. NNC; PPL.   35224

---- The new federal calculator;
or, Scholar's assistant. Philadelphia, J. Grigg, 1828. 180 p.
DAU; DLC; ICMcC; IaDuC; OMC;
PPi; TxU-T.   35225

Smith, Benjamin Bosworth
    Memoir of Herbert Marshall.
Boston, R. P. and C. Williams,
1828. 126 p. CtY; MB; MBD;
MNF.   35226

---- Thoughts on revivals. Middlebury, Pr. by J. W. Copeland,
1828. 23 p. CSmH; DLC.   35227

[Smith, James] 1775-1839
    Rejected addresses; or, The
new Theatrum poetarum... 2d
Amer. ed. Philadelphia, Neal &
Mackenzie [Mifflin & Parry, prs.]
1828. 144 p. PU.   35228

Smith, John, 1766-1831
    A sermon delivered September
25, 1827, at the ordination of the
Rev. Nathaniel Wales, as pastor
of the First Church in Belfast,
Maine... Belfast [Me.] Pr. by

Ephraim Fellowes, 1828. 32 p.
CSmH; MB; MBC; MH; MeB;
MeLB; NN; RPB.   35229

Smith, John Augustine
    Eulogium on the late Wright
Post, M. D. delivered in the
chapel of Columbia college...
New York, Charles S. Francis
[Geo. H. Evans, pr.] 1828. 21 p.
MB; MBAt; NNNAM; NbU; PHi.
                              35230
[Smith, Mrs. Margaret (Bayard)]
1778-1844
    What is gentility? A moral
tale... Washington, D. C., P.
Thompson, 1828. 257 p. DLC;
ICU; IObB; PU; RPB.   35231

Smith, Nathan Ryno, 1792-1877
    An address pronounced before
the medical graduates of the University of Maryland, April 7,
1828... Baltimore, Pr. by Benjamin Edes, 1828. 24 p. CtHT-W;
MBCo; MdHi; MdUM; NNNAM;
OC; OCHP; PU.   35232

Smith, Stephen Rensselaer, 1788-
1850
    An appeal to the public, in
vindication of Universalists and
others. Philadelphia, Atkinson &
Alexander, 1828. 21 p. MBC;
MMeT.   35233

---- The nature and object of
punishment. A discourse, delivered at the hall of the Franklin
Institute, Philadelphia. Wednesday evening, March 5, 1828.
Utica, Pr. by Dauby & Maynard,
1828. 11 p. MMet; NUtHi.
                              35234
---- True believers, hated by the
world. A discourse, delivered in
the "Free Church," Clinton,
N. Y., in the afternoon of the
third Sunday in November, 1828,
and in Utica the first Sunday in
December. Utica [N. Y.] Pr. by
Dauby & Maynard, 1828. 15 p.
CSmH; N; NUtHi.   35235

Smith, William, 1762-1840
  Speech of the Hon. William
Smith, of South-Carolina, in the
Senate of the United States, on the
bill making appropriation for internal improvements, delivered
on the 11th April, 1828. Charleston, Pr. and sold by A. E. Miller, 1828. 28 p. CSmH; ICU;
MiU; PPAmP; RPB; ScCC; ScU;
TxU; WHi.   35236

Smollett, Tobias George, 1721-
1771
  The history of England, from
the revolution in 1688, to the
death of George II. Designed as
a continuaton of Mr. Hume's history. In two volumes. By T.
Smollett, M. D. A new edition,
with the author's last corrections
and improvements... The library
ed. E. Littell, Philadelphia, Pr.
by S. Parker, 1828. 2 vols. Ar-
Hi; CBDP; CtB; CtHT; GMM;
KHi; KyLo; LN; MH; MoSU; NdHi;
OClW; OU; PP; PU (vol. I only);
PWc; ScCC; ScDuE; TBriK;
TxDaM; ViL; WvU.   35237

---- ---- A new ed., with the
author's last corrections and improvements. Philadelphia, Bennett & Walton, 1828. 2 v. CtHT;
GEU; GHi; InGrD; KyWA; LHL;
MoSpD; OHi; TMC; ViU.   35238

Smyth, Alexander, 1765-1830
  Speech of Alexander Smyth, of
Virginia, on the resolution amendatory of the constitution, delivered in the House of Representatives, on the 18th December,
1828. Washington, Pr. by Duff
Green, 1828. 12, 8 p. MWA;
PPAmP.   35239

Snider, Benjamin S.
  A New Year's address, delivered to the citizens of Center-
ville... comprising the origin,
titles and attributes of speculative Free-masonry... Geneseo,

[N. Y.] Pr. for the author, 1828.
23 p. CSmH.   35240

Snow, Caleb Hopkins
  A history of Boston, the me-
tropolis of Massachusetts, from
its origin to the present period,
with some account of the envir-
ons... 2d ed. Boston, Pub. by
Abel Bowen, 1828. iv, 427 p.
CtSoP; ICMe; ICN; MB; MDeeP;
MH; MPeaS; MdBP; NH; NIC;
PPi; RNR; BrMus.   35241

Snyder, Simon
  Letters to the people of the
United States, upon the subject of
presidential election. Originally
published in the United States
Gazette, by Simon Snyder... Phila-
delphia, Pr. at the United States
Office, 1828. 27 p. PHi; PPAmP.
                             35242

Soane, George
  The innkeeper's daughter; a
melo-drama, in two acts. Philadelphia, Neal & Mackenzie, 1828.
46 p. MH; NcU.   35243

Social and camp-meeting songs
for the pious... 12th ed. enl.
Baltimore, Armstrong & Plaskitt,
and J. Plaskitt & co., 1828. 215
p. MdBE.   35244

Society for Promoting the Gospel
among Seamen, in the Port of
New-York.
  Report of the Society for Pro-
moting the Gospel among Seamen,
in the Port of New-York... New-
York, Pr. by J. & J. Harper,
1828. 24 p. MiD-B; PPPrHi.
                             35245
Society for the Encouragement of
Faithful Domestic Servants in
New-York.
  Third annual report of the
managers of the Society for the
Encouragement of Faithful Domes-
tic Servants in New-York. New
York, Pr. by D. Fanshaw, at
the American Tract Society's

House, 1828. 32 p. NNG;
PPAmP; BrMus.   35246

Society for the Promotion of
Temperance. Bridgewater, Mass.
Constitution... Taunton, Danforth and Thurber, prs., 1828.
8 p. MBrid.   35247

Society for the Reformation of
Juvenile Delinquents in the City
of New York.
  Third annual report of the
managers of the Society for the
Reformation of Juvenile Delin-
quents in the City and State of
New York. New York, Pr. by
Mahlon Day, 1828. 64 p. DLC;
MH; OClW; TNJ; TxU; BrMus.
                             35248
Socio, Clio Convivius, pseud.,
comp.
  The post-chaise companion,
and magazine of wit. Original and
selected from the most favourite
literary authors. 2d ed., with
corrections and additions. By
Clio Convivius Socio... Baltimore,
Pub. for the purchaser, 1828.
224 p. DLC; MWA.   35249

Soler, Mariano Cubi y. See
Cubi y Soler, Mariano.

Solis, Jacob S.
  Calendar of the festivals and
lunar months of every year, observed by the Israelites. Commencing A.M. 5589 and ending in
the year 5612, being a period of
24 years. New Orleans, F. De-
laup, pr. of the Congregation,
1828. 4 p. Dr. Meyer Solis-
Cohen.   35250

Some account of General Jackson,
drawn up from the Hon. Mr. Eaton's very circumstantial narrative, and other well-established
information respecting him. By a
gentleman of the Baltimore bar...
Baltimore, H. Vicary, Matchett,
pr., 1828. viii, [7]-272 p. CtY;

DLC; LNHT; MB; MH; MdBP;
MdHi; O; PLFM; WHi.   35251

Some account of some of the
bloody deeds of Gen. Jackson...
[1828?] 1 p. DLC.   35252

Some notices of Kentucky. See
Carey, Mathew.
No entries.   35253-35352

Some of the memorable events.
See Mitchill, Samuel Latham.

Some remarks made before the
joint committee on rivers and
canals, relating to the proposed
improvements of Connecticut
River and the extension of the
Hampshire and Hampden canal.
February, 1828. Boston, Dutton
& Wentworth, state prs., 1828.
24 p. CtHC; CtSoP; DBRE; DLC;
MB; MBAT; MH-BA; MNF; MWA;
MdBJ; MiU-T; NIC; NN; NhHi.
                             35353
Some remarks on education. See
Furbish, James.

Some remarks upon a publication
by the Philadelphia Medical Society. See Swaim, William.

[Somerset, Charles A.]
  A day after the fair; a bur-
letta, in one act. New-York, Elton's dramatic repository, 1828.
24 p. MH; PU.   35354

Sophia: or, The bandit of the forest. A play, in three acts. By a
gentleman of this City. New-
York, 1828. 16 p. RPB. 35355

Soule, Joshua
  Substance of a sermon preached
in Augusta, Georgia, before the
South Carolina conference, January 14, 1827. Pub. at the request
of the conference. 2d ed., with an
appendix by the author. Baltimore,
J.D. Toy, 1828. 48 p. CLU;
GEU; IEG; KyU; NjR.   35356

South Carolina
    Acts and resolutions of the
General Assembly of the state of
South Carolina, passed in De-
cember, 1827 and January, 1828.
Columbia, Pr. by D. & J. M.
Faust, 1828. 97, 96, [4] p. C;
IaU-L; In-SC; MdBB; Mo; Nb; Nj.
                                    35357
---- Report of a special commit-
tee appointed by the Chamber of
commerce, to inquire into the
cost, revenue and advantages of
a rail road communication be-
tween the city of Charleston and
the towns of Hamburg & Augusta.
Charleston, Pr. by A. E. Miller,
1828. 32 p. CSmH; DBRE; DLC;
MBAt; MiU-T; NHi; NIC; NN;
RBR; ScCC; ScHi; ScU; WM; WU.
                                    35358
---- Report of the superintendent of public works. [Pr. at the
State Gazette Office. D. & J. M.
Faust, prs., Columbia, 1828]
15 p. MCM; NN.   35359

---- Resolutions [denouncing the
tariff acts of 1824 and 1828 as
infractions of the U. S., and proposing that a convention be called
for the purpose of amending said
constitution... [Charleston?
1828] Bdsd. NN.   35360

South Carolina Canal and Rail-
road Company.
    By laws of the South Carolina
Canal and Railroad Company, a-
dopted by the stockholders, May
13, 1828. [Charleston, J. S. Burges, pr., 1828] 8 p. DLC. 35361

---- ---- Together with the act
of incorporation. Granted by the
state legislature. Charleston, Pr.
by James S. Burges, 1828. 16
p. CSmH; DBRE; DLC; DNA;
MB; MH-BA; NN; ScU; WM.
                                    35362

---- First semi-annual report,

to the president and directors of
the South Carolina Canal and
Railroad Company, by their committee of inquiry. Charleston,
Pr. by A. E. Miller, 1828. 24,
[4] p. CSmH; DLC; MB; MH-BA;
NN; NNC; ScHi; ScU; WM.
                                    35363
South Carolina. Colleton District.
Citizens
    An address of sundry citizens
of Colleton district, to the people
of South Carolina [relative to the
late tariff bill, passed by the
Congress of the U. S.] [Charles-
ton, A. E. Miller] 1828. 8 p.
NcD.   35364

South Carolina. Kershaw District.
Citizens.
    An adjourned meeting of the
citizens of Kershaw District was
held, in Camden, on the 18th
instant to receive the report of
the committee appointed to draft
a Memorial and Resolutions to
Congress, in opposition to the
proposed tariff on woolens...
[Camden? 1828] 9 p. PHi.
                                    35365
South Carolina. Richland District.
Citizens.
    Address of the citizens of
Richland dist. to the citizens of
South Carolina. Columbia, S. C.,
Pr. by David W. Sims, 1828.
14 p. NHi; ScU.   35366

South Western Theological Seminary. See Appeal to the Northern and Eastern Churches.

Southard, Samuel Lewis
    Anniversary address, deliver-
ed before the Columbian Institute, at Washington, on the
twenty-first December, one thousand eight hundred and twenty-
seven. Pr. by order of the Institute. Washington, 1828. 29 p.
CSmH; DLC; NHC-S; NN; NNC;
NjP; PHi; PPL; PPPrHi; TNJ.
                                    35367

Southington, First Church.
The confession of faith, and covenant of the First Church in Southington. To which is added A catalogue of the members from 1780 to 1828. New-Haven, Pr. by Treadway and Adams, 1828. 21 p. CtY; DLC; MWA; MiD-B; NHi; NNUT.   35368

Southmayd, Jonathan Coleman, 1798-1838
A discourse on the duty of Christians with regard to the use of distilled spirits. Preached at Montpelier, March 16th, 1828. Montpelier, Pr. by E. P. Walton, 1828. 16 p. CSmH; GDC; MH; NCH; VtU.   35369

Southwick, Solomon, 1773-1859
An oration: delivered by appointment on the fourth day of July, A. D. 1828, in presence of the convention of the seceeding free Masons...at the Presbyterian Church in the village of Le Roy, in the county of Genesee, and state of New York. Albany, Wood and Webster, 1828. 81 p. CSmH; DLC; ICU; IaCrM; MB; MDeeP; MH-AH; MHi; MWA; NN; PHi; PPFM; RPB.   35370

---- A solemn warning against free-masonry, addressed to the young men of the United States... With an appendix, containing the correspondence between Eliphalet Murdock...and the author, relating to the supposed murder of Mr. Murdock's father, through masonic vengeance, at Rensselaerville, in the county of Albany, in October, 1803...2d ed.; rev. and cor. by the author. Albany, Pr. by G. Galpin, 1828. 129 p. DLC; NNFM; PPFM.   35371

Sparks, Jared, 1789-1866
The life of John Ledyard, the American traveller; comprising selections from his journals and correspondence...Cambridge [Mass.] Pub. by Hilliard and Brown; New York, G. & C. Carvill [etc., etc.] [Hilliard, Metcalf & Co., prs. to the University] 1828. xii, 325 p. CSmH; ICN; MA; Mi; MoSM; PPL; RHi; RPB; TNJ; ViU.   35372

Spicer, Tobias
Camp-Meetings defended, or A brief review of a pamphlet lately published, entitled "Camp-meetings described and exposed, and strange things stated."... New Haven, Pr. by T. G. Woodward, 1828. 24 p. CtHi. 35373

The spirit of orthodoxy. See Eddowes, Ralph.

Spofford, Jeremiah
A gazetteer of Massachusetts: containing a general view of the state... By Jeremiah Spofford, counsellor of the Massachusetts Medical Society. With a map of the state. Newburyport, Pub. by Charles Whipple, 1828. 348 p. DLC; ICJ; MB; MBAt; MH; MH-BA; MWA; N; NN; BrMus.   35374

The spoil'd child. See Bickerstaffe, Isaac.

Sprague, Peleg
Speech of Mr. Sprague, of Maine on the tariff bill, delivered in the House of Representatives, March 31, 1828. Washington, Peter Force, 1828. 38 p. DLC; LU; MWA; PHi.   35375

[Sprague, William Buell] 1795-1876
Letters from Europe, in 1828; first published in the New York Observer. New York, J. Leavitt, 1828. 135, [1] p. CBPac; CtHT; DLC; KU; LNP; MB; MBC; MiD; NGH; NNUT; NhD; NjP; OClWHi; PPPrHi; PU; BrMus.   35376

Spring, Gardiner
 A dissertation on the means of
regeneration... New York, Pr. by
John T. West, New-York Observer
Office, 1828. 47 p. ArCH; GDC;
MB; MH-AH; MWA; MeHi; MiD-
B; MnSM; NjR; OClWHi; PPL;
PPPrHi.   35377

Spring, Gardiner, 1785-1873
 The doctrine of election illus-
trated and established in a ser-
mon. By the Rev. Gardiner
Spring... Richmond [Va.], Pr. at
the Franklin Press, 1828. 24 p.
CSmH; NjR; PPPrHi; ScCliJ.
                                 35378
Sproat, P. W.
 General Welfare: an investi-
gation of the powers vested in the
Congress of the United States, by
the constitution. Philadelphia, Pr.
for the Proprietor, 1828. 36 p.
MB; MBAt; NN; OClWHi.   35379

The spy.   See Cooper, James
Fenimore.

[Staats, Cuyler]
 Tribute to the memory of De
Witt Clinton, late governor of the
state of New York. Being a com-
prehensive sketch of his life, together with the proceedings of the
New-York Legislature, and of
various corporate and public bod-
ies: By a citizen of Albany. Albany, Pr. by Webster and Wood,
1828. 204 p. CSmH; CtB; DLC;
ICN; MBFM; MH; MWA; MdBE;
MdBJ; MiD-B; MnHi; NBLiHi;
NBuG; NCH; NN; NNC; NRHi;
NjR; OClWHi; OO; PHi; PPL;
PPPrHi; RNR; WHi; BrMus.
                                 35380
Stacy, Nathaniel
 A discourse delivered at Hamilton Centre, July 4, 1828. Hamilton [N.Y.] Pr. by Geo. Williams
& co., 1828. 21 p. CSmH.35381

Stanford, John
 Addresses delivered on laying

the corner stone of the intended
penitentiary, on the island in the
East River, (The Blackwell's,)
in presence of the Hon. the May-
or, and Common Council, of the
city of New-York: September 10,
1828... New-York, Pr. by Peter
Van Pelt, 1828. 7 p. NHi; NN;
NNC.   35382

Stanhope, Philip Dormer, 4th
earl of Chesterfield, 1694-1773
 The beauties of Chesterfield,
consisting of selections from his
works. By Alfred Howard. Stereotyped at the Boston Type and
Stereotype Foundry. Boston, Pub.
by Charles Ewer [Pr. by J.H.A.
Frost] 1828. 261 p. CSmH;
KyDC; LNHT; MB; MH; NCH;
PPL.   35383

---- Practical morality, or, A
guide to men and manners: consisting of Lord Chesterfield's advice to his son. To which is added, a supplement containing extracts from various books, recommended by Lord Chesterfield
to Mr. Stanhope... New York, Pr.
and pub. by G. Long, 1828. 275
p. MBB; MHingH; OO.   35384

Stansbury, Arthur J., 1781-1848
 Elementary catechism on the
constitution of the United States.
For the use of schools. Boston,
Hilliard, Gray, Little and Wil-
kins, 1828. 78 p. CU; MBAt; MH;
NNC.   35385

Starck, Johann Friedrich, 1680-
1756
 Johann Friedrich Starcks...
Tägliches handbuch in guten und
bösen Tagen... Stereotypirt von J.
Howe, Philadelphia. Philadelphia,
Herausgegeben von Georg W.
Mentz, 1828. 538 p. PPL.
                                 35386
Starkie, Thomas, 1782-1849
 A practical treatise on the law
of evidence and digest on proofs

in civil and criminal proceedings,
... with references to American
decisions, by Theron Metcalf.
With additional notes, by Edward
D. Ingraham. Boston, Wells &
Lilly; Philadelphia, P. H. Nick-
lin, 1828. 3 vol. Ct; LNT-L;
MH-L; MdBP; MoSU-L; MoU;
NcD; Nj; WaPS; WaU.   35387

State Bank of North Carolina,
Raleigh, N. C.
An act to redeem the paper
currency in circulation, and to
establish a bank, by the name
and title of the State Bank of
North-Carolina, passed Decem-
ber, 1810; an act in addition to
the preceding, passed December,
1811. Also, an act to amend the
charter, passed in 1816. To which
are subjoined the by-laws of the
corporation. Raleigh, Pr. by J.
Gales & son, 1828. 36 p. CSmH.
                         35388
Statesman and Gazette, Natchez,
Miss.
The carrier's address, to the
Patrons of the Statesman and
Gazette 1st January 1828. [Na-
tchez, Miss., 1828] 1 p. DLC.
                         35389
Statistical tables of the state of
New-York; containing complete
lists of the counties, towns, sen-
atorial and congressional districts,
population... Compiled from the
best authorities. New-York, J.
Seymour, 1828. 24 p. MBC;
NBLiHi; BrMus.   35390

Stearns, John Glazier, 1795-1874
An appendix to "An inquiry into the nature and tendency of
speculative free-masonry." In
which is proved the true character of Morgan's "Illustrations of
Masonry." Cazenovia, Pr. by J.
F. Fairchild, 1828. 54 p. DLC;
MiU-C; N; PHi.   35391

---- A dialogue, on the effectual
means of separating Free Mason-

ry from the Church of Christ.
[Utica, N. Y., Pr. by D. Bennett
& Co., 1828] 12 p. CSmH; DLC.
                         35392
---- An inquiry into the nature
and tendency of speculative free-
masonry, with an appendix, in
which is proved the true character of Morgan's Illustrations of
masonry... 2d ed., enl. Westfield [N. Y.] H. Newcomb, 1828.
191 p. DLC; ICU; MBFM; MdHi;
OClWHi; PLFM.   35393

---- Plain truth: containing remarks on various subjects, relative to the institution of speculative Free Masonry. Cazenovia
[N. Y.] Pr. by J. F. Fairchild,
1828. 82 p. CSmH; IaCrM;
MBFM.   35394

Steel, Samuel
A sermon on Christian bap-
tism, shewing the apostolic prac-
tice, both as to subjects and
mode. Lexington, Ky., Pr. by
Joseph G. Norwood, 1828. 50 p.
KyLoF; KyU; MB; MBAt; Ms-Ar;
NHC; NN; OCHP; PPPrHi;
TxU.   35395

---- Two letters on baptism, addressed to a friend. Intended as
an answer to a pamphlet entitled,
"A blow at the root of Popery,
&c." Lexington, Ky., Pr. by
Thos. T. Skillman. At the Office
of the Western Luminary, 1828.
24 p. OC; PPPrHi.   35396

Steele's Albany almanack for
1829. By Edwin E. Prentiss. Albany, Oliver Steele [1828] 12 l.
CLU; DLC; N; NN; NR; NcD.
                         35397
---- ---- Albany, Oliver Steele
[1828] 13 l. MWA; NCooHi.
                         35398
Sterne, Laurence
The beauties of Sterne, consisting of selections from his
works. Boston, N. H. Whitaker,

1828. 160 p. MB; MDeeP; MH;
PSC-Hi; ViRUT.   35399

[----] A sentimental journey
through France and Italy, by Mr.
Yorick [pseud.] Four volumes
comprised in one. Campe's ed.
Nurnburg and New York, F.
Campe and co. [1828?] 118 p.
DLC.   35400

[Stetson, Caleb] 1793-1870
   No. 19. The Apostle Paul a
Unitarian. Pr. for the American
Unitarian Association. Boston,
Bowles & Dearborn, [Press of I.
R. Butts & Co.] 1828. 35 p.
CBPac; ICMe; ICU; IEG; M;
MBAU; MBC; MH-AH; MHi;
MMeT-Hi; MNF.   35401

Stevenson, Andrew, 1784-1857
   Speech... on the proposition to
amend the constitution of the
United States respecting the election of president and vice president. Washington, Gales & Seaton, 1828. BrMus.   35402

Stevenson, James S. d 1831
   Speech of Mr. Stevenson, of
Pennsylvania, on the proposed increase of the tariff: delivered
in the House of Representatives
of the United States, March 5,
1828. Washington, 1828. 22 p.
MWA; NNC.   35403

[Stevenson, William]
   ...Life of William Caxton.
Pub. under the superintendence
of the Soc., for the Diffusion of
Useful Knowledge... New York,
G. and C. Carvill [etc., etc.]
1828. 32 p. ICN; MiU.   35404

Stewart, Andrew, 1791-1872
   Mr. Stewart's speech on the
tariff, delivered in the House of
Representatives on the 8th of Ap-
ril, 1828. [n.p., 1828?] 24 p.
MdBP.   35405

---- Washington City, May 23,
1828. Sir. As I am about to re-
tire from public life, and from
the service of a people who have
so long honored me with their
continued and unwavering confi-
dence I deem it my duty, at the
close of my political career to
tender you my sincere and heart-
felt thanks... Andrew Stewart.
3 p. DLC.   35406

Stewart, Charles Samuel, 1795-
1870
   Journal of a residence in the
Sandwich Islands, during the
years 1823-1825... 2d ed... with
an introduction and notes by Rev.
William Ellis. From 1st London
ed. New York, John P. Haven,
and G. & C. Carvill; Philadelphia, Towar and Hogan, Carey,
Lea & Carey; Baltimore, Cushing & Jewitt; Washington, Pishey
Thompson; Boston, Hilliard, Gray,
and co.; Portland, Shirley &
Hyde, 1828. 320 p. CSmH; ICMcC;
LNT; MH; MdBP; MnHi; MoSp;
NNS; OClWHi.   35407

---- ---- 3d ed. cor. and enl.
with an introduction and notes by
Rev. Wm. Ellis, from the 1st
London ed. New York, John P.
Haven [Sleight & George, prs.]
1828. 2 vols. CtMW; MWA; MiHi;
NN; NSyU.   35408

---- Private journal of a voyage
to the Pacific Ocean, and resi-
dence at the Sandwich Islands,
in the years 1822, 1823, 1824
and 1825. By C.S. Stewart...
New York, John P. Haven [Sleight
& George, prs.] 1828.   406 p.
CL; GHi; ICN; Ia; MH; Me; MiU;
MnU; NNG; NRU; NjP; NjR;
OClW; OMC; PPL; PU; Tx; ViRUT;
BrMus.   35409

Stewart, Dugald, 1753-1828
   The philosophy of the active
and moral powers of man...

Boston, Wells and Lilly, 1828.
2 v. CBPac; CtHC; CtW; DLC;
ICN; KU; KyLx; MBAt; MH; MoS;
NcD; NjP; PU; ScCC; WBB.
35410

Stewart, John G.
An address, delivered on the
5th day of July, 1828, to the
people of colour, on the first anniversary of their emancipation
from slavery, in the state of
New-York. Albany, 1828. 11 p.
N. 35411

Stockton, Joseph, 1779-1832
The western calculator; or, A
new and compendious system of
practical arithmetic; containing
the elementary principles and
rules of calculation, in whole,
mixed, and decimal numbers. Arranged, defined, and illustrated
in a plain and natural order, and
adapted to the use of schools,
throughout the western country,
and the present commerce of the
United States. In eight parts. 5th
ed. Pittsburgh, Johnston & Stockton, Market Street, 1828. 203,
[1] p. MH; OClWHi; P; PPiU.
35412
Stoddard's diary; or Columbia almanack for 1829. By Edwin E.
Prentiss. Hudson, A. Stoddard
[1828] 18 l. CtNhHi; InU; MWA;
NHi; NN; NjR; PHi. 35413

[Stoddart, Isabella]
Arthur Monteith: a moral tale,
founded on an historical fact...
To which is added, The Young
West Indian. By Mrs. Blackford
[pseud] 2d Amer. ed. New York,
W. Burgess, jun., 1828. 144 p.
DLC; KU. 35414

[----] The Eskdale herd-boy, a
Scottish tale for the instruction
and amusement of young persons
...1st Amer. ed. New York, [Pr.
by Vanderpool & Cole] Pub. by
Wm. Burgess, Jun., 1828. xi,
184, [2] p. CtHT-W; MB; MPB;

PP; PPL. 35415

[----] The Scottish orphans: ...
by Mrs. Blackford [pseud.]...
3d Amer. ed. New York, Pub.
by Wm. Burgess, jun. [Vander-
pool & Cole, prs.] 1828. 144 p.
DLC; IU; NNC. 35416

Stone, Micah
The character, trials, and security of the church. A sermon
preached at the dedication of the
meeting house of the Evangelical
Society in South Brookfield, Aug.
13, 1828. Brookfield, Pr. by E.
& G. Merriam, 1828. 31 p.
CSmH. 35417

The storm. See Dix, Dorothea
Lynde.

Storrs, Henry Randolph
Sentinel & Gazette, Extra.
Substance of Mr. Storrs' remarks, at the meeting of the
friends of the administration,
held at Whitesboro', July fourth,
1828, for the purpose of nominating an elector of president, and
vice-president, for the county of
Oneida. Utica, Pr. by Northway
& Porter, [1828] 23 p. CSmH;
DLC; MH (28 p.); MiD-B; MnHi;
MdBJ; NCH. 35418

---- Substance of Mr. Storrs'
remarks, at the meeting of the
friends of the administration, held
at Whitesboro; July fourth, 1828,
for the purpose of nominating an
elector of president and vice-
president, for the county of Oneida. Utica, Pr. by Northway &
Porter, 1828. 23 p. NjR.
35419
Story, Joseph, 1779-1845
A discourse pronounced at the
request of the Essex Historical
Society on the 18th of September,
1828, in commemoration of the
first settlement of Salem. Boston, Hilliard, Gray, Little, and

Wilkins, publishers [Cambridge, Hilliard, Metcalf & Co., prs.] 1828. 90 p. CBPac; CLSU; CSmH; CtHT; CtSoP; DLC; ICN; ICU; IaU; MB; MBAt; MBC; MH; MHi; MnHi; MdBJ; MiD-B; MnM; MoSHi; NBLiHi; NCH; NNC; NcU; NhHi; OCHP; OClWHi; PHi; PPL; RHi; RPB; ScCC; WHi; BrMus.
35420

The story of Ahmed the cobler or, The great astrologer. Canton, Pr. by W. W. Wyman, 1828. 56 p. DLC.   35421

The story of Aladdin; or, The wonderful lamp. New York, S. King [c1828] 10 l. PP.   35422

The story of William and Ellen. Wendell, Mass., Pr. and sold by J. Metcalf, 1828. 16 p. DLC; MH; MWA.   35423

The stranger's guide. See Tanner, Henry Schenck.

The stray lamb. Wendell, J. Metcalf, 1828. 8 p. MNF. 35424

Streeter, Russell
    A Christmas sermon in the Universalist meeting house, Watertown, Mass., December 25, 1827. Boston, Henry Bowen, pr., 1828. 16 p. CtSoP; MH-AH; PPL; RPB.   35425

Strickland, Joe, pseud. See Dekay, Joseph E.

The striking similitude between the reign of terror of the elder Adams, and the reign of corruption of the younger Adams. See Democratic Party. New York.

Strong, Joseph, 1753-1834
    Sermons preached March 23, A. D. 1828, on the completion of the fiftieth year of the author's ministry. Norwich [Conn.] Pr. by J. Dunham, 1828. 26 p.

CSmH.   35426

Strong, Solomon, 1780-1850
    A sketch of the character of the late Hon. Samuel Howe, delivered at the opening of the Court of Common Pleas in Lenox, on the twenty-sixth day of February, 1828. Williamstown, Bannister, 1828. 8 p. MWiW.
35427

[Strong, Titus] 1787-1855
    ...A candid examination of the Episcopal Church; in two letters to a friend. 2d ed. Pub. by the "Episcopal Female Tract Society of Philadelphia." for the "Society of the Protestant Episcopal Church for the Advancement of Christianity in Pennsylvania. Philadelphia, Pr. by Wm. Stavely, 1828. (Religious tracts, No. 57) 24 p. NNG; PPL.   35428

[----] ---- 11th ed. To which is added, A consideration of some popular objections. Boston, R. P. & C. Williams, 1828. 90 p. Ct; CtY; MBD; MWA; NNG.   35429

[----] The cypress wreath; or, Mourner's friend. A selection of pieces, adapted to the consolation of the afflicted... Greenfield, Mass., Phelps & Clark, 1828. 108 p. CSmH; DLC.   35430

Strong, William L.
    Sermon, delivered Lord's Day, January 6, 1828, soon after the one hundredth anniversary of the organization of the church in Somers. With a sketch of some leading events in the history of the church and congregation... Hartford, Pr. by Peter B. Gleason, & Co., 1828. 24 p. CtHi.
35431

Stuart, Gilbert. See Catalogue of an exhibition...

Stuart, Moses, 1780-1852
    Grammar of the Hebrew lan-

guage; 3d ed. Hanover, Flagg &
Gould, publishers & prs., Cod-
man press, 1828. 240 p. DLC;
MA.   35432

---- A Hebrew Chrestomathy designed as an introduction to a
course of Hebrew study. 3d ed.
with corr. and additions. Andover, Gould & Newman, publishers & prs., New York, Codman
Press, 1828. 63 p. NN.   35433

---- Two discourses on the atonement... 2d ed. Andover, Pub. by
Mark Newman, Flag & Gould,
prs., 1828. 46, [2] p. CoU; DLC;
PPPrHi.   35434

A student, pseud. See To Mr.
Charles Adams.

The student's walk. See Grierson, Miss.

Sugden, Edward Burtenshaw
    A practical treatise of the law
of vendors and purchasers of estates... 1st Amer., from the 7th
London ed.; with notes and references to American decisions.
By Thos. Huntington, Counsellor
at Law. Brookfield, Pub. by E.
and G. Merriam; Boston, Hilliard, Gray, Little and Wilkins;
New York, Collins and Hannay;
Philadelphia, John Grigg, 1828.
lxxxiv, 600, xxxviii, [2] p. CoU;
MoU; NcD.   35435

Suit, Pleasant
    The farmers' accountant and
instructions for overseers; to
which is added, the mode of cal-
culating interest on bonds, making up executors', administra-
tors' and guardians' accounts, according to the rules of the Superior Court of Chancery, founded
on the decision of the Court of
Appeals. Richmond, J. Macfarlan, 1828. [39 p.] DAU; ICJ;
NcD; Vi; ViU.   35436

Sullivan, John Langdon, 1777-
1865
    Refutation of Mr. Colden's
"Answer to Mr. Sullivan's report
to the Society for Establishing
Useful Manufactories in New Jersey, upon the intended encroachments of the Morris Canal Company in diverting from their natural course the waters of the
Passaic. [Boston?] 1828. 56 p.
CtY; DBRE; DLC; MH; NN; NNE;
BrMus.   35437

[----] Report, on the origin and
increase of the Paterson manufactories, and the intended diver-
sion of their waters by the Morris Canal Company: also on post
rail roads, as the means of
cheap conveyance throughout New-
Jersey, of bringing Susquehanna
coal to the iron mines and
forges, and to supply Paterson
and New-York: also on a method
of supplying the city of New-York
with water from the great falls
of the Passaic. Paterson, Pr. by
Day & Burnett, 1828. 60, [2] p.
CSmH; DBRE; DLC; DeGE; MWA;
NN; NNE; NjR.   35438

Sullivan, Thomas Russell
    A brief exposure of Rev. Mr.
Robinson's evasion, perversions,
and general unfairness in controversy. Keene, N.H., Pr. by J.
and J.W. Prentiss, 1828. 27 p.
MBAU; MBAt; MBC; NhHi.
                             35439

Sumner, Bradford
    Oration delivered Friday, July
4, 1828, in commemoration of
American independence, before
the supreme executive of the
commonwealth, and the city council and inhabitants of the city of
Boston. Boston, Nathan Hale, pr.
1828. 29 p. CSmH; CtSoP; CtY;
DLC; ICN; MBB; MBC; MH; MHi;
MdW; MiD-B; MiU-C; NHi; NN;
NhHi; RPB; BrMus.   35440

The Sunday school hymn book...
Philadelphia, American Sunday
School Union, 1828. 128 p.
CtHT-W; KU (with appendix of
64 p.); M; MHi; MoSC; PPL;
PPPrHi; RPB; TxU.   35441

A Sunday school teacher. See
Morris, Helen.

Sundry experienced teachers.
See The United States spelling
book.

A Superintendant of a Sabbath
School in New Jersey, pseud.
See Fisk, Harvey.

Supplement to Andrew Jackson's
negro speculations. See Erwin,
Andrew.

Sure methods of improving health.
See Graham, Thomas John.

Surr, Thomas Skinner, 1770-1847
  George Barnwell. A novel.
Boston, N.H. Whitaker [Pr. by
J.H.A. Frost] 1828. 2 vols. MB;
MiGr; OClW; PU.   35442

[Swaim, William]
  Some remarks upon a publica-
tion by the Philadelphia Medical
Society concerning Swaim's pana-
cea... Philadelphia, 1828.
52 p. DLC; ICJ; MB; MBCo;
NNNAM; NbU-M; PHi; PPL.
                         35443
Swan, Jabez S.
  Funeral sermon, occasioned
by the death of Mr. Henry Miner.
Delivered at Stonington, Conn.
May 11, 1828. Stonington, Pr. by
W. & J.B. Storer, 1828. 21 p.
CSmH; CtHi; NN.   35444

Swedenborg, Emanuel, 1688-1772
  The Athanasian creed, ex-
tracted from the Apocalypse or
Book of Revelations explained, of
Emanuel Swedenborg. Boston,
Adonis Howard, 1828. iv, 232 p.

CtHT; CtMW; MB; MH-AH;
MeBaT; NNUT; NjP; NjR; PU;
RPA; RPB; ScC.   35445

---- Concerning the earths in the
solar system which are called
planets and concerning the earths
in the starry system... translated
from the Latin of Emanuel Swedenborg. Pub. at London by the
author, 1758. Boston, Adonis
Howard. Press of the New Jerusalem Magazine. Freeman &
Bolles, prs., 1828. 4, 197 p.
CtMW; ICN; MH-AH; MeBaT;
NjR.   35446

---- The doctrine of the New
Jerusalem concerning faith.
Trans. from the Latin of Eman-
uel Swedenborg. Boston, Adonis
Howard, 1828. [Press of the
New Jerusalem Magazine. Free-
man and Bolles, prs.] [2], 52 p.
CtMW; KyLxT; MB; MH-AH;
MeBaT; MiD; NjR.   35447

---- The heavenly doctrine of the
New Jerusalem, as revealed from
Heaven. ...4th Amer., from the
latest London ed. Philadelphia,
Pub. by Daniel Harrington. Thos. S.
Manning, pr., 1828. 114 p.
PHi; PLT; PPL; PU.   35448

---- On the intercourse between
the soul and the body, which is
supposed to take place either by
physical influx, or by spiritual
influx, or by pre-established harmony. From the Latin of Emanuel Swedenborg. Boston, Adonis
Howard, 1828. iv, 56 p. MB.
                         35449
---- A treatise concerning divine
love and divine wisdom. Boston,
Adonis Howard [Freeman &
Bolles, prs.] 1828. 179 p. CtMW;
MA; MNe; MeBaT; NNUT; NjP;
NjR.   35450

---- A treatise concerning the
last judgement and the destruc-

tion of Babylon... Boston, Hilliard, Gray, Little and Wilkins, and Adonis Howard [Freeman & Bolles, prs.] 1828. 143, 74 p. CtMW; MB; MH-AH; MeBaT; NjR; ScC.   35451

Swift, Elisha Pope, 1792-1865
Duties and responsibilities of the professional office in theological seminaries. A sermon, delivered in the First Presbyterian Church in Pittsburgh, October 16, 1828, at the inauguration of the Rev. Jacob J. Janeway, D. D. as professor of theology in the Western Theological Seminary of the Presbyterian Church in the United States... Pittsburgh, Pr. by Johnston and Stockton, 1828. 71 p. MBC; MH; MiD-B; NNUT; NjPT; OCHP; PHi; PLT; PPPrHi; PPiPT; BrMus.   35452

Swift, William Henry
Report of the survey of the route of the Ithaca and Owego Rail-Road. Ithaca, Pr. by Mack & Andrus, 1828. 16 p. DBRE; MWA; NIC; NN; NNE.   35453

Swords's pocket almanack, Christian's calendar for 1829. New-York, T. & J. Swords [1828] 48 l. MBAt; MHi; MWA; NHi; NNG; NNS; NjR; PHi.   35454

A system of Bible questions, historical, doctrinal and practical for the use of children and youth in Sabbath-school, Bible classes, and private families. By four clergymen. 2nd ed. corr. and imp. Ithaca, Pr. by Pew & Mathewson, 1828. 179 p. DLC; NIC.
35455

T

Tales and selections from the English souvenirs for MDCCCXXVIII. Philadelphia, Pr.

by J. Kay, jun. for Carey, Lea & Carey [etc., etc.] 1828. 300 p. MH; NRU.   35456

Tales of a grandfather. See Scott, Walter.

Tales of Peter Parley. See Goodrich, Samuel Griswold.

Tales of the Emerald Isle; or, Legends of Ireland. By a lady of Boston, author of "Tales of the fireside," and "Stories for children"... New York, W. Borradaile, 1828. 2 p. l., 258 p. DLC; MH; MWA; PU; RPB.
35457

Tales of the west. See Carne, John.

Taliaferro, John
Supplemental account of some of the bloody deeds of General Jackson, being a supplement to the "Coffin handbill." John Taliaferro. Member of Congress from Northern Neck, Va. [1828] 1 p. DLC.   35458

The talisman for 1829. New York, Elam Bliss [J. Seymour, pr.] 1828. x, [2] 342 p. DLC; KHi; LU; MH; MWA; NNP; ScCliTO; TxU; WU.   35459

Tanner, Henry Schenck, 1786-1858
A new pocket atlas of the United States, with the roads and distances, designed for the use of travelers... Philadelphia, Pub. by the author, 1828. 2 p., 12 maps. DLC.   35460

[----] The stranger's guide to the public buildings, places of amusement, streets... steam boat landings, stage offices, etc., etc. of the city of Philadelphia and adjoining districts... Philadelphia, H. S. Tanner, 1828. 38, 10 p. DLC; MB; PHi; PPL; PU. 35461

Tappan, Benjamin, 1788-1863
Song of the angels at the birth
of Christ. A sermon delivered
in Augusta, on the evening of
December 25, 1827. Augusta, Pr.
by Eaton & Severance, 1828. 23
p. MB; MBC; MH-AH; MWA;
MeLB.   35462

[Tappan, Lewis] 1788-1873
Letter from a gentleman in
Boston to a Unitarian clergyman
of that city... Boston, T. R. Mar-
vin, pr., 1828. 20 p. CSmH;
CtHC; DLC; ICMe; ICU; MB;
MBC; MH; MWA; MiD-B; MiU;
Nh; RPB; WHi.   35463

[----] ---- 2d ed. Boston, T. R.
Marvin, pr., 1828. 20 p. CtHC;
MBAt; MNF; MWA; MiD-B;
OClWHi; PPL; TxDaM.   35464

[----] ---- 3rd ed. Boston, T. R.
Marvin, pr., 1828. 20 p. DLC;
MH; MWA; NNUT; PPL.   35465

[----] ---- 4th ed. Boston, T.
R. Marvin, pr., 1828. 20 p.
CBPac; CtHC; MH; MeBaT;
MoSpD; N; NNC.   35466

Tariff; or rates of duties payable,
according to the existing laws
and Treasury decisions, on the
first day of July, 1828... Washington, Pr. by E. DeKrafft,
1828. 1 p. l., [35]-111 p. DLC.
                             35467

Taylor, Benjamin Cook
A sermon delivered in the Reformed Dutch Church at English
Neighbourhood, N. J. before the
Education Society of the Classis
of Bergen, on Tuesday, November 25, 1828. New York, Vanderpool & Cole, 1828. 20 p. [i. e.
[1]-17 [18] bl. 19-20 "Constitution of the Education Society"]
CtHC; N; NjP; PPPrHi (17 p.)
                             35468
Taylor, Ben
To the freemen of Kentucky...

Ben Taylor Woodford County
[Ky.] Oct. 1st 1828. 2 p. DLC.
                             35469
Taylor, Jane, 1783-1824
Poetical remains of the late
Jane Taylor; with extracts from
her correspondence. Stereotyped
by L. Johnson. Philadelphia, Pr.
& pub. by Wm. Stavely, 1828.
144 p. MWA; PPAmS.   35470

Taylor, Joseph
The wonders of the horse, re-
corded in anecdotes, and inter-
spersed with poetry... New York,
G. G. Sickels, 1828. 144 p. MH;
OMC; VtU.   35471

Taylor, Nathaniel William, 1786-
1858
Concio ad clerum. A sermon
delivered in the chapel of Yale
College, September 10, 1828.
New Haven, Pr. by H. Howe,
1828. 38 p. CSmH; CU; CtY;
DLC; ICN; MB; MH; MWA;
MiD-B; NN; NNC; OO; PPPrHi;
RPB; WHi; BrMus.   35472

Taylor, Thomas House, 1799-
1867
Address delivered in St.
Paul's Church, Radcliffeborough,
before the Charleston Protestant
Episcopal Sunday School Society
... at their 9th anniversary, May
27... 1828. Charleston, A. E.
Miller, 1828. 10 p. ScC. 35473

A teacher, pseud. See Dix,
Dorothea Lynde.

A teacher, pseud. See Scholar's
guide to chirography.

A teacher of little children in
Philadelphia. See The child's
instructer.

Teackle, Mr.
... Sketch of Mr. Teackles remarks, in the House of Delegates,
in the debate upon sales by public

auction. House of Delegates. Thursday, Feb. 14, 1828. (Carrolltonian-Extra. Wednesday, February 20, 1828. Annapolis, Md.) [Annapolis, 1828] 1 p. DLC.
35474

Teissier, J. A.
Projected salt works in Boston Bay. [Boston, 1828] 8 p. DLC; MB.
35475

Temperate Society of Canandaigua
(Circular) [Canandaigua, 1828] Bdsd. NCanHi.
35476

Templi carmina. See Brown, Bartholomew.

The Tennesseean [pseud.] See Armstrong, James L.

Tenney, Caleb Jewett, 1780-1847
New England distinguished. A discourse, preached in Wethersfield, Nov. 29, 1827, being the day of annual thanksgiving, with an appendix. Wethersfield, A. Francis, pr., 1828. 16 p. CtHi; MBC; MH; NN; RPB.
35477

The terpsichorina, or, The companion to the opera. Being a choice collection of sentimental songs and duets... [No. 2] New York, Pub. at Whale's Theatrical, Play, Print, and Song Repository, and to be had of Bourne of Neal & Mackenzie, Philadelphia; and of Richardson & Lord, Boston, Evans, pr., 1828. [4] 68-96 p. MH; RPB.
35478

Testimonials, in favour of the Carstarian system of writing, as taught by Mr. Foster, at his establishment No. 84 Broadway, New-York. New York, Pr. by Elliott and Palmer, 1828. 24 p. N.
35479

Thacher, James, 1754-1844
American medical biography;

or, Memoirs of eminent physicians who have flourished in America. Boston, Richardson & Lord, [etc.] 1828. 2 v. in 1. CSmH; CtB; CtMW; DNLM; DeGE; GEU-M; GU-M; ICU; InU-M; KyLo; MB; MBAt; MHi; MWA; MdBJ; MoSM; NBu; NIC; NN; NNNAM; NNUT; NWM; NbU-M; NhD; NhHi; NjP; NjR; OCHP; PHi; PPAmP; PU; RHi; RPB; ScCM; TNJ; ViRA; VtU; WBB; WHi; BrMus.
35480

[Thacher, Samuel Cooper] 1785-1818
No. 18. On the evidence necessary to establish the doctrine of the Trinity, Printed for the American Unitarian Association. Boston, Bowles & Dearborn [Press of Isaac R. Butts & Co.] 1828. 16 p. CBPac; DLC; ICMe; ICU; IEG; MB; MBC; MH-AH; ScCC.
35481

[----] ---- 2d ed. Boston, Bowles & Dearborn, 1828. 16 p. KyHi; MB; MBAt; MH-AH; MMeT; MMeT-Hi; MeB; MeBaT;
35482

Thanksgiving ball. The pleasure , of your company, is requested at the Hall of T. L. Reed, this evening. E. Johnson, W. M. Bixby, H. Shaw, T. H. Kidder. (Managers) Wallingford, Dec. 4, 1828. Bdsd. Vt Arlington Historical Society.
35483

Thayer, Caroline Matilda (Warren) d. 1840
First lessons in the history of the United States... New York, J. F. Sibell, 1828. 147 p. DLC; NjP; PHi; TNJ.
35484

---- The gamesters: or, Ruins of innocence. An original novel, founded in truth. By Caroline Matilda Warren... Boston, J. Shaw, 1828. iv, 300 p. CSmH; DLC; ICU; IU; IUC; KU; MB;

MH; MWA; MdAS; MnU; RNHi; WHi. 35485

Thayer, Gideon F.
An address delivered at the opening of Chauncy-hall, on Monday, Aug. 18, 1828. [Boston] 1828. 12 p. DLC. 35486

Thayer, Nathaniel, 1769-1840
The Christian doctrine and ordinances. A discourse, delivered at Hubbardston, at the ordination of Reverend Abner D. Jones, November 13, 1828. Lancaster, Pr. by Carter, Andrews & Co., 1828. 24 p. DLC; PPL. 35487

---- A discourse, delivered at Lancaster, on the day of annual thanksgiving, Nov. 27, 1828. Lancaster, Pr. by Carter, Andrews and Co., 1828. 16 p. DLC. 35488

---- Means by which Unitarian Christians may refute misrepresentations of their faith. A discourse delivered at Townsend, Massachusetts, Feb. 10, 1828. Lancaster [Mass.] Pr. by Ferdinand and Joseph Andrews, 1828. 15 p. CSmH; DLC. 35489

Theatrical comicalities, whimsicalities, oddities and drolleries. New-York, Elton's theatrical, play, print and song store, 1828. 24 p. MH. 35490

Theodora; a dramatic piece in two acts. New-York, Pub. by John M. Danforth, 1828. 26 p. NNC. 35491

Theological Scholarship Society of St. Thomas's Church, New York. See New York. St. Thomas's Church. Theological Scholarship Society.

The third class book; comprising reading lessons for young scholars... 2d ed., greatly improved.

Boston, Hilliard, Gray, Little and Wilkins, 1828. 216 p. CtHT-W; DLC; MH; MeHi; BrMus. 35492

Thirteen letters. See England, John.

Thomas, Elijah
The young lady's piece book; or, A selection of elegant pieces in verse and prose, from various authors, designed for the use of schools, &c. Philadelphia, E. Thomas, 1828. 162 p. DLC; NNC. 35493

Thomas, M., auctioneer.
Library at auction. Catalogue of rare and valuable books; the library of the late Richard Peters, Esq. to be sold by order of the executor on Monday 15th December, 1828 at the auction store, No. 87 Chestnut St. M. Thomas, Auctioneer. Philadelphia, 1828. 39 p. PPAmP; BrMus. 35494

[Thomas, William]
Address to the freemen of Morgan County. [Springfield? 1828] 12 p. IHi. 35495

Thomas à Kempis, 1380-1471
An extract of the Christian's pattern, or a treatise on the Imitation of Christ, written in Latin by Thomas a Kempis. By John Wesley, A.M. Stereotype ed. Philadelphia, Pr. for the publisher, 1828. 208 p. OMC. 35496

---- The following of Christ; in four books. By Thomas a Kempis. With reflections at the conclusion of each chapter by the Albe F. de la Mennais. Baltimore, Pub. by Fielding Lucas, Jun., 1828. 341 p. DGU; ICN; PLT. 35497

---- Der Kleine Kempis, oder kurze Sprüche und Gebelhlein, aus denen meistens unbekannten

Werklein des Thomae a Kempis, zusammengetragen, zur Erbauung der Kleinen. Harrisburg, Bey Gustav S. Peters, 1828. 256 p. PHi; PPL. 35498

Thompson, John C.
An oration, pronounced at Burlington, Vermont, July 4, 1828. Burlington, Pr. at the Free press office, 1828. 32 p. NNUT; VtHi. 35499

Thompson, John Samuel, b. 1787
Unitarianism the religion of Jesus, or Critical lectures on the Unity of God, and Salvation of all Men. Philadelphia, Pub. by Edwin T. Scott, 1828. 60 p. MBAU; MMeT-Hi. 35500

---- Universalism vindicated, and the refuter refuted; by the Rev. John S. Thompson, A. M., being a reply to "The doctrine of universal salvation considered and refuted, in a letter to Mr. Thompson," by Lewis W. Covell. [Rochester, N. Y., 1828?] 15 p. MB. 35501

Thompson, Pishey, bookseller, Washington, D. C.
Catalogue of books on sale by Pishey Thompson... Washington city... Washington, Pr. by Gales & Seaton, 1828. 51 p. DLC. 35502

Thompson, Zadock, 1796-1856
Thompson's new arithmetic. The youth's assistant in theoretic and practical arithmetic. Designed for the use of schools in the United State.[!] Improved ed. Woodstock, Vt., Pr. by David Watson, 1828. 225 p. VtHi. 35503

---- ---- Improved ed. Woodstock, Vt., Pr. by David Watson, 1828. 216 p. MH; MiU; Vt; VtHi. 35504

---- The youth's assistant in theoretic and practical arithmetic. Designed for the use of the

schools in the United States. Burlington, Pr. by E. & T. Mills, 1828. 216 p. DAU; MH; MiU; VtU. 35505

Thomson, Charles West, 1798-1879
The sylph, and other poems. By Charles West Thomson... Philadelphia, Carey, Lea & Carey, 1828. 2 p. l., 110 p. DLC; LNHT; MB; MnU; PHi; PPL; PU; RPB. 35506

Thomson, James, 1700-1748
The seasons by James Thomson, to which is prefixed the life of the author by P. Murdoch, D. D. F. R. S. Concord, Pub. by Manahan, Hoag & Co., 1828. 204 p. MB; NN; NhHi; NjP. 35507

---- ---- Philadelphia, Pub. by Edwin T. Scott, 1828. 192 p. CSt; MH; MW; PPL. 35508

Thomson, Samuel, 1769-1843
Eine beschreibung von dem leben und medicinischen erfindungen von Samuel Thomson, enthaltend eine erklärung seines systems in seinem praxis, oder gewohneit, und die art und weise um krankheiten zu kuriren mit gekräuter-medicinen, auf einen ganz neuen plan... 1. deutsche, von der 4. englischen ausg. Geschrieben von ihm selbst. Lancaster, O., Gedruckt für H. Howard, bey J. Herman, 1828. 228 p. DLC; DNLM. 35509

---- Neue anweisung zur Gesundheit; oder, botanischer familien arzt, enthaltend ein vellständiges system von practistren, auf einen ganz neuen plan. ... Erste Deutsche, von der vierten Englischen ausgabe. Lancaster, O., Gedruckt für Horton Howard, bey Johann Herman, 1828. 144, [2] p. PPL. 35510

Thornton, Abel
  The life of Elder Abel Thornton, late of Johnston, Rhode Island, a preacher in the Freewill Baptist connexion and a member of the R.I.Q. Meeting. Written by himself. Pub. by the R.I.
Q. meeting. Providence, Office
of the Investigator, J.B. Yer-
rington, pr., 1828. 132 p. CU;
DLC; ICU; MeLB; NHi; NN;
NNC; PHi; RHi; RNHi; RPB;
                                 35511
Thornton, John
  Repentance explained and en-
forced... 2d Amer. ed. Baltimore, Pr. for Rev'd. G. Leidy.
[By J. T. Hanzsehe?] 1828. 189
p. MdBP; PLT.   35512

  Thoughts selected from the ancient and modern poets...Boston,
Hilliard, Gray, Little, and Wilkins, 1828. 258 p. CtB; ICU;
MB; MH; NNP.   35513

Tidd, William
  The practice of the courts of
Kings bench, and common pleas,
in personal actions, and ejectment;
to which are added the law and
practice of extents; and the rules
of court, and modern decisions,
in the exchequer of pleas. In two
volumes... By Wm. Tidd... 2d
Amer. from 8th London ed. Philadelphia, Towar & Hogan, 1828.
2 vols. Az; KyLxT; LNT-L; MH-
L; N-L; OCLaw; OClW; PU-L;
                                 35514
Tilghman, Benjamin
  Sir. The outrage committed
on Wednesday last on my person,
is doubtless known to you. You
may easily imagine that the re-
dress ordinarily given among
gentlemen was immediately
sought... Benjamin Tilghman.
Philadelphia, March 28, 1828.
1 p. DLC.   35515

Time's almanac for 1829. Baltimore, Plaskitt & Co., Wooddy,

pr. [1828] 11 l. MdBE.   35516

Timpson, Thomas, 1790-1860?
  Elizabeth C...; or, Early pi-
ety, an authentic memoir. By T.
Timpson, minister of Union
Chapel, Lewishorn, Kent. 1st
Amer. ed. Hartford, D.F. Rob-
inson, publisher, 1828. 107 p.
IObB.   35517

'Tis all a farce. See Allingham,
John Till.

To Messrs. N. Goddard. See
Carey, Mathew.

To Mr. Charles Adams, editor
of the "New Haven Chronicle."
Sir -- It is not from any merit
of your own, that I condescend
to address you ... Your conduct,
in regard to the recent disturb-
ances at Yale College, has ex-
cited the surprize of those who
could boast the honour of your
acquaintance, and earned for you
the scorn of the public...
[Signed] A student. August 19th,
1828. P.S. the above letter...
was written about a week ago...
you have retracted a part of your
calumnies. Go on, Sir, and re-
tract the whole... August 25,
1828. [New Haven? 1828] 1 l.
CtY.   35518

To sweep the Augean stable.
See Democratic Party. Ohio.

To the calm, considerate and reflecting; to the lovers of truth,
mercy and justice; to the Christian, of whatsoever denomination;
to the patriot, who loves his
country more than men; to the
Pennsylvanian, who is seeking to
advance his own and his country's
welfare - These pages are respectfully inscribed. Butler, Pa.
1828. 16 p. P.   35519

To the catholic voters of the

city of Baltimore. [Baltimore, 1828] 6 p. DLC.   35520

To the citizens of Ohio county. See Davis, William M.

To the citizens of the ninth congressional district. See Wickliffe, Charles Anderson.

To the citizens of the United States. See Carey, Mathew.

To the Commissioners of the Albany Basin... The memorial of the subscribers, owners of ground lying on the inland side of the upper part of the Albany Basin... [Albany? 1828?] 16 p. NN.   35521

To the farmers and mechanics of New-Hampshire. In a few days you may be called upon to decide, whether you will live under a monarchial government, or a republican government... [1828] 2 p. DLC.   35522

To the Federalists of the United States. See Catullus, pseud.

To the free voters of the state of Maryland. The present crisis of affairs as respects not only the United States, but the relative position of every potentate of Europe, calls loudly upon the inhabitants of the only Republic in the world to attend to their interest... [Signed Independence, Oct. ? 1828] 1 p. DLC.   35523

To the friends of Ireland. See Carey, Mathew.

To the honourable Senate and House of Representatives of the United States, in Congress assembled. The memorial of the undersigned, merchant tailors of the city of New-York, respectfully showeth... [New York, 1828]

Bdsd. DNA.   35524

To the honourable the Legislature of the state of New York... The petition of Felix Pascalis, M. D., of Samuel L. Mitchill, M. D. ... New York, Jan. 31, 1828. 4 p. NjR.   35525

To the independent electors of the Somerset and Penobscot congressional district. [Bangor? 1828?] 8 p. DLC; MH.   35526

To the members of the Pennsylvania Society. See Carey, Mathew.

To the members of the Roman Catholic Church. [Baltimore? 1828] 12 p. DLC; MdHi. 35527

...To the members of the Society of Friends. See Rickman, William.

To the memory of Mrs. Ann Carter Francis, Life of John Brown Francis of Warwick... [Providence, 1828] Bdsd. RPJCB.   35528

To the people. The real state of the case. [Washington, Mar. 24, 1828] 4 p. DLC.   35529

To the people of Cayuga County. See National Republican Party. North Carolina.

To the people of Kentucky. See Junius, pseud.

To the people of Kentucky. See Democratic Party. Kentucky.

To the public. See Benton Jesse.

To the public. See Gibson, John.

To the public. See Giles, William Branch.

To the public. ("The following papers contain all the publications which have appeared in the newspapers, from the parties, in relation to the publication of Mr. Jefferson's letter to Governor Giles of the 25th of December, 1825...") [Richmond, T. W. White, pr., 1828?] 17 p. MH; NN; ViU; WHi.   35530

To the voters of the third congressional district. See Brent, William L.

... To thinking men. He who will not reason, is a bigot; he who cannot, is a fool; and he who dare not is a slave... Any person, by applying to Marshall & Dean, bookseller, Rochester, N. Y., can learn the name of the writer of these remarks. He however assumes to the publick, the cognomen of Exploder. Plain Truth-Extra. Rochester (N. Y.) June 5, 1828. [Rochester, 1828] Bdsd. MNBedf.   35531

To William Jenkins, Esq. [Baltimore, 1828] [Signed Well Wisher] 8 p. DLC.   35532

Todd, David
    Judge Todd's answer and the court's decision, upon the article of impeachment preferred against him by the House of Representatives of Missouri, in session, 1828. The public is presented with my answer to the article of impeachment. David Todd, Jan. 22, 1828. [early Missouri press] 11 p. DLC.   35533

Todd, John
    An address delivered in the chapel of Amherst college before the Alexandrian Society, the Tuesday preceding commencement. Aug. 26, 1828. Amherst, J. S. and C. Adams, prs., 1828. 31 p. CBPac; CSmH; Ct; GDC;

M; MAJ; MB; MBAt; MBC; MH; MHi; MWA; NCH; NN; NNUT; OClW; RPB.   35534

The token, a Christmas and New Year's present. Ed. by N. P. Willis. Boston, S. G. Goodrich [Examiner Press, Hiram Tupper, pr.] 1829. [i. e. 1828] x, 348 p. CSmH; DLC; ICN; KU; MB; MH; MWA; NNC; PU.   35535

A token for children. See Janeway, James.

Tomline, Harold Nuttall
    Digested index to the crown law containing all the points relating to criminal matters... New York, Gould, 1828. 264 p. NjP.   35536

Tommy Wellwood or a few days of incident and instruction. New York, American Tract Society, 1828. 48 p. MB. (missing '67).   35537

Tonna, Mrs. Charlotte Elizabeth (Browne) 1790-1846
    Rachel. Boston, Crocker & Brewster, 1828. MB (unavailable 1970)   35538

Tooker, Mary M.
    A brief account of the religious experience, sickness and death of the late pious Miss Mary M. Tooker: Taken from her own mouth by two female friends. A. E. and P. B. a few weeks before her departure. New York, Pr. & pub. by J. C. Totten, 1828, 72 p. PPL.   35539

Tosca, William Augustus
    The Christmas gift; ... Boston, Bowles & Dearborn, Press of Isaac R. Butts and co., 1828. 20 p. MB; NNC.   35540

Totten, John C., comp.
    Selections of hymns and spiritual songs... To which is added,

an appendix containing funeral hymns. 20th ed. New York, Pr. and sold by John C. Totten, 1828. [191] p. RPB.   35541

The tourist's map of the state of New York, compiled from the latest authorities, Engraved by V. Balch & S. Stiles. Utica, W. Williams, 1828. 19 3/4 x 20 1/2. DLC.   35542

Tower, David
Four lectures on the Thomsonian practice of medicine. By David Tower... Canandaigua, Pr. by Bemis, Morse and Ward (for the author) 1828. 72 p. DLC.   35543

Towne, J.
An address delivered on the fifty-second anniversary of American independence... [Hanover, N. H. ? 1828?] 12 p. Nh.   35544

Townsend, John
An address delivered on Edisto Island, before the Agricultural Society of St. John's Colleton, at it's anniversary meeting on Wednesday, the 9th of July, 1828. Charleston, Pr. by A. E. Miller, 1828. 51 p. NHi; PHi.   35545

---- What is the character of the late tariff law? And what are the measures best calculated to meet it? Considered in a reply, addressed to a committee representing the citizens of St. John's, Colleton. Charleston, A. E. Miller, 1828. 24 p. CtY; ICU.   35546

Townshend, Vt. Congregational Church
Articles of faith, and form of covenant adopted by the Congregational Church of Christ, in Townshend, Va. [!], Apr. 25, 1828. With scripture proofs and illustrations. To which are added resolutions of President Edwards. Bellows Falls, Pr. by James I.

Cutler, 1828. 12 p. MBC; MHi.   35547

The tragical comedy, or Comical tragedy, of Punch and Judy. Extracted from the London ed. With a design, by G. Cruikshank. New-York, Neal & Mackenzie, at the Circulating Library, and Dramatic Repository, and Philadelphia [S. H. Jackson, pr.] 1828. 24 p. MH; MWA.   35548

Trah, Siuol
All hail old hickory!! Headquarters, Baltimore. November 8th, 1828... [Signed] Siuol Trah. 1 p. DLC.   35549

---- General orders. Headquarters, Baltimore, Oct. 28th, 1828. My fellow citizens- Behold I am unfaithful and true and in righteousness I will judge and make war. Behold my sign the Hickory tree! Look how he is shaking the great man, and make them fall; and you will all likewise perish if you do not partake of his leaves and receive my watchword. Jackson and Calhoun... [Signed] Siuol Trah. Baltimore, 1828. 1 p. DLC.   35550

---- Headquarters, Baltimore. 1st December 1828. Great official news. [Signed] Siuol Trah. 1 p. DLC.   35551

Transylvania University
A catalogue of the trustees and faculty of Transylvania University: together with the course of study in the institution. [Lexington, Kentucky. Joseph G. Norwood, pr., 1828] 4 p. KyBgW; KyLxT.   35552

---- Transylvania journal of medicine, Extra. Catalogue of the officers of the medical department of Transylvania University, and of the graduates of 1828. Lexington, Ky., Pr. by

Albert G. Meriwether, 1828. 8 p.
KyLxT; KyU.   35553

Treadwell, Daniel
    To S. C. Phillips, Benja.
Hankes and Perley Putnam, Esq's,
committee of the directors of the
Salem Mill Dam Corporation. By
Daniel Treadwell. Boston, 1828.
16 p. NjR.   35554

A treatise concerning religious
affections. See Edwards, Jonathan.

A treatise on the patriarchal, or
co-operative system of society.
See Kingsley, Zephaniah.

Trenck, Friedrich, freiherr von
der, 1726-1794
    The life of Baron Frederick
Trenck containing his adventures,
his cruel and excessive sufferings,
during ten years imprisonment at
the fortress of Magdebury, by the
command of the late King of Prussia. Also, anecdotes: historical,
political and personal. Exeter,
N. H. , Pub. by Laban A. Tyler,
1828. 2 vols. MB; MNe; NGH;
VtB.   35555

---- ---- Stereotyped at the Boston Type and Stereotype Foundry.
Boston, Pub. by T. Bedlington,
1828. 264 p. IObB; MH; MoSpD;
NIC; NT; NcD; NhHi; PPL; PU.
                              35556
Trenor, J.
    A physiological inquiry into
the structure, organization, and
nourishment of the human teeth,
...J. Seymour, pr. , New York,
1828. 25 p. NNNAM.   35557

Trial and dying confession of
Henry Evans...executed on Fri-
day the 22d day of August, 1828.
Watertown, Jeff. Co. , New York,
Pr. and pub. by S. A. Abbey
[1828?] NN.   35558

Tribute to the memory of De
Witt Clinton. See Staats, Cuyler.

Trimble, David, 1782-1842
    The address of David Trimble,
to the public, containing proof
that he did not make statements
attributed to him, in relation to
the charges against the President
of the United States, and Mr.
Henry Clay. Frankfort [Ky.] Pr.
by J. H. Holeman, 1828. 40 p.
CSmH; DLC; ICU; KyLoF; NN;
NjR; WHi.   35559

Trinitarian Society, Castine, Me.
    Correspondence between the
committee of the Trinitarian Society and the committee of the
First Society in Castine, on the
subject of a union of said societies, with some remarks by the
latter committee, and an appendix. Pr. by B. G. Bond, American Office, 1828. 24 p. MH.
                              35560
[Triolus,] pseud.
    The boarding school. A poem.
Brooklyn, Pr. by Piercy and
Burling, 1828. 8 p. NN. 35561

Troy Budget - extra. See Democratic Party. New York.

True Reformed Dutch Church
    The acts and proceedings of the
general synod of the True Re-
formed Dutch Church in the United
States of America, at the City of
New York, June, 1828. New York,
Pr. at the Conference Office, A.
Hoyt, pr. , 1828. 57 p. IaDuU.
                              35562
Trumbull, Henry
    History of the discovery of
America; of the landing of our
forefathers at Plymouth, and of
their most remarkable engage-
ments with the Indians in New
England, from their first landing
in 1620, until the final subjugation
of the natives in 1679. Boston,
J. P. Peaslee, 1828. 256 p.

ArBaA; CSt; Ct; CtHT; CtMW; CtSoP; DLC; ICN; MH; MdBP; MiU; MoS; NIC; NN; PP; VtB.
35563

Truth, pseud.
Review of a pamphlet, entitled "An epistle and testimony, from the Yearly Meeting of Friends, held in New-York," &c. &c. signed by Sam'l. Parsons & Anne Mott. New-York, Pr. by A. Ming, jr., 1828. 16 p. CSmH; MH; PHi; PSC-Hi.   35564

[Tucker, George] 1775-1861
The valley of Shenandoah; or, Memoirs of the Graysons... 2d ed. New York, O. A. Roorbach, 1828. 2 v. CSmH; DLC; ViU.
35565

Tuckerman, Joseph
Mr. Tuckerman's first semi-annual report of the second year, as minister at large. Boston, Bowles & Dearborn, 1828. [Press of Isaac R. Butts & Co.] 20 p. CtSoP; ICU; MB; MBAt; MH; MHi; MWA; NN; PPL.   35566

---- Mr. Tuckerman's second semiannual report of the second year of his service as a minister at large in Boston. Boston, Bowles & Dearborn [Boston, Press of Isaac R. Butts & Co.] 1828. 35 p. CtSoP; ICU; KWiU; MH; MWA; MiD.   35567

[Tuckerman, Joseph] 1778-1840
A word to fathers and mothers. [Boston, 1828] [Signed: A parent.] 4 p. MH; NN.   35568

Tuke, Henry
The faith of the people called Quakers, in our Lord and Saviour Jesus Christ, set forth in various extracts from their writings, by Henry Tuke. From the 3d York ed. Philadelphia, S. W. Conrad, pr., 1828. 81 p. InRE; N; NcD; PHC; PHi; PSC-Hi.   35569

Turner, Edward, 1798-1837
Elements of chemistry, including the recent discoveries and doctrines of the science. 1st Amer., from the 1st London ed. Philadelphia, J. Grigg, 1828. 499, [1] p. CtMW; MdBM; MiU; NBuU-M; NNC-P; NcU; OClW; PPC; PU; ViU; VtMiM. 35570

[Turner, William] 1761-1859
An abstract of the Bible history. 3d Amer. from the 7th English ed. with alterations and additions. Boston, Bowles & Dearborn, 1828. 216 p. MB; MH; MWA.   35571

[Turnor, John]
Price 6 1/4 cents. Observations, on the efficacy of white mustard seed, (sinapis alba) taken whole. From the 10th London ed., rev. and imp. [Stoke Rockford... Oct. 1827] [The above article, may be had of Joseph Callender, - J. B. Russell. New England Farmer Office. Boston, and of G. Thorburn & Son, New York] 8 p. [Boston, 1828] PPL.
35572

[Tuthill, Louisa Caroline (Huggins)?]
Love of admiration, or Mary's visit to B----. A moral tale. By a Lady. New Haven, Pub. by A. H. Maltby [Sold by Hilliard, Gray, Little and Wilkins, and Crocker & Brewster, Boston; also by Jonathan Leavitt and J. P. Haven, New York, [Durrie, Peck & Co., prs.] 1828. 160 p. CSmH; CtHi; CtSoP; CtY; NN; OMC; PP; PU.
35573

Twenty-two plain reasons for not being a Roman Catholic. Pub. by the American Tract Society and sold at their depository... New York, [1828?] 24 p. At head of title: (No. 62) MoS.   35574

The twin sisters; or, Two girls of nineteen: being the interesting

adventures of Sophia and Charlotte
Melford. An affecting narrative.
Written by Charlotte, one of the
sisters. New-York, S. King,
1828. 36 p. DLC.   35575

The twins. See Crocker, Sophia.

The two goats. Wendell, J. Metcalf, 1828. 8 p. MWA.   35576

The two lambs. See Cameron,
Mrs. Lucy Lyttleton (Butt).

Tyson, John S.
    Second edition. To Honorable
men. The attention of honorable
men is requested to the annexed
note. To Dabney S. Car. You
have without the slightest provo-
cation, repeatedly assailed my
character... I John S. Tyson, do
unhesitatingly pronounce you,
Dabney S. Carr, a political as-
sassin an unprincipled villian, a
liar and a coward; --a disgrace
to your party and a stigma to
the town. John S. Tyson July 8
1828. 1 p. DLC.   35577

Tytler, Alexander Frazer
    Elements of general history,
ancient and modern. By Alexander Frazer Tytler, F. R. S. E.
With a continuation, terminating
at the demise of King George III,
1820. By Rev. Edward Nares,
D. D. To which are added a succinct history of the United States;
with additions and alterations by
an American gentleman... Concord, N. H. , Pr. and pub. by
Horatio Hill & Co. , 1828. 527,
44 p. CLSU; CoD; IaDmD; KyDC;
MB; MDeeP; NSyHi; NjR; PAtM.
                          35578

U

Ude, Louis Eustache
    The French cook. By Louis
Eustache Ude... Philadelphia,

Carey, Lea and Carey, 1828.
439 p. LNHT; MW; MeHi.
                          35579
Uncle Sam's almanack for 1829.
By Joseph Cramer. Philadelphia,
Denny & Walker [1828] 18 l.
DLC; MB; MWA.   35580

An uncompromising Friend of
reform. See Cooke, John
Rogers.

Underhill, Daniel C.
    Tables of arithmetic made
easy... 3d stereotype from the
5th imp. ed. New York, Pr. and
sold by Mahlon Day, Stereotyped
by James Conner, 1828. 23 p.
MH; MnHi; NFred.   35581

Union College
    Catalogue of the members of
the class graduating at Union
College, July 23, 1828. [1828]
6 p. MWA; NSchU.   35582

---- Catalogus senatus academici,
et eorum, qui munera et officia
academici gesserunt, quique ali-
quovis gradu exornati fuerunt in
collegio Concordiae, Schenectadiae, in republica Novi Eboraci.
Schenectadiae, Typis Isaaci
Riggs, 1828. 26 p. N; NSchU;
PPL; WHi.   35583

Unitarian Association in the
County of Worcester
    Constitution of the Unitarian
Association, in the County of
Worcester. Worcester, Aegis
Press, 1828. 7 p. ICN; MeBaT;
MH; MWA; MWHi; NNUT.
                          35584
United States
    Abigail Appleton. Feb. 18,
1828. Mr. Ripley, from the
Committee on Naval Affairs, to
which was referred the petition
of Abigail Appleton, made the
following report: Washington,
Gales & Seaton, 1828. 2 p. (Rep.
No. 148) DLC; NjR.   35585

---- Abstract of American seamen. Letter from the Secretary of State transmitting an abstract of American seamen in the several districts of the United States for the year 1827. April 7, 1828. Read, and laid upon the table. Washington, Pr. by Gales & Seaton, 1828. 19 p. (Doc. No. 252) DLC; NjR.   35586

---- Act - state of Maryland. An act of the General Assembly of Maryland, entitled a Further supplement to the act entitled "An act for the promotion of internal improvement." March 17, 1828. Referred to the Committee of the Whole House to which is committed the bill authorizing a subscription of stock in the Chesapeake and Ohio Canal Company. Washington, Pr. by Gales & Seaton, 1828. 5 p. (Doc. No. 205) DLC; NjR.   35587

---- An act authorizing a subscription for the statistical tables prepared by George Watterston and Nicholas B. Van Zandt. Feb. 12, 1828. [Washington, 1828] 1 p. (H. R. 76) DNA.   35588

---- An act authorizing a subscription to the stock of the Chesapeake and Ohio Canal Company. May 9, 1828--Received. May 10 --Read twice, and referred to the Committee on Roads and Canals. [Washington, 1828] 3 p. (H. R. 41) DNA.   35589

---- An act confirming the reports of the Register and Receiver of the Land Office for the District of St. Stephen's, in the state of Alabama, and for other purposes. May 17, 1828. [Washington, 1828] 3 p. (H. R. 297) DNA.   35590

---- An act explanatory of an act, entitled "An act to reduce and fix the military peace establishment of the United States," passed March 2d, 1821. Feb. 20, 1828. Pr. by order of the House of Representatives. [Washington, 1828] 1 p. (S. 4) DNA.   35591

---- An act for ascertaining the latitude of the southerly bend or extreme of Lake Michigan, and of certain other points, for the purpose, thereafter, of fixing the true northern boundary lines of the States of Ohio, Indiana, and Illinois. May 5, 1828. Read, and passed to a second reading. [Washington, 1828] 3 p. (H. R. 230) DNA.   35592

---- An act for the benefit of Andrew Westbrook. April 28, 1828. Read, and passed to a second reading. [Washington, 1828] 1 p. (H. R. 16) DNA.   35593

---- An act for the punishment of contraventions of the fifth article of the Treaty between the United States and Russia. May 5th, 1828. Read twice, and referred to the Committee on Foreign Relations. [Washington, 1828] 1 p. (H. R. 290) DNA.   35594

---- An act for the relief of certain surviving officers and soldiers of the Army of the Revolution. May 1, 1828. Committed to the Committee of the Whole House on the state of the Union. [Washington, 1828] 3 p. (S. 44) DNA; MB.   35595

---- An act for the relief of Cyrus Sibley, agent of George M. Brooke. April 23, 1828. Pr. by order of the House of Representatives. [Washington, 1828] 1 p. (S. 136) DNA.   35596

---- An act for the relief of John B. Lemaitre, junior, and Robertson and Barnwell of Mobile. May 19, 1828. Read twice, and referred to the Committee on Finance. [Washington, 1828] 1 p. (H. R. 174) DNA.   35597

---- An act for the relief of Nancy Dolan. May 19, 1828. Read twice, and referred to the Committee of Claims. [Washington, 1828] 1 p. (H. R. 173) DNA.
                                    35598

---- An act for the relief of purchasers of the public lands, that have reverted for non-payment of the purchase money. April 28, 1828. The following bill having been amended, was reported to the Senate, and ordered to be printed with the amendments. [Washington, 1828] 3 p. (H. R. 13) DNA.   35599

---- An act for the relief of Samuel Ward. May 6, 1828. -- Received. May 7 --Read twice and referred to the Committee on Finance. [Washington, 1828] 1 p. (H. R. 75) DNA.   35600

---- An act for the relief of Sarah Chitwood. May 6, received --May 7, read twice, and referred to the Committee on Pensions. [Washington, 1828] 1 p. (H. R. 135) DNA.   35601

---- An act for the relief of Simeon Broadmeadow. Jan. 11, 1828, Received. Jan. 14, read, and passed to a second reading. [Washington, 1828] 1 p. (H. R. 57) DNA.   35602

---- An act for the relief of the legal representatives of General Moses Hazen, deceased. March 28, 1828. Pr. by order of the House of Representatives. Mr. Wolf, from the Committee on Revolutionary Claims, to which was referred the bill from the Senate, entitled "An act for the relief of legal representatives of

General Moses Hazen, deceased, reported the same, with amendments. [Washington, 1828] 1 p. (S. 66) DNA.   35603

---- An act for the relief of William Benning. Feb. 12, 1828. Received. [Washington, 1828] 3 p. (H. R. 32) DNA.   35604

---- An act granting compensation to Rebecca Blodget, for her right of dower in the property therein mentioned. April 25, 1828. Read twice, and referred to the Committee on the Judiciary. [Washington, 1828] 1 p. (H. R. 180) DNA.   35605

---- An act in addition to "An act making an appropriation for the support of the Navy of the United States, for the year one thousand eight hundred and twenty-eight." April 23, 1828. Pr. by order of the House of Representatives. [Washington, 1828] 1 p. (S. 135) DNA.   35606

---- An act in addition to the act, entitled "An act to provide for the sale of lands conveyed to the United States, in certain cases, and for other purposes," passed the twenty-sixth day of May, eighteen hundred and twenty-four. March 31, 1828. Received. [Washington, 1828] 1 p. (H. R. 4) DNA.   35607

---- An act in alteration of the several acts imposing duties on imports. [Washington, 1828] [4] p. DLC.   35608

---- An act in alteration of the several acts imposing duties on imports. May 13, 1828. Pr. by order of the House of Representatives. [Washington, 1828] 3 p. (H. R. 132, as amended by the Senate) DNA.   35609

---- An act making appropriations for certain fortifications of
the United States, for the year
one thousand eight hundred and
twenty-eight. Feb. 25, 1828.
Read twice, and referred to the
Committee on Finance. [Wash-
ington, 1828] 1 p. (H. R. 96)
DNA.   35610

---- An act making appropriations for internal improvements.
March 10, 1828. Read, and
passed to a second reading.
[Washington, 1828] 3 p. (H. R.
119) DNA.   35611

---- An act making appropriations for the Indian Department,
for the year one thousand eight
hundred and twenty-eight. April
24, 1828. Read, and passed to
a second reading. [Washington,
1828] 3 p. (H. R. 120) DNA.
                              35612
---- An act making appropriations for the military service of
the United States, for the year
one thousand eight hundred and
twenty-eight. Feb. 25, 1828.
Read twice, and referred to the
Committee on Finance. [Wash-
ington, 1828] 5 p. (H. R. 142)
DNA.   35613

---- An act making appropriations for the Public Buildings,
and for other purposes. April 29,
1828. Read twice, and referred
to the Committee on the District
of Columbia. [Washington, 1828]
3 p. (H. R. 158) DNA.   35614

---- An act making appropriations for the support of the Navy
of the United States, for the year
eighteen hundred and twenty-
eight. Feb. 18, 1828. Received.
[Washington, 1828] 5 p. (H. R.
91) DNA.   35615

---- An act regulating commercial intercourse with the islands

of Martinique and Guadaloupe.
April 8, 1828. Pr. by order of
the House of Representatives.
[Washington, 1828] 1 p. (S. 122)
DNA.   35616

---- An act supplementary to an
act, entitled "An act providing
for the correction of errors in
making entries of lands at the
Land Offices," passed March
third, one thousand eight hundred
and nineteen. Jan. 11, 1828--
Pr. by order of the House of
Representatives. Mr. Isacks,
from the Committee on the Public Lands, to which was referred
the bill from the Senate, entitled
"An act supplementary to an act,
entitled 'An act providing for the
correction of errors in making
entries of lands at the Land Offices," passed March 3, 1819,
reported the same, with an
amendment; which was read, and,
with the bill, committed to a
Committee of the Whole House
to-morrow. [Washington, 1828]
1 p. (S. 32) DNA.   35617

---- An act supplementary to
"An act for enrolling and licensing ships or vessels to be employed in the Coasting Trade and
Fisheries, and for regulating the
same." Mar. 31, 1828. Pr. by
order of the House of Representatives. [Washington, 1828] 3 p.
(S. 9) DNA.   35618

---- An act supplementary to
"An act to provide for the adjustment of claims of persons entitled to indemnification, under
the first article of the treaty of
Ghent, and for the distribution
among such claimants of the sum
paid, and to be paid, by the government of Great Britain, under
a convention between the United
States and His Britannic Majesty,
concluded at London, on the thirteenth of November, one thousand

eight hundred and twenty-six,"
passed on the second day of
March, one thousand eight hundred and twenty-seven. March 22,
1828. Pr. by order of the House
of Representatives. [Washington,
1828] 1 p. (S. 96) DNA.   35619

---- An act supplementary to the
several acts providing for the
settlement and confirmation of
private land claims in Florida.
March 31, 1828. Pr. by order
of the House of Representatives.
[Washington, 1828] 7 p. (S. 49)
DNA.   35620

---- An act to abolish imprisonment for debt. Feb. 11, 1828.
Mr. Wickliffe, from the Committee on the Judiciary, to which
had been referred the bill from
the Senate to abolish imprisonment for debt, reported the same,
with amendments; which were
read, and committed to a Committee of the Whole House to-
morrow. [Washington, 1828] 17 p.
(S. 1) DNA.   35621

---- An act to abolish the office
of Major General in the army of
the United States. May 15, 1828.
Read twice, and referred to the
Committee on Military Affairs.
[Washington, 1828] 1 p. (H.R.
280) DNA.   35622

---- An act to admit iron and
machinery necessary for rail
roads, duty free. Apr. 30, 1828.
Committed to the Committee of
the Whole House on the state of
the Union, and printed by order
of the House of Representatives.
[Washington, 1828] 1 p. (S. 132)
DNA.   35623

---- An act to aid the state of
Ohio in extending the Miami Canal from Dayton to Lake Erie.
May 20, 1828. --Received. [Wash-
ington, 1828] 3 p. (H.R. 94)

DNA.   35624

---- An act to alter and establish post roads, and discontinue
others. May 19, 1828. The following bill of the Senate, passed
by the House of Representatives,
with amendments, was referred
to the Committee on the Post Office and Post Roads, and ordered
to be printed, with said amendments. [Washington, 1828] 19 p.
(S. 133) DNA.   35625

---- An act to amend and explain an act, entitled "An act
confirming an act of the legislature of Virginia, incorporating
the Chesapeake and Ohio Canal
Company, and an act of the state
of Maryland, for the same purpose." May 8, 1828. --Received.
[Washington, 1828] 3 p. (H.R.
40) DNA.   35626

---- An act to authorize the appointment of a surveyor for the
Virginia Military District, within
the state of Ohio. May 20, 1828.
--Received. [Washington, 1828]
3 p. (H.R. 49) DNA.   35627

---- An act to authorize the
building of light-houses, and for
other purposes. May 5, 1828.
Read, and passed to a second
reading. [Washington, 1828] 5 p.
(H.R. 177) DNA.   35628

---- An act to authorize the improving of certain harbors, the
building of piers, and for other
purposes. May 5, 1828. Read
twice, and referred to the Committee on Commerce. [Washing-
ton, 1828] 3 p. (H.R. 228) DNA.
                             35629

---- An act to authorize the legislature of the state of Indiana to
sell the lands heretofore appropriated for the use of schools in
that state January 2, 1828. -Pr.
by order of the House of Repre-

sentatives. In Senate of the
United States. December 6, 1827.
[Washington, 1828] 1 p. (S. 2)
DNA.   35630

---- An act to authorize the
President to appoint a Superintendent and Receiver at the Fever
river lead mines, and for other
purposes. Apr. 9, 1828. Read,
and with the original bill, committed to a Committee of the
Whole House to-morrow. Mr.
Duncan, from the Committee on
the Public Lands, to which was
referred the bill from the Senate,
entitled "An act to authorize the
President to lease lots in the
town of Galena, and lead mines
on the Upper Mississippi," reported the same, with the following amendments, viz: Amend the
title to read-- [Washington,
1828] 5 p. (S. 51.) DNA. 35631

---- An act to authorize the purchase of a site, and the erection
of barracks, in the vicinity of
New Orleans. March 15, 1828.
Pr. by order of the House of
Representatives. [Washington,
1828] 1 p. (S. 74) DNA.   35632

---- An act to compensate Susan
Decatur, widow and representative of Captain Stephen Decatur,
deceased, and others. Mar. 18,
1828. Pr. by order of the House
of Representatives. [Washington,
1828] 3 p. (S. 50) DNA.   35633

---- An act to confirm certain
claims to lands in the territory
of Michigan. Feb. 25, 1828.
Read, and passed to a second
reading. [Washington, 1828] 3 p.
(H. R. 34) DNA.   35634

---- An act to enlarge the powers
of the several corporations of the
District of Columbia, and for other purposes. May 15, 1828.
Read twice, and referred to the

Committee on the District of
Columbia. [Washington, 1828] 9
p. (H. R. 128) DNA.   35635

---- An act to revive and continue in force, for a limited
time, an act, entitled "An act
authorizing the payment of certain certificates." May 17, 1828.
Read twice, and referred to the
Committee on Finance. [Washing-
ton, 1828] 1 p. (H. R. 193) DNA.
                          35636

---- An additional supplement to
the Catalogue of the Library of
Congress. Washington, Pr. by
Rothwell & Ustick, 1828. 16 p.
DLC; M; PP.   35637

---- Adjust claims of South
Carolina. May 5, 1828. Read,
and, with the bill, committed to
a Committee of the Whole House
to-morrow. Mr. McCoy, from
the Committee of Claims, to
which was referred the bill from
the Senate "for adjusting the
claims of the state of South Carolina against the United States,"
made the following report: Washington, Gales & Seaton, 1828.
86 p. (Rep. No. 246) DLC; NjR.
                          35638

---- Africans at Key West. Message from the President of the
United States relative to the disposition of the Africans landed
at Key West from a stranded
Spanish vessel. April 30, 1828.
Read, and referred to the Committee on the Judiciary. Washington, Pr. by Gales & Seaton,
1828. 10 p. (Doc. No. 262)
DLC; NjR.   35639

---- Agent--lead mines, Missouri and Illinois, &c. Message
from the President of the United
States transmitting the information required by a resolution of
the House of Representatives of
the 10th inst. in relation to instructions given for the govern-

ment of the agent of the United States' Superintendent of the lead mines in Missouri and Illinois; also, a report from the Secretary of War setting forth the reasons for not nominating the Commissioners to treat with the Choctaw Indians, &c. December 23, 1828. Read, and laid upon the table. Washington, Pr. by Gales & Seaton, 1828. 8 p. (Doc. No. 30) DLC; NjR.   35640

---- Alexander Garden. January 11, 1828. Mr. Creighton, from the Committee on Revolutionary Claims, to which was referred the petition of Alexander Garden, made the following report: Washington, Pr. by Gales & Seaton, 1828. 1 p. (Rep. No. 65) DLC; NjR.   35641

---- Alexander Scott. March 7, 1828. Read, and laid upon the table. Mr. Everett, from the Committee on Foreign Affairs, to which was referred the claim of Alexander Scott, made the following report: Washington, Gales & Seaton, 1828. 17 p. 1 bdsd. (Rep. No. 182) DLC; NjR. 35642

---- Allen B. McAlhany. April 3, 1828. Mr. Moore, of Alabama, from the Committee on Private Land Claims, to which the subject had been referred, made the following report: Washington, Gales & Seaton, 1828. 1 p. (Rep. No. 222) DLC; NjR.   35643

---- Amendment: The bill to graduate the price of the public lands, to make donations thereof to actual settlers, and to cede the refuse to the states in which they lie, being under consideration in Committee of the Whole, Mr. Tazewell proposed further to amend the original bill, by striking out the third section, and inserting the following in lieu there-

of. April 16, 1828. [Washington, 1828] 1 p. (S. 33) DNA. 35644

---- Amendment: Mr. Bates, of Missouri, submitted the following, which, when the bill [No. 144] further to amend the Judicial System of the United States, shall be taken up for consideration, he will move as an amendment of the same. Feb. 18, 1828. Read, and referred to the Committee of the Whole House to which the said bill is committed. [Washington, 1828] 3 p. (H. R. 144) DNA.   35645

---- Amendment: Mr. Bates submitted the following, to be proposed as an amendment to the above bill: When the bill [No. 219] "further to extend the laws on the subject of land claims in the state of Mississippi and the territory of Arkansas," shall be taken up for consideration, the following will be proposed. April 22, 1828. Committed to the Committee of the Whole House to which the said bill is committed. [Washington, 1828] 3 p. (H. R. 219) DNA.   35646

---- Amendment: Mr. Berrien offered the following amendment to the bill to provide for the final settlement of private land claims in the several states and territories. March 20, 1828. [Washington, 1828] 5 p. (S. 49) DNA.   35647

---- Amendment: Mr. Cambreleng, from the Committee on Commerce, to which was referred the bill from the Senate, entitled "An act to establish a port of entry at St. Mark's, in Florida, reported the same: March 31, 1828. Pr. by order of the House of Representatives. [Washington, 1828] 1 p. (S. 64) DNA.   35648

---- Amendment. Mr. Chilton submitted the following, which, when the bill to establish an armory on the western waters shall be taken up for consideration, he will move as an amendment thereto. Feb. 15, 1828. Read, and committed to the Committee of the Whole House to which the said bill is committed. [Washington, 1828] 1 p. (H. R. 150) DNA. 35649

---- Amendment. Mr. Crockett submitted the following, which, when the Bill H. R. No. 27, "to amend an act, entitled an act to authorize the state of Tennessee to issue grants and perfect titles, to certain lands therein described, and to settle the claims to vacant and unappropriated lands in the same," passed 18th April, 1806, comes up for consideration, he will move as an amendment. Dec. 11, 1828. Read and committed to the Committee of the Whole House, to which said Bill is committed. [Washington, 1828] 3 p. (H. R. 27) DNA. 35650

---- Amendment. Mr. Drayton, from the Committee on Military Affairs, to which had been referred the bill from the Senate, [No. 6,] entitled "An act explanatory of an act, entitled An act to reduce and fix the military peace establishment of the United States, passed March second, one thousand eight hundred and twenty-one," reported the same with the following amendment. [Washington, 1828] 3 p. (S. 6) DNA. 35651

---- Amendment. Mr. Isacks, from the Committee on the Public Lands, to which was referred the bill from the Senate, entitled "An act for the benefit of the Trustees of the Lafayette Academy, in Alabama," reported the same with an amendment.

April 28, 1828. Pr. by order of the House of Representatives. [Washington, 1828] 1 p. (S. 67) DNA. 35652

---- Amendment. Mr. Smith, of Indiana, submitted the following, which, when the bill to graduate the price of public lands, to make donations thereof to actual settlers, and to cede the refuse to the states in which they may lie, upon equitable terms, shall be taken up for consideration, he proposes to move as an amendment of the same. Mar. 27, 1828. Read, and committed to the Committee of the Whole House, to which the said bill is committed. [Washington, 1828] 3 p. (H. R. 145) DNA. 35653

---- Amendment: Mr. Van Buren, from the Committee on the Judiciary, to whom was recommitted the "bill for regulating processes in the courts of the United States in the states admitted into the Union since the 29th of September, 1789," reported the same with the following amendment. March 17, 1828. [Washington, 1828] 1 p. (S. 11) DNA. 35654

---- Amendment: Mr. Vinton submitted the following, which, when the "Bill (No. 145) to graduate the price of the Public Lands; to make donations thereof to actual settlers; and to cede the refuse to the States in which they lie, upon equitable terms," shall be taken up for consideration, he will propose as an amendment. Feb. 7, 1828. Read, and committed to the Committee of the Whole House to which the said bill is committed. [Washington, 1828] 1 p. (H. R. 145) DNA. 35655

---- Amendment. Mr. White submitted the following as an amendment to be proposed to the bill

[No. 132] in alteration of the several acts imposing duties on imports, when that bill shall be taken up for consideration by the House. Feb. 29, 1828. Referred to the Committee of the Whole House to which the said bill is committed. [Washington, 1828] 1 p. (H. R. 132) DNA.   35656

---- Amendment: Mr. Whittlesey, from the Committee of Claims, to which was recommitted the bill for the relief of Marigny D'Auterive, reported the same, with the following amendment. Marigny D'Auterive. March 24, 1828. [Washington, 1828] 1 p. (H. R. 19) DNA.   35657

---- Amendment. Mr. Williams, from the Committee of Claims, to which was recommitted the bill for the relief of Richard Harris and Nimrod Farrow, reported the same with the following amendment. March 12, 1828. Read, and with the Bill, committed to a Committee of the Whole House to-morrow. [Washington, 1828] 1 p. (H. R. 210) DNA.   35658

---- Amendment: Mr. Woodbury offered the following as an amendment to the bill for the relief of certain surviving Officers of the Army of the Revolution. March 27, 1828. [Washington, 1828] 1 p. (S. 44) DNA.   35659

---- Amendment. Mr. Woods, of Ohio, submitted the following, which when the bill making an appropriation to defray the expenses of certain Indians who propose to emigrate, shall be taken up for consideration, he will move as a substitute for the said bill: March 22, 1828. Referred to the Committee of the Whole House on the State of the Union to which the said bill is committed. [Washington, 1828]

3 p. (H. R. 55) DNA.   35660

---- Amendment. Mr. Wright, of Ohio, submitted the following amendment to the bill in alteration of the several acts imposing duties on imports. April 2, 1828. [Washington, 1828] 3 p. (H. R. 132) DNA.   35661

---- Amendment proposed by Mr. Kane, to the bill, entitled "An act in alteration of the several acts imposing duties on imports:" May 5, 1828. [Washington, 1828] 1 p. (H. R. 132) DNA.   35662

---- Amendment proposed to be offered to the bill in alteration of the several acts imposing duties on imports. Mr. Wolf submitted the following: March 3, 1828. Read, and laid upon the table. [Washington, 1828] 1 p. (H. R. 132) DNA.   35663

---- Amendment to a bill to amend and consolidate the acts respecting copy-rights. Mr. Verplanck submitted the following, which, when the "bill to amend the act for the encouragement of learning, by securing the copies of maps, charts, and books, to the authors and proprietors of such copies, during the times therein mentioned," shall be taken up for consideration, he will move as an amendment of the same. Feb. 21, 1828. [Washington, 1828] 7 p. (H. R. 140) DNA.   35664

---- Amendment to be proposed by Mr. Noble, to the bill more effectually to provide for the national defence, by establishing an uniform militia throughout the United States, and providing for the discipline thereof. March 21, 1828. [Washington, 1828] 3 p. (S. 53) DNA.   35665

---- Amendment to the bill "to

amend the acts concerning naturalization." Mr. Verplanck submitted the following, which, when the Bill to amend the acts concerning naturalization, shall be taken up for consideration, he will move as an amendment to the same. Feb. 15, 1828. Read, and committed to the Committee of the Whole House to which the said bill is committed. [Washington, 1828] 1 p. (H. R. 121) DNA. 35666

---- Amendments: The "bill to graduate the price of the Public Lands, to make donations thereof to actual settlers, and to cede the refuse to the States in which they lie," being under consideration, Mr. Barton proposed the following amendments. April 9, 1828. [Washington, 1828] 1 p. (S. 33) DNA. 35667

---- Amendments: The Committee on Finance, to which was referred the bill, entitled "An act making appropriations for Internal Improvements," report the same with the following amendments. March 20, 1828. [Washington, 1828] 1 p. (H. R. 119) DNA. 35668

---- Amendments: The Committee on Finance, to which was referred the bill entitled "An act making appropriations for the support of the Navy of the United States, for the year 1828, reported the same with the following amendments. March 3, 1828. [Washington, 1828] 1 p. (H. R. 91) DNA. 35669

---- Amendments: Mr. Hendricks, from the Select Committee on Roads and Canals, to whom was referred "the bill for the preservation and repair of the Cumberland road," reported the same, with the following amendments. March 17, 1828. [Washington,

1828] 3 p. (S. 6) DNA. 35670

---- Amendments: Mr. Hoffman, from the Committee on Naval Affairs, to which was referred the bill from the Senate, entitled, "An act for the better organization of the Medical Department of the Navy of the United States, reported the same with the following amendments. April 8, 1828. Read, and committed to the Committee of the Whole House to which is committed the bill [H. R. No. 162] regulating the appointment and pay of surgeons and surgeons' mates in the Navy of the United States. [Washington, 1828] 3 p. (S. 72) DNA. 35671

---- Amendments: Mr. Magee from the Committee on the Post Office and Post Roads, to whom was referred the bill from the Senate, entitled "An act to alter and establish Post Roads," reported the same with the following amendments. May 6, 1828. Pr. by order of the House of Representatives. [Washington, 1828] 19 p. (S. 133) DNA. 35672

---- Amendments: Mr. Mercer, from the Committee on Roads and Canals, to which was referred the bill from the Senate, entitled "An act to provide for opening and making a Military Road in the state of Maine," reported the same with the following amendments. April 12, 1828. Read, and committed to the Committee of the Whole House. [Washington, 1828] 1 p. (S. 113) DNA. 35673

---- American hemp, flax, and cotton. Letter from the Secretary of the Navy transmitting the information required by a resolution of the House of Representatives of the 12th May last, in relation to connecting with two or more

Navy Yards of the United States as many establishments for purchasing, water-rotting, and preparing for manufacture, American hemp, flax, and cotton, &c. &c. December 22, 1828. Read, and laid upon the table. Washington, Pr. by Gales & Seaton, 1828. 3 p. (Doc. No. 28) DLC; NjR. 35674

---- American water-rotted hemp, &c. &c. Reports from the Navy Department, in relation to experiments on American water-rotted hemp, when made into canvass, cables, and cordage. January 18, 1828. Pr. by order of the House of Representatives. Washington, Pr. by Gales & Seaton, 1828. 35 p. (Doc. No. 68). DLC; NhHi; NjR. 35675

---- Amos Edwards. Feb. 29, 1828. Read, and laid upon the table. Mr. M'Duffie, from the Committee of Ways and Means, to which was referred the case of Amos Edwards, made the following report: Washington, Gales & Seaton, 1828. 1 p. (Rep. No. 166) DLC; NjR. 35676

---- Amos Sweet and others. Feb. 29, 1828. Mr. Whittlesey, from the Committee of Claims, to which was referred the petition of Amos Sweet, made the following report: Washington, Gales & Seaton, 1828. 1 p. (Rep. No. 168) DLC; NjR. 35677

---- Angelia Cutaw and Cecille Boyer. Feb. 5, 1828. Mr. Smith, from the Committee on Indian Affairs, to which had been referred the petition of Angelia Cutaw and Cecille Boyer, made the following report: Washington, Pr. by Gales & Seaton, 1828. 2 p. (Rep. No. 127) DLC; NjR. 35678

---- Ann Brashears. Feb. 12,

1828. Mr. Buckner, from the Committee on Private Land Claims, to which the subject had been referred, made the following report: Washington, Gales & Seaton, 1828. 4 p. (Rep. No. 142) DLC; NjR. 35679

---- Anna Dubord. January 14, 1828. Read, and, with the bill, committed to a Committee of the Whole House to-morrow. Mr. Livingston, from the Committee on the Judiciary, to which had been referred the bill from the Senate for the relief of Anna Dubord, made the following report: Washington, Gales & Seaton, 1828. 1 p. (Rep. No. 70) DLC; NjR. 35680

---- Annual report - Commissioner of Public Buildings. Message from the President of the United States, transmitting the annual report of the Commissioner of the Public Buildings. Jan. 4, 1828. Read, and referred to the Committee on Public Buildings. Washington, Pr. by Gales & Seaton, 1828. 8 p. (Doc. No. 41) DLC; NjR. 35681

---- Annual report on the state of finances. Letter from the Secretary of the Treasury transmitting the annual report on the state of finances. Dec. 9, 1828. Read, and laid upon the table. Washington, Pr. by Gales & Seaton, 1828. 40 p. (Doc. No. 9) DLC; DeGE; NjR. 35682

---- Appropriations - first session, twentieth Congress. Statement of appropriations made during the first session of the twentieth Congress of the United States of America, specifying the amount and object of each. May 30, 1828. Pr. by order of the House of Representatives. Washington, Pr. by Gales & Seaton,

1828. 35 p. (Doc. No. 288) DLC; NjR.   35683

---- Appropriations - Naval service, for 1827. Letter from the Secretary of the Navy, transmitting a statement of the appropriations for the naval service, for the year 1827, the amount expended, and the balance remaining on the 31st December, 1827. Feb. 18, 1828. Read, and laid upon the table. Washington, Pr. by Gales & Seaton, 1828. 3 p. 2 bdsds. (Doc. No. 222) DLC; NjR.   35684

---- Appropriations and expenditures--War department 1827. Letter from the Secretary of War transmitting a statement of appropriations for the War Department for 1827; the expenditures of the same, and the balance in the treasury on the 31st December last. February 8, 1828. Read, and laid upon the table. Washington, Pr. by Gales and Seaton. 4 p. 7 bdsds. (Doc. No. 129) DLC; NjR.   35685

---- Appropriations for internal improvement. May 14, 1828. Read, and laid upon the table. Mr. McDuffie, from the Committee on Conference, on the part of the House of Representatives, appointed to confer with a Committee on the part of the Senate, upon the disagreeing vote of the two Houses on the amendments proposed by the Senate to the bill making appropriations for internal improvements, made the following report: Washington, Gales & Seaton, 1828. 1 p. (Rep. No. 257) DLC; NjR.   35686

---- Archibald W. Hamilton. March 14, 1828. Mr. Williams, from the Committee of Claims, to which was referred the petition of Archibald W. Hamilton,

made the following report: Washington, Gales & Seaton, 1828. 1 p. (Rep. No. 190) DLC; NjR.   35687

---- Asa Herring. Jan. 3, 1828. Mr. Ingham, from the Committee on the Post Office and Post Roads, to which was referred the petition of Asa Herring, made the following report: Washington, Gales & Seaton, 1828. 2 p. (Rep. No. 50) DLC; NjR.   35688

---- Assays of foreign coins-- Mint U. S. Letter from the Secretary of the Treasury transmitting a report of assays of foreign coins at the Mint of the United States during the past year. Apr. 16, 1828. Referred to the Committee of Ways and Means. Washington, Pr. by Gales & Seaton, 1828. 6 p. (Doc. No. 251) DLC; NjR.   35689

---- Attach part of Chicksaw Country to Monroe County--Mississippi. Feb. 11, 1828. Read, and laid upon the table. Mr. M' Lean, from the Committee on Indian Affairs, to which the subject had been referred, made the following report: Washington, Pr. by Gales & Seaton, 1828. 1 p. (Rep. No. 135) DLC; NjR.   35690

---- Augustus Aspinwall. Feb. 22, 1828. Mr. Alexander Smyth, from the Committee of Ways and Means, to which was referred the petition of Augustus Aspinwall, made the following report: Washington, Gales & Seaton, 1828. 1 p. (Rep. No. 155) DLC; NjR.   35691

---- Balances--collectors customs and receivers for land sold. Letter from the Comptroller of the Treasury transmitting a list of the balances standing on the books of the revenue which have remained unsettled by the collectors of the customs and others more than three years prior to the 30th September last; and a similar list in the case of receivers of public moneys for the sales of the public land. January 30, 1828. Read, and laid upon the table. Washington, Pr. by Gales & Seaton, 1828. 3 p., 4 bdsds. (Doc. No. 224) DLC; NjR.   35692

---- Balances on books of the revenue. Letter from the Comptroller of the Treasury transmitting a list of balances standing on the books of the revenue which have remained unsettled by the collectors of the late internal taxes more than three years prior to Sept. 30, 1827. January 30, 1828. Read, and laid upon the table. Washington, Pr. by Gales & Seaton, 1828. 3 p., 2 bdsds. (Doc. No. 224) DLC; NjR.   35693

---- Balances on the books of the register of the treasury. Letter from the Comptroller of the Treasury transmitting statements of balances on account of internal revenue on the books of the register of more than three years' standing; also, a list of balances on account of direct tax of 1815 and 1816. December 24, 1828. Read, and laid upon the table. Washington, Pr. by Gales & Seaton, 1828. 9 p. (Doc. No. 34) DLC; NjR. 35694

---- Baltimore and Ohio Railroad Company. Documents accompanying a memorial of the President and directors of the Baltimore and Ohio Rail Road Company. May 19, 1828. Pr. by order of the House of Representatives. Washington, Pr. by Gales & Seaton, 1828. 5 p. (Doc. No. 272) CtY; DBRE; DLC; DeGE; MB; MH; NN; NjR;

P.   35695

---- Baltimore and Ohio Railroad - iron. Mr. Buchanan submitted the following letter, &c. Upon the subject of obtaining a supply of iron for the Baltimore and Ohio Rail road. May 16, 1828. Pr. by order of the House of Representatives. Washington, Pr. by Gales & Seaton, 1828. 7 p. (Doc. No. 271) CtY; DBRE; DLC; DeGE; MB; MH; NN; NjR; P.   35696

---- Baltimore Chamber of Commerce. Memorial of the Chamber of Commerce of the city of Baltimore. January 22, 1828. Referred to the Committee on Manufactures. Washington, Pr. by Gales & Seaton, 1828. 3 p. (Doc. No. 82) DLC; NjR.   35697

---- Bank of the United States. Letter from the Secretary of the Treasury transmitting (in compliance with a resolution of the House of Representatives, of the 3d instant) the monthly statements of the affairs of the Bank of the United States for the year 1827. March 6, 1828. Read, and laid upon the table. Washington, Pr. by Gales & Seaton, 1828. 12 bdsds. (Doc. No. 100) DLC; NjR.   35698

---- Banks of the District of Columbia. Letter from the Secretary of the Treasury, transmitting the returns of the incorporated banks within the District of Columbia. Jan. 14, 1828. Read, and laid upon the table. Washington, Pr. by Gales & Seaton, 1828. 13 p. (Doc. No. 59) DLC; NjR.   35699

---- Bannister Stone. January 28, 1828. Mr. P. P. Barbour, from the Committee on the Judiciary, to which was referred the petition of Bannister Stone, made the following report: Washington, Pr. by Gales & Seaton, 1828. 1 p. (Rep. No. 104) DLC; NjR.   35700

---- Baptist Missionary Convention. April 1, 1828. Read, and laid upon the table. Mr. Lumpkin, from the Committee on Indian Affairs, to which was referred the petition of the Baptist General Missionary Convention of the United States, made the following report: Washington, Gales & Seaton, 1828. 1 p. (Rep. No. 219) DLC; NjR.   35701

---- Barracks at Carlisle, Penn. May 21, 1828. Read, and laid upon the table. Mr. Orr, from the Committee on Military Affairs, to which the subject had been referred, made the following report: Washington, Gales & Seaton, 1828. 1 p. (Rep. No. 266) DLC; NjR.   35702

---- Barracks at New Orleans. Letter from the Secretary of War transmitting the information required by a resolution of the House of Representatives, of 14th inst. in relation to the erection of barracks at New Orleans, and the sale of the old barracks at the same place, &c. March 31, 1828. Read and referred to the Committee of the Whole House, to which is committed the bill from the Senate to authorize the purchase of a site, and the erection of barracks in the vicinity of New Orleans. Washington, Pr. by Gales & Seaton, 1828. 8 p. (Doc. No. 230) DLC; NjR.   35703

---- Barrataria. Documents accompanying the amendment proposed by the Senate to the Bill (H. R. No. 96) making appropriations for certain fortifications of the United States, for the year

1828. March 7, 1828. Pr. by order of the House of Representatives. Washington, Pr. by Gales & Seaton, 1828. 6 p. (Doc. No. 186) DLC; NjR.   35704

---- Benajah Wolcott. March 20, 1828. Read, and laid upon the table. Mr. Ramsey, from the Committee of Claims, to which was referred the petition of Benajah Wolcott, made the following report: Washington, Gales & Seaton, 1828. 8 p. (Rep. No. 202) DLC; NjR.   35705

---- Benjamin Freeland. January 14, 1828. Mr. Isacks, from the Committee on the Public Lands, to which had been referred the petition of Benjamin Freeland, of Indiana, made the following report: Washington, Pr. by Gales & Seaton, 1828. 2 p. (Rep. No. 73) DLC; NjR. 35706

---- Benjamin Simmons. January 28, 1828. Mr. Dickinson, from the Committee on Revolutionary Claims, to which was referred the petition of Benjamin Simmons, made the following report: Washington, Pr. by Gales & Seaton, 1828. 8 p. (Rep. No. 103) DLC; NjR.   35707

---- Bezaleel Wells. Petition for increased protection to woollen manufactures. January 22, 1828. Referred to the Committee on Manufactures. Washington, Pr. by Gales & Seaton, 1828. 4 p. (Doc. No. 83) DLC; MH; NjR. 35708

---- A bill allowing an additional drawback on sugar refined in the United States, and exported therefrom. Jan. 3, 1828. Read twice, and committed to a Committee of the Whole House to-morrow. Mr. Cambreleng, from the Committee on Commerce, to which was referred the petition

of sundry sugar refiners, reported the following bill: [Washington, 1828] 1 p. (H. R. 47) DNA.
35709

---- ---- Jan. 3, 1828. Read twice, and committed to a Committee of the Whole House to-morrow. Dec. 10, 1828. Repr. by order of the House of Representatives. Dec. 10, 1828. Passed through the Committee of the Whole House without amendment, and postponed until Monday next. Mr. Cambreleng, from the Committee on Commerce, to which was referred the petiton of sundry sugar refiners, reported the following bill: [Washington, 1828] 1 p. (H. R. 47) DNA.
35710

---- A bill allowing compensation to certain registers of land offices, and receivers of public moneys, for extra services, in the territory of Arkansas. Apr. 12, 1828. Read twice, and committed to a Committee of the Whole House to-morrow. Mr. Jennings, from the Committee on the Public Lands, to which the subject had been referred, reported the following bill: [Washington, 1828] 2 p. (H. R. 265) DNA.
35711

---- A bill allowing compensation to the members of the Legislature of the territory of Arkansas. Mar. 21, 1828. Read twice, and committed to a Committee of the Whole House to-morrow. Mr. Strong, from the Committee on the Territories, to which the subject had been referred, reported the following bill: [Washington, 1828] 1 p. (H. R. 234) DNA.
35712

---- A bill allowing the duties on foreign merchandise, imported into Louisville, Pittsburg, Cincinnati, and St. Louis, to be secured and paid at those places. Feb. 29, 1828. Mr. Woodbury, from the Committee on Finance,

reported the following bill; which was read, and passed to a second reading. [Washington, 1828] 3 p. (S. 110) DNA.   35713

---- ---- Dec. 8, 1828. Agreeably to notice given, Mr. Benton asked and obtained leave to introduce the following bill; which was read, and passed to a second reading. Dec. 10, read second time, and referred to the Committee on Commerce. Dec. 22, reported without amendment. [Washington, 1828] 3 p. (S. 10) DNA.   35714

---- A bill allowing to certain persons in the territory of Florida the right of pre-emption. Dec. 19, 1828. Read twice, and committed to a Committee of the Whole House to-morrow. Mr. Isacks, from the Committee on the Public Lands, to which the subject had been referred, reported the following bill: [Washington, 1828] 1 p. (H. R. 320) DNA.   35715

---- A bill altering the duties on wines imported into the United States. Jan. 30, 1828. Read twice, and committed to a Committee of the Whole House on the state of the Union. Mr. Cambreleng, from the Committee on Commerce, to which the subject had been referred, reported the following bill: [Washington, 1828] 1 p. (H. R. 130) DNA.   35716

---- A bill authorizing a subscription for the statistical tables, prepared by George Watterston and Nicholas B. Van Zandt. Jan. 14, 1828. Read twice, and committed to a Committee of the Whole House to-morrow. Mr. Wood, of New York, from the Committee on the Library, to which the subject had been referred, reported the following

bill: [Washington, 1828] 1 p.
(H. R. 76) DNA.   35717

---- A bill authorizing a subscription of stock for the establishment of a permanent post
road between the cities of Baltimore and Philadelphia. May 13,
1828. Read twice, and committed
to the Committee of the Whole
House on the State of the Union.
Mr. Mercer, from the Committee on Roads and Canals, to which
the subject had been referred,
reported the following bill.
[Washington, 1828] 3 p. (H. R.
301) DNA.   35718

---- A bill authorizing a subscription of stock in the Washington Turnpike Road Company. Jan.
30, 1828. Read twice, and committed to a Committee of the
Whole House to-morrow. Mr.
Mercer, from the Committee on
Roads and Canals, to which the
subject had been referred, reported the following bill: [Wash-
ington, 1828] 2 p. (H. R. 129)
DNA.   35719

---- A bill authorizing a subscription to the stock of the
Chesapeake and Ohio Canal Company. Jan. 2, 1828. Read twice,
and committed to the Committee
of the Whole House to which is
committed the bill (No. 40) to
amend and explain an act, entitled "An act confirming an act
of the Legislature of Virginia,
incorporating the Chesapeake and
Ohio Canal Company, and an act
of the state of Maryland, for the
same purpose." Mr. Mercer,
from the Committee on Roads
and Canals, reported the following bill: [Washington, 1828] 1 p.
(H. R. 41) DNA.   35720

---- A bill authorizing the corporation of Georgetown to erect
a bridge over the river Potomac,

within the District of Columbia.
Mar. 17, 1828. Read twice, and
committed to a Committee of
the Whole House to-morrow.
Mr. Alexander, from the Committee for the District of Columbia, to which the subject had
been referred, reported the following bill: [Washington, 1828]
3 p. (H. R. 223) DNA.   35721

---- A bill authorizing the establishment of an arsenal at or
near Pensacola, in Florida. Jan.
11, 1828. Agreeably to notice,
Mr. Johnston, of Louisiana,
asked and obtained leave to bring
in the following bill; which was
read, and passed to a second
reading. [Washington, 1828] 1 p.
(S. 55) DNA.   35722

---- A bill authorizing the laying
off a town on Bean river, in the
state of Illinois, and for other
purposes. Dec. 24, 1828. Mr.
Kane, from the Committee on
Public Lands, reported the following bill; which was read, and
passed to a second reading.
[Washington, 1828] 3 p. (S. 37)
DNA.   35723

---- A bill authorizing the Legislative Council of Florida, to
meet in October instead of December; and repealing the provi-
so in the sixth section of the
act entitled "An act to amend
"An act for the establishment of
a Territorial government in Florida," and for other purposes;"
approved, March third, one thousand eight hundred and twenty-
three. Apr. 8, 1828. Engrossed
for a third reading to-morrow.
Mr. Strong, from the Committee
on the Territories, to which the
subject had been referred, reported the following bill: [Wash-
ington, 1828] 1 p. (H. R. 257)
DNA.   35724

---- A bill authorizing the Legislative Council of the territory of Michigan to take charge of school lands in said territory. Jan. 14, 1828. Read twice, and committed to a Committee of the Whole House to-morrow. Mr. Haile, from the Committee on the Public Lands, to which the subject had been referred, reported the following bill: [Washington, 1828] 1 p. (H. R. 73) DNA.   35725

---- A bill authorizing the President of the United States, to appoint certain agents therein mentioned. Mar. 31, 1828. Mr. Macon, from the Committee on Foreign Relations, reported the following bill; which was read, and passed to a second reading. [Washington, 1828] 1 p. (S. 130) DNA.   35726

---- A bill authorizing the President of the United States to cause experiments to be made, to test the utility and practicability of a fire-ship, the invention of Uriah Brown. May 10, 1828. Read twice, and committed to a Committee of the Whole House to-morrow. Mr. Dorsey, from the Committee on Naval Affairs, reported the following bill: [Washington, 1828] 1 p. (H. R. 296) DNA.   35727

---- A bill authorizing the President of the United States to cause the boundary lines between the Pattawatima Indians and the United States to be surveyed and established. Feb. 11, 1828. Read twice, and committed to a Committee of the Whole House to-morrow. Mr. McLean, from the Committee on Indian Affairs, to which the subject had been referred, reported the following bill: [Washington, 1828] 3 p. (H. R. 159) DNA.   35728

---- A bill authorizing the refund-ing of certain moneys paid by the state of North Carolina for the purchase of certain Indian reservations. Jan. 22, 1828. Read twice, and committed to a Committee of the Whole House to-morrow. Mr. Carson, from the Committee on Indian Affairs, to which the subject had been referred, reported the following bill: [Washington, 1828] 1 p. (H. R. 102) DNA.   35729

---- A bill authorizing the relinquishment of the sixteenth sections, granted for the use of schools, in the state of Alabama; and the entry of other lands in lieu thereof. Feb. 22, 1828. Mr. King, from the Committee on Public Lands, reported the following bill; which was read, and passed to a second reading. [Washington, 1828] 1 p. (S. 98) DNA.   35730

---- ---- Dec. 17, 1828. Agreeably to notice given, Mr. King asked and obtained leave to bring in the following bill; which was read twice, and referred to the Committee on Public Lands. Dec. 22d, reported without amendment. [Washington, 1828] 1 p. (S. 32) DNA.   35731

---- A bill authorizing the Secretary of State to issue a patent to Elizabeth H. Bulkley, widow of Chauncey Bulkley, deceased. Jan. 7, 1828. Mr. Seymour, from the Committee on the Judiciary, reported the following bill; which was read, and passed to a second reading. [Washington, 1828] 1 p. (S. 47) DNA. 35732

---- A bill authorizing the Secretary of the Treasury to remove the collector's office, in the district of Passamaquoddy. Mar. 4, 1828. Read twice, and committed to a Committee of the Whole House to-morrow. Mr. Cambreleng, from the Committee on Commerce, to which the subject had been referred, reported the following bill: [Washington, 1828] 1 p. (H. R. 204) DNA.   35733

---- A bill concerning free persons of color in the District of Columbia, and for other purposes. Feb. 1, 1828. Read twice, and committed to a Committee of the Whole House to-morrow. Mr. Varnum, from the Committee for the District of Columbia, to which the subject had been referred, reported the following bill: [Washington, 1828] 1 p. (H. R. 139) DNA.   35734

---- A bill concerning the government and discipline of the penitentiary in the District of Columbia. Jan. 31, 1828. Read twice, and committed to a Committee of the Whole House to-morrow. Mr. Alexander, from the Committee for the District of Columbia, to which the subject had been referred, reported the following bill: [Washington, 1828] 11 p. (H. R. 134) DNA.   35735

---- A bill concerning the Orphan's Court of Alexandria County, in the District of Columbia. Mar. 12, 1828. Mr. Eaton, from the Committee on the District of Columbia, reported the following bill; which was read, and passed to a second reading. [Washington, 1828] 1 p. (S. 121) DNA. 35736

---- A bill concerning the selection of school-lands, in the several territories of the United States. Jan. 10, 1828. Mr. Barton, from the Committee on Public Lands, reported the following bill; which was read, and passed to a second reading. [Washington, 1828] 1 p. (S. 54) DNA.   35737

---- A bill concerning the Washington City College in the District of Columbia. Jan. 2, 1828. Read twice, and committed to a Committee of the Whole House to-morrow. Mr. Alexander, from the Committee for the District of Columbia, to which had been referred the petition of Jeremiah Keily, reported the following bill: [Washington, 1828] 1 p. (H. R. 31) DNA.   35738

---- A bill confirming the reports of the Register and Receiver of the Land Office for the District of St. Stephen's, in the state of Alabama, and for other purposes. May 10, 1828. Read twice, and committed to the Committee of the Whole House to which is committed the bill [H. R. No. 141,] supplementary to the several acts providing for the settlement and confirmation of private land claims in Florida. Mr. Isacks, from the Committee on the Public Lands, to which the subject had been referred, reported the following bill: [Washington, 1828] 3 p. (H. R. 297) DNA.   35739

---- ---- Dec. 10, 1828. Agreeably to notice, Mr. King asked and obtained leave to bring in the following bill; which was read twice, and referred to the Committee on Public Lands. Dec. 15, reported without amendment. [Washington, 1828] 3 p. (S. 13) DNA.   35740

---- A bill confirming to Francis Valle, Jean Baptiste Valle, Jean Baptiste Pratte, and St. James Beauvois, or to their heirs or legal representatives, of the county of Madison, in the state of Missouri, certain lands. Jan. 16, 1828. Read twice, and committed to a Committee of the Whole House to-morrow. Mr.

Whipple, from the Committee on the Public Lands, to which had been referred the petition of Francis Valle, et al. reported the following bill: [Washington, 1828] 1 p. (H. R. 80) DNA.   35741

---- A bill declaring the consent of Congress to an act of the General Assembly of the state of North Carolina, entitled, An act to incorporate the Occacock Navigation Company. Feb. 6, 1828. Mr. Branch, from the Committee on Finance, reported the following bill; which was read, and passed to a second reading. [Washington, 1828] 1 p. (S. 83) DNA.   35742

---- A bill establishing the territorial government of Huron. Jan. 15, 1828. Read twice, and committed to a Committee of the Whole House on the state of the Union. Mr. Strong, from the Committee on the Territories, to which the subject had been referred, reported the following bill: [Washington, 1828] 10 p. (H. R. 77) DNA.   35743

---- ---- Jan. 15, 1828. Read twice, and committed to a Committee of the Whole House on the state of the Union. Dec. 9, 1828. Repr. by order of the House of Representatives, with amendments. [Note.--The parts to be stricken out are pr. in brackets--the amendments in italics. Mr. Strong from the Committee on the Territories, to which the subject had been referred, reported the following bill: [Washington, 1828] 11 p. (H. R. 77) DNA.   35744

---- A bill explanatory of an act, entitled "An act to reduce and fix the military peace establishment of the United States," passed March 2d, 1821. Dec. 8, 1828. Agreeably to notice given,

Mr. Benton asked and obtained leave to bring in the following bill; which was read, and passed to a second reading. Dec. 10, read second time, and referred to Committee on Military Affairs --December 15, reported without amendment. [Washington, 1828] 1 p. (S. 6) DNA.   35745

---- A bill explanatory of "An act to compensate the Registers and Receivers of the Land Offices, for extra services rendered under the provisions of the act of the second of March, one thousand eight hundred and twenty-one." Apr. 24, 1828. Read twice, and committed to the Committee of the Whole House to which is committed the bill from the Senate, [No. 76] entitled "An act for the relief of John Brahan. Mr. Vinton, from the Committee on the Public Lands, reported the following bill: [Washington, 1828] 1 p. (H. R. 278) DNA.   35746

---- A bill explanatory of "An act to grant a certain quantity of land to the state of Ohio, for the purpose of making a road from Columbus to Sandusky." Mar. 10, 1828. Mr. Hendricks, from the Select Committee on Roads and Canals, reported the following bill; which was read, and passed to a second reading. [Washington, 1828] 1 p. (S. 118) DNA.   35747

---- A bill extending the limits of certain land offices in Indiana, and for other purposes. Feb. 25, 1828. Mr. Barton, from the Committee on Public Lands, reported the following bill; which was read, and passed to a second reading. [Washington, 1828] 1 p. (S. 100) DNA.   35748

---- A bill fixing and graduating

the pay of the surgeons and assistant surgeons of the Army. Jan. 11, 1828. Read twice, and committed to a Committee of the Whole House to-morrow. Mr. Hamilton, from the Committee on Military Affairs, to which the subject had been referred, reported the following bill: [Washington, 1828] 1 p. (H. R. 66) DNA.   35749

---- A bill for adjusting the claims of the state of South Carolina against the United States. Jan. 22, 1828. Mr. Harrison, from the Committee on Military Affairs, reported the following bill; which was read, and passed to a second reading. [Washington, 1828] 3 p. (S. 65) DNA.   35750

---- A bill for ascertaining the latitude of the southerly bend or extreme of Lake Michigan, and of certain other points, for the purpose, thereafter, of fixing the true northern boundary lines of the states of Ohio, Indiana, and Illinois. Mar. 18, 1828. Read twice, and committed to the Committee of the Whole House on the State of the Union. Mr. Strong, from the Committee on the Territories, to which the subject had been referred, reported the following bill: [Washington, 1828] 3 p. (H. R. 230) DNA.   35751

---- ---- May 10, 1828. Read twice, and committed to a Committee of the Whole House to-morrow. Mr. Strong, from the Committee on the Territories, reported the following bill: [Washington, 1828] 3 p. (H. R. 307) DNA.   35752

---- A bill for improving the inland navigation between the St. Mary's River and the entrance of the River St. John's, in Florida, and for other purposes. Jan. 11,

1828. Read twice, and committed to a Committee of the Whole House to-morrow. Mr. Mercer, from the Committee on Roads and Canals, to which the subject had been referred, reported the following bill: [Washington, 1828] 1 p. (H. R. 67) DNA.   35753

---- A bill for improving the post road leading from New York to Albany, in the state of New York, between Mesier's Mills, in the county of Dutchess, and Croton river, in the county of West Chester. May 21, 1828. Read twice, and committed to the Committee of the Whole House on the state of the Union. Mr. Marvin, from the Committee on Roads and Canals, to which the subject had been referred, reported the following bill: [Washington, 1828] 3 p. (H. R. 303) DNA.   35754

---- A bill for increasing the pay of the captains and master commandant in the Navy of the United States. Dec. 24, 1828. Read twice, and committed to a Committee of the Whole House on the state of the Union. Mr. Hoffman, from the Committee on Naval Affairs, to which the subject had been referred, reported the following bill: [Washington, 1828] 1 p. (H. R. 332) DNA.   35755

---- A bill for the benefit of Doctor Eliakim Crosby. May 8, 1828. Read twice, and committed to a Committee of the Whole House to-morrow. Mr. Sterigere, from the Committee on Private Land Claims, to which was referred the case of Doctor Eliakim Crosby, reported the following bill. [Washington, 1828] 1 p. (H. R. 295) DNA.   35756

---- A bill for the benefit of Elijah L. Clarke, of Louisiana. Apr. 1, 1828. Read twice, and

committed to a Committee of the
Whole House to-morrow. Mr.
Buckner, from the Committee on
Private Land Claims, to which
was referred the petition of Elijah L. Clarke, reported the following bill: [Washington, 1828]
1 p. (H. R. 251) DNA.   35757

---- A bill for the benefit of
George P. Frost, of Rochester,
and state of New York, Dec. 31,
1828. Read twice, and committed to a Committee of the Whole
House to-morrow. Mr. Buckner,
from the Committee on Private
Land Claims, to which was referred the petition of George P.
Frost, reported the following
bill: [Washington, 1828] 1 p.
(H. R. 348) DNA.   35758

---- A bill for the benefit of
John B. Dupuis. Jan. 7, 1828.
Read twice, and committed to a
Committee of the Whole House
to-morrow. Mr. Buckner, from
the Committee on Private Land
Claims, to which had been re-
ferred the petition of Joseph
Smith, reported the following
bill: [Washington, 1828] 1 p.
(H. R. 56) DNA.   35759

---- A bill for the benefit of
John Winton, of the state of Tennessee. Jan. 11, 1828. Read
twice, and committed to a Committee of the Whole House to-
morrow. Mr. Buckner, from the
Committee on Private Land
Claims, reported the following
bill: [Washington, 1828] 1 p.
(H. R. 63) DNA.   35760

---- A bill for the benefit of
Mary Ann Bond and Mary Loveless. Jan. 4, 1828. Read twice,
and committed to a Committee of
the Whole House to-morrow. Mr.
Shepperd, from the Committee
on Private Land Claims, to which
the subject was referred, re-

ported the following bill: [Wash-
ington, 1828] 1 p. (H. R. 50)
DNA.   35761

---- A bill for the benefit of
Samuel Blyth. Jan. 3, 1828.
Read twice, and committed to a
Committee of the Whole House
to-morrow. Mr. Burges, from
the Committee on Military Pensions, to which was referred the
petition of Samuel Blyth, reported the following bill: [Washing-
ton, 1828] 1 p. (H. R. 45) DNA.
                            35762
---- A bill for the benefit of
Samuel Sprigg, of Virginia. Jan.
17, 1828. Read twice, and committed to a Committee of the
Whole House to-morrow. Mr.
Buckner, from the Committee on
Private Land Claims, to which
was referred the petition of Samuel Sprigg, reported the following bill: [Washington, 1828] 1 p.
(H. R. 88) DNA.   35763

---- A bill for the benefit of the
North Carolina Institution for the
instruction of Deaf and Dumb.
Jan. 23, 1828. Mr. Barton, from
the Committee on Public Lands,
reported the following bill; which
was read, and passed to a second reading. [Washington, 1828]
1 p. (S. 68) DNA.   35764

---- A bill for the benefit of the
Pennsylvania Institution for the
Deaf and Dumb. Mar. 5, 1828.
Agreeably to notice given, Mr.
Marks asked, and obtained,
leave to bring in the following
bill; which was read twice, and
referred to the Committee on
Public Lands. Mar. 7--Reported.
[Washington, 1828] 1 p. (S. 114)
DNA.   35765

---- A bill for the benefit of the
Trustees of the Lafayette Acad-
emy, in Alabama. Jan. 23, 1828.
Mr. King reported the following

bill from the Committee on Public Lands; which was read, and passed to a second reading. [Washington, 1828] 1 p. (S. 67) DNA.   35766

---- A bill for the better organization of the Medical Department of the Navy of the United States. Jan. 25, 1828. Mr. Hayne, from the Committee on Naval Affairs, reported the following bill; which was read, and passed to a second reading. [Washington, 1828] 3 p. (S. 72) DNA.   35767

---- A bill for the continuation of the Cumberland Road. Jan. 2, 1828. Read twice, and committed to a Committee of the Whole House to-morrow. Mr. Mercer, from the Committee on Roads and Canals, reported the following bill: [Washington, 1828] 1 p. (H. R. 43) DNA.   35768

---- A bill for the continuation of the Cumberland Road. Dec. 4, 1828. Agreeably to notice given, Mr. Noble asked and obtained leave to bring in the following bill; which was read, and passed to a second reading. Dec. 5, read 2d time, and ordered to lie: --Dec. 11, referred to Committee on Roads and Canals:--Dec. 30, reported without amendment. [Washington, 1828] 3 p. (S. 1) DNA.   35769

---- A bill for the establishment of a General Superintendency of Indian Affairs in the Department of War. Jan. 2, 1828. Read twice, and committed to a Committee of the Whole House to-morrow. Mr. M'Lean, from the Committee on Indian Affairs, reported the following bill: [Washington, 1828] 3 p. (H. R. 29) DNA.   35770

---- A bill for the improvement of Pennsylvania Avenue, in the city of Washington. Feb. 22, 1828. Mr. Eaton, from the Committee on the District of Columbia, reported the following bill; which was read, and passed to a second reading. [Washington, 1828] 1 p. (S. 97) DNA. 35771

---- A bill for the improvement of the post road leading from Natchez to New Orleans. Jan. 24, 1828. Read twice, and committed to a Committee of the Whole House to-morrow. Mr. Stewart from the Committee on Roads and Canals, to which the subject had been referred, reported the following bill: [Washington, 1828] 1 p. (H. R. 108) DNA.   35772

---- A bill for the indemnity of William Stewart. Mar. 22, 1828. Read twice, and committed to a Committee of the Whole House tomorrow. Mr. Isacks, from the Committee on the Public Lands, to which was referred the case of William Stewart, reported the following bill: [Washington, 1828] 1 p. (H. R. 237) DNA.   35773

---- A bill for the preservation and repair of the Cumberland Road. Jan. 2, 1828. Read twice, and committed to a Committee of the Whole House to-morrow. Mr. Mercer, from the Committee on Roads and Canals, reported the following bill: [Washington, 1828] 5 p. (H. R. 42) DNA.   35774

---- A bill for the preservation and repair of the Cumberland Road. Jan. 2, 1828. Read twice, and committed to a Committee of the Whole House to-morrow. Dec. 13, 1828. Repr. by order of the House of Representatives. Mr. Mercer, from the Committee on Roads and Canals, reported the following bill: [Washington, 1828]

5 p. (H. R. 42) DNA.   35775

---- A bill for the relief of Abigail Appleton, of Ipswich, in the state of Massachusetts. Feb. 18, 1828. Read twice, and committed to a Committee of the Whole House to-morrow. Mr. Ripley, from the Committee on Naval Affairs, to which was referred the petition of Abigail Appleton, reported the following bill: [Washington, 1828] 1 p. (H. R. 171) DNA.   35776

---- ---- Dec. 22, 1828. Read and committed to the Committee of the Whole House to which is committed the bill for the relief of Elizabeth Mays. Mr. Ripley, from the Committee on Naval Affairs, to which was referred the petition of Abigail Appleton, reported the following bill: [Washington, 1828] 1 p. (H. R. 325) DNA.   35777

---- A bill for the relief of Abraham C. Truax. Jan. 30, 1828. Mr. Ruggles, from the Committee of Claims, reported the following bill; which was read, and passed to a second reading. [Washington, 1828] 1 p. (S. 78) DNA.   35778

---- A bill for the relief of Alexander Garden. Jan. 11, 1828. Read twice, and committed to a Committee of the Whole House to-morrow. Mr. Creighton, from the Committee on Revolutionary Claims, to which was referred the petition of Alexander Garden, reported the following bill: [Washington, 1828] 1 p. (H. R. 64) DNA.   35779

---- A bill for the relief of Allen B. McAlhany. Apr. 3, 1828. Read twice, and committed to the Committee of the Whole House to which is committed the bill for

the relief of Matthias Roll. Mr. Moore, of Alabama, from the Committee on Private Land Claims, to which was referred the case of Allen B. McAlhany, reported the following bill: [Washington, 1828] 1 p. (H. R. 253) DNA.   35780

---- A bill for the relief of Amasa Stetson. Feb. 1, 1828. Mr. Ruggles, from the Committee of Claims, reported the following bill; which was read, and passed to a second reading. [Washington, 1828] 3 p. (S. 80) DNA.   35781

---- A bill for the relief of Amos Binney. Dec. 30, 1828. Read twice, and committed to a Committee of the Whole House to-morrow. Mr. Bartlett, from the Committee on Naval Affairs, to which was referred the case of Amos Binney, reported the following bill: [Washington, 1828] 1 p. (H. R. 342) DNA.   35782

---- A bill for the relief of Amos Sweet, Stephen Jenks, Arnold Jenks, David Jenks, and Betsey Jenks, widow of George Jenks, second, deceased. Feb. 29, 1828. Read twice, and committed to the Committee of the Whole House to which is committed the bill for the relief of Wm. Shannon and Hugh Shannon. Mr. Whittlesey, from the Committee of Claims, to which was referred the petition of Amos Sweet, reported the following bill: [Washington, 1828] 1 p. (H. R. 197) DNA.   35783

---- A bill for the relief of Ann Brashears, of Mississippi. Feb. 12, 1828. Read twice, and committed to a Committee of the Whole House to-morrow. Mr. Buckner, from the Committee on Private Land Claims, to which was referred the petition of Thomas B. Magruder and Ann Brashears, reported the following bill: [Washington, 1828] 1 p. (H. R. 163) DNA.   35784

---- A bill for the relief of Anthony Hermange. Feb. 25, 1828. Read twice, and committed to a Committee of the Whole House to-morrow. Mr. Kerr, from the Committee on the Judiciary, to which was referred the case of Anthony Hermange, reported the following bill: [Washington, 1828] 1 p. (H. R. 187) DNA.
35785

---- A bill for the relief of Archibald Bard and John Findlay, executors of the last will and testament of Doctor Robert Johnson, deceased. Jan. 11, 1828. Read twice, and committed to a Committee of the Whole House to-morrow. Mr. Wolf, from the Committee on Revolutionary Claims, to which was referred the petition of the Executors of Robert Johnson, reported the following bill: [Washington, 1828] 1 p. (H. R. 62) DNA.
35786

---- A bill for the relief of Archibald W. Hamilton. Mar. 14, 1828. Read twice, and committed to a Committee of the Whole House to-morrow. Mr. Williams, from the Committee of Claims, reported the following bill: [Washington, 1828] 1 p. (H. R. 218) DNA.   35787

---- A bill for the relief of Asa Herring. Jan. 3, 1828. Read twice, and committed to a Committee of the Whole House to-morrow. Mr. Ingham, from the Committee on the Post Office and Post Roads, to which was referred the petition of Asa Herring, reported the following bill: [Washington, 1828] 1 p. (H. R. 48) DNA.   35788

---- A bill for the relief of Augustus Aspinwall. Feb. 22, 1828. Read twice, and committed to the Committee of the Whole House to-morrow. Mr. Smyth, from the Committee of Ways and Means, to which was referred the petition of Augustus Aspinwall, reported the following bill: [Washington, 1828] 1 p. (H. R. 179) DNA.   35789

---- A bill for the relief of Bannister Stone. Jan. 28, 1828. Read twice, and committed to a Committee of the Whole House to-morrow. Mr. P. P. Barbour, from the Committee on the Judiciary, to which was referred petition of Bannister Stone, reported the following bill: [Washington, 1828] 1 p. (H. R. 114) DNA.   35790

---- A bill for the relief of Benedict Joseph Flaget, Bishop of Bardstown. Mar. 14, 1828. Read twice, and committed to a Committee of the Whole House to-morrow. Mr. McDuffie, from the Committee of Ways and Means, to which the subject had been referred, reported the following bill: [Washington, 1828] 1 p. (H. R. 221) DNA.   35791

---- A bill for the relief of Benjamin Freeland, of Indiana. Jan. 14, 1828. Read twice, and committed to a Committee of the Whole House to-morrow. Mr. Isacks, from the Committee on the Public Lands, to which had been referred the petition of Benjamin Freeland, reported the following bill: [Washington, 1828] 1 p. (H. R. 71) DNA.   35792

---- A bill for the relief of Benjamin Reynolds, of Tennessee. Feb. 15, 1828. Mr. Eaton, from the Committee on Public Lands, reported the following bill; which was read, and passed to a second reading. [Washington, 1828] 1 p. (S. 87) DNA.   35793

---- A bill for the relief of Benjamin Simmons. Jan. 28, 1828. Read twice, and committed to a Committee of the Whole House to-morrow. Mr. Dickinson, from the Committee on Revolutionary Claims, to which had been referred the petition of Benjamin Simmons, reported the following bill: [Washington, 1828] 1 p. (H. R. 116) DNA.   35794

---- A bill for the relief of Caleb Stark. Jan. 28, 1828. Mr. Bell, from the Committee of Claims, reported the following bill; which was read, and passed to a second reading. [Washington, 1828] 1 p. (S. 73) DNA.   35795

---- A bill for the relief of Cecille Boyer, and the children of Muta-ma-go-quo, all of Indian descent. Feb. 5, 1828. Read twice, and committed to a Committee of the Whole House to-morrow. Mr. Smith, from the Committee on Indian Affairs, to which was referred the petition of Cecille Boyer, reported the following bill: [Washington, 1828] 1 p. (H. R. 146) DNA.   35796

---- ---- Dec. 15, 1828. Read twice, and committed to a Committee of the Whole House to-morrow. Mr. Smith, of Indiana, from the Committee on Indian Affairs, to which was referred the petition of Cecille Boyer and Angelia Cutaw, reported the following bill: [Washington, 1828] 1 p. (H. R. 315) DNA.   35797

---- A bill for the relief of certain surviving Officers of the Army of the Revolution. Jan. 3, 1828. Mr. Woodbury, from the select committee appointed on

the subject, reported the following bill; which was read, and passed to a second reading. [Washington, 1828] 1 p. (S. 44) DNA.   35798

---- A bill for the relief of Charles A. Burnett. Feb. 25, 1828. Read twice, and committed to a Committee of the Whole House to-morrow. Mr. Sprigg, from the Committee on Expenditures on the Public Buildings, to which was referred the petition of Charles A. Burnett, reported the following bill: [Washington, 1828] 1 p. (H. R. 192) DNA.   35799

---- A bill for the relief of Cyrus Sibley, agent of George M. Brooke. Apr. 8, 1828. Mr. Smith, of Maryland, from the Committee on Finance, reported the following bill; which was read, and passed to a second reading. [Washington, 1828] 1 p. (S. 136) DNA.   35800

---- A bill for the relief of Daniel Goodwin, executor of Benjamin Goodwin, deceased. Feb. 21, 1828. Read twice, and committed to a Committee of the Whole House to-morrow. Mr. Wolf, from the Committee on Revolutionary Claims, to which was referred the petition of Daniel Goodwin, executor of Benjamin Goodwin, deceased, reported the following bill: [Washington, 1828] 1 p. (H. R. 178) DNA.   35801

---- A bill for the relief of David Ellis. Feb. 20, 1828. Mr. Parris, from the Committee on Finance, reported the following bill; which was read, and passed to a second reading. [Washington, 1828] 1 p. (S. 93) DNA. 35802

---- A bill for the relief of Dillon Buell. Feb. 29, 1828. Mr. Ruggles, from the Committee of

Claims, reported the following bill; which was read, and passed to a second reading. [Washington, 1828] 1 p. (S. 108) DNA. 35803

---- A bill for the relief of Dodd and Barnard, and others. Jan. 10, 1828. Mr. Smith of Maryland, from the Committee on Finance, reported the following bill; which was read, and passed to a second reading. [Washington, 1828] 1 p. (S. 52) DNA. 35804

---- A bill for the relief of Ebenezer Cooley, of Louisiana. Dec. 31, 1828. Read twice and committed to a Committee of the Whole House to-morrow. Mr. Vinton, from the Committee on the Public Lands, to which was referred the petition of Ebenezer Cooley, reported the following bill: [Washington, 1828] 1 p. (H. R. 350) DNA. 35805

---- A bill for the relief of Edward Allen Talbot. May 13, 1828. Mr. Rowan, from the Committee on the Judiciary, reported the following bill; which was read, and passed to a second reading. [Washington, 1828] 1 p. (S. 149) DNA. 35806

---- A bill for the relief of Elihu Hall Bay, and others, confirming grants to lands in the district west of Pearl River, derived from the British Government of West Florida, and not subsequently granted by Spain or the United States. Feb. 25, 1828. Agreeably to notice, Mr. Smith of South Carolina, asked, and obtained leave to bring in the following bill; which was read, and passed to a second reading. [Washington, 1828] 1 p. (S. 102) DNA. 35807

---- A bill for the relief of Elijah Carr. Dec. 15, 1828. Read twice, and committed to a Com-

mitee of the Whole House to-morrow. Mr. Jennings, from the Committee on the Public Lands, to which was referred the petition of Elijah Carr, reported the following bill: [Washington, 1828] 1 p. (H. R. 316) DNA. 35808

---- A bill for the relief of Elisha Tracy. Feb. 18, 1828. Mr. Ruggles, from the Committee of Claims, reported the following bill; which was read, and passed to a second reading. [Washington, 1828] 1 p. (S. 88) DNA. 35809

---- A bill for the relief of Elizabeth Mays. Mar. 7, 1828. Read twice, and committed to the Committee of the Whole House to which is committed the bill for the relief of Abigail Appleton, &c. Mr. Hoffman, from the Committee on Naval Affairs, to which was referred the petition of Elizabeth Mays, reported the following bill. [Washington, 1828] 1 p. (H. R. 209) DNA. 35810

---- ---- Dec. 11, 1828. Read twice, and committed to a Committee of the Whole House to-morrow. Mr. Hoffman, from the Committee on Naval Affairs, to which was referred the petition of Elizabeth Mays, reported the following bill: [Washington, 1828] 1 p. (H. R. 310) DNA. 35811

---- A bill for the relief of Elizabeth Shaw. Jan. 16, 1828. Read twice, and committed to a Committee of the Whole House to-morrow. Mr. Lawrence, from the Committee on Military Pensions, to which had been referred the petition of Elizabeth Shaw, reported the following bill: [Washington, 1828] 1 p. (H. R. 83) DNA. 35812

---- A bill for the relief of

Ezekiel Foster and Co. of Eastport, state of Maine. Jan. 17, 1828. Mr. Smith, of Maryland, from the Committee on Finance, reported the following bill; which was read, and passed to a second reading. [Washington, 1828] 1 p. (S. 62) DNA.   35813

---- A bill for the relief of Ezra Thurbur, and the legal representatives of Gideon King. Dec. 29, 1828. Read twice, and committed to a Committee of the Whole House to-morrow. Mr. Clark, of New York, from the Committee of Claims, to which was referred the case of King and Thurbur, reported the following bill: [Washington, 1828] 1 p. (H. R. 338) DNA.   35814

---- A bill for the relief of Francis English, of Indiana. Feb. 26, 1828. Mr. Barton, from the Committee on Public Lands, reported the following bill; which was read, and passed to a second reading. [Washington, 1828] 1 p. (S. 105) DNA.   35815

----- A bill for the relief of Francis H. Gregory. Feb. 26, 1828. Mr. Hayne, from the Committee on Naval Affairs, reported the following bill; which was read, and passed to a second reading. [Washington, 1828] 1 p. (S. 104) DNA.   35816

---- A bill for the relief of Francis Preston. Mar. 22, 1828. Read twice, and committed to a Committee of the Whole House to-morrow. Mr. Bates of Missouri, from the Committee on Private Land Claims, to which was referred the petition of Francis Preston, reported the following bill: [Washington, 1828] 2 p. (H. R. 236) DNA.   35817

---- A bill for the relief of Fred-

erick Onstine. Jan. 30, 1828. Read twice, and committed to a Committee of the Whole House to-morrow. Mr. Earll, from the Committee on Private Land Claims, to which had been referred the petition of Frederick Onstine, reported the following bill: [Washington, 1828] 1 p. (H. R. 124) DNA.   35818

---- A bill for the relief of Gabriel Godfrey. Mar. 10, 1828. Mr. Ruggles, from the Committee of Claims, reported the following bill; which was read, and passed to a second reading. [Washington, 1828] 1 p. (S. 119) DNA.   35819

---- A bill for the relief of George Johnston, Jonathan W. Ford, Josiah Mason, and John English. Jan. 2, 1828. Read twice, and committed to a Committee of the Whole House to-morrow. Mr. Whittlesey, from the Committee of Claims, to which was referred the petition of George Johnston, and others, reported the following bill: [Washington, 1828] 1 p. (H. R. 30) DNA.   35820

---- A bill for the relief of George Wilson. Feb. 19, 1828. Mr. Van Buren, from the Committee on the Judiciary, reported the following bill; which was read, and passed to a second reading. [Washington, 1828] 1 p. (S. 91) DNA.   35821

---- A bill for the relief of Hampton L. Boone, of Missouri. Jan. 3, 1828. Mr. Barton, from the Committee on Public Lands, reported the following bill; which was read, and passed to a second reading. [Washington, 1828] 1 p. (S. 43) DNA.   35822

---- A bill for the relief of Henry

Case. May 1, 1828. Mr. King, from the Committee on Public Lands, reported the following bill; which was read, and passed to a second reading. [Washington, 1828] 1 p. (S. 148) DNA. 35823

---- ---- Dec. 9, 1828. Agreeably to notice given, Mr. Noble asked and obtained leave to bring in the following bill; which was read, and passed to a second reading. Dec. 10, read second time, and referred to the Committee on Public Lands--Dec. 17, reported without amendment. [Washington, 1828] 1 p. (S. 11) DNA. 35824

---- A bill for the relief of Hyacinth Bernard. Dec. 29, 1828. Read twice, and committed to a Committee of the Whole House to-morrow. Mr. Gurley, from the Committee on the Public Lands, reported the following bill: [Washington, 1828] 1 p. (H. R. 339) DNA. 35825

---- A bill for the relief of James Fraser. Feb. 8, 1828. Mr. Eaton, from the Committee on the District of Columbia, reported the following bill; which was read, and passed to a second reading. [Washington, 1828] 1 p. (S. 84) DNA. 35826

---- A bill for the relief of James Russel. Mar. 22, 1828. Read twice, and committed to a Committee of the Whole House to-morrow. Mr. Bates, of Missouri, from the Committee on Private Land Claims, to which was referred the petition of James Russel, reported the following bill: [Washington, 1828] 1 p. (H. R. 238) DNA. 35827

---- A bill for the relief of Jane Mary Lawrence. Feb. 1, 1828. Read twice, and committed to a Committee of the Whole House to-morrow. Mr. Bates of Missouri, from the Committee on Military Pensions, to which was referred the petition of Jane Mary Lawrence, reported the following bill: [Washington, 1828] 1 p. (H. R. 141) DNA. 35828

---- A bill for the relief of Jared E. Groce, of the state of Alabama. Apr. 9, 1828. Read twice, and committed to a Committee of the Whole House to-morrow. Mr. Jennings, from the Committee on the Public Lands, to which was referred the case of Jared E. Groce, reported the following bill: [Washington, 1828] 1 p. (H. R. 261) DNA. 35829

---- A bill for the relief of Jeremiah Walker, of the state of Louisiana. Mar. 25, 1828. Read twice, and committed to a Committee of the Whole House to-morrow. Mr. Moore, of Alabama, from the Committee on Private Land Claims, to which was referred the petition of Jeremiah Walker, reported the following bill: [Washington, 1828] 1 p. (H. R. 241) DNA. 35830

---- A bill for the relief of Jesse Wilkinson. Mar. 14, 1828. Read twice, and committed to a Committee of the Whole House to-morrow. Mr. Miller, from the Committee on Naval Affairs, reported the following bill: [Washington, 1828] 1 p. (H. R. 220) DNA. 35831

---- A bill for the relief of Joel Byington. Apr. 14, 1828. Read twice, and committed to a Committee of the Whole House to-morrow. Mr. Whittlesey, from the Committee of Claims, to which was referred the case of Joel Byington, reported the following bill: [Washington, 1828]

1 p. (H. R. 266) DNA.   35832

---- A bill for the relief of John B. Lemaitre, junior. Feb. 19, 1828. Read twice, and committed to a Committee of the Whole House to-morrow. Mr. McDuffie, from the Committee of Ways and Means, to which was referred the petition of John B. Lemaitre, junior, reported the following bill: [Washington, 1828] 1 p. (H. R. 174) DNA.   35833

---- ---- Dec. 10, 1828. Read twice, and ordered to be engrossed, and read the third time to-morrow. Mr. McDuffie, from the Committee of Ways and Means, to which was referred the petition of John B. Lemaitre, junior, reported the following bill: [Washington, 1828] 1 p. (H. R. 305) DNA.   35834

---- A bill for the relief of John Brahan. Jan. 29, 1828. Mr. King, from the Committee on Public Lands, reported the following bill; which was read, and passed to a second reading. [Washington, 1828] 1 p. (S. 76) DNA.   35835

---- A bill for the relief of John Culbertson, and for the payment of an interpreter for the District Court of the United States, for the Eastern District in Louisiana. Jan. 23, 1828. Mr. Van Buren, from the Committee on the Judiciary, reported the following bill; which was read, and passed to a second reading. [Washington, 1828] 1 p. (S. 69) DNA.   35836

---- ---- Dec. 16, 1828. Mr. Berrien, from the Committee on the Judiciary, reported the following bill; which was read, and passed to a second reading. [Washington, 1828] 1 p. (S. 27) DNA.   35837

---- A bill for the relief of John F. Ohl. Feb. 29, 1828. Read twice, and committed to a Committee of the Whole House to-morrow. Mr. Dwight, from the Committee of Ways and Means, to which was referred the petition of John F. Ohl, reported the following bill: [Washington, 1828] 1 p. (H. R. 195) DNA.   35838

---- A bill for the relief of John Gates, junior. Mar. 31, 1828. Read twice, and committed to a Committee of the Whole House to-morrow. Mr. Whittlesey, from the Committee of Claims, to which was referred the petition of John Gates, junior, reported the following bill: [Washington, 1828] 1 p. (H. R. 248) DNA.   35839

---- A bill for the relief of John Heard, junior, surviving assignee of Amasa Davis, junior. Mar. 10, 1828. Read twice, and committed to a Committee of the Whole House to-morrow. Mr. Dwight, from the Committee of Ways and Means, to which the subject had been referred, reported the following bill: [Washington, 1828] 1 p. (H. R. 211) DNA.   35840

---- A bill for the relief of John Hunter. Jan. 4, 1828. Read twice, and committed to a Committee of the Whole House to-morrow. Mr. Stewart, from the Committee on Roads and Canals, to which was referred the petition of John Hunter, reported the following bill: [Washington, 1828] 1 p. (H. R. 54) DNA.   35841

---- A bill for the relief of John Long. Dec. 24, 1828. Read twice, and committed to a Committee of the Whole House to-morrow. Mr. McCoy, from the Committee of Claims, to which was referred the petition of John Long, reported the following bill: [Washington, 1828] 1 p. (H. R. 333) DNA.   35842

---- A bill for the relief of John Miles. Feb. 29, 1828. Read twice, and committed to the Committee of the Whole House to which is committed the bill for the relief of the legal representatives of Wm. Shannon and Hugh Shannon. Mr. Whittlesey, from the Committee of Claims, to which was referred the petiton of John Miles, reported the following bill. [Washington, 1828] 1 p. (H. R. 198) DNA.   35843

---- A bill for the relief of John Moffit. Feb. 1, 1828. Read twice, and committed to a Committee of the Whole House to-morrow. Mr. Wolf, from the Committee on Revolutionary Claims, to which had been referred the petition of John Moffit, reported the following bill: [Washington, 1828] 1 p. (H. R. 137) DNA.   35844

---- A bill for the relief of John Shirkey. Jan. 2, 1828. Read twice, and committed to a Committee of the Whole House to-morrow. Mr. Long, from the Committee on Military Pensions, to which was referred the petition of John Shirkey, reported the following bill: [Washington, 1828] 1 p. (H. R. 33) DNA.   35845

---- A bill for the relief of John Smith T. and Wilson P. Hunt. Dec. 8, 1828. Agreeably to notice given, Mr. Benton asked and obtained leave to bring in the following bill; which was read, and passed to a second reading. Dec. 10, read second time, and referred to the Committee on Military Affairs. Dec. 15, reported without amendment. [Washington, 1828] 1 p. (S. 8) DNA.   35846

---- A bill for the relief of John T. Ross. Feb. 14, 1828. Read twice, and committed to a Committee of the Whole House to-morrow. Mr. Cambreleng, from the Committee on Commerce, to which was referred the petition of John T. Ross, reported the following bill: [Washington, 1828] 1 p. (H. R. 167) DNA.   35847

---- A bill for the relief of John Willard and Thomas P. Baldwin. Jan. 23, 1828. Read twice, and committed to a Committee of the Whole House to-morrow. Mr. Whittlesey, from the Committee of Claims, to which was referred the petition of John Willard, reported the following bill: [Washington, 1828] 1 p. (H. R. 105) DNA.   35848

---- A bill for the relief of Jonathan Chapman. Mar. 27, 1828. Mr. Parris, from the Committee on Finance, reported the following bill; which was read, and passed to a second reading. [Washington, 1828] 1 p. (S. 129) DNA.   35849

---- A bill for the relief of Jonathan Taylor, of Kentucky. Feb. 18, 1828. Mr. Johnson, of Kentucky, from the Committee on Military Affairs, reported the following bill; which was read, and passed to a second reading. [Washington, 1828] 1 p. (S. 89) DNA.   35850

---- A bill for the relief of Jonathan W. Brown. Feb. 5, 1828. Mr. Kane, from the Committee on Public Lands, reported the following bill; which was read, and passed to a second reading. [Washington, 1828] 1 p. (S. 82) DNA.   35851

---- A bill for the relief of Joseph Dixon. May 1, 1828. Read twice, and committed to a Committee of the Whole House tomorrow. Mr. Ramsey, from the Committee of Claims, to which was referred the petition of Joseph Dixon, reported the following bill: [Washington, 1828] 1 p. (H. R. 287) DNA.   35852

---- A bill for the relief of Joseph Pierce and Company. Feb. 5, 1828. Read twice, and committed to a Committee of the Whole House to-morrow. Mr. Buckner, from the Committee on Private Land Claims, to which was referred the petition of the heirs of Joseph Pierce, reported the following bill: [Washington, 1828] 1 p. (H. R. 147) DNA.
                                     35853
---- ---- Dec. 28, 1828. Read twice, and committed to a Committee of the Whole House tomorrow. Mr. Buckner, from the Committee on Private Land Claims, to which was referred the petition of the heirs of Joseph Pierce, reported the following bill: [Washington, 1828] 1 p. (H. R. 337) DNA.   35854

---- A bill for the relief of Joseph Young. Jan. 30, 1828. Read twice, and committed to a Committee of the Whole House to-morrow. Mr. Conner, from the Committee on the Post Office and Post Roads, to which was referred the petition of Joseph Young, reported the following bill: [Washington, 1828] 1 p. (H. R. 126) DNA.   35855

---- A bill for the relief of Joshua Foltz. Feb. 22, 1828. Read twice, and committed to a Committee of the Whole House to-morrow. Mr. Creighton, from the Committee on Revolutionary Claims, to which was referred the petition of Joshua Foltz, reported the following bill: [Wash-

ington, 1828.] 1 p. (H. R. 182) DNA.   35856

---- A bill for the relief of Judah Alden. Jan. 29, 1828. Read twice, and committed to a Committee of the Whole House to-morrow. Mr. Wolf, from the Committee on Revolutionary Claims, to which had been referred the petition of Judah Alden, reported the following bill: [Washington, 1828] 1 p. (H. R. 118) DNA.   35857

---- A bill for the relief of Judith Thomas. Feb. 13, 1828. Read twice, and committed to the Committee of the Whole House to which is committed the bill for the relief of John Shirkey. Mr. Long, from the Committee on Military Pensions, to which was referred the petition of Judith Thomas, reported the following bill: [Washington, 1828] 1 p. (H. R. 164) DNA.   35858

---- A bill for the relief of Lewis Schrack. Apr. 9, 1828. Read twice, and committed to a Committee of the Whole House to-morrow. Mr. Whittlesey, from the Committee of Claims, to which was referred the petition of Lewis Schrack, reported the following bill: [Washington, 1828] 1 p. (H. R. 260) DNA.
                                     35859
---- A bill for the relief of Luther Chapin. Feb. 20, 1828. Read twice, and committed to a Committee of the Whole House to-morrow. Mr. Whittlesey, from the Committee of Claims, to which was referred the petition of Luther Chapin, reported the following bill: [Washington, 1828] 1 p. (H. R. 175) DNA.
                                     35860
---- ---- Dec. 22, 1828. Read twice, and committed to a Committee of the Whole House to-

morrow. Mr. Whittlesey, from the Committee of Claims, to which was referred the petition of Luther Chapin, reported the following bill: [Washington, 1828] 1 p. (H. R. 330) DNA.   35861

---- A bill for the relief of Mary James, of Bedford county, Virginia. Jan. 16, 1828. Read twice, and committed to a Committee of the Whole House to-morrow. Mr. Mitchell, of Tennessee, from the Committee on Revolutionary Claims, to which had been referred the petition of Mary James, reported the following bill: [Washington, 1828] 1 p. (H. R. 84) DNA.   35862

---- A bill for the relief of Mary Reynolds. Jan. 21, 1828. Read twice, and committed to a Committee of the Whole House to-morrow. Mr. Wolf, from the Committee on Revolutionary Claims, to which the subject had been referred, reported the following bill: [Washington, 1828] 1 p. (H. R. 97) DNA.   35863

---- A bill for the relief of Matthias Roll. Jan. 17, 1828. Read twice, and committed to a Committee of the Whole House to-morrow. Mr. Sterigere, from the Committee on Private Land Claims, to which had been referred the petition of Matthias Roll, reported the following bill: [Washington, 1828] 1 p. (H. R. 89) DNA.   35864

---- ---- Dec. 12, 1828. Read twice and committed to a Committee of the Whole House to-morrow. Mr. Sterigere, from the Committee on Private Lands Claims, to which was referred the petition of Matthias Roll, reported the following bill: [Washington, 1828] 1 p. (H. R. 314) DNA.   35865

---- A bill for the relief of Michael Lewis. May 6, 1823[!] Read twice, and committed to a Committee of the Whole House to-morrow. Mr. Miller, from the Committee on Naval Affairs, to which was referred the petition of Michael Lewis, reported the following bill: [Washington, 1828] 1 p. (H. R. 292) DNA.   35866

---- A bill for the relief of Mrs. Brown, widow of the late Major General Brown. Mar. 3, 1828. The following bill, having been introduced on leave, was read twice, and referred to the Committee on Military Affairs, who this day reported it without amendment. [Washington, 1828] 1 p. (S. 111) DNA.   35867

---- A bill for the relief of Moses Shepherd. Mar. 3, 1828. Mr. Hendricks, from the Select Committee on Roads and Canals, reported the following bill; which was read, and passed to a second reading. [Washington, 1828] 1 p. (S. 112) DNA.   35868

---- A bill for the relief of Nancy Dolan. Feb. 19, 1828. Read twice, and committed to a Committee of the Whole House to-morrow. Mr. Isacks, from the Committee on the Public Lands, to which was referred the petition of Nancy Dolan, reported the following bill: [Washington, 1828] 1 p. (H. R. 173) DNA.   35869

---- A bill for the relief of Nathaniel B. Wood. Dec. 17, 1828. Read twice, and committed to a Committee of the Whole House to-morrow. Mr. Whittlesey, from the Committee of Claims, to which was referred the case of Nathaniel B. Wood, reported the following bill: [Washington, 1828] 1 p. (H. R. 318) DNA.   35870

---- A bill for the relief of Nathaniel Blake. Jan. 4, 1828. Read twice, and committed to a Committee of the Whole House to-morrow. Mr. McDuffie, from the Committee of Ways and Means, to which was referred the case of Nathaniel Blake, reported the following bill: [Washington, 1828] 1 p. (H. R. 53) DNA.   35871

---- ---- Dec. 31, 1828. Read twice, and committed to a Committee of the Whole House to-morrow. Mr. McDuffie, from the Committee of Ways and Means, to which was referred the case of Nathaniel Blake, reported the following bill: [Washington, 1828] 1 p. (H. R. 352) DNA.   35872

---- A bill for the relief of Nathaniel Briggs. Jan. 24, 1828. Read twice, and committed to a Committee of the Whole House to-morrow. Mr. Cambreleng, from the Committee on Commerce, to which was referred the petition of Nathaniel Briggs, reported the following bill: [Washington, 1828] 1 p. (H. R. 107) DNA.
35873

---- A bill for the relief of Nathaniel Patten. Dec. 8, 1828. Agreeably to notice given, Mr. Benton asked and obtained leave to bring in the following bill; which was read, and passed to a second reading. Dec. 10, read a second time, and referred to the Committee on Post Offices and Post Roads--Dec. 15, reported without amendment. [Washington, 1828] 1 p. (S. 9) DNA.
35874

---- A bill for the relief of Nehemiah Parsons. Feb. 8, 1828. Read twice, and committed to a Committee of the Whole House to-morrow. Mr. Gorham, from the Committee on Commerce, to which was referred the petition of Nehemiah Parsons, reported the fol-

lowing bill: [Washington, 1828] 1 p. (H. R. 151) DNA.   35875

---- A bill for the relief of Orson Sparks and John Watson. Dec. 31, 1828. Read twice, and committed to a Committee of the Whole House, to which is committed the bill [No. 334] for the relief of Thomas Wheatley. Mr. Whittlesey from the Committee of Claims, reported the following bill: [Washington, 1828] 1 p. (H. R. 343) DNA.   35876

---- A bill for the relief of Payson Perrin. Feb. 25, 1828. Mr. Parris, from the Committee on Finance, reported the following bill; which was read, and passed to a second reading. [Washington, 1828] 1 p. (S. 99) DNA. 35877

---- A bill for the relief of Peter Ford. May 2, 1828. Read twice, and committed to a Committee of the Whole House to-morrow. Mr. Whittlesey, from the Committee of Claims, to which was referred the petition of Peter Ford, reported the following bill: [Washington, 1828] 1 p. (H. R. 289) DNA.   35878

---- A bill for the relief of Peter P. M'Cormack. Dec. 22, 1828. Read twice, and committed to a Committee of the Whole House to-morrow. Mr. Bates, of Missouri, from the Committee on Private Land Claims, to which the case of Peter P. M'Cormack had been referred, reported the following bill: [Washington, 1828] 1 p. (H. R. 328) DNA.   35879

---- A bill for the relief of Peters and Pond. Jan. 30, 1828. Read twice, and committed to a Committee of the Whole House to-morrow. Mr. Gorham, from the Committee on Commerce, to which had been referred the peti-

tion of Peters and Pond, reported the following bill: [Washing-
ton, 1828] 1 p. (H. R. 122) DNA.
35880
---- A bill for the relief of Philip Coombs and others. Jan. 22,
1828. Read twice, and committed
to a Committee of the Whole
House to-morrow. Mr. Cambreleng, from the Committee on
Commerce, to which was referred the petition of Philip
Coombs, reported the following
bill: [Washington, 1828] 1 p.
(H. R. 101) DNA.   35881

---- A bill for the relief of Philip Slaughter. Feb. 15, 1828.
Read twice, and committed to a
Committee of the Whole House
to-morrow. Mr. Wolf, from the
Committee on Revolutionary
Claims, to which was referred the
petition of Philip Slaughter, reported the following bill: [Wash-
ington, 1828] 1 p. (H. R. 168)
DNA.   35882

---- A bill for the relief of Richard Biddle, administrator of John
Wilkins, Jr. formerly Quarter-
master General of the Army of
the United States. Feb. 4, 1828.
Mr. Johnson, of Kentucky, from
the Committee on Military Affairs, reported the following bill;
which was read, and passed to
a second reading. [Washington,
1828] 1 p. (S. 81) DNA.   35883

---- ---- Dec. 12, 1828. Read
twice, and committed to a Committee of the Whole House to-
morrow. Mr. Whittlesey, from
the Committee of Claims, to
which was referred the petition
of Richard Biddle, administrator
of John Wilkins, reported the
following bill: [Washington, 1828]
1 p. (H. R. 313) DNA.   35884

---- A bill for the relief of
Richard Eppes. Mar. 12, 1828.

Read twice, and committed to a
Committee of the Whole House
to-morrow. Mr. Whittlesey,
from the Committee of Claims,
to which was referred the petition of Richard Eppes, reported
the following bill: [Washington,
1828] 1 p. (H. R. 215) DNA.
35885
---- A bill for the relief of
Richard Harris and Nimrod Farrow. Mar. 7, 1828. Read twice,
and committed to a Committee
of the Whole House to-morrow.
Mr. Williams, from the Committee of Claims, to which was
referred the case of Harris and
Farrow, reported the following
bill: [Washington, 1828] 1 p.
(H. R. 210) DNA.   35886

---- A bill for the relief of
Richard Taylor. Mar. 23, 1828.
Pursuant to instructions, Mr.
Noble, from the Committee on
Pensions, reported the following
bill; which was read, and passed
to a second reading. [Washing-
ton, 1828] 1 p. (S. 127) DNA.
35887
---- A bill for the relief of
Richard Taylor, of Kentucky.
Jan. 29, 1828. Mr. Johnson, of
Kentucky, from the Committee
on Military Affairs, reported the
following bill; which was read,
and passed to a second reading.
[Washington, 1828] 1 p. (S. 75)
DNA.   35888

---- A bill for the relief of
Richard W. Meade. Jan. 4, 1828.
Read twice, and committed to a
Committee of the Whole House
to-morrow. Mr. Everett, from
the Committee on Foreign Affairs, to which had been referred the petition of Richard W.
Meade, reported the following
bill: [Washington, 1828] 1 p.
(H. R. 51) DNA.   35889

---- A bill for the relief of Rid-

dle, Becktill, and Headington.
Mar. 3, 1828. Read twice, and
committed to a Committee of the
Whole House to-morrow. Mr.
Ramsey, from the Committee of
Claims, to which was referred
the case of Riddle, Becktill, and
Headington, reported the follow-
ing bill: [Washington, 1828] 1 p.
(H. R. 199) DNA.   35890

---- A bill for the relief of Robert Barclay, of Missouri. Jan.
14, 1828. Mr. Barton reported
the following bill from the Committee on Public Lands, which
was read, and passed to a second reading. [Washington, 1828]
1 p. (S. 57) DNA.   35891

---- A bill for the relief of Robert Huston. Feb. 11, 1828.
Read twice, and committed to a
Committee of the Whole House
to-morrow. Mr. Whittlesey,
from the Committee of Claims,
to which was referred the petition of Robert Huston, reported
the following bill: [Washington,
1828] 1 p. (H. R. 157) DNA.
                                    35892
---- A bill for the relief of Robert L. Kennon. Feb. 25, 1828.
Read twice, and committed to a
Committee of the Whole House to-
morrow. Mr. William R. Davis,
from the Committee on the Public Lands, to which was referred the petition of Robert L.
Kennon, reported the following
bill: [Washington, 1828] 1 p.
(H. R. 189) DNA.   35893

---- A bill for the relief of Robertson and Barnwell. Mar. 24,
1828. Read twice, and committed
to a Committee of the Whole
House to-morrow. Mr. McDuffie,
from the Committee of Ways and
Means, to which was referred
the petition of Robertson and
Barnwell, reported the following
bill: [Washington, 1828] 1 p.

DNA.   35894

---- A bill for the relief of Samuel Chesnut. Feb. 22, 1828.
Read twice, and committed to a
Committee of the Whole House
to-morrow. Mr. Whittlesey,
from the Committee of Claims,
to which was referred the petition of Samuel Chesnut, reported
the following bill: [Washington,
1828] 1 p. (H. R. 181) DNA.
                                    35895
---- A bill for the relief of
Samuel Cobun, of Mississippi.
Jan. 15, 1828. Mr. Ellis, from
the Committee on Public Lands,
reported the following bill; which
was read, and passed to a second reading. [Washington, 1828]
1 p. (S. 58) DNA.   35896

---- A bill for the relief of
Samuel Dubose, administrator of
Elias D. Dick, deceased. Feb. 6,
1828. Read twice, and committed to a Committee of the Whole
House to-morrow. Mr. Ramsey,
from the Committee of Claims,
to which had been referred the
petition of Samuel Dubose, reported the following bill: [Wash-
ington, 1828] 1 p. (H. R. 148)
DNA.   35897

---- ---- Dec. 31, 1828. Read
twice, and committed to a Committee of the Whole House to-
morrow. Mr. Ramsay, from the
Committee of Claims, to which
was referred the case of Samuel
Dubose, administrator of Elias
D. Dick, reported the following
bill: [Washington, 1828] 1 p.
(H. R. 347) DNA.   35898

---- A bill for the relief of
Samuel Ward. Jan. 14, 1828.
Read twice, and committed to a
Committee of the Whole House
to-morrow. Mr. Wolf, from the
Committee on Revolutionary
Claims, to which had been re-

ferred the petition of Samuel Ward, reported the following bill: [Washington, 1828] 1 p. (H.R. 75) DNA. 35899

---- A bill for the relief of Sandy Walker. Mar. 3, 1828. Read twice, and committed to a Committee of the Whole House tomorrow. Mr. Bates of Massachusetts, from the Committee on Military Pensions, to which was referred the petition of Sandy Walker, reported the following bill: [Washington, 1828] 1 p. (H.R. 202) DNA. 35900

---- A bill for the relief of Sarah Chitwood. Jan. 31, 1828. Read twice, and committed to the Committee of the Whole House to which is referred the bill for the relief of Mary James, of Bedford county, Virginia. Mr. Forward, from the Committee on Military Pensions, to which was referred the petition of Sarah Chitwood, reported the following bill: [Washington, 1828] 1 p. (H.R. 135) DNA. 35901

---- A bill for the relief of Sarah Jones. May 13, 1828. Read twice, and committed to a Committee of the Whole House tomorrow. Mr. Bates, of Massachusetts, from the Committee on Military Pensions, to which was referred the petition of Sarah Jones, reported the following bill: [Washington, 1828] 1 p. (H.R. 298) DNA. 35902

---- A bill for the relief of Seth Knowles. Feb. 8, 1828. Read twice, and committed to a Committee of the Whole House tomorrow. Mr. McDuffie, from the Committee of Ways and Means, to which the petition of Seth Knowles has been referred, reported the following bill: [Washington, 1828] 1 p. (H.R. 152) DNA. 35903

---- A bill for the relief of Simeon Broadmeadow. Jan. 7, 1828. Read twice, and ordered to be engrossed, and read the third time to-morrow. Mr. P.P. Barbour, from the Committee on the Judiciary, to which was referred the petition of Simeon Broadmeadow, reported the following bill: [Washington, 1828] 1 p. (H.R. 57) DNA. 35904

---- A bill for the relief of sundry citizens of Baltimore. Jan. 24, 1828. Mr. Ruggles, from the Committee of Claims, to whom the subject was referred, reported the following bill; which was read and passed to a second reading. [Washington, 1828] 1 p. (S. 71) DNA. 35905

---- A bill for the relief of sundry citizens of the United States, who have lost property by the depredations of certain Indian tribes. Dec. 8, 1828. Agreeably to notice given, Mr. Benton asked and obtained leave to bring in the following bill; which was read, and passed to a second reading. Dec. 10, read second time, and referred to Committee on Indian Affairs--Dec. 15, reported without amendment. [Washington, 1828] 1 p. (S. 7) DNA. 35906

---- A bill for the relief of sundry officers, soldiers, and widows. Feb. 13, 1828. Read twice, and committed to a Committee of the Whole House to-morrow. Mr. Forward, from the Committee on Military Pensions, to which the subject had been referred, reported the following bill: [Washington, 1828] 3 p. (H.R. 166) DNA. 35907

---- A bill for the relief of sundry Revolutionary and other offi-

cers and soldiers, and for other purposes. Apr. 29, 1828. Read twice, and committed to the Committee of the Whole House to which is committed the bill [H. R. No. 166] for the relief of sundry officers, soldiers, and widows. Mr. Forward, from the Committee on Military Pensions, reported the following bill: [Washington, 1828] 5 p. (H. R. 283) DNA.
35908

---- ---- Dec. 12, 1828. Read twice, and committed to a Committee of the Whole House to-morrow. Mr. Mitchell, of Tennessee, from the Committee on Military Pensions, to which the subject had been referred, reported the following bill: [Washington, 1828] 7 p. (H. R. 311) DNA. 35909

---- A bill for the relief of the assignees of Jacob Clements, deceased. Jan. 2, 1828. Read twice, and committed to a Committee of the Whole House to-morrow. Mr. Cambreleng, from the Committee on Commerce, to which was referred the petition of Potts and Clements, assignees of Jacob Clements, reported the following bill: [Washington, 1828] 1 p. (H. R. 35) DNA. 35910

---- A bill for the relief of the Collectors of the customs for the ports of Norfolk and Portsmouth, and of Petersburg, in Virginia. Apr. 18, 1828. Read twice, and committed to the Committee of the Whole House to which is committed the bill [H. R. No. 92] to authorize the licensing of vessels to be employed in the mackerel fishery. Mr. Newton, from the Committee on Commerce, to which the subject had been referred, reported the following bill: [Washington, 1828] 1 p. (H. R. 274) DNA. 35911

---- A bill for the relief of the heirs and legal representatives of Antonio Bonnabel, deceased. Dec. 29, 1828. Read twice, and committed to a Committee of the Whole House to-morrow. Mr. Gurley, from the Committee on the Public Lands, reported the following bill: [Washington, 1828] 1 p. (H. R. 340) DNA.
35912

---- A bill for the relief of the heirs and legal representatives of Lewis Clarke, deceased. Apr. 1, 1828. Read twice, and committed to a Committee of the Whole House to-morrow. Mr. Buckner, from the Committee on Private Land Claims, to which was referred the petition of Lewis Clarke, reported the following bill: [Washington, 1828] 1 p. (H. R. 250) DNA. 35913

---- A bill for the relief of the heirs of Caron de Beaumarchais. Apr. 1, 1828. Read twice, and committed to a Committee of the Whole House to-morrow. Mr. Everett, from the Committee on Foreign Affairs, to which the claim of the heirs of Caron de Beaumarchais had been referred, reported the following bill: [Washington, 1828] 1 p. (H. R. 252) DNA. 35914

---- A bill for the relief of the heirs of Colonel John Ellis, deceased. Dec. 29, 1828. Read twice, and committed to a Committee of the Whole House to-morrow. Mr. Buckner, from the Committee on Private Land Claims, to which the subject had been referred, reported the following bill: [Washington, 1828] 1 p. (H. R. 336) DNA. 35915

---- A bill for the relief of the heirs of John Gwynn. Jan. 18, 1828. Read twice, and committed

to a Committee of the Whole
House to-morrow. Mr. Hunt, from
the Committee on Revolutionary
Claims, to which the subject had
been referred, reported the following bill: [Washington, 1828] 1
p. (H. R. 93) DNA.   35916

---- A bill for the relief of the
heirs of John Pierre Landerau,
deceased. Dec. 31, 1828. Read
twice, and committed to a Committee of the Whole House, to
which is committed the bill for
the relief of the heirs of Philip
Renaut. Mr. Blake, from the Committee on Private Land Claims, to
which was referred the petition
of the heirs of John Pierre Landerau, reported the following bill:
[Washington, 1828] 1 p. (H. R.
349) DNA.   35917

---- A bill for the relief of the
heirs of Philip Renant. Feb. 1,
1828. Read twice, and committed
to a Committee of the Whole
House to-morrow. Mr. Bates, of
Missouri, from the Committee on
Private Land Claims, to which
was referred the petition of the
heirs of Philip Renant, reported
the following bill: [Washington,
1828] 1 p. (H. R. 138) DNA.
                            35918
---- A bill for the relief of the
legal representatives of Balthazar
Kramar, and the legal representatives of Captain Richard Taylor,
and of John McKenney. Feb. 20,
1828. Agreeably to notice, Mr.
Johnson, of Kentucky, asked and
obtained leave to bring in the following bill; which was read, and
passed to a second reading. [Wash-
ington, 1828] 1 p. (S. 94) DNA.
                            35919
---- A bill for the relief of the
legal representatives of General
Moses Hazen, deceased. Jan. 23,
1828. Mr. Bell, from the Committee of Claims, reported the
following bill; which was read,

and passed to a second reading.
[Washington, 1828] 1 p. (S. 66)
DNA.   35920

---- A bill for the relief of the
legal representatives of James
Davenport, deceased. Apr. 23,
1828. Read twice, and committed to the Committee of the
Whole House to which is committed the bill for the relief of William Tipton. Mr. Long, from the
Committee on Military Pensions,
to which was referred the petition of the representatives of
James Davenport, deceased, reported the following bill: [Wash-
ington, 1828] 1 p. (H. R. 277)
DNA.   35921

---- A bill for the relief of the
legal representatives of John
Guest, deceased. Mar. 12, 1828.
Read twice, and committed to a
Committee of the Whole House
to-morrow. Mr. Ramsey, from
the Committee of Claims, to
which was referred the petition
of Rebecca Guest, reported the
following bill: [Washington, 1828]
1 p. (H. R. 214) DNA.   35922

---- A bill for the relief of the
legal representatives of Joseph
Jeans, deceased. Mar. 21, 1828.
Read twice, and committed to a
Committee of the Whole House
to-morrow. Mr. Ramsay, from
the Committee of Claims, to
which was referred the case of
the representatives of Joseph
Jeans, deceased, reported the
following bill: [Washington, 1828]
1 p. (H. R. 235) DNA.   35923

---- A bill for the relief of the
legal representatives of Joseph
Summerl and Israel Brown, deceased. Jan. 26, 1828. Read
twice, and committed to a Committee of the Whole House to-
morrow. Mr. Cambreleng, from
the Committee on Commerce, to

which had been referred the petition of Isaac W. Norris, administrator of Joseph Summerl, deceased, reported the following bill: [Washington, 1828] 1 p. (H. R. 112) DNA.   35924

---- A bill for the relief of the legal representatives of Meriwether Lewis. Apr. 28, 1828. Read twice, and ordered to be engrossed, and read the third time to-morrow. Mr. Isacks, from the Committee on the Public Lands, reported the following bill: [Washington, 1828] 1 p. (H. R. 282) DNA.   35925

---- A bill for the relief of the legal representatives of Walter Livingston. Apr. 5, 1828. Read twice, and committed to a Committee of the Whole House on Monday next. Mr. Hunt, from the Committee on Revolutionary Claims, to which was referred the case of Robert L. Livingston, surviving executor of Walter Livingston, deceased, reported the following bill: [Washington, 1828] 1 p. (H. R. 255) DNA.   35926

---- A bill for the relief of the legal representatives of William Scott, deceased, citizens of the state of Mississippi. Jan. 15, 1828. Mr. Ellis, from the Committee on Public Lands, reported the following bill; which was read, and passed to a second reading. [Washington, 1828] 1 p. (S. 59) DNA.   35927

---- A bill for the relief of the legal representatives of William Shannon and Hugh Shannon. Jan. 9, 1828. Read twice, and committed to a Committee of the Whole House to-morrow. Mr. Whittlesey, from the Committee of Claims, to which was referred the petition of William and Hugh Shannon, reported the following

bill: [Washington, 1828] 1 p. (H. R. 61) DNA.   35928

---- A bill for the relief of the mayor and city council of Baltimore. Mar. 31, 1828. Read twice, and committed to a Committee of the Whole House to-morrow. Mr. McCoy, from the Committee of Claims, to which the subject had been referred, reported the following bill: [Washington, 1828] 1 p. (H. R. 249) DNA.   35929

---- A bill for the relief of the representatives of Elias Earle, deceased. Dec. 31, 1828. Mr. Berrien, from the Committee on the Judiciary, reported the following bill; which was read, and passed to a second reading. [Washington, 1828] 1 p. (S. 41) DNA.   35930

---- A bill for the relief of the representatives of James A. Harper, deceased. Mar. 5, 1828. Read twice, and committed to a Committee of the Whole House to-morrow. Mr. Whittlesey, from the Committee of Claims, to which was referred the case of the representatives of James A. Harper, reported the following bill. [Washington, 1828] 1 p. (H. R. 206) DNA.   35931

---- A bill for the relief of the representatives of John P. Cox. Jan. 4, 1828. Read twice, and committed to a Committee of the Whole House to-morrow. Mr. McIntire, from the Committee of Claims, to which had been referred the petition of Emelie Cox, reported the following bill: [Washington, 1828] 1 p. (H. R. 52) DNA.   35932

---- A bill for the relief of the representatives of Patience Gordon, widow, deceased. Jan. 3,

1828. Mr. Ruggles, from the Committee of Claims, reported the following bill; which was read, and passed to a second reading. [Washington, 1828] 1 p. (S. 42) DNA.   35933

---- A bill for the relief of the state of Pennsylvania. Apr. 4, 1828. Read twice, and committed to a Committee of the Whole House to-morrow. Mr. Ramsey, from the Committee of Claims, to which the subject had been referred, reported the following bill: [Washington, 1828] 1 p. (H. R. 254) DNA.   35934

---- A bill for the relief of the surviving officers of the army of the Revolution, and others. Feb. 11, 1828. Read twice, and committed to the Committee of the Whole House, on the state of the Union. Mr. Burges, from the select committee to whom the subject had been referred, reported the following bill: [Washington, 1828] 3 p. (H. R. 160) DNA.   35935

---- A bill for the relief of the widow and children of Captain William Beckham. Apr. 9, 1828. Read twice, and committed to the Committee of the Whole House to which is committed the bills for the relief of Mary James and for the relief of Sarah Chitwood. Mr. Long, from the Committee on Military Pensions, to which was referred the petition of Polly Campbell, reported the following bill: [Washington, 1828] 1 p. (H. R. 259) DNA.   35936

---- A bill for the relief of Theophilus Cooksey. Dec. 24, 1828. Read twice, and committed to a Committee of the Whole House to-morrow. Mr. McIntire, from the Committee of Claims, to which was referred the petition of The-ophilus Cooksey, reported the following bill: [Washington, 1828] 1 p. (H. R. 335) DNA.   35937

---- A bill for the relief of Thomas Blackwell. Mar. 18, 1828. Read twice, and committed to a Committee of the Whole House to-morrow. Mr. Tucker, of New Jersey, from the Committee on Revolutionary Claims, to which was referred the petition of Thomas Blackwell, reported the following bill: [Washington, 1828] 1 p. (H. R. 231) DNA.   35938

---- A bill for the relief of Thomas Constantine. Mar. 26, 1828. Mr. Eaton, from the Committee on the District of Columbia, reported the following bill; which was read, and passed to a second reading. [Washington, 1828] 1 p. (S. 128) DNA. 35939

---- A bill for the relief of Thomas Cutts. Feb. 12, 1828. Read twice, and committed to a Committee of the Whole House to-morrow. Mr. Wolf, from the Committee on Revolutionary Claims, to which was referred the case of Thomas Cutts, reported the following bill: [Washington, 1828] 1 p. (H. R. 161) DNA.   35940

---- A bill for the relief of Thomas F. Cornell. Jan. 29, 1828. Read twice, and committed to a Committee of the Whole House to-morrow. Mr. Strong, from the Committee on the Territories, to which had been referred the case of Thomas F. Cornell, reported the following bill: [Washington, 1828] 1 p. (H. R. 117) DNA.   35941

---- A bill for the relief of Thomas Flowers. Feb. 29, 1828. Read twice, and ordered to be engrossed, and read the third time to-morrow. Mr. Isacks, from the Committee on the Public Lands, to which had been referred the case of Thomas Flowers, reported the following bill: [Washington, 1828] 1 p. (H. R. 194) DNA.   35942

---- A bill for the relief of Thomas Griffin. Dec. 22, 1828. Mr. Berrien, from the Committee on the Judiciary, reported the following bill which was read; and passed to a second reading. [Washington, 1828] 1 p. (S. 33) DNA.   35943

---- A bill for the relief of Thomas Hunt. Mar. 6, 1828. Read twice, and committed to a Committee of the Whole House to-morrow. Mr. Ramsey, from the Committee of Claims, to which was referred the petition of Thomas Hunt, reported the following bill: [Washington, 1828] 1 p. (H. R. 207) DNA.   35944

---- A bill for the relief of Thomas L. McKenney. Feb. 14, 1828. Mr. Eaton reported the following bill, from the Committee on the District of Columbia; which was read, and passed to a second reading. [Washington, 1828] 1 p. (S. 86) DNA.   35945

---- A bill for the relief of Thomas L. Winthrop and others, directors of an association, called the New England Mississippi Land Company. Dec. 31, 1828. Mr. Berrien, from the Committee on the Judiciary, reported the following bill; which was read and passed to a second reading. [Washington, 1828] 1 p. (S. 40) DNA.   35946

---- A bill for the relief of Thomas Wheatley. Dec. 24, 1828. Read twice, and committed to a Committee of the Whole House

to-morrow. Mr. Whittlesey, from the Committee of Claims, reported the following bill: [Washington, 1828] 1 p. (H. R. 334) DNA.   35947

---- A bill for the relief of Wallace Robinson. Mar. 28, 1828. Read twice, and committed to a Committee of the Whole House to-morrow. Mr. Isacks, from the Committee on the Public Lands, to which was referred the petition of Wallace Robinson, reported the following bill: [Washington, 1828] 2 p. (H. R. 245) DNA.   35948

---- A bill for the relief of William Augustus Archbold. Mar. 21, 1828. Read twice, and ordered to be engrossed and read the third time to-morrow. Mr. P. P. Barbour, from the Committee on the Judiciary, to which was referred the case of William Augustus Archbald, reported the following bill: [Washington, 1828] 1 p. (H. R. 233) DNA.
35949
---- A bill for the relief of William Bell. Mar. 17, 1828. Mr. Hayne, from the Committee on Naval Affairs, reported the following bill; which was read, and passed to a second reading. [Washington, 1828] 1 p. (S. 123) DNA.   35950

----A bill for the relief of William Benning. Jan. 2, 1828. Read twice, and committed to a Committee of the Whole House to-morrow. Mr. Alexander, from the Committee for the District of Columbia, to which was referred the petition of William Benning, reported the following bill: [Washington, 1828] 3 p. (H. R. 32) DNA.   35951

---- A bill for the relief of William J. Quincy and Charles E.

Quincy. Feb. 25, 1828. Read twice, and committed to the Committee of the Whole House, to which is committed the bill for the relief of Seth Knowles. Mr. Sprague, from the Committee of Ways and Means, to which was referred the case of William J. Quincy and Charles E. Quincy, reported the following bill: [Washington, 1828] 1 p. (H. R. 185) DNA.   35952

---- ---- Dec. 10, 1828. Read twice, and committed to a Committee of the Whole House to-morrow. Mr. Dwight, from the Committee of Ways and Means, to which was referred the case of William J. Quincy and Charles E. Quincy, reported the following bill: [Washington, 1828] 1 p. (H. R. 306) DNA.   35953

---- A bill for the relief of William M. Sneed, and the executors of Stephen Sneed, sen'r. deceased. Feb. 19, 1828. Mr. Harrison, from the Committee on Military Affairs, reported the following bill; which was read, and passed to a second reading. [Washington, 1828] 1 p. (S. 90) DNA.   35954

---- A bill for the relief of William McClure. Jan. 23, 1828. Read twice, and committed to a Committee of the Whole House to-morrow. Mr. Clark, of New York, from the Committee of Claims, to which the petition of William McClure had been referred, reported the following bill: [Washington, 1828.] 1 p. (H. R. 104) DNA.   35955

---- A bill for the relief of William Morrisson. Feb. 25, 1828. Read twice, and committed to a Committee of the Whole House to-morrow. Mr. Whittlesey, from the Committee of Claims,

to which was referred the petition of William Morrisson, reported the following bill: [Washington, 1828] 1 p. (H. R. 188) DNA.   35956

---- A bill for the relief of William Otis. Feb. 29, 1828. Mr. Parris, from the Committee on Finance, reported the following bill; which was read, and passed to a second reading. [Washington, 1828] 1 p. (S. 107) DNA.   35957

---- ---- Dec. 10, 1828. Read twice, and committed to a Committee of the Whole House to-morrow. Mr. Whittlesey, from the Committee of Claims, to which was referred the petition of William Otis, reported the following bill: [Washington, 1828] 1 p. (H. R. 309) DNA.   35958

---- A bill for the relief of William R. Maddox. Mar. 3, 1828. Read twice, and committed to a Committee of the Whole House to-morrow. Mr. Sprigg, from the Committee on Expenditures on the Public Buildings, to which was referred the petition of William R. Maddox, reported the following bill: [Washington, 1828] 1 p. (H. R. 203) DNA.   35959

---- A bill for the relief of William Tipton. Apr. 21, 1828. Read twice, and committed to a Committee of the Whole House to-morrow. Mr. Mitchell, of Tennessee, from the Committee on Military Pensions, to which was referred the petition of William Tipton, reported the following bill: [Washington, 1828] 1 p. (H. R. 275) DNA.   35960

---- A bill for the relief of William W. Montgomery. Apr. 24, 1828. Mr. Van Buren, from the Committee on the Judiciary, reported the following bill; which was read, and passed to a second reading. [Washington, 1828] 1 p. (S. 144) DNA.   35961

---- A bill for the relief of Willoughby Barton. Apr. 28, 1828. Mr. Cobb, from the Committee of Claims, reported the following bill; which was read, and passed to a second reading. [Washington, 1828] 1 p. (S. 146) DNA.   35962

---- A bill for the relief of Wilson and Hallett, merchants, of Mobile. Dec. 31, 1828. Read twice, and committed to a Committee of the Whole House to-morrow. Mr. McDuffie, from the Committee of Ways and Means, to which was referred the case of Wilson and Hallett, merchants of Mobile, reported the following bill: [Washington, 1828] 1 p. (H. R. 351) DNA.   35963

---- A bill for the restoration of Simeon Webster, a soldier of the Revolution, to the list of Revolutionary pensioners. Jan. 14, 1828. Mr. Foot, from the Committee on Pensions, reported the following bill; which was read, and passed to a second reading. [Washington, 1828] 1 p. (S. 56) DNA.   35964

---- A bill further to amend the judicial system of the United States. Feb. 4, 1828. Read twice, and committed to the Committee of the Whole House on the state of the Union. Mr. P. P. Barbour, from the Committee on the Judiciary, reported the following bill: [Washington, 1828] 1 p. (H. R. 144) DNA.   35965

---- A bill further to extend the laws on the subject of land claims in the state of Missouri and territory of Arkansas. Mar. 14, 1828. Read twice, and com-

mited to a Committee of the Whole House to-morrow. Mr. Isacks, from the Committee on the Public Lands, to which was referred the petition of Chad Miller, reported the following bill: [Washington, 1828] 1 p. (H. R. 219) DNA.   35966

---- A bill further to indemnify the owner and underwriters of the British ship Union, and her cargo. Feb. 26, 1828. Mr. Smith, of Maryland, from the Committee on Finance, reported the following bill; which was read, and passed to a second reading. [Washington, 1828] 1 p. (S. 103) DNA.   35967

---- A bill giving the right of pre-emption, in the purchase of land, to certain settlers contiguous to the Big St. Joseph's river, in the southern limits of the territory of Michigan, and in the northern limits of the state of Indiana. Feb. 29, 1828. Read twice, and committed to the Committee of the Whole House to which is committed the bill giving the right of pre-emption, in the purchase of land, to certain settlers in the Choctaw District, in the state of Mississippi. [Washington, 1828] 1 p. (H. R. 196) DNA.   35968

---- A bill giving the right of pre-emption, in the purchase of land, to certain settlers in the Choctaw District, state of Mississippi. Jan. 28, 1828. Read twice, and committed to a Committee of the Whole House to-morrow. Mr. Haile, from the Committee on the Public Lands, to which the subject had been referred, reported the following bill. [Washington, 1828] 1 p. (H. R. 115) DNA.   35969

---- A bill granting a quantity of

land to the state of Indiana, to aid in making a road from Lawrenceburgh to Fort Wayne. Apr. 15, 1828. Read twice, and committed to the Committee of the Whole House to which is committed the Bill [No. 224] to aid the state of Louisiana in constructing a road from Franklinton to St. Francisville, and from Covington to Opelousas, in said state. Mr. Woods, of Ohio, from the Committee on Roads, and Canals, to which the subject had been referred, reported the following bill: [Washington, 1828] 1 p. (H. R. 271) DNA.   35970

---- A bill granting a quantity of land to the state of Ohio to aid in the construction of the canals authorized by the laws of that state. Feb. 11, 1828. Read twice, and committed to a Committee of the Whole House tomorrow. Mr. Isacks, from the Committee on the Public Lands, to which the subject had been referred, reported the following bill: [Washington, 1828] 3 p. (H. R. 155) DNA.   35971

---- A bill granting a township of land to Kenyon College, in Ohio. Feb. 20, 1828. Mr. Kane, from the Committee on Public Lands, reported the following bill; which was read, and passed to a second reading. [Washington, 1828] 1 p. (S. 92) DNA.   35972

---- A bill granting certain lands to the state of Missouri, to aid in making a road from Cape Girardeau to Clay Court House. Feb. 22, 1828. Mr. Hendricks, from the Select Committee on Roads and Canals, reported the following bill; which was read, and passed to a second reading. [Washington, 1828] 1 p. (S. 95) DNA.   35973

---- A bill granting certain quarter sections of land to the territory of Florida, and directing the manner in which the quarter sections heretofore reserved shall be disposed of, and for other purposes. Jan. 11, 1828. Read twice, and committed to a Committee of the Whole House tomorrow. Mr. W. R. Davis, from the Committee on the Public Lands, to which the subject had been referred, reported the following bill: [Washington, 1828] 3 p. (H. R. 65) DNA.   35974

---- A bill granting compensation to Rebecca Blodget, for her right of dower in the property therein mentioned. Feb. 22, 1828. Read twice, and committed to a Committee of the Whole House to-morrow. Mr. Livingston, from the Committee on the Judiciary, to which was referred the petition of Rebecca Blodget, reported the following bill: [Washington, 1828] 1 p. (H. R. 180) DNA.   35975

---- A bill granting to William Conner the right of pre-emption to six hundred and forty-eight acres of land. Jan. 29, 1828. Mr. Van Buren, from the Committee on the Judiciary, reported the following bill; which was read, and passed to a second reading. [Washington, 1828] 1 p. (S. 77) DNA.   35976

---- A bill in addition to an act, entitled "An act concerning discriminating duties of tonnage and impost." Jan. 9, 1828. Mr. Woodbury reported the following bill from the Committee on Commerce; which was read, and passed to a second reading. [Washington, 1828] 1 p. (S. 48) DNA.   35977

---- A bill in addition to "An

act making an appropriation for the support of the Navy of the United States, for the year 1828." Apr. 7, 1828. Mr. Smith of Maryland, from the Committee|on Finance, reported the following bill; which was read, and passed to a second reading. [Washington, 1828] 1 p. (S. 135) DNA.   35978

---- A bill in alteration of the several acts imposing duties on imports. [Washington, 1828] 10 p. DeGE.   35979

---- The bill in alteration of the several acts imposing duties on imports, as proposed to be a-mended by Mr. Mallary and Mr. Buchanan. Mar. 27, 1828. Pr. by order of the House of Representatives. [Washington, 1828] 11 p. (H. R. 132) DNA.   35980

---- A bill in alteration of the several acts imposing duties on imports. As reported from the Committee of the Whole on the State of the Union. Apr. 4, 1828. [Washington, 1828] 20 p. (H. R. 132) DNA.   35981

---- A bill in favor of Richard W. Steele. Apr. 8, 1828. Read twice, and committed to a Committee of the Whole House to-morrow. Mr. Buckner, from the Committee on Private Land Claims, to which was referred the petition of Richard W. Steele, reported the following bill: [Washington, 1828] 1 p. (H. R. 258) DNA.   35982

---- A bill in relation to the banks in the District of Columbia. Apr. 15, 1828. Mr. Van Buren, from the Committee on the Judiciary, reported the following bill; which was read, and passed to a second reading. [Washington, 1828] 1 p. (S. 139) DNA. 35983

---- A bill making a donation of a quarter section of land to the county of Washington, in Mississippi. Apr. 2, 1828. Mr. Ellis, from the Committee on Public Lands, reported the following bill; which was read, and passed to a second reading. [Washington, 1828] 1 p. (S. 131) DNA.
                                35984
---- A bill making a grant of land to aid in improving the navigation of rivers Teche, Vermillion, Plaquemine, and other water courses in the state of Louisiana. Mar. 12, 1828. Read twice, and committed to a Committee of the Whole House to-morrow. Mr. Gurley, from the Committee on Roads and Canals, to which the subject had been referred, reported the following bill: [Washington, 1828] 1 p. (H. R. 216) DNA.   35985

---- A bill making a supplementary appropriation for the military service of the year one thousand eight hundred and twenty-eight. Apr. 14, 1828. Read twice, and committed to the Committee of the Whole House on the state of the Union. Mr. McDuffie, from the Committee of Ways and Means, reported the following bill: [Washington, 1828] 1 p. (H. R. 267) DNA.   35986

---- A bill making an appropriation for building a marine hospital at or near Charleston, in South Carolina. Jan. 16, 1828. Read twice, and committed to a Committee of the Whole House to-morrow. Mr. Cambreleng, from the Committee on Commerce, to which the subject had been referred, reported the following bill: [Washington, 1828] 1 p. (H. R. 82) DNA.   35987

---- A bill making an appropriation for removing the bar at the east pass of the mouth of Pascagoula river, and for improving the harbor thereof. Feb. 13, 1828. Read twice, and committed to a Committee of the Whole House to-morrow. Mr. Gurley, from the Committee on Roads and Canals, to which the subject had been referred, reported the following bill: [Washington, 1828] 1 p. (H. R. 165) DNA. 35988

---- A bill making an appropriation for the erection of a breakwater, near the island of Nantucket. May 21, 1828. Mr. Silsbee from the Committee on Commerce, reported the following bill; which was read, and passed to a second reading: [Washington, 1828] 1 p. (S. 150) DNA. 35989

---- A bill making an appropriation for the erection of a breakwater near the mouth of Delaware Bay. Jan. 30, 1828. Read twice, and committed to a Committee of the Whole House to-morrow. Mr. Sutherland, from the Committee on Commerce, to which the subject had been referred, reported the following bill: [Washington, 1828] 1 p. (H. R. 131) DNA. 35990

---- A bill making an appropriation for the improvement of the navigation of the Ohio and Mississippi rivers. Mar. 27, 1828. Read twice, and committed to a Committee of the Whole House to-morrow. Mr. Woods, of Ohio, from the Committee on Roads and Canals, to which the subject had been referred, reported the following bill: [Washington, 1828] 1 p. (H. R. 244) DNA. 35991

---- A bill making an appropriation for the Navy Hospital Fund. Jan. 2, 1828. Read twice, and committed to a Committee of the Whole House to-morrow. Mr. McDuffie, from the Committee of Ways and Means, to which the subject had been referred, reported the following bill: [Washington, 1828] 1 p. (H. R. 36) DNA. 35992

---- A bill making an appropriation to defray the expenses of certain Indians, who propose to emigrate. Jan. 7, 1828. Read twice, and committed to a Committee of the Whole House to-morrow. Mr. McLean, from the Committee on Indian Affairs, to which the subject had been referred, reported the following bill: [Washington, 1828] 1 p. (H. R. 55) DNA. 35993

---- A bill making an appropriation to extinguish the Indian title to a reserve allowed to John Lynch, of the Cherokee Tribe of Indians, within the limits of the state of Georgia, by the treaty of 1819, between the United States and said tribe of Indians. Jan. 16, 1828. Read twice, and committed to a Committee of the Whole House to-morrow. Mr. M'Lean, from the Committee on Indian Affairs, to which the subject had been referred, reported the following bill: [Washington, 1828.] 1 p. (H. R. 81) DNA. 35994

---- A bill making an appropriation to pay the claims of certain citizens of Louisiana and Mississippi, formerly inhabitants of West Florida. Feb. 20, 1828. Read twice, and committed to a Committee of the Whole House to-morrow. Mr. McDuffie, from the Committee of Ways and Means, to which the subject had been referred, reported the following bill: [Washington, 1828] 1 p. (H. R. 176) DNA. 35995

---- A bill making an appropriation to pay the claims of certain citizens of Louisiana and Mississippi, formerly inhabitants of West Florida. Dec. 22, 1828. Read twice, and committed to a Committee of the Whole House to-morrow. Mr. McDuffie, from the Committee of Ways and Means, to which the subject had been referred, reported the following bill: [Washington, 1828] 1 p. (H. R. 329) DNA.   35996

---- A bill making appropriations for certain fortifications of the United States, for the first quarter of the year one thousand eight hundred and twenty-nine. Apr. 17, 1828. Read twice, and committed to the Committee of the Whole House on the State of the Union. Mr. McDuffie, from the Committee of Ways and Means, reported the following bill: [Washington, 1828] 1 p. (H. R. 272) DNA.   35997

---- A bill making appropriations for certain fortifications of the United States, for the year one thousand eight hundred and twenty-eight. Jan. 21, 1828. Read twice, and committed to a Committee of the Whole House on the state of the Union. Mr. McDuffie, from the Committee of Ways and Means, to which the subject had been referred, reported the following bill: [Washington, 1828] 1 p. (H. R. 96) DNA.   35998

---- A bill making appropriations for internal improvements. Jan. 30, 1828. Read twice, and committed to a Committee of the Whole House on the state of the Union. Mr. McDuffie, from the Committee of Ways and Means, to which the subject had been referred, reported the following bill: [Washington, 1828] 3 p. (H. R. 119) DNA.   35999

---- A bill making appropriations for the Indian Department,

for the year one thousand eight hundred and twenty-eight. Jan. 30, 1828. Read twice, and committed to the Committee of the Whole House on the State of the Union. Mr. McDuffie, from the Committee of Ways and Means, to which the subject had been referred, reported the following bill: [Washington, 1828] 1 p. (H. R. 120) DNA.   36000

---- A bill making appropriations for the military service of the United States, for the first quarter of the year one thousand eight hundred and twenty-nine. Apr. 11, 1828. Read twice, and committed to the Committee of the Whole House on the state of the Union. Mr. McDuffie, from the Committee of Ways and Means, reported the following bill: [Washington, 1828] 1 p. (H. R. 264) DNA.   36001

---- A bill making appropriations for the military service of the United States for the year one thousand eight hundred and twenty-eight. Feb. 2, 1828. Read twice, and committed to the Committee of the Whole House on the state of the Union. Mr. McDuffie, from the Committee of Ways and Means, to which the subject had been referred, reported the following bill: [Washington, 1828] 3 p. (H. R. 142) DNA.   36002

---- A bill making appropriations for the payment of the Revolutionary and other pensioners of the United States, for the first quarter of the year one thousand eight hundred and twenty-nine. Apr. 29, 1828. Read twice, and committed to the Committee of the Whole House on the state of the Union. Mr. McDuffie, from the Committee of Ways and Means, reported the following bill: [Washington, 1828] 1 p. (H. R. 285)

United States 355

DNA. 36003

---- A bill making appropriations for the public buildings, and for other purposes. Feb. 11, 1828. Read twice, and committed to the Committee of the Whole House on the state of the Union. Mr. Van Rensselaer, from the Committee on the Public Buildings, to which the subject had been referred, reported the following bill: [Washington, 1828] 1 p. (H. R. 158) DNA. 36004

---- A bill making appropriations for the purchase of books, and for other purposes. May 5, 1828. Read twice, and committed to the Committee of the Whole House on the state of the Union. Mr. Everett, from the Committee on the Library, reported the following bill: [Washington, 1828] 1 p. (H. R. 291) DNA. 36005

---- A bill making appropriations for the support of government, for the first quarter of the year one thousand eight hundred and twenty-nine. Apr. 29, 1828. Read twice, and committed to the Committee of the Whole House on the state of the Union. Mr. Mc Duffie, from the Committee of Ways and Means, reported the following bill: [Washington, 1828] 17 p. (H. R. 284) DNA. 36006

---- A bill making appropriations for the support of government for the year one thousand eight hundred and twenty-eight. Jan. 14, 1828. Read twice, and committed to a Committee of the Whole House to-morrow. Mr. McDuffie, from the Committee of Ways and Means, reported the following bill: [Washington, 1828] 19 p. (H. R. 70) DNA. 36007

---- A bill making appropriations for the support of the Navy

of the United States, for the first quarter of the year one thousand eight hundred and twenty-nine. Apr. 11, 1828. Read twice, and committed to the Committee of the Whole House on the state of the Union. Mr. McDuffie, from the Committee of Ways and Means, reported the following bill: [Washington, 1828] 3 p. (H. R. 263) DNA. 36008

---- A bill making appropriations for the support of the Navy of the United States, for the year eighteen hundred and twenty-eight. Jan. 18, 1828. Read twice, and committed to a Committee of the Whole House on the state of the Union. Mr. McDuffie, from the Committee of Ways and Means, to which the subject had been referred, reported the following bill: [Washington, 1828] 3 p. (H. R. 91) DNA. 36009

---- A bill making appropriations to carry into effect certain Indian Treaties. May 7, 1828. Read twice, and committed to the Committee of the Whole House on the state of the Union. Mr. Mc Duffie, from the Committee of Ways and Means, reported the following bill: [Washington, 1828] 1 p. (H. R. 293) DNA. 36010

---- A bill making appropriations to enable the President of the United States to defray the expenses of a delegation of the Choctaw and Chickasaw Nations of Indians to explore the country west of the Mississippi. Mar. 24, 1828. Introduced by Mr. Ellis, on leave, and read, Mar. 25, 1828. Read second time and referred to the Committee on Indian Affairs, Mar. 27, 1828. Reported without amendment. [Washington, 1828] 1 p. (S. 126) DNA. 36011

---- A bill making further provision for the Military Academy of West Point. Jan. 15, 1828. Read twice, and committed to a Committee of the Whole House tomorrow. Mr. Hamilton, from the Committee on Military Affairs, to which the subject had been referred, reported the following bill: [Washington, 1828] 1 p. (H. R. 79) DNA.   36012

---- A bill more effectually to provide for the national defence, by establishing an uniform militia throughout the United States, and providing for the discipline thereof. Jan. 10, 1828. Mr. Chandler, from the Committee on the Militia, reported the following bill; which was read, and passed to a second reading. [Washington, 1828] 17 p. (S. 53) DNA. 36013

---- A bill prescribing the modes of commencing, prosecuting, and deciding controversies between States. Dec. 11, 1828. Agreeably to notice given, Mr. Robbins asked and obtained leave to bring in the following bill; which was read twice, and referred to the Committee on the Judiciary. Dec. 31, reported without amendment. [Washington, 1828] 7 p. (S. 15) DNA.   36014

---- A bill providing for the appointment of a surveyor of the public lands in the states of Louisiana and Mississippi, and to regulate the price of surveying. Apr. 24, 1828. Read twice, and committed to a Committee of the Whole House tomorrow. Mr. Vinton, from the Committee on the Public Lands, reported the following bill: [Washington, 1828] 3 p. (H. R. 279) DNA.   36015

---- A bill providing for the appointment of an additional Judge of the Superior Court for the territory of Arkansas, and for other purposes. Mar. 7, 1828. Mr. Seymour, from the Committee on the Judiciary, reported the following bill; which was read, and passed to a second reading. [Washington, 1828] 3 p. (S. 116) DNA.   36016

---- A bill providing for the gradual increase of the Corps of Engineers and for other purposes. Jan. 25, 1828. Read twice, and committed to a Committee of the Whole House to-morrow. Mr. Hamilton, from the Committee on Military Affairs, to which the subject had been referred, reported the following bill: [Washington, 1828] 1 p. (H. R. 110) DNA.   36017

---- A bill providing for the printing and binding sixty thousand copies of the abstract of infantry tactics; including exercises and manoeuvres of light infantry and riflemen, and for other purposes. Dec. 15, 1828. Mr. Chandler, from the Committee on the Militia, reported the following bill; which was read, and passed to a second reading. [Washington, 1828] 1 p. (S. 19) DNA.   36018

---- A bill regulating commercial intercourse with the islands of Martinique and Guadaloupe. Mar. 14, 1828. Mr. Woodbury, from the Committee on Commerce, reported the following bill; which was read, and passed to a second reading. [Washington, 1828.] 1 p. (S. 122) DNA.   36019

---- A bill regulating the appointment and pay of Surgeons and Surgeons Mates in the Navy of the United States. Feb. 12, 1828. Read twice, and committed to the Committee of the Whole House to which is committed the bill fixing and graduating the pay of the Surgeons and Assistant Surgeons of the Army. Mr. Carter, from the Committee on Naval Affairs, to which the subject had been referred, reported the following bill: [Washington, 1828] 3 p. (H. R. 162) DNA.   36020

---- A bill releasing the lien of the United States, upon a part of the land of Benjamin Owens, in Anne Arundel county, state of Maryland, to the trustees of Mount Zion meeting-house, in said county and state. Dec. 22, 1828. Read twice, and committed to a Committee of the Whole House to-morrow. Mr. P. P. Barbour, from the Committee on the Judiciary, to which the subject had been referred, reported the following bill: [Washington, 1828] 1 p. (H. R. 323) DNA.   36021

---- A bill relinquishing the right of the United States to certain Indian reservations under the treaty of Fort Jackson. May 13, 1828. Read twice, and committed to a Committee of the Whole House to-morrow. Mr. Isacks, from the Committee on the Public Lands, to which was referred the petitions of George Stiggins, William Hardridge, and David and Samuel Hale, reported the following bill: [Washington, 1828] 1 p. (H. R. 299) DNA.   36022

---- A bill repealing the law requiring annual examinations of the several land offices. Jan. 24, 1828. Mr. Barton, from the Committee on Public Lands, reported the following bill; which was read, and passed to a second reading. [Washington, 1828] 1 p. (S. 70) DNA.   36023

---- ---- Dec. 31, 1828. Mr. Barton, from the Committee on Public Lands, reported the following bill; which was read, and passed to a second reading. [Washington, 1828] 1 p. (S. 39) DNA.   36024

---- A bill requiring and providing for the publication and distribution of a certain number of copies of an abstract of infantry tactics, including exercises and manoeuvres of light infantry and riflemen, and for other purposes. Dec. 19, 1828. Read twice, and committed to the Committee of the Whole House on the state of the Union. Mr. Thompson, from the Committee on the Militia, to which the subject had been referred, reported the following bill: [Washington, 1828] 3 p. (H. R. 321) DNA.   36025

---- A bill respecting the conveyance of real estate, by deed, in the District of Columbia. Jan. 15, 1828. Read twice, and committed to a Committee of the Whole House to-morrow. Mr. Varnum, from the Committee for the District of Columbia, to which the subject had been referred, reported the following bill: [Washington, 1828] 3 p. (H. R. 78) DNA.   36026

---- A bill restricting the location of certain land claims in the territory of Arkansas; and for other purposes. Dec. 15, 1828. Mr. Barton, from the Committee on Public Lands, reported the following bill; which was read and passed to a second reading. [Washington, 1828] 1 p. (S. 18) DNA.   36027

---- A bill supplemental to an act, to set apart and dispose of certain public lands for the encouragement of the cultivation of the vine and olive, passed on the third of March, one thousand eight hundred and seventeen. Mar. 11, 1828. Mr. King, from the Committee on Public Lands, reported the following bill; which was read, and passed to a second reading. [Washington, 1828] 1 p. (S. 120) DNA.   36028

---- A bill supplementary to an act, entitled "An act granting certain grounds in the city of Detroit, to the mayor, recorder, aldermen, and freemen, of that city." Mar. 7, 1828. Mr. Harrison, from the Committee on Military Affairs, reported the following bill; which was read, and passed to a second reading. [Washington, 1828] 1 p. (S. 115) DNA.   36029

---- A bill supplementary to an act, entitled "An act to complete the survey of the southern and western boundaries of the state of Missouri." Jan. 17, 1828. Read twice, and committed to a Committee of the Whole House to-morrow. Mr. Bates, of Missouri, from the Select Committee, to which the subject had been referred, reported the following bill: [Washington, 1828] 1 p. (H. R. 90) DNA.   36030

---- A bill supplementary to "An act to authorize the Secretary of State to liquidate certain claims therein mentioned," passed upon eighteenth of April, one thousand eight hundred and fourteen. May 1, 1828. Read twice, and committed to the Committee of the Whole House to which is committed the bill making an appropriation to pay the claims of certain citizens of Louisiana and Mississippi, formerly inhabitants of West Florida. Mr. McDuffie, from the Committee of Ways and Means, to which was referred the petition of Joseph de la Francin, and a report of the Secretary of State upon the same, reported the following bill: [Wash-

inton, 1828] 1 p. (H. R. 286) DNA.   36031

---- A bill supplementary to "An act to provide for the adjustment of claims of persons entitled to indemnification, under the first article of the Treaty of Ghent, and for the distribution among such claimants, of the sum paid, and to be paid, by the government of Great Britain, under a Convention between the United States and His Britannic Majesty, concluded at London, on the thirteenth of November, one thousand eight hundred and twenty-six," passed on the second day of March, one thousand eight hundred and twenty-seven. Feb. 22, 1828. Mr. Seymour, from the Committee on the Judiciary, reported the following bill; which was read, and passed to a second reading. [Washington, 1828] 1 p. (S. 96) DNA.   36032

---- A bill supplementary to certain acts authorizing the payment of interest due to the states of New York, Pennsylvania, Delaware, Maryland, and Virginia. Feb. 25, 1828. Agreeably to notice given, Mr. Chambers asked and obtained leave to bring in the following bill; which was read, and passed to a second reading. [Washington, 1828] 1 p. (S. 101) DNA.   36033

---- A bill supplementary to the several acts providing for the adjustment of land claims in the state of Mississippi. Feb. 1, 1828. Mr. Ellis, from the Committee on Public Lands, reported the following bill; which was read, and passed to a second reading. [Washington, 1828] 3 p. (S. 79) DNA.   36034

---- A bill supplementary to the several acts providing for the adjustment of land claims in the state of Mississippi. Feb. 18, 1828. Read twice, and committed to a Committee of the Whole House to-morrow. Mr. Isacks, from the Committee on the Public Lands, to which the subject had been referred, reported the following bill: [Washington, 1828] 3 p. (H. R. 169) DNA.   36035

---- A bill supplementary to the several acts providing for the settlement and confirmation of private land claims in Florida. Feb. 7, 1828. Read twice, and committed to a Committee of the Whole House to-morrow. Mr. Isacks, from the Committee on the Public Lands, to which the subject had been referred, reported the following bill: [Washington, 1828] 1 p. (H. R. 149) DNA.   36036

---- ---- Feb. 29, 1828. Mr. King, from the Committee on Public Lands, reported the following bill; which was read, and passed to a second reading. [Washington, 1828] 3 p. (S. 109) DNA.   36037

---- A bill to abolish imprisonment for debt. Jan. 14, 1828. Repr. as amended in Senate, and made the order of the day for Tuesday, the 15th inst. [Washington, 1828] 9 p. (S. 1) DNA.   36038

---- ---- Jan. 15, 1828. Mr. Noble proposed the following as amendments... [Washington, 1828] 6 p. (S. 1) DNA.   36039

---- A bill to abolish the agency of the United States on the coast of Africa, to provide other means of carrying into effect the laws prohibiting the slave trade, and for other purposes. Feb. 25, 1828. Read twice, and committed to a Committee of the Whole

House on the state of the Union. Mr. McDuffie, from the Committee of Ways and Means, to which the subject had been referred, reported the following bill: [Washington, 1828] 1 p. (H. R. 190) DNA.   36040

---- A bill to abolish the office of Major General, in the military peace establishment of the United States. Apr. 26, 1828. Read twice, and committed to a Committee of the Whole House on the state of the Union. Mr. Alexander Smyth, from the Committee on Military Affairs, to which the subject had been referred, reported the following bill: [Washington, 1828] 1 p. (H. R. 280) DNA.   36041

---- A bill to admit iron and machinery necessary for rail roads, duty free. Apr. 2, 1828. Mr. Smith, of Maryland, from the Committee on Finance, reported the following bill; which was read, and passed to a second reading. [Washington, 1828] 1 p. (S. 132) DNA.   36042

---- A bill to aid in the education of indigent deaf and dumb persons. Jan. 31, 1828. Read twice, and committed to a Committee of the Whole House to-morrow. Mr. Wright, of Ohio, from the Select Committee appointed on the fourteenth of December last, and to which the subject was referred, reported the following bill: [Washington, 1828] 1 p. (H. R. 136) DNA.   36043

---- A bill to aid the state of Louisiana in constructing a road from Franklinton to St. Francisville, and from Covington to Opelousus, in said state. Mar. 17, 1828. Read twice, and committed to a Committee of the Whole House to-morrow. Mr. Gurley, from the Committee on Roads, and Canals, to which the subject had been referred, reported the following bill: [Washington, 1828] 1 p. (H. R. 224) DNA.   36044

---- A bill to aid the state of Ohio in extending the Miami Canal from Dayton to Lake Erie. Jan. 18, 1828. Read twice, and committed to a Committee of the Whole House to-morrow. Mr. Woods, of Ohio, from the Committee on Roads and Canals, to which the subject had been referred, reported the following bill: [Washington, 1828] 3 p. (H. R. 94) DNA.   36045

---- A bill to aid the states of Mississippi and Louisiana in improving the navigation of Pearl river. Mar. 3, 1828. Read twice, and committed to the Committee of the Whole House to which is committed the bill making an appropriation for removing the bar at the East Pass of the mouth of Pascagoula river, and for improving the harbor thereof. Mr. Gurley, from the Committee on Roads and Canals, to which the subject had been referred, reported the following bill: [Washington, 1828] 1 p. (H. R. 201) DNA.   36046

---- A bill to allow a salary to the marshal of the district of Connecticut. Feb. 11, 1828. Read twice, and committed to a Committee of the Whole House to-morrow. Mr. P. P. Barbour, from the Committee on the Judiciary, to which the subject had been referred, reported the following bill: [Washington, 1828] 1 p. (H. R. 156) DNA.   36047

---- ---- Dec. 11, 1828. Agreeably to notice given, Mr. Foot asked and obtained leave to bring in the following bill; which was

read, and passed to a second reading. Dec. 15. --Read the second time, and referred to the Committee on the Judiciary. Dec. 22. --Reported without amendment. [Washington, 1828] 1 p. (S. 17) DNA.   36048

---- A bill to allow a salary to the marshal of the eastern district of Virginia. Apr. 11, 1828. Read twice, and committed to the Committee of the Whole House to which is committed the bill to allow a salary to the marshal of the district of Connecticut. Mr. P. P. Barbour, from the Committee on the Judiciary, to which was referred the case of John Pegram, Marshal of the Eastern District of the state of Virginia, reported the following bill: [Washington, 1828] 1 p. (H. R. 262) DNA.   36049

---- A bill to allow further time to complete the issuing and locating of military land warrants. Dec. 31, 1828. Ordered to be engrossed for to-morrow. [Washington, 1828] 1 p. (H. R. 344) DNA.   36050

---- A bill to allow ships and vessels, from beyond the Cape of Good Hope, to make entry at Edgartown. Feb. 23, 1828. Read twice, and committed to a Committee of the Whole House to-morrow. Mr. Gorham, from the Committee on Commerce, to which the subject had been referred, reported the following bill: [Washington, 1828] 1 p. (H. R. 183) DNA.   36051

---- A bill to alter and amend the sinking fund act of 1817, and to secure more effectually the application of the surplus money in the Treasury, to the payment of the public debt. May 1, 1828, read, and passed to a second

reading--May 5, read the second time, and referred to the Committee on Finance--May 7, reported without amendment. [Washington, 1828] 1 p. (S. 147) DNA.
36052

---- A bill to alter and establish post roads. Apr. 4, 1828. Mr. Johnson, of Kentucky, from the Committee on the Post Office and Post Roads, reported the following bill; which was read, and passed to a second reading. [Washington, 1828] 3 p. (S. 133) DNA.   36053

---- A bill to alter the bridge and draw across the Potomac, from Washington City to Alexandria. Apr. 23, 1828. Mr. Eaton, from the Committee on the District of Columbia, reported the following bill; which was read, and passed to a second reading. [Washington, 1828] 1 p. (S. 143) DNA.   36054

---- A bill to alter the time of holding the District Court of the United States for the Western District of Louisiana. Jan. 21, 1828. Read twice, and committed to a Committee of the Whole House to-morrow. Mr. P. P. Barbour, from the Committee on the Judiciary, to which the subject had been referred, reported the following bill: [Washington, 1828] 1 p. (H. R. 95) DNA.
36055

---- A bill to amend an act entitled "An act for the better organization of the Medical Department of the Navy," approved 24th May, 1828. Dec. 17, 1828. Mr. Hayne, from the Committee on Naval Affairs, reported the following bill; which, was read, and passed to a second reading. [Washington, 1828] 1 p. (S. 31) DNA.   36056

---- A bill to amend an act, en-

titled "An act for the better regulation of the Ordnance Department," approved February 8th, 1815. Jan. 8, 1828. Read twice, and committed to a Committee of the Whole House to-morrow. Mr. Vance, from the Committee on Military Affairs, reported the following bill: [Washington, 1828] 1 p. (H. R. 60) DNA.
36057

---- A bill to amend an act, entitled "An act to authorize the register or enrolment, and license to be issued in the name of the President or Secretary of any incorporated company owning a steam-boat or vessel." May 8, 1828. Read twice, and laid upon the table. Mr. Cambreleng, from the Committee on Commerce, reported the following bill: [Washington, 1828] 1 p. (H. R. 294) DNA.   36058

---- A bill to amend an act, entitled "An act to grant certain relinquished and unappropriated lands to the state of Alabama, for the purpose of improving the navigation of the Tennessee, Coosa, Cahawba, and Black Warrior rivers, approved the twenty-third day of May, one thousand eight hundred and twenty-eight. Dec. 22, 1828. Read twice, and committed to the Committee of the Whole House to which is committed the "bill to authorize those persons who have relinquished lands under the provisions of the several acts for the relief of purchasers of public land, to purchase the same at private sale, at a fixed price." Mr. Isacks, from the Committee on the Public Lands, to which the subject had been referred, reported the following bill: [Washington, 1828] 1 p. (H. R. 322) DNA.   36059

---- A bill to amend an Act, entitled "An Act to provide for certain persons engaged in the land and naval service of the United States in the Revolutionary war, and of the several acts made in amendment thereof." Jan. 3, 1828. Read twice, and committed to a Committee of the Whole House to-morrow. Mr. Burges, from the Committee on Military Pensions, to which the subject was referred, reported the following bill: [Washington, 1828] 3 p. (H. R. 46) DNA.   36060

---- A bill to amend an act, entitled "An act to provide for certain persons engaged in the land and naval service of the United States in the Revolutionary war, and the several acts made in amendment thereof, and for other purposes. Dec. 16, 1828. Read twice, and committed to a Committee of the Whole House to-morrow. Mr. Mitchell, of Tennessee, from the Committee on Military Pensions, to which the subject had been referred, reported the following bill: [Washington, 1828] 5 p. (H. R. 317) DNA.   36061

---- A bill to amend an act, entitled "An act to provide for the appointment of an additional Judge for the Michigan Territory, and for other purposes," passed January thirtieth, one thousand eight hundred and twenty-three. Mar. 18, 1828. Read twice, and committed to a Committee of the Whole House to-morrow. Mr. Strong, from the Committee on the Territories, reported the following bill: [Washington, 1828] 3 p. (H. R. 229) DNA.   36062

---- A bill to amend and explain an act, entitled "An act confirming an act of the Legislature of Virginia, incorporating the Chesapeake and Ohio Canal Company, and an act of the state of Mary-

land, for the same purpose." Jan. 2, 1828. Read twice, and committed to a Committee of the Whole House to-morrow. Mr. Mercer, from the Committee on Roads and Canals, reported the following bill: [Washington, 1828] 1 p. (H. R. 40) DNA.   36063

---- A bill to amend the act, entitled "An act for the relief of purchasers of public lands that have reverted for non-payment of the purchase money." Dec. 22, 1828. Read twice, and committed to a Committee of the Whole House to-morrow. Mr. Vinton, from the Committee on the Public Lands, to which the subject had been referred, reported the following bill: [Washington, 1828] 1 p. (H. R. 326) DNA.
36064

---- A bill to amend the act for the encouragement of learning, by securing the copies of maps, charts, and books, to the authors and proprietors of such copies, during the times therein mentioned. Feb. 1, 1828. Read twice, and committed to a Committee of the Whole House to-morrow. Mr. P. P. Barbour, from the Committee on the Judiciary, to which the subject had been referred, reported the following bill: [Washington, 1828] 1 p. (H. R. 140) DNA.   36065

---- A bill to amend the acts concerning naturalization. Jan. 30, 1828. Read twice, and committed to the Committee of the Whole House on the state of the Union. Mr. Buchanan, from the Committee on the Judiciary, to which the subject had been referred, reported the following bill: [Washington, 1828] 1 p. (H. R. 121) DNA.   36066

---- A bill to amend the acts to provide for surveying the coasts of the United States. May 1, 1828. Read twice, and committed to a Committee of the Whole House to-morrow. Mr. Carter, from the Committee on Naval Affairs, reported the following bill: [Washington, 1828] 1 p. (H. R. 288) DNA.   36067

---- A bill to ascertain and survey the northern boundary of the state of Illinois. Jan. 7, 1828. Read twice, and committed to a Committee of the Whole House to-morrow. Mr. P. P. Barbour, from the Committee on the Judiciary, to which the subject had been referred, reported the following bill: [Washington, 1828] 1 p. (H. R. 58) DNA.   36068

---- A bill to authorize a Rail road within the District of Columbia. Apr. 15, 1828. Mr. Eaton, from the Committee on the District of Columbia, reported the following bill; which was read, and passed to a second reading. [Washington, 1828] 1 p. (S. 140) DNA.   36069

---- A bill to authorize a subscription by the United States to the stock of the Tenth Turnpike Road Company, in the state of New Hampshire. Apr. 11, 1828. Read twice, and committed to a Committee of the Whole House to-morrow. Mr. Davis, of Massachusetts, from the Committee on Roads and Canals, to which the subject had been referred, reported the following bill: [Washington, 1828] 1 p. (H. R. 269) DNA.   36070

---- A bill to authorize certain companies to import iron and machinery for rail roads, free of duty. Apr. 11, 1828. Read twice, and committed to the Committee of the Whole House on the state of the Union. Mr. McDuffie,

from the Committee of Ways and Means, to which the subject had been referred, reported the following bill: [Washington, 1828] 1 p. (H. R. 268) DNA.   36071

---- A bill to authorize the appointment of a Surveyor for the Virginia Military District, within the state of Ohio. Jan. 4, 1828. Read twice, and committed to a Committee of the Whole House to-morrow. Mr. Vinton, from the Committee on the Public Lands, to which the subject had been referred, reported the following bill: [Washington, 1828] 3 p. (H. R. 49) DNA.   36072

---- A bill to authorize the appointment of a Surveyor for the Virginia Military District within the state of Ohio. Dec. 9, 1828. Read twice, and committed to a Committee of the Whole House, to-morrow. [Washington, 1828] 3 p. (H. R. 301) DLC; DNA.   36073

---- A bill to authorize the building of light-houses, and for other purposes. Feb. 20, 1828. Read twice, and committed to the Committee of the Whole House on the state of the Union. Mr. Newton, from the Committee on Commerce, to which the subject had been referred, reported the following bill: [Washington, 1828] 5 p. (H. R. 177) DNA.   36074

---- A bill to authorize the citizens of Arkansas Territory to elect certain officers. Dec. 22, 1828. Ordered to be engrossed for to-morrow. [Washington, 1828] 1 p. (H. R. 324) DNA.   36075

---- A bill to authorize the claimants of land in Florida, commonly called Forbes's Purchase, to institute a suit in a Court of the United States, with intent of procuring an adjudica-

tion on their claim. Feb. 25,
1828. Read twice, and committed
to a Committee of the Whole
House to-morrow. Mr. Buckner,
from the Committee on Private
Land Claims, to which the subject was referred, reported the
following bill: [Washington, 1828]
5 p. (H. R. 186) DNA.   36076

---- A bill to authorize the construction of additional dry docks.
Jan. 25, 1828. Read twice, and
committed to a Committee of the
Whole House to-morrow. Mr.
Hoffman, from the Committee on
Naval Affairs, to which the subject had been referred, reported
the following bill: [Washington,
1828] 1 p. (H. R. 111) DNA.
                             36077
---- A bill to authorize the establishment of a National Road
from the junction of the Penobscot and Matanawcook rivers, in
the state of Maine, to the boundary line between the United
States and the Province of New
Brunswick. Mar. 27, 1828. Read
twice, and committed to a Committee of the Whole House to-
morrow. Mr. Davis, of Massachusetts, from the Committee on
Roads and Canals, to which the
subject had been referred, reported the following bill: [Wash-
ington, 1828] 1 p. (H. R. 243)
DNA.   36078

---- A bill to authorize the improvement of a road through the
lands of the Chickasaw Nation,
in the direction between Memphis
and Tuscumbia, in the state of
Alabama. May 13, 1828. Read
twice, and committed to the Committee of the Whole House on the
state of the Union. [Washington,
1828] 1 p. (H. R. 300) DNA.
                             36079
---- A bill to authorize the improving of certain harbors, the
building of piers, and for other

purposes. Mar. 18, 1828. Read
twice, and committed to the
Committee of the Whole House
on the state of the Union. Mr.
Newton, from the Committee on
Commerce, to which the subjects had been referred, reported the following bill: [Washing-
ton, 1828] 3 p. (H. R. 228)
DNA.   36080

---- A bill to authorize the laying out and construction of a
road from La Plaisance Harbor
to the road leading from Detroit
to Chicago, in the Territory of
Michigan. Jan. 11, 1828. Read
twice, and committed to a Committee of the Whole House to-
morrow. Mr. Mercer, from the
Committee on Roads and Canals,
to which the subject had been
referred, reported the following
bill: [Washington, 1828] 1 p.
(H. R. 69) DNA.   36081

---- A bill to authorize the laying out and making one or more
roads from the City of Washington, towards the Northwestern
Frontier of the states of New
York and Pennsylvania. Jan. 21,
1828. Read twice, and committed
to the Committee of the Whole
House to which is committed the
bill for laying out and making a
national road from the City of
Washington, in the District of
Columbia, to New Orleans, in
the state of Louisiana. Mr. Mercer, from the Committee on
Roads and Canals, to which the
subject had been referred, reported the following bill: [Wash-
ington, 1828] 5 p. (H. R. 100)
DNA.   36082

---- A bill to authorize the legal representatives of the Baron
de Bastrop, to institute process
in the Courts of the United
States, with intent to the settlement of their claims to certain

lands in the state of Louisiana, and for other purposes. Jan. 25, 1828. Read twice, and committed to a Committee of the Whole House to-morrow. Mr. Whipple, from the Committee on the Public Lands, to which the subject had been referred, reported the following bill: [Washington, 1828] 5 p. (H. R. 109) DNA.   36083

---- A bill to authorize the Legislature of the state of Indiana to sell and convey certain lands granted to said state. Jan. 21, 1828. Read twice, and committed to a Committee of the Whole House to-morrow. Mr. Jennings, from the Committee on the Public Lands, to which the subject had been referred, reported the following bill: [Washington, 1828] 1 p. (H. R. 99) DNA.   36084

---- A bill to authorize the Legislature of the state of Ohio to sell certain lands heretofore appropriated for the support of religion in the Ohio Company's and John Cleves Symmes' purchases. Jan. 21, 1828. Read twice, and committed to a Committee of the Whole House to-morrow. Mr. Vinton, from the Committee on the Public Lands, to which the subject had been referred, reported the following bill: [Washington, 1828] 1 p. (H. R. 98) DNA.   36085

---- A bill to authorize the licensing of vessels to be employed in the Mackerel Fishery. Jan. 18, 1828. Read twice, and committed to a Committee of the Whole House to-morrow. Mr. Cambreleng, from the Committee on Commerce, to which the subject had been referred, reported the following bill: [Washington, 1828] 1 p. (H. R. 92) DNA.   36086

---- A bill to authorize the oc-cupation of the Oregon River. Dec. 18, 1827. Read twice and committed to a Committee of the Whole House on the state of the Union. Dec. 23, 1828. Repr. by order of the House of Representatives. [Washington, 1828] 3 p. (H. R. 12) DNA.   36087

---- The bill to authorize the occupation of the Oregon river, being under consideration in Committee of the Whole House on the state of the Union, Mr. Drayton submitted the following as an a-mendment of the same: Dec. 24, 1828. [Washington, 1828] 2 p. (H. R. 12) DNA.   36088

---- A bill to authorize the Postmaster General to erect a suitable building for a Post-Office, in the city of New-Orleans. Apr. 9, 1828. Mr. Johnson, of Kentucky, from the Committee on the Post Office and Post Roads, reported the following bill; which was read, and passed to a second reading. [Washington, 1828] 1 p. (S. 138) DNA.   36089

--- A bill to authorize the Postmaster General to erect an additional building, and employ five additional clerks. Feb. 8, 1828. Read twice, and committed to a Committee of the Whole House to-morrow. Mr. McDuffie, from the Committee of Ways and Means, to which the subject had been referred, reported the following bill: [Washington, 1828] 1 p. (H. R. 153) DNA.   36090

---- A bill to authorize the President to appoint a Superintendent and Receiver at the Fever river lead mines, and for other purposes. Dec. 31, 1828. Read twice, and committed to the Committee of the Whole House on the state of the Union. Mr. Duncan, from the Committee on the Public Lands, to which the subject had been referred, reported the following bill: [Washington, 1828] 3 p. (H. R. 346) DNA.   36091

---- A bill to authorize the President of the United States to cause the reserved Lead Mines, in the state of Missouri, to be exposed to public sale, and for other purposes. Dec. 8, 1828. Agreeably to notice given, Mr. Benton asked and obtained leave to bring in the following bill; which was read, and passed to a second reading. Dec. 10, read second time, and referred to the Committee on Public Lands--Dec. 15, reported with amendments. [Washington, 1828] 1 p. (S. 5) DNA.   36092

---- A bill to authorize the President of the United States to cause the reserved Salt Springs in the state of Missouri to be exposed to public sale. Dec. 8, 1828. Agreeably to notice, Mr. Benton asked and obtained leave to bring in the following bill; which was read, and passed to a second reading. Dec. 10, read second time, and referred to the Committee on Public Lands. Dec. 15, reported without amendment. [Washington, 1828] 1 p. (S. 4) DNA.   36093

---- A bill to authorize the President of the United States to employ an Agent to procure from the Plantation Office, and other offices in England, copies of such documents as will serve to illustrate the early history of the states of this Union. Feb. 8, 1828. Read twice, and committed to a Committee of the Whole House to-morrow. Mr. McDuffie, from the Committee of Ways and Means, to which the subject had been referred, reported the following bill: [Washington, 1828]

1 p. (H. R. 154) DNA.   36094

---- A bill to authorize the President of the United States to lease certain lots of ground, therein mentioned. Jan. 9, 1828. Mr. Kane, from the Committee on Public Lands, reported the following bill; which was read, and passed to a second reading. [Washington, 1828] 1 p. (S. 51) DNA.   36095

---- A bill to authorize the President of the United States to run and mark a line, dividing the territory of Arkansas from the state of Louisiana. Mar. 14, 1828. Read twice, and committed to a Committee of the Whole House to-morrow. Mr. P. P. Barbour, from the Committee on the Judiciary, to which the subject had been referred, reported the following bill: [Washington, 1828] 1 p. (H. R. 217) DNA.   36096

---- A bill to authorize the purchase and distribution of the seventh volume of the Laws of the United States, and the General Index to the Laws of the United States. Jan. 15, 1828. Mr. Dickerson, from the Committee on the Library of Congress, reported the following bill; which was read, and passed to a second reading. [Washington, 1828] 1 p. (S. 61) DNA. 36097

---- A bill to authorize the purchase of a site, and the erection of barracks, in the vicinity of New Orleans. Jan. 28, 1828. Mr. Harrison, from the Committee on Military Affairs, reported the following bill; which was read, and passed to a second reading. [Washington, 1828] 1 p. (S. 74) DNA.   36098

---- ---- Dec. 16, 1828. Agreeably to notice given, Mr. Johnston, of Louisiana, asked and obtained leave to bring in the following bill; which was read, and passed to a second reading. Dec. 17--Read second time, and referred to the Committee on Military Affairs. Dec. 22--Reported without amendment. [Washington, 1828] 1 p. (S. 24) DNA.   36099

---- A bill to authorize the sale of Public Lands containing Lead Mines, and which have been reserved from sale, in the state of Missouri. Jan. 30, 1828. Read twice, and committed to a Committee of the Whole House tomorrow. Mr. Jennings, from the Committee on the Public Lands to which the subject had been referred, reported the following bill: [Washington, 1828] 1 p. (H. R. 125) DNA.   36100

---- A bill to authorize the Secretary of War to purchase additional land, whereon to erect needful buildings at Fort Washington. Mar. 18, 1828. Read twice, and committed to a Committee of the Whole House tomorrow. Mr. Smyth of Virginia, from the Committee on Military Affairs, to which the subject had been referred, reported the following bill: [Washington, 1828] 1 p. (H. R. 226) DNA.   36101

---- A bill to authorize the survey and opening of a road from St. Louis, on the river Mississippi, to Washington, in the Territory of Arkansas. Apr. 5, 1828. Read twice, and committed to the Committee of the Whole House to which is committed the bill to authorize the survey and opening of a road from Wiggins's Ferry. , on the river Mississippi, to the Lead Mines, on Fever river. Mr. Mercer, from the Committee on Roads and Canals, to which the subject

had been referred, reported the following bill: [Washington, 1828] 3 p. (H. R. 256) DNA.   36102

---- A bill to authorize the survey and opening of a road from Wiggins' Ferry, on the river Mississippi to the Lead Mines, on Fever river. Mar. 4, 1828. Read twice, and committed to the Committee of the Whole House to which is committed the bill to authorize the laying out and construction of a road from La Plaisance harbor to the road leading from Detroit to Chicago, &c. Mr. Mercer, from the Committee on Roads and Canals, to which the subject had been referred reported the following bill: [Washington, 1828] 3 p. (H. R. 205) DNA.   36103

---- A bill to authorize the surveying and opening a Road within the Territory of Michigan, from Detroit, westwardly, to Lake Michigan. Jan. 11, 1828. Read twice, and committed to a Committee of the Whole House tomorrow. Mr. Mercer, from the Committee on Roads and Canals, to which the subject had been referred, reported the following bill: [Washington, 1828] 3 p. (H. R. 68) DNA.   36104

---- A bill to authorize those persons who have relinquished lands, under the provisions of the several acts for the relief of purchasers of public lands, to purchase the same, at private sale, at a fixed price. Jan. 17, 1828. Read twice, and committed to a Committee of the Whole House to-morrow. Mr. Isacks, from the Committee on the Public Lands, to which the subject had been referred, reported the following bill: [Washington, 1828] 5 p. (H. R. 86) DNA.   36105

---- A bill to cede to the State of South Carolina the jurisdiction over, and the title to, a certain tract of land, called Mount Dearborn, in the said State. Jan. 30, 1828. Read twice, and committed to a Committee of the Whole House to-morrow. Mr. Hamilton, from the Committee on Military Affairs, to which the subject had been referred, reported the following bill: [Washington, 1828] 1 p. (H. R. 127) DNA.   36106

---- A bill to compensate Susan Decatur, widow and representative of Captain Stephen Decatur, deceased, and others. Jan. 9, 1828. Mr. Hayne, from the Committee on Naval Affairs, reported the following bill; which was read, and passed to a second reading. [Washington, 1828] 1 p. (S. 50) DNA.   36107

---- ---- Dec. 17, 1828. Mr. Hayne, from the Committee on Naval Affairs, reported the following bill; which was read, and passed to a second reading. [Washington, 1828] 3 p. (S. 30) DNA.   36108

---- A bill to compensate the Register and Receiver at Augusta, Mississippi, for services performed in Mobile. Mar. 31, 1828. Read twice, and committed to a Committee of the Whole House to-morrow. Mr. Isacks, from the Committee on the Public Lands, to which the subject had been referred, reported the following bill: [Washington, 1828] 1 p. (H. R. 246) DNA.   36109

---- A bill to confirm certain claims to lands in the territory of Michigan. Jan. 2, 1828. Read twice, and committed to a Committee of the Whole House to-morrow. Mr. Whipple, from the Committee on the Public Lands,

to which was referred the report of the Commissioners of Land Claims in the Territory of Michigan, reported the following bill: [Washington, 1828] 1 p. (H. R. 34) DNA.   36110

---- A bill to confirm certain claims to lands in the territory of Michigan. Jan. 11, 1828. Mr. Whipple submitted the following, which he proposes, when the bill of the above title is taken up for consideration, to move as amendments: [Washington, 1828] 1 p. (H. R. 34) DNA.   36111

---- A bill to confirm claims to lands in the District between the Rio Hondo and Sabine Rivers, founded on habitation and cultivation. Feb. 29, 1828. Mr. Ellis, from the Committee on Public Lands, reported the following bill; which was read, and passed to a second reading. [Washington, 1828] 1 p. (S. 106) DNA. 36112

---- A bill to confirm claims to lands in the District between the Rio Hondo and Sabine rivers, in the state of Louisiana, founded on habitation and cultivation. Feb. 25, 1828. Read twice, and committed to a Committee of the Whole House to-morrow. Mr. Whipple, from the Committee on the Public Lands, to which the subject had been referred, reported the following bill: [Washington, 1828] 1 p. (H. R. 184) DNA.   36113

---- A bill to continue a copyright to John Rowlett. Apr. 17, 1828. Mr. Seymour, from the Committee on the Judiciary, reported the following bill; which was read, and passed to a second reading. [Washington, 1828] 1 p. (S. 141) DNA.   36114

---- A bill to continue in force,

for a limited time, and to amend, an act entitled "An act to enable claimants to lands within the limits of the state of Missouri and Territory of Arkansas, to institute proceedings to try the validity of their claims. Apr. 4, 1828. Mr. Berrien, from the Committee on Private Land Claims, reported the following bill; which was read, and passed to a second reading. [Washington, 1828] 1 p. (S. 134) DNA.   36115

---- A bill to continue in force the provisions of "An act to authorize the Corporation of the City of Washington to draw Lotteries." Mar. 3, 1828. Read twice, and committed to a Committee of the Whole House to-morrow. Mr. Varnum, from the Committee for the District of Columbia, to which the subject had been referred, reported the following bill: [Washington, 1828] 1 p. (H. R. 200) DNA.   36116

---- A bill to continue the Mint at the City of Philadelphia, and for other purposes. Jan. 23, 1828. Read twice, and committed to a Committee of the Whole House to-morrow. Mr. Sergeant, from the Select Committee, to which the subject had been referred, reported the following bill: [Washington, 1828] 3 p. (H. R. 106) DNA.   36117

---- A bill to continue the present mode of supplying the Army of the United States, and for other purposes, appertaining to the same. Jan. 2, 1828. Read twice, and committed to a Committee of the Whole House to-morrow. Mr. Hamilton, from the Committee on Military Affairs, reported the following bill: [Washington, 1828] 1 p. (H. R. 39) DNA.   36118

---- A bill to enable the Presi-

dent of the United States to hold a treaty with the Chippewas, Ottowas, Pattawattimas, Winnebagoes, Fox, and Sacs nations of Indians. Jan. 23, 1828. Read twice, and committed to a Committee of the Whole House to-morrow. Mr. McLean, from Committee on Indian Affairs, to which the subject had been referred, reported the following bill: [Washington, 1828] 1 p. (H. R. 103) DNA.   36119

---- A bill to enable Walter Wilson and John Tipton to purchase the ground whereon the battle of Tippecanoe was fought, on the seventh day of November, eighteen hundred and eleven. Mar. 31, 1828. Read twice, and committed to a Committee of the Whole House to-morrow. Mr. Jennings, from the Committee on the Public Lands, to which was referred the petition of Walter Wilson and John Tipton, reported the following bill: [Washington, 1828] 1 p. (H. R. 247) DNA.   36120

---- A bill to encourage vaccination. Jan. 21, 1828. Agreeably to notice given, Mr. Bateman asked and obtained leave to bring in the following bill; which was read, and passed to a second reading. [Washington, 1828] 1 p. (S. 63) DNA.   36121

---- A bill to enlarge the powers of the several Corporations of the District of Columbia, and for other purposes. Jan. 30, 1828. Read twice, and committed to the Committee of the Whole House, to which is committed the "bill to amend and explain an act, entitled 'An act of the Legislature of Virginia, incorporating the Chesapeake and Ohio Canal Company; and an act of the State of Maryland for the same purpose." Mr. Mercer, from the Committee on Roads and Canals, to which the subject had been referred, reported the following bill: [Washington, 1828] 9 p. (H. R. 128) DNA. 36122

---- ---- As amended. The parts stricken out are in brackets. The insertions in Italics. May 9, 1828. Pr. by order of the House of Representatives. Mr. Mercer, from the Committee on Roads and Canals, to which the subject had been referred, reported the following bill: [Washington, 1828] 11 p. (H. R. 128) DNA. 36123

---- A bill to equalize and reduce the duties on imported teas. Feb. 18, 1828. Read twice, and committed to a Committee of the Whole House to-morrow. Mr. McDuffie, from the Committee of Ways and Means, to which the subject had been referred, reported the following bill: [Washington, 1828] 2 p. (H. R. 172) DNA. 36124

---- A bill to equalize the duties on Prussian vessels and their cargoes. May 21, 1828. Read twice, and committed to the Committee of the Whole House on the state of the Union. Mr. Cambreleng, from the Committee on Commerce, to which the subject had been referred, reported the following bill: [Washington, 1828] 1 p. (H. R. 302) DNA. 36125

---- A bill to establish a Port of Entry at Magnolia, in Florida. Dec. 23, 1828. Read twice, and ordered to be engrossed, and read the third time to-morrow. Mr. Cambreleng, from the Committee on Commerce, to which the subject had been referred, reported the following bill: [Washington, 1828] 1 p. (H. R. 331) DNA. 36126

---- A bill to establish a Port of Entry, at St. Marks, in Florida. Jan. 21, 1828. Mr. Woodbury, from the Committee on Commerce, reported the following bill; which was read, and passed to a second reading. [Washington, 1828] 1 p. (S. 64) DNA. 36127

---- A bill to establish a system of Quarantine for the District of Columbia, and for other purposes. Jan. 14, 1828. Read twice, and committed to a Committee of the Whole House to-morrow. Mr. Alexander, from the Committee for the District of Columbia, to which the subject had been referred, reported the following bill: [Washington, 1828] 1 p. (H. R. 72) DNA. 36128

---- A bill to establish an Armory on the Western Waters. Feb. 7, 1828. Read twice, and committed to a Committee of the Whole House to-morrow. Mr. Orr, from the Committee on Military Affairs, to which the subject had been referred, reported the following bill: [Washington, 1828] 1 p. (H. R. 150) DNA. 36129

---- A bill to establish sundry Post Roads, and discontinue others. Apr. 21, 1828. Read twice, and committed to a Committee of the Whole House to-morrow. Mr. McKean, from the Committee on the Post Office and Post Roads, reported the following bill: [Washington, 1828] 15 p. (H. R. 276) DNA. 36130

---- A bill to graduate the price of the Public Lands, to make donation thereof to actual settlers, and to cede the refuse to the States in which they lie. Apr. 14, 1828. Ordered to be printed as amended in Committee of the Whole. [Washington, 1828] 3 p.

(S. 33) DNA.   36131

---- ---- Apr. 18, 1828. Repr.
as amended in Committee of the
Whole. [Washington, 1828] 5 p.
(S. 33) DNA.   36132

---- A bill to graduate the price
of the Public Lands, to make donations thereof to actual settlers,
and to cede the refuse to the
States in which they lie, upon
equitable terms. Feb. 5, 1828.
Read twice, and committed to the
Committee of the Whole House
on the state of the Union. Mr.
Duncan, from the Committee on
the Public Lands, to which the
subject has been referred, reported the following bill: [Wash-
ington, 1828] 3 p. (H.R. 145)
DNA.   36133

---- ---- Feb. 5, 1828. Read
twice, and committed to the Committee of the Whole House on the
state of the Union. Mr. Duncan,
from the Committee on the Public Lands, to which the subject
had been referred, reported the
following bill: [Washington, 1828]
9 p. (H.R. 145) DNA.   36134

---- A bill to graduate the price
of the Public Lands, to make provision for actual settlers, and to
cede the refuse upon equitable
terms, and for meritorious objects, to the States in which they
lie. Dec. 8, 1828. Read, and
passed to second reading, Dec.
10, read second time, referred
to Committee on Public Lands,
and ordered to be printed. [Wash-
ington, 1828] 5 p. (S. 3) DNA.
                              36135
---- A bill to grant certain relinquished and unappropriated
lands to the State of Alabama,
for the purpose of improving the
navigation of the Tennessee,
Coosa, Cahawba, and Black Warrior rivers. Jan. 7, 1828. Agree-

ably to notice given, Mr. Mc
Kinley asked and obtained leave
to bring in the following bill;
which was read, and passed to a
second reading. [Washington,
1828] 3 p. (S. 46) DNA. 36136

---- A bill to grant to the state
of Ohio certain lands for the support of Schools in the Connecticut Western Reserve. Jan. 30,
1828. Read twice, and committed to a Committee of the Whole
House to-morrow. Mr. Vinton,
from the Committee on the Public Lands, to which the subject
had been referred, reported the
following bill: [Washington, 1828]
1 p. (H.R. 123) DNA.   36137

---- A bill to hasten the estin-
guishment of the Public Debt.
Apr. 28, 1828. Read twice, and
committed to the Committee of
the Whole House on the state of
the Union. Mr. McDuffie, from
the Committee of Ways and Means,
reported the following bill:
[Washington, 1828] 1 p. (H.R.
281) DNA.   36138

---- A bill to improve the condition of the office of the Surveyor
General for the States of Illinois,
Missouri, and Territory of Arkansas. Mar. 11, 1828. Read
twice, and committed to a Committee of the Whole House to-
morrow. Mr. Isacks, from the
Committee on the Public Lands,
to which the subject had been referred, reported the following
bill: [Washington, 1828] 1 p.
(H.R. 213) DNA.   36139

---- A bill to incorporate the
Alexandria Canal Company. Dec.
29, 1828. Read twice, and com-
mitted to a Committee of the
Whole House to-morrow. Mr.
Mercer, from the Committee on
Roads and Canals, reported the
following bill: [Washington,

1828] 19 p. (H. R. 341) DNA.
                                    36140
---- A bill to incorporate the
Sisters of Charity of St.
Joseph; and the Sisters of the Visitation,
of Georgetown, in the District of
Columbia. Apr. 22, 1828. Mr.
Eaton, from the Committee on the
District of Columbia, reported the
following bill; which was read,
and passed to a second reading.
[Washington, 1828] 3 p. (S. 142)
DNA.   36141

---- A bill to incorporate the
Trustees of the Female Orphan
Asylum in Georgetown, in the
District of Columbia. Feb. 11,
1828. Mr. Eaton, from the Committee on the District of Columbia, reported the following bill;
which was read, and passed to a
second reading. [Washington,
1828] 3 p. (S. 85) DNA.   36142

---- A bill to incorporate the
Washington, Alexandria, and Baltimore Steam Packet Company.
Mar. 7, 1828. Read twice, and
committed to a Committee of the
Whole House to-morrow. Mr.
Bryan, from the Committee for
the District of Columbia, to which
the subject had been referred,
reported the following bill: [Wash-
ington, 1828] 5 p. (H. R. 208)
DNA.   36143

---- A bill to increase the pay of
Lieutenants in the Navy, who
shall have served ten years, or
upwards, as such. Jan. 3, 1828.
Mr. Hayne, from the Committee
on Naval Affairs, reported the
following bill; which was read,
and passed to a second reading.
[Washington, 1828] 1 p. (S. 45)
DNA.   36144

---- A bill to increase the pay
of the Master Armorer in the
Armories of the United States.
Jan. 17, 1828. Read twice, and

committed to a Committee of the
Whole House to-morrow. Mr.
Hamilton, from the Committee on
Military Affairs, to which the
subject had been referred re-
ported the following bill: [Wash-
ington, 1828] 1 p. (H. R. 87)
DNA.   36145

---- A bill to preserve from in-
jury and waste the school lands
in the Territory of Arkansas.
Dec. 12, 1828. Ordered to engrossed[sic] for Monday next.
[Washington, 1828] 1 p. (H. R. 312)
DNA.   36146

---- A bill to prevent defalca-
tions on the part of the Disbursing Agents of the Government,
and for other purposes. Jan. 2,
1828. Read twice, and committed
to a Committee of the Whole
House to-morrow. Mr. M'Duffie,
from the Committee of Ways and
Means, reported the following
bill: [Washington, 1828] 1 p.
(H. R. 37) DNA.   36147

---- A bill to privilege Soldiers
from arrest, in certain cases.
Mar. 18, 1828. Read twice, and
committed to a Committee of the
Whole House to-morrow. Mr.
Smith, from the Committee on
Military Affairs, to which the
subject had been referred, reported the following bill: [Wash-
ington, 1828] 1 p. (H. R. 227)
DNA.   36148

---- A bill to provide for an exploring expedition to the Pacific
Ocean and South Seas. Mar. 25,
1828. Read the first and second
time, and committed to a Committee of the Whole House to-
morrow. Mr. Ripley, from the
Committee on Naval Affairs, to
which the subject was referred,
reported the following bill: [Wash-
ington, 1828] 1 p. (H. R. 240)
DNA.   36149

---- A bill to provide for extending the term for the pensions of certain persons. Apr. 15, 1828. Read twice, and committed to a Committee of the Whole House to-morrow. Mr. Hoffman, from the Committee on Naval Affairs, to which the subject had been referred, reported the following bill: [Washington, 1828] 1 p. (H. R. 270) DNA.   36150

---- A bill to provide for opening and making a Military Road in the State of Maine. Mar. 4, 1828. Mr. Chandler, from the Committee on Military Affairs, reported the following bill; which was read, and passed to a second reading. [Washington, 1828] 1 p. (S. 113) DNA.   36151

---- A bill to provide for persons disabled by wounds, or otherwise, while in the service of the United States. Mar. 10, 1828. Mr. Noble reported the following bill, from the Committee on Pensions; which was read, and passed to a second reading. [Washington, 1828] 1 p. (S. 117) DNA.   36152

---- A bill to provide for the appointment of a Translator for the District Courts of the United States in the Eastern and Western Districts of Louisiana, and for compensating the person who has heretofore performed the duty of Translator of the said Court in the Eastern District. Jan. 23, 1828. Read twice, and committed to a Committee of the Whole House to-morrow. Mr. Livingston, from the Committee on the Judiciary, to which was referred the petition of John Culbertson, reported the following bill: [Washington, 1828] 1 p. (H. R. 113) DNA.   36153

---- A bill to provide for the

distribution of a part of the revenues of the United States among the several States. Dec. 17, 1828. Agreeably to notice given, Mr. Dickerson asked and obtained leave to bring in the following bill; which was read, and passed to a second reading. Dec. 18, read the second time, and ordered to lie on the table and be printed. [Washington, 1828] 1 p. (S. 29) DNA.   36154

---- A bill to provide for the final settlement of Private Land Claims in the several States and Territories. Jan. 9, 1828. Mr. Berrien, from the Committee on Private Land Claims, reported the following bill; which was read, and passed to a second reading. [Washington, 1828] 7 p. (S. 49) DNA.   36155

---- A bill to provide for the legal adjudication and settlement of the claim of the Marquis de Maison Rouge, or his legal representatives, to certain lands in the State of Louisiana. Feb. 4, 1828. Read twice, and committed to the Committee of the Whole House to which is committed the "Bill to authorize the legal Representatives of the Baron de Bastrop, to institute process in the Courts of the United States, with intent to the settlement of their claims in certain lands in the State of Louisiana, and for other purposes." Mr. Whipple, from the Committee on the Public Lands, to which the subject had been referred, reported the following bill: [Washington, 1828] 3 p. (H. R. 143) DNA.   36156

---- A bill to provide for the legal adjudication and settlement of the claims to land therein mentioned. Mar. 18, 1828. Introduced by Mr. Johnston, of Louisiana, on leave; read twice, and referred to the Committee on Private Land Claims. Apr. 3, 1828. --Reported without amendment. [Washington, 1828] 3 p. (S. 124) DNA.   36157

---- A bill to provide for the purchase and distribution of certain copies of the Digest of the Laws of the United States, by Thomas F. Gordon. Dec. 11, 1828. Agreeably to notice given, Mr. Marks asked and obtained leave to bring in the following bill; which was twice read, and referred to the Committee on the Judiciary. Dec. 22, reported without amendment. [Washington, 1828] 1 p. (S. 16) DNA.   36158

---- A bill to provide for the purchase of certain copies of the Digest of the Laws of the United States, by Thomas F. Gordon. Jan. 15, 1828. Mr. Van Buren, from the Committee on the Judiciary, reported the following bill; which was read, and passed to a second reading. [Washington, 1828] 1 p. (S. 60) DNA.   36159

---- A bill to reduce the rates of postage on pamphlets for public schools. Mar. 25, 1828. Read twice, and ordered to be engrossed, and read the third time to-morrow. Mr. Ingham, from the Committee on the Post Office and Post Roads, to which the subject had been referred, reported the following bill: [Washington, 1828] 1 p. (H. R. 242) DNA.   36160

---- A bill to reform the Penal Laws of the District of Columbia, and for other purposes. Jan. 31, 1828. Read twice, and committed to a Committee of the Whole House to-morrow. Mr. Alexander, from the Committee for the District of Columbia, to which the subject had been referred, re-

ported the following bill: [Washington, 1828] 21 p. (H. R. 133) DNA.   36161

---- A bill to refund the moiety of the forfeiture upon the schooner Volant. Feb. 18, 1828. Read twice, and committed to a Committee of the Whole House to-morrow. Mr. Verplanck, from the Committee of Ways and Means, to which the subject had been referred, reported the following bill: [Washington, 1828] 1 p. (H. R. 170) DNA.   36162

---- ---- Dec. 10, 1828. Read twice, and committed to a Committee of the Whole House to-morrow. Mr. Verplanck, from the Committee of Ways and Means, to which the subject had been referred, reported the following bill: [Washington, 1828] 1 p. (H. R. 308) DNA.   36163

---- A bill to refund to George and William Bangs the amount of duties on certain goods, destroyed by fire. Jan. 2, 1828. Read twice, and committed to the Committee of the Whole House to which is committed the bill for the benefit of Sewall, Williams, & Co. Mr. Dwight, from the Committee of Ways and Means, reported the following bill: [Washington, 1828] 1 p. (H. R. 38) DNA.   36164

---- A bill to regulate the foreign and coasting trade on the Northern and Northwestern frontiers of the United States, and for other purposes. Apr. 18, 1828. Read twice, and committed to the Committee of the Whole House to which is committed the Bill [H. R. No. 92] authorizing the licensing of vessels to be employed in the mackerel fishery. Mr. Cambreleng, from the Committee on Commerce, to which the subject had been referred, reported the following bill: [Washington, 1828] 1 p. (H. R. 273) DNA. 36165

---- A bill to regulate the laying out and making of a National Road from the city of Washington, in the District of Columbia, to New Orleans, in the State of Louisiana. Jan. 2, 1828. Read twice, and committed to a Committee of the Whole House tomorrow. Mr. Mercer, from the Committee on Roads and Canals, reported the following bill: [Washington, 1828] 7 p. (H. R. 44) DNA. 36166

---- A bill to release the right of the United States to cetain lands in East Florida, to the heirs-at-law and devisees of William Drayton, deceased. Mar. 19, 1828. Read twice, and committed to a Committee of the Whole House to-morrow. Mr. W. R. Davis, from the Committee on the Public Lands, to which was referred the petition of the heirs of William Drayton, deceased, reported the following bill: [Washington, 1828] 1 p. (H. R. 232) DNA. 36167

---- A bill to repair the Post Road from Cincinnati to Portland, in the State of Ohio. Mar. 17, 1828. Read twice, and committed to the Committee of the Whole House to which is committed the bill for the improvement of the post road leading from Natchez to New Orleans. Mr. Woods, of Ohio, from the Committee on Roads and Canals, to which the subject had been referred, reported the following bill: [Washington, 1828] 1 p. (H. R. 225) DNA. 36168

---- A bill to repeal so much of the Acts of December 12, 1813,

and April 16, 1818, as provides for the conferring of Brevet Rank. Apr. 28, 1828. Mr. Harrison, from the Committee on Military Affairs, reported the following bill; which was read, and passed to a second reading. [Washington, 1828] 1 p. (S. 145) DNA. 36169

---- A bill to repeal the thirty-seventh section of an act regulating the collection of duties on Imports and Tonnage, passed the first of March, one thousand eight hundred and twenty-three, and to amend the twenty-eighth section of said act. Jan. 14, 1828. Read twice, and committed to a Committee of the Whole House to-morrow. Mr. Cambreleng, from the Committee on Commerce, to which the subject had been referred, reported the following bill: [Washington, 1828] 1 p. (H. R. 74) DNA. 36170

---- A bill to repeal the tonnage duties upon ships and vessels of the United States, and upon certain foreign vessels. Dec. 31, 1828. Read twice, and committed to the Committee of the Whole House on the state of the Union. Mr. Sprague, from the Committee of Ways and Means, to which the subject had been referred, reported the following bill: [Washington, 1828] 1 p. (H. R. 345) DNA. 36171

---- A bill to revive and continue in force "An act declaring the assent of Congress to a certain act of Maryland." Jan. 8, 1828. Read twice, and committed to a Committee of the Whole House to-morrow. Mr. Barney, from the Committee on Commerce, to which the subject had been referred, reported the following bill: [Washington, 1828] 1 p. (H. R. 59) DNA. 36172

---- A bill to revive and continue
in force, an act entitled "An act
to provide for persons who were
disabled by known wounds, received in the Revolutionary War."
Apr. 8, 1828. Mr. Noble, from
the Committee on Pensions, reported the following bill; which
was read, and passed to a second
reading. [Washington, 1828] 3 p.
(S. 137) DNA.   36173

---- A bill to revive and continue
in force, for a limited time, an
act entitled "An act authorizing
the payment of certain certificates." Feb. 26, 1828. Read
twice, and committed to a Committee of the Whole House to-
morrow. Mr. Wolf, from the
Committee on Revolutionary
Claims, to which the subject had
been referred, reported the following bill: [Washington, 1828]
1 p. (H. R. 193) DNA.   36174

---- ---- Dec. 19, 1828. Read
twice, and committed to a Committee of the Whole House to-day.
Mr. Wolf, from the Committee
on Revolutionary Claims, to which
the subject had been referred, reported the following bill: [Wash-
ington, 1828] 1 p. (H. R. 319)
DNA.   36175

---- A bill to vest the title of
certain lots of ground in the
Board of Trustees for the regula-
tion of schools in the town of St.
Louis. Dec. 22, 1828. Read twice
and committed to a Committee of
the Whole House to-morrow. Mr.
Bates, of Missouri, from the
Committee on Private Land
Claims, to which was referred
the petition of a Committee of the
Board of Trustees for the regula-
tion of schools in the town of St.
Louis, reported the following bill:
[Washington, 1828] 1 p. (H. R.
327) DNA.   36176

---- Boundary - Georgia and
Florida. Message from the President of the United States, transmitting documents relative to the
boundary line between Georgia
and Florida. Mar. 3, 1828.
Read, and laid on the table.
Washington, Pr. by Gales & Seaton, 1828. 9 p. (Doc. No. 170)
DLC; NjR.   36177

---- Boundary line - U. S. and
Great Britain. Message from the
President of the United States,
In reply to a resolution of the
House of Representatives, of the
25th ultimo, requesting copies of
instructions given by the govern-
ment of the confederations to its
Ministers, in relation to the set-
tlement of boundaries with Great
Britain, &c. March 25, 1828.
Read, and laid upon the table.
Washington, Pr. by Gales & Sea-
ton, 1828. 4 p. (Doc. No. 217)
CSmH; DLC; NjR.   36178

---- Breakwater - Delaware Bay.
Resolution of the Legislature of
Pennsylvania, on the construction
of a breakwater in the Delaware
Bay. Feb. 11, 1828. Referred to
the Committee of the Whole House
to which is committed the bill of
the House of Representatives (No.
131) for the accomplishment of
that object. Washington, Pr. by
Gales & Seaton, 1828. 3 p. (Doc.
No. 134) DLC; DeGE; NjR.
                            36179

---- Breakwater in Delaware Bay.
Jan. 30, 1828. Mr. Sutherland,
from the Committee on Commerce,
to which the subject had been referred, made the following report:
Washington, Pr. by Gales & Seaton,
1828. 8 p. (Rep. No. 118) DLC; NjR.
                            36180

---- Business to be acted upon.
May 3, 1828. Read, and laid up-
on the table. Mr. Tucker, of
South Carolina, from the Joint
Committee of the two Houses

of Congress, appointed to consider and report what business is necessary to be acted upon at the present Session, &c. &c., made the following report: Washington, Gales & Seaton, 1828. 19 p. (Rep. No. 243) DLC; NjR. 36181

---- By the President of the United States of America: a proclamation [Re. duties on the tonnage of ships and vessels] Given under my hand, at the city of Washington, this first day of July, in the year of our Lord one thousand eight hundred and twenty-eight and the fifty-second of the independence of the United States. John Quincy Adams. [n. p. 1828] 1 p. DLC. 36182

---- ---- Whereas a convention, between the United States of America and His Majesty the King of the United Kingdom of Great Britain and Ireland, was concluded and signed by the Plenipotentiaries at London, on the 29th day of September, one thousand eight hundred and twenty-seven, which convention is, word for word, as follows...Done at the City of Washington, this fifteenth day of May, in the year of our Lord, one thousand eight hundred and twenty eight...John Quincy Adams. [Washington, 1828] 3 p. DLC. 36183

---- Cadets. Letter from the Secretary of War transmitting the information required by a resolution of the House in relation to the annual appointments made in the Army of the United States since the 31st of December, 1820; the number of Cadets who have received appointments of the lowest grade, by brevet, during the same period; and also the number of officers now in the Army who entered it as Cadets from the Military Academy.

Dec. 31, 1828. Referred to the Committee on Military Affairs. Washington, Pr. by Gales & Seaton, 1828. 4 p. (Doc. No. 41) DLC; NjR. 36184

---- Cadets at West Point. Letter from the Secretary of War, transmitting a list of the cadets now at West Point; their names, the state and county from whence sent, &c. &c. Feb. 29, 1828. Read, and laid upon the table. Washington, Pr. by Gales & Seaton, 1828. 9 p., 4 bdsds. (Doc. No. 167) DLC; MH; NjR. 36185

---- Canal - Baltimore to contemplated Chesapeake & Ohio Canal. Letter from the Secretary of War, transmitting, pursuant to a resolution of the House of Representatives of the 12th ultimo, a report and plans of the survey of a route for a canal from the city of Baltimore to the contemplated Chesapeake and Ohio Canal. Jan. 14, 1828. Referred to the Committee on Roads and Canals. Washington, Pr. by Gales & Seaton, 1828. 31 p. (Doc. No. 58) DLC; DeGE; NjR. 36186

---- Canal - Dayton to Lake Erie. Jan. 18, 1828. Mr. Woods, of Ohio, from the Committee on Roads and Canals, to which the subject had been referred, made the following report: Washington, Pr. by Gales & Seaton, 1828. 3 p. (Rep. No. 88) DLC; NjR. 36187

---- Caron de Beaumarchais. Apr. 1, 1828. Mr. Everett, from the Committee on Foreign Affairs, to which was referred the claim of Caron de Beaumarchais, made the following report: Washington, Gales & Seaton, 1828. 125 p. (Rep. No. 220) DLC; NjR. 36188

---- Case of Francis Larche (to accompany Senate bill No. 37); Mr. Livingston submitted the following depositions relative to the claim of Francis Larche. Apr. 30, 1828. Read, and laid upon the table. Washington, Pr. by Gales & Seaton, 1828. 4 p. (Doc. No. 265) DLC; NjR.   36189

---- Case of Henry Lee. Dec. 30, 1828. Mr. Taliaferro submitted the following as an amendment of the report of the Committee of Claims on the petition of Henry Lee. Washington, Pr. by Gales & Seaton, 1828. 2 p. (Rep. No. 26) DLC; NjR.   36190

---- Case of Russell Jarvis. May 16, 1828. Read, and laid upon the table. Mr. McDuffie, from the Select Committee to which was referred the message of the President of the United States of the 17th ultimo, relative to an assault upon his Private Secretary, made the following report: Washington, Gales & Seaton, 1828. 43 p. (Rep. No. 260) DLC; NjR.   36191

---- Change of stations of troops U.S. Letter from the Secretary of War, transmitting reports of change of stations of the troops of the United States, during the year 1827. Jan. 7, 1827[sic] 1828. Read, and laid on the table. Washington, Pr. by Gales & Seaton, 1828. 7 p. (Doc. No. 46) DLC; NjR.   36192

---- Charges against the Creek agent since Jan. 1, 1826. Message from the President of the United States transmitting the information required by a resolution of the House of Representatives, of the 9th inst. in relation to charges preferred against the agent of the United States for the Creek tribe of Indians, since

Jan. 1, 1826.   Apr. 16, 1828. Read, and laid upon the table. Washington, Pr. by Gales & Seaton, 1828. 30 p. (Doc. No. 248) DLC; NjR.   36193

---- Cherokee Council to Col. H. Montgomery. Message from the President of the United States transmitting a copy of the letter from the Cherokee Council to Col. Hugh Montgomery, &c. December 8, 1828. Read, and laid upon the table. Washington, Pr. by Gales & Seaton, 1828. 13 p. (Doc. No. 6) DLC; NjR. 36194

---- Cherokee government. Message from the President of the United States, transmitting the information required by a Resolution of the House of Representatives, of the 3d inst., in relation to the formation of a new government by the Cherokee tribe of Indians, within the state of North Carolina, Georgia, Tennessee, and Alabama, &c. Mar. 22, 1828. Read, and laid upon the table. Washington, Pr. by Gales & Seaton, 1828. 19 p. (Doc. No. 211) DLC; NjR.   36195

---- Cherokee lands - North Carolina. Jan. 22, 1828. Mr. Carson, from the Committee on Indian Affairs, to which the subject had been referred, made the following report: Washington, Pr. by Gales & Seaton, 1828. 8 p. (Rep. No. 92) DLC; NjR.   36196

---- Chesapeake and Ohio Canal - extension of. Letter from the Secretary of War transmitting a report, map, and estimate of the Chesapeake and Ohio Canal to Alexandria in the District of Columbia. Apr. 21, 1828. Referred to the Committee on Roads and Canals. Washington, Pr. by Gales & Seaton, 1828. 14 p. 1 map. (Doc. No. 254) DLC;

NjR. 36197

---- Chesapeake and Ohio Canal. Jan. 2, 1828. Mr. Mercer, from the Committee on Roads and Canals, made the following report: Washington, Gales & Seaton, 1828. 136 p. 2 bdsds. (Rep. No. 47) DLC; MiU-T; NN; NjR. 36198

---- ---- Feb. 11, 1828. Read, and referred to the Committee of the Whole House to which is committed the "Bill to amend and explain an act, 'An act confirming an act of the Legislature of Virginia, incorporating the Chesapeake and Ohio Canal Company, and an act of the state of Maryland for the same purpose' " Washington, Gales & Seaton, 1828. 146 p. 9 bdsds. (Rep. No. 141) DLC; NjR. 36199

---- ---- Letter from the Secretary of War, transmitting estimates of the cost of making a canal from Cumberland to Georgetown. Mar. 10, 1828. Read, and laid on the table. Washington, Pr. by Gales & Seaton, 1828. 100 p. (Doc. No. 192) DLC; DeGE; NjR; RPB; TxU. 36200

---- Chesapeake and Ohio Canal Company. Memorial of the central committee of the Chesapeake and Ohio Canal Convention to the Congress of the United States. Jan. 28, 1828. Read, and referred to the Committee of the Whole House to which is committed the "bill to explain an act entitled 'An Act of the Legislature of Virginia, incorporating the Chesapeake and Ohio Canal Company, and an act of the state of Maryland for the same purpose.'" Washington, 1828. 8 p. (Doc. No. 101) DLC; DeGE; NjR. 36201

---- ---- Memorial of the Ches-

apeake and Ohio Canal Company. Dec. 5, 1828. Referred to the Committee on Roads and Canals. Washington, Pr. by Gales & Seaton, 1828. 32 p. (Doc. No. 12) DLC; NjR. 36202

---- Chipola Canal Company - Act Council, Florida. Copy of an act to incorporate the Chipola Canal Company, with powers to construct a canal or rail-way between the Chipola River and the eastern arm of St. Andrews Bay. Feb. 22, 1828. Referred to the Committee on Roads and Canals. Feb. 29, 1828. Pr. by order of the House of Representatives. Washington, Pr. by Gales & Seaton, 1828. 7 p. (Doc. No. 166) CtY; DBRE; DLC; MB; MBAt; MH; NN; NjR; P. 36203

---- ---- Mar. 14, 1828. Mr. Mercer, from the Committee on Roads and Canals, to which the subject had been referred, made the following report: Washington, Gales & Seaton, 1828. 8 p. (Rep. No. 191) DLC; NN; NjR. 36204

---- Citizens of Georgia - claim on Creek Indians. Memorial of the Legislature of Georgia, on the subject of the claims of the citizens of that state, against the Creek Nation, under the Treaty of the Indian Springs, of 1821. Feb. 12, 1828. Referred to the Committee of the Whole House to which is committed the report of the Committee on Indian Affairs, of the 5th inst. on the same subject. Washington, Pr. by Gales & Seaton, 1828. 8 p. (Doc. No. 135) DLC; DeGE; NjR. 36205

---- ---- Feb. 5, 1828. Read, and committed to a Committee of the Whole House to-morrow. Mr. McLean, from the Committee on Indian Affairs, to which the subject had been referred, made the following report: Washington, Pr. by Gales & Seaton, 1828. 23 p. (Rep. No. 128) DLC; NjR.   36206

---- Claim of Maryland for interest, &c. Mar. 12, 1828. Read, and laid upon the table. Mr. Williams, from the Committee of Claims, to which the subject had been referred, made the following report: Washington, Gales & Seaton, 1828. 2 p. (Rep. No. 189) DLC; NjR.   36207

---- Claim of the Marquis de Maison Rouge. Feb. 4, 1828. Mr. Whipple, from the Committee on the Public Lands, to which the subject had been referred, made the following report: Washington, Pr. by Gales & Seaton, 1828. 4 p. (Rep. No. 123) DLC; NjR.   36208

---- Claim of the state of Pennsylvania. Apr. 4, 1828. Mr. Ramsey, from the Committee of Claims, to which was referred the claim of the state of Pennsylvania, made the following report: Washington, Gales & Seaton, 1828. 5 p. (Rep. No. 223) DLC; NjR.   36209

---- Claims under eleventh article of Treaty with Spain. Letter from the Secretary of State, transmitting a list of such claims as were rejected by the Board of Commissioners, under the eleventh article of the treaty between Spain and the United States, &c. Mar. 24, 1828. Read, and laid upon the table. Washington, Pr. by Gales & Seaton, 1828. 3 p. (Doc. No. 212) DLC; NjR. 36210

---- Clerks - Navy Department. Letter from the Secretary of the Navy, transmitting lists of the clerks employed in his office, and in the office of the Navy

Commissioners, during the year 1827. Jan. 7, 1828. Read, and laid upon the table. Washington, Pr. by Gales & Seaton, 1828. 6 p. (Doc. No. 47) DLC; NjR.   36211

---- Clerks - State Department. Letter from the Secretary of State, transmitting statement of the names of the clerks in the State Department and the Patent Office, during the year 1827, and the compensation of each. Feb. 12, 1828. Read, and laid upon the table. Washington, Pr. by Gales & Seaton, 1828. 4 p. (Doc. No. 136) DLC; NjR.   36212

---- Clerks in the Post Office Department. Letter from the Postmaster General, transmitting a list of the clerks employed in the Department, during the year 1827, and the salary of each. Jan. 3, 1828. Read, and laid upon the table. Washington, Pr. by Gales & Seaton, 1828. 4 p. (Doc. No. 37) DLC; NjR.   36213

---- Clerks in the War Department. Letter from the Secretary of War, transmitting a list of the names of the clerks employed in the War Department, during the year 1827, and the salary of each. Jan. 21, 1828. Read, and laid upon the table. Washington, Pr. by Gales & Seaton, 1828. 6 p. DLC; NjR.   36214

---- Coasting trade through Delaware Bay. Mr. Sergeant submitted the following estimate of the annual coasting trade, to and from ports within the limits of the United States, passing in and out of the Delaware Bay, &c. Jan. 15, 1828. Pr. by order of the House of Representatives. Washington, Pr. by Gales & Seaton, 1828. 4 p. 1 bdsd. (Doc. No. 67) DLC; NjR.   36215

---- Col. Pipkin's regiment Tennessee Militia. Apr. 5, 1828. Read, and laid upon the table. Mr. Hamilton, from the Committee on Military Affairs, made the following report: Washington, Gales & Seaton, 1828. 2 p. (Rep. No. 225) DLC; NjR.   36216

---- Colonization Society. Memorial of the American Society for Colonizing the Free People of Color of the United States. Jan. 28, 1828. Read, and referred to a Select Committee, to wit: Mr. Mercer, Mr. Gorham, Mr. Shepperd, Mr. Weems, Mr. Johns, Mr. Vinton, and Mr. Fort. Washington, Pr. by Gales & Seaton, 1828. 79 p. 2 bdsds. (Doc. No. 99) CSmH; DLC; ICN; NjR.   36217

---- Commerce and navigation of the United States. Letter from the Secretary of the Treasury transmitting statements of the commerce and navigation of the United States during the year ending on the 30th day of September, 1828. Apr. 21, 1828. Read, and laid upon the table. Washington, Pr. by Gales & Seaton, 1828. 308 p. 3 bdsds. (Doc. 253) DLC; NjR.   36218

---- Commission under the Treaty of Ghent. Communication presented by Mr. Wickliffe from the commissioners under the Treaty of Ghent. Apr. 25, 1828. Pr. by order of the House of Representatives. Washington, Pr. by Gales & Seaton, 1828. 3 p. (Doc. No. 257) DLC; NjR.   36219

---- Communication from the delegate of Florida, enclosing an extract from the governor's message containing a statement of the qualities of the public land in Florida, and showing the necessity for a graduation of prices.

Jan. 14, 1828. Pr. by order of the Senate of the United States. Washington, Pr. by Duff Green. 1828. 12 p. (Doc. No. 33) DLC; NjR.   36220

---- Comparative statement of duties, under the "Bill altering the several acts imposing duties on imports," and the present rate of duties. Apr. 30, 1828. Pr. by order of the Senate of the United States. Washington, Duff Green, 1828. 6 p. (Doc. No. 186) DLC; NjR.   36221

---- Compensate registers and receivers - Arkansas. Documents to accompany the bill (H. R. No. 265) allowing compensation to the registers of land offices and receivers of public moneys for extra services in the territory of Arkansas. Washington, Pr. by Gales & Seaton, 1828. 4 p. (Doc. No. 243) DLC; NjR; P.   36222

---- Compensation of collectors, &c. Letter from the Secretary of the Treasury, transmitting a statement of the compensation received by each collector, naval officer, & surveyor of the customs, for the years 1824, 1825, and 1826. Feb. 12, 1828. Read, and laid upon the table. Washington, Pr. by Gales & Seaton, 1828. 3 p. 6 bdsds. (Doc. No. 141) DLC; NjR.   36223

---- Comptroller General South Carolina. Memorial of the Comptroller General of S. Carolina, praying that certain balances due for military works and the purchase of arms, during the late war, may be paid, with interest, to the state of South Carolina. Jan. 3, 1828. Referred to the Committee on Military Affairs. Washington, Pr. by Gales & Seaton, 1828. 7 p. (Doc. No. 38)

DLC; NjR.   36224

---- Condition of the Cumberland
Road. Letter from the Postmaster General, in reply to a resolution of the House of Representatives, requiring information in
relation to the present state and
condition of the Cumberland Road.
May 10, 1828. Read, and referred to the Committee on the
Post Office and Post Roads.
Washington, Pr. by Gales & Seaton, 1828. 3 p. (Doc. No. 269)
DLC; NjR.   36225

---- Condy Raguet. Mar. 25,
1828. Read, and laid upon the
table. Mr. Everett, from the
Committee on Foreign Affairs, to
which was referred the communication of Condy Raguet, late
Charge d'Affairs of the United
States at the Court of Brazil,
made the following report: Washington, Gales & Seaton, 1828. 4
p. (Rep. No. 212) DLC; NjR.
                         36226
---- Connecticut. Memorial of
sundry inhabitants of the counties
of Windham and Tolland, state of
Connecticut, praying for the aid
of government in the cultivation
of the mulberry tree and of silk.
Feb. 25, 1828. Referred to the
Committee on Agriculture. Washington, Pr. by Gales & Seaton,
1828. 6 p. (Doc. No. 159) DLC;
NjR.   36227

---- ---- Statement of the clerk
of the District Court of Connecticut, showing the amount of fees
received by the Marshal, in 1827.
Feb. 11, 1828. Read, and laid on
the table. Washington, Pr. by
Gales & Seaton, 1828. 3 p. (Doc.
No. 131) DLC; NjR.   36228

---- The Constitution of the
United States of America: The
rules of the Senate and of the
House of Representatives: with

Jefferson's Manual. Pr. by order
of the Senate of the United States.
Washington, Pr. by Duff Green,
1828. 216 p. CtHT; GU; NNC;
NhHi; RPB.   36229

---- The Constitution of the
United States; together with the
census of 1820; and the actual
vote of 1824, for President of
the United States. Knoxville,
Ten., Pr. by Hyram Barry,
1828. 24 p. THi.   36230

---- Contingent expenses - House
of Reps. &c. Annual report of
the clerk of the House of Representatives of the names of the
clerks, messengers, &c. in the
service of the House and of the
expenditure of the contingent fund
of 1828. Dec. 5, 1828. Washington, Pr. by Gales & Seaton,
1828. 5 p. (Doc. No. 4) DLC;
NjR.   36231

---- Contingent expenses - military establishment, 1827. Letter
from the Secretary of War, transmitting a statement, showing the
expenditure of the money appropriated for the contingent expenses of the military establishment of the United States, for
the year 1827. Jan. 7, 1828.
Read, and laid upon the table.
Washington, Pr. by Gales & Seaton, 1828. 4 p. 2 bdsds. (Doc.
No. 49) DLC; NjR.   36232

---- Contingent expenses, Navy
Department. Letter from the
Secretary of the Navy transmit-
ting an abstract of the expendi-
tures of the appropriations for
the contingent expenses of the
Navy for the year ending 30th
Sept. 1828. Dec. 18, 1828.
Read, and laid upon the table.
Washington, Pr. by Gales &
Seaton, 1828. 14 p. (Doc. No.
24) DLC; NjR.   36233

---- Contingent expenses of the Navy. Letter from the Secretary of the Navy, transmitting an abstract of the expenditures of the appropriations for the contingent expenses of the Navy, from 1st, Oct., 1826, to 30th Sept., 1827. Jan. 7, 1828. Referred to the Committee of Ways and Means. Washington, Pr. by Gales & Seaton, 1828. 3 p. 6 bdsds. (Doc. No. 50) DLC; NjR.   36234

---- Continuation of Cumberland Road. Letter from the Secretary of War, transmitting (in compliance with a resolution of the House of Representatives, of the 11th instant,) a report of Commissioners, appointed to locate the National Road, under the act of March 3, 1825. Feb. 19, 1828. Read, and laid upon the table. Washington, Pr. by Gales & Seaton, 1828. 16 p. 1 bdsd. (Doc. No. 149) DLC; NjR.   36235

---- Contracts - Post Office Department, 1827. Letter from the Postmaster General transmitting a statement of contracts made by the department during the year 1827. Apr. 25, 1828. Read, and laid upon the table. Washington, Pr. by Gales & Seaton, 1828. 36 p. (Doc. No. 258) DLC; NjR.   36236

---- Contracts - War Department - 1827. Letter from the Secretary of War, transmitting statement of contracts made by that department, during the year 1827. Jan. 30, 1828. Read, and laid upon the table. Washington, Pr. by Gales & Seaton, 1828. 3 p. 15 bdsds. (Doc. No. 221) DLC; NjR.   36237

---- Contracts by Navy Commissioners. Letter from the Secretary of the Navy transmitting a statement of contracts made by the Commissioners of the Navy

during the year 1827. Feb. 8, 1828. Read, and laid upon the table. Washington, Pr. by Gales & Seaton, 1828. 3 p. 3 bdsds. (Doc. No. 128) DLC; NjR.   36238

---- Conventions with Great Britain. Message from the President of the United States, transmitting copies of three conventions with Great Britain: 1. For continuing in force the provisions of the Convention of 3d July, 1815. 2. For continuing in force the provisions of the third article of the Convention of 20th Oct. 1818, 3. A Convention, concluded 29th Sept. 1827, for carrying into effect the provisions of the fifth article of the Treaty of Ghent, in relation to the Northeastern Boundary of the United States. May 19, 1828. Read, and laid upon the table. Washington, Pr. by Gales & Seaton, 1828. 13 p. (Doc. No. 275) DLC; NjR.   36239

---- Corporation of Baltimore. Report of the Secretary of the Treasury on the memorial of the Mayor and City Council of Baltimore, for pay and allowance for money advanced and supplies furnished during the late war. Jan. 2, 1828. Referred to the Committee of Claims. Washington, Pr. by Gales & Seaton, 1828. 44 p. (Doc. No. 39) DLC; NjR.   36240

---- Corporation of Washington. Memorial of the Mayor, Aldermen, and Common Council, of the city of Washington. Jan. 7, 1828. Referred to the Committee on Commerce. Washington, Pr. by Gales & Seaton, 1828. 5 p. (Doc. No. 51) DLC; NjR. 36241

---- Corporations - Washington, Georgetown, and Alexandria. Jan. 30, 1828. Mr. Mercer, from the Committee on Roads and Canals, to which was referred a memorial of the corporations of Washington, Georgetown, and Alexandria, in the District of Columbia, made the following report: Washington, Pr. by Gales & Seaton, 1828. 32 p., 2 bdsds. (Rep. No. 112) DLC; NjR.   36242

---- Correspondence - Secretary of War and General Jackson. Letter from the Secretary of War, transmitting copies of all the letters and correspondence between the Secretary of War and Gen. Andrew Jackson, from the commencement of the Creek War, to 1st March, 1815. Feb. 18, 1828. Read, and laid upon the table. Washington, Pr. by Gales & Seaton, 1828. 22 p. (Doc. No. 146) DLC; NjR.   36243

---- Correspondence with Brazilian government. Message from the President of the United States, transmitting copies of a correspondence with the government of Brazil in relation to an alleged blockade by the naval force of Brazil, the imprisonment of American citizens, and the demand made by the Charge d'Affaires of the U. S. of his passports, and the cause thereof. May 23, 1828. Read, and laid upon the table. Washington, Pr. by Gales & Seaton, 1828. 232 p. (Doc. No. 281) DLC; MH-L; NjR.   36244

---- Creek Indian broke, &c. Letter from the Secretary of War, transmitting the information in part required by a resolution of the House of Representatives, 21st inst. in relation to the breaking an individual, and depriving him of his authority among the Creeks; also, in relation to the appointment of an Indian chief in the territory of Michigan, during the year 1827. Mar. 28, 1828. Read, and laid

upon the table. Washington, Pr. by Gales & Seaton, 1828. 20 p. (Doc. No. 219) DLC; NjR.   36245

---- Creek treaty - Nov. 15, 1827. Message from the President of the United States transmitting the information required by a resolution of the House of Representatives of the 22d ultimo in relation to the treaty with the Creek nation of Indians, of the 15th of November last. Apr. 8, 1828. Read, and laid upon the table. Washington, Pr. by Gales & Seaton, 1828. 26 p. (Doc. No. 238) DLC; NjR.   36246

---- Creeks removed west of the Mississippi. Letter from the Secretary of War transmitting the information required by a resolution of the House of Representatives of the 15th inst. in relation to the number of Creek Indians which have removed west of the Mississippi, and the expense attending the same. Jan. 21, 1828. Read and laid upon the table. Washington, Pr. by Gales & Seaton, 1828. 4 p. (Doc. No. 74) DLC; NjR.   36247

---- Cumberland Road. Letter from the Secretary of War transmitting a copy of the last annual report of the Superintendent of the Cumberland Road. Dec. 11, 1828. Read, and laid upon the table. Washington, Pr. by Gales & Seaton, 1828. 9 p. (Doc. No. 14) DLC; DeGE; NjR.   36248

---- ---- Message from the President of the United States, transmitting copies of resolutions of the Legislature of Pennsylvania, in relation to the Cumberland Road. Feb. 22, 1828. Read, and committed to the Committee of the Whole House to which is committed the Bill for the preservation and repair of the Cum-

berland Road. Washington, Pr. by
Gales & Seaton, 1828. 7 p. (Doc.
No. 152) DLC; NjR.   36249

---- Custom-house bonds - unpaid. Letter from the Secretary
of the Treasury, transmitting the
information required by a resolution of the House of Representatives of 18th ult. in relation to
bonds taken to secure the payment of duties on imports, at the
several custom-houses which have
become due, and remain unpaid,
&c. May 12, 1828. Read, and
laid upon the table. Washington,
Pr. by Gales & Seaton, 1828.
149 p. (Doc. No. 287) DLC; NjR;
OO.   36250

---- D. Bouligny and J. E. Frost.
Memorial of D. Bouligny & John
E. Frost. Apr. 12, 1828. Referred to the Committee of the
Whole House to which is committed the bill from the Senate
(No. 96) entitled "An act supplementary to an act to provide for
the adjustment of claims of persons entitled to indemnification
under the first article of the
treaty of Ghent, and for the distribution, among such claimants,
of the sum paid by the government of Great Britain, under a
convention between the United
States and His Britannic Majesty,
concluded at London, on the 13th
of November, 1826," passed on
the 2d day of March, 1827.
Washington, Pr. by Gales & Seaton, 1828. 28 p. (Doc. No. 242)
DLC; NjR.   36251

---- Daniel Goodwin, executor of
Benjamin. Feb. 21, 1828. Mr.
Wolf, from the Committee on
Revolutionary Claims, to which
was referred the petition of Daniel Goodwin, executor of Benjamin Goodwin, deceased, made the
following report: Washington,
Gales & Seaton, 1828. 3 p. (Rep.

No. 154) DLC; NjR.   36252

---- Death of officers on the
Gulf frontier. Letter from the
Secretary of War transmitting the
information required by a resolution of the House of Representatives of the 14th inst. in relation
to the death of officers of the
army on the Gulf frontier, &c.
&c. Jan. 21, 1821. Read and
laid upon the table. Washington,
Pr. by Gales & Seaton, 1828. 5
p. 1 bdsd. (Doc. No. 75) DLC;
NjR.   36253

---- Delaware and Hudson Canal.
Memorial of the Delaware and
Hudson Canal Company. Apr. 7,
1828. Referred to the Committee
of Ways and Means. Apr. 14,
1828. Bill reported, No. 268.
Washington, Pr. by Gales & Seaton, 1828. 20 p. (Doc. No. 247)
CtY; DBRE; DLC; DeGE; MB;
MBAt; MH; NN; NjR; PPL; RPB.
                            36254
---- Denison Douglass. Dec. 19,
1827. Read, and laid upon the
table. Apr. 26, 1828. Committed
to a Committee of the Whole
House to-morrow. Mr. McCoy,
from the Committee of Claims,
to which was referred the petition of Denison Douglass, made
the following report: Washington,
Gales & Seaton, 1828. 5 p. (Rep.
No. 238) DLC; NjR.   36255

---- Discriminating duties -
Prussia. Message from the President of the United States, transmitting information on the abolition of discriminating duties by
the government of Prussia, since
the 15th April, 1826, so far as
they affected the vessels of the
U. States and their cargoes, &c.
&c. Apr. 16, 1828. Read, and
laid upon the table. Washington,
Pr. by Gales & Seaton, 1828. 6
p. (Doc. No. 274) DLC; NjR.
                            36256

---- Distribution of the laws. May 16, 1828. Read, and laid upon the table. Mr. Everett, from the Committee on the Library, to which the subject had been referred, made the following report: Washington, Gales & Seaton, 1828. 4 p. (Rep. No. 261) DLC; NjR.   36257

---- District of Columbia. Memorial of inhabitants of the District of Columbia, praying for the gradual abolition of slavery in the District of Columbia. Mar. 24, 1828. Referred to the Committee for the District of Columbia. Washington, Pr. by Gales & Seaton, 1828. 5 p. (Doc. No. 215) DLC; NjR. 36258

---- District tonnage of the United States, Dec. 31, 1826. Letter from the Secretary of the Treasury, transmitting a statement of the district tonnage of the United States. On the 31, Dec. 1826, &c. &c. Jan. 7, 1828. Read, and laid on the table. Washington, Pr. by Gales & Seaton, 1828. 4 p. 7 bdsds. (Doc. No. 48) DLC; NjR. 36259

---- Dividing line - Florida and Georgia. Message from the President of the United States transmitting copies of communications from the Governor of Georgia relating to the line dividing that state from the territory of Florida. Jan. 23, 1828. Read, and referred to the Committee on the Judiciary. Washington, Pr. by Gales & Seaton, 1828. 16 p. (Doc. No. 87) DLC; NjR.   36260

---- Dividing line between Georgia and Florida. Mar. 21, 1828. Read, and laid upon the table. Mr. P. P. Barbour, from the Committee on the Judiciary, to which the subject had been referred, made the following report: Washington, Gales & Seaton, 1828. 7 p. (Rep. No. 204) DLC; NjR.   36261

---- Doctor Eliakim Crosby. May 8, 1828. Mr. Sterifer, from the Committee on Private Land Claims, to which was referred the petition of Dr. Eliakim Crosby, made the following report: Washington, Gales & Seaton, 1828. 2 p. (Rep. No. 249) DLC; NjR.   36262

---- Document relating to bill number fifty-eight for the relief of Samuel Cobun of Mississippi. January 15, 1828. Pr. by order of the United States. Washington, Pr. by Duff Green, 1828. 3 p. (Doc. No. 39) DLC; NjR. 36263

---- Drawback, 1825, 1826, & 1827. Letter from the Secretary of the Treasury transmitting a statement by the register, of drawbacks on merchandise exported in the years 1825, 1826, and 1827. Dec. 18, 1828. Read, and laid upon the table. Washington, Pr. by Gales & Seaton, 1828. 8 p. (Doc. No. 25) DLC; NjR.   36264

---- Drawback on exports - 1824, 1825, and 1826. Letter from the Secretary of the Treasury, transmitting a statement of the amount of drawback on exports in the years 1824, 1825, and 1826, compared with the amount of duties which accrued in the same respectively. May 16, 1828. Read, and laid upon the table. Washington, Pr. by Gales & Seaton, 1828. 12 p. (Doc. No. 280) DLC; NjR.   36265

---- Drawback on refined sugar. Jan. 3, 1828. Mr. Cambreleng, from the Committee on Commerce, to which was referred the petition of sundry sugar refiners, made the following report: Washington, Gales & Seaton, 1828. 6 p. (Rep. No. 51) DLC; NjR.   36266

---- Dry docks. Jan. 25, 1828.
Mr. Hoffman, from the Committee on Naval Affairs, to which the
subject had been referred, made
the following report: Washington,
Pr. by Gales & Seaton, 1828. 9
p. (Rep. No. 100) DLC; NjR.
36267
---- ---- Jan. 25, 1828. Dec. 17,
1828. Repr. by order of the
House of Representatives. Mr.
Hoffman, from the Committee on
Naval Affairs, to which the subject had been referred, made the
following report: Washington, Pr.
by Gales & Seaton, 1828. 8 p.
(Rep. No. 8) DLC; NjR. 36268

---- Duncan McArthur. Letter
from Duncan McArthur, to the
Speaker of the House of Representatives accompanied with documents, calculated to sustain his
claim to lands between the lines
of Ludlow & Roberts, &c. &c.
Feb. 12, 1828. Referred to the
Committee on the Public Lands.
Washington, Pr. by Gales & Seaton, 1828. 68 p. (Doc. No. 137)
DLC; NjR. 36269

---- Duties on imported teas.
Feb. 18, 1828. Mr. McDuffie,
from the Committee of Ways and
Means, to which the subject had
been referred, made the following
report: Washington, Gales &
Seaton, 1828. 2 p. (Rep. No. 149)
DLC; NjR. 36270

---- Duties on imports. Jan. 31,
1828. Mr. Mallary, from the
Committee on Manufactures, made
the following report: Washington,
Pr. by Gales & Seaton, 1828.
160 p. (Rep. No. 115) DLC; NjR.
36271
---- Duties on merchandise, tonnage, &c. Letter from the Secretary of the Treasury, transmitting a statement exhibiting the
details of duties on merchandise
and tonnage, referred to in the

annual report on the state of the
finances; of eighth Dec. last;
also, a statement of the tonnage
employed in the foreign trade of
the United States, for the year
1826. May 16, 1828. Read, and
laid upon the table. Washington,
Pr. by Gales & Seaton, 1828.
12 p. (Doc. No. 282) DLC; NjR.
36272
---- Duties on teas. Letter from
the Secretary of the Treasury,
transmitting a statement, showing
the duties actually received on
teas, during the years 1823,
1824, 1825, 1826, and 1827. Feb.
28, 1828. Read, and laid upon
the table. Washington, Pr. by
Gales & Seaton, 1828. 4 p. (Doc.
No. 165) DLC; NjR. 36273

---- Duties on woollens. Statement, made by Mr. Cambreleng,
of the duties, ad valorem, which
would be charged on woollens of
various descriptions, under the
amendment proposed to be made
by Mr. Mallary to the Bill no.
132, according to the 2d, 3d, and
4th provisions of that amendment.
Feb. 18, 1828. Washington, Pr. by
Gales & Seaton, 1828. 7 p. (Doc.
no. 143) DLC; NjR. 36274

---- Ebenezer Cooley. Dec. 31,
1828. Mr. Vinton, from the Committee on the Public Lands, to
which was referred the case of
Ebenezer Cooley, made the following report: Washington, Pr.
by Gales & Seaton, 1828. 3 p.
(Rep. No. 28) DLC; NjR. 36275

---- Edmund Brooke. Jan. 25,
1828. Read, and laid upon the
table. Jan. 29, 1828. Committed
to a Committee of the Whole
House to-morrow. Mr. Hunt,
from the Committee on Revolutionary Claims to which was referred the petition of Edmund
Brooke, made the following report: Washington, Pr. by Gales

& Seaton, 1828. 2 p. (Rep. No. 107) DLC; NjR.   36276

---- ---- Mar. 18, 1828. Read, and laid upon the table. Mar. 20, 1828. Committed to a Committee of the Whole House to-morrow. Mr. Wolf, from the Committee on Revolutionary Claims, to which was recommitted the report made on the petition of Edmund Brooke, made the following report: Washington, Gales & Seaton, 1828. 10 p. (Rep. No. 205) DLC; NjR.   36277

---- Edward Cary. Feb. 15, 1828. Read, and laid upon the table. Feb. 19, 1828. Committed to a Committee of the Whole House to-morrow. Mr. Williams, from the Committee of Claims, to which was referred the petition of Edward Cary, made the following report: Washington, Gales & Seaton, 1828. 8 p. 1 bdsd. (Rep. No. 153) DLC; NjR.   36278

---- Eleanor Simpson. Feb. 25, 1828. Read, and laid upon the table. Mr. McDuffie, from the Committee of Ways and Means, to which was referred the petition of Eleanor Simpson, made the following report: Washington, Gales & Seaton, 1828. 1 p. (Rep. No. 165) DLC; NjR.   36279

---- Elijah Carr. Dec. 15, 1828. Mr. Jennings, from the Committee on the Public Lands, to which was referred the petition of Elijah Carr, made the following report: Washington, Pr. by Gales & Seaton, 1828. 1 p. (Rep. No. 4) DLC; NjR.   36280

---- Elizabeth Mays. Mar. 7, 1828. Mr. Hoffman, from the Committee on Naval Affairs, to which was referred the petition of Elizabeth Mays, made the fol-

lowing report: Washington, Gales & Seaton, 1828. 1 p. (Rep. No. 180) DLC; NjR.   36281

---- Elizabeth Shaw. Jan. 16, 1828. Mr. Lawrence, from the Committee on Military Pensions, to which was referred the petition of Elizabeth Shaw, made the following report: Washington, Pr. by Gales & Seaton, 1828. 1 p. (Rep. No. 81) DLC; NjR. 36282

---- Elvington Roberts. Memorial of Elvington Roberts, to be permitted to surrender his patent and obtain a new one, for the land he intended to purchase. Jan. 11, 1828. Pr. by order of the House of Representatives. Washington, Pr. by Gales & Seaton, 1828. 6 p. (Doc. No. 55) DLC; NjR.   36283

---- Emigrating Indians, Feb. 6, 1828. Read, and referred to the Committee of Ways and Means. Mr. McLean from the Committee on Indian Affairs, to which had been referred the subject of affording aid to Indians emigrating to places without the limits of the United States and territories thereof, and so much of the estimates of appropriations as relates to that subject, made the following report: Washington, Pr. by Gales & Seaton, 1828. 2 p. (Rep. No. 130) DLC; NjR.   36284

---- Emigrating Indians. Letter from the Secretary of War, transmitting information of the inadequacy of the fund for defraying the expenses attending the emigration of the Creek Indians. Jan. 7, 1828. Referred to the Committee of Ways and Means. Washington, Pr. by Gales & Seaton, 1828. 11 p. (Doc. No. 44) DLC; NjR.   36285

---- Emoluments of officers of

customs, &c. Letter from the Secretary of the Treasury transmitting a statement of the official emoluments of the officers of the customs, for the year 1827. Also, abstracts of fees received in the case of certificates to accompany distilled spirits, wines, &c. &c. Mar. 18, 1828. Read, and laid upon the table. Washington, Pr. by Gales & Seaton, 1828. 4 p. 6 bdsds. (Doc. No. 226) DLC; NjR.   36286

---- (Engineer orders No. 5) Engineer department, Washington, May 28, 1828... Alexander Macomb. Maj. Gen., Chief engineer of the United States. [Washington, 1828] 1 p. DLC.   36287

---- Estimate of appropriations for 1828. Letter from the Secretary of the Treasury transmitting an estimate of appropriations necessary for the service of the year 1828. Jan. 4, 1828. Read, and referred to the Committee of Ways and Means. Washington, Pr. by Gales & Seaton, 1828. 57 p. (Doc. No. 40) DLC; NjR. 36288

---- Estimates of appropriations for the first quarter of the year 1829. Letter from the Secretary of the Treasury transmitting estimates of appropriations for the service of the first quarter of the year 1829. Apr. 11, 1828. Committed to a Committee of the Whole House on the State of the Union. Washington, Pr. by Gales & Seaton, 1828. 34 p. (Doc. No. 241) DLC; NjR.   36289

---- Examination - land offices. Letter from the Secretary of the Treasury transmitting a list of the persons employed to examine the land offices for the years 1823, 1824, 1825, 1826, and 1827, and the compensation allowed to each. April 4, 1828.

Referred to the Committee on Public Lands. Washington, Pr. by Gales & Seaton, 1828. 8 p. (Doc. No. 235) DLC; NjR.
                                        36290
---- Expenditures - Military Academy at West Point. Letter from the Secretary of War, transmitting the information required by a resolution of the House of Representatives of the United States, of the 29th ultimo, in relation to the expenditures at the Military Academy at West Point, from its organization in 1802, to the present time. Mar. 13, 1828. Read, and laid upon the table. Washington, Pr. by Gales & Seaton, 1828. 8 p. 2 bdsds. (Doc. No. 194) DLC; NjR.   36291

---- Expenditures - Public buildings. May 14, 1828. Read, and laid upon the table. Mr. Sprigg, from the Committee on Expenditures on the Public Buildings, made the following report: Washington, Gales & Seaton, 1828. 7 p. 1 bdsd. (Rep. No. 258) DLC; NjR.   36292

---- Expenditures in the Department of State. Apr. 5, 1828. Read, and laid upon the table. Mr. Blair, from the Committee on so much of the Public Accounts and Expenditures as relates to the State Department, made the following report: Washington, Gales & Seaton, 1828. 99 p. (Rep. No. 226) DLC; NjR.
                                        36293
---- Expenditures of public departments. Jan. 31, 1828. Read, and referred to the Select Committee appointed, on the 15th instant, to revise the rules, &c. Mr. Jounson, from the Committee on Public Expenditures, to which the subject had been referred, made the following report: Washington, Pr. by Gales & Seaton, 1828. 2 p. (Rep. No.

116) DLC; NjR.   36294

---- Explore South Seas. Mar.
25, 1828. Accompanied by a bill,
(No. 240) which was twice read,
and committed for to-morrow.
Mr. Ripley, from the Committee
on Naval Affairs, made the following report: Washington, Gales
& Seaton, 1828. 18 p. (Rep. No.
209) CSmH; DLC; NjR.   36295

---- Explore the southern polar
regions. Letter from J. N. Reynolds to the Speaker of the House
of Representatives upon the subject of an Antarctic expedition,
accompanied with petitions from
inhabitants of several states praying the aid of the government in
carrying the same into effect.
Jan. 22, 1828. Read, and referred to the Committee on Naval Affairs. Washington, Pr. by
Gales & Seaton, 1828. 4 p. (Doc.
No. 88) DLC; NjR.   36296

---- Extend Cumberland Road.
Letter from the Secretary of War
transmitting a report of the engineer engaged to survey the route
of the extension of the national
road from Cumberland to Washington City. Dec. 29, 1828. Referred to the Committee on
Roads and Canals. Washington,
Pr. by Gales & Seaton, 1828. 7
p. (Doc. No. 39) DLC; DeGE;
NjR.   36297

---- The Farmers' Register and
Maryland Herald - Extra. Hagerstown, Thursday morning. Dec. 4,
1828. [President's message to
both houses of Congress, Dec. 2]
[Hagerstown, 1828] Bdsd. DLC.
                            36298
---- Farrow and Harris. Documents, &c. relating to the claim
of Farrow and Harris. Dec. 18,
1828. Pr. by order of the House
of Representatives. Washington,
Pr. by Gales & Seaton, 1828. 5

p. (Doc. No. 21) DLC; NjR.
                            36299
---- ---- Letter from the Secretary of War transmitting a memorial from Nimrod Farrow upon the subject of the claim of
Farrow and Harris. Dec. 29,
1828. Read, and laid upon the
table. Washington, Pr. by Gales
& Seaton, 1828. 11 p. (Doc. No.
36) DLC; NjR.   36300

---- ---- Letter from the Secretary of War transmitting further information in relation to
the settlement of the claim of
Farrow and Harris against the
United States. Dec. 19, 1828.
Read, and referred to the Committee of the Whole House to
which is committed a bill for
their relief. Washington, Pr. by
Gales & Seaton, 1828. 2 p. (Doc.
No. 27) DLC; NjR.   36301

---- Florida Indians. Letter
from the Secretary of War transmitting a report made by the
Agent of Indian Affairs in Florida, in relation to the wish of
those Indians to send a deputa-
tion to examine the country west
of the Mississippi. Dec. 23,
1828. Read, and referred to the
Committee on Indian Affairs.
Washington, Pr. by Gales & Seaton, 1828. 3 p. (Doc. No. 31)
DLC; NjR.   36302

---- Florida, resolutions legislature of - Georgia boundary.
Dec. 15, 1828. Read, and laid
upon the table. Washington, Pr.
by Gales & Seaton, 1828. 1 p.
(Doc. No. 17) DLC; NjR.
                            36303
---- Fortifications at Pensacola.
Feb. 1, 1828. Read, and referred to the Committee of the
Whole House on the state of the
Union, to which is referred the
bill (No. 96) making appropriations for certain fortifications of

the United States, for the year 1828. Mr. Hamilton, from the Committee on Military Affairs, to which had been referred the estimate of appropriations in relation to fortifications, made the following report: Washington, Pr. by Gales & Seaton, 1828. 1 p. (Rep. No. 119) DLC; NjR. 36304

---- Frances Felix. Jan. 23, 1828. Read, and laid upon the table. Mr. Clark of New York, from the Committee of Claims, to which had been referred the petition of Frances Felix, made the following report: Washington, Pr. by Gales & Seaton, 1828. 1 p. (Rep. No. 93) DLC; NjR. 36305

---- Francis Henderson and Francis Henderson Jr. Mar. 7, 1828. Read, and laid upon the table. Mr. Everett, from the Committee on Foreign Affairs, to which was referred the claim of Francis Henderson and Francis Henderson, Jr. made the following report: Washington, Gales & Seaton, 1828. 2 p. (Rep. No. 183) DLC; NjR. 36306

---- Francis Larche. Apr. 14, 1828. Read, and laid upon the table. Mr. Williams, from the Committee of Claims, to which was referred the bill from the Senate, entitled "An act for the relief of Francis Larche, of New Orleans," made the following report: Washington, Gales & Seaton, 1828. 2 p. (Rep. No. 236) DLC; NjR. 36307

---- Francis Preston. Mar. 22, 1828. Mr. Bates, of Missouri, from the Committee on Private Land Claims, to which was referred the petition of Francis Preston, made the following report: Washington, Gales & Seaton, 1828. 4 p. (Rep. No. 207) DLC; NjR. 36308

---- Francis Valle, et al. Jan. 16, 1828. Mr. Whipple, from the Committee on the Public Lands, to which had been referred the petition of Francis Valle and others, made the following report: Washington, Pr. by Gales & Seaton, 1828. 1 p. (Rep. No. 82) DLC; NjR. 36309

---- Frederick Onstine. Jan. 30, 1828. Mr. Earll, from the Committee on Private Land Claims, to which was referred the petition of Frederick Onstine, made the following report: Washington, Pr. by Gales & Seaton, 1828. 3 p. (Rep. No. 108) DLC; NjR. 36310

---- Fugitive slaves. Message from the President of the United States transmitting the information required by a resolution of the House of Representatives of the 10th of May last, in relation to negotiations with G. Britain upon the subject of fugitive slaves. Dec. 15, 1828. Read, and referred to the Committee on Foreign Affairs. Washington, Pr. by Gales & Seaton, 1828. 6 p. (Doc. No. 19) DLC; NjR. 36311

---- Fugitives from the United States to Mexico, &c. &c. Message from the President of the United States, transmitting the information required by a resolution of the House of Representatives of 2nd instant, respecting the recovery of debts, &c. in the Mexican states, from persons absconding from the United States and the province of Texas. Jan. 15, 1828. Read and laid upon the table. Washington, Pr. by Gales & Seaton, 1828. 4 p. (Doc. No. 61) DLC; NjR. 36312

---- G. T. Beyer. Dec. 30, 1828. Read, and laid upon the table. Mr. Everett, from the Committee on Foreign Affairs, to which was referred the case of G. T. Beyer, made the following report: Washington, Pr. by Gales & Seaton, 1828. 1 p. (Rep. No. 25) DLC; NjR.   36313

---- General Assembly of Ohio. Resolutions of the General Assembly of Ohio, in reply to the resolutions of the General Assembly of South Carolina, respecting the Constitutional powers of the general government. Feb. 25, 1828. Read, and laid upon the table. Washington, Pr. by Gales & Seaton, 1828. 4 p. (Doc. No. 161) DLC; NjR.   36314

---- General index to the laws of the United States of America, from March 4th 1789, to March 3rd, 1827, including all treaties entered into between those periods; in which the principles involved in acts for the relief of individuals or of a private or local nature, are arranged under general heads, to which such principles appropriately belong. Arranged to the edition commenced by Bioren, Duane, and Weightman, in 1815, and subsequently continued by Davis & Force and William A. Davis. Compiled in pursuance of an order of the House of Representatives of the United States, of May 15th, 1824, by Samuel Burch, chief clerk in office of that House. Washington City, Pub. by Wm. A. Davis, P. Force, pr., 1828. 331 p. Ct; GU; IaU-L; MdBP; MdHi; MiD; NWM.   36315

---- George and William Bangs. Jan. 2, 1828. Mr. Dwight, from the Committee of Ways and Means, made the following report: Washington, Gales & Seaton, 1828. 1 p. (Rep. No. 46) DLC; NjR.
36316
---- George Blenkinship. May 21, 1828. Read, and laid upon the table. Mr. Everett, from the Committee on Foreign Affairs, to which was referred the case of George Blenkinship, for a claim on France prior to 1800, made the following report: Washington, Gales & Seaton, 1828. 2 p. (Rep. No. 264) DLC; NjR.
36317
---- George Johnston and others. Jan. 2, 1828. Mr. Whittlesey, from the Committee of Claims, to which was referred the petition of George Johnston, et al. made the following report: Washington, Gales & Seaton, 1828. 4 p. (Rep. No. 44) DLC; NjR.
36318
---- George P. Frost. Dec. 31, 1828. Mr. Buckner, from the Committee on Private Land Claims, to which was referred the petition of Geo. P. Frost, of the state of New York, made the following report: Washington, Pr. by Gales & Seaton, 1828. 1 p. (Rep. No. 32) DLC; NjR.
36319
---- Georgia. Report adopted by the Legislature of Georgia on African colonization. Feb. 8, 1828. Referred to the Select Committee appointed on the 28th ultimo, on the memorial of the American Colonization Society. Washington, Pr. by Gales & Seaton, 1828. 9 p. (Doc. No. 126) DLC; NjR; PHi; RPB.   36320

---- Georgia and Florida. Resolutions and documents relating to the boundary line between the state of Georgia and the territory of Florida. Jan. 28, 1828. Referred to the Committee on the Judiciary. Washington, Pr. by Gales & Seaton, 1828. 21 p. (Doc. No. 103) DLC; FU; NhHi; NjR.   36321

---- Georgia lands occupied by the Cherokee Indians. Report of a committee and resolutions of the Legislature of the state of Georgia in relation to certain lands occupied by the Cherokee Indians belonging to the said state. Jan. 28, 1828. Referred to the Committee on Indian Affairs. Washington, Pr. by Gales & Seaton, 1828. 13 p. (Doc. No. 102) DLC; NhHi; NjR; WHi. 36322

---- Graduate price of public lands. Feb. 5, 1828. Mr. Duncan, from the Committee on the Public Lands, to which the subject had been referred, made the following report: Washington, Pr. by Gales & Seaton, 1828. 8 p. (Rep. No. 125) DLC; NjR. 37323

---- Growth and manufacture of silk. Letter from the Secretary of the Treasury, transmitting the information required by a resolution of the House of Representatives, of May 11, 1826, in relation to the growth and manufacture of silk, adapted to the different parts of the Union. Feb. 7, 1828. Referred to the Committee of Agriculture. Washington, Pr. by Gales & Seaton, 1828. 8, viii, 9-220 p., 7 bdsds. (Doc. No. 158) CtHT; DLC; DeGE; NjR. 36324

---- H. P. Cathell. Jan. 11, 1828. Read, and laid upon the table. Mr. P. P. Barbour, from the Committee on the Judiciary, to which had been referred the petition of H. P. Cathell, made the following report: Washington, Pr. by Gales & Seaton, 1828. 3 p. (Rep. No. 77) DLC; NjR. 36325

---- Harbor of Stonington. Letter from the Secretary of War, transmitting, in compliance with a resolution of the House of Representatives of the 27th Dec., last, a report of a survey of the harbor of Stonington, with a view to the erection of a sea-wall, for the protection of said harbor. Feb. 23, 1828. Referred to the Committee on Commerce. Washington, Pr. by Gales & Seaton, 1828. 9 p. (Doc. No. 153) DLC; NN; NjR. 36326

---- Harris and Farrow. Mar. 7, 1828. Mr. Williams, from the Committee of Claims, to which had been referred the case of Richard Harris and Nimrod Farrow, made the following report: Washington, Gales & Seaton, 1828. 8 p. (Rep. No. 181) DLC; NjR. 36327

---- Heirs, &c. of William Drayton, deceased. Mar. 19, 1828. Mr. Wm. R. Davis, from the Committee on the Public Lands, to which was referred the petition of the heirs-at-law and devisees of Wm. Drayton, deceased, praying for a relinquishment of the right of the United States to certain lands in East Florida, made the following report: Washington, Gales & Seaton, 1828. 2 p. (Rep. No. 200) DLC; NjR. 36328

---- Heirs of Philip Renaut, Feb. 1, 1828. Mr. Bates of Missouri, from the Committee on Private Land Claims, to which had been referred the petition of the heirs of Philip Renaut, made the following report: Washington, Pr. by Gales & Seaton, 1828. 2 p. (Rep. No. 120) DLC; NjR. 36329

---- Henry Bedinger. Feb. 11, 1828. Read, and laid upon the table. Feb. 18, 1828. Committed to a Committee of the Whole House to-morrow. Mr. Ingham, from the Committee on the Post Office and Post Roads, to which had been referred the petition of Henry Bedinger, made the following report: Washington, Gales & Seaton, 1828. 2 p. (Rep. No. 151) DLC; NjR. 36330

---- Henry Huttleston. May 21, 1828. Read, and laid upon the table. Mr. Everett, from the Committee on Foreign Affairs, to which was referred the case of Henry Huttleston, a claimant on the government of Naples, made the following report: Washington, Gales & Seaton, 1828. 2 p. (Rep. No. 265) DLC; NjR. 36331

---- Hiwasse and Conesauga Rivers. Letter from the Secretary of War transmitting a communication from the chief engineer on the subject of a communication between the Hiwasse and Conesauga Rivers, &c. December 11, 1828. Read, and laid upon the table. Dec. 12, 1828. Referred to the Committee on Roads and Canals. Washington, Pr. by Gales & Seaton, 1828. 10 p. (Doc. No. 15) DLC; NN; NjR. 36332

---- Hunters of Oregon. Memorial of James M. Bradford and others. Dec. 10, 1828. Read, and committed to the Committee of the Whole House to which was committed the bill (H. R. No. 12) to authorize the occupation of the Orgon River. Washington, Pr. by Gales & Seaton, 1828. 6 p. (Doc. No. 13) CSmH; DLC; NjR. 36333

---- Hyacinth Bernard. Dec. 29, 1828. Mr. Gurley, from the Committee on the Public Lands, to which was referred the case of Hyacinth Bernard, made the following report: Washington, Pr. by Gales & Seaton, 1828. 2 p. (Rep. No. 22) DLC; NjR. 36334

---- In Senate of the United States. Jan. 3, 1828. Mr. Woodbury, from the Select Committee to whom was referred the memorial on behalf of the surviving officers of the Army of the Revolution, made the following report: Washington, Pr. by Duff Green, 1828. 7 p. (Doc. No. 18) DLC; NjR. 36335

---- ---- Jan. 9, 1828. Mr. Berrien made the following report: Washington, Pr. by Duff Green, 1828. 3 p. (Doc. No. 22) DLC; NjR. 36336

---- ---- Jan. 9, 1828. Mr. Hayne, from the Committee on Naval Affairs, made the following report, accompanied by a bill for the relief of Susan Decatur, widow of Captain Stephen Decatur, and others. Washington, Pr. by Duff Green, 1828. 15 p. (Doc. No. 23) DLC; NjR. 36337

---- ---- Jan. 10, 1828. Mr. Harrison, from the Committee on Military Affairs, to whom was referred the bill to prevent desertions in the army, and for other purposes, reported it with the following amendment. [Washington, 1828] 1 p. (S. 28) DNA. 36338

---- ---- Jan. 14, 1828. Mr. Foot, made the following report: Washington, Pr. by Duff Green, 1828. 2 p. (Doc. No. 34) DLC; NjR. 36339

---- ---- Jan. 15, 1828. Mr. Cobb made the following report: Washington, Pr. by Duff Green, 1828. 2 p. (Doc. No. 41) DLC; NjR. 36340

---- ---- Jan. 15, 1828. Mr. Ellis, from the Committee on Public Lands, to which was referred the petition of the representatives of William Scott, deceased, with the accompanying documents, made the following report: Washington, Pr. by Duff Green, 1828. 1 p. (Doc. No. 38) DLC; NjR. 36341

---- ---- Jan. 16, 1828. Mr.

Parris, from the Committee on Finance, to which was committed the bill supplementary to "An act for enrolling and licensing ships or vessels to be employed in the coasting trade and fisheries, and for regulating the same," reported it with the following amendment: [Washington, 1828] 3 p. (S. 9) DNA.   36342

---- ---- Jan. 21, 1828. Mr. Dickerson made the following report: Washington, Pr. by Duff Green, 1828. 4 p. (Doc. No. 51) DLC; NjR.   36343

---- ---- Jan. 21, 1828. Mr. Woodbury, from the Committee on Commerce, to whom was referred a resolution of the 31st ult. concerning the expediency of an appropriation to deepen the harbor of St. Marks, in Florida, and to erect a light house near it; and also a resolution of the 15th inst. concerning the establishment of a port of entry at St. Marks, and the removal of obstructions in the Apalachicola and Ocalla rivers in Florida, made a report: Washington, Pr. by Duff Green, 1828. 7 p. (Doc. No. 50) DLC; NjR.   36344

---- ---- Jan. 22, 1828. Mr. Cobb made the following report. Washington, Pr. by Duff Green, 1828. 2 p. (Doc. No. 52) DLC; NjR.   36345

---- ---- Jan. 22, 1828. Mr. Harrison made the following report: Washington, Pr. by Duff Green, 1828. 80 p. 1 bdsd. (Doc. No. 54) DLC; NjR.   36346

---- ---- Jan. 23, 1828. Mr. Bell made the following report: Washington, Pr. by Duff Green, 1828. 9 p. (Doc. No. 57) DLC; NjR.   36347

---- ---- Jan. 23, 1828. Mr.

Cobb made the following report: Washington, Pr. by Duff Green, 1828. 15 p. (Doc. No. 58) DLC; NjR.   36348

---- ---- Jan. 23, 1828. Mr. Harrison made the following report: Washington, Pr. by Duff Green, 1828. 8 p. (Doc. No. 59) DLC; NjR.   36349

---- ---- Jan. 24, 1828. Mr. Ruggles made the following report: Washington, Pr. by Duff Green, 1828. 18 p. (Doc. No. 61) DLC; NjR.   36350

---- ---- Jan. 28, 1828. Mr. Bell made the following report: Washington, Pr. by Duff Green, 1828. 9 p. (Doc. No. 65) DLC; NjR.   36351

---- ---- Jan. 28, 1828. Mr. Harrison made the following report: Washington, Pr. by Duff Green, 1828. 3 p. (Doc. No. 66) DLC; NjR.   36352

---- ---- Jan. 28, 1828. Resolved, that an act of the British Parliament, passed the 2d day of July in the year 1821, entitled, "An act for regulating the fur trade, and establishing a civil and criminal jurisdiction in certain parts of North America," be printed for the use of the Senate. Washington, Pr. by Duff Green, 1828. 7 p. (Doc. No. 67) DLC; NjR.   36353

---- ---- Jan. 29, 1828. Mr. Johnson, of Kentucky, made the following report: Washington, Duff Green, 1828. 10 p. (Rep. No. 74) DLC; NjR.   36354

---- ---- Jan. 29, 1828. Mr. Smith, of Maryland, made the following report: Washington, Duff Green, 1828. 7 p. (Doc. No. 75) DLC; NjR.   36355

---- ---- Jan. 30, 1828. Mr. Rowan proposed the following amendment to the "Bill for regulating processes in the Courts of the United States, in states admitted into the Union since the 29th of September, 1789." [Washington, 1828] 1 p. (S. 11) DNA.   36356

---- ---- Feb. 1, 1828. The following amendment was proposed by Mr. Bell, to the bill for the relief of certain surviving officers of the army of the Revolution. [Washington, 1828] 3 p. (S. 44) DNA.   36357

---- ---- Feb. 4, 1828. Mr. Johnson, of Kentucky, made the following report: Washington, Duff Green, 1828. 37 p. (Doc. No. 84) DLC; NjR.   36358

---- ---- Feb. 5, 1828. Mr. Smith, of Maryland, made the following report: Washington, Duff Green, 1828. 6 p. 1 bdsd. (Doc. No. 87) DLC; NjR.   36359

---- ---- Feb. 5, 1828. Resolved, That the Committee on the Post Office and Post Roads... Washington, Duff Green, 1828. 21 p. 7 bdsds. (Doc. No. 88) DLC; NjR.   36360

---- ---- Feb. 6, 1828. Documents relating to the Senate Bill 28, to prevent desertion... Washington, Duff Green, 1828. 5 p. (Doc. No. 92) DLC; NjR. 36361

---- ---- Feb. 8, 1828. Mr. Smith, of Maryland, made the following report: Washington, Duff Green, 1828. 4 p. (Doc. No. 95) DLC; NjR.   36361a

---- ---- Feb. 14, 1828. Mr. Eaton, from the Committee on the District of Columbia, to whom was re-committed the "Bill for the relief of the Columbian College in the District of Columbia," reported the following amendment: [Washington, 1828] 1 p. (S. 7) DNA.   36362

---- ---- Feb. 14, 1828. Mr. Eaton made the following report: The Committee on the District of Columbia, to whom was recommitted a bill for the relief of the Columbian College, with instructions to ascertain particular facts or information, Report: [Washington, 1828] 17 p. (Doc. No. 103) DLC; NjR.   36363

---- ---- Feb. 15, 1828. Resolved, that the report on the subject of the militia, made in the year 1790, by Henry Knox, Secretary of War, and submitted to Congress by the President of the United States, be printed for the use of the Senate. Washington, Duff Green, 1828. 26 p. (Doc. No. 106) DLC; NjR.   36364

---- ---- Feb. 18, 1828. Mr. Cobb made the following report: The Committee of Claims, to which was referred the petition of Catherine McNiff... Washington, Duff Green, 1828. 1 p. (Doc. No. 107) DLC; NjR.   36365

---- ---- Feb. 18, 1828. Mr. Johnson, of Kentucky, made the following report: The Committee on Military Affairs, to whom was referred the resolution... Washington, Duff Green, 1828. 4 p., 1 bdsd. (Doc. No. 108) DLC; NjR.   36366

---- ---- Feb. 18, 1828. Mr. Ruggles made the following report: The Committee of Claims, to whom was referred the petition of Elisha Tracy... report: Washington, Pr. by Duff Green, 1828. 1 p. (Doc. No. 116) DLC; NjR.   36367

---- ---- Feb. 19, 1828. Amendment proposed by Mr. Barton, to the "Bill to graduate the price of the Public Lands, to make donations thereof to actual settlers, and to cede the refuse to the states in which they lie." [Washington, 1828] 1 p. (S. 33) DNA.
36368

---- ---- Feb. 19, 1828. Mr. Cobb made the following report: The Committee of Claims, to which was referred the memorial of Willie Blount... respectfully report: Washington, Pr. by Duff Green, 1828. 68 p. 2 bdsds. (Doc. No. 110) DLC; NjR.
36369

---- ---- Feb. 22, 1828. Mr. Eaton made the following report: The Committee... on a bill for the improvement of Pennsylvania Avenue, consider it proper to present the grounds on which they have acted: Washington, Pr. by Duff Green, 1828. 7 p. (Doc. No. 119) DLC; NjR.
36370

---- ---- Feb. 26, 1828. Mr. Benton submitted the following motion for consideration: resolved, that the Committee on Finance be instructed to inquire whether any error had occurred in the construction of the 4th section of an act entitled, "An act to provide for the redemption of the public debt"... Washington, Pr. by Duff Green, 1828. 1 p. (Doc. No. 122) DLC; NjR.
36371

---- ---- Feb. 26, 1828. Mr. Harrison made the following report: The Committee on Military Affairs, to whom was referred a resolution relative to the Arsenal at Augusta in the state of Maine ... report: Washington, Pr. by Duff Green, 1828. 2 p. (Doc. No. 121) DLC; NjR.
36372

---- ---- Feb. 26, 1828. Mr. Smith of Maryland made the following report: The Committee on Finance, to which was referred a resolution of the Senate dated the 31st December, 1827... report: Washington, Pr. by Duff Green, 1828. 5 p. (Doc. No. 125) DLC; NjR.
36373

---- ---- Feb. 29, 1828. Mr. King made the following report: The Committee on the Public Lands, to whom was referred the reports of the Commissioners appointed to ascertain claims and title to land in Florida... report: Washington, Pr. by Duff Green, 1828. 2 p. (Doc. No. 126) DLC; NjR.
36374

---- ---- Mar. 10, 1828. Mr. Barton made the following report: The Committee on Public Lands have considered the resolution of the Senate of the 28th January last... Washington, Pr. by Duff Green, 1828. 1 p. (Doc. No. 135) DLC; NjR.
36375

---- ---- Mar. 10, 1828. Mr. Cobb made the following report: The Committee of Claims, to whom was referred the petition of Robert Robbins... report: Washington, Pr. by Duff Green, 1828. 2 p. (Doc. No. 134) DLC; NjR.
36376

---- ---- Mar. 11, 1828. Mr. Benton submitted the following motion for consideration: Resolved. That the Committee on Military Affairs be instructed to prepare and bring in a bill, to make the following reforms and alterations in the laws and regulations for the government of the Military Academy... Washington, Pr. by Duff Green, 1828. 1 p. (Doc. No. 136) DLC; NjR. 36377

---- ---- Mar. 18, 1828. Mr. Johnson of Kentucky made the following report: The Committee on the Post Offices and Post Roads, to whom was referred the petition of William Mickler, report: Washington, Pr. by Duff Green, 1828. 5 p. (Doc. No. 143) DLC; NjR.   36378

---- ---- Mar. 18, 1828. Mr. Noble made the following report: The Committee on Pensions, to whom was referred that part of the memorial of Richard Taylor ...report... Washington, Pr. by Duff Green, 1828. 7 p. (Doc. No. 142) DLC; NjR.   36379

---- ---- Mar. 19, 1828. Mr. Harrison made the following report: The Committee on Military Affairs, to whom was referred the resolution of the Senate directing them to inquire into the expediency of continuing or abolishing the office of Major General in the Army of the United States, report: Washington, Pr. by Duff Green, 1828. 7 p. (Doc. No. 144) DLC; NjR.   36380

---- ---- Mar. 20, 1828. The following motion, submitted by Mr. Benton, was considered, and ordered to lie on the table and be printed. Resolved, that the Committee on Pensions be directed to prepare and bring in a bill to authorize the commutation of the pensions now payable by the United States... 1 p. (Doc. No. 149) DLC; NjR.   36381

---- ---- Mar. 27, 1828. Mr. Woodbury submitted the following as an amendment to the "Bill for the relief of certain surviving Officers of the Army of the Revolution." [Washington, 1828] 3 p. (S. 44) DNA.   36382

---- ---- Apr. 2, 1828. Mr. Smith, from the Committee on Finance, to which was referred the memorial of the Baltimore

and Ohio Rail Road Company, praying that they may be permitted to import iron and iron machinery for said road free of duty, reported a bill to admit iron and machinery necessary for rail roads, duty free; and laid on the table the following document, which, with the memorial (Doc. 140) heretofore printed, were ordered to be printed. Washington, Pr. by Duff Green, 1828. 5 p. (Doc. No. 161) DLC; NjR. 36383

---- ---- Apr. 4, 1828. Mr. Williams, from the Committee on Commerce, to which was referred the resolution of the Senate, of the 1st inst. directing that committee to "inquire into the expediency of making further appropriation for removing obstructions at the mouth of the Pascagoula River "laid the following letters from Silas Dinsmore and W. Bartou, on the table, which were ordered to be printed. Washington, Pr. by Duff Green, 1828. 7 p. (Doc. No. 164) DLC; NjR. 36384

---- ---- Apr. 14, 1828. Resolved, that the report of the Joint Select Committee of the Senate and House of Representatives of the state of Maine, in relation to the north-eastern boundary of the state... Washington, Duff Green, 1828. 126 p. (Doc. No. 171) DLC; NjR.   36385

---- ---- Apr. 21, 1828. Mr. Smith, of Maryland, made the following report: The Committee on Finance, to which was referred the following resolution, offered by Mr. Benton... report. Washington, Duff Green, 1828. 12p. 2 bdsd. (Doc. No. 173) DLC; NjR. 36386

---- ---- Apr. 25, 1828. Mr. Woodbury's amendment, as amended, to the "Bill for the relief of certain surviving Officers

of the Army of the Revolution."
[Washington, 1828] 3 p. (S. 44)
DNA.   36387

---- ---- Apr. 28, 1828. Mr.
Tazewell made the following report: The Committee on Foreign
Relations, to whom were referred sundry petitions and the resolution of several legislatures...
Washington, Duff Green, 1828. 15
p. (Doc. No. 178) DLC; NjR.
                            36388
---- ---- Apr. 28, 1828. Mr.
Williams made the following report: The Committee on Commerce, who were instructed by a
resolution of the Senate, date the
13th ultimo... Washington, Duff
Green, 1828. 8 p. (Doc. No. 179)
DLC; NjR.   36389

---- ---- Apr. 29, 1828. Mr.
Van Buren made the following report: The report of the Committee on the Judiciary, on the resolution... Washington, Duff Green,
1828. 1 p. (Doc. No. 183) DLC;
NjR.   36390

---- ---- Apr. 30, 1828. Mr.
Benton submitted the following
resolutions: Resolved, that no
right of soil or of jurisdiction...
Washington, Duff Green, 1828. 1
p. (Doc. No. 187) DLC; NjR.
                            36391
---- ---- May 6, 1828. The following letters were laid upon the
table by Mr. Smith, of Maryland,
and ordered to be printed. Washington, Duff Green, 1828. 4 p.
(Doc. No. 192) DLC; NjR. 36392

---- ---- May 12, 1828. Mr.
Webster submitted the following
motion for consideration: Washington, Duff Green, 1828. 1 p.
(Doc. No. 194) DLC; NjR. 36393

---- ---- May 13, 1828. Mr.
Smith, of Maryland, made the
following report: The Committee

on Finance, to which was referred the... Washington, Duff
Green, 1828. 10 p. (Doc. No.
195) DLC; NjR.   36394

---- ---- May 17, 1828. Mr.
Dickerson made the following report: The Joint Library Committee beg leave to report: Washington, Duff Green, 1828. 2 p.
(Doc. No. 198) DLC; NjR. 36395

---- ---- May 21, 1828. Mr.
Silbee made the following report:
The Committee on Commerce, to
whom was referred a report and
plan of the survey of the island
of Nantucket... Washington, Duff
Green, 1828. 2 p. (Doc. No. 199)
DLC; NjR.   36396

---- ---- May 22, 1828. Mr.
Berrien made the following report: The Select Committee, to
whom was referred the memorial of sundry citizens of New Jersey... Washington, Duff Green,
1828. 21 p. (Doc. No. 202) DLC;
NjR.   36397

---- ---- May 22, 1828. Mr.
Van Buren made the following report: The Committee on the Judiciary, to which was referred
the message... Washington, Duff
Green, 1828. 2 p. (Doc. No. 201)
DLC; NjR.   36398

---- ---- May 24, 1828. Mr.
Chambers submitted the following
report: The Select Committee, to
whom were referred the several
petitions and memorials of those
persons... Washington, Duff
Green, 1828. 14 p. (Doc. No.
206) CSmH; DLC; NjR.   36399

---- ---- Dec. 3, 1828. Report
from the commissioner of the
General Land Office. With one
from the register and receiver of
the Land Office at Washington,
Mississippi... Washington, Duff

Green, 1828. 5 p. (Doc. No. 3) DLC; NjR.   36400

---- ---- Dec. 8, 1828. Read, and passed to a second reading, and ordered to be printed. A Joint Resolution for the care and preservation of the Cumberland Road. Washington, Duff Green, 1828. 1 p. (Doc. No. 6) DLC; NjR.   36401

---- ---- Dec. 22, 1828. Mr. Berrien made the following report: The Committee on the Judiciary, to which was referred the petition of John C. Herbert, Report: Washington, Duff Green, 1828. 2 p. (Doc. No. 16) DLC; NjR.   36402

---- ---- Dec. 22, 1828. Mr. Berrian made the following report: The Judiciary Committee, to whom was referred the petition of Thomas Griffin, administrator of Lawrence Gibbons. . . Washington, Duff Green, 1828. 2 p. (Doc. No. 15) DLC; NjR.   36403

---- ---- Dec. 23, 1828. Mr. Benton's resolution on the public debt, the sinking fund, the abolition of duties, and the balances of public money in the hands of the Bank of the United States. Considered, made the order of the day for Monday next, and ordered to be printed. Washington, Duff Green, 1828. 1 p. (Doc. No. 17) DLC; DeGE; NjR.   36404

---- ---- Dec. 23, 1828. Motion by Mr. Eaton, to refer to the Committee on Finance, the subject of a change in the mode of compensating, and in the duties of the Officers of the Customs. Dec. 23, 1828. Agreed to, and ordered to be printed. Washington, Duff Green, 1828. 1 p. (Doc. No. 18) DLC; NjR.   36405

---- ---- Dec. 31, 1828. Mr. Berrien made the following report: The Committee on the Judiciary, to whom was referred the petition of Elias Earle, Executor of Elias Earle, deceased, Report: Washington, Duff Green, 1828. 1 p. (Doc. No. 22) DLC; NjR.   36406

---- ---- Dec. 31, 1828. Read, and ordered to be printed. Mr. Berrien, from the Committee on the Judiciary, to whom was referred the petition of Thomas L. Winthrop . . .   Washington, Duff Green, 1828. 7 p. (Doc. No. 21) DLC; NjR.   36407

---- The inaugural address of President Jefferson, constitution and rules of the Jefferson Debating Society, and the names of the members. Hingham [Mass.] Farmer & Brown, prs., 1828. 23 p. CSmH.   36408

---- Indemnity for damages by Creek Indians. Letter from the Secretary of the Treasury, transmitting the information required by a resolution of the House of Representatives, of the 3d inst., relative to the execution of an act for the relief of Samuel Menac, passed 27th of April, 1816. Also, of an act for the relief of certain Creek Indians, passed 3d March 1817, &c. &c. Mar. 15, 1828. Read, and laid upon the table. Washington, Pr. by Gales & Seaton, 1828. 35 p. (Doc. No. 200) DLC; NjR.   36409

---- Index to bills and resolutions of the House of Representatives: First session, Twentieth Congress. [Washington, 1828] 12 p. DNA.   36410

---- Index to printed resolutions and bills of the Senate of the United States, First session of the 20th Congress, 1827-8. [Washington, 1828] 9 p. DNA.   36411

United States 401

---- Indian governments. Jan. 14, 1828. Read, and laid upon the table. Mr. Lumpkin, from the Committee on Indian Affairs, to which the subject had been referred, made the following report: Washington, Pr. by Gales & Seaton, 1828. 2 p. (Rep. No. 67) DLC; NjR. 36412

---- Indian removing westward. Jan. 7, 1828. Mr. McLean, from the Committee on Indian Affairs, to which the subject had been referred made the following report: Washington, Gales & Seaton, 1828. 4 p. (Rep. No. 56) DLC; NjR. 36413

---- Indian reserved land in Indiana. Letter from the Secretary of the Treasury in reply to a resolution of the House of Representatives of the 12th inst. in relation to the sale of Indian reserved land in the state of Indiana to individuals. Dec. 18, 1828. Read, and laid upon the table. Washington, Pr. by Gales & Seaton, 1828. 2 p. (Doc. No. 22) DLC; NjR. 36414

---- Indian tribes - Northwestern frontier. Letter from the Secretary of War, transmitting the information required by a Resolution of the House of Representatives, of 12th inst. in relation to the hostile disposition of Indian tribes on the northwestern frontier. May 21, 1828. Read, and referred to the Committee on Military Affairs. Washington, Pr. by Gales & Seaton, 1828. 18 p. (Doc. No. 278) DLC; NjR. 36415

---- Indians removed to the west of the Mississippi. Letter from the Secretary of War transmitting the information required by a resolution of the House of Representatives of the 22d ultimo in relation to the tribes and parts of tribes of Indians that have re-moved to the west of the Mississippi River, their location, &c. Apr. 1, 1828. Read, and laid upon the table. Washington, Pr. by Gales & Seaton, 1828. 6 p. (Doc. No. 233) DLC; NjR. 36416

---- Infantry drill, being an abridgment of the system of tactics for the infantry of the United States, lately revised by order of the War department, and sanctioned by the President of the United States. With explanatory plates. Baltimore, F. Lucas, jun'r., 1828. xii, [9]-196 p. CSmH; TNJ. 36417

---- Internal improvement. Letter from the Secretary of War, transmitting the information required by a resolution of the House of Representatives of 19th Dec. 1826, in relation to the works of internal improvement which have been undertaken or projected by the general government, from the year 1824 to the year 1826, inclusive, &c. Mar. 4, 1828. Read, and laid upon the table. Washington, Pr. by Gales & Seaton, 1828. 4 p. 1 bdsd. (Doc. No. 172) DLC; DeGE; NjR; PU. 36418

---- ---- Letter from the Secretary of War transmitting the information required by a resolution of the House of Representatives of the 3d inst. (so far as is now practicable) in relation to the amount deemed necessary in the execution and completion of each work of internal improvement specified in the report made on the 4th of March, 1828, &c. &c. Apr. 29, 1828. Read, and laid upon the table. Washington, Pr. by Gales & Seaton, 1828. 4 p. 2 bdsds. (Doc. No. 261) DLC; NjR. 36419

---- Internal improvements since

1824. Message from the President of the United States transmitting a report from the Secretary of War in relation to harbors, roads, and other works of internal improvement, undertaken and projected since 30th April, 1824. December 8, 1828. Read, and referred to the Committee on Roads and Canals. Washington, Pr. by Gales & Seaton, 1828. 5 p. 5 bdsds. (Doc. No. 7) CtY; DLC; MB; MBAt; MH; NN; NjR. 36420

---- Isaac W. Norris - Sammerl & Brown. Jan. 26, 1828. Mr. Cambreleng, from the Committee on Commerce, to which was referred the petition of Isaac W. Norris, administrator of Joseph Sammerl, deceased, made the following report: Washington, Pr. by Gales & Seaton, 1828. 2 p. (Rep. No. 101) DLC; NjR. 36421

---- J. F. Carmichael. Made Jan. 4, 1828. Jan. 7, 1828. Pr. by order of the House of Representatives. Mr. Moore, of Alabama, from the Committee on Private Land Claims, to which was referred the petition of J. F. Carmichael, made the following report: Washington, Gales & Seaton, 1828. 1 p. (Rep. No. 57) DLC; NjR.   36422

---- J. F. Ohl. Feb. 29, 1828. Mr. Dwight, from the Committee of Ways and Means, to which was referred the petition of John F. Ohl, made the following report: Washington, Gales & Seaton, 1828. 1 p. (Rep. No. 170) DLC; NjR. 36423

---- Jacob Clements' assignees. Jan. 2, 1828. Mr. Cambreleng, from the Committee on Commerce, to which had been referred the petition of Potts & Clements, assignees of Jacob Clements, made the following report: Washington, Gales & Seaton,

1828. 1 p. (Rep. No. 41) DLC; NjR. 36424

---- James A. Harper. Mar. 4, 1828. Mr. Whittlesey, from the Committee of Claims, to which the subject had been referred, made the following report: Washington, Gales & Seaton, 1828. 2 p. (Rep. No. 178) DLC; NjR. 36425

---- James D. Barry, and Bailey & Torrey. May 21, 1828. Read, and laid upon the table. Mr. Everett, from the Committee on Foreign Affairs, to which were referred the cases of James D. Barry, and of Bailey and Torrey, made the following report: Washington, Gales & Seaton, 1828. 2 p. (Rep. No. 262) DLC; NjR. 36426

---- James Devereux. Dec. 30, 1828. Read, and laid upon the table. Mr. Everett, from the Committee on Foreign Affairs, to which was referred the case of James Devereux, et al, made the following report: Washington, Pr. by Gales & Seaton, 1828. 28 p. (Rep. No. 24) DLC; NjR. 36427

---- James McCarty. Jan. 21, 1828. Read, and laid upon the table. Apr. 22, 1828. Committed to a Committee of the Whole House to-morrow. Dec. 5, 1828. Committee of the Whole discharged and recommitted to the Committee of Claims. Report of the Committee of Claims in the case of James McCarty. Washington, Pr. by Gales & Seaton, 1828. 13 p. (Rep. No. 1) DLC; NjR. 36428

---- James M'ilvain. Memorial of James M'ilvain, praying that the aid of government may be extended to the growers of wool, and the manufacturers of woollen goods. Feb. 20, 1828. Referred to the Committee of the Whole House on the state of the Union, to which is committed the Bill

(No. 132) in alteration of the several acts imposing duties on imports. Washington, Pr. by Gales & Seaton, 1828. 10 p. (Doc. No. 151) DLC; NjR.   36429

---- James Mitchell. Dec. 19, 1828. Read, and committed to a Committee of the Whole House tomorrow. Mr. Whittlesey, from the Committee of Claims, to which was referred the petition of James Mitchell, made the following report: Washington, Pr. by Gales & Seaton, 1828. 2 p. (Rep. No. 10) DLC; NjR. 36430

---- James Ray. May 6, 1828. Read, and laid upon the table. Mr. Everett, from the Committee on Foreign Affairs, to which was referred the case of James Ray and others, made the following report: Washington, Gales & Seaton, 1828. 16 p. (Rep. No. 247) DLC; NjR.   36431

---- James Riley, et al., and Groning & Kelley. May 21, 1828. Read, and laid upon the table. Mr. Everett, from the Committee on Foreign Affairs, to which were referred the cases of James Riley and others, and of Groning & Kelley, claimants on France for spoliations, made the following report: Washington, Gales & Seaton, 1828. 3 p. (Rep. No. 263) DLC; NjR.   36432

---- James River and Kenhawa Canal route. Letter from the Secretary of War, transmitting a report on the James River and Kenhawa Canal route. Mar. 24, 1828. Read, and laid upon the table. Washington, Pr. by Gales & Seaton, 1828. 68 p. 2 bdsds. (Doc. No. 216) DLC; NjR.   36433

---- James Russel. Mar. 22, 1828. Mr. Bates, of Missouri, from the Committee on Private Land Claims, to which was referred the petition of James Russel, made the following report: Washington, Gales & Seaton, 1828. 2 p. (Rep. No. 206) DLC; NjR. 36434

---- James Scull. Dec. 16, 1828. Read, and laid upon the table. Mr. McDuffie, from the Committee of Ways and Means, to which was referred the petition of James Scull, made the following report: Washington, Pr. by Gales & Seaton, 1828. 5 p. (Rep. No. 5) DLC; NjR.   36435

---- Jane Mary Lawrence. Feb. 1, 1828. Mr. Bates, of Missouri, from the Committee on Military Pensions, to which had been referred the petition of Jane Mary Lawrence, made the following report: Washington, Pr. by Gales & Seaton, 1828. 1 p. (Rep. No. 122) DLC; NjR.   36436

---- Jared E. Groce. Apr. 9, 1828. Mr. Jennings, from the Committee on the Public Lands, to which was referred the petition of Jared E. Groce, made the following report: Washington, Gales & Seaton, 1828. 1 p. (Rep. No. 230) DLC; NjR.   36437

---- Jeremiah Walker. Mar. 25, 1828. Mr. Moore, of Alabama, from the Committee on Private Land Claims, to which was referred the petition of Jeremiah Walker, made the following report: Washington, Gales & Seaton, 1828. 1 p. (Rep. No. 211) DLC; NjR.   36438

---- Jesse Wilkinson. Mar. 14, 1828. Mr. Miller, from the Committee on Naval Affairs, to which was referred the petition of Jesse Wilkinson, made the following report: Washington, Gales & Seaton, 1828. 21 p. (Rep. No. 192) DLC; NjR.   36439

---- Joel Byington. Apr. 14, 1828.
Mr. Whittlesey, from the Committee of Claims, to which was
referred the petition of Joel Byington, made the following report:
Washington, Gales & Seaton, 1828.
2 p. (Rep. No. 224) DLC; NjR.
                                 36440
---- John Brest and al, heirs
of John P. Landerau. Dec. 31,
1828. Mr. Blake, from the Committee on Private Land Claims,
to which was referred the case of
John Brest, one of the heirs of
John Pierre Landerau, made the
following report: Washington, Pr.
by Gales & Seaton, 1828. 2 p.
(Rep. No. 33) DLC; NjR. 36441

---- John Bruce, administrator
of Philip Bush. Feb. 23, 1828.
Committed to a Committee of the
Whole House to-morrow. Mr.
Hunt, from the Committee on
Revolutionary Claims, to which
was recommitted its report of the
4th ultimo, in the case of John
Bruce, Administrator of Philip
Bush, made the following report:
Washington, Gales & Seaton, 1828.
3 p. (Rep. No. 159) DLC; NjR.
                                 36442
---- John Burton et al. - Schoon-
er Volant. Feb. 18, 1828. Mr.
Verplanck, from the Committee
of Ways and Means, to which the
subject had been referred, made
the following report: Washington,
Gales & Seaton, 1828. 2 p. (Rep.
No. 147) DLC; NjR.   36443

---- John Culbertson [To accompany Bill H. R. No. 113] Memorial of John Culbertson. Jan. 14,
1828. Referred to the Committee
on the Judiciary. Jan. 28, 1828.
Pr. by order of the House of
Representatives. Washington, Pr.
by Gales & Seaton, 1828. 7 p.
(Doc. No. 92) DLC; NjR. 36444

---- John F. Carmichael. Letter
from the Commissioner of the

General Land Office transmitting
a report of the register and receiver of the Land Office at Washington, Mississippi, on the claims
to land of John F. Carmichael.
Dec. 5, 1828. Read, and laid upon the table. Washington, Pr. by
Gales & Seaton, 1828. 5 p. (Doc.
No. 5) DLC; NjR.   36445

---- John Gates, Jr. Mar. 31,
1828. Mr. Whittlesey, from the
Committee of Claims, to which
was referred the petition of John
Gates, Jr., made the following
report: Washington, Gales &
Seaton, 1828. 18 p. (Rep. No.
217) DLC; NjR.   36446

---- John Good. Jan. 14, 1828.
Read, and laid upon the table.
Mr. McCoy, from the Committee
of Claims, to which had been referred the petition of John Good,
made the following report: Washington, Pr. by Gales & Seaton,
1828. 6 p. (Rep. No. 75) DLC;
NjR.   36447

---- ---- May 5, 1828. Read,
and laid upon the table. Mr.
Ramsey, from the Committee of
Claims, to which was referred
the petition of John Good, made
the following report: Washington,
Gales & Seaton, 1828. 3 p. (Rep.
No. 245) DLC; NjR.   36448

---- John Gwynn - heirs of. Jan.
18, 1828. Mr. Hunt, from the
Committee on Revolutionary
Claims, to which was referred
the petition of Julia Gwynn, made
the following report: Washington,
Pr. by Gales & Seaton, 1828. 1
p. (Rep. No. 87) DLC; NjR.
                                 36449
---- John Heard, Jr. Mar. 10,
1828. Mr. Dwight, from the Committee of Ways and Means, to
which was referred the petition
of John Heard, Jr. surviving assignee of Amasa Davis, Jr. made

the following report: Washington, Gales & Seaton, 1828. 1 p. (Rep. No. 184) DLC; NjR.   36450

---- John Long. Dec. 24, 1828. Mr. McCoy, from the Committee of Claims, to which was referred the petition of John Long, made the following report: Washington, Pr. by Gales & Seaton, 1828. 1 p. (Rep. No. 17) DLC; NjR.   36451

---- John M'Donnell. Jan. 14, 1828. Read, and laid upon the table. Mr. McDuffie, from the Committee of Ways and Means, to which was referred the petition of John M'Donnell, of Detroit, made the following report: Washington, Pr. by Gales & Seaton, 1828. 1 p. (Rep. No. 69) DLC; NjR.   36452

---- John Miles. Feb. 29, 1828. Mr. Whittlesey, from the Committee of Claims, to which was referred the petition of John Miles, made the following report: Washington, Gales & Seaton, 1828. 1 p. (Rep. No. 169) DLC; NjR.   36453

---- John Moffit. Feb. 1, 1828. Mr. Wolf, from the Committee on Revolutionary Claims, to which was referred the petition of John Moffit, made the following report: Washington, Pr. by Gales & Seaton, 1828. 1 p. (Rep. No. 121) DLC; NjR.   36454

---- John Shirkey. Jan. 2, 1828. Mr. Long, from the Committee on Military Pensions, to which was referred the petition of John Shirkey, made the following report: Washington, Gales & Seaton, 1828. 1 p. (Rep. No. 40) DLC; NjR.   36455

---- John Thompson, Christ. Adams, and S. Spraggins. Dec. 31, 1828. Read, and laid upon the table. Mr. Moore of Alabama, from the Committee on Private Land Claims, to which was referred the petition of John Thompson, Christopher Adams, and Samuel Spraggins, made the following report: Washington, Pr. by Gales & Seaton, 1828. 1 p. (Rep. No. 31) DLC; NjR.   36456

---- John Willard. January 23, 1828. Mr. Whittlesey, from the Committee of Claims, to which had been referred the petition of John Willard, made the following report: Washington, Pr. by Gales & Seaton, 1828. 2 p. (Rep. No. 95) DLC; NjR.   36457

---- John Winton. Jan. 11, 1828. Mr. Buckner, from the Committee on Private Land Claims, to which was referred the petition of John Winton of Tennessee, made the following report: Washington, Pr. by Gales & Seaton, 1828. 2 p. (Rep. No. 66) DLC; NjR.   36458

---- Joint resolution authorizing an examination of the claims to land of John F. Carmichael. Jan. 4, 1828. Read the first time. Jan. 7, 1828. Read the second time, and committed to a Committee of the Whole House to-morrow. [Washington, 1828] 1 p. (H. R. 5) DNA.   36459

---- Joint resolution providing for the care and preservation of the public buildings. Feb. 4, 1828. Read twice, and committed to the Committee of the Whole House on the state of the Union. [Washington, 1828] 1 p. (H. R. 7) DNA.   36460

---- Joint resolutions, providing for the distribution of certain public documents, and the removal of certain books from the library. Feb. 22, 1828. Read, and laid upon the table. Mr. Everett, from the Committee on the Library, reported... [Washington,

1828] 3 p. (H. R. 8) DNA. 36461

---- Jonathan M. Blaisdell. Dec. 16, 1828. Read, and laid upon the table. Mr. McDuffie, from the Committee of Ways and Means, to which was referred the petition of Jonathan M. Blaisdell, made the following report: Washington, Pr. by Gales & Seaton, 1828. 5 p. (Rep. No. 6) DLC; NjR.   36462

---- Jonathan S. Smith. Apr. 29, 1828. Read, and laid upon the table. Mr. Everett, from the Committee of Foreign Affairs, to which was referred the memorial of Jonathan S. Smith, made the following report: Washington, Gales & Seaton, 1828. 2 p. (Rep. No. 239) DLC; NjR.   36463

---- Joseph Burnett. Mar. 18, 1828. Read, and laid upon the table. Mr. Everett from the Committee on Foreign Affairs, to which had been referred the petition of Joseph Burnett, made the following report: Washington, Gales & Seaton, 1828. 2 p. (Rep. No. 198) DLC; NjR.   36464

---- Joseph Dixon. May 1, 1828. Read, and with the bill, committed to a Committee of the Whole House to-morrow. Mr. Ramsey, from the Committee of Claims, to which was referred the petition of Joseph Dixon, made the following report: Washington, Gales & Seaton, 1828. 1 p. (Rep. No. 241) DLC; NjR.   36465

---- Joseph G. Nancrede. Memorial of Joseph G. Nancrede, vaccine physician, Philadelphia. January 14, 1828. Read and laid upon the table. Washington, Pr. by Gales & Seaton, 1828. 5 p. (Doc. No. 66) DLC; NjR. 36466

---- Joseph Jeans - representatives of. Mar. 21, 1828. Mr.

Ramsay, from the Committee of Claims, to which was referred the case of the representatives of Joseph Jeans, made the following report: Washington, Gales & Seaton, 1828. 1 p. (Rep. No. 203) DLC; NjR.   36467

---- Joseph Smith and John B. Dupuis. Jan. 7, 1828. Mr. Buckner, from the Committee on Private Land Claims, to which was referred the petition of Joseph Smith, made the following report: Washington, Gales & Seaton, 1828. 2 p. (Rep. No. 55) DLC; NjR. 36468

---- Joseph Young. Jan. 30, 1828. Mr. Conner, from the Committee on the Post Office and Post Roads, to which was referred the petition of Joseph Young, made the following report: Washington, Pr. by Gales & Seaton, 1828. 1 p. (Rep. No. 113) DLC; NjR. 36469

---- Joshua Foltz. Feb. 22, 1828. Mr. Creighton, from the Committee on Revolutionary Claims, to which was referred the petition of Joshua Foltz, made the following report: Washington, Gales & Seaton, 1828. 2 p. (Rep. No. 156) DLC; NjR.   36470

---- Journal of the House of Representatives of the United States, being the first session of the twentieth Congress: Begun and held at the city of Washington, Dec. 3, 1827. And in the fifty-second year of the independence of the United States. Washington, Pr. by Gales & Seaton, 1827 [i. e. 1828] 1043 p. DLC; NjR. 36471

---- Journal of the Senate of the United States of America: being the first session of the twentieth Congress; begun and held at the city of Washington, Dec. 3, 1827 ... Washington, Pr. by Duff Green, 1827 [i. e. 1828] 586 p.

NN. 36472

---- Judah Alden. Jan. 29, 1828.
Mr. Wolf, from the Committee on
Revolutionary Claims, to which
had been referred the petition of
Judah Alden, made the following
report: Washington, Pr. by Gales
& Seaton, 1828. 1 p. (Rep. No.
106) DLC; NjR. 36473

---- Judge - Michigan. Mar. 18,
1828. Mr. Strong, from the Committee on the Territories, to
which the subject had been referred, made the following report: Washington, Gales & Seaton, 1828. 1 p. (Rep. No. 197)
DLC; NjR. 36474

---- Judiciary system, United
States. May 12, 1826. Read, and
laid upon the table. Feb. 8, 1828.
Reprinted by order of the House
of Representatives. Mr. Webster,
from the Committee on the Judiciary, to which had been referred
the message from the Senate, declining a conference upon the subject of the disagreeing votes of
the two Houses on the amendments proposed by the Senate to
the bill to amend the Judicial
system of the United States, made
the following report: Washington,
Pr. by Gales & Seaton, 1828. 5
p. (Doc. No. 135) DLC; NjR.
36475

---- Land claims in Michigan.
Report of the Committee on Public Lands, of the House of Representatives of the U. States, in
relation to claim to lands in the
territory of Michigan. Jan. 2,
1828. Pr. by order of the House
of Representatives. Washington,
Gales & Seaton, 1828. 515 p.
(Rep. No. 42) DLC; NjR. 36476

---- Land claims in Mississippi.
Documents accompanying the Bill
(No. 169) supplementary to the
several acts, for the adjustment
of land claims, in the state of
Mississippi. Feb. 18, 1828. Pr.
by order of the House of Repre-
sentatives. Washington, Pr. by
Gales & Seaton, 1828. 5 p. (Doc.
No. 144) DLC; NjR. 36477

---- Land district - south of
Tennessee. Letter from the Secretary of the Treasury transmitting the information required by
a resolution of the House of Representatives of the U. States in
relation to the survey of the public lands south of Tennessee.
February 2, 1828. Read, and referred to the Committee on the
Public Lands. Washington, Pr.
by Gales & Seaton, 1828. 22 p.
(Doc. No. 110) DLC; NjR. 36478

---- Land for Fort Washington.
Mar. 18, 1828. Mr. Smyth, of
Virginia, from the Committee of
Military Affairs, to which the
subject had been referred, made
the following report: Washington,
Gales & Seaton, 1828. 2 p. (Rep.
No. 195) DLC; NjR. 36479

---- Land relinquished - provision for repurchase of. Jan. 17,
1828. Mr. Isacks, from the Committee of the Public Lands, to
which the subject had been referred, made the following report:
Washington, Pr. by Gales & Seaton, 1828. 28 p. (Rep. No. 86)
DLC; NjR. 36480

---- Land to Kentucky Asylum -
deaf and dumb. Letter from the
Secretary of the Treasury, transmitting the information required
by a Resolution of the House of
Representatives of the 8th inst.
upon the subject of a township of
land granted to the Kentucky
Asylum for teaching the deaf and
dumb. Mar. 20, 1828. Read, and
laid upon the table. Washington,
Pr. by Gales & Seaton, 1828. 30
p. (Doc. No. 208) DLC; NjR. 36481

---- Lands for schools and seat of government - Florida. Jan. 11, 1828. Mr. W. R. Davis, from the Committee on the Public Lands, to which the subject had been referred, made the following report: Washington, Pr. by Gales & Seaton, 1828. 5 p. (Rep. No. 64) DLC; NjR.   36482

---- Lands for support of colleges in Ohio. Feb. 4, 1828. Read, and committed to a Committee of the Whole House tomorrow. Mr. Isacks, from the Committee on the Public Lands, to which the subject had been referred, made the following report: Washington, Pr. by Gales and Seaton, 1828. 2 p. (Rep. No. 124) DLC; NjR.   36483

---- Lands granted to Indiana. Documents to accompany Bill H. R. No. 99 to authorize the Legislature of the state of Indiana to sell and convey certain tracts of land granted to said state. Jan. 21, 1828. Pr. by order of the House of Representatives. Washington, Pr. by Gales & Seaton, 1828. 6 p. (Doc. No. 71) DLC; NjR.   36484

---- Lands in Alabama. Documents submitted by Mr. Owen and referred to the Committee of the Whole House to which is committed the bill (No. 86) to authorize the persons who have relinquished lands under the provisions of the several acts for the relief of purchasers of public lands to purchase the same at private sale at a fixed price. Mar. 31, 1828. Washington, Pr. by Gales & Seaton, 1828. 6 p. (Doc. No. 231) DLC; NjR.   36485

---- Lands to Alabama, &c. December 22, 1828. Mr. Isacks, from the Committee on the Public Lands, to which the subject

had been referred, made the following report: Washington, Pr. by Gales & Seaton, 1828. 4 p. (Rep. No. 11) DLC; NjR. 36486

---- Lands to Ohio - for canals. Feb. 11, 1828. Mr. Isacks, from the Committee on the Public Lands, to which the subject had been referred, made the following report: Washington, Pr. by Gales & Seaton, 1828. 2 p. (Rep. No. 139) DLC; NjR.   36487

---- Laws of the United States, resolutions of Congress under the Confederation, treaties, proclamations, Spanish regulations, and other documents respecting the public lands. Comp. in obedience to a resolution of the House of Representatives of the United States, passed first March 1826, and printed by an order dated nineteenth Feb. , 1827. Washington, Pr. by Gales & Seaton, 1828-36. 2 v. CSmH; DLC.   36488

---- Lead mines. Letter from the Secretary of War, transmitting the information required by a resolution of the House of Representatives of the 2d inst. In relation to the lead mines of the United States. Jan. 7, 1828. Read, and referred to the Committee on the Public Lands. Washington, Pr. by Gales & Seaton, 1828. 10 p. (Doc. No. 45) DLC; NjR.   36489

---- Legislature of Georgia on tariff and internal improvement. Letter from the Governor of Georgia transmitting a report of a committee of the General Assembly of said state on the subject of the powers of the general government for the purposes of encouraging domestic manufactures, and effecting a system of internal improvement. Feb. 6, 1828. Read, and referred to the

Committee of the Whole House to which is committed the bill (No. 132) in alteration of the several acts imposing duties on imports. Washington, Pr. by Gales & Seaton, 1828. 13 p. (Doc. No. 120) DLC; NjR.   36490

---- Legislature of the state of Alabama. Resolution of the Legislature of the state of Alabama proposing amendments to the Constitution of the United States. Feb. 4, 1828. Read, and committed to the Committee of the Whole House on the state of the Union. Washington, Pr. by Gales & Seaton, 1828. 4 p. (Doc. No. 116) DLC; NjR.   36491

---- Letter from James Mease transmitting a treatise on the rearing of silkworms by Mr. De Hazzi, of Munich, with plates, etc., etc. Apr. 21, 1828. Pr. by order of the Senate of the United States. Washington, Duff Green, 1828. 106 p. (Doc. No. 175 - pt 2) DLC; KU.   36492

---- Letter from Nathaniel Smith, laid on the table by Hon. Mr. Benton, showing the operation of the graduating system of Tennessee, in relation to the sale of the state lands, &c. Mar. 28, 1828. Pr. by order of the Senate of the United States. Washington, Pr. by Duff Green, 1828. 4 p. (Doc. No. 156) DLC; NjR.   36493

---- Letter from the Commissioner of the General Land Office, to the Hon. Mr. Barton, chairman of the Committee on Public Lands, with statements showing the amount of payments by the purchasers of Public Lands, and the mode in which those payments are accounted for, to the 30th June, 1827. Mar. 12, 1828. Pr. by order of the Senate of the United States. Washington, Pr. by

Duff Green, 1828. 6 p. (Doc. No. 138) DLC; NjR.   36494

---- Letter from the Commissioners of the General Land Office, to the| Hon. Powhatan Ellis, on the subject of private land claims. Feb. 1, 1828. Pr. by order of the Senate of the United States. Washington, Duff Green, 1828. 3 p. (Doc. No. 78) CSmH; DLC; NjR.   36495

---- Letter from the Governor of Georgia, with a report adopted by the Legislature of that state, on the tariff and internal improvement. Feb. 6, 1828. Referred to the Committees on Manufactures and Roads and Canals, and ordered to be printed. Washington, Duff Green, 1828. 15 p. (Doc. No. 90) DLC; NjR.   36496

---- Letter from the Hon. Mr. Mitchell, of Tennessee, laid on the table by the Hon. Mr. Benton, showing the operation of the graduating system of Tennessee, in relation to the sale of state lands, &c. April 2, 1828. Pr. by order of the Senate of the United States. Washington, Pr. by Duff Green, 1828. 6 p. (Doc. No. 160) DLC; NjR.   36497

---- Letter from the Postmaster General to the Hon. R. M. Johnson, on the subject of pamphlet postage. Apr. 3, 1828. Pr. by order of the Senate of the United States. Washington, Pr. by Duff Green, 1828. 3 p. (Doc. No. 162) DLC; NjR.   36498

---- Letter from the Postmaster General to the Hon. Richard M. Johnson, chairman of the Committee on the Post Office and Post Roads, in relation to the erection of a suitable building for a post office at New Orleans, April 9, 1828. Pr. by order of the Senate of the United States. Washington, Pr. by Duff Green, 1828. 3 p. (Doc. No. 170) DLC; NjR. 36499

---- Letter from the Secretary of the Treasury to the Hon. David Barton, in relation to the bill to graduate the price of relinquished lands to be sold to the original purchasers. Jan. 23, 1828. Pr. by order of the Senate of the United States. Washington, Pr. by Duff Green, 1828. 3 p. (Doc. No. 60) DLC; NjR. 36500

---- Letter from the Secretary of the Treasury, transmitting 1. A statement of payments made during the year 1827, for the discharge of miscellaneous claims, not otherwise provided for: 2. Of contracts and purchases by the collectors, for the Revenue Service, during the year 1826: 3. Of expenditures on account of sick and disabled seamen, during the year 1826. 4. Of contracts made relative to oil, light-vessels, Jan. 30, 1828. Read, and laid upon the table. Washington, Pr. by Gales & Seaton, 1828. 12 p. 5 bdsds. (Doc. No. 185) DLC; NjR. 36501

---- Letter from the Secretary of the Treasury transmitting statements from the incorporated banks in the District of Columbia exhibiting a statement of their affairs at the close of the year 1827. Jan. 14, 1828. Pr. by order of the Senate of the United States. Washington, Pr. by Duff Green, 1828. 13 p. (Doc. No. 35) DLC; NjR. 36502

---- Letter from the Secretary of the Treasury, transmitting the information required by a resolution of the House of Representatives of May 11, 1826 in relation to the growth and manufacture of silk, adapted to the different parts of the Union; Feb. 7, 1828, referred to the Committee on agriculture. [Washington, Pr. by Gales & Seaton, 1828] 220 p. (Doc. No. 158) MDeeP. 36503

---- Letter from the Secretary of the Treasury transmitting the information required by a resolution of the House of Representatives, of May 11, 1826, in relation to the growth and manufacture of silk, adapted to the different parts of the Union. Feb. 7, 1828... Washington, Pr. by D. Green, 1828. 224 p. (Doc. No. 175) DeGE; MBHo. 36504

---- Letter from the Secretary of the Treasury, transmitting the information required by a resolution of the House of Representatives, of the 8th ult. in relation to the nett revenue collected annually, from the year 1790 to 1826, inclusive, on ironware, wool, hemp, flax, sail-cloth, mollasses, foreign distilled spirits, and cotton and woollen manufactures, &c. Mar. 1, 1828. Read, and laid upon the table. Washington, Pr. by Gales & Seaton, 1828. 17 p. (Doc. No. 168) DLC; NjR. 36505

---- Letter from the Secretary of the Treasury, with a report from the Director of the Mint, showing the assays of foreign coins made at that institution in 1827. Apr. 14, 1828. Pr. by order of the Senate of the United States. Washington, Duff Green, 1828. 4 p. (Doc. No. 172) DLC; NjR. 36506

---- Letter from the Secretary of War to the Hon. Samuel Smith, chairman of the Committee on Finance, in relation to the expense of visitors to the Military Academy at West Point. Mar. 10, 1828. Pr. by order of the Senate of the United States. Washington, Pr. by Duff Green, 1828. 16 p. (Doc. No. 132) DLC; NjR. 36507

---- Letter from Tho. M. Bayly. Letter from Thomas M. Bayly, to the Speaker of the House of Representatives. May 19, 1828. Pr. by order of the House of Representatives. Washington, Pr. by Gales & Seaton, 1828. 4 p. (Doc. No. 273) DLC; NjR.   36508

---- Lewis Rouse. Jan. 2, 1828. Read, and laid upon the table. Mr. Ramsey, from the Committee of Claims, to which was referred the petition of Lewis Rouse, made the following report: Washington, Gales & Seaton, 1828. 25 p. (Rep. No. 45) DLC; NjR.
36509

---- Lewis Schrack. Apr. 9, 1828. Mr. Whittlesey, from the Committee of Claims, to which was referred the petition of Lewis Schrack, made the following report: Washington, Gales & Seaton, 1828. 2 p. (Rep. No. 231) DLC; NjR.   36510

---- Licenses granted to trade with Indians. Letter from the Secretary of War, transmitting an abstract of all licenses granted by the superintendents and agents for Indian affairs, to trade with Indians, &c. Feb. 12, 1828. Read, and laid upon the table. Washington, Pr. by Gales & Seaton, 1828. 3 p. 5 bdsds. (Doc. No. 140) DLC; NjR; PU.   36511

---- Light vessel - Brandywine Shoal. Letter from the Secretary of the Treasury, communicating information in relation to the removal of the light vessel from Brandywine Shoal to Tuckanuck Shoal. Jan. 2, 1828. Read, and laid upon the table. Washington, Pr. by Gales & Seaton, 1828. 7 p. (Doc. No. 32) DLC; DeGE; NjR.   36512

---- List of Committee of the Senate of the United States. Twen-

tieth Congress - Second session - 1828-'9. Washington, Duff Green, 1828. 3 p. (Doc. No. 23) DLC; NjR.   36513

---- A list of patents granted by the United States, for the encouragement of arts and sciences, alphabetically arranged, from 1790 to 1828, [To be continued by supplements:] Containing the names of the patentees, their places of residence, and the dates of their patents... City of Washington, D.C., Pr. and sold by S. Alfred Elliot, 1828. 72 p. IObB. 36514

---- A list of reports to be made to the House of Representatives at the second session of the twentieth Congress, by the executive departments. Prepared by the clerk, in obedience to a standing order of the House of Representatives. Dec. 1, 1828. Washington, Pr. by Gales & Seaton, 1828. 14 p. (Doc. No. 1) DLC; NjR.
36515

---- List of Select Committees. A list of the Select Committees of the House of Representatives, First session, twentieth Congress. Jan. 3, 1828. Pr. by order of the House of Representatives. Washington, Pr. by Gales & Seaton, 1828. 4 p. (Doc. No. 35) DLC; NjR.   36516

---- List of the names of such officers and soldiers of the Revolutionary Army as have acquired a right to lands from the United States, and who have not yet applied therefore. Jan. 16, 1828. Pr. by order of the Senate of the United States. Washington, Pr. by Duff Green, 1828. 94 p. (Doc. No. 42) DLC; NjR.   36517

---- Lotteries in the District of Columbia. Mar. 3, 1828. Mr. Varnum, from the Committee for the District of Columbia, to which the subject had been referred, made the following report. [Washington, 1828] 1 p. (Rep. No. 174) DLC; NjR.   36518

---- Louisiana. Memorial of the Legislature of Louisiana praying for the final adjustment of land titles in the state of Louisiana, and particularly for the settlement of the land claims in said state, known by the names of the De Bastrop and Maison Rouge Grants. Also, praying for the grant of lands, in certain cases, to aid the internal improvement of said state, and for other purposes. Jan. 7, 1828. Referred, part to the Committee on the Public Lands; the residue to the Committee on Roads and Canals. Washington, Pr. by Gales & Seaton, 1828. 5 p. (Doc. No. 90) DLC; NjR.   36519

---- ---- Memorial of the Mayor, Aldermen, and inhabitants, of New Orleans. Dec. 31, 1827. Referred to the Committee on Private Land Claims. Washington, Gales & Seaton, 1828. 25 p. 3 bdsds. (Doc. No. 26) CSmH; DLC; NjR.   36520

---- Lovely's Purchase - Arkansas. Letter from the Secretary of War transmitting correspondence relative to settlement of Lovely's Purchase in territory of Arkansas. Apr. 30, 1828. Read, and laid upon the table. Washington, Pr. by Gales & Seaton, 1828. 39 p. (Doc. No. 263) DLC; NjR.   36521

---- Luther Chapin. Feb. 20, 1828. Mr. Whittlesey, from the Committee of Claims, to which was referred the petition of Luther Chapin, made the following report: Washington, Gales & Seaton, 1828. 1 p. (Rep. No. 152) DLC; NjR.   36522

---- ---- Dec. 22, 1828. Mr. Whittlesey, from the Committee of Claims, to which the case of Luther Chapin had been referred, made the following report: Washington, Pr. by Gales & Seaton, 1828. 14 p. (Rep. No. 14) DLC; NjR.   36523

---- Maine. Memorial of merchants and others of Portland, in the state of Maine against an increase of duty on imported hemp, iron, molasses, and woollen goods. Jan. 28, 1828. Referred to the Committee on Manufactures. Washington, Pr. by Gales & Seaton, 1828. 5 p. (Doc. No. 91) DLC; NjR.   36524

---- Marcellin Bonnabel. Dec. 29, 1828. Mr. Gurley, from the Committee on the Public Lands, to which was referred the case of the heirs of Antonio Bonnabel, made the following report: Washington, Pr. by Gales & Seaton, 1828. 1 p. (Rep. No. 21) DLC; NjR.   36525

---- Marigny D'Auterive. Mar. 24, 1828. Mr. Whittlesey, from the Committee of Claims, to which was recommitted the bill (No. 19) for the relief of Marigny D'Auterive, made the following report: Washington, Gales & Seaton, 1828. 1 p. (Rep. No. 210) DLC; NjR.   36526

---- Marine hospital - Charleston, S. C. Jan. 16, 1828. Mr. Cambreleng, from the Committee on Commerce, to which the subject had been referred, made the following report: Washington, Pr. by Gales & Seaton, 1828. 5 p. (Rep. No. 83) DLC; NjR.   36527

---- Martinique and Guadaloupe. Documents to accompany the bill from the Senate (No. 122) regulating the commercial intercourse with the islands of Martinique and Guadaloupe. Apr. 8, 1828. Pr. by order of the House of Representatives. Washington, Pr. by Gales & Seaton, 1828. 13 p. (Doc. No. 240) DLC; NjR.   36528

---- Mary Ann Bond and Mary Loveless. Jan. 4, 1828. Mr. Shepperd, from the Committee on Private Land Claims, to which was referred the petition of Mary Ann Bond and Mary Loveless, made the following report: Washington, Gales & Seaton, 1828. 2 p. (Rep. No. 54) DLC; NjR.
36529

---- Mary James. Jan. 16, 1828. Mr. Mitchell, of Tennessee, from the Committee on Military Pensions, to which was referred the petition of Mary James, of Bedford county, Virginia, made the following report: Washington, Pr. by Gales & Seaton, 1828. 1 p. (Rep. No. 80) DLC; NjR. 36530

---- Mary Reynolds. Jan. 21, 1828. Mr. Wolf, from the Committee on Revolutionary Claims, to which the subject had been referred, made the following report: Washington, Pr. by Gales & Seaton, 1828. 2 p. (Rep. No. 89) DLC; NjR.   89) 36531

---- Maryland. Memorial of farmers, mechanics, and others, of Anne Arundel and Baltimore counties, against an increase of duty on imported manufactures. Mar. 10, 1828. Referred to the Committee of the Whole House to which is referred the bill in alteration of the several acts imposing duties on imports. Washington, Pr. by Gales & Seaton, 1828. 5 p. (Doc. No. 188) DLC; NjR.   36532

---- ---- Memorial of the Baltimore and Ohio Railroad Company, praying to import iron and ma-

chinery, free of duty. Mar. 17, 1828. Referred to the Committee on Roads and Canals. Washington, Pr. by Gales & Seaton, 1828. 4 p. (Doc. No. 206) CtY; DBRE; DLC; DeGE; MB; MH; NN; NjR; P.
36533

---- ---- Memorial of the Chamber of Commerce of the city of Baltimore upon the subject of protested bills of exchange. Feb. 4, 1828. Referred to the Committee on Commerce. Washington, Pr. by Gales & Seaton, 1828. 5 p. (Doc. No. 119) DLC; NjR. 36534

---- Massachusetts. Memorial of citizens of Boston, &c. in favor of further protection to manufactures. Jan. 22, 1828. Referred to the Committee on Manufactures. Washington, Pr. by Gales & Seaton, 1828. 9 p. (Doc. No. 84) DLC; NjR.   36535

---- ---- Memorial of citizens of Duxbury in the state of Massachusetts. Jan. 14, 1828. Referred to the Committee on Commerce. Jan. 29, 1828. Pr. by order of the House of Representatives. Washington, Pr. by Gales & Seaton, 1828. 4 p. (Doc. No. 96) DLC; NjR.   36536

---- ---- Memorial of inhabitants of Nantucket, in the state of Massachusetts, praying that an expedition may be fitted out under the sanction of government, to survey and explore the islands and coasts of the Pacific. Feb. 18, 1828. Referred to the Committee on Naval Affairs. Washington, Pr. by Gales & Seaton, 1828. 3 p. (Doc. No. 179) DLC; NjR. 36537

---- ---- Memorial of inhabitants of Scituate, Pembroke, Hancock, &c. in the state of Massachusetts praying for the improvement of North River Channel. May 5, 1828. Referred to the Committee

on Commerce. Washington, Pr. by
Gales & Seaton, 1828. 4 p. (Doc.
No. 266) DLC; NjR.   36538

---- ---- Memorial of the proprietors of the Hingham Umbrella
Manufactory. Mar. 3, 1828. Read,
and referred to the Committee of
the Whole House to which is committed the bill in alteration of the
several acts imposing duties on
imports. Washington, Pr. by
Gales & Seaton, 1828. 3 p. (Doc.
No. 176) DLC; NjR.   36539

---- ---- Petition of citizens of
New Bedford, praying that a naval
expedition may be undertaken, for
the exploration of the north and
south Pacific Ocean, and other
seas, visited by whale ships and
others. Mar. 17, 1828. Referred
to the Committee on Naval Affairs. Washington, Pr. by Gales
& Seaton, 1828. 3 p. (Doc. No.
201) CSmH; DLC; NjR.   36540

---- ---- Petition of sundry
farmers and landholders of the
town of Westborough, county of
Wooster, commonwealth of Massachusetts, against a further increase of duties on imported
manufactures. Jan. 28, 1828. Referred to the Committee on Manufactures. Washington, Pr. by
Gales & Seaton, 1828. 5 p. (Doc.
No. 95) DLC; NjR.   36541

---- Massachusetts - wool growers of Berkshire. Memorial of
the wool growers and manufacturers of Berkshire, state of Massachusetts. Dec. 31, 1827. Referred to the Committee on Manufactures. Washington, Gales &
Seaton, 1828. 5 p. (Doc. No. 29)
DLC; NjR.   36542

---- Massachusetts militia claims.
Letter from the Secretary of War
transmitting, in pursuance of a
resolution of the House of Repre-

sentatives of the 15th of Dec.
1826, a report upon the subject
of the claims of the state of Massachusetts for certain services
rendered during the late wars.
May 10, 1828. Read, and laid upon the table. Dec. 5, 1828. Pr. by
order of the House of Representatives. Washington, Pr. by Gales
& Seaton, 1828. 181 p. (Doc. No.
3) DLC; MB; NjR.   36543

---- Masters commandant - Navy
United States. Statement submitted by the Committee on Naval Affairs to accompany the bill to increase the pay of the captains
and masters commandant in the
Navy of the United States. Dec.
20, 1828. Washington, Pr. by
Gales & Seaton, 1828. 4 p. (Doc.
No. 32) DLC; NjR.   36544

---- Matthias Roll. Jan. 17, 1828.
Mr. Sterigere, from the Committee on Private Land Claims, to
which was referred the petition of
Matthias Roll, made the following
report: Washington, Pr. by Gales
& Seaton, 1828. 1 p. (Rep. No.
85) DLC; NjR.   36545

---- Mayor and common council
of Baltimore. Mar. 31, 1828. Mr.
McCoy, from the Committee of
Claims, to which the subject had
been referred, made the following
report: Washington, Gales & Seaton, 1828. 2 p. (Rep. No. 218)
DLC; NjR.   36546

---- Memorial and resolutions
adopted at the anti-tariff meeting
held at Sumter District, South
Carolina, on Monday, Sept. 3,
1827. Mar. 21, 1828. Referred to
the Committee on Manufactures,
and ordered to be printed. Washington, Pr. by Duff Green, 1828.
9 p. (Doc. No. 150) DLC; NjR.
                         36547

---- Memorial and resolutions of
merchants and others, of the city

of Philadelphia, remonstrating against the further increase of duties on imports. Jan. 29, 1828. Referred to the Committee on Manufactures, and ordered to be printed. Washington, Pr. by Duff Green, 1828. 16 p. (Doc. No. 68) DLC; NjR. 36548

---- Memorial of certain hardware manufacturers, smiths and iron founders of Philadelphia, praying that the duties on imported iron and steel may be reduced. Mar. 19, 1828. Referred to the Committee on Manufactures and ordered to be printed. Washington, Pr. by Duff Green, 1828. 9 p. (Doc. No. 145) DLC; NjR. 36549

---- Memorial of certain merchant tailors of Boston, praying that additional duty be imposed on ready made clothing, when imported into United States. May 5, 1828. Pr. by order of the Senate of the United States. Washington, Duff Green, 1828. 5 p. (Doc. No. 190) DLC; DeGE; NjR. 36550

---- Memorial of certain surgeons of the United States Navy, praying that certain regulations be adopted for the admission of candidates and that the pay of surgeons in the navy be increased. Jan. 25, 1828. Pr. by order of the Senate of the United States. Washington, Pr. by Duff Green, 1828. 10 p. (Doc. No. 62) DLC; NjR. 36551

---- Memorial of Garsed, Raines, and Co. of Frankford, Philadelphia County, Pennsylvania, praying that an additional duty be laid on yarns, threads, and twines, made of flax, when imported. April 30, 1828. Pr. by order of the Senate of the United States. Washington, Duff Green, 1828. 6 p. (Doc. No. 184) DLC; NjR. 36552

---- Memorial of General Winfield Scott. Dec. 29, 1828. Referred to the Committee on Military Affairs. Washington, Pr. by Gales & Seaton, 1828. 2 p. (Doc. No. 40) DLC; NjR. 36553

---- Memorial of sundry citizens of Alleghany County in the state of Pennsylvania in favor of an increase of the tariff for the protection of domestic manufactures. Jan. 11, 1828. Pr. by order of the Senate of the United States. Washington, Pr. by Duff Green, 1828. 11 p. (Doc. No. 31) DLC; NjR. 36554

---- Memorial of sundry citizens of Elizabeth city and county of Pasquotank in North Carolina praying that an appropriation may be made for the purpose of opening a water communication from Albemarle Sound to the Atlantic Ocean. Jan. 21, 1828. Pr. by order of the Senate of the United States. Washington, Pr. by Duff Green, 1828. 4 p. (Doc. No. 49) DLC; NjR. 36555

---- Memorial of sundry citizens of Missouri, praying that further provision be made for the confirmation of land titles derived from the French and Spanish governments, &c. Feb. 13, 1828. Pr. by order of the Senate of the United States. Washington, Duff Green, 1828. 8 p. (Doc. No. 101) DLC; NjR. 36556

---- Memorial of sundry citizens of Northumberland County, Pennsylvania, in favor of an increase of duties for the protection of domestic manufactures. January 29, 1828. Referred to the Committee on Manufactures, and ordered to be printed. Washington, Pr. by Duff Green, 1828. 3 p. (Doc. No. 69) DLC; NjR. 36557

---- Memorial of sundry citizens
of Orangeburgh District, S. C. adverse to the increase of duties
on woollens and other imports.
Jan. 14, 1828. Pr. by order of
the Senate of the United States.
Washington, Pr. by Duff Green,
1828. 4 p. (Doc. No. 32) DLC;
MH; NjR.   36558

---- Memorial of sundry citizens
of Philadelphia, praying to be
protected from the injurious operation of the auction system, &c.
Dec. 18, 1828. Referred to the
Committee on Finance, and ordered to be printed. Washington,
Duff Green, 1828. 2 p. (Doc. No.
13) DLC; DeGE; NjR.   36559

---- Memorial of sundry citizens
of the districts of Chesterfield,
Marlborough, and Darlington,
South Carolina, in opposition to
increasing the duties on foreign
manufactures. Mar. 12, 1828.
Referred to the Committee on
Manufactures, and ordered to be
printed. Washington, Pr. by Duff
Green, 1828. 8 p. (Doc. No. 137)
DLC; NjR.   36560

---- Memorial of sundry inhabitants of Michigan, remonstrating
against the passage of the bill to
graduate the price of public
lands, make donations thereof to
actual settlers, and to cede the
refuse to the states in which they
lie. Apr. 4, 1828. Pr. by order
of the Senate of the United States.
Washington, Pr. by Duff Green,
1828. 4 p. (Doc. No. 163) DLC;
NjR.   36561

---- Memorial of sundry inhabitants of Murfreesborough, N.
Carolina, praying that a passage
be made between Ocracock Inlet
and the Atlantic Ocean. Apr. 4,
1828. Pr. by order of the Senate
of the United States. Washington,
Pr. by Duff Green, 1828. 4 p.

(Doc. No. 165) DLC; NjR. 36562

---- Memorial of sundry journeymen tailors, of Philadelphia, praying that protection be extended to
them, by the regulation of the
duty on ready made clothing, &c.
May 1, 1828. Pr. by order of
the Senate of the United States.
Washington, Duff Green, 1828. 4
p. (Doc. No. 188) DLC; NjR.
                              36563
---- Memorial of sundry merchant tailors, of New York, praying that an additional duty be imposed on ready made clothing,
when imported into the United
States. May 5, 1828. Pr. by order of the Senate of the United
States. Washington, Duff Green,
1828. 4 p. (Doc. No. 191) DLC;
NjR.   36564

---- Memorial of sundry persons,
master tailors, of Philadelphia,
praying that additional duty be
laid on ready made clothing, when
imported, &c. April 28, 1828.
Referred to the Committee on
Manufactures, and ordered to be
printed. Washington, Duff Green,
1828. 3 p. (Doc. No. 182) DLC;
NjR.   36565

---- Memorial of sundry persons,
merchant tailors, of Philadelphia,
praying that additional duty be
laid on ready made clothing. Apr.
28, 1828. Referred to the Committee on Manufactures, and ordered to be printed. Washington,
Duff Green, 1828. 4 p. (Doc. No.
181) DLC; NjR.   36566

---- Memorial of sundry residents of the city and county of
Philadelphia, praying that additional duties may be imposed on
certain manufactured articles,
when imported. Jan. 9, 1828.
Printed by order of the Senate of
the United States. Washington, Pr.
by Duff Green, 1828. 4 p. (Doc.

No. 24) DLC; NjR.   36567

---- Memorial of sundry umbrella-makers of Philadelphia, praying that protection be extended to the manufacture of cotton umbrellas. Feb. 11, 1828. Referred to the Committee on Manufactures, and ordered to be printed. Washington, Duff Green, 1828. 3 p. (Doc. No. 97) DLC; NjR; PHi.   36568

---- Memorial of the Agricultural Society of South Carolina adverse to an increase of duties on coarse woollens and other imports. Jan. 8, 1828. Pr. by order of the Senate of the United States. Washington, Pr. by Duff Green, 1828. 4 p. (Doc. No. 26) DLC; NjR.   36569

---- Memorial of the Baltimore and Ohio Rail Road Company, praying that they may be permitted to import iron and iron machinery for said road free of duty. Mar. 17, 1828. Referred to the Committee on Finance, ordered to be printed. Washington, Pr. by Duff Green, 1828. 4 p. (Doc. No. 140) CtY; DBRE; DLC; MBAt; MH; NN; NjR; P.   36570

---- Memorial of the Baltimore Chamber of Commerce, praying that a law may be passed to regulate the settlement of protested bills of exchange. Feb. 4, 1828. Referred to the Committee on Commerce, and ordered to be printed. Washington, Duff Green, 1828. 5 p. (Doc. No. 83) DLC; DeGE; NjR.   36571

---- Memorial of the Chamber of Commerce, and of other citizens of Charleston, South Carolina, adverse to the increase of duties on imports, &c. Jan. 4, 1828. Pr. by order of the Senate of the United States. Washington, Pr. by Duff Green, 1828. 10 p. (Doc. No. 21) DLC; NjR.   36572

---- Memorial of the citizens of Boston, and its vicinity in favor of the increase of duty on woollen goods, as contemplated by the woollens bill. Jan. 21, 1828. Pr. by order of the Senate of the United States. Washington, Pr. by Duff Green, 1828. 59 p. (Doc. No. 45) DLC; NjR.   36573

---- Memorial of the citizens of Chester District, South Carolina, adverse to an increase of duty on woollen goods, as contemplated by the woollens bill. Jan. 29, 1828. Referred to the Committee on Manufactures, and ordered to be printed. Washington, Pr. by Duff Green, 1828. 5 p. (Doc. No. 70) DLC; MH; NjR.   36574

---- Memorial of the citizens of Georgetown, South Carolina, adverse to the increase of duties on coarse woollens and other imports. Jan. 9, 1828. Pr. by order of the Senate of the United States. Washington, Pr. by Duff Green, 1828. 7 p. (Doc. No. 25) DLC; NjR.   36575

---- Memorial of the citizens of Kershaw District, South Carolina, adverse to the proposed tariff on woollens. Mar. 21, 1828. Referred to the Committee on Manufactures and ordered to be printed. Washington, Pr. by Duff Green, 1828. 10 p. (Doc. No. 153) DLC; NjR.   36576

---- Memorial of the citizens of Lancaster District, South Carolina adverse to the system of protecting duties in favor of domestic manufactures. Jan. 15, 1828. Pr. by order of the Senate of the United States. Washington, Pr. by Duff Green, 1828. 4 p. (Doc. No. 37) DLC; NjR.   36577

---- Memorial of the citizens of Laurens District, South Carolina, adverse to the present tariff, and to the passage of the woollens bill. Jan. 10, 1828. Pr. by order of the Senate of the United States. Washington, Pr. by Duff Green, 1828. 8 p. (Doc. No. 28) DLC; NjR.   36578

---- Memorial of the citizens of Plymouth and Kingston, Mass. adverse to an increase of duty on woollen goods, as contemplated by the woollens bill. Jan. 21, 1828. Referred to the Committee on Manufactures, and ordered to be printed. Washington, Pr. by Duff Green, 1828. 8 p. (Doc. No. 46) DLC; NjR.   36579

---- Memorial of the citizens of Savannah, stating the advantages that would result to the government, from establishing a naval depot at that place. Apr. 28, 1828. Referred to the Committee on Naval Affairs, and ordered to be printed. Washington, Duff Green, 1828. 7 p. (Doc. No. 180) DLC; NjR.   36580

---- Memorial of the citizens of Union District, South Carolina, against the system of protecting duties adopted by Congress. Mar. 21, 1828. Referred to the Committee on Manufactures, and ordered to be printed. Washington, Pr. by Duff Green, 1828. 4 p. (Doc. No. 152) DLC; MH; NjR.   36581

---- Memorial of the citizens of Westborough, Massachusetts protesting against any increase of duties on imports and especially on woollen goods. Jan. 28, 1828. Referred to the Committee on Manufactures, and ordered to be printed. Washington, Pr. by Duff Green, 1828. 7 p. (Doc. No. 64) DLC; NjR.   36582

---- Memorial of the city council of Charleston, praying that the South Carolina Canal and Rail Road Company be authorized to import, free of duty, iron and machinery to be used in effecting the objects of their incorporation. Apr. 7, 1828. Pr. by order of the Senate of the United States. Washington, Pr. by Duff Green, 1828. 4 p. (Doc. No. 166) CtY; DBRE; DLC; MB; MBAt; MH; NN; NjR; P.   36583

---- Memorial of the Comptroller General of South Carolina, praying that certain balances due for military works the purchase of arms, during the late war, may be paid with interest to the State of South Carolina, January 3, 1828. Washington, Pr. by Gales & Seaton, 1828. 7 p. (Doc. No. 38) Sabin 87410.   36584

---- Memorial of the General Assembly of Indiana, expressive of the advantages resulting from the Cumberland Road and the desire of that state for its completion. Feb. 20, 1828. Referred to the Committee on Roads and Canals, and ordered to be printed. Washington, Pr. by Duff Green, 1828. 6 p. (Doc. No. 111) DLC; NjR.   36585

---- Memorial of the inhabitants of Richland District, in the state of South Carolina. Jan. 3, 1828. Pr. by order of the Senate of the United States. Washington, Pr. by Duff Green, 1828. 4 p. (Doc. No. 17) DLC; NjR.   36586

---- Memorial of the inhabitants of Thomaston, and its vicinity, adverse to a further increase of duties on imports, for the protection of domestic manufactures. Feb. 1, 1828. Referred to the Committees on Manufactures and Finances, and ordered to be printed. Washington, Duff Green,

1828. 5 p. (Doc. No. 79) DLC;
NjR.   36587

---- Memorial of the Legislature
of Alabama, on the subject of the
public lands within the said state.
Feb. 4, 1828. Referred, part to
a Select Committee, and part to
the Committee on Public Lands,
and ordered to be printed. Washington, Duff Green, 1828. 7 p.
(Doc. No. 82) DLC; NjR. 36588

---- Memorial of the Legislature
of Louisiana, in relation to the
public lands in that state. Washington, Duff Green, 1828. 3 p.
(Doc. No. 10) DLC; NjR. 36589

---- Memorial of the Legislature
of the state of South Carolina,
remonstrating against the passing
of laws by Congress, increasing
the duties upon the importations,
for the encouragement of domestic manufactures: against the exercise of the general power to
construct roads and canals, either
with or without the consent of the
states, ... Washington, Pr. by
Gales & Seaton, 1828. 19 p. (Doc.
No. 65) DLC; MH; MWA; NN.
                            36590
---- Memorial of the manufacturers of salt, of Barnstable,
Massachusetts praying that the
duty on imported salt may not be
repealed. Mar. 6, 1828. Pr. by
order of the Senate of the United
States. Washington, Pr. by Duff
Green, 1828. 3 p. (Doc. No. 131)
DLC; NjR.   36591

---- Memorial of the manufacturers of salt of the county of
Kanawha, Virginia against the repeal of the duty on imported salt.
Jan. 21, 1828. Pr. by order of
the Senate of the United States.
Washington, Pr. by Duff Green,
1828. 21 p. 1 bdsd. (Doc. No.
47) DLC; NjR.   36592

---- Memorial of the merchants
of Boston, representing their views
in relation to the system of credit
duties on imports. Dec. 17, 1828.
Referred to the Committee on
Commerce, and ordered to be
printed. Washington, Duff Green,
1828. 3 p. (Doc. No. 12) DLC;
NjR.   36593

---- Memorial of the merchants
of Savannah, Georgia praying that
certain regulations be made for
the settlements of bills of exchange. Feb. 22, 1828. Referred
to the Committee on Commerce,
and ordered to be printed. Washington, Pr. by Duff Green, 1828.
4 p. (Doc. No. 118) DLC; NjR.
                            36594
----Memorial of the merchants
of the city of Philadelphia, engaged in the China trade, on the
subject of a regulation of the duty
on tea. Jan. 31, 1828. Referred
to the Committee on Finance, and
ordered to be printed. Washington,
Duff Green, 1828. 6 p. (Doc. No.
77) DLC; DeGE; NjR.   36595

---- Memorial of the New York
Chamber of Commerce adverse
to an increase of duties on im-
ported woollens. Jan. 22, 1828.
Pr. by order of the Senate of the
United States. Washington, Pr. by
Duff Green, 1828. 4 p. (Doc. No.
53) DLC; NjR.   36596

---- Memorial of the New York
Chamber of Commerce praying
that an uniform mode of settling
protested bills of exchange by an
act of Congress. Mar. 20, 1828.
Pr. by order of the Senate of the
United States. Washington, Pr. by
Duff Green, 1828. 9 p. (Doc. No.
148) DLC; NjR.   36597

---- Memorial of the Northampton Slate Quarry Company in
Pennsylvania, praying that further
protecting duty be laid on import-

ed slate for roofing. Mar. 19, 1828. Referred to the Committee on Manufactures, and ordered to be printed. Washington, Pr. by Duff Green, 1828. 3 p. (Doc. No. 146) DLC; NjR.   36598

---- Memorial of the Philadelphia Chamber of Commerce, praying for a revision of the revenue laws, and the establishment of warehouses at the principle ports. Washington, Duff Green, 1828. 2 p. (Doc. No. 11) DLC; DeGE; NjR; PHi.   36599

---- Memorial of the salt manufacturers in the town of Salina, Onondaga County, New York against the repeal of duty on imported salt. Jan. 21, 1828. Pr. by order of the Senate of the United States. Washington, Pr. by Duff Green, 1828. 4 p. (Doc. No. 48) DLC; NjR.   36600

---- Memorial of the Sisters of Charity of St. Joseph, praying to be incorporated within the District of Columbia. Apr. 8, 1828. Referred to the Committee on the District of Columbia, and ordered to be printed. Washington, Pr. by Duff Green, 1828. 5 p. (Doc. No. 167) DLC; NjR.   36601

---- Memorial of the South Carolina Canal and Railroad Company, Apr. 7, 1828. Referred to the Committee of Ways and Means, April 14th, 1828. Bill reported. No. 268. Washington, Pr. by Duff Green, 1828. 4 p. (Doc. No. 246) MB; MBAt; MHi; NN. 36602

---- Memorial on behalf of the Pittsburgh Manufacturing Association. Jan. 3, 1828. Pr. by order of the Senate of the Unites States. Washington, Pr. by Duff Green, 1828. 5 p. (Doc. No. 16) DLC; NjR.   36603

---- Memorial with the resolutions adopted at the anti-tariff meeting held at Abbeville Courthouse, South Carolina on Monday, the 3d of September, 1827. Mar. 21, 1828. Referred to the Committee on Manufactures, and ordered to be printed. Washington, Pr. by Duff Green, 1828. 17 p. (Doc. No. 151) DLC; NjR. 36604

---- Merchants of Alexandria - District of Columbia. Dec. 29, 1828. Read, and laid upon the table. Mr. P. P. Barbour, from the Committee on the Judiciary, to which was referred the petition of merchants of Alexandria, praying for indemnity under the Treaty of Ghent, made the following report: Washington, Pr. by Gales & Seaton, 1828. 1 p. (Rep. No. 18) DLC; NjR.   36605

---- Message from the President of the United States, communicating information relative to the trade between the United States and the colonies of France. Feb. 5, 1828. Pr. by order of the Senate of the United States. Washington, Duff Green, 1828. 11 p. (Doc. No. 89) DLC; NjR. 36606

---- Message from the President of the United States, in compliance with a resolution of the Senate of the 26th May, 1828, showing, by a report from the Treasury Department, the estimates for the year 1828, and the appropriations for all purposes, including public lands made during the last session of Congress. Washington, Duff Green, 1828. 15 p. (Doc. No. 4) DLC; NjR.   36607

---- Message from the President of the United States, in compliance with a resolution of the Senate, relating to the accounts and official conduct of Thomas A. Smith, receiver of public moneys,

Franklin, Missouri. May 24, 1828.
Pr. by order of the Senate of the
United States. Washington, Duff
Green, 1828. 6 p. (Doc. No. 205)
DLC; NjR.   36608

---- Message from the President
of the United States, relative to
commercial regulations with Prussia. May 16, 1828. Read, and referred to the Committee on Commerce, and ordered to be printed.
Washington, Duff Green, 1828.
6 p. (Doc. No. 196) DLC; NjR.
                            36609
---- Message from the President
of the United States to both
houses of Congress at the commencement of the second session
of the twentieth Congress. Dec.
2, 1828. Read, and committed to
the Committee of the Whole House
on the state of the union. Washington, Pr. by Gales & Seaton,
1828. 176 p. 9 bdsds. (Doc. No.
2) DLC; DeGE; NjR.   36610

---- Message from the President
of the United States, to the two
houses of Congress, at the commencement of the second session
of the twentieth Congress. Dec.
2, 1828. Pr. by order of the
Senate of the United States. Washington, Duff Green, 1828. 188 p.
(Doc. No. 1) DLC; NjR.   36611

---- Message from the President
of the United States, transmitting
a report from the Secretary of
War, in relation to the removal
of the Indian agency from Fort
Wayne, in Indiana. May 1, 1828.
Pr. by order of the Senate of the
United States. Washington, Duff
Green, 1828. 27 p. (Doc. No.
189) DLC; NjR.   36612

---- Message from the President
of the United States transmitting
communications from the Governor of Georgia, in relation to the
subject of running and marking

the line dividing the territory of
Florida from the state of Georgia.
Jan. 23, 1828. Pr. by order of
the Senate of the United States.
Washington, Pr. by Duff Green,
1828. 16 p. (Doc. No. 55) DLC;
NjR.   36613

---- Message from the President
of the United States transmitting
(in compliance with a resolution
of the 19th ult.) the correspondence with the British government
relative to the improvement to
the navigation within their jurisdiction, opposite to the coast of
Florida. Jan. 4, 1828. Pr. by
order of the Senate of the United
States. Washington, Pr. by Duff
Green, 1828. 15 p. (Doc. No. 19)
CSmH; DLC; NjR.   36614

---- Message from the President
of the United States, transmitting,
in compliance with a resolution
of the Senate, of the eleventh
instant, a report from the Secretary of State, with copies of instructions, &c. to Andrew Elli-
cott, commissioner for running
the line between the United States
and Spain. Feb. 15, 1828. Referred to the Committee on the
Judiciary, and ordered to be
printed. Washington, Duff Green,
1828. 10 p. (Doc. No. 105) DLC;
NjR.   36615

---- Message from the President
of the United States transmitting
the annual report of the Commissioner of the Public Buildings,
in compliance with a resolution
of the Senate of the 28th of Jan.
1818. Jan. 4, 1828. Pr. by order
of the Senate of the United States.
Washington, Pr. by Duff Green,
1828. 20 p. (Doc. No. 20) DLC;
NjR.   36616

---- Message from the President
of the United States transmitting
to Congress copies of a commu-

nication from the Governor of Pennsylvania, and resolutions of the Legislature of that Commonwealth relative to the permanent preservation and repair of so much of the Cumberland Road as passes through that state. Feb. 25, 1828. Referred to the Committee on Roads and Canals, and ordered to be printed. Washington, Pr. by Duff Green, 1828. 7 p. (Doc. No. 120) DLC; NjR.
                                        36617

---- Message from the President of the United States, with documents relating to alleged aggressions on the rights of citizens of the United States by the authorities of New Brunswick, on the territory dispute between the United States and Great Britain. Mar. 4, 1828. Pr. by order of the Senate of the United States. Washington, Pr. by Duff Green, 1828. 49 p. (Doc. No. 130) DLC; NjR.   36618

---- Message from the President of the United States, with a report from the Secretary of State, showing the number of free taxable inhabitants who are not freeholders, in Ohio, Missouri, Mississippi, and the western district of Louisiana, and in the territory of Florida: Made in compliance with a resolution of the Senate, of 25th April, 1828. Washington, Duff Green, 1828. 3 p. (Doc. No. 8) DLC; NjR.   36619

---- Message from the President of the United States, with a report from the Secretary of War, (In compliance with a resolution of the Senate, of the 26th May, 1828,) relative to the practicability and probable cost of constructing an artificial harbor or breakwater at the mouth of Mississippi. Dec. 8, 1828. Read, and ordered to be printed. Washington, Duff Green, 1828. 4 p. (Doc. No. 5)

DLC; NjR.   36620

---- Michael Lewis. May 6, 1828. Mr. Miller, from the Committee on Naval Affairs, to which was referred the case of Michael Lewis, made the following report: Washington, Gales & Seaton, 1828. 1 p. (Rep. No. 248) DLC; NjR.   36621

---- Military road - defence of northwestern frontier - Michigan. Letter from the Secretary of War transmitting the information required by a resolution of the House of Representatives, of the eighth instant, relative to the proceedings under the act of 2d Mar. 1827, for the defence of the northwestern frontier, &c. December 23, 1828. Read, and referred to the Committee of Ways and Means. Washington, Pr. by Gales & Seaton, 1828. 3 p. (Doc. No. 29) DLC; NjR.   36622

---- Militia United States. Letter from the Secretary of War, transmitting an abstract of the general annual returns of the militia of the United States, their arms, accoutrements, and ammunition, by states and territories, from the latest returns. Feb. 3, 1828. Read, and referred to the Committee on the Militia. Washington, Pr. by Gales & Seaton, 1828. 3 p., 2 bdsds. (Doc. No. 130) DLC; NjR.   36623

---- Minor Thomas. Jan. 8, 1828. Read, and laid upon the table. Mr. Earll, from the Committee on Private Land Claims, to which was referred the petition of Minor Thomas, of the state of Indiana, made the following report: Washington, Pr. by Gales & Seaton, 1828. 2 p. (Rep. No. 60) DLC; NjR.   36624

---- Mint of the United States. Letter from the Secretary of the Treasury transmitting statements in relation to the operations of the Mint of the U. S. during the year 1827. Apr. 16, 1828. Read, and laid upon the table. Washington, Pr. by Gales & Seaton, 1828. 3 bdsds. (Doc. No. 250) DLC; NjR.   36625

---- Minutes of evidence, taken before the Committee on Manufactures, first session of the Twentieth Congress. Ordered to be printed, 31st January, 1828. [Washington, 1828] [2], 19-160 p. (House Rep. No. 115) DeGE; PHC; RPB.   36626

---- Mr. Gorham submitted the following, to be by him proposed as amendments to the report of the Select Committee appointed on the seventeenth ultimo, on the message of the President of the United States in relation to an assault committed on the person of his Private Secretary. Russell Jarvis. May 23, 1828. Pr. by order of the House of Representatives. [Washington, 1828] 1 p. (H. R.) DNA.   36627

---- Mr. Mallary submitted the following, which, when the bill [No. 132] in alteration of the several acts imposing duties on imports shall be taken up for consideration, he will move as amendments to the same. Feb. 12, 1828. Referred to the Committee of the Whole on the said bill. [Washington, 1828] 1 p. (H. R. 132) DNA.   36628

---- Mr. Strong submitted the following, which, when the Bill [No. 145,] to graduate the price of public lands, to make donations thereof to actual settlers, and to cede the refuse to the States in which they lie, upon equitable terms, shall be taken

up for consideration, he will move as an amendment to the amendment proposed by Mr. Vinton to said bill. Feb. 12, 1828. Read twice, and committed to the Committee of the Whole House to which the above bill is committed. [Washington, 1828] 1 p. (H. R. 145) DNA.   36629

---- Mr. Wilde's resolution. Feb. 21, 1828. Laid on the table for consideration. Feb. 22, 1828. Considered, modified, and laid on the table. Feb. 29, 1828. Considered, modified to read as follows, and again laid on the table. [Washington, 1828] 1 p. (H. R. 9) DNA.   36630

---- Mr. Wright submitted the following, with intention, when the "Bill further to amend the judicial system of the United States," shall be taken up for consideration, to move it as an amendment to the said bill. Feb. 8, 1828. Read twice, and committed to a Committee of the Whole House, to which the said bill is committed. [Washington, 1828] 1 p. (H. R. 144) DNA.   36631

---- Moritz Furst. Feb. 8, 1828. Read, and laid upon the table. Mr. Whittlesey, from the Committee of Claims, to which had been referred the petition of Moritz Furst, made the following report: Washington, Pr. by Gales & Seaton, 1828. 5 p. (Rep. No. 133) DLC; NjR.   36632

---- Moses Hazen. Mar. 28, 1828. Read, and, with the bill, committed to a Committee of the Whole House to-morrow. Mr. Wolf, from the Committee on Revolutionary Claims, to which was referred the bill from the Senate, entitled "An act for the relief of the legal representatives of General Moses Hazen, deceased," made the following report: Washington, Gales & Seaton, 1828. 4 p. (Rep. No. 216) DLC; NjR.   36633

---- Moses Shepherd. May 10, 1828. Read, and laid upon the table. Mr. McIntire, from the Committee of Claims, to which was referred the bill from the Senate, (No. 112) for the relief of Moses Shepherd, made the following report. Washington, Gales & Seaton, 1828. 185 p. (Rep. No. 253) DLC; NjR.   36634

---- Nancy Dolan. Feb. 19, 1828. Mr. Isacks, from the Committee on the Public Lands, to which was referred the petition of Nancy Dolan, made the following report: Washington, Gales & Seaton, 1828. 2 p. (Rep. No. 150) DLC; NjR.   36635

---- Nathaniel B. Wood. Dec. 17, 1828. Mr. Whittlesey, from the Committee of Claims, to which was referred the petition of Nathaniel B. Wood, made the following report: Washington, Pr. by Gales & Seaton, 1828. 1 p. (Rep. No. 7) DLC; NjR.   36636

---- Nathaniel Briggs. Jan. 24, 1828. Mr. Cambreleng, from the Committee on Commerce, to which had been referred the petition of Nathaniel Briggs, made the following report: Washington, Pr. by Gales & Seaton, 1828. 1 p. (Rep. No. 96) DLC; NjR.
36637
---- National debt. Letter from the Secretary of the Treasury, transmitting the information required by a resolution of the House of Representatives, of the 8th instant, in relation to the sum which will be required annually to discharge the whole of the national debt in the year 1835, &c. Mar. 13, 1828. Read, and refer-

red to the Committee of Ways and Means. Washington, Pr. by Gales & Seaton, 1828. 8 p. (Doc. No. 195) DLC; NjR.   36638

---- National paintings. Letter from John Trumbull to the Speaker of the House of Representatives on the subject of the national paintings in the rotunda of the Capitol. Dec. 9, 1828. Read, and laid upon the table. Washington, Pr. by Gales & Seaton, 1828. 3 p. (Doc. No. 10) DLC; NjR.
36639
---- National road. Memorial of the General Assembly of the state of Indiana, upon the subject of the Cumberland or Wester, national road. Feb. 25, 1828. Referred to the Committee of the Whole House, to which is committed the bill for the continuation of the Cumberland Road. Washington, Pr. by Gales & Seaton, 1828. 3 p. (Doc. No. 163) DLC; NjR.   36640

---- National road - Washington to New Orleans. Letter from the Secretary of War transmitting a report of the chief engineer accompanied by a report upon the reconnoissance of a route across the Cumberland Mountain of the national road contemplated from Washington to New Orleans, and a map of the country between those two cities. Jan. 30, 1828. Read, and laid upon the table. Feb. 7, 1828. Referred to the Committee of the Whole House to which is committed the bill (No. 44) to regulate the laying out and making a national road from the city of Washington in the District of Columbia, to New Orleans, in the state of Louisiana. Washington, Pr. by Gales & Seaton, 1828. 19 p. 9 bdsds. (Doc. No. 125) DLC; NN; NjR; PU.   36641

---- Navigation between St. Mary's

and St. John's River, Florida. Jan. 11, 1828. Mr. Mercer, from the Committee on Roads and Canals to which the subject had been referred, made the following report: Washington, Pr. by Gales & Seaton, 1828. 5 p. (Rep. No. 61) DLC; NjR.   36642

---- Navigation of Pearl River. Mar. 3, 1828. Mr. Gurley, from the Committee on Roads and Canals, to which the subject had been referred made the following report: Washington, Gales & Seaton, 1828. 2 p. (Rep. No. 175) DLC; NjR.   36643

---- Navigation of rivers Teche, Vermillion, &c. -Lou. Mar. 12, 1828. Mr. Gurley, from the Committee on Roads and Canals, to which the subject had been referred, made the following report: Washington, Gales & Seaton, 1828. 5 p. (Rep. No. 188) DLC; NjR.   36644

---- Navigation of the St. Lawrence. Message from the President of the United States, transmitting a report from the Secretary of State, and the correspondence with the government of Great Britain, relative to the free navigation of the River St. Lawrence. Jan. 7, 1828. Read, and referred to the Committee on Foreign Affairs. Washington, Pr. by Gales & Seaton, 1828. 54 p. (Doc. No. 43) DLC; DeGE; NjR.   36645

---- Navy of the United States. Memorial of the Lieutenants of the Navy of the United States. Dec. 14, 1827. Referred to the Committee on Naval Affairs. Jan. 25, 1828. Pr. by order of the House of Representatives. Washington, Pr. by Gales & Seaton, 1828. 7 p. (Doc. No. 89) DLC; NjR.   36646

---- Navy pension fund. Letter from the Secretary of the Navy, transmitting the annual report in relation to the Navy pension fund. Mar. 14, 1828. Read, and referred to the Committee on Naval Affairs. Washington, Pr. by Gales & Seaton, 1828. 23 p. 2 bdsds. (Doc. No. 197) DLC; NjR. 36647

---- Negotiation for Cherokee land. Letter from the Secretary of War transmitting the report of the commissioners appointed to negotiate with the Cherokee Indians for a certain portion of their country. Jan. 30, 1828. Read, and laid upon the table. Washington, Pr. by Gales & Seaton, 1828. 40 p. (Doc. No. 106) DLC; NjR.   36648

---- Nehemiah Parsons. Feb. 8, 1828. Mr. Gorham, from the Committee on Commerce, to which was referred the petition of Nehemiah Parsons, made the following report: Washington, Pr. by Gales & Seaton, 1828. 2 p. (Rep. No. 132) DLC; NjR.
                                  36649
---- Nett amount of postage for 1827. Letter from the Postmaster General, transmitting a statement of the nett amount of postage accruing at each office, in each state and territory of the U. States, for the year ending 31st March, 1827. Jan. 14, 1828. Read, and laid upon the table. Washington, Gales & Seaton, 1828. 76 p. (Doc. No. 60) DLC; NjR.   36650

---- New Hampshire. Memorial of citizens of New Hampshire in favor of further protection to domestic manufactures. Jan. 22, 1828. Referred to the Committee on Manufactures. Washington, Pr. by Gales & Seaton, 1828. 5 p. (Doc. No. 80) DLC; NjR. 36651

---- ---- Petition of farmers of New Hampshire praying for the interests of agriculture and manufactures. Jan. 22, 1828. Referred to the Committee on Manufactures. Washington, Pr. by Gales & Seaton, 1828. 5 p. (Doc. No. 81) DLC; NjR.   36652

---- New Jersey. Petition of the manufacturers of Paterson, in the state of New Jersey. Dec. 31, 1827. Referred to the Committee on Manufactures. Washington, Gales & Seaton, 1828. 12 p. (Doc. No. 27) DLC; NjR.   36653

---- New York Chamber of Commerce. Memorial of the New York Chamber of Commerce against an increase of duty on woollens, &c. Jan. 28, 1828. Referred to the Committee on Manufactures. Washington, Pr. by Gales & Seaton, 1828. 4 p. (Doc. No. 94) DLC; NjR.   36654

---- New York. Memorial of agriculturists and manufacturers of the state of New York, friendly to the encouragement and protection of American industry. Jan. 3, 1828. Referred to the Committee on Manufactures. Washington, Pr. by Gales & Seaton, 1828. 13 p. (Doc. No. 33) DLC; DeGE; NjR.   36655

---- ---- Memorial of inhabitants of Herkimer County, New York, for further protection to farmers and manufacturers, by additional duties on imports. Feb. 18, 1828. Referred to the Committee of the Whole House to which is referred the Bill (No. 132) in alteration of the several acts imposing duties on imports. Washington, Pr. by Gales & Seaton, 1828. 3 p. (Doc. No. 147) DLC; NjR. 36656

---- ---- Memorial of inhabitants of Otsego County, upon the sub-

ject of an increase of duties on certain imported manufactures, &c. &c. Mar. 3, 1828. Referred to the Committee of the Whole House on the State of the Union. Washington, Pr. by Gales & Seaton, 1828. 5 p. (Doc. No. 178) DLC; NjR.   36657

---- ---- Memorial of inhabitants of the city of Albany, and county of Sullivan; on the subject of affording further protecting duties, to domestic manufactures. Feb. 11, 1828. Referred to the Committee of the Whole House to which is committed the Bill (No. 132) in alteration of the several acts imposing duties on imports. Washington, Pr. by Gales & Seaton, 1828. 5 p. (Doc. No. 132) DLC; NjR.   36658

---- ---- Memorial of inhabitants of the city of Albany, in the state of New-York, praying further protection to agricultural and manufacturing interests. Dec. 31, 1827. Referred to the Committee on Manufactures. Jan. 3, 1828. Pr. by order of the House of Representatives. Washington, Pr. by Gales & Seaton, 1828. 6 p. (Doc. No. 42) DLC; NjR. 36659

---- ---- Memorial of the inhabitants of Dutchess County, in the state of New York, against an increase of duty on imported merchandise, &c. Mar. 3, 1828. Referred to the Committee of the Whole House on the State of the Union. Washington, Pr. by Gales & Seaton, 1828. 7 p. (Doc. No. 175) DLC; NjR.   36660

---- ---- Memorial of the inhabitants of Dutchess County in the state of New York upon the subject of the bill now before the House of Representatives entitled A bill in alteration of the several acts imposing duties on im-

ports. Apr. 8, 1828. Read, and
laid upon the table. Washington,
Pr. by Gales & Seaton, 1828. 7
p. (Doc. No. 239) DLC; NjR.
                              36661
---- ---- Memorial of the Ontario Agricultural Society of the
state of New York, praying further protecting duties on certain
domestic manufactures. Jan. 14,
1828. Referred to the Committee
on Manufactures. Washington, Pr.
by Gales & Seaton, 1828. 3 p.
(Doc. No. 63) DLC; NjR. 36662

---- ---- Memorial to merchants,
traders, &c. of the city of New
York praying that a duty of ten
per cent may be imposed by law
upon sales at auction. Apr. 28,
1828. Read, and laid upon the
table. Washington, Pr. by Gales
& Seaton, 1828. 4 p. (Doc. No.
260) DLC; NjR.   36663

---- ---- Petition of inhabitants
of Red Hook in the county of
Dutchess, and the state of New
York, against a further increase
of duties on imported manufactures, &c. Mar. 31, 1828. Referred to the Committee of the
Whole House to which is committed the bill in alteration of the
several acts imposing duties on
imports. Washington, Pr. by
Gales & Seaton, 1828. 5 p. (Doc.
No. 228) DLC; NjR.   36664

---- ---- Petition of sundry inhabitants of the county of Delaware, in the state of New York,
praying for the passage of a law
imposing additional duties on certain imported materials and fab-
rics therein mentioned. Mar. 31,
1828. Referred to the Committee
of the Whole House to which is
committed the bill in alteration
of the several acts imposing duties on imports. Washington, Pr.
by Gales & Seaton, 1828. 4 p.
(Doc. No. 229) DLC; NjR. 36665

---- ---- Petition of the wool
growers and manufacturers of
Madison County praying further
protection to the growers of wool
and manufacturers of woollen
goods. Feb. 4, 1828. Referred to
the Committee of the Whole House
on the State of the Union. Washington, Pr. by Gales & Seaton,
1828. 6 p. (Doc. No. 112) DLC;
NjR.   36666

---- ---- Resolutions of the Legislature of the state of New York
upon the subject of an increase
of duties upon certain articles
imported into the United States.
Feb. 7, 1828. Read, and referred
to the Committee of the Whole
House to which is committed the
bill (No. 132) in alteration of the
several acts imposing duties on
imports. Washington, Pr. by
Gales & Seaton, 1828. 3 p. (Doc.
No. 123) DLC; NjR.   36667

---- North Carolina. Resolution
of the Legislature of North Carolina, against an increase of duties on imports. Jan. 14, 1828.
Referred to the Committee on
Manufactures. Washington, Pr.
by Gales & Seaton, 1828. 5 p.
(Doc. No. 62) DLC; NjR. 36668

---- Northern and northwestern
boundary line. Letter from the
Secretary of State, transmitting
pursuant to a resolution of the
House of Representatives, of the
19th ultimo. A copy of the maps
and report of Commissioners under the Treaty of Ghent, for ascertaining the northern and northwestern boundary, between the U.
States and Great Britain. Mar.
18, 1828. Read, and laid upon the
table. Washington, Pr. by Gales
& Seaton, 1828. 3 p. (Doc. No.
218) CSmH; DLC; NjR.   36669

---- Northern boundary of Indiana. Message from the President

of the United States, with a plot of the survey of the northern boundary of the state of Indiana. Dec. 12, 1827. Read, and referred to the Committee on the Judiciary. Washington, Pr. by Gales & Seaton, 1828. 4 p. (Doc. No. 187) CSmH; DLC; NjR.   36670

---- Note - Minister U. S. to Spain, of 20th Jan. 1826. Message from the President of the United States, transmitting, in pursuance of a resolution of the House of Representatives of the 19th instant, a copy of the note of the minister of the United States to Spain, dated 20th Jan., 1826. May 21, 1828. Read, and laid upon the table. Washington, Pr. by Gales & Seaton, 1828. 25 p. (Doc. No. 276) DLC; NjR.   36671

---- Obstructions - The Ohio River. Apr. 4, 1828. Read, and laid upon the table. Mr. Woods, from the Committee on Roads and Canals, to which the subject had been referred, made the following report: Washington, Gales & Seaton, 1828. 2 p. (Rep. No. 269) DLC; NjR.   36672

---- Obstructions in the river Ohio. Mar. 27, 1828. Mr. Woods, of Ohio, from the Committee on Roads and Canals, to which the subject had been referred, made the following report: Washington, Gales & Seaton, 1828. 4 p. (Rep. No. 213) DLC; NjR.   36673

---- Obstructions to navigation, Wabash. Letter from the Secretary of War in reply to a resolution of the House of Representatives, of the 15th instant, requiring information in relation to the survey of the obstructions to the navigation of the Wabash River. Dec. 18, 1828. Read, and laid upon the table. Washington, Pr. by Gales & Seaton, 1828. 1 p.

(Doc. No. 26) DLC; NjR.   36674

---- Of the state of the finances. Mar. 12, 1828. Read, and laid upon the table. Mr. McDuffie, from the Committee of Ways and Means, made the following report: Washington, Gales & Seaton, 1828. 35 p. 1 bdsd. (Rep. No. 185) DLC; NjR.   36675

---- Officers of Revolutionary Army. Feb. 11, 1828. Mr. Burgess, from the Select Committee to which the subject had been referred, made the following report: Washington, Pr. by Gales & Seaton, 1828. 21 p. (Rep. No. 136) DLC; NjR.   36676

---- Officers on the pension list. Letter from the Secretary of War transmitting a list of officers on the pension roll of the U. S. designating the states to which the officers severally belong. Jan. 30, 1828. Read, and laid upon the table. Washington, Pr. by Gales & Seaton, 1828. 29 p. (Doc. No. 124) DLC; NjR.   36677

---- Official army register for 1828. Adjutant General's office, Washington, Jan., 1828. Way & Gideon, prs. 32 p. MdHi. 36678

---- Official record from the War Department of the proceedings of the court martial which tried, and the orders of General Jackson for shooting the six militia men, together with official letters from the War Department showing that these American citizens were inhumanly and illegally massacred. Albany, N. Y., Webster & Wood, 1828. 47 p. CLU; MiD-B; NRHi; NSyHi; OClWHi; T; WHi.   36679

---- Official record from the War Department of the court martial which tried, and the orders of

General Jackson for shooting the six militia men, together with official letters from the War Department, ordered to be printed by Congress, showing that these American citizens were inhumanly massacred. Concord [N. H.] Pr. by J. B. Moore, 1828. 52 p. CSmH; DLC; ICN; MH; MiD-B; Nh; NhHi. 36680

---- ---- Washington, Pr. at the office of J. Elliot, 1828. 32 p. CSmH; CtHT-W; DLC; ICU; MH; MWA; MdHi; MiD-B; MnHi; NIC; NjR; OClWHi; OO; PPFM; RPB; TxU. 36681

---- Ohio. Memorial of the inhabitants of Montgomery County in the state of Ohio upon the subject of free people of color. Jan. 21, 1828. Read, and laid upon the table. Washington, Pr. by Gales & Seaton, 1828. 4 p. (Doc. No. 79) DLC; NjR. 36682

---- ---- Resolutions of the General Assembly of the state of Ohio, in relation to the right of the general government, to levy tonnage and impose duties, to protect domestic industry, &c. Feb. 28, 1828. Referred to the Committee of the Whole House to which is committed the Bill in alteration of the several acts imposing duties on imports. Washington, Pr. by Gales & Seaton, 1828. 4 p. (Doc. No. 156) DLC; NjR. 36683

---- Old continental money. Letter from the Secretary of the Treasury transmitting the information required by a resolution of the House of Representatives, of the 16th instant, in relation to the amount of continental money issued during the Revolutionary War, and the depreciation of the same, &c. Jan. 30, 1828. Read, and laid upon the table. Washington, Pr. by Gales & Seaton,

1828. 33 p. (Doc. No. 107) DLC; NjR. 36684

---- On civilization of the Indians. Supplemental report from the Bureau of Indian Affairs. Dec. 9, 1828. Read, and laid upon the table. Washington, Pr. by Gales & Seaton, 1828. 8 p. (Doc. No. 11) DLC; NjR. 36685

---- On retrenchment. May 15, 1828. Read, and committed to the Committee of the Whole House on the state of the Union. Mr. Hamilton, from the Select Committee to whom the subject was referred, made the following report: Washington, Gales & Seaton, 1828. 190 p., 2 bdsds. (Rep. No. 259) DLC; NjR. 36686

---- On Senate Bill No. 50 - Susan Decatur, et al. Mar. 18, 1828. Read, and, with the bill, committed to a Committee of the Whole House to-morrow. Mr. Hoffman, from the Committee on Naval Affairs, to which was referred the bill from the Senate entitled "An act to compensate Susan Decatur, widow and representative of Captain Stephen Decatur, deceased, and others; "also, the memorials of Charles Stewart, Robert Thornton, F. C. De Krafft, and Michael Carrol, made the following report: Washington, Gales & Seaton, 1828. 29 p. (Rep. No. 201) DLC; NjR. 36687

---- On Senate Bill, No. 101. Dec. 8, 1828. Committed, with the bill, to a Committee of the Whole House to-morrow. May 5, 1828. Read, and laid upon the table. Mr. Williams, from the Committee of Claims, to which was referred the bill from the Senate, entitled "An act providing for the final settlement of the claims of certain states therein mentioned, for interest on their

advances during the late war,"
made the following report: Washington, Gales & Seaton, 1828. 3
p. (Rep. No. 250) DLC; NjR.
                              36688
---- On Senate Bill, No. 108 -
Dillon Buell. Apr. 7, 1828.
Read, and, with the bill, committed to a Committee of the Whole
House to-morrow. Mr. Whittlesey, from the Committee of
Claims, to which had been referred the bill from the Senate (No.
108) for the relief of Dillon Buell, made the following report:
Washington, Gales & Seaton,
1828. 1 p. (Rep. No. 228) DLC;
NjR.   36689

---- Operations of the Mint.
Message from the President of
the United States transmitting a
report of the director of the Mint,
and a statement of the operations
of that institution during the year
1827. Jan. 21, 1828. Read and
laid upon the table. Washington,
Pr. by Gales & Seaton, 1828. 6
p. 1 bdsd. (Doc. No. 70) DLC;
NjR.   36690

---- Opinion - Attorney General -
Treaty of Ghent. Message from
the President of the United States
transmitting a copy of the opinion
of the Attorney General upon the
construction of the award of the
Emperor of Russia under the
Treaty of Ghent, &c. &c. Apr.
22, 1828. Read, and laid upon
the table. Washington, Pr. by
Gales & Seaton, 1828. 9 p. (Doc.
No. 256) DLC; NjR.   36691

---- Orleans Navigation Company. Feb. 11, 1828. Read, and
committed to a Committee of the
Whole House to-morrow. Mr. P.
P. Barbour, from the Committee
on the Judiciary, to which the
subject had been referred, made
the following report: Washington,
Pr. by Gales & Seaton, 1828.

22 p. (Rep. No. 138) DLC; NjR.
                              36692
---- Orson Sparks and John Watson. Dec. 31, 1828. Mr. Whittlesey, from the Committee of
Claims, made the following report: Washington, Pr. by Gales
& Seaton, 1828. 4 p. (Rep. No.
27) DLC; NjR.   36693

---- Pascagoula River. Feb. 13,
1828. Mr. Gurley, from the
Committee on Roads and Canals,
to which the subject had been referred, made the following report: Washington, Gales & Seaton, 1828. 7 p. (Rep. No. 145)
DLC; NjR.   36694

---- Passengers in 1827. Letter
from the Secretary of State,
transmitting the annual statement
of the number and description of
passengers arriving in the United
States, on ship board, for the
year ending on the 30th Sept.
1827. May 16, 1828. Read, and
laid upon the table. Washington,
Pr. by Gales & Seaton, 1828. 3
p. 19 bdsds. (Doc. No. 286)
DLC; NjR.   36695

---- Patents - 1827. Letter from
the Secretary of State, transmitting a list of the names of the
persons to whom patents have
been granted for the invention of
any new or useful art, or ma-
chine, manufacture, or composition of matter, or any improvement thereon, from Jan. 1, 1827,
to Dec. 31, 1827. Jan. 2, 1828.
Read, and laid upon the table.
Washington, Pr. by Gales & Seaton, 1828. 23 p. (Doc. No. 34)
DLC; NjR.   36696

---- Payments to citizens of
Georgia. Message from the President of the United States, transmitting the information required
by a resolution of the House of
Representatives, of the 3d April

last, relating to payments made to the citizens of Georgia, under the 4th article of the Treaty with the Creek Nation, of the 8th Feb. 1821, and the disallowance of certain claims exhibited under that treaty, &c. May 9, 1828. Read, and laid upon the table. Washington, Pr. by Gales & Seaton, 1828. 70 p. (Doc. No. 268) DLC; NjR.							36697

---- Payments to jurors United States' Courts. Letter from the Secretary of the Treasury, transmitting a statement of money paid by the United States to jurors for attendance at the district and circuit courts of the United States, for the years 1824, 1825, and 1826, &c. Feb. 28, 1828. Read, and laid upon the table. Washington, Pr. by Gales & Seaton, 1828. 3 p. 1 bdsd. (Doc. No. 164) DLC; NjR.							36698

---- Payments to Major General Brown. Letter from the Secretary of War transmitting the information required by a resolution of the House, of 28th ultimo, in relation to the sums of money which have been received by Major General Brown; and also, what sums have been received by his aids in each year since 1820, &c. May 9, 1828. Read, and laid upon the table. Washington, Pr. by Gales & Seaton, 1828. 11 p. (Doc. No. 267) DLC; NjR.							36699

---- Pennsylvania - Chamber of Commerce, Philadelphia - cash duties. Dec. 11, 1828. Referred to the Committee on Commerce. Washington, Pr. by Gales & Seaton, 1828. 2 p. (Doc. No. 16) DLC; NjR.							36700

---- Pennsylvania. Memorial and resolutions of citizens of Philadelphia, in the state of Pennsylvania, against a further increase of duties on imported manufactures, &c. &c. Jan. 28, 1828. Referred to the Committee on Manufactures. Washington, Pr. by Gales & Seaton, 1828. 15 p. (Doc. No. 93) DLC; DeGE; NjR.							36701

---- ---- Memorial from citizens of Adams County, Penn., praying for additional duties on woollen goods, &c. with a view to the protection of domestic industry. Mar. 10, 1828. Referred to the Committee of the Whole House to which is committed the bill in alteration of the several acts imposing duties on imports. Washington, Pr. by Gales & Seaton, 1828. 4 p. (Doc. No. 191) DLC; NjR.							36702

---- ---- Memorial of citizens of Alleghany County, in the state of Pennsylvania, praying that the amendment proposed by Mr. Mallary, to the Tariff bill now before the House, may be adopted. Mar. 20, 1828. Read, and referred to the Committee of the Whole House to which is committed the bill in alteration of the several acts imposing duties on imports. Washington, Pr. by Gales & Seaton, 1828. 5 p. (Doc. No. 207) DLC; NjR.							36703

---- ---- Memorial of citizens of the city and county of Philadelphia, upon the subject of a post route, between the cities of Philadelphia and Baltimore. Mar. 17, 1828. Read, and referred to the Committee on Roads and Canals. Washington, Pr. by Gales & Seaton, 1828. 5 p. (Doc. No. 203) DLC; DeGE; NjR.							36704

---- ---- Memorial of citizens of the state of Pennsylvania praying for the enactment of a law that all colored children born in the Dis't of Columbia after a certain day, shall be free. Jan. 21, 1828.

Referred to the Committee for the District of Columbia. Washington, Pr. by Gales & Seaton, 1828. 4 p. (Doc. No. 86) DLC; NjR.
36705

---- ---- Memorial of inhabitants of Blairsville, upon the subject of an armory, &c. Mar. 24, 1828. Read, and laid upon the table. Washington, Pr. by Gales & Seaton, 1828. 3 p. (Doc. No. 214) DLC; NjR.   36706

---- ---- Memorial of inhabitants of Pennsylvania praying further protection of the national industry. Jan. 3, 1828. Referred to the Committee on Manufactures. Washington, Gales & Seaton, 1828. 9 p. (Doc. No. 36) DLC; NjR.
36707

---- ---- Memorial of inhabitants of Philadelphia, praying that the Baltimore and Ohio Railroad Company may not be permitted to import iron free of duty. May 12, 1828. Read, and committed to the Committee of the Whole House on the State of the Union. Washington, Pr. by Gales & Seaton, 1828. 6 p. (Doc. No. 270) CtY; DBRE; DLC; MB; MBAt; MH; MWA; NjR.   36708

---- ---- Memorial of manufacturers of hardware, smiths and iron-founders, of the city of Philadelphia. Mar. 17, 1828. Referred to the Committee of the Whole House to which is committed the bill in alteration of the several acts imposing duties on imports. Washington, Pr. by Gales & Seaton, 1828. 8 p. (Doc. No. 202) DLC; DeGE; NjR.
36709

---- ---- Petition from inhabitants of Beaver County, Pa. for an increased tariff. Mar. 24, 1828. Referred to the Committee of the Whole House on the State of the Union. Washington, Pr. by Gales & Seaton, 1828. 3 p. (Doc.

No. 213) DLC; NjR.   36710

---- ---- Petition of inhabitants of Northampton County, state of Pennsylvania, praying for an additional and specific duty on imported roofing and ciphering slate. Feb. 4, 1828. Referred to the Committee of the Whole House on the State of the Union to which is committed the bill in alteration of the several acts imposing duty on imports. Washington, Pr. by Gales & Seaton, 1828. 3 p. (Doc. No. 114) DLC; NjR.   36711

---- ---- Resolutions and memorial, of inhabitants of the county of Washington, in the state of Pennsylvania, upon the subject of an increase of duty, on certain manufactured articles imported, and on unmanufactured wool. Mar. 5, 1828. Read, and laid upon the table. Washington, Pr. by Gales & Seaton. 1828. 6 p. (Doc. No. 181) DLC; NjR.   36712

---- ---- Resolutions of the Legislature of Pennsylvania in favor of further protection to domestic manufactures. Jan. 28, 1828. Read, and laid upon the table. Washington, Pr. by Gales & Seaton, 1828. 4 p. (Doc. No. 97) DLC; DeGE; NjR.   36713

---- Pensions to widows, &c. of deceased seamen. Documents submitted by the chairman of the Committee on Naval Affairs to accompany the bill (H. R. No. 270) to provide for extending the term of the pensions of certain persons. Apr. 15, 1828. Washington, Pr. by Gales & Seaton, 1828. 5 p. (Doc. No. 244) DLC; NjR.   36714

---- Peter Ford. May 2, 1828. Mr. Whittlesey, from the Committee of Claims, to which was referred [the petition of?] Peter

Ford, made the following report: Washington, Gales & Seaton, 1828. 2 p. (Rep. No. 242) DLC; NjR. 36715

---- Peter P. M'Cormack. December 22, 1828. Mr. Bates of Missouri, from the Committee on Private Land Claims, to which was referred the petition of Peter P. M'Cormack, made the following report: Washington, Pr. by Gales & Seaton, 1828. 2 p. (Rep. No. 13) DLC; NjR. 36716

---- Peters and Pond. Jan. 30, 1828. Mr. Gorham, from the Committee on Commerce, to which was referred the petition of Peters and Pond, made the following report: Washington, Pr. by Gales & Seaton, 1828. 2 p. (Rep. No. 110) DLC; NjR. 36717

---- Petition of John Adlum, stating that he had prepared a treatise on the cultivation of the vine, and the manufacture of wine therefrom; and praying that encouragement be extended to him, by rendering said treatise useful to the United States, and of advantage to himself. April 30, 1828. Referred to the Committee on Agriculture, and ordered to be printed. Washington, Duff Green, 1828. 3 p. (Doc. No. 185) DLC; NjR. 36718

---- Petition of Philander Chase, President of Kenyon College, Ohio, praying for a donation of land, for the benefit of that institution. Feb. 6, 1828. Referred to the Committee on Public Lands, and ordered to be printed. Washington, Duff Green, 1828. 10 p. (Doc. No. 91) DLC; NjR. 36719

---- Petition of sundry residents of Hertford, N. Carolina, praying that an appropriation be made for opening an outlet for commerce to the ocean, at or near "Roanoke Inlet." Mar. 3, 1828. Referred to the Committee on Commerce, and ordered to be printed. Washington, Pr. by Duff Green, 1828. 4 p. (Doc. No. 129) DLC; NjR. 36720

---- Petition of the Sisters of Visitation of Georgetown, D. C. praying that an act of incorporation may be passed in their favor. Apr. 8, 1828. Referred to the Committee on the District of Columbia, and ordered to be printed. Washington, Pr. by Duff Green, 1828. 9 p. (Doc. No. 168) DLC; NjR. 36721

---- Philip Slaughter. Feb. 15, 1828. Mr. Wolf, from the Committee on Revolutionary Claims, to which had been referred the petition of Philip Slaughter, made the following report: Washington, Gales & Seaton, 1828. 7 p. (Rep. No. 146) DLC; NjR. 36722

---- Polly Campbell. Apr. 9, 1828. Mr. Long, from the Committee on Military Pensions, to which was referred the petition of Polly Campbell, made the following report: Washington, Gales & Seaton, 1828. 2 p. (Rep. No. 232) DLC; NjR. 36723

---- Ports of entry - Florida. December 30, 1828. Read, and laid upon the table. Mr. Cambreleng, from the Committee on Commerce, to which the subject had been referred made the following report: Washington, Pr. by Gales & Seaton, 1828. 1 p. (Rep. No. 23) DLC; NjR. 36724

---- Post-office laws, instructions and forms, published for the regulations of the Post-Office. Pr. for the Post-Office Department. Washington, Pr. by Way & Gideon, 1828. 63 p. DLC; MH; MdHi; PPAmP; PPL. 36725

---- Pre-emption to certain persons in Florida. December 19, 1828. Mr. Isacks, from the Committee on the Public Lands, to which the subject had been referred, made the following report: Washington, Pr. by Gales & Seaton, 1828. 1 p. (Rep. No. 9) DLC; NjR.   36726

---- Private claims of Florida. Letter from the Secretary of the Treasury, transmitting the reports and decisions of the register and receiver of public moneys in the District of East Florida, upon private land claims in said district. Jan. 30, 1828. Read and referred to the Committee on the Public Lands. Feb. 7, 1828. Pr. by order of the House of Representatives. Washington, Pr. by Gales & Seaton, 1828. 53 p. 5 bdsds. (Doc. No. 169) DLC; NjR.   36727

---- Private property taken for public use. Jan. 21, 1828. Read, and laid upon the table. Mr. P. P. Barbour, from the Committee on the Judiciary, to which the subject had been referred, made the following report: Washington, Pr. by Gales & Seaton, 1828. 1 p. (Rep. No. 90) DLC; NjR.   36728

---- Protested bills of exchange. Memorial of the New York Chamber of Commerce, relative to protested bills of exchange. Mar. 17, 1828. Referred to the Committee on Commerce. Washington, Pr. by Gales & Seaton, 1828. 8 p. (Doc. No. 204) DLC; NjR. 36729

---- The public and general statutes passed by the Congress of the United States of America from 1789 to 1827 inclusive... Pub. under the inspection of Joseph Story. Boston, Wells & Lilly, 1828. 3 vols. ICN; MH-L; PP; TNJ; WHi.   36730

---- Public lands. Letter from the Commissioner of the General Land Office to the Hon. Mr. Haile, of the House of Representatives. Jan. 10, 1828. Pr. by order of the House of Representatives. Washington, Pr. by Gales & Seaton, 1828. 6 p. (Doc. No. 53) DLC; NjR.   36731

---- Public lands in market from five to twenty years. Letter from the Secretary of the Treasury transmitting the information required by a resolution of the House of Representatives of 18th February last in relation to the public land now unsold which has been in market for five years and under; from five to ten years; from ten to fifteen years; and from fifteen to twenty years, and upwards &c. Feb. 21, 1828. Read, and laid upon the table. Washington, Pr. by Gales & Seaton, 1828. 13 p. 1 bdsd. (Doc. No. 255) DLC; NjR.   36732

---- Rail road company - Baltimore and Ohio. Dec. 23, 1828. Referred to the Committee on Roads and Canals. Memorial. Washington, Pr. by Gales & Seaton, 1828. 2 p. (Doc. No. 48) CtY; DBRE; DLC; DeGE; MB; MH; NN; NjR; P.   36733

---- Rebecca Blodget. Feb. 22, 1828. Mr. Livingston, from the Committee on the Judiciary, to which was referred the petition of Rebecca Blodget, made the following report: Washington, Gales & Seaton, 1828. 3 p. (Rep. No. 157) DLC; NjR.   36734

---- Rebecca Guest. Mar. 12, 1828. Mr. Ramsey, from the Committee of Claims, to which was referred the petition of Rebecca Guest, made the following report: Washington, Gales & Seaton, 1828. 2 p. (Rep. No. 186) DLC; NjR.   36735

---- Recaptured Africans. Letter from the Secretary of the Navy, transmitting the information required by a resolution of the House of Representatives, of the 5th instant, in relation to the present condition and probable annual expense of the United States Agency for Recaptured Africans on the coast of Africa, &c. &c. Mar. 12, 1828. Referred to Committee of Ways and Means. Washington, Pr. by Gales & Seaton, 1828. 15 p. (Doc. No. 193) DLC; NjR. 36736

---- Reduce duties on wines. Jan. 30, 1828. Mr. Cambreleng, from the Committee on Commerce, to which the subject had been referred, made the following report: Washington, Pr. by Gales & Seaton, 1828. 5 p. (Rep. No. 111) DLC; NjR. 36737

---- Reduction of duty on tea. Memorial of merchants of Philadelphia respecting a reduction of duty on teas. Jan. 21, 1828. Read, and referred to the Committee on Commerce. Jan. 30, 1828. Referred to the Committee on Ways and Means. Washington, Pr. by Gales & Seaton, 1828. 4 p. (Doc. No. 109) DLC; NjR. 36738

---- Register of the commissioned and warrant officers of the Navy of the United States; including officers of the Marine Corps, &c. for the year 1829. Pr. by order of the Secretary of the Navy, in compliance with a resolution of the Senate of the United States, of August 2, 1813. City of Washington, S. A. Elliot, pr., 1828 62 p. MdHi. 36739

---- Remonstrance of the General Assembly of Alabama, on the subject of protecting duties, and adverse to an increase. Feb. 5, 1828. Referred to the Committee on Manufactures, and ordered to be printed. Washington, Duff Green, 1828. 6 p. (Doc. No. 86) DLC; NjR. 36740

---- Repair Cumberland Road. Letter from the Secretary of War, transmitting a report of the superintendent of the Cumberland Road, relative to the mode of repairing the same. Jan. 14, 1828. Read, and referred to the Committee on Roads and Canals. Washington, Pr. by Gales & Seaton, 1828. 8 p. (Doc. No. 57) DLC; NjR. 36741

---- Report - Commissioners Sinking Fund. Annual report of the Commissioners of the Sinking Fund. Feb. 6, 1828. Read, and laid upon the table. Washington, Pr. by Gales & Seaton, 1828. 18 p. (Doc. No. 121) DLC; NjR. 36742

---- Report from the commissioner of the General Land Office, made in compliance with a resolution of the Senate, of the 25th April, 1828... Washington, Duff Green, 1828. 84 p. (Rep. No. 9) DLC; NjR. 36743

---- Report from the commissioner of the General Land Office, relative to a quarter section of land purchased by Henry Case. Made in compliance with a resolution of the Senate of the 21st instant. Apr. 24, 1828. Referred to the Committee on Public Lands, and ordered to be printed. Washington, Duff Green, 1828. 4 p. (Doc. No. 176) DLC; NjR. 36744

---- Report from the Postmaster General, with a list of the post roads established more than two years, and which do not produce one-third of the expense of transporting the mail on the same. Dec. 30, 1828. Read, and ordered to be printed. Washington,

Duff Green, 1828. 13 p. (Doc. No. 20) DLC; DeGE (14 p.); NjR.

36745

---- Report from the Postmaster General, with a statement of the contracts made by that department in 1827. Apr. 25, 1828. Pr. by order of the Senate of the United States. Washington, Pr. by Duff Green, 1828. 36 p. (Doc. No. 177) DLC; NjR.   36746

---- Report from the Secretary of the Navy, in compliance with a resolution of the Senate of 20th May, 1826, in relation to the difficulties in obtaining seamen for the Navy, the cause of such difficulties, and the measures necessary to remove them. May 26, 1828. Pr. by order of the Senate of the United States. Washington, Duff Green, 1828. 11 p. (Doc. No. 207) DLC; NjR.   36747

---- Report from the Secretary of the Treasury (in compliance with a resolution of the Senate of the 10th instant) showing unexpended balances of appropriation on the first day of each year, from 1817 to 1827; amount of surplus money, above sums appropriated, at the adjournment of Congress, from 1817 to 1827; and in what years of said term any part of said surplus, and how much, was paid into the Sinking Fund. Mar. 26, 1828. Referred to the Committee on Finance, and ordered to be printed. Washington, Pr. by Duff Green, 1828. 5 p. 2 bdsds. (Doc. No. 155) DLC; NjR.   36748

---- Report from the Secretary of the Treasury, on the state of the finances.   Made 9th December, 1828.   Washington, Duff Green, 1828.   38 p. (Doc. No. 7) DLC; NjR.   36749

---- Report from the Secretary of the Treasury, with a statement of the value and amount of duties on certain cotton goods imported into the U. S. from 1817 to 1827, inclusive, made in compliance with a resolution of the Senate of the 5th of March 1828. Mar. 10, 1828. Pr. by order of the Senate of the United States. Washington, Pr. by Duff Green, 1828. 5 p. (Doc. No. 133) DLC; NjR.   36750

---- Report from the Secretary of the Treasury, with statements showing the disbursements of that Department, for the purposes therein mentioned. Jan. 29, 1828. Pr. by order of the Senate of the United States. Washington, Duff Green, 1828. 12 p. 6 bdsds. (Doc. No. 73) DLC; NjR. 36751

---- Report from the Secretary of the Treasury, with the annual statement of the commerce and navigation of the United States, for the year ending on the 30th of September, 1827. April 21, 1828. Pr. by order of the Senate of the United States. Washington, Duff Green, 1828. 308 p. 2 bdsds. (Doc. No. 174) DLC; NjR. 36752

---- Report from the Secretary of War (in compliance with a resolution of the Senate of the 10th instant) with report and plan of the survey of the harbor of Marblehead, Massachusetts. Jan. 15, 1828. Pr. by order of the Senate of the United States. Washington, Pr. by Duff Green, 1828. 8 p. (Doc. No. 40) DLC; NjR.

36753

---- Report from the Secretary of War, in compliance with a resolution of the Senate of the 11th instant, with statements showing amount paid to officers of the army, on account of Brevet Rank, in 1827, &c. March 28, 1828. Pr. by order of the Senate of the

United States. Washington, Pr. by Duff Green, 1828. 11 p. (Doc. No. 157) DLC; NjR.   36754

---- Report from the Secretary of War, in relation to lead and lead mines in Missouri. Apr. 8, 1828. Pr. by order of the Senate of the United States. Washington, Pr. by Duff Green, 1828. 7 p. 2 bdsds. (Doc. No. 169) DLC; NjR.   36755

---- Report from the Secretary of War with a report and plan of the survey of the Island of Nantucket, in compliance with a resolution of the Senate of the 10th instant. Jan. 18, 1828. Pr. by order of the Senate of the United States. Washington, Pr. by Duff Green, 1828. 20 p. (Doc. No. 44) DLC; NjR.   36756

---- Report from the Secretary of War, with abstract of licenses granted to trade with the Indians, during the year ending on the 1st September, 1827. Feb. 8, 1828. Pr. by order of the Senate of the United States. Washington, Duff Green, 1828. 3 p. 4 bdsds. (Doc. No. 96) DLC; NjR.   36757

---- Report from the Secretary of War with statements showing the different sums paid to persons appointed as visitors of the Military Academy at West Point from 1817 to 1827, to defray their expenses, &c. Mar. 3, 1828. Pr. by order of the Senate of the United States. Washington, Pr. by Duff Green, 1828. 7 p. (Doc. No. 128) DLC; NjR.   36758

---- Report of a joint committee of the Legislature of Georgia on the subject of running and marking the line dividing the territory of Florida from the state of Georgia. Jan. 29, 1828. Pr. by order of the Senate of the United States. Washington, Pr. by Duff Green, 1828. 7 p. (Doc. No. 56) DLC; NjR.   36759

---- Report of a special committee of the Senate of South Carolina on the resolutions submitted by Mr. Ramsay on the subject of state rights. Jan. 11, 1828. Pr. by order of the Senate of the United States. Washington, Pr. by Duff Green, 1828. 19 p. (Doc. No. 29) DLC; NjR.   36760

---- Report of the Joint Committee on the state of the Republic, on the Florida boundary, and the documents on which the report is founded in the House of Representatives; Dec. 4, 1828 - Read and ordered to be printed. Milledgeville, Camak & Bagland, prs., 1828. 21 p. MB.   36761

---- Report of the Joint Select Committee of the Legislature of the state of North Carolina on the alteration of the tariff contemplated by the woollens bill. Jan. 11, 1828. Pr. by order of the Senate of the United States. Washington, Pr. by Duff Green, 1828. 5 p. (Doc. No. 30) DLC; NjR.   36762

---- Report of the Postmaster General, with a statement showing the Post Roads which have been established more than two years, and which do not produce one-third of the expense incurred by transporting the mail on the same. Feb. 13, 1828. Referred to the Committee on the Post Office and Post Roads, and ordered to be printed. Washington, Duff Green, 1828. 45 p. (Doc. No. 102) DLC; NjR.   36763

---- Report of the Secretary of State, showing the names and salaries of the clerks employed in the department, in the year 1827. Feb. 12, 1828. Pr. by order of

the Senate of the United States. Washington, Duff Green, 1828. 4 p. (Doc. No. 98) DLC; NjR.
36764

---- Report of the Secretary of the Navy, (In compliance with a resolution of the Senate,) showing the number of midshipmen appointed during the present session of Congress. May 23, 1828. Pr. by order of the Senate of the United States. Washington, Duff Green, 1828. 6 p. (Doc. No. 204) DLC; NjR.   36765

---- Report of the Secretary of the Navy, with a plan for a naval peace establishment of the United States. (In compliance with a resolution of the Senate, of the 28th Feb., 1827.) Jan. 15, 1828. Pr. by order of the Senate of the United States. Washington, Pr. by Duff Green, 1828. 9 p. (Doc. No. 36) DLC; NjR.   36766

---- Report of the Secretary of the Navy, with a statement of the contracts made by the Commissioners of the Navy Board, during the year 1827. Feb. 12, 1828. Pr. by order of the Senate of the United States. Washington, Duff Green 1828. 8 p. 1 bdsd. (Doc. No. 100) DLC; DeGE (10 p.); NjR.   36767

---- Report of the Secretary of the Navy, with statements showing the appropriations for the naval service for 1827; the expenditures under each specific head; and the balances remaining unexpended under each head, on the 31st of Dec. 1827. Feb. 15, 1828. Pr. by order of the Senate of the United States. Washington, Duff Green, 1828. 6 p. 2 bdsds. (Doc. No. 105) DLC; NjR. 36768

---- Report of the Secretary of the Navy, with statements showing the operations of the Navy

Pension Fund, and relief afforded thereby in 1827. Mar. 14, 1828. Pr. by order of the Senate of the United States. Washington, Pr. by Duff Green, 1828. 24 p. 1 bdsd. (Doc. No. 139) DLC; NjR. 36769

---- Report of the Secretary of the Senate, showing the expenditures of the contingent fund of the Senate, for the year 1828. Washington, Duff Green, 1828. 4 p. (Doc. No. 2) DLC; NjR.   36770

---- Report of the Secretary of the Treasury, in compliance with a resolution of the Senate of the 12th instant, showing the average annual amount of moneys in the bank of the United States, and its branches, from the year 1817 to 1827 inclusive. Mar. 24, 1828. Referred to the Committee on Finance, and ordered to be printed. Washington, Pr. by Duff Green, 1828. 4 p. (Doc. No. 154) DLC; NjR.   36771

---- Report of the Secretary of the Treasury, showing the moneys in the hands of Thomas A. Smith, Receiver of Public Moneys, at Franklin, Missouri; and amounts of deposites, and instructions given to him on the subject. Apr. 3, 1828. Read, and referred to the Committee on the Judiciary - April 29, report made - May 6, ordered to be printed. Washington, Duff Green, 1828. 61 p. (Doc. No. 193) DLC; NjR. 36772

---- Report of the Secretary of the Treasury. Supplemental to the annual report on the state of the finances of the United States, from that department, dated 8th Dec. last. May 16, 1828. Pr. by order of the Senate of the United States. Washington, Duff Green, 1828. 9 p. (Doc. No. 197) DLC; NjR.   36773

---- Report of the Secretary of the Treasury with a letter from the Register and Receiver of Public Moneys for the district of East Florida; transmitting their report and decisions upon private land claims, under the fifth section of the act of Feb. 8, 1827. Jan. 30, 1828... Washington, Duff Green, 1828. 16 p. (Doc. No. 164) Nj; NjR.   36774

---- ---- Referred to the Committee on Public Lands, and ordered to be printed. Washington, Duff Green, 1828. 59 p. 6 bdsds. (Doc. No. 76) DLC; NjR.   36775

---- Report of the Secretary of the Treasury, with statements of emoluments of the officers of the customs, in 1827. Mar. 17, 1828. Referred to the Committee on Commerce, and ordered to be printed. Washington, Pr. by Duff Green, 1828. 4 p. 6 bdsds. (Doc. No. 141) DLC; NjR.   36776

---- Report of the Secretary of the Treasury, with statements of the register and receiver of the land office at St. Stephen's, in Alabama, relative to land claims in that district; with a supplemental report on the claim of Lewis Judson, and the names of the Spanish commandments of Mobile. Mar. 28, 1828. Read, and ordered to be printed - Apr. 2d, 1828, referred to the Committee on Public Lands. Washington, Pr. by Duff Green, 1828. 19 p. 13 bdsds. DLC; NjR.   36777

---- Report of the Secretary of the Treasury, with statements showing the product of the customs for the years 1824, '5 and '6. Also, an average of the same. Prepared in obedience to a resolution of the Senate of the 12th instant. Mar. 28, 1828. Referred to the Committee on Finance, and ordered to be printed. Washington, Pr. by Duff Green, 1828. 13 p. (Doc. No. 158) DLC; NjR.   36778

---- Report of the Secretary of War, in compliance with a resolution of the Senate, of the eighth instant, transmitting a report of the commissioner for locating the continuation of the Cumberland road, under act of Mar. 3, 1825. Feb. 12, 1828. Referred to the Committee on Roads and Canals, and ordered to be printed. Washington, Duff Green, 1828. 18 p. 1 bdsd. (Doc. No. 99) DLC; NjR.   36779

---- Report of the Secretary of War, in compliance with the resolution of the Senate of the 13th instant, with statements showing the reasons that induced the department to postpone the expenditure of the appropriation of the last session, for the removal of obstructions at the mouth of the Pascagoula Bay. Mar. 19, 1828. Pr. by order of the Senate of the United States. Washington, Pr. by Duff Green, 1828. 9 p. (Doc. No. 147) DLC; NjR.   36780

---- Report of the Secretary of War, showing that progress has been made in deepening and clearing the channel, at a place called the Grand Chain. May 22, 1828. Pr. by order of the Senate of the United States. Washington, Duff Green, 1828. 7 p. (Doc. No. 203) DLC; NjR.   36781

---- Report of the Secretary of War, showing the appropriations for 1827, the amount expended, and the balance remaining unexpended, under each specific head, on the 31st of Dec. last. Feb. 8, 1828. Pr. by order of the Senate of the United States. Washington, Duff Green, 1828. 5 p. 4 bdsds. (Doc. No. 93) DLC; NjR. 36782

---- Report of the Secretary of War, with a statement of contracts made by that department in 1827. Jan. 29, 1828. Pr. by order of the Senate of the United States. Washington, Pr. by Duff Green, 1828. 3 p. 18 bdsds. (Doc. No. 72) DLC; NjR.   36783

---- Report of the Secretary of War, with an abstract of the annual returns of the Militia of the United States. Feb. 8, 1828. Pr. by order of the Senate of the United States. Washington, Duff Green, 1828. 3 p. 2 bdsds. (Doc. No. 94) DLC; NjR.   36784

---- Reports and proceedings of Col. McKenney on the subject of his recent tour among the southern Indians, as submitted to Congress with the message of the President U. S.   Washington, Pr. by Gales & Seaton, 1828. 37 p. DeGE; MH; MWA.   36785

---- Reports of cases argued and adjudged in the Supreme court of the United States. January term, 1828--January term, 1843. By Richard Peters, junior ... Philadelphia, P. H. Nicklin, L. R. Bailey, pr., 1828-43. 17 v. CtY; DLC; IU; IaHi; KyLxT; M; MB; MdBB; Me-LR; Mi-L; Ms; NNLI; OCHP; PPiU-L; PU-L; RPB; RPL; ViU; WaU.   36786

---- Reports - registers &c. St. Stephen's. Letter from the Secretary of the Treasury, transmitting two reports made by the register and receiver of the land office for the District of St. Stephen's, in the state of Alabama. Mar. 28, 1828. Read, and referred to the Committee on the Public Lands. May 10, 1828. Bill reported, No. 297, and printed by order of the House of Representatives. Washington, Pr. by Gales & Seaton, 1828. 19 p.

8 bdsds. (Doc. No. 285) DLC; NjR.   36787

---- Representatives of James Davenport. Apr. 23, 1828. Read, and with the bill committed to the Committee of the Whole House to which is committed the bill for the relief of William Tipton. Mr. Long, from the Committee on Military Pensions, to which was referred the petition of the legal representatives of James Davenport, deceased, made the following report: Washington, Gales & Seaton, 1828. 2 p. (Rep. No. 237) DLC; NjR.   36788

---- Representatives of John P. Cox. Jan. 4, 1828. Mr. McIntire, from the Committee of Claims, to which had been referred the petition of Emilie Cox, made the following report: Washington, Gales & Seaton, 1828. 3 p. (Rep. No. 52) DLC; NjR.
36789

---- Reps. John Ellis, deceased. Dec. 29, 1828. Mr. Buckner, from the Committee on Private Land Claims, to which was referred the petition of the heirs and representatives of John Ellis, deceased, made the following report: Washington, Pr. by Gales & Seaton, 1828. 2 p. (Rep. No. 20) DLC; NjR.   36790

---- Reservations under the Cherokee treaty. Letter from the Secretary of War transmitting a list of persons entitled to reservations under the treaty with the Cherokees on the 27th February, 1819, &c. Jan. 23, 1828. Read, and laid on the table. Washington, Pr. by Gales & Seaton, 1828. 7 p. (Doc. No. 104) DLC; NjR.
36791

---- Resolution amendatory of a joint resolution, passed on the third of March, one thousand eight hundred and nineteen. Dec.

17, 1828. Referred to the Committee on the Judiciary. [Washington, 1828] 1 p. (S. 2) DNA.
36792

---- Resolution amendatory of a joint resolution, passed 3d of March, 1819. Introduced on leave by Mr. Eaton. --Dec. 15th, 1828, read and passed to second reading--Dec. 16th, read second time, and considered in Committee of the Whole, and ordered to be printed, with the following offered as an amendment, by Mr. Knight. [Washington, 1828] 1 p. (S. 2) DNA.
36793

---- Resolution, authorizing the Speaker of the House of Representatives to frank letters and packages. [Washington, 1828] 1 p. (H. R. 8) DNA.
36794

---- Resolution directing an examination of the printing of Congress, with a view to correct the errors in the same. May 22, 1828. Read the first time, and laid on the table. Mr. Wickliffe, from the Committee on Retrenchment, reported the following resolution: [Washington, 1828] 3 p. (H. R. 11) DNA.
36795

---- Resolution, directing the Secretary of War to publish a list of the officers and soldiers of the Revolution entitled to land, who have not applied therefor. Jan. 15, 1828. Mr. Van Buren, from the Committee on the Judiciary, to whom the subject was referred, reported the following. [Washington, 1828] 1 p. (S. 1) DNA.
36796

---- Resolution in relation to the mail route between the cities of New Orleans and Mobile. May 20, 1828. --Received. [Washington, 1828] 1 p. (H. R. 12) DNA.
36797

---- Resolution in relation to the powers of the general government, on the subject of internal improvement. Dec. 16, 1828. Read the first time, and laid upon the table. Dec. 17, 1828. Read twice, and laid upon the table. [Washington, 1828] 1 p. (H. R. 1) DNA.
36798

No entry.
36799

---- Resolution. Jan. 11, 1828. Mr. Sloane submitted the following resolution, which was read, and ordered to lie upon the table for one day: [Washington, 1828] 2 p. (H. R. 6) DNA.
36800

---- Resolution of the General Assembly of Indiana in favor of the encouragement of domestic manufactures and internal improvements. Feb. 20, 1828. Referred to the Committees on Manufactures, and on Roads and Canals, and ordered to be printed. Washington, Pr. by Duff Green, 1828. 3 p. (Doc. No. 113) DLC; NjR.
36801

---- Resolution of the General Assembly of Indiana, relative to the western mail route from Louisville, Kentucky to St. Louis, Missouri... Feb. 20, 1828. Referred to the Committee on Roads and Canals, and ordered to be printed. Washington, Pr. by Duff Green, 1828. 3 p. (Doc. No. 112) DLC; NjR.
36802

---- Resolution of the Legislative Council of Florida on the expediency of providing for the graduation of the price of public lands in that territory. Jan. 17, 1828.

Pr. by order of the Senate of the United States. Washington, Pr. by Duff Green, 1828. 4 p. (Doc. No. 43) DLC; NjR; PU. 36803

---- Resolution of the Legislature of Alabama, proposing amendments to the Constitution of the United States. Feb. 5, 1828. Pr. by order of the Senate of the United States. Washington, Duff Green, 1828. 4 p. (Doc. No. 85) DLC; NjR. 36804

---- Resolution of the Legislature of Indiana requesting from the government, copies of the Journal of the Federal Convention, Journals of the two Houses of Congress, and printed documents, &c. Feb. 21, 1828. Referred to the Committee on the Library, and ordered to be printed. Washington, Pr. by Duff Green, 1828. 3 p. (Doc. No. 117) DLC; NjR. 36805

---- Resolution of the Legislature of Pennsylvania instructing their senators, and requesting their representatives in Congress to procure the establishment of such a tariff as will afford additional protection to domestic manufactures. Jan. 29, 1828. Referred to a Committee on Manufactures, and ordered to be printed. Washington, Pr. by Duff Green, 1828. 4 p. (Doc. No. 71) DLC; NjR. 36806

---- Resolution of the state of Rhode Island and Providence Plantations on the subject of protecting duties, &c. Jan. 28, 1828. Referred to the Committee on Manufactures, and ordered to be printed. Washington, Pr. by Duff Green, 1828. 3 p. (Doc. No. 63) DLC; NjR. 36807

---- Resolution submitted by Mr. Gilmer. Treaties with Creek Indians. Mar. 21, 1828. Laid on the table for consideration. [Washington, 1828] 1 p. (H. R. 10) DNA. 36808

---- Resolution to amend the Constitution. Dec. 19, 1827. Read, and committed to a Committee of the Whole House on the state of the Union. Dec. 12, 1828. Repr. by order of the House of Representatives. Mr. Smyth of Virginia, submitted the following proposition to amend the Constitution of the United States. [Washington, 1828] 3 p. (H. R. 2) DNA. 36809

---- Resolution to amend the Constitution. Dec. 19, 1827. Read, and committed to the Committee of the Whole House on the state of the Union. Dec. 12, 1828. Repr. by order of the House of Representatives. Dec. 18, 1828. Considered in Committee of the Whole House on the state of the Union. Dec. 19, 1828. Committee of the Whole discharged, and resolution laid on the table. Mr. Smyth, of Virginia, submitted the following proposition to amend the Constitution of the United States. [Washington, 1828] 3 p. (H. R. 2) DNA. 36810

---- Resolution to authorize the President to loan the barracks at Sackett's Harbor, to the trustees of a scientific and military school to be established there. May 1st. --Received. May 2d--Read, and passed to a second reading. [Washington, 1828] 1 p. (H. R. 10) DNA. 36811

---- Resolution to provide for the repair and preservation of the Cumberland Road, and other roads made by the federal government within the limits of the different states. May 6, 1828. Agreeably to notice given, Mr. Benton asked and obtained leave to bring in the following resolution; which was read, and passed to a second reading. [Washington, 1828] 1 p. (S. 2) DNA.   36812

---- Resolutions - Legislature New Jersey - tariff. Report of a committee, and resolutions of the General Assembly of New Jersey, upon the subject of the constitutional power of the general government to enact laws for the protection of manufactures, &c. &c. Mar. 15, 1828. Referred to the Committee of the Whole House on the State of the Union to which is committed the bill in alteration of the several acts imposing duties on imports. Washington, Pr. by Gales & Seaton, 1828. 4 p. (Doc. No. 198) DLC; NjR.
36813

---- Resolutions and report of a Committee of the General Assembly of Ohio favorable to the exercise, by the General Government of the power to protect domestic manufactures. Feb. 26, 1828. Referred to the Committee on Manufactures and ordered to be printed. Washington, Pr. by Duff Green, 1828. 12 p. (Doc. No. 124) DLC; NjR.   36814

---- Resolutions of the citizens of York District, South Carolina, opposed to increase of duties on imports, &c. &c. Feb. 20, 1828. Referred to the Committee on Manufactures, and ordered to be printed. Washington, Pr. by Duff Green, 1828. 4 p. (Doc. No. 115) DLC; NjR.   36815

---- Resolutions of the General Assembly of Indiana, that further relief be extended to purchasers of public lands. Feb. 20, 1828. Referred to the Committee on Public Lands, and ordered to be printed. Washington, Pr. by Duff Green, 1828. 4 p. (Doc. No. 114) DLC; NjR.   36816

---- Resolutions of the General Assembly of Ohio dissenting from the opinions contained in certain resolutions of the Legislature of South Carolina, denying the power of the general government over internal improvements and protection of domestic manufactures. Feb. 26, 1828. Pr. by order of the Senate of the United States. Washington, Pr. by order of the Senate of the United States. Washington, Pr. by Duff Green, 1828. 5 p. (Doc. No. 123) DLC; NjR.
36817

---- Resolutions of the Legislature of Georgia, in relation to the American Colonization Society. Feb. 4, 1828. Pr. by order of the Senate of the United States. Washington, Duff Green, 1828. 11 p. (Doc. No. 81) DLC; NjR.
36818

---- Resolutions of the Legislature of Georgia, requesting the senators and representatives from that state, in Congress, to use their best exertions to obtain the extinguishment of the title of the Cherokee Indians to land in the state of Georgia. Feb. 4, 1828. Referred to the Committee on Indian Affairs, and ordered to be printed. Washington, Duff Green, 1828. 13 p. (Doc. No. 80) DLC; NjR.   36819

---- Resolutions passed at a meeting of certain manufactures of Philadelphia and others of the city and county of Philadelphia in favor of an increase of duties on imports for the protection of domestic manufactures. Mar. 3, 1828. Referred to the Committee on Manufactures, and ordered to be printed. Washington, Pr. by Duff Green, 1828. 4 p. (Doc. No. 127) DLC; NjR.   36820

---- Resolutions: public lands for popular education. May 26th, 1828. Read and laid upon the table. Mr. Mercer submitted the

following. [Washington, 1828] 1 p.
(H. R. 13) DNA.   36821

---- Resolutions submitted by Mr.
Davis, of S. C. May 26th, 1828.
Read, and laid upon the table.
Mr. Davis, of South Carolina,
submitted the following resolu-
tions: [Washington, 1828] 1 p.
(H. R. 14) DNA.   36822

---- Rhode Island - citizens of
Bristol. Memorial of citizens of
Bristol, in the state of Rhode Is-
land, against an increase of duty
on certain imported manufactures.
Mar. 3, 1828. Read, and laid up-
on the table. Washington, Pr. by
Gales & Seaton, 1828. 4 p. (Doc.
No. 177) DLC; NjR.   36823

---- Rhode Island. Memorial of
a committee in behalf of cotton
manufacturers, of Providence, in
the state of Rhode Island. Feb.
11, 1828. Referred to the Committee of the Whole House, to
which is committed the bill (No.
132) in alteration of the several
acts imposing duties on imports.
Washington, Pr. by Gales & Seaton, 1828. 4 p. (Doc. No. 133)
DLC; NjR.   36824

---- ---- Memorial of citizens
of the town of Warren, in the
state of Rhode Island, against an
increase of duty on molasses imported, &c. Feb. 25, 1828. Read,
and laid upon the table. Washington, Pr. by Gales & Seaton, 1828.
5 p. (Doc. No. 160) DLC; NjR.
                              36825
---- ---- Memorial of the farmers and manufacturers of the
county of Kent, in the state of
Rhode Island, praying for further
protection to domestic manufactures. Jan. 14, 1828. Referred
to the committee on manufactures.
Washington, Pr. by Gales & Seaton, 1828. 4 p. (Doc. No. 64)
DLC; NjR.   36826

---- ---- Petition of inhabitants
of Newport, Rhode Island, distil-
lers of rum and importers of molasses, against an increase of duty on molasses. Feb. 4, 1828.
Read, and laid upon the table.
Washington, Pr. by Gales & Seaton, 1828. 3 p. (Doc. No. 118)
DLC; NjR.   36827

---- ---- Representation of sundry citizens of Providence, in the
state of Rhode Island, upon the
subject of an increased duty on
certain imports. Mar. 3, 1828.
Read, and laid upon the table.
Washington, Pr. by Gales & Seaton, 1828. 5 p. (Doc. No. 174)
DLC; NjR.   36828

---- ---- Resolution of the General Assembly of Rhode Island in
favor of further protection to domestic manufactures. Jan. 28,
1828. Read, and laid upon the
table. Washington, Pr. by Gales
& Seaton, 1828. 3 p. (Doc. No.
98) DLC; NjR.   36829

---- Richard Biddle, administrator of John Wilkins. Dec. 12,
1828. Mr. Whittlesey, from the
Committee of Claims, to which
was referred the petition of Richard Biddle, administrator of General John Wilkins, made the following report: Washington, Pr.
by Gales & Seaton, 1828. 1 p.
(Rep. No. 3) DLC; NjR.   36830

---- Richard Drummond. Mar. 3,
1828. Read, and laid upon the
table. Mr. Williams, from the
Committee of Claims to which was
referred the petition of Richard
Drummond, made the following
report: Washington, Gales & Seaton, 1828. 3 p. (Rep. No. 176)
DLC; NjR.   36831

---- Richard Eppes. Mar. 12,
1828. Mr. Whittlesey from the
Committee of Claims, to which

was referred the petition of Richard Eppes, made the following report: Washington, Gales & Seaton, 1828. 2 p. (Rep. No. 187) DLC; NjR. 36832

---- Richard G. Morriss. Feb. 5, 1828. Read, and committed to the Committee of the Whole House to which is committed the bill for the relief of Benjamin Simmons. Mr. Wolf, from the Committee on Revolutionary Claims, to which was referred the petition of Richard G. Morriss made the following report: Washington, Pr. by Gales & Seaton, 1828. 3 p. (Rep. No. 127) DLC; NjR. 36833

---- Richard H. Wilde. Jan. 14, 1828. Read, and, with the bill, laid upon the table. Mr. Wickliffe, from the Committee on the Judiciary, to which had been referred the bill from the Senate entitled "An act to authorize the cancelling of a bond, therein mentioned" made the following report: Washington, Pr. by Gales & Seaton, 1828. 4 p. (Rep. No. 76) DLC; NjR. 36834

---- ---- Petition of Richard H. Wilde. Dec. 17, 1827. Referred to the Committee on the Judiciary. Dec. 20, 1827. Bill reported, No. 17. Jan. 14, 1828. Pr. by order of the House of Representatives. Washington, Pr. by Gales & Seaton, 1828. 8 p. (Doc. No. 56) DLC; NjR. 36835

---- Richard Peacock. Feb. 15, 1828. Read, and laid upon the table. Mar. 14, 1828. Committed to a Committee of the Whole House to-morrow. Mr. Hunt, from the Committee on Revolutionary Claims, to which was referred the petition of Richard Peacock, made the following report: Washington, Gales & Seaton, 1828. 4 p. (Rep. No. 193) DLC; NjR. 36836

---- Richard W. Meade. Jan. 8, 1828. Mr. Everett, from the Committee on Foreign Affairs, to which had been referred the petition of Richard W. Meade, made the following report: Washington, Gales & Seaton, 1828. 101 p. (Rep. No. 58) CSmH (88 p.); DLC; NjR. 36837

---- Richard W. Steele. Apr. 8, 1828. Mr. Buckner, from the Committee on Private Land Claims, to which was referred the petition of Richard W. Steele, made the following report: Washington, Gales & Seaton, 1828. 3 p. (Rep. No. 229) DLC; NjR. 36838

---- Richard Wall. Jan. 7, 1828. Read, and laid upon the table. April 28, 1828. Recommitted to the Committee on Revolutionary Claims. May 5, 1828. Second report, to lie. May 9, 1828. Committed to a Committee of the Whole House to-morrow. Mr. Wolf, from the Committee on Revolutionary Claims, to which was referred the case of Richard Wall, made the following report: Washington, Gales & Seaton, 1828. 9 p. (Rep. No. 251) DLC; NjR. 36839

---- Riddle, Becktill, and Headington. Mar. 3, 1828. Mr. Ramsey, from the Committee of Claims, to which was referred the petition of Riddle, Becktill, and Headington, made the following report: Washington, Gales & Seaton, 1828. 2 p. (Rep. No. 173) DLC; NjR. 36840

---- Road - Baltimore to Philadelphia. May 13, 1828. Mr. Mercer, from the Committee on Roads and Canals, to which the subject had been referred, made the following report: Washington, Gales & Seaton, 1828. 2 p. (Rep.

No. 254) DLC; N̲j̲R̲.   36841

---- Road - Homochitto Swamp.
Jan. 24, 1828. Mr. Stewart, from
the Committee on Roads and Canals, to which the subject had
been referred, made the following report: Washington, Pr. by
Gales & Seaton, 1828. 10 p. (Rep.
No. 97) DLC; N̲j̲R̲.   36842

---- Road - Lawrenceburg to
Fort Wayne, Indiana. Apr. 15,
1828. Mr. Woods, of Ohio, from
the Committee on Roads and Canals, to which the subject had
been referred, made the following report: Washington, Gales
& Seaton, 1828. 3 p. (Rep. No.
234) DLC; N̲j̲R̲.   36843

---- Road - Memphis to Tuscumbia. May 13, 1828. Mr. Mercer,
from the Committee on Roads
and Canals, to which the subject
had been referred, made the following report: Washington, Gales
& Seaton, 1828. 1 p. (Rep. No.
256) DLC; N̲j̲R̲.   36844

---- Road - Penobscot River to
New Brunswick. Mar. 27, 1828.
Mr. Davis, of Massachusetts,
from the Committee on Roads and
Canals, to which the subject had
been referred, made the follow-
ing report: Washington, Gales &
Seaton, 1828. 2 p. (Rep. No. 214)
DLC; N̲j̲R̲.   36845

---- Road - Union town, through
Pittsburg, to Lake Erie. May 21,
1828. Read, and laid upon the
table. Mr. Stewart, from the
Committee on Roads and Canals,
to which the subject had been referred, made the following report:
Washington, Gales & Seaton, 1828.
6 p. (Rep. No. 267) DLC; DeGE;
N̲j̲R̲.   36846

---- Road - Washington to New
Orleans. Jan. 2, 1828. Mr. Mercer, from the Committee on
Roads and Canals, to which the
subject had been referred, made
the following report: Washington,
Gales & Seaton, 1828. 26 p. 1
bdsd. (Rep. No. 48) DLC; DeGE;
N̲j̲R̲.   36847

---- Road - Washington to northwest part of New York. Letter
from the Secretary of War transmitting a report from the engineer appointed to examine a route
for a national road from the city
of Washington to the northwestern
frontier of the state of New York.
Dec. 29, 1828. Referred to the
Committee on Roads and Canals.
Washington, Pr. by Gales & Seaton, 1828. 22 p. 1 bdsd. (Doc.
No. 38) DLC; N̲j̲R̲.   36848

---- Road - Washington to north-
western parts of New York and
Pennsylvania. Jan. 21, 1828. Mr.
Mercer, from the Committee on
Roads and Canals, to which the
subject had been referred, made
the following report: Washington,
Pr. by Gales & Seaton, 1828. 43
p. 3 bdsds. (Rep. No. 91) DLC;
DeGE; N̲j̲R̲.   36849

---- Road - Wiggins' Ferry to
lead mines on Fever River. Mar.
4, 1828. Mr. Mercer, from the
Committee on Roads and Canals,
to which the subject had been referred, made the following report: Washington, Gales & Seaton, 1828. 3 p. (Rep. No. 177)
DLC; N̲j̲R̲.   36850

---- Road - Zaneville, Ohio, to
Florence, Alabama. Letter from
the Secretary of War, transmitting a report of the reconnoissance of a route for a national
road, from Zaneville, Ohio, to
Florence, Alabama. Mar. 18,
1828. Read, and laid upon the
table. Washington, Pr. by Gales
& Seaton, 1828. 44 p. (Doc. No.

209) DLC; NjR.   36851

---- Road from Columbus to New
Orleans. Letter from the Postmaster General in reply to a
resolution of the House of Representatives of the last session in
relation to the probable cost required for the repairs of the road
from Columbus passing through
the Choctaw nation to New Orleans, &c. &c. Dec. 22, 1828.
Read, and referred to the Committee on the Post Office and
Post Roads. Washington, Pr. by
Gales & Seaton, 1828. 4 p. (Doc.
No. 23) DLC; NjR.   36852

---- Road through the Wyandot
Reservation, &c. Letter from the
Postmaster General transmitting
the information required by a resolution of the House of Representatives of the 8th inst. in relation to a road through the Wyandot Reservation, between Cincinnati and Portland in the state
of Ohio, &c. &c. Jan. 21, 1828.
Read, and referred to the Committee on roads and canals.
Washington, Pr. by Gales & Seaton, 1828. 3 p. (Doc. No. 73)
DLC; NjR.   36853

---- Roads and canals. May 26,
1828. Read, and laid upon the
table. Mr. Mercer, from the
Committee on Roads and Canals,
made the following report: Washington, Gales & Seaton, 1828. 16
p. (Rep. No. 270) DLC; NjR.
                         36854

---- Roads in Louisiana. Mar. 17,
1828. Mr. Gurley, from the Committee on Roads and Canals, to
which the subject had been referred, made the following report: Washington, Gales & Seaton, 1828. 2 p. (Rep. No. 194)
DLC; NjR.   36855

---- Robert Campbell and George
B. Cumming. Memorial of Robert

Campbell and Geo. B. Cumming.
Feb. 11, 1828. Referred to the
Committee of the Whole House, to
which is committed the Bill (No.
17) to authorize the cancelling a
certain bond therein mentioned.
Washington, Pr. by Gales & Seaton, 1828. 6 p. (Doc. No. 138)
DLC; NjR.   36856

---- Robert Huston. Feb. 11,
1828. Mr. Whittlesey, from the
Committee of Claims, to which
was referred the petition of Robert Huston, made the following
report: Washington, Pr. by
Gales & Seaton, 1828. 3 p. (Rep.
No. 137) DLC; NjR.   36857

---- Robert Irvin. Feb. 13, 1828.
Read, and committed to a Committee of the Whole House to-
morrow. Mr. McCoy, from the
Committee of Claims, to which
was recommitted the petition of
Robert Irvin, made the following
report: Washington, Gales & Seaton, 1828. 2 p. (Rep. No. 144)
DLC; NjR.   36858

---- Robert Johnston's executors.
Jan. 11, 1828. Mr. Wolfe, from
the Committee on Revolutionary
Claims, to which was referred
the petition of the executors of
Dr. Robert Johnston, made the
following report: Washington, Pr.
by Gales & Seaton, 1828. 3 p.
(Rep. No. 63) DLC; NjR. 36859

---- Robert L. Kennon. Feb. 25,
1828. Mr. Wm. R. Davis, from
the Committee on the Public
Lands, to which was referred the
petition of Robert L. Kennon,
made the following report: Washington, Gales & Seaton, 1828. 1
p. (Rep. No. 160) DLC; NjR.
                         36860

---- Robert L. Livingston, execu-
tor of Walter. Apr. 5, 1828. Mr.
Hunt, from the Committee on
Revolutionary Claims, to which

was referred the petition of Robert L. Livingston, surviving executor of Walter Livingston, made the following report: Washington, Gales & Seaton, 1828. 20 p. (Rep. No. 227) DLC; NjR.   36861

---- ---- Report of the Secretary of the Treasury, on the petition of Robert L. Livingston, surviving executor of Walter Livingston, deceased. Feb. 29, 1828. Read, and laid upon the table. Mar. 3, 1828. Pr. by order of the House of Representatives. Washington, Pr. by Gales & Seaton, 1828. 6 p. (Doc. No. 171) DLC; NjR.   36862

---- Rules and orders of the House of Representatives. Apr. 26, 1828. Read, and laid upon the table. Washington, Gales & Seaton, 1828. 2 p. (Rep. No. 240) DLC; NjR.   36863

---- Sales of lands - lead mines Missouri. Jan. 30, 1828. Mr. Jennings, from the Committee on the Public Lands, to which the subject had been referred, made the following report: Washington, Pr. by Gales & Seaton, 1828. 2 p. (Rep. No. 114) DLC; NjR.
                                    36864
---- Samuel Chesnut. Feb. 22, 1828. Mr. Whittlesey, from the Committee of Claims, to which was referred the petition of Samuel Chesnut, made the following report: Washington, Gales & Seaton, 1828. 1 p. (Rep. No. 158) DLC; NjR.   36865

---- Samuel D. Walker. Report of the Secretary of the Treasury on the case of Samuel D. Walker. Dec. 23, 1828. Read, and laid upon the table. Washington, Pr. by Gales & Seaton, 1828. 2 p. (Doc. No. 33) DLC; NjR. 36866

---- Samuel Dubose administra-

tor of E. D. Dick. Feb. 6, 1828. Mr. Ramsey, from the Committee of Claims, to which was referred the petition of Samuel Dubose, administrator of Elias D. Dick, deceased, made the following report: Washington, Pr. by Gales & Seaton, 1828. 2 p. (Rep. No. 129) DLC; NjR.   36867

---- ---- Dec. 31, 1828. Mr. Ramsey, from the Committee of Claims, to which was referred the petition of Samuel Dubose, administrator of Elias D. Dick, deceased, made the following report: Washington, Pr. by Gales & Seaton, 1828. 2 p. (Rep. No. 30) DLC; NjR.   36868

---- Samuel Sprigg. Jan. 17, 1828. Mr. Buckner, from the Committee on Private Land Claims, to which was referred the petition of Samuel Sprigg, made the following report: Washington, Pr. by Gales & Seaton, 1828. 2 p. (Rep. No. 84) DLC; NjR.   36869

---- Samuel Ward. Jan. 14, 1828. Mr. Wolfe, from the Committee on Revolutionary Claims, to which was referred the petition of Samuel Ward, made the following report: Washington, Pr. by Gales & Seaton, 1828. 4 p. (Rep. No. 74) DLC; NjR.   36870

---- Sandy Walker. Mar. 3, 1828. Mr. Bates, of Massachusetts, from the Committee on Military Pensions, to which was referred the petition of Sandy Walker, made the following report: Washington, Gales & Seaton, 1828. 1 p. (Rep. No. 171) DLC; NjR.   36871

---- Sarah Chitwood. Jan. 31, 1828. Mr. Forward, from the Committee on Military Pensions, to which had been referred the petition of Sarah Chitwood, made the following report: Washington,

Pr. by Gales & Seaton, 1828. 1
p. (Rep. No. 117) DLC; NjR.
                                36872
---- Sarah Jones. May 13, 1828.
Mr. Bates, of Massachusetts,
from the Committee on Military
Pensions, to which was referred
the petition of Sarah Jones, made
the following report: Washington, Gales & Seaton, 1828. 1 p.
(Rep. No. 255) DLC; NjR. 36873

---- School lands - Michigan.
Jan. 14, 1828. Mr. Haile, from
the Committee on the Public
Lands, to which the subject had
been referred, made the follow-
ing report: Washington, Pr. by
Gales & Seaton, 1828. 1 p.
(Rep. No. 71) DLC; NjR. 36874

---- School lands - Ohio. Jan.
30, 1828. Mr. Vinton, from the
Committee on the Public Lands,
to which the subject had been referred, made the following report: Washington, Pr. by Gales
& Seaton, 1828. 1 p. (Rep. No.
109) DLC; NjR.   36875

---- School lands - Union County, Indiana. Jan. 14, 1828.
Read, and the Committee discharged from further considera-
tion of the subject. Mr. Jen-
nings, from the Committee on
Public Lands, to which the sub-
ject had been referred, made the
following report: Washington,
Pr. by Gales & Seaton, 1828. 1
p. (Rep. No. 68) DLC; NjR.
                                36876
---- School lands, St. Louis,
Missouri. Dec. 22, 1828. Mr.
Bates of Missouri, from the
Committee on Private Land
Claims, to which the subject had
been referred, made the follow-
ing report: Washington, Pr. by
Gales & Seaton, 1828. 2 p. (Rep.
No. 12) DLC; NjR.   36877

---- Selection of commissioned
and warrant officers - Navy.
Letter from the Secretary of the
Navy, transmitting the information required by a resolution of
the House of Representatives, of
the 18th ultimo, in relation to the
rule adopted by the Navy Department, in selecting from the list
of candidates for commission or
warrants, such as the service
may require, &c. Mar. 14, 1828.
Read, and laid upon the table.
Washington, Pr. by Gales & Seaton, 1828. 11 p. (Doc. No. 196)
DLC; NjR.   36878

---- Selling spirits to Indian
tribes. Letter from the Secretary
of War, transmitting a report,
containing the regulations which
have been adopted to give effect
to the 22d section of an act of
Congress, passed in the year
1802, regulating trade amongst
the Indian tribes, which 22d section gives the President power
to prevent the introduction of ardent spirit amongst the Indians.
Feb. 19, 1828. Read and laid
upon the table. Washington, Pr.
by Gales & Seaton, 1828. 3 p.
(Doc. No. 146) DLC; NjR.
                                36879
---- Senate Bill No. 96 -Claims
- Treaty of Ghent. Mar. 22,
1828. Read, and, with the said
bill, committed to a Committee
of the Whole House to-morrow.
Washington, Gales & Seaton,
1828. 8 p. (Rep. No. 208) DLC;
NjR.   36880

---- Seth Knowles. Feb. 8,
1828. Mr. McDuffie, from the
Committee of Ways and Means,
to which was referred the petition of Seth Knowles, made the
following report: Washington,
Pr. by Gales & Seaton, 1828. 1
p. (Rep. No. 131) DLC; NjR.
                                36881
---- Settlement on the Oregon
River. Memorial of citizens of

the United States, praying for a grant of land, and the aid of government in forming a colony on the northwest coast of the United States. Feb. 11, 1828. Read, and referred to the Committee of the Whole House, to which is committed the Bill (No. 12) to authorize the occupation of the Oregon River. Washington, Pr. by Gales & Seaton, 1828. 4 p. (Doc. No. 139) DLC; NjR.   36882

---- Settlers - Michigan and Indiana. Feb. 29, 1828. Mr. Jennings, from the Committee on the Public Lands, to which the subject had been referred, made the following report: Washington, Gales & Seaton, 1828. 1 p. (Rep. No. 167) DLC; NjR.   36883

---- Settlers on land - Choctaw district - Mississippi. Jan. 28, 1828. Mr. Haile, from the Committee on the Public Lands, to which the subject had been referred, made the following report: Washington, Pr. by Gales & Seaton, 1828. 5 p. (Rep. No. 102) DLC; NjR. 36884

---- Silk-worms. Letter from James Mease, transmitting a treatise on the rearing of silkworms, by Mr. de Hazzi, of Munich, with plates, &c. &c. Feb. 2, 1828. Read, and referred to the Committee on Agriculture. Washington, Pr. by Gales & Seaton, 1828. 108 p. 1 bdsd. (Doc. No. 226) CSmH; DLC; DeGE; MB; NjR.   36885

---- Slaves, &c. captured during the late war. Memorial of Aug. Neale, agent for claimants, before the Commissioners to award indemnity for slaves, and other property, under the Treaty of Ghent. Mar.

10, 1828. Read, and laid on the table. Washington, Pr. by Gales & Seaton, 1828. 7 p. (Doc. No. 190) DLC; NjR.   36886

---- South Carolina. Memorial of citizens of Chesterfield, Marlborough, and Darlington assembled at Cheraw in South Carolina against a further increase of duties on imported articles. Feb. 4, 1828. Referred to the Committee of the Whole House on the state of the Union. Washington, Pr. by Gales & Seaton, 1828. 8 p. (Doc. No. 111) DLC; NjR.
                                   36887
---- ---- Memorial of inhabitants of Newberry District, in the state of South Carolina, against further protecting duties to domestic manufactures, and that all laws heretofore passed for that purpose, may be repealed. Feb. 25, 1828. Referred to the Committee of the Whole House to which is referred the Bill in alteration of the several laws imposing duties on imports. Washington, Pr. by Gales & Seaton, 1828. 6 p. (Doc. No. 157) DLC; NjR.   36888

---- ---- Memorial of the canal and rail road company. Apr. 7, 1828. Referred to the Committee of Ways and Means. Apr. 14, 1828. Bill reported--No. 268. Washington, Pr. by Gales & Seaton, 1828. 4 p. (Doc. No. 246) CtY; DBRE; DLC; IU; MBAt; MH; NN; NjR; P.   36889

---- ---- Memorial of the Charleston Chamber of Commerce, and of other citizens of South Carolina, against an increase of duty on woollens. Dec. 11, 1827. Referred to the Committee on Manufactures. Feb. 22, 1828. Ordered to be printed by House of Representatives. Washington, Pr. by Gales & Seaton, 1828. 10 p.

(Doc. No. 155) DLC; NjR. 36890

---- ---- Memorial of the citizens of Laurens District, South Carolina, against any increase of the tariff, &c. January 22, 1828. Referred to the Committee on Commerce and Manufactures. Washington, Pr. by Gales & Seaton, 1828. 6 p. (Doc. No. 85) DLC; NjR.   36891

---- ---- Memorial of the Legislature of the state of South Carolina, remonstrating against the passing of laws by Congress, increasing the duties upon importations for the encouragement of domestic manufactures: Against the exercise of the general power to construct roads and canals, either with or without the consent of the states; and against the appropriation of moneys, by Congress, for the Colonization Society... Jan. 14, 1828. Read and laid upon the table. Washington, Pr. by Gales & Seaton, 1828. 19 p. (Doc. No. 65) DLC; NjR.   36892

---- ---- Remonstrance of the citizens of Beaufort District, S. C. against any further increase of the duties on imports. Dec. 31, 1827. Referred to the Committee on Manufactures. Washington, Pr. by Gales & Seaton, 1828. 7 p. (Doc. No. 28) DLC; NjR.   36893

---- Southern bend of Lake Michigan. Dec. 10, 1828. Mr. Strong, from the Committee on the Territories, to which the subject had been referred, made the following report: Washington, Pr. by Gales & Seaton, 1828. 3 p. (Rep. No. 2) DLC; MiD-B; NjR.   36894

---- Southern boundary - Lake Michigan. Mar. 18, 1828. Mr.

Strong, from the Committee on the Territories, to which the subject had been referred, made the following report: Washington, Gales & Seaton, 1828. 3 p. (Rep. No. 196) DLC; NjR.   36895

---- State of Alabama. A remonstrance of the General Assembly of Alabama on the subject of protecting duties. Feb. 4, 1828. Referred to the Committee of the Whole House on the State of the Union. Washington, Pr. by Gales & Seaton, 1828. 6 p. (Doc. No. 113) DLC; NjR.   36896

---- Statement from Thomas L. McKenney, declining the acceptance of the provisions of the "Bill for the relief of Thomas L. McKenney," for reasons therein mentioned. Feb. 19, 1828. Pr. by order of the Senate of the United States. Washington, Duff Green, 1828. 3 p. (Doc. No. 109) DLC; NjR.   36897

---- ... Statement of the appropriations and expenditures of the general government of the United States for the years 1817, 1822, 1823, 1824, 1825, 1826, and 1827, arranged under sundry general heads or objects. [Washington, 1828] 1 table. DeGE. 36898

---- Statement showing the quantity, and average value of the unsold and unsaleable public lands, which would fall under the operation of the graduation bill, &c. Dec. 30, 1828. Laid on the table by Mr. Benton, and ordered to be printed. Washington, Duff Green, 1828. 3 p. (Doc. No. 19) DLC; NjR.   36899

---- Stationery - Custom House, Philadelphia. Letter from the Secretary of the Treasury transmitting the information required by a resolution of the House of

Representatives of the 22d instant in relation to supplying the Custom-House at Philadelphia with stationery, &c. January 30, 1828. Read, and laid upon the table. Washington, Pr. by Gales & Seaton, 1828. 3 p. (Doc. No. 105) DLC; NjR.   36900

---- Steamboat tonnage United States. Letter from the Secretary of the Treasury transmitting a statement of the steamboat tonnage of the United States and the duty collected upon the same. April 16, 1828. Read, and laid upon the table. Washington, Pr. by Gales & Seaton, 1828. 4 p. (Doc. No. 249) DLC; NjR. 36901

---- Stephen Hook's statement and oath. Dec. 5, 1828. Referred to the Committee on the Judiciary. Dec. 10, 1828. Committee discharged. Ordered to lie on the table. Dec. 12, 1828. Committed to a Committee of the Whole House to-morrow. Washington, Pr. by Gales & Seaton, 1828. 2 p. (Doc. No. 18) DLC; NjR.   36902

---- Submitted by Mr. Buchanan, as an amendment to the bill for the preservation and repair of the Cumberland Road, to be considered when that bill shall be taken up by the House. Jan. 14, 1828. [Washington, 1828] 2 p. (H. R. 42) DNA.   36903

---- ---- Jan. 14, 1828. Dec. 15, 1828. Repr. by order of the House of Representatives. [Washington, 1828] 1 p. (H. R. 42) DNA.   36904

---- Subscribe stock Tenth Turnpike Road Company, N. H. Apr. 14, 1828. Mr. Davis, of Massachusetts, from the Committee on Roads, and Canals, to which was referred the petition of the pro-

prietors of the Tenth Turnpike Road Company, in the state of New Hampshire, made the following report: Washington, Gales & Seaton, 1828. 8 p. (Rep. No. 233) DLC; NjR.   36905

---- Sufferers of the late war - Michigan. May 24, 1828. Read, and laid upon the table. Mr. Whittlesey, from the Committee of Claims, to which was referred the memorial of the Legislative Council of the territory of Michigan, in behalf of inhabitants of said territory, who suffered by the destruction of their property during the late war, made the following report. Washington, Gales & Seaton, 1828. 2 p. (Rep. No. 268) DLC; NjR.   36906

---- Suffering condition of the emigrant Indians. Letter from the Secretary of War, to the Chairman of the Committee on Indian Affairs, upon the subject of the suffering conditions of the emigrant Indians. Jan. 21, 1828. Read, and referred to the Committee of Ways and Means. Washington, Pr. by Gales & Seaton, 1828. 4 p. (Doc. No. 283) DLC; NjR.   36907

---- Sundry memorials, resolutions, and petitions from states, territories, and individuals, on the subject of graduating the prices of the public lands. Jan. 9, 1828. Pr. by order of the Senate of the United States. Washington, Pr. by Duff Green, 1828. 17 p. (Doc. No. 27) DLC; NjR.   36908

---- Superintendent Armory - Harper's Ferry. Letter from the Secretary of War transmitting the information required by a resolution of the House of Representatives, of the 14th instant, in relation to coal and gunstocks purchased since 1st Jan., 1820, for the use of said armory. Jan. 22, 1828. Read, and laid upon the table. Washington, Pr. by Gales & Seaton, 1828. 21 p. (Doc. No. 78) DLC; DeGE; NjR.   36909

---- Supplementary appropriation (military) for 1828. Documents laid before the House of Representatives by the chairman of the Committee of Ways and Means. To accompany the bill (No. 267) making a supplementary appropriation for the military service of the year 1828. Washington, Pr. by Gales & Seaton, 1828. 8 p. (Doc. No. 245) DLC; NjR.   36910

---- Surgeons of the Navy. Memorial of the surgeons of the Navy of the United States. Jan. 14, 1828. Referred to the Committee on Naval Affairs. Feb. 12, 1828. Bill reported - No. 162. Washington, Pr. by Gales & Seaton, 1828. 8 p. (Doc. No. 182) DLC; NNNAM; NjR.   36911

---- Survey - swash in Pamlico Sound. Letter from the Secretary of War, transmitting, in obedience to a resolution of the House of Representatives, a report and plan of the survey of the swash in Pamlico Sound. January 18, 1828. Referred to the Committee on Commerce. Washington, Pr. by Gales & Seaton, 1828. 12 p. (Doc. No. 69) DLC; NjR.   36912

---- Survey harbor of Black Rock. Letter from the Secretary of War, transmitting a report of the survey of the harbor of Black Rock, in the state of Connecticut. Jan. 10, 1828. Referred to the Committee on Commerce. Washington, Gales & Seaton, 1828. 8 p. (Doc. No. 52) DLC; NjR.   36913

---- Survey of Cape Fear River. Letter from the Secretary of War transmitting a report and plan of the survey of Cape Fear River below the town of Wilmington. Feb. 8, 1828. Referred to the Committee on Commerce. Washington, Pr. by Gales & Seaton, 1828. 14 p. (Doc. No. 127) DLC; NjR.   36914

---- Survey of Ocracock Inlet. Letter from the Secretary of War transmitting a report in relation to the improvement of the navigation of Ocracock Inlet in the state of North Carolina. Dec. 29, 1828. Referred to the Committee on Commerce. Washington, Pr. by Gales & Seaton, 1828. 10 p. (Doc. No. 37) DLC; NjR.   36915

---- Survey of Sandusky Bay, Ohio. Letter from the Secretary of War, transmitting a report and plan of the survey of Sandusky Bay in the state of Ohio. Jan. 21, 1828. Read and referred to the Committee on Commerce. Washington, Pr. by Gales & Seaton, 1828. 5 p. (Doc. No. 72) DLC; NjR.   36916

---- Survey of the island of Nantucket. Letter from the Secretary of War transmitting a report and plan of the survey of the island of Nantucket. Jan. 22, 1828. Read, and laid upon the table. Washington, Pr. by Gales & Seaton, 1828. 18 p. (Doc. No. 77) DLC; NjR.   36917

---- Survey of the Muscle Shoals. Letter from the Secretary of War, transmitting the information required by a resolution of the House of Representatives of the 16th Jan. last, in relation to an examination of the Muscle Shoals in Tennessee River, with a view to removing the obstructions to the navigation thereof, and the construction of a canal around the same. May 14, 1828. Read, and referred to the Committee of the Whole House to which is committed the bill from the Senate (No. 46) to grant certain relinquished and unappropriate lands to the state of Alabama, for the purpose of improving the navigation of the Tennessee, Coosa, Cahawba, and Black Warrior rivers. Washington, Pr. by Gales & Seaton, 1828. 20 p. (Doc. No. 284) DLC; NjR.   36918

---- Survey the coasts of the United States. Documents submitted by Mr. Carter from the Committee on Naval Affairs to accompany the bill (No. 288) to amend the acts to provide for surveying the coasts of the United States. May 1, 1828. Pr. by order of the House of Representatives. Washington, Pr. by Gales & Seaton, 1828. 12 p. (Doc. No. 264) DLC; DeGE (11 p.); NjR.   36919

---- Surveyor for Virginia military district in Ohio. Jan. 4, 1828. Mr. Vinton, from the Committee on the Public Lands, to which the subject had been referred, made the following report: Washington, Gales & Seaton, 1828. 2 p. (Rep. No. 53) DLC; NjR.   36920

---- Surveyor's office - Illinois, Missouri, and Arkansas. Letter from the Secretary of the Treasury, transmitting the information required by a resolution of the House of Representatives, of the 11th instant, in relation to the actual condition of the office of the surveyor of the public lands, in the state of Illinois and Missouri, and the territory of Arkansas, &c. &c. Feb. 18, 1828. Referred to the Committee on the

Public Lands. Washington, Pr. by Gales & Seaton, 1828. 13 p. (Doc. No. 145) DLC; NjR.   36921

---- Surveys - Kennebec River, &c. Letter from the Secretary of War, transmitting a report of the surveys of the Kennebec River, and of contemplated routes for canals, connected with the waters of the said rivers. Feb. 22, 1828. Referred to the Committee on Roads and Canals. March 4, 1828. Ordered to be printed. Washington, Pr. by Gales & Seaton, 1828. 58 p. (Doc. No. 173) DLC; NjR.   36922

---- ---- Concord, Pr. by Jacob B. Moore, 1828. 28 p. NN; NhHi.   36923

---- Surveys of harbors - Rhode Island. Letter from the Secretary of War, transmitting reports of surveys of Church's Cove Harbor; of the shores north end of Goat Island, and the river and harbor of Warren, all in the state of Rhode Island. Feb. 23, 1828. Referred to the Committee on Commerce. Washington, Pr. by Gales & Seaton, 1828. 10 p. (Doc. No. 154) DLC; NjR.   36924

---- Tax on domestic spirits of 1813. Jan. 2, 1828. Read, and laid upon the table. Mr. McDuffie, from the Committee of Ways and Means, to which the subject had been referred, made the following report: Washington, Gales & Seaton, 1828. 1 p. (Rep. No. 43) DLC; NjR.   36925

---- Tennessee militiamen. Report of the Committee on Military Affairs to which were referred the correspondence and documents from the War Department, in relation to the proceedings of a court martial ordered for the trial of certain Tennessee militia-men. Feb. 11, 1828. Read, and laid upon the table. Washington, Pr. by Gales & Seaton, 1828. 63 p. 37 bdsds. (Rep. No. 140) CSmH; DLC; NjR.   36926

---- Territorial government - Huron. Jan. 15, 1828. Mr. Strong, from the Committee on the Territories, to which was referred the memorial of the Legislative Council of the territory of Michigan, &c., made the following report: Washington, Pr. by Gales & Seaton, 1828. 13 p. (Rep. No. 79) DLC; NjR.
36927

---- Territory of Huron. Memorial of inhabitants of the town of Galena, in the state of Illinois. Dec. 29, 1828. Read, and laid upon the table. Washington, Pr. by Gales & Seaton, 1828. 6 p. (Doc. No. 35) DLC; NjR.
36928

---- Territory west of the Rocky Mountains. Message from the President of the United States transmitting the correspondence between this government and that of Great Britain, on the subject of the claims of the two governments to the territory west of the Rocky Mountains. Mar. 15, 1828. Read, and laid upon the table. Washington, Pr. by Gales & Seaton, 1828. 77 p. (Doc. No. 199) CSmH; DLC; NjR.   36929

---- Theophilus Cooksey. Dec. 24, 1828. Mr. McIntire from the Committee of Claims, to which was referred the petition of Theophilus Cooksey, made the following report: Washington, Pr. by Gales & Seaton, 1828. 1 p. (Rep. No. 16) DLC; NjR.
36930

---- Thirty-seventh section of act to collect duties on imports. Jan. 14, 1828. Mr. Cambreleng, from the Committee on Commerce, to which the subject had

been referred, made the following report: Washington, Pr. by Gales & Seaton, 1828. 3 p. (Rep. No. 72) DLC; NjR.   36931

---- Thomas Blackwell. Mar. 16, 1828. Mr. Tucker of New Jersey, from the Committee on Revolutionary Claims, to which was referred the petition of Thomas Blackwell, made the following report: Washington, Gales & Seaton, 1828. 1 p. (Rep. No. 199) DLC; NjR.   36932

---- Thomas F. Cornell. Jan. 29, 1828. Mr. Strong, from the Committee on the Territories, to which had been referred the case of Thomas Cornell, made the following report: Washington, Pr. by Gales & Seaton, 1828. 1 p. (Rep. No. 105) DLC; NjR.   36933

---- Thomas Hunt. Mar. 6, 1828. Mr. Ramsey, from the Committee of Claims, to which was referred the petition of Thomas Hunt, made the following report: Washington, Gales & Seaton, 1828. 11 p. (Rep. No. 179) DLC; NjR.   36934

---- Thomas R. Williams. Jan. 11, 1828. Read, and laid upon the table. Mr. P. P. Barbour, from the Committee on the Judiciary, to which was referred the petition of Thomas R. Williams, made the following report: Washington, Pr. by Gales & Seaton, 1828. 1 p. (Rep. No. 62) DLC; NjR.   36935

---- Thomas Wheatley. Dec. 24, 1828. Mr. Whittlesey, from the Committee of Claims, to which was referred the case of Thomas Wheatley, made the following report: Washington, Pr. by Gales & Seaton, 1828. 3 p. (Rep. No. 15) DLC; NjR.   36936

---- Thurber and King. Dec. 29, 1828. Mr. Clark, of New York, from the Committee of Claims, to which was referred the case of King and Thurber, made the following report: Washington, Pr. by Gales & Seaton, 1828. 7 p. (Rep. No. 19) DLC; NjR. 36937

---- To accompany Bill No. 158 - appropriation public buildings. Estimate of appropriations necessary to complete the public buildings. Feb. 11, 1828. Accompanying bill (No. 158) making appropriations for the public buildings, and for other purposes. Washington, Pr. by Gales & Seaton, 1828. 8 p. (Doc. No. 180) DLC; NjR. 36938

---- Tonnage duties - to repeal. Dec. 31, 1828. Mr. Sprague, from the Committee of Ways and Means, to which the subject had been referred, made the following report: Washington, Pr. by Gales & Seaton, 1828. 4 p. (Rep. No. 29) DLC; DeGE; NjR. 36939

---- Trade -United States and British colonies. Message from the President of the United States transmitting, pursuant to a resolution of the House of Representatives of the 9th inst. , the correspondence between the U. States and G. Britain, upon the subject of the trade between the United States and the British colonial possessions in the West Indies and North America, &c. April 28, 1828. Read, and laid upon the table. Washington, Pr. by Gales & Seaton, 1828. 57 p. (Doc. No. 259) DLC; NjR. 36940

---- Transfer real estate - District of Columbia. Jan. 15, 1828. Mr. Varnum, from the Committee to which the subject had been referred, made the following report: Washington, Pr. by Gales

& Seaton, 1828. 1 p. (Rep. No. 78) DLC; NjR. 36941

---- Treasury clerks. Letter from the Secretary of the Treasury, transmitting a report of the names of the clerks employed in the Treasury Department, during the year 1827, and the compensation of each. Jan. 10, 1828. Read, laid upon the table. Washington, Pr. by Gales & Seaton, 1828. 13 p. (Doc. No. 54) DLC; NjR. 36942

---- ... Treaty between the United States of America, and the Eel river or Thorntown party of Miami Indians. .. made and concluded, on the eleventh day of February, one thousand eight hundred and twenty eight, at the Wyandot village, near the Wabash, within the United States, by John Tipton, commissioner on the part of the United States, and certain chiefs and warriors of said nation, on the part, and in behalf of, said nation ... [Washington, 1828] 2 l. [2nd leaf & verso of 1st leaf blank] DLC. 36943

---- Treaty of limits between the United States of America, and the united Mexican states. [Washington, 1828] 4 [i. e. 7] p. DLC. 36944

---- Treaty with Eel River Indians. Message from the President of the United States, transmitting a copy of a treaty concluded on the 11th of Feb. last, with the Eel River or Thorntown Party of Miami Indians. May 23, 1828. Read, and laid upon the table. Washington, Pr. by Gales & Seaton, 1828. 7 p. (Doc. No. 270) DLC; NjR. 36945

---- Treaty with Sweden. Message from the President of the United States transmitting a copy of a treaty of commerce and navigation between the United States and His Majesty the King of Sweden and Norway. Feb. 7, 1828. Read, and laid upon the table. Washington, Pr. by Gales & Seaton, 1828. 20 p. (Doc. No. 122) DLC; NjR.   36946

---- Treaty with the Creek Indians. Message from the President of the United States, transmitting a copy of a treaty, concluded on the 15th day of November, 1827, between the United States and the Creek Nation of Indians. Mar. 22, 1828. Read, and laid upon the table. Washington, Pr. by Gales & Seaton, 1828. 8 p. (Doc. No. 210) DLC; NjR.   36947

---- Twentieth Congress. 1st Session. Wednesday January 30-31, 1828. [Washington] National Journal, January 30-31, 1828. 2 p. DLC.   36948

---- United States and Brazil. Message from the President of the United States transmitting copies of a correspondence between the Secretary of State and the Charge d'Affaires from Brazil on the subjects of the discussions between that government and the government of the United States. Rendered in obedience to a resolution of the House of Representatives, of the 2d instant. Jan. 30, 1828. Read, and referred to the Committee on Foreign Affairs. Washington, Pr. by Gales & Seaton, 1828. 8 p. (Doc. No. 108) DLC; NjR.   36949

---- United States' armories. Letter from the Secretary of War, transmitting a statement of expenditures at the armories and the arms, &c. made therein, during the year 1827. Mar. 6, 1828. Read, and laid on the table. Washington, Pr. by Gales & Seaton, 1828. 8 p. (Doc. No. 183)

DLC; NjR.   36950

---- Unproductive post roads. Letter from the Postmaster General, transmitting a list of post-roads which have been established more than two years, and do not produce one-third of the expense incurred by the department for the transportation of the mail on the route. Feb. 12, 1828. Referred to the Committee on the Post Office and Post Roads. Washington, Pr. by Gales & Seaton, 1828. 75 p. (Doc. No. 220) DLC; NjR.   36951

---- ---- Letter from the Postmaster General transmitting a list of post-roads which have been established more than two years, and which do not produce one-third of the expense incurred for the transportation of the mail on the same. Dec. 31, 1828. Read, and laid upon the table. Washington, Pr. by Gales & Seaton, 1828. 15 p. (Doc. No. 42) DLC; NjR.   36952

---- Unsettled accounts, &c. Third Auditor. Letter from the Comptroller of the Treasury transmitting reports of the Third Auditor. 1st. Of officers who have not rendered their accounts within the year, according to law; 2d. Abatement of accounts which have remained unsettled for more than three years, prior to the 30th of September last; 3d. Abstract of moneys advanced prior to 3d March 1809, which remained unaccounted for on the books of his office on the 30th September last. Dec. 15, Read, and laid upon the table. Washington, Pr. by Gales & Seaton, 1828. 95 p. (Doc. No. 20) DLC; NjR.   36953

---- Unsettled balances - register of Treasury. Letter from the Comptroller of the Treasury transmitting a list of balances on the books of the register, which have remained unsettled three years prior to the 30th September last. Dec. 16, 1828. Read, and laid upon the table. Washington, Pr. by Gales & Seaton, 1828. 7 p. (Doc. No. 47) DLC; NjR.   36954

---- Unsettled balances, &c. &c. Letter from the Comptroller of the Treasury transmitting a list of balances on the books of the Register of the Treasury which have remained unsettled three years, prior to 30th September, 1828; a similar list rendered by the Fourth Auditor of the Treasury; and a list of the names of officers who have failed to render their accounts to the Fourth Auditor for adjustment, pursuant to law. Dec. 5, 1828. Read, and laid upon the table. Washington, Pr. by Gales & Seaton, 1828. 30 p. (Doc. No. 8) DLC; DeGE; (39 p); NjR.   36955

---- Uriah Brown. Communication of Uriah Brown. Feb. 18, 1828. Referred to the Committee on Naval Affairs. Washington, Pr. by Gales & Seaton, 1828. 5 p. (Doc. No. 150) DLC; NjR. 36956

---- ---- May 10, 1828. Mr. Dorsey, from the Committee on Naval Affairs, to which was referred the petition of Uriah Brown, relative to a system of coast and harbor defence, by means of "impregnable and invincible fire ships," made the following report: Washington, Gales & Seaton, 1828. 8 p. (Rep. No. 252) DLC; NjR.   36957

---- Vacant lands in Tennessee. Documents submitted by Mr. Polk and referred to the Committee of the Whole House to which is committed the bill (H. R. No.

27) to amend the act entitled "An act to authorize the state of Tennessee to issue grants and perfect titles to certain lands therein described, and to settle the claims to vacant and unappropriated lands in the same" passed on the 18th day of April, 1806. Washington, Pr. by Gales & Seaton, 1828. 7 p. (Doc. No. 232) DLC; NjR.   36958

---- ---- Letter from the Secretary of the Treasury transmitting the information required by a resolution of the House of Representatives of the 14th instant, in relation to the quantity and quality of the vacant and unappropriated public lands in the state of Tennessee, south and west of the Congressional Reservation Line. Jan. 22, 1828. Read and laid upon the table. Washington, Pr. by Gales & Seaton, 1828. 7 p. (Doc. No. 76) DLC; NjR. 36959

---- Varioloid, or small pox, in Washington. Mar. 27, 1828. Read, and laid upon the table. Mr. Alexander, from the Committee for the District of Columbia, to which the subject had been referred, made the following report: Washington, Gales & Seaton, 1828. 3 p. (Rep. No. 215) DLC; NjR.   36960

---- Vermont. Memorial of Samuel C. Crafts and others, citizens of the state of Vermont, praying for further protection to domestic industry. Jan. 2, 1828. Read, and referred to the Committee on Manufactures. Washington, Pr. by Gales & Seaton, 1828. 6 p. (Doc. No. 31) DLC; NjR.
                                       36961
---- Vessels sunk in Baltimore Harbor. Apr. 2, 1828. Read, and, with the bill, committed to a Committee of the Whole House to-morrow. Mr. Williams, from

the Committee of Claims, to which was referred the bill from the Senate, entitled "An act for the relief of sundry citizens of Baltimore," made the following report: Washington, Gales & Seaton, 1828. 21 p. (Rep. No. 221) DLC; NjR. 36962

---- Virginia - Mecklenburg County. Memorial of inhabitants of Mecklenburg County, in the state of Virginia, against any increase of duty on imported goods. Jan. 2, 1828. Referred to the Committee on Manufactures. Washington, Pr. by Gales & Seaton, 1828. 10 p. (Doc. No. 30) DLC; NjR. 36963

---- Volunteer mounted gunmen. Documents in relation to the employment of volunteer mounted gunmen on the western frontier of the United States. Apr. 1, 1828. Pr. by order of the House of Representatives. Washington, Pr. by Gales & Seaton, 1828. 5 p. (Doc. No. 234) DLC; NjR. 36964

---- William A. Tennille. Petition of Colonel William A. Tennille. Feb. 4, 1828. Referred to the Committee on the Judiciary. Washington, Pr. by Gales & Seaton, 1828. 5 p. (Doc. No. 115) DLC; NjR. 36965

---- William and Hugh Shannon. Jan. 9, 1828. Mr. Whittlesey, from the Committee of Claims, to which was referred the petition of William and Hugh Shannon, made the following report: Washington, Gales & Seaton, 1828. 1 p. (Rep. No. 59) DLC; NjR. 36966

---- William Hubble and Daniel Gano. Jan. 25, 1828. Read, and laid upon the table. Mr. Wolf, from the Committee on Revolutionary Claims, to which were referred the petitions of William

Hubble and Daniel Gano, made the following report: Washington, Pr. by Gales & Seaton, 1828. 1 p. (Rep. No. 99) DLC; NjR. 36967

---- Wm. J. Quincy and Charles E. Quincy. Feb. 25, 1828. Mr. Sprague, from the Committee of Ways and Means, to which was referred the petition of Wm. J. Quincy and Charles E. Quincy, made the following report: Washington, Gales & Seaton, 1828. 1 p. (Rep. No. 161) DLC; NjR. 36968

---- William M'Clure. Jan. 23, 1828. Mr. Clark of New York, from the Committee of Claims, to which had been referred the petition of William M'Clure, made the following report: Washington, Pr. by Gales & Seaton, 1828. 4 p. 2 bdsds. (Rep. No. 94) DLC; NjR. 36969

---- William Morrisson. Feb. 25, 1828. Mr. Whittlesey, from the Committee of Claims, to which was referred the petition of William Morrisson made the following report: Washington, Gales & Seaton, 1828. 1 p. (Rep. No. 164) DLC; NjR. 36970

---- William Otis. May 5, 1828. Read, and with the bill, committed to a Committee of the Whole House to-morrow. Mr. Whittlesey, from the Committee of Claims, to which was referred the bill from the Senate for the relief of William Otis, made the following report: Washington, Gales & Seaton, 1828. 3 p. (Rep. No. 244) DLC; NjR. 36971

---- William R. Maddox. Mar. 3, 1828. Mr. Sprigg, from the Committee on Expenditures on the Public Buildings, to which had been referred the petition of William R. Maddox, made the following report: Washington, Gales

& Seaton, 1828. 2 p. (Rep. No. 172) DLC; NjR. 36972

---- William Tipton. Apr. 21, 1828. Mr. Mitchell of Tennessee, from the Committee on Military Pensions, made the following report: Washington, Gales & Seaton, 1828. 2 p. (Rep. No. 235) DLC; NjR. 36973

---- Wines imported, and duties thereon. Statement submitted by Mr. Cambreleng, of wines imported, and the duties accruing on the same, from 1801 to 1826, also, a statement of the aggregate value of exports to Madeira, from 1st Oct., 1800, to 30th Sept., 1827. Feb. 26, 1828. Referred to the Committee of the Whole House to which is committed the Bill (No. 130) to alter the duties on wine imported into the United States. Washington, Pr. by Gales & Seaton, 1828. 4 p. 1 bdsd. (Doc. No. 162) DLC; NjR. 36974

---- Winnebago Indians. Letter from the Secretary of War transmitting a report of Gov. Cass and Col. McKenney on the subject of the complaints of the Winnebago Indians, &c. Feb. 5, 1828. Read, and referred to the Committee of the Whole House to which is committed the bill (No. 103) to enable the President of the United States to hold a treaty with the Chippewas, Ottawas, Pattawatimas, Winnebagoes, Fox, and Sacs Nations of Indians. Washington, Pr. by Gales and Seaton, 1828. 7 p. (Doc. No. 117) DLC; NjR. 36975

---- Wool and woollens. Statement submitted by Mr. Wright, of Ohio, in relation to the effects to be produced by the bill reported to the House in alteration of the several acts imposing duties on imports in reference to wool and woollens. Mar. 10, 1828. Pr. by order of the House of Representatives. Washington, Pr. by Gales & Seaton, 1828. 6 p. (Doc. No. 189) DLC; NjR. 36976

---- Wool-growers and farmers - New York. Resolutions adopted at a meeting of wool-growers and farmers, convened, pursuant to public notice, in Columbia County, New York. Feb. 13, 1828. Referred to the Committee of the Whole House to which is committed the Bill (No. 132) in alteration of the several acts imposing duties on imports. Washington, Pr. by Gales & Seaton, 1828. 11 p. (Doc. No. 142) DLC; NjR. 36977

---- Ysabel Osorno de Valverde. Jan. 3, 1828. Read, and laid upon the table. Mr. Everett, from the Committee of Foreign Affairs, to which was referred the petition of Ysabel Osorno de Valverde, made the following report: Washington, Gales & Seaton, 1828. 6 p. (Rep. No. 49) DLC; NjR. 36978

The United States almanac, comprising calculations for the latitude, and meridians of the Northern Southern and Western states ...Philadelphia, R. Desilver, 1828. 54 p. DLC; MB; P. 36979

United States Military Academy, West Point.
   Register of graduates of the United States Military Academy, who have been commissioned in the army of the United States, from June, 1802, to July 1828, inclusive [West Point, N.Y.] 1828. 12 p. DLC; DeGE; PPL. 36980

---- Register of the officers and cadets of the U.S. Military Academy. June, 1828. 22 p. MBAt. 36981

The United States spelling book,
with appropriate reading lessons:
being an easy standard for spelling, reading & pronouncing the
English language, according to
the rules established by John
Walker, in his critical and pronouncing dictionary. By sundry
experienced teachers... 28th ed.
Pittsburgh, Pr. and pub. by
Cramer & Spear, 1828. 156 p.
NN; OClWHi.   36982

United States' Telegraph, Washington, D. C.
    Address: of the carriers of
the United States' Telegraph, to
their patrons. Jan. 1st, 1828.
[Washington, D. C. 1828] 1 p.
DLC.   36983

A universal biographical dictionary. See Baldwin, Charles N.

A universal history of the United
States of America embracing the
whole period from the earliest
discovery down to the present
time... by a citizen of the United
States. Hartford, E. Strong,
1828. 456 p. DLC.   36984

The universal letter-writer; or,
Whole art of polite correspondence: containing a great variety
of plain, easy, entertaining, and
familiar original letters, adapted
to every age and situation in life,
but more particularly on business,
education, and love. Together
with various forms of petitions,
suitable to the different wants
and exigencies of life: proper
methods of addressing superiors
and persons of all ranks... to
which is added, a model collection of genteel complimentary
cards. Likewise, useful forms in
law, such as wills, bonds, &c.
To which is subjoined an index
... New ed. , cor. and enl.
Philadelphia, M. Carey, 1828.
124 p. DLC; OHi.   36985

Universalist tract. See Counterpart to "A strange thing."

Der Unterschied Zwischen wahren
und falschen Bekehrungen. See
American Tract Society, New
York.

[Updike, Wilkens] 1784-1867
    An address to the people of
Rhode Island; proving that more
than eight millions of the public
money has been wasted by the
present administration. By a
Land Holder. Providence, Office
of the Republican Herald, John
S. Greene, pr. , 1828. 28 p.
CSmH; MH; MWA; NN; RHi; RP;
RPB.   36986

Upham, Charles Wentworth,
1802-1875
    Letters on the logos. ... Bos-
ton, Bowles & Dearborn [Hiram
Tupper, pr.] 1828. 215 p.
CtMW; DLC; ICMe; IEG; IU; MB;
MBAU; MBC; MH-AH; MHi;
MMeT-Hi; MWA; MeBaT; MnHi;
NNG; NNUT; NbOP; PPLT;
PPPrHi; RPB; VtU.   36987

Upham, Thomas Cogswell
    Elements of intellectual phi-
losophy, designed as a textbook,
by Thomas C. Upham, professor
of moral and intellectual philoso-
phy and instructor of Hebrew in
Bowdoin College. 2d ed. Port-
land, Pub. by Shirley & Hyde,
Pr. by J. Griffin, 1828. 576 p.
CSmH; GAU; GDC; GU; IJI;
KyLx; LU; MB; MH; MMeT; MNe;
Md; MeLB; MoSpD; MtH; NNUT;
OClW; OkEP; OMC; PU.   36988

Utica. Citizens.
    At a numerous meeting of the
citizens of the village of Utica,
held at the court room, on Tuesday the 5th day of August, 1828
... for the purpose of expressing
their sentiments upon the measures now in progress for enforc-

ing the observance of the Sabbath
... [Utica, 1828] 1 l. DLC.
                                36989
---- A brief statement of the
proceedings of the citizens of
Utica, touching certain measures
for enforcing the observance of
the Sabbath. Utica, Northway &
Porter, prs., 1828. 11 p. NUt;
PHi; WHi.   36990

Utica. Central Corresponding
Committee. See National Republican Party. New York.

The Utica [City] directory: to
which is added a brief historical,
topographical and statistical account of the village and its neighbourhood; accompanied by a map
of the village. Utica, Pub. by
Elisha Harrington. Dauby & Maynard, prs., 1828. 99 [16] p.
DLC; MWA; NN; NUt; NUtHi.
                                36991

V

A valedictory address. See
Carey, Mathew.

Valentine and Orson
    Valentine and Orson; or, The
surprising adventures of two
sons of the Emperor of Greece.
A new ed., embellished with cuts.
New York, Pub. by S. King
[c 1828] 18 l. PP.   36992

The valley of Shenandoah. See
Tucker, George.

Value, Victor. See Académie
Classique et Militaire de Mantua.

Van Buren, Martin
    Substance of Mr. Van Buren's
observations on Mr. Foot's
amendment to the rules of the
Senate, by which it was proposed
to give the Vice-President the
right to call to order for words

spoken in debate. Washington, Pr.
by Green & Jarvis, 1828. 23 p.
DLC; MBC; MiD-B; N.   36993

Van Doren, Isaac
    Messers. Van Doren's Insti-
tute for Young Ladies. Removed
from Newark, New Jersey, to
Brooklyn Heights, Near the city
of New-York. [Newark, N. J.,
Feb. 12, 1828] 12 p. Washington's Headquarters Museum,
Newburg, N. Y.   36994

Van Dyck, Leonard B.
    An examination of certain pro-
ceedings of the board of superintendents, of the Theological Seminary of the Reformed Dutch
Church, at New-Brunswick. Schenectady, Pr. by Isaac Riggs,
1828. 20 p. PPL.   36995

[Van Ness, William Peter] 1778-
1826
    A concise narrative of Gen.
Jackson's first invasion of Florida, and of his immortal defence
of New-Orleans: with remarks
...5th ed. Albany, Pr. at the
Argus Office by order of the Republican General Committee,
1828. 24 p. IaU; N; NRHi.
                             36996
[----] ---- 6th ed. [New York,
1828?] 24 p. DLC.   36997

[Van Slyck, Albert]
    Broad grins of Rochester, con-
sisting of conversations between
the genius of the Genesee River,
and the guardian of the Erie Canal, which took place near the
aqueduct crossing the river at
Rochester. Rochester, Pr. for
the author by E. Scrantom, 1828.
47 p. RPB.   36998

Vanuxem, Lardner
    Observations on the geology
and organic remains of the secondary, tersiary, and alluvial
formations of the Atlantic coast of

the United States of North America... Extracted from the sixth volume of the Journal of the Academy of Natural Sciences of Philadelphia. Philadelphia, Mifflin and Parry, prs., 1828. 44 p. NNM; PU.   36999

Variety; or, Stories for children. With 24 engravings founded on Friends Kate and Fanny. 1st Amer. from the 2d London ed. New York, Gray & Bunce for W. B. Gilley, 1828. 66 l. PP.
37000

[Vaux, James]
From the Franklin Journal. Remarks upon the use of anthracite, and its application to the various purposes of domestic economy. [Philadelphia, 1828] [5] p. **PPL.**   37001

Verhandlungen und addresse von der Convention der Delegaten, welche sich den 28sten December, 1827. See National Republican Party. Ohio.

Vergilius Maro, Publius
P. Virgilii Maronis Opera. Interpretatione et notis illustravit carolus Ruaens, Soc. Jesu ... huic editioni accesit Clavis Virgiliana. E. Stereotypis A. D. & G. Bruce Fabricatis, Novi-eboraci, Philadelphiae, Pub. by Joseph Allen, sold by J. Grigg, 1828. xxii, 567, 105 p. CtHT-W; InHan; InNd.   37002

Vermont
Acts passed by the Legislature of the state of Vermont, at their October session, 1828. Pub. by authority. Woodstock, Pr. by Rufus Colton [1828] 72 p. CSmH; IaU; InSC; Ky; MdBB; NB; NNLI; Nj; Nv; R; TxU; W-L.   37003

---- Governor's speech. Gentlemen of the Council, and gentlemen of the House of Representa-

tives... Montpelier, Oct. 10, 1828. Bdsd. VtU.   37004

---- Journal of the Convention of Vermont, convened at the State House at Montpelier, June 26, A. D. 1828. Pub. by order of the Convention. Royalton, Pr. by W. Spooner [1828] 22 p. DLC; ICJ; ICN; M; MH-L; MiU-L; NcD; NjP; RPB.   37005

---- Journal of the Council of Censors, at their sessions at Montpelier and Burlington, in June, October and November, 1827. Pub. by order of the Council. Montpelier, Pr. by E. P. Walton, 1828. 48 p. DLC; IaHi; ICLaw; ICN; IU; M; MH; Mi; MnU; NB; OCLloyd; VtMiM.   37006

---- Journal of the General Assembly of the state of Vermont, at their session begun and held at Montpelier, Washington County, on Thursday, 9th October, A. D. 1828. Woodstock, Pr. by Rufus Colton, [1828] 203 p. VtU; BrMus.   37007

---- Report of the Board of Commissioners for Common Schools, submitted to the Legislature of the state of Vermont, Oct. 25, 1828. Ordered to be printed and circulated to each school district in the state. Woodstock, Pr. by Rufus Colton, 1828. 12 p. DHEW; IU; M.   37008

---- Reports of cases argued and determined in the Supreme Court of the state of Vermont. Prepared and published in pursuance of a statute law of the State. By Asa Aikens. Vol. II. Windsor, Pub. for the reporter by Simeon Ide, 1828. 458 p. Ct; CtU; DLC; ICLaw; Ia; In-SC; M; MBS; MH-L; MdBB; MiD-B; Mn; MoKB; NCH; NNLI; Nb; Nj; Nv; OcPW; PU-L; RPL; W; Wy.   37009

Vermont Bible Society
   Sixteenth annual report of the
Vermont Bible Society, communicated at their meeting, at Montpelier, Oct. 15, 1828. Montpelier, Pr. by E. P. Walton, Watchman Office, 1828. 16 p. VtU.
                                 37010
Vermont Colonization Society
   Ninth report of the Vermont
Colonization Society, communicated at the annual meeting, at
Montpelier, Oct. 17, 1828. Montpelier, Pr. by E. P. Walton,
1828. 8 p. MBC.   37011

Vermont Domestic Missionary
Society
   Annual report of the Vermont
Domestic Missionary Society,
presented at Burlington, Sept. 11,
1828. Burlington, Free Press
[1828] 24 p. Nh.   37012

Vermont Republican Convention.
See Democratic Party. Vermont.

Vermont Sabbath School Union
   Third annual report of the Vermont Sabbath School Union. Rutland, Pr. by Wm. Fay, 1828.
12 p. MHi.   37013

Vermont. University.
   University of Vermont. Commencement. Aug. 6, 1828. Order
of exercises. [Burlington] Pr. at
the Free Press Office [1828]
Bdsd. VtU.   37014

---- ---- Junior exhibition. Aug.
5, 1828. Order of exercises.
[Burlington] Pr. at the Free
Press Office [1828] Bdsd. VtU.
                                 37015
Vernon, William Henry
   A methodical treatise on the
cultivation of the mulberry tree,
on the raising of silk worms,
and on winding the silk from the
cocoons. United to an accurate
description of the winding mill.
With plates. Abridged from the
French of M. de la Brousse; with
notes and an appendix. By Wm.
H. Vernon. Boston, Hilliard,
Gray & Company. Eastman &
Bridgham, prs., Providence,
1828. 174 p. CSt; CUAL; DLC;
ICJ; MB; MBAt; MH; MS; NIC;
OCLloyd; PPAmP; PPF; PU;
PU-V; RHi; RNHi; RNR.   37016

Verren, Antoine
   La tache du minstre, ambas-
sadeur de Christ: Sermon D'en-
trée prononcé a New-York, dans
l'eglise Episcopale Protestante
Francaise du Saint - Esprit, le
12 Octobre, 1828 ... New-York,
T. & J. Swords, 1828. 20 p.
MiD-B.   37017

Vidaurre y Encalada, Manuel
Lorenzo de, 1773-1841
   Efectos de las facciones en
los gobiernos nacientes. En este
libro se recopilan los principios
fundamentales del gobierno demo-
cratico constitucional representa-
tivo. Obra escrita por el cuida-
dano M. L. Vidaurre ... Boston,
Impresa por W. W. Clapp, ano
1828. 280 p. MB; MH; MHi;
MdBJ; MeBa; PPL; ViU; BrMus.
                                 37018
---- Proyecto de un codigo penal;
contiene una explicacion prolija
de la entidad de los delitos en
general, y de la particular natur-
aleza de las penas que parecen
proporcionadas. Al ultimo se
agrega una disertacion sobre la
necesaria reforma del clero. Obra escrita por el ciudadano M.
L. de Vidaurre ... Boston, Impresa por H. Tupper, 1828. 230,
[2] p. DLC; MH-L; MHi; NhHi.
                                 37019
View of General Jackson's domestic relations. See Hammond,
Charles.

A view of South America and
Mexico. See Niles, John Milton.

The village in the mountains...
Utica, Pr. by C. Bennett, 1828.
60 p. Historical Records Survey,
Utica Imprints. Amer. Imprints
Inventory, No. 36, 1942.   37020

Villarino, José J.
A practical method of learning
to speak correctly the Castilian
language. New York, Pr. by
Lanuza, Mendia & Co. [etc.]
1828. viii, 484, [4] p. CtHT;
CtMW; InCW; IaDuU.   37021

Vindex, pseud.
A review and refutation of the
statements made in the late report of the canal commissioners,
to the Legislature of this state.
By Vindex. Albany, 1828. 8+ p.
MWA.   37022

Vindication of An address. See
Jenkins, William.

Vindication of the land agent.
See Austin, Benjamin.

Vindication of the rights of the
Churches of Christ. First printed
in the Spirit of the Pilgrims.
Boston, Peirce & Williams, 1828.
47 p. (Variously attributed to
John Lowell and Enoch Pond).
CtHC; ICN; MH; MHi; MiD-B;
N; NjPT; NjR; PPL; RPB. 37023

A vindication of the truth, being
a review of a sermon delivered
by Joshua L. Wilson, D. D. By
a member of the Enon Baptist
Church, in Cincinnati. Cincinnati, Morgan, Fisher & L'Hommedieu, prs. , Feb. , 1828. 38 p.
OCHP; OClWHi; PMA.   37024

Vinton, Samuel Finley, 1792-
1862
Speech of Mr. Vinton on the
emigration of Indians. Delivered
in the House of Representatives,
Feb. 20, 1828. Washington, Pr.
by Gales & Seaton, 1828. 28 p.

MB; MBAt; MdHi; MeB; MiD-B;
OO.   37025

The violin instructor, containing
a plain and easy introduction to
the rules and principles of the
violin; together with a choice and
extensive selection of new and
valuable music, consisting of pre-
ludes, and duets, songs, waltzes,
&c. , many of which have never
before been published in this
country. 2d ed. , corr. and imp.
Hallowell, Glazier & Co. , 1828.
52 p. Williamson: 10, 156. 37026

Virginia
Acts passed at a General Assembly of the Commonwealth of
Virginia, begun and held at the
capitol, in the city of Richmond,
on Monday the third day of December, in the year of our Lord
one thousand eight hundred and
twenty-seven. Richmond, Pr. by
Thomas Ritchie, pr. for the commonwealth, 1828. 142 p. Vi.
37027
---- A bill, concerning the Baltimore and Ohio Rail-Road.
[Richmond, Pr. by Thomas
Ritchie, pr. for the commonwealth, 1828] 2 p. DBRE; NN; V.
37028
---- A catalogue of the library of
the state of Virginia, arranged
alphabetically, under different
heads, with the number and size
of the volume of each work, and
its edition specified. To which is
prefixed, the rules and regulations provided for its government,
in conformity with the third section of "An act concerning the
public library," passed Feb. 11th,
1828. Richmond, Pr. by S. Shepherd & Co. , 1828. 31 p. Vi;
ViU; ViW.   37029

---- Journal of the House of Delegates of the commonwealth of
Virginia, begun and held at the
capitol, in the city of Richmond,

on Monday, the third day of December, one thousand eight hundred and twenty-seven. Richmond, Pr. by Thomas Ritchie, pr. for the commonwealth, 1827 [i. e. 1828] 210 p. Vi.   37030

---- Journal of the House of Delegates of Virginia, Anno Domini, 1776. [7 October-21 December 1776] Richmond, Pr. by Samuel Sheperd & Co., 1828. 108 p. DLC; Vi.   37031

---- Journal of the Senate of the commonwealth of Virginia, begun and held at the capitol, in the city of Richmond, on Monday the third day of December, in the year one thousand eight hundred and twenty seven. Richmond, Pr. by John Warrock, pr. to the Senate, 1827 [i. e. 1828] 154, [1] p. Vi.   37032

---- Journal of the Senate of the commonwealth of Virginia, begun and held in the city of Williamsburg, on Monday, the 5th day of October, in the year of our Lord 1778 [-1779]. Richmond, Pr. by Thomas W. White, 1828. v. p.; separate titles for each session of the Senate. Vi.   37033

---- Report of the principal engineer, on the rail-way from the coal-pits to James river. [Richmond, Pr. by Thomas Ritchie, pr. for the commonwealth, 1828] 6 p. DBRE; MiU-T; NN; Vi.   37034

---- Twelfth annual report of the Board of Public Works, to the General Assembly of Virginia. 24th January, 1828. Richmond, Pr. by Thomas Ritchie, pr. for the commonwealth, 1828. 29 p. CtY; DBRE; DLC; Vi.   37035

---- Twelfth annual report of the president and directors of the Board of Public Works, to the General Assembly of Virginia, January 24th, 1828. Richmond, Pr. by Samuel Shepherd & Co., 1828. [171]-410 p. CtY; DLC; IU; MiU-T; NN; Vi.   37036

The Virginia address. See National Republican Party. Virginia.

The Virginia almanac for 1829. Richmond [1828] DLC (22 l. ntp).   37037

Virginia and North Carolina almanack for 1829. By David Richardson. Richmond, John Warrock [1828] 18 l. CSmH; DLC; MWA; NcU; ViHi.   37038

Virginia electoral ticket. See Democratic Party. Virginia.

Virginia. Richmond Fayette Light Artillery.
    By-laws of the Richmond Fayette Light Artillery, commissioned on the 29th of May, 1821. Richmond, Pr. by Samuel Shepherd & Co., 1828. 8 p. CSmH.   37039

Virginia. University.
    ... Catalogue of the library of the University of Virginia... Also, a notice of such donations as have been made to the university. Charlottesville, Va., Gilmer, Davis & co., 1828. 114 p. CSmH; MH; NN; RPB; Vi; ViU.   37040

---- The course of examination and questions propounded in the several schools of the University of Virginia, at the late public examination in July, 1828. [Charlottesville, 1828] 3 p. DLC; ViU.   37041

---- University of Virginia, May 1, 1828. Sir, You will perceive by the subjoined resolution of the faculty of this institution... [Charlottesville, 1828. [p. [1] of 4 p. folder. ViU.   37042

---- Supplementary enactments
... [Verso: By-laws of the faculty of the University of Virginia]
[Charlottesville, 1828] [2] p.
ViU.   37043

A Virginian. See Heath, James
Ewell.

The visit concluded: or The second part of A visit to the seaside... Worcester, Pub. by Clarendon Harris, 1828. 275 p. MWA.
                           37044
A visit to my birth-place. See
Bunbury, Selina.

A visit to the Isle of Wight. See
Grierson, Miss.

A visit to the sea-side... Worcester, Pub. by Clarendon Harris. Wm. Manning, pr. [1828?]
275 p. MWA.   37045

---- In two parts. Boston,
Bowles & Dearborn, Press of
Isaac R. Butts & Co., 1828. 286
p. KU; MH.   37046

A voice from Kentucky. Concord,
Monday, Oct. 20, 1828. New
Hampshire Patriot - Extra. 8 p.
MdBJ; NhHi.   37047

A voice from the interior. Who
shall be president? The hero of
New-Orleans, or John the second,
of the House of Braintree. By a
republican of the Jefferson School.
Boston, True & Greene, prs.,
1828. 20 p. DLC; MiD-B. 37048

The voice of truth. To the citizens of Pennsylvania. Read for
yourselves. Reflect for yourselves. To you is committed the
safety of your country. Harrisburg, Argus office [1828] 24 p.
MB.   37049

The voice of Virginia! See National Republican Party. Virginia.

Der volksfreund und Hagerstauner
calender auf 1829. Hagerstaun,
Maryland, J. Gruber und D. May,
[1828] 15 l. MWA; PPAmP;
PPeSchw; PU.   37050

Volney, Constantin François
Chassebeuf comte de, 1757-1820
    Volney's ruins; or, Meditations
on the revolutions of empires.
Trans. from the 6th Paris ed. to
which is added the law of nature
and a short biographical notice,
by Count Daru. New York, Dixon
and Sickles, 1828. 247 p. CSmH;
CoU; MB; MBC; MCM; MdBS-P;
NRU; NT; PHi; RPB.   37051

Voltair, François Marie Arouet
de, 1694-1778
    Historie de Charles XII, Roi
de Suede. Par Voltaire, D'une
edition stéréotype De Paris. New
York, Collins & Co. [Imprint par
W. E. Dean] 1828. 308 p. MWalp;
NOg; ViL.   37052

---- The history of Charles the
Twelfth, King of Sweden. A new
translation, from the last Paris
ed. Hartford, S. Andrus, pub.,
1828. 276 p. IU; FS; MoSU; NcU;
TNJ-P.   37053

Vox populi vox Dei. In honor of
the election of our distinguished
fellow-citizen General Andrew
Jackson, to the Presidency of the
United States, You are respectfully invited to attend a ball in
Nashville, to be given at Mr. Edmondson's Hotel, on the 23 inst.
Nashville, Dec. 10, 1828. Bdsd.,
pr. on white silk. DLC.   37054

The voyage of Captain Popanilla.
See Beaconsfield, Benjamin Disraeli.

The voyages and adventures of
Capt. Robert Boyle. See Chetwood, William Rufus.

W

[Wade, Deborah B.]
The Burman slave girl also letters of Christian Burmans and a description of the Burman School a visit to the Burman Emperor. Boston, Pub. at James Lorings, 1828. 110 p. ViHaI. 37055

Wagler, F. A.
The celebrated Washington waltz, arranged for the piano forte by F. A. Wagler... Baltimore, Geo. Willig, Jr. c 1828. [2] p. ViU. 37056

Wainwright, Jonathan Mayhew, bp. , 1792-1854
A discourse on the occasion of forming the African Mission School Society, delivered in Christ Church in Hartford, Conn. , on Sunday evening, Aug. 10, 1828. Hartford, H. and F. J. Huntington [Hudson & Skinner, prs.] 1828. 24 p. CSmH; CtHT-W; CtHi; DLC; ICMe; MBAt; MWA; MiU-C; NHi; NN; OClWHi; PPPrHi; RPB; TxU. 37057

[----] Music of the church; a collection of psalm, hymn, and chant tunes, adapted to the worship of the Protestant Episcopal Church in the United States. Stereotyped by Peter C. Smith. New York, Pub. by Samuel F. Bradford, Philadelphia, Pr. by P. C. Smith, 1828. xxiii [i. e. xxxi], 238 p. CtHT-W; MBC; MH; NNG; NjR; PPPrHi; RPB. 37058

---- A sermon preached before the board of directors of the Domestic and Foreign Missionary Society of the Protestant Episcopal Church in the United States of America, in St. James' Church, Philadelphia, on Tuesday, May 13, 1828. New-York, Pr. by J. Seymore, 1828. 24 p. CSmH; CtHT; MB; MH; NCH; NGH; NIC; NNG; NcU; NjN; PPL; RPB; VtMiM. 37059

[Waldo, Samuel Putnam] 1780-1826
Memoirs of the illustrious citizen and patriot, Andrew Jackson ... By a citizen of Hagers Town, Md. Chambersburg [Pa.], Pr. for subscribers, 1828, 306 p. DLC; ICN; KyBgW-K; MBAt; MdBP; MdHi; NcD; NcU; OClWHi; PPFM; PPPrHi. 37060

Walker, James, 1794-1874
The exclusive system. A discourse delivered in Saco, on the evening of the twenty-first of November, 1827. Kennebunk, Pr. by James K. Remich, 1828. 34 p. MH; MeHi. 37061

---- A sermon delivered before His Excellency Levi Lincoln, governor, his honor Thomas L. Winthrop, lieut. governor, the hon. council, the Senate, and House of Representatives of the commonwealth of Massachusetts, on the day of general election, May 28, 1828. Boston, Dutton & Wentworth, prs. to the state, 1828. 16 p. CBPac; CLU; CSmH; CtSoP; DLC; ICMe; ICN; MBAt; MBC; MDeeP; MH; MH-AH; MHi; MMeT-Hi; MWA; MiD-B; MnU; NCH; NIC; NhHi; NjR; OClWHi; PHi; PPL; RPB; WHi; BrMus. 37062

Walker, John, 1732-1807
Cobb's abridgment of J. Walker's Critical pronouncing dictionary, and expositor of the English language, carefully compiled from the London quarto editions, published under the inspection of the author; in which Mr. Walker's principles of orthography and pronunciation are strictly followed ... Particularly designed for the use of schools. By Lyman Cobb, author of The spelling-book. Stereotyped by A. Chandler. Ithaca, N. Y. , Pr. and pub. by Mack & Andrus, 1828. 440 p. NIC; WHi. 37063

----Walker's critical pronouncing dictionary and expositor of the English language, abridged for the use of schools, containing a compendium of the principles of English pronunciation... Stereotype ed. Boston, Chas. Ewer, 1828. 447 p. MB; MH; NNC; OClWHi; OrSaW. 37064

---- Walker's critical pronouncing dictionary and expositor of the English language. Abridged. By the Rev. Thos. Smith, London. To which is added, a chronological table, containing the principal events of the late war between the United States and Great Britain... Coopertown, Stereotyped and pr. by H. & E. Phinney, 1828. 400 p. NBatHL. 37065

---- A critical pronouncing dictionary and expositor of the English language... 1st pocket ed. Hartford, S. Andrus, 1828. 336 p. MB; NNC (imp.); PHi. 37066

---- ---- To which are prefixed principals of English pronunciation and rules to be observed by the nations of Scotland, Ireland and London. Pub. by Collins & Hannay, New York, 1828. [2], 609, 102 p. AMob; CU; DLC; IEG; IU; InLW; MFiHi; MH; MdBE; NjMD; RP; WHi. 37067

---- Critical pronouncing dictionary and expositor of the English language, abridged for the use of schools by an American citizen. Philadelphia, Pr. and pub. by Griggs & Dickson for E. T. Scott, 1828. 413 p. DLC; MoS; OPosm. 37068

---- A rhyming dictionary, containing all the perfect rhymes of a different orthography, and allowable rhymes of a different sound, throughout the language... 2d Amer. ed. Boston, N. H. Whitaker, 1828. 128 p. IEG; KU;

KyLo; MHi; MShM; NjHoS. 37069

Walker, Joseph
    A glance at Dean's 120 reasons for being a Universalist. Portland, Shirley & Hyde, prs., 1828. 107 p. DLC; KU; MBC; MeBaT; MeHi; NNUT. 37070

[Wall, William G.] b. 1792
    The Hudson river port folio. [New York, Pub. by H. I. Megarey, 1828?] 20 col. pl. 50 x 68 cm. CSmH. 37071

Wallack, William H.
    Paul Jones; or The pilot of the German ocean. A melo drama in three acts. Adapted to the New-York Theatres. New York, Pub. at Elton's Dramatic repository and print store and W. Whale, Messrs. Richardson and Lord, Boston. Thos. Desliver, Philadelphia. W. Applegate, pr., 1828. 52 p. DLC; ICU; MH; PU. 37072

Walsh, Michael, 1763-1840
    The mercantile arithmetic adapted to the commerce of the United States in its domestic and foreign relations, with an appendix containing practical systems of mensuration, gauging, and bookkeeping; a new ed. rev. and imp. Boston, Richardson & Lord, 1828. 239, 76 p. CtMW; DAU; MH; NcGW; TxU-T. 37073

[Walsh, Robert] 1784-1859
    Biographical sketch of Andrew Jackson. [Albany, 1828] 16 p. DLC. 37074

[----] Biographical sketch of the life of Andrew Jackson, major-general of the armies of the United States, the hero of New-Orleans... Hudson, N. Y., W. E. Norman, 1828. 65 p. CSmH; DLC; ICHi; MBAt; MH; MWA; NN; NbU; PHi; T; WHi; BrMus. 37075

Walsh, Robert, 1772-1852
  Narrative of a journey from
Constantinople to England. Phila-
delphia, Carey, Lea & Carey,
1828. iv, 270 p. CtMW; GHi;
MB; MH; MoS; NNG; NcU; NjR;
OO; P; PPL; RNR; RPA; ScSoh;
ScU; VtU; WBB.   37076

Walton's Vermont register and
farmer's almanac for 1829. By
Zadock Thompson. Montpelier,
E. P. Walton [1828] 72 l. CLU;
InU; M; MB; MHi; MWA; N; NHi;
NNC; NhHi; OCLloyd; OO; P;
VtHi; WHi.   37077

The warbler, containing a collec-
tion of modern and popular songs
...By an Amateur. Baltimore,
Pub. by H. W. Bool, Jr., and
Henry Vicary, 1828. 216 p. RPB.
                           37078
[Ward, Henry Dana]
  Free masonry. Its pretensions
exposed in faithful extracts of its
standard authors; with a review
of Town's Speculative masonry...
its dangerous tendency exhibited
in extracts from the Abbé Bar-
ruel and Professor Robison...
New York, 1828. xvi, 399 p.
DeWI; GU; ICMe; ICU; IaCrM;
KyBC; MB; MH; MHi; MdHi;
MeB; MiU; NNF; NT; OCM;
OClWHi; OHi; PHi; PPFM; RPMA;
ScU; TNJ; TxU; UPB; WMFM;
BrMus.   37079

Ware, Henry, 1794-1843
  An address delivered at Ken-
nebunk before the York County
Unitarian Association Oct. 24,
1827. ...Kennebunk, Pr. by
James K. Remich, 1828. 35 p.
CBPac; CSmH; DLC; ICMe; MB;
MBC; MH; MiD-B; OClWHi; RPB.
                           37080
---- The recollections of Jotham
Anderson. With other pieces. 2d
ed. enl. Boston, Christian Regis-
ter [S. B. Manning, pr.] 1828. 3
l., 189 p. DLC; IEG; IU; MB;

MBAU; MBAt; MH-AH; MWA;
PU; BrMus.   37081

---- Two letters on the genuineness of the verse, 1 John, v. 7,
and on the scriptural argument
for Unitarianism; addressed to
the Rev. Alexander M'Leod, D. D.
of New York. Boston, Pub. by
J. W. Burditt, 1828. 36 p. MBAU.
                           37082
Ware, James
  The pocket farrier; or Gentleman's guide in the mangement of
horses under various diseases.
With an explanation of the symp-
toms attending the different dis-
orders, and the shortest, plain-
est, and most humane methods of
curing them. Directions for the
judging of the horse's age, and
useful observations on the breed-
ing, raising, and training of
colts... Richmond, T. W. White,
pr. 1828. 192 p. CSmH; DLC;
MBCo; Vi; ViU.   37083

Ware, William
  Three sermons, illustrative of
the principles of Unitarian Chris-
tianity, preached in Utica, on
Sunday, the 12th of October, 1828.
Utica, Pr. by Northway & Porter,
1828. 41 p. MH-AH; MHi; NN;
NUt.   37084

Warehousing system. See Aurora.

[Warfield, Charles]
  In relation to the Baltimore
and Ohio Rail Road Company. [a
protest against the taking of his
land]. [Baltimore, 1828] 8 p.
MdBJ-G.   37085

Warren, Mr.
  Mr. Warren, wishing to establish a well regulated Winter Theatre and such a one as may be
an ornament to the city of Washington proposes to the present
stockholders an advance of not
more than $60 on each and every

share of their stock... The favor or your company is requested, to attend a meeting of the stockholders, in the theatre, on Wednesday next, the 27th inst., at 4 o'clock P.M. city of Washington, Aug. 25th, 1828. 1 p. DLC.
37086

Warren, Caroline Matilda. See Thayer, Mrs. Caroline Matilda (Warren).

Warton, John
Death-bed scenes, and pastoral conversations, by the late John Warton, D.D. Edited by his sons. Philadelphia, Carey and Lea, 1828. 2 v. in 1. CtHC; GDC; ICU; KyLx; MA; MB; MBC; MDeeP; NGH; OSW; ScC; VtMiM.
37087

Washington, Thomas
Argument delivered in the Supreme court of errors and appeals, for the state of Tennessee, at Nashville, January term, 1828. In the case of David Ivey vs. Nathan G. Pinson and Danl. Harkins; involving the question in controversy between the University of North Carolina and the claimants of western lands, whose warrants have been attempted to be escheated by said state. Nashville, Pr. by John S. Simpson, 1828. 56 p. MB; TNJ.   37088

Washington, D.C.
A proclamation. Mayor's office, Washington. Dec. 23, 1828. Whereas it has been too much the habit of idle and inconsiderable persons, on Christmas and New Year's day and Eve, to indulge firing off guns, pistols, squibs, and crackers, and burning of gun-powder in divers other ways, to the great annoyance of the peaceable inhabitants of this city... [Requesting police to preserve peace and apprehend all offenders] [Dated] 23d day of December 1828. Jo. Gales, jr.,

Mayor. [Washington, 1828] 1 p. DLC.   37089

Washington almanac for 1829. By Nathan Bassett. Baltimore, Cushing & Jewett [1828] 35 p. CtY.   37090

Washington Orphan Asylum Society
Thirteenth annual report of the Washington Orphan Asylum Society: instituted on the tenth of October, 1815. Washington, E. De Krafft, pr., 1828. 7 p. DLC.
37091

Washington Republican, Washington, D.C.
The carrier's address to the patrons of the "Washington Republican." Washington, Gurnsey co., Jan. 1, 1828. 1 p. DLC.
37092

Washington. Trinity Church
Ceremonies on laying the corner stone of Trinity Church in the city of Washington, on Saturday, 31st May, 1828. Washington, Pr. by Way & Gideon, 1828. 14 p. DLC; RPB.   37093

Watkins, Lucy
Henry and Eliza, a pathetic tale: founded on a well known recent event. ... To which is added, Mary, the maid of the inn, an affecting narrative. The singular way she discovers her lover to be a robber and murderer; who is convicted and executed, she loses her reason, and is frozen to death. Philadelphia, Freeman Scott, 1828. 70 p. IObB; P.
37094

Watson, Richard
An address delivered at the ordination of the Reverend John Bell, Jonathan Crowther, and others, at the conference of Wesleyan Methodist ministers, held in Manchester, August 1827. New-York, Pub. by N. Bangs & J. Emory, for the Methodist Episco-

pal Church, at the Conference office, A. Hoyt, pr., 1828. 27 p. GEU; MiD; NRAB.   37095

---- An apology for the Bible, in a series of letters, addressed to Thomas Paine. Cambridge, Pub. by Hilliard and Brown [Cambridge, Hilliard, Metcalf, & Co.] 1828. 173 p. PPL.   37096

---- ---- Also, Leslie's Short and easy method with the deists. New York, Azor Hoyt, pr., Pub. by N. Bangs & J. Emory, 1828. 226 p. CSmH; CtMW; MB; MiMu; USlC.   37097

Watterston, George
Tabular statistical views of the population, commerce, navigation, public lands, post office establishment, revenue, mint, military & naval establishments, expenditures, and public debt of the United States. Washington, J. Elliot, 1828. 132 [i.e. 136] p. ICJ; MdBE; MiD-B; MoSW; NIC; RPA; RPB.   37098

Watts, Alarie Alexander, 1797-1864, ed.
The poetical album; and register of modern fugitive poetry, ed. by Alarie A. Watts... Boston, Wells and Lilly, 1828. xvi, 395 p. DLC; MB; NjR; OO; WOccR.   37099

Watts, Isaac, 1674-1748
Hymns and spiritual songs in three books... Stereotyped by J. Reed. Elizabeth-Town, N.J., Booth, 1828. 246 p. NjP. 37100

---- ---- Philadelphia, H. Adams, 1828. 240 p. CSmH; NN.   37101

---- ---- Philadelphia, M'Carty & Davis, 1828. 274 p. CU.   37102

---- ---- [Sandbornton, N.H.] D.V. Moulton [Stereotyped by T. H. Carter & co., Boston] 1828.

272 p. MB; NN.   37103

---- The world to come; or, Discourses on the joys and sorrows of departed souls of death, and the glory or terror of the resurrection... A new ed., embellished with a fine portrait of the author. New York, Pub. by J. McGowan, 1828. 561 p. IaIndianS.   37104

Watts, Joseph
The tailor's instructor, or, A comprehensive analysis of the elements of cutting garments of every kind. Pr. at the Advocate Office. Hallowell, 1828. 12 p. DLC.   37105

Wauch, Mansie. See Moir, David Macbeth.

Waverly Circulating Library, Waverly, Me.
Catalogue of the Waverly Circulating Library, No. 8, Mussey's Row Middle Street. Portland, Pr. by J. Adams, 1828. 12 p. MiD-B.   37106

The way to be good and happy. Wendell, J. Metcalf, 1828. 16 p. MH.   37107

Wayne, Anthony
To the freemen of Maryland. Read, pause, and reflect. facts! stubborn facts!...[Signed] Anthony Wayne [1828] 1 p. DLC; MH.   37108

[Webbe, Cornelius]
Posthumous papers, facetious and fanciful, of a person lately about town... New-York, Pr. by J. & J. Harper, sold by Collins & Hannay [etc.] 1828. 243 p. DLC; IEN; MB; MH; NCH; NRU; NjP; NjR; PU.   37109

[----] ---- Another issue. Imprint differs slightly. DLC.   37110

Webster 473

Webster, Daniel, 1782-1852
Remarks of Mr. Webster in
the Senate of the United States,
May 9, 1828, on the tarriff bill.
Boston, Press of the Boston
Daily Advertiser, W. L. Lewis,
pr. , 1828. 32 p. CoD; IEN-M;
M; MB; MBAt; MH-AH; MHi;
NhHi; PHi; RP; WHi.   37111

---- ---- Boston, Press of the
Boston daily advertiser, 1828.
48 p. CSmH; DeGE.   37112

[Webster, Ezekiel]
A defence of the national administration in an address to the
people of New-Hampshire. By
Cato. Concord, Pr. by H. E.
Moore, 1828. 18 p. DLC; MiD-B;
Nh; NhHi; NjR; OClWHi; WHi.
      37113
Webster, John White, 1793-1850
A manual of chemistry on the
basis of Professor Brande's; containing the principal facts of the
science... compiled from the
works of the most distinguished
chemists. Designed as a text
book for the use of students, and
persons attending lectures on
chemistry. 2d ed. Boston, Pub.
by Richardson & Lord, 1828. xi,
[1] 619, [1] p. CtHT; CtMW;
IGK; LShC; MB; MH; MHi; MdBS;
NCH; NNNAM; NRU-M; NSyU;
OClM; PPF; PPL; PU-S; RPB;
TNJ; WM.   37114

Webster, Noah, 1758-1843
An American dictionary of the
English language...In two vols.
New York, Pub. by S. Converse,
Pr. by Hezekiah Howe, New
Haven, 1828. 2 vols. AzU;
CSmH; CU; CtHC; CtHT; CtHT-
W; CtY; CoU; DLC; GU; ICHi;
ICN; InCW; KU; MB; MBC; MH;
MHi; MShM; MdBJ; MdBP; MdBS;
MiD; MnU; MoSM; NCH; NNC;
NUt; NcU; NhD; NjP; OClWHi; P;
PHC; PP; PPAmP; RPB; ScC;
TxGR; ViU; VtMiM; WHi; WU;

WM; WaU.   37115

---- The American spelling book;
containing the rudiments of the
English language, for the use of
schools in the United States...
Rev. impression. Canandaigua,
Pr. by Bemis, Morse & Ward,
1828. 168 p. NBuG.   37116

---- ---- Cincinnati, Pub. by
Morgan & Sanxay, Stereotyped by
J. Howe, Philadelphia, 1828.
168 p. OHi.   37117

---- ---- Concord, N. H. , Pub.
by Manahan, Hoag & co. , 1828.
168 p. MWA; NNC.   37118

---- ---- Concord, N. H. , Pub.
by Horatio Hill & Co. , 1828. 168
p. MH; MnU; NhD; NhHi.   37119

---- ---- Middletown, Conn. ,
Pub. by Wm. H. Niles. Stereotyped by A. Chandler, 1828. 168
p. CSmH; CtHT-W; CtHi; CtY;
MB; MH; MWA; NN; NNC. 37120

---- ---- New Brunswick, N. J. ,
Pr. by Terhune & Letson, 1828.
168 p. CtY; OClWHi.   37121

---- ---- Philadelphia, Pub. by
Robert H. Sherburne, Stereotyped
by J. Howe, 1828. 168 p. CtSoP;
MH; MNS; MWA; NN; OClWHi;
OMC; RPB; VtU; WHi.   37122

Webster's calendar: or the Albany
almanack for 1829. By Edwin E.
Prentiss. Albany, Websters &
Skinners [1828] 18 l. MWA; MiU-
C; N; NCooHi; NN; WHi.   37123

---- ---- Albany, Websters &
Skinners [1828] [2d ed.] 18 l.
DLC; MWA; N; NCooHi; NN;
OClWHi; PHi.   37124

Weeden, J.
A summary view of the houses
for public worship in the city and

county of New York, A. D. 1828...
New York, M. Day, 1828. 2 p.
NNG.   37125

The week; or, The practical duties of the fourth commandment,
exhibited in a series of tracts,
entitled The last day of the week,
The first day of the week & The
week completed. New York,
Bangs & Emory, 1828. 92+ 93+
97 p. CtMW; MoSV.   37126

Week days and Sunday. Designed
for very little children. By the
author of 'Fruit and Flowers'.
Boston, Hilliard, Gray, Little,
and Wilkins, 1828. 8 p. MH.
                                  37127

Weems, Mason Locke, 1759-1825
    God's revenge against adultery,
awfully [!] exemplified in the following cases of American crim.
con. Philadelphia, Pub. by Jos.
Allen, sold by John Grigg, 1828.
71 p. PHi.   37128

---- The life of Gen. Francis
Marion, a celebrated partisan officer in the revolutionary war,
against the British and Tories in
South Carolina and Georgia. By
Brig. Gen. P. Horry, of Marion's
brigade: and M. L. Weems...
Philadelphia, J. Allen, 1828.
252 p. DLC; PU.   37129

---- The life of George Washington: with curious anecdotes, equal-
ly honourable to himself, and ex-
emplary to his young countrymen
...Philadelphia, Joseph Allen,
1828. 228 p. KWiU; PHi; Vi;
ViU.   37130

Weighty considerations. Come let
us reason together. People of
Kentucky...A free citizen. July
1828. 1 p. DLC.   37131

Welch, Jonathan Ashley, 1792-
1859
    Address delivered before the

Windham County Peace Society,
at their semi-annual meeting,
held at Plainfield, Feb. 13, 1828.
Brooklyn, Con. , Advertiser
press, John Gray, jr. , 1828. 28
p. CSmH; CtHi; ICMe; MBAt;
MeB; PHi; RP; BrMus.   37132

Weld, Lewis
    An address delivered in the
capitol, in Washington City, Feb.
16th, 1828, at an exhibition of
three of the pupils of the Pennsylvania Institution for the Education of the Deaf and Dumb. Pub.
by request. Washington, Way &
Gideon, prs. , 1828. 11 p. CtY;
MB; MH; MHi; MWA; Md;
PPAmP; PPL; RPB; BrMus.
                                  37133
A well wisher, pseud. See A
brief summary of Baptist sentiments.

Well-wisher, pseud. See To William Jenkins.

Wells, Albert
    A compendium of general his-
tory. 1st ed. Pub. by Collins &
Co. New York, Pr. by W. E.
Dean, 1828. viii [1], 215 p.
CtHC; NcDaD.   37134

Wernwag, Lewis
    Memorial of Lewis Wernwag,
to the Senate and House of Representatives, praying an extension of his patent for his improvement in bridge architecture. Pr.
by John S. Gallaher, 1828. [Pre-
face dated "Harper's Ferry, Feb.
10, 1828] 12 p. NIC.   37135

Wesley, John
    The miscellaneous works of
the Rev. John Wesley. Containing
a plain account of Christian per-
fection... Principles of the Methodists [etc.] New York, Pr. and
sold by J. & J. Harper, 1828. 3
v. GAGTh; GEU-T; In; InGr;
NNUT.   37136

---- A plain account of Christian prefection. By the Rev. John Wesley. New York, J. Emory and B. Waugh, 1828. 60 p. ICU. 37137

Wesleyan Academy. Wilbraham, Mass.
Catalogue of the officers and students of the Wesleyan Academy, Wilbraham, Mass. Fall term, Nov. 1828. Springfield, S. Bowles, pr., 1828. 8 p. CSmH. 37138

West Parish Sewing Society
Constitution of the West Parish Sewing Society. Instituted April, 1820. Boston, Beals, Homer & Co., prs., 1828. 8 p. MWA. 37139

Westchester and Putnam farmers' almanac for 1829. By David Young. Peekskill, S. Marks & Son [1828] 18 1. NjR. 37140

Western, Henry M.
Address on domestic manufactures delivered before The American Institute, in the City of New York, on the 4th of July,... New York, Pub. by the American Institute, Pr. by John Dixon, 1828. 14 p. TxDaM. 37141

The Western almanack, and Michigan register for 1829. By Hiram Wilmarth. Detroit, J.W. Seymour, [1828] 12 1. MiD-B. 37142

Western almanack for 1829. By Oliver Loud. Buffalo, Day, Follett & Haskins [1828] 12 1. WHi. 37143

---- ---- Fredonia, Henry C. Frisbee [1828] 18 1. DLC; ICHi. 37144

---- ---- Rochester, E. Peck & Co. [1828] 12 1. MWA; N; NBuHi; NHi; NR; NRMA; NRU. 37145

Western Education Society, N.Y.
Tenth report of the directors of the Western Education Society of the state of New York, presented at their anniversary meeting, Aug. 2, 1828. Utica, Pr. by Hastings & Tracy, 1828. 16 p. PPPrHi. 37146

The Western farmers' almanac for 1829. By Rev. John Taylor. Pittsburgh, H. Holdship & Son; D. & M. Maclean, prs. [1828] 18 1. N; OHi; WvU. 37147

---- ---- Issue with added "Magazine." 36 1. DLC; InU; MWA; NBuHi; OClWHi; OMC; P; PHi; PPi; PPiU; Wv-Ar. 37148

Western Railway
Report of the commissioners on the Western Railway. Boston, Springfield, 1828. 56 p. ICJ; NIC. 37149

The Western souvenir, a Christmas and New Year's gift for 1829. Ed. by James Hall. Cincinnati, Pub. by N. & G. Guilford [W. M. Farnsworth, pr.] [1828] 324 p. CSmH; DLC; IGK; IU; InHi; InU; KyLoF; MnHi; NNC; OClWHi; OHi; PP; PPi; PPiU; RPB; WHi; BrMus. 37150

Western Sunday School Union. N.Y.
The third report of the Western Sunday School Union of the state of New York: presented at the annual meeting in Utica, Aug. 28, 1828. Utica, Pr. for the Society by Colwell & Ely, 1828. 24 p. MWA; N; NUt; OO. 37151

Der Westliche Menschenfreund u. Schellsburger Calender auf 1829. Von Carl Friedrich Egelmann. Schellsburg, Friedrich Goeb [1828] 18 1. Drake 11656. 37152

Westminster Assembly of Divines
The Westminster Shorter Catechism with the Scripture proofs in words at length. Lexington,

Ky., Pr. and pub. by Thomas T. Skillman, 1828. 46 p. ICU. 37153

Wetherill, Samuel P. & Co.
A treatise on the diseases of seamen. Medicine chests carefully put up by Samuel P. Wetherill & Co. chemists and druggists. No. 65 North Front Street, Philadelphia. Philadelphia, Mifflin and Parry, prs., 1828. 24 p. PHi. 37154

What is gentility? See Smith, Mrs. Margaret (Bayard).

Wheaton, Eber
Analytical arithmetic, being a natural and easy introduction to the elementary rules of the science... New York, J. F. Sibell, [1828] 108 p. NN; BrMus. 37155

---- Oration delivered July 4, 1828. By Eber Wheaton, esq., of the New-York Journeymen Coopers' Society, at Masonichall, before the several civic societies of New-York, Peter Van Pelt, pr., 1828. 17 p. DLC; PHi; PPL. 37156

Wheaton, Nathaniel Sheldon, 1792-1862
The providence of God displayed in the rise and fall of nations. A sermon, delivered at the annual election, in Trinity Church, New-Haven, on Wednesday the 7th of May, 1828. ... New-Haven, Pub. by order of the Legislature, J. Barber, pr., 1828. 18 p. CSmH; Ct; CtHi; CtSoP; DLC; MH; MHi; MiD-B; N; NNP; OClWHi. 37157

Wheeling Gazette. Wheeling, W. Va.
New Year's address to the patrons of the Wheeling Gazette. January 1st, 1828. [Wheeling, W. Va. 1828] 1 p. DLC. 37158

Whelpley, Samuel, 1766-1817
A compend of history from the earliest times, comprehending a general view of the present state of the world with respect to civilization, religion, and government. 10th ed. Boston, Richardson & Lord, 1828. 2 v. in 1. CL; CtHT-W; MB; MH; MdBL; MeBaT; MiD; MnU; OClWHi; PAtM; TxU-T; ViAlTh. 37159

When the following letter was written... See Carey, Mathew.

Which society shall you join, liberal or orthodox? A letter to a friend... 2d ed. Boston, Peirce and Williams, 1828. 24 p. CBPac; CtHC; MBC; NNUT; OClWHi; PHi; PPL. 37160

Whimwhams, by four of us... Boston, S. G. Goodrich, 1828. ix p., 1l., 104 [i. e. 204] p. DLC; ICU; MH; MWHi; NHi; PU; BrMus. 37160a

Whipple, Thomas
To the editor of the National Journal. Sir: In your journal of the 7th February, you say "Mr. Whipple asked if it was to be allowed that the private character of members was to be referred to on this floor." ... Thos. Whipple. Thursday February 7th, 1828. 1 p. DLC. 37161

Whitaker, Daniel Kimball, 1801-1881
Christian perseverance: a sermon delivered in the Second Independent Church in Charleston S. C. Pub. by the Charleston Unitarian Book Society. Charleston, Pr. by James S. Burges, 1828. 42 p. DLC; ICMe; MB; MBAU; MBC; MWA; NNUT; RPB; ScU; BrMus. 37162

[White, Charles] 1793-1861
Almack's revisited; or Herbert

Milton... In two volumes. New
York, Pr. by J. & J. Harper, for
Collins and Hannay, Collins and
Co., and G. and C. Carvill;
Philadelphia, Carey, Lea and
Carey, Towar and Hogan, and R.
H. Small; Boston, Hilliard, Gray
and Co., and Richardson and
Lord, 1828. 2 vols. MB; MH; Mi;
NCH; NNS; NSyHi; NcU; NjR; OAU;
RPB.   37163

White, William, 1748-1836
    An address delivered at the
commencement of the General
Theological Seminary of the Prot-
estant Episcopal Church in the
United States; held in St. John's
Chapel, in the city of New York
... New York, Pr. by T. & J.
Swords, 1828. 19 p. CtHT; NCH;
NGH; NIC; NNG; NNUT; PHi.
                             37164
Whitehouse, Elizabeth S.
    Kingdom stories for juniors;
Stories of the Kingdom of Israel,
arranged for story-tellers... with
introd. by Alberta Munkres and
Neilson C. Haunay... N.Y. Chi-
cago etc. Fleming H. Revell.
Co., [c1828] 221 p. DLC; MBU.
                             37165
Whitman, Bernard, 1796-1834
    A discourse on regeneration.
Boston, Bowles and Dearborn,
Press of Isaac R. Butts & Co.,
1828. 57 p. CtHC; ICMe; ICU;
MBAU; MBAt; MBC; MH; MeHi;
MiD-B; Nh; RPB; BrMus. 37166

---- ---- 2d ed. Boston, Bowles
and Dearborn, Press of Isaac R.
Butts and Co., 1828. 57 p.
CtSoP; ICN; MDovC; MH; PPL.
                             37167
---- ---- 3d ed. Boston, Bowles
& Dearborn. Press of Isaac R.
Butts and Co., 1828. 57 p. IEG;
MBAU; MMeT.   37168

---- ---- 4th ed. Boston, Bowles
and Dearborn, Press of Isaac R.
Butts and Co., 1828. 57 p.

CBPac; ICMcC; MH; MHi; WHi.
                             37169
---- A thanksgiving discourse, on
the means of increasing public
happiness. Cambridge, Pub. by
Hilliard and Brown. Boston,
Bowles and Dearborn [Boston,
Press of Isaac R. Butts & Co.]
1828. 35 p. ICMe; MB; MBAU;
MBAt; MWA; MeHi.   37170

Whitman, John W., reporter.
See Report of a trial in the su-
preme judicial court, holden at
Boston.

Whittemore, Thomas
    A discourse delivered in the
Central Universalist Church Boston, before the Female Samari-
tan Society. Oct. 26, 1828. Boston, Pr. and pub. at the Trumpet Office, George N. Bazin, pr.
[1828] 16 p. MBC; BrMus.
                             37171
Wickliffe, Charles Anderson,
1788-1869
    Address of C. A. Wickliffe,
esq. on the presidential election.
Published by the Jackson Club of
the city and county of Philadelphia. Bardstown, June 10, 1828.
To the citizens of the Ninth Congressional District. [Philadel-
phia, 1828] 8 p. PHi.   37172

---- Speech of Mr. Wickliffe in
the House of Representatives, on
the 30th of January, 1828, in
favor of the adoption of the resolutions proposing an inquiry into
the expediency of reducing the
public expenditures, and providing,
by further legislation, against the
abuses in the misapplication of
public money. City of Washington, Pr. by F. S. Myer, 1828.
20 p. CSmH; MH.   37173

[----] To the citizens of the ninth
congressional district. Fellow
citizens - [Louisville? S. Penn,
jr., pr., 1828?] 12 p.

KyLoF.   37174

Wigglesworth, Michael, 1631-1705
The day of doom: or, A poetical description of the great and
last judgement. With a short discourse about eternity... From the
6th ed., 1715. Boston, C. Ewer,
1828. 95 p. CBPac; DLC; ICMe;
ICN; IaU; MA; MB; MH; MHi;
Nh; PLFM; RPB; WU.   37175

Wilbur, Hervey
Useful tables of Scripture
names, Scripture geography,
Scripture chronology, Scripture
references, &c. Prepared to ac-
company the Reference Testa-
ment. Amherst, Mass., J. S. &
C. Adams, 1828. 18 p. MB; NN.
                           37176
---- ---- Prepared to accom-
pany the Reference Bible. New-
York, H. C. Sleight, 1828. 31 p.
NN.   37177

Wilcox, A. F.
A catechetical and practical
grammar, of the English language. For the use of schools.
New Haven, Pub. by S. Wadsworth and R. Lockwood. New
York, Pr. by Hezekiah Howe,
1828. vi, 110 p. CtSoP; CtY;
MB; MH; NNC; VtMiM.   37178

Wilcox, Carlos, 1794-1823
Remains of the Rev. Carlos
Wilcox, late pastor of the North
Congregational Church in Hart-
ford, with a memoir of his life.
Hartford, E. Hopkins, publisher,
[P. Canfield, pr.] 1828. 431 p.
CSaT; CtHi; DLC; IEG; IP; MWA;
NBuG; NjP; OClWHi; PU; RHi;
RPB; VtMiS.   37179

Wilde, Richard Henry, 1789-1847
Speeches of Mr. Wilde, of
Georgia, on internal improve-
ments. Delivered in the House of
Representatives of the United
States, Feb. 29, and March 7,

1828. Washington, Pr. by Gales
& Seaton, 1828. 14 p. DLC;
MiD-B.   37180

Wilkins, John Howard
Elements of astronomy, illustrated with plates, for the use of
schools and academies. With
questions... 5th ed., stereotyped.
Boston, Hilliard, Gray, Little,
and Wilkins, 1828. viii, 152 p.
InCW; MB; MBAt; MH; MHi;
MoSpD; PPF; TNJ.   37181

[Wilkinson, Edward] 1728-1809
Wisdom, a poem... Greens-
borough [Vt.] Pr. by T. Early
Strange, 1828. 14 p. CSmH.
                           37182
Willard, Emma (Hart)
History of the United States,
or Republic of America: exhibited
in connexion with its chronology
and progressive geography by
means of a series of maps; designed for schools and private libraries... New York, White, Gallaher & White, 1828. xvi, vii,
426 p. Ct; ICU; MB; MHi;
MsJMC; MsSM; NcDaD; NjP; NjR;
PU; RNR; RPA; RPJCB; TNJ.
                           37183
---- A series of maps to Willard's History of the U. S.; or,
Republic of America. Designed
for schools and private libraries.
New York, White, Gallaher and
White, 1828. 12 maps. ICU; MH;
MoSHi; NjR; ViU.   37184

[Willard, Samuel] 1776-1859
The general class-book, or interesting lessons in prose and
verse, on a great variety of subjects; combined with an epitome
of English orthography and pronunciation, and intended as the
third book in a course of reading
for the use of schools. By the
author of the Franklin primer and
the Improved reader. Greenfield,
Mass., A. Phelps & A. Clark,
1828. 312 p. DLC.   37185

[----] Secondary lessons, or The improved reader; intended as a sequel to the Franklin Primer. By a friend of youth... New Haven, Durrie & Peck, and New York, R. Lockwood, 1828. 184 p. CtY.   37186

---- Simple hymns for children. Index to passages of Scripture... Lessons for aid of parents and instructors of Sunday schools. Keene, N. H. , J. Prentiss, 1828. 31 p. MDeeP (not located 1970).
                                37187

Willetts, Jacob
   Easy grammar of geography. Poughkeepsie, Paraclete Potter, 1828. 215 p. NP.   37188

William Vance's oath of allegiance to the king of Great Britain. [New York?] 1828. Bdsd. MB.   37188a

Williams, Catherine R. (Arnold), 1790-1872
   Original poems, on various subjects... Providence, Pr. by H. H. Brown, 1828. 107 p. CSmH; CtSoP; MB; MH; MWA; NIC; NNC; PU; RHi; RLa; RP; RPA; ViU; BrMus.   37189

Williams, H.
   Elements of drawing, exemplified in a variety of figures and sketches of parts of the human form... 4th ed. , enl. Boston, R. P. & C. Williams. S. W. Allen, pr. , Newburyport, 1828. 10 p. MNF.   37190

Williams, John D.
   The mathematical companion; containing new researches and improvements in the mathematics; with collections of questions proposed and resolved by ingenious correspondents. Conducted by J. D. Williams. New York, 1828. [A prospectus] 8 p. MH.   37191

Williams, John Mason, 1780-1868
   A sketch of the character of the late Hon. Samuel Howe, delivered at the opening of the Court of Common Pleas, at Worcester, on the third day of March 1828, after the usual charge to the grand jury. Published by request of the Bar of the county. Worcester, from the Aegis Press, Griffin and Morrill, prs. , 1828. 16 p. CLU; CSmH; Ct; CtSoP; CtY; DLC; ICU; KHi; MBAt; MBC; MDeeP; MH; MHi; MNF; MWA; MiD-B; MoU; NN; NbHi; Nh; NjR; OClWHi; PPAmP; PPL; RPB; ScHi; WHi; BrMus.   37192

Williams, Joshua Lewis
   Sermon preached before the North Society of Greenwich, July 25th, 1828; at the ordination and installation of Rev. Chauncey Wilcox... Norwalk, Conn. , Pr. by Albert Hanford, 1828. 19 p. CSmH; CtHi.   37193

Williams, R. P. & C. , firm.
   Advertisement. Candid examination of the Episcopal Church, in two letters to a friend. In strong paper covers, 19 cents each. $1. 50 per doz. $10 per hundred. [Ad for the "Eleventh edition... Boston, R. P. & C. Williams, 1828.] MBC.   37194

Williams, William
   Journal of the life, travels and gospel labours, of William Williams, dec. A minister of the Society of Friends. Late of White-Water, Indiana. Cincinnati, Lodge, L'Hommedieu, and Hammond, prs. , 1828. 272 p. CSmH; DLC; ICN; IEG; In; InU; KWiU; MH; MnHi; NN; NNUT; NbOP; NcU; OClWHi; PSC-Hi; RNHi; T; TxU; WHi.   37195

Williams' calendar, or the Utica almanack for 1829. By Edwin E.

Prentiss. Buffalo, Sargent & Wilgus [1828] 18 l. CSmH; NBuHi; NRMA.   37196

---- ---- Utica, William Williams [1828] 18 l. CLU; CSmH; InU; MWA; NBuHi; NHi; NIC; NN; NUtHi.   37197

---- ---- Watertown, Knowlton and Rice [1828] 18 l. NHC.
                                 37198
Williams College
Catalogue of books, in the library of Williams College, Williamstown, Williamstown, Pr. by Ridley Bannister, 1828. 40 p. MWiW.   37199

---- Catalogue of the officers and students of Williams College, and the Berkshire Medical Institute, connected with it. 1828. [Williamstown, R. Bannister? 1828] 20 p. MWiW; PPL. 37200

---- Commencement. Williams College, September 3, 1828. [Williamstown, R. Bannister? 1828] 4 p. MWiW.   37201

---- Exhibition of the Junior class. Williams College, May 20, 1828. [Williamstown, R. Bannister? 1828] 2 l. MWiW. 37202

---- Senior exhibition. Williams College, December 30, 1828. [Williamstown, R. Bannister? 1828] 2 l. MWiW.   37203

---- Adelphic Union.
Exhibition of the Adelphic Union Society. Williams College, August 6, 1828. [Williamstown, R. Bannister? 1828] 2 l. MWiW.
                                 37204
Willis, Nathaniel Parker, ed.
The legendary, consisting of original pieces, principally illustrative of American history, scenery, and manners. Boston, Saml. G. Goodrich, 1828. 2 vols.

CSmH; CU; CtHT-W; DLC; GDC; ICN; IU; Ia; MB; MH; MdBP; MiD-B; MiU; MnHi; MnU; NBuG; NN; NNS; NjR; PU; RNR; TxU; WHi.   37205

Williston, Seth, 1770-1851
Sermons adapted to revivals: being designed to promote both their power and purity. New York, Sold by John P. Haven, American Tract House, 1828. 220 p. ICU.   37206

Wilson, Alexander, 1766-1813
American ornithology; or The natural history of the birds of the United States. Illustrated with plates engraved and coloured from original drawings taken from nature... In three vols. ... Pub. by Collins & co., New York, and Harrison Hall, Philadelphia. 1828-[1829] 3 vols. + vol. of plates. CtMW; DeWI; IaU; In; MB; MBH; MH-Z; MdBJ; MdBP; MnU; NcU; NjN; PHC; PHi; PPAmP; PPF; PU-Z; T; WHi.
                                 37207
Wilson, Bird, 1777-1859
A sermon, delivered in the chapel of the General Theological Seminary... on Sunday, December 9th, 1827. New York, Elam Bliss [Pr. by Vanderpool & Cole] 1828. 29 p. CtHT; MBD; MiD-B; N; NCH; NGH; NNG; PHi.   37208

Wilson, James, 1760-1839
Dissertation on the future restoration of the Jews, the overthrow of the papal civil authority, and on other interesting events of prophecy. In two sections. Providence, H. H. Brown, pr., 1828. 22 p. MBC; MWA; NNUT; OCH; PPPrHi; RHi; RPB.   37209

[Wilson, Samuel]
The life and death of Isabella Turnbull and Ann Wade. New York, Pub. by N. Bangs and J. Emory for the Methodist Episco-

pal Church, at the Conference office, A. Hoyt, pr., 1828. 12 p. NBLiHi.   37210

Wilson, William
   Economy of the kitchen-garden, the orchard, and the vinery, with plain practical directions, for their management. New York, Pub. by Anderson, Davis & Co., 1828. 206 p. CSmH; Nh; NjR; PPL.
                                  37211
Wines, Abijah, 1766-1833
   The merely amiable, moral man, no Christian. A discourse, ...Portland, Shirley & Hyde, prs., 1828. 26 p. MBAt; MBC; MH; Me; MeHi; Nh; NhHi; NjR; RPB.   37212

Winships' Nursery, Brighton, Mass.
   Catalogue of fruit trees, ornamental and flowering shrubs, herbaceous plants, and bulbous roots, at Messrs. Winship's Brighton Nursery. Boston, Pr. at the New England Farmer office, by John B. Russell, 1828. 12 p. MB.   37213

Winter evenings conversations... between a father and his children, on the works of God. 3d ed. Philadelphia, 1828. BrMus.
                                  37214
[Wirt, William] 1772-1834
   Case of the ship James Birckhead. [Baltimore, 1828] 7 p. MdHi (20 p.); PPL.   37215

Wiscasset, Me. Second Congregational Church.
   Confession of faith and church covenance and rules, adopted by the Second Congregational Church in Wiscasset as their articles of Christian fellowship and union. Church formed Oct. 9, 1828. Wiscasset, John Herrick, pr., 1828. 19 p. MBC; MBH.   37216

Wisdom, a poem. See Wilkin-

son, Edward.

Wisner, William
   Review of a sermon, entitled, "The Christian bishop approving himself unto God: in reference to the present state of the Protestant Episcopal Church in the United States." Preached by Bishop Hobart, at the consecration of Henry U. Onderdonk, D.D., assistant bishop of Pennsylvania. Ithaca, Pr. by D.D. Spencer, 1828. 32 p. CSmH (20 p); MH; NHi; NIC.   37217

Witherspoon, John
   A letter from a blacksmith to the ministers and elders of the church of Scotland. 3d ed. Boston, R.P. & C. Williams, 1828. 90 p. MH.   37218

Woburn, Mass. First Congregational Church
   Rules and regulations of the First Congregational Church in Woburn, Ms. ...[Boston, Crocker & Brewster, 1828] 12, 4 p. MWo.   37219

Wolfe, Charles A., 1791-1823
   Remains of the late Rev. Charles Wolfe, A.B. curate of Donoughmore, Diocese of Armagh; with a brief memoir of his life. By the Rev. John A. Russell, chaplain to his excellency the Lord Lieutenant of Ireland and curate of St. Werburgh's, Dublin. Hartford, Pub. by H. and F.J. Huntington [P. Canfield, pr.] 1828. 294 p. DLC; GDC; ICMcC; LNB; MA; MBC; MiD-B; NCH; NNG; NNUT; NUt; NhHi; PHi; PPL; PPiU; RNR; RP; Vi; ViRUT; VtMiM; WHi.   37220

Wood, Benjamin, 1772-1849
   A discourse delivered Feb. 26, 1828, at the funeral of Mr. Pearly Hunt, aged 25 years, son of Mr. Joseph Hunt... Pub. by the

request of the connections of the deceased. Worcester, Pr. by S. H. Colton and Co., 1828. 11 p. ICN; M; MWA; MWHi; NN.
37221

Wood, Daniel
An epistle to Friends of the New York yearly meeting... New York, Pr. by Samuel Wood & son, 1828. 8 p. InRE; NjR; PHC.
37222

Wood, Jacob, 1793?-1853
Two sermons, originally delivered in Shrewsbury, Mass., and published in the "Gospel Preacher." Sermon I. On the Character of God. Sermon II. On the duty of men to declare their religious faith. Providence, John S. Greene, pr., 1828. 15 p. MMeT-Hi; BrMus.
37223

Wood, Silas
A sketch of the first settlement of the several towns on Long-Island, with their political condition, to the end of the American revolution. A new ed. Brooklyn, N. Y., Pr. by Alden Spooner, 1828. 181, [2] p. CSmH; CtSoP; ICN; IU; LNHT; MH; MHi; MiD-B; MoSM; NHi; NN; NjR; OClWHi; PHi; WHi; BrMus.
37224

Woodbine Institute
A prospectus of Woodbine Institute, for Practical Education, and Agriculture; Including some of the prominent points of Fellemberg's Institutions in Switzerland. Under the superintendence of John M. Keagy, M. D. Harrisburg, Pr. by John S. Wiestling, 1828. 8 p. **PPL**.
37225

Woodbridge, John
The mutability of the world, and the permanency of the Gospel. A sermon, preached Mar. 31, 1828, at the interment of the Rev. Joseph Lyman, D. D. ... who died, Mar. 27, 1828, in the

79th year of his age... Amherst, J. S. & C. Adams, prs., 1828. 25 p. ICN; MA; MB; MBC; MH; MNF; MPiB; MWA; N; NBLiHi; NjR; PPPrHi; RPB.
37226

Woodbridge, William C.
Rudiments of geography on a new plan. Designed to assist the memory by comparison and classification: with numerous engravings of manners, customs and curiosities. Accompanied with an atlas... 9th ed., from the 3d imp. ed., with corrections. Hartford, Oliver D. Cooke & Co., 1828. 208 p. CtHi.
37227

Woodbury, Levi
Remarks by Mr. Woodbury, of New Hampshire, on the first decision of the bill for the relief of the surviving officers of the revolution. Washington, Pr. by Green & Jarvis, 1828. 12 p. DLC; MBAt; Nh.
37228

Woodman, Jonathan
A discourse, delivered before the Legislature of Vermont, on the day of election at Montpelier, Oct. 9, 1828. Montpelier, Pr. by E. P. Walton, Watchman Office, 1828. 23 p. MBC; MeLB; OCHP; VtMiM; BrMus.
37229

Woods, Alva, 1794-1887
Intellectual and moral culture. A discourse delivered at his inauguration as president of Transylvania University, Oct. 13th, 1828. Lexington, Ky., J. G. Norwood, pr., 1828. 20, 4 p. CBPac; CSmH; DLC; ICU; KyBgW; KyLxT; MBAt; MBC; MH; MWA; NN; NjP; NjR; OCHP; PHi; PPAmP; RHi; TxU; BrMus.
37230

Woods, John, 1794-1855
Speech of Mr. Woods of Ohio on the emigration of Indians delivered in the House of Representatives, Feb. 19, 1828. Washing-

ton, Gales & Seaton, 1828. 20 p. LU.   37231

Woods, Leonard
Lectures on infant baptism. Andover, Pub. by Mark Newman, Flagg & Gould, prs., 1828. 174 p. CtHi; DLC; NjR.   37232

Wood's almanac for 1829. By Joshua Sharp. New York, Samuel Wood & Sons; Richard & George S. Wood, prs., [1828] 18 l. DLC; InU; MWA; N; NHi; NN.   37233

[Woolman, John] 1720-1772
An epistle to the quarterly & monthly meetings of Friends. New York, Pr. by Mahlon Day, 1828. 24 p. PHC.   37234

Worcester, Joseph Emerson, 1784-1865
An atlas accompanying Worcester's Epitome of geography; comprising .. maps and tables. New York, Pub. by R. Lockwood. Boston, Hilliard, Gray, Little and Wilkins, 1828. 17 l. CtHT-W; MB; MH; NcWsM.   37235

---- Elements of geography, ancient and modern, with an atlas. Stereotype ed. Boston, Hilliard Gray, Little & Wilkins [T. R. Marvin, pr.] 1828. x, 9-294, [2] p. MDeeP; MH; MHi.   37236

---- Elements of history, ancient and modern: with historical charts. 3d ed. Boston, Hilliard, Gray, Little, and Wilkins, 1828. xii, 339 p. CtHT-W; ICN; ICU; InCW; MH; MHi; MWHi; NjR; PPAmP; RPB; TNJ; TxU-T.
37237
---- Stereotype ed. An epitome of geography, with an atlas. By J. E. Worcester. Philadelphia, Pub. by Uriah Hunt. Boston, Hilliard, Gray, Little, and Wilkins [Stereotyped at the Boston type and stereotype foundry] 1828.

viii, 165, 6 p. KyHi; MH; NNC.
37238
---- An epitome of history, with historical and chronological charts. 2d ed. Boston, Pub. by Hilliard, Gray, Little and Wilkins, 1828. [Lancaster, Pr. by F. & J. Andrews] v, [1] 135 p. CSt; PPL.   37239

---- An historical atlas, containing the following charts...3d ed. Boston, Hilliard, Gray, Little, and Wilkins [etc., etc.] 1828. 1 p. l., 9 fold. charts. Ct; DLC; LNT; MH; MdBP; MiD; NhHi; PV.   37240

---- Outlines of Scripture geography, with an atlas. Boston, Hilliard, Gray, Little, and Wilkins, and Bowles and Dearborn, 1828. 44 p. MBC; MH; OO; PPAmS; RPB; TxU-T.   37241

---- Questions adapted to the use of the third edition of Worcester's Elements of history. Boston, Hilliard, Gray, Little, and Wilkins, 1828. 60 p. MH.   37242

---- Worcester's modern atlas. Boston, Hilliard, Gray, Little & Wilkins [1828] xvi p. maps & tables. MH.   37243

[Worcester, Noah] 1758-1837
Pacific overtures for Christian Harmony. No. 1. By the editor of the Friend of peace. [n. p., 1828] 24 p. CSmH.   37244

Worcester, Samuel, 1793-1844
An address, delivered at the twelfth anniversary of the Massachusetts Peace Society, Dec. 25, 1827... Cambridge, Hilliard, Metcalf, and co., prs. to the university, 1828. 12, 8 p. [8 p. is "Twelfth annual report..." of the Society, also entered as a separate.] CSmH.   37245

---- A primer of the English language for the use of families and schools. Stereotype ed. Boston, Hilliard, Gray, Little & Wilkins, 1828. 72 p. DLC.   37246

Worcester County Bar Association.
Rules of the Bar of the county of Worcester, 1828. [Worcester, 1828] 18 p. DLC; MB; MH-L; NbHi; OClWHi; WHi.   37247

Worcester County Institution for Savings
Constitution and by-laws of the Worcester County Institution for Savings, in the town of Worcester. Worcester, Pr. by S. H. Colton & Co., 1828. 12 p. MH-BA; MWA.
                                        37248
Worcester village register. Apr. 1828. [Worcester, Dorr & Howland] [4] p. MWA; NIC.   37249

A word to fathers and mothers.
See Tuckerman, Joseph.

Worse and worse!! Fellow citizens. Every statement in the hand bill of the 8th instant, entitled, "Look to your interest," is now officially confirmed...
[Boston, 1828] Bdsd. MB. 37250

Worth, W. I.
[Letter to Hon. P. B. Porter, Secretary of War, in defense of the conduct of Major W. I. Worth] [New York, G. F. Hopkins, prs., 1828] 8 p. NbU.   37251

The wreath.   See Littleford, Mrs.

Wright, Akins
A history of the principal and most distinguished martyrs in the different ages of the world; giving an account of their birth, sufferings, and death; and particularly their dying words in testimony of that religion which they professed. Cincinnati, Pub. by A. Wright; Hatch, Nichols & Buxton,

prs., 1828. 503, [1] p. ICU; OCX; OMC; OUrC; TNJ.   37252

Wright, John Crafts, 1784?-1861
Speech of Mr. John C. Wright, on the subject of retrenchment. Delivered in the House of Representatives, Feb. 6, 1828. Washington, Pr. by Gales & Seaton, 1828. 44 p. DLC; IU; MWA; MiD-B; OCHP; PPL.   37253

Wright, John Flannel
Substance of a sermon preached in Cincinnati, Ohio, Feb. 10, 1828... Cincinnati, Wm. M. Farnsworth, pr., 1828. 23 p. MiD; OClWHi.   37254

Wright, Silas, 1795-1847
Speech of Hon. Silas Wright, jun. in the House of Representatives of the United States, in support of the bill to establish a national tariff. Albany, Croswell & Van Benthuysen, by Webster and Wood, 1828. 40 p. N.   37255

---- Speech of Mr. Silas Wright, of New-York, on the proposition to amend the tariff; delivered in the House of Representatives of the United States, Mar. 7, 1828. Washington, Pr. by Green & Jarvis, 1828. 64 p. CSmH; IU; MWA; N; RNR.   37256

[Wright, Thomas]
Farewell to time, or Last views of life, and prospects of immortality. Including devotional exercises, a great variety of which are in the language of Scripture, -to be used by the sick, or by those who minister to them. By the author of "The Morning and Evening Sacrifice." New-York, W. B. Gilley; G. & C. Carvill; Collins & Co.; Collins & Hannay; Wm. Burgess, Jun.; Elam Bliss; Jon. Leavitt; Caleb Bartlett, Philadelphia, Towar & Hogan, John Grigg [New York, J.

Seymour, pr.] 1828. 328 p. GDC; IU; MH-AH; MW; NSyU. 37257

Wylie, Andrew, 1789-1851
An address delivered to the graduates of Washington College, Sept. 25th, 1828. Washington, Pennsylvania, [1828] 11 p. PHi.
37258
---- Godliness the nation's hope. A sermon, preached on the 4th of July, 1828... Washington, Pa., [1828] 12 p. PPPrHi.
37259
---- A sermon on the sin of duelling, preached at Washington, Pa., April, 1827. Pittsburgh, Pr. by D. & M. Maclean, 1828. 22 p. CSmH; MsWJ; PWcHi.
37260

X-Y-Z

Xenophon
...Xenophontis De Ciri Institutione. Libre octo. Ex recensione ex cum notis. Thomas Hutchinson, A. M. Philadelphia, Pub. and sold by H. Cowperthwait, 1828. 500 p. ArU; CtHT-W; CtMW; InU; MsCLiM; OMC; ScCliTO; ViAlTh; ViL; WMM.
37261
Yale, Cyrus
Life of Rev. Jeremiah Hallock, late pastor of the Congregational Church in Canton, Conn. ... New-York, John P. Haven, 1828. 316 p. CBPac; Ct; ICMcC; ICU; MA; MFiHi; MH-AH; MWA; NN; NNUT; NhHi; OClW; OO. 37262

---- Plea for union in erecting a house of God. A discourse delivered at New-Hartford, Feb. 3, 1828. ...Hartford, Pr. by Philemon Canfield, 1828. 31 p. CtHi. 37263

Yale University
Order of exercises at commencement, Yale College, Sept.

10, 1828. New-Haven, Pr. by Charles Adams, 1828. 4 p. DLC.
37264
---- Reports on the course of instruction in Yale College, by a committee of the corporation, and the academical faculty. New Haven, Pr. by Hezekiah Howe, 1828. 56 p. Ct; DLC; MB; MH; MiU; NB; NNS; OClWHi; OO; PPAmP; PPPrHi. 37265

---- Yale college, New-Haven, Aug. 1, 1828. On Monday morning of this week... [Statement transmitted to the parent of each student concerned, apropos of the "bread and butter rebellion." New Haven? 1828] 1 l. (Pr. on p. [1] of folded sheet; p. [2-4] blank.) 37266

---- ----[New Haven? 1828] 2 l. (Pr. on p. [2-3] of folded sheet.)
37267
---- ---- Another issue. (Pr. on p. [1-2] of folded sheet; p. [3-4] blank.) 37268

---- Calliopean Society. Library. Catalogue of books belonging to the Calliopean Society: Yale college. Mar. 1828. [New Haven, Treadway & Adams, pr., 1828] 26 p. CtY. 37269

---- Faculty.
[Statement transmitted to the parent of each student concerned, Aug. 1, 1828, and now given to the public, apropos of the "bread and butter rebellion." Dated Aug. 6, 1828] [New Haven? 1828] 2 l. (Pr. on opposite pages.) 37270

---- Medical School.
Laws of the medical institution of Yale College. New Haven, Hezekiah Howe, 1828. 8 p. Ct; MB; NNNAM. 37271

---- Students.
Yale college, Aug. 1, 1828...

Events of an important nature
having recently taken place...
[Circular, signed by 134 students,
sent to their respective parents
apropos of the "bread and butter
rebellion." New Haven? 1828]
2 l. (Pr. on p. [2-3] of a folded
sheet.) CtY.   37272

The yankee. The farmer's almanack, and annual register for
1829. By Thomas Spofford. Boston, David Felt & Co. [1828] 18 l.
CLU; CU; CtY; DLC; MBAt; MBC;
MH; MHi; MWA; MeHi; N; NbHi;
OClWHi; WHi.   37273

The Yankee in London; or A
short trip to America. Cincinnati, Pub. and sold by Robbins &
Wright, Hatch, Nichols & Buxton,
prs., 1828. 140 p. IU; OC; ViU.
                           37274

Yates, John B.
   Address delivered before the
alumni of Union College, on the
24th day of July, 1827. Schenectady, Pr. by Isaac Riggs, 1828.
23 p. CSmH; MB; N; NN. 37275

The yellow shoe-strings. See
Pedder, James.

Yes and no: A tale. See
Phipps, Constantine Henry of
Normandy, 1st marquis.

Yorick, Mr., pseud. See Sterne,
Laurence.

You are requested to attend the
funeral of Mr. Robert Douthat,
from the residence of Major
William Price, this afternoon at
1/2 past 3 o'clock. Wednesday,
May 21, 1828. [Richmond? 1828]
Bdsd. ViU.   37276

No entry   37277

Young, Augustus
   An oration, delivered at Crafts-
bury on the anniversary of the
nativity of St. John the Baptist.
Montpelier, E. P. Walton, 1828.
VtHi; BrMus.   37278

Young, Edward, 1684-1765
   The complaint; or, Night
thoughts. Hartford, S. Andrus,
1828. 324 p. MMilt.   37279

Young, James Hamilton
   Map of Asia, carefully compiled from the latest maps and
charts and other geographical
publications. Drawn & engraved
by J. H. Young. Philadelphia, Pub.
by A. Finley, 1828. 108 x 140
cm. RPB.   37280

The young clergyman... Cambridge, Hilliard and Brown, 1828.
18 p. MB; MH; MWA.   37281

A young lady of Virginia, pseud.
See Lorraine, A. M.

Young men of Cortland county.
See Democratic Party. New York.

Young Men's Association of Trenton, N. J. See National Republican Party. New Jersey.

Young Men's Bible Association
of Philadelphia
   Constitution, proceedings, and
address of the Young Men's Bible
Association of the City and Coun-
ty of Philadelphia. For the
Spread of the Scriptures in South
America. Philadelphia, W. Pil-
kington & Co., pr., 1828. 8 p.
P; PPPrHi.   37282

Young Men's Bible Society of
Baltimore
    The eighth report of the Young
Men's Bible Society of Baltimore,
auxiliary to the American Bible
Society, including the seventh report of the Ladies Branch Bible
Society, presented at their annual meeting, Nov. 26, 1827. To
which is added a list of subscribers. Baltimore, Pr. by John D.
Toy, 1828. 35 p. MdHi.   37283

---- Report of the Young Men's
Bible Society of Baltimore, presented March 24, 1828. Detailing
the progress made by the Committee of Management, in carrying into effect the resolution
adopted by the society at their
late annual meeting, to "undertake, with a firm reliance upon
Divine Providence, to supply each
destitute family in the State of
Maryland with a copy of the Sacred Scriptures within one year."
Baltimore, Pr. by John D. Toy,
1828. 12 p. MdHi.   37284

Young Men's Temperance Society
    Address of the executive com-
mittee of the Young Men's Temperance Society, to the young men
of Philadelphia. Philadelphia, I.
Ashmead & Co. , prs. , 1828. 16 p.
P; PPPrHi; RPB; ScCC.   37285

The youth's almanack for 1829.
Brookfield, E. & G. Merriam;
Boston, Pierce & Williams
[1828] 12 1. MWA; OMC.   37286

The youth's library. See American Sunday School Union.

Yvonnet, Francis V.
    An oration delivered at the
Baptist Church in the city of
Troy, on the eighth day of January, 1828, in commemoration of
the victory obtained at New-Orleans, on the eighth of January,
1815, by Gen. Andrew Jackson,
and the forces under his command. Troy, Pr. by Francis
Adancourt, 1828. 46 p. PPL.
                            37287

Zum neuen Jahr 1828 bringt der
Herumträger des Unabhängigen
Republicaners seinen Lesern
folgenden Glücks-Wunsch dar.
[1828] Lancaster County Historical Society.   37288

Addenda

Addresses, delivered at the celebration of the thirteenth anniversary of the victory of New Orleans...Philadelphia, Pr. by Wm.
Stavely, 1828. 16 p. Sabin
35391.   37289

Associated Methodist Reformers
    Instrument of Association...
prepared in Baltimore. Baltimore,
R. J. Matchett, 1828. 7, [1] p.
MdHi.   37290

A brief inquiry into some of the
objections urged against the election of Andrew Jackson to the office of President of the United
States. Sustained by official documents. [1828?-latest date mentioned is June 30, 1827] 35 p.
KU.   37291

The Cabinet or philosopher's
masterpiece. New-York, S. King,
1828. 24 p. MH.   37292

Claims of Sunday Schools upon
churchmen. 2d ed. With thoughts
on Sunday Schools. Hartford, H.
and F. J. Huntington, P. Canfield,
pr., 1828. 66 p. CtY; MH-AH.
                                37293
Democratic Party. New Jersey.
    Presidential election, 1776.
Independence, liberty, and glory!
Washington, La Fayette, and
Jackson. Brandywine, York-
Town, and New-Orleans. Hearts
of Oak, to the Polls; Support Old
Hickory, the defender of his
country, and the man of the
people. [New Jersey, 1828?] 8
p. KU.   37294

---- Pennsylvania.

A refutation of the charges
made against the public conduct
of Gen. Andrew Jackson, and also a detail of the most prominent
objections to the election of J.
Quincy Adams to the Presidency.
By the Dauphin County Committee. Harrisburg, 1828. 36 p.
PHi; BrMus.   37295

Dickinson College
    Catalogue of the officers &
students of Dickinson College...
Carlisle, 1828. 16 p. NjR.
                                37296
Freemasons. Kentucky.
    Proceedings of a convention of
Select Masters, held at Masons'
Hall in the town of Frankfort...
Frankfort, Pr. by Amos Kendall
and company, 1828. 10 p. NNFM.
                                37297
Johnson, Samuel
    The Rambler. By Samuel John-
son...with an essay of his life
and genius by Arthur Murphy...
Princeton, Borrenstein, 1828. 4
v. MnU; NNUT; NjP; PU; OO.
                                37298
Krebs, William
    Reply of [William] Krebs and
[Richard] Cromwell to the remon-
strance of Seth Sweetser...[Bal-
timore? 1828] 10 p. MdBP.
                                37299
Lloyd, W. F.
    The teacher's manual; or,
Hints to a teacher on being appointed to the charge of the Sunday school class. Philadelphia,
American Sunday School Union,
1828. 108 p. GDC.   37300

Maryland
    Communication from the ex-

488

ecutive enclosing reports of the several armorers in this state. Annapolis, Pr. by Jeremiah Hughes, 1828. 36 p. MdBP. 37301

---- Communication from the executive enclosing resolutions from the legislatures of the states of South Carolina and Georgia. Annapolis, Pr. by Jeremiah Hughes, 1828. 36 p. MdBP. 37302

---- A communication from the Register in Chancery in reply to an order of the House of Delegates... Annapolis, Pr. by Jeremiah Hughes, 1828. 4 p. MdBP. 37303

---- Communication from the Treasurer of the Western Shore relative to the [American] Colonization Society. [Annapolis? 1828] 8 p. MdBP. 37304

---- Document No. 1 accompanying[!] the message of [the governor]... to the General Assembly... Annapolis, Pr. by Jeremiah Hughes, 1828. 23 p. MdBP; MdHi. 37305

---- Letter from Judge Brice relative to crimes and criminal law. Annapolis, Pr. by Jeremiah Hughes, 1828. [Document No. 2 accompanying the message of Governor Kent to the General Assembly, January 2, 1828] 1 l., 8 p. MdBP. 37306

---- Message from the executive ... to the Legislature, enclosing communications from the executives of the states of Maine, Connecticut and Virginia. Annapolis, Pr. by Jeremiah Hughes, 1828. 18 p. MdBP. 37307

---- A report from the Treasurer of the Western Shore relative to the amount of revenue received... for the last three years. Annapolis, Pr. by Jeremiah

Hughes, 1828. 2 l., 1 folding table. MdBP. 37308

---- Report from the Treasurer of the Western Shore relative to the several banks in this state. Annapolis, Pr. by Jeremiah Hughes, 1828. 2 l., 2 folding tables. MdBP. 37309

---- Report of the committee appointed to examine the accounts of the Treasurer, and the general state of the finances of the city of Annapolis. Annapolis, Jeremiah Hughes, pr., 1828. 28 p. MdBJ-G. 37310

---- Report of the Committee on Claims. Annapolis, J. Hughes, pr., 1828. 8 p. MdBP. 37311

---- Report of the Committee on Claims, on the accounts and proceedings of... [the] Treasurer of the Eastern Shore. Annapolis, Pr. by Jeremiah Hughes, 1828. 1 l., 3 fold. tables. MdBP. 37312

---- Report of the Committee on Ways and Means... Annapolis, Pr. by Jeremiah Hughes, 1828. 15 p. MdBP. 37313

---- Report of the Treasurer of the Eastern Shore... in reply to an order of the House of Delegates. Annapolis, Pr. by Jeremiah Hughes, 1828. 4 p. MdBP. 37314

---- Report of the Treasurer of the Western Shore in obedience to an order of the House of Delegates. [Annapolis] Pr. by Jeremiah Hughes, 1828. 8 p. MdBP. 37315

---- Rules and regulations adopted for the government of the House of Delegates... in the conduct of business. Annapolis, Prnited[!] by Jeremiah Hughes, 1828. 8 p. MdBP. 37316

---- Statement from the Late States[!] Agent of the Western Shore, relative to his account with the state of Maryland. Annapolis, Pr. by Wm. M'Neir, 1828. 7, [1] p. MdBP.   37317

Massachusetts (Commonwealth)
Resolves of the General Court of the commonwealth of Massachusetts, passed at the several sessions of the General Court, commencing May, 1824, and ending March, 1828. Published agreeably to a Resolve of 16th Jan. 1812. Boston, Dutton and Wentworth, prs., to the state, 1828. 736, xxxii p. IaU-L; MBevHi; Mi-L; NNLI; Nb.   37318

Mott, John, fl. 1827
Copy of a letter written by John Mott to an Orthodox Friend. [Rensselaerville, [sic] 1828] MBC; MH; PHC.   37319

Mrs. Colvin's Messenger.
The carrier's address to the patrons of Mrs. Colvin's Messenger, January 1, 1828. [Washington, D. C.] Myer, pr., [1828] 1 p. DLC.   37320

National Republican Party. New Jersey.
The truth teller, the people's ticket. For President, John Quincy Adams, for Vice President Richard Rush... Salem, 1828. 24 p. NjR.   37321

New York (State)
Journal of the Assembly of the state of New-York; at their fifty-first session. Begun and held at the capitol, in the city of Albany, the 1st day of January, 1828. Albany, Pr. by E. Croswell, pr. to the state, 1828. 1209, 66, 111, xlviii p. NNLI.   37322

---- Journal of the Assembly of the state of New-York, at their fifty-first session, second meeting: begun and held at the capitol, in the city of Albany, Tuesday, September 9th, 1828. Albany, Pr. by E. Croswell, pr. to the state, 1828. 134, vi p. NNLI.   37323

---- Journal of the Senate of the state of New-York; at their fifty-first session, begun and held at the capitol, in the city of Albany, the 1st day of January, 1828. Albany, Pr. by E. Croswell, Pr. to the state, 1828. 523, 38, 36, 43, xix p. NNLI.   37324

---- Journal of the Senate of the state of New York, at their fifty-first session, second meeting; begun and held at the capitol, in the city of Albany, Tuesday, September 9th, 1828. Albany, Pr. by E. Croswell, pr. to the state, 1828. 99, iv p. NNLI.   37325

---- Laws of the state of New York, passed at the fifty-first session of the Legislature, begun and held at the city of Albany, the first day of January, 1828. Albany, Pr. by E. Croswell, 1828. 544 p. Ar-SC; In-SC; MdBB; Mi-L; Ms; N; NNIA; NNLI; Nb; Nj; NjR; R; RPL; TxU-L; Wa-L.   37326

---- Laws of the state of New York, passed at the second meeting of the fifty-first session of the Legislature, begun and held at the city of Albany, the ninth day of September, 1828. Albany, Pr. by E. Croswell, pr. to the state, 1828. 70 p. In-SC; Nj; OCLaw; TxU-L; W; Wa-L.   37327

New York Asylum for Lying in Women.
Fifth annual report of the managers of the New York Asylum for Lying-in Women; March 13, 1828. New York, Pr. by Gray & Bunce,

1828. NjR.   37328

Otis, Job
    Medicine chests, with suitable
directions, faithfully prepared by
Job Otis, druggist and apothecary,
Water-Street, New-Bedford. Ships,
vessels, and families, supplied
at short notice. New Bedford,
Benjamin T. Congdon, 1828. 32
p. Donahue.   37329

Pennsylvania
    Tagebuch des Senats der Re-
publik Pennsylvanien, 1827-1828.
Libanon, Pr. by Jacob Stover,
1828. Seidensticker p. 238.
                               37330
[Pratt, Samuel Jackson] 1749-
1814
    The sublime and beautiful of
Scripture: being essays on select passages of sacred composition, by Courtney Melmoth. Harrisburg, Pub. by Henry Sprigman,
John S. Wiestling, pr., 1828. vi,
227 [2] p. GDC.   37331

Preston's cure for intemperance.
New York, 1828. 12 p. NjR.
                               37332
Review. The Reverend Rector of
the Roman Church in Frederick-
Town, vs. The Young Men's Bible
Society. [Frederick-Town] Pub.
for the Reader, 1828. 15 p.
MdBJ-G.   37333

Riley, James, 1777-1840
    An authentic narrative of the
loss of the American brig Commerce...; with an account of the
sufferings of the surviving officers and crew...; and observations historical, geographical,
etc. made during the travels...;
preceded by a brief sketch of the
author's life...Hartford, S. Andrus, publisher, stereotyped by A.
Chandler, 1828. 271 p. C; CLCO;
CSmH; CtHT; CtHi; DLC; ICHi;
IP; InGrD; KTW; KyDC; MDeeP;
MLow; MdAN; MdBE; NGH; NNF;
NR; NcElon; P; PFal; PRA-T;
PWb; PWmDS; TJoS; TNJ. 37334

---- ---- Hartford, Con., And-
rus & Judd [1828?] 271 p. DLC.
                               37335
Shakespeare William
    Richard the Third, a tragedy.
Adapted to the stage by Colley
Cibber. [Oxberry's edition] New
York, W. Whale, [etc.] 1828. 90
p. MH.   37336

Shaw, John Angier, 1792-1873
    An address delivered before
the Bridgewater Society for the
Promotion of Temperance, Feb.
22, 1828. Boston, Munroe and
Francis, 1828. 24 p. M; MBC;
MH; BrMus.   37337

[Smith, James]
    Appeal. To the citizens of
Baltimore in his own vindication.
[Baltimore, 1828] 96 p. MdBP.
                               37338
Steel, John Honeywood, 1780-
1838
    An analysis of the mineral
waters of Saratoga and Ballston,
with practical remarks on their
use in various diseases containing observations on the geology
and mineralogy of the surrounding
country with a geological map.
2d ed., imp. Saratoga Springs,
1828. 118 p. MBC; MWA; RPM;
BrMus.   37339

Sweetser, Seth
    Remonstrances of Seth Sweet-
ser. Sen. against the plan of
William Krebs and others. Baltimore, Pr. by R. J. Matchett,
1828. 8 p. Md; MdBP.   37340

The theatrical budget. New York,
Elton's theatrical play, print and
song store, 1828. New Ser. No.
1-6. [Series of 6 pamphlets -
each with same general title and
imprint] MH; NIC.   37341

Transylvania Journal of Medicine
    Suum crique - (Let each have
his own) Lexington, Ky. , August
15th, 1828. [Dissertation regarding criticism of the first number
of the Transylvania Journal of
Medicine by the Medical Recorder.] 7 p. KyLoF.   37342